LADYBUG

C. J. Michaels

Strategic Book Publishing and Rights Co.

Every effort has been made within the author's ability, to respect copyright law and trace copyright holders to obtain permission for the use of their work. All artistic work that is ex libris of the artists who are recognised in this book, is also acknowledged in an appendix to the book.

The author apologises for any errors or omissions and would be grateful if notified of any corrections that should be incorporated in future reprints or editions of this book.

Copyright © 2017 C. J. Michaels. All rights reserved.
E.U. Copyright © 2007, 2008.

No part of this book may be reproduced or transmitted in any form or by any means, graphic, electronic, or mechanical, including photocopying, recording, taping, or by any information storage retrieval system, without the permission, in writing, of the publisher and author. For more information, send an email to cjm@mystromediation.com, Attention Subsidiary Rights Department.

Strategic Book Publishing and Rights Co., LLC
USA | Singapore
www.sbpra.com

For information about special discounts for bulk purchases, please contact Strategic Book Publishing and Rights Co., LLC Special Sales, at bookorder@sbpra.net.

ISBN: 978-1-68181-510-7

L-*IF*-E
Just because one doesn't see it, doesn't mean that it's not there – BUDDHA.

生活
せい かつ

Life number
The sum of all digits in one's date of birth.

Destiny number
Forecasts relationships from a karmic lineage.

Renewal number
Highlights new beginnings.

Courage number
Defender of courage and respect.

Love number
Tests patience and forgiveness.

Truth number
Responds candidly to questions.

Strength number
Warrior for inner power and protection.

PRECURSOR

"Row, row, row your boat gently down the stream
Merrily, merrily, merrily, merrily
Life
Is
Not
A dream."

How well do you know your life? How closely have you ever really examined it? If you could trace a timeline from the moment that you were born until now, what dates, events and interludes of time would fall in tandem with one another and suddenly highlight new meaning and perspective to you? What hidden messages or secrets would unfold in your name; birth date, an unconscious habit, people's passing comments to you, the purpose of undesired events that possibly led to unexpected glory? If you took a pen and paper and sat to delve into your past would you suddenly see the apparition of a path or a line of coincidences to highlight your current truth? – What do you *see*? That the universe knows what it's doing is no longer a feel-good notion, but the *truth*? Use your imagination and discover how *real* it is; for the truth is a pure notion that is conceived only in the world of idealism. Once you have discovered it there then you may make it real. Realism then becomes a notion for all to see… Never lose sight of your truth and your reality shall be exactly where and what you are meant to be.

A PATH TO EQUINOX

January 28, 1967 (7)*
THE NAME DAY
She was born Canadian to English-speaking parents; baptised with a French name, the one the Beatles' loved, and translated from her father's middle name; christened with a Spanish middle name supported by a versatile surname, bestowed an effective nickname, while the small but mighty "M" was pronounced her maxim and beacon to lead her right, along her way...

March 5, 1979 (7)
A PRELUDE TO FREEDOM
..The day she hugged her mother, who then left her father – all in the name of love...

January 28, 1980 (2)
THE MAGIC
..The day pen and paper began to whisper her way...

December 25, 1980 (1)
THE WONDER
.. *Montego* Bay. She saw a cruise ship, and felt a wonder...

January 28, 1981 (3)
A HINT TO LOVE
..Her parents gave her a Spanish guitar and something else still undiscovered...

June 27, 1981 (7)
LE PRIX D'EXCELLENCE

..Unannounced to her she won. The gift was a gold *cross* that slipped and fell when they handed it to her. Yet, she picked it up despite the fear, faced the crowd to spite the fear and said: "Thank you," without it...

January *28*, 1982 (4)
A VOCATION

.. She was fifteen when it was surreptitiously hinted to her. It arrived in a greeting card dedicated to her: "To *maestro* – Happy Birthday!"...

October *22*, 1994 (1)
THE DEPARTURE

..The day her dad died and became a divine messenger...

1995 to1997
CLUES

..A timely phone call that allowed her to see the world through her father's eyes. A friend from *M*adrid and a Spanish word game, "mayor "K" " and "menor "k"" that shed light on watchwords that went unnoticed...

---

*The sum of all the digits in the date

April 7, 1998 (2)
REASONS

..The day she arrived at *Mayūrqa* and noticed the prophecy from the Spanish word game. The day she acquitted her heart's reasons from her head for loving and leaving a few good men. When the last of the clues became clear, and scribbled notes of a man and his dog turned real...

February 18, 2003 (7)
AN ANSWER

..She was Assistant Cruise Director when the ship docked into *Montego Bay*. Thus she finally understood the wonder...

June 17, 2003 (1)
THE SUBLIMINAL

..The day her mother felt prompted, and took a photo of her daughter's future, present and past...

October 25, 2003 (4)
THE MESSENGER

.. In some cultures it is believed that a bird that enters a house is a messenger from the spirit world notifying that a death in the home is destined to join it in the near future. It was at the siesta hour when the small sparrow came to the house and began to tap feverishly with its beak at the small glass window pane next to the front door. She and Jesy tried to convince the bird to tap somewhere else, but it remained there for a few days instead, chirping and tapping incessantly. The presence of the little creature disconcerted the couple who said nothing about the superstition as if it would deny giving it possibility or even permission to exist...

November 23, 2003 (3)
A PHILOSOPHY

.. "For every death there is a birth and for every birth there is a death." Jesy's niece was born and the young woman, who was Jesy's mate, wondered if the little sparrow at the pane of glass had chosen the wrong house? So she asked Life, if it had not gone already, to bless the life that might be leaving...

December 22, 2003 (3)
DIVINE WIND

.. Canada. She was clearing the snow from her mum's front porch. It was midday, cold but clear. The snow had fallen the night before and all was calm when the sudden sound of a crash and broken glass invaded the quiet. An adult grouse had flown like a Kamikaze into the side porch window shattering the window into a zillion pieces. The bird lay dead on the white snow bank next to the porch steps. The young woman looked at the grouse with a heavy heart of dismay. This time the message was made clear. It had not gone into her mother's home so she felt relieved. Then she instantly remembered the persistent little sparrow at Jesy's house, and almost as quickly shunned the notion and told Life not to listen to her silly fears. Instead she whispered an apology to the bird for the glass porch being in its way. Then gently moved the creature onto her snowy shovel, carried it well into the forest and buried it deep beneath the warmth of the snow...

December 28, 2003 (9)
TRUTH

.. In *vitae* veritas. The Day of the Innocent in Spain. The same day when two souls were reunited as one. The day her Jesy died and went on his way...

August 7, 2004 (3)
SOLSTITIUM
.. Life heard the man in Barcelona speaking to the woman: 'Nahh. I've finished with that now. No more. Never again,' he said dryly. 'Nahh, I want to go home, take English classes from a native speaker, then find me a girlfriend,' he added a bit more enthused.

'A girlfriend!? – You?' questioned the woman.

'Yea,' he said with a smile. 'I'll buy her one of those Minis, they're cool...'

..Meanwhile, the cruise ship was at sea in the Mediterranean. Only 20 kilometres from the port of Barcelona, when the heavy-set man suddenly swivelled around on his office chair looked at his colleague: 'Michèle? ...'

'.. Hmm, yes Hal?'

'I hope that whatever is looking for you – finds you...'

'..?? Thank you Hal...'

Don't let Time and Space *invade* the Memory

"He's a cocaine addict for *Christ-of-her's* sake!

Everything
But everything
Is against the odds – me
Everything *except* what
I *THINK*, I *FEEL* and *SEE*
Within the ambiguity of it all
It's All against me!
Even them, facts, Reality!!
THIS world.
Everything except
Possibility and Imagination
Destiny
Energy
Truth…
And a bit of Einstein, I hope."

INDUCTION

I'll protect you from the hooded claw
Keep the vampires from your door
The power of love
A force from above
Cleaning my soul
Flame on burn desire
Love with tongues of fire
Purge the soul
Make love your goal.

'THE POWER OF LOVE' – FRANKIE GOES TO HOLLYWOOD
LYRICS ADAPTED

Destiny

I've never done this before. I can't even type; always done it by pen or pencil. The Luddite way, you know. Am waiting, and wasting my time waiting. Anxiety levels in my stomach are high. Definitely not able to focus or concentrate on much else and really don't want to either. Tired of being alone and that seems to be my fate so get over it – right? Charlie – Carles, is also alone; on his couch like a vegetable after taking 3grams of it. He's getting ready to leave and I want him to know about the other place before he decides. I have to wait for the right moment and I am tired of that. I want to act now. I want to go there and talk to him and can't – will but shouldn't. Who's more ill now? Totally vexed by her too; the prostitute that has become his refuge because he *can't* have her. Because he can when he wants and because she can't harass him like I guess I do. The Eagle's song *Desperado* comes to mind… "When will you come to your senses? …The queen of diamonds will take you for everything that she can get – the queen of hearts is your best bet…" The more he *takes* the least he wants me, yet on Monday he asked me to stay with him.

Even though I know that he went with her on the Friday… Yadi-yadi ya. I am doing this just to kill time. Waiting, like that movie *The Hours*. Typing sucks. It really does. The whole psychology of it all exhausts me. I can see it and talk it out, but typing it out is overwhelming for me. He crossed the limits and now she is no longer professional. She's personal. She looks to him as her possible saviour, a possible boyfriend – hell, he takes care of her better than anyone in his life. How messed up is that? He has her sex, she gets coke, his money, knows his vulnerabilities, even gets his ring from France which of course he does not even ask back. She knows how to please him sexually and she can always be ready for him… Not like in the real world… How can a woman who wants to be with Carles compete with that? (Why she would want to, is a better question.) Emotional provocations now: shit. Precisely the area, I did not want to get into. Great. The more I think of it the more I don't want him around. I just want him to get better and away from me. I want him to know about Narconon, and Tavad, before he decides on Hipócrates… I just want to feel like I helped him get there, then I want to focus on me. I want him away so that I can be free. He came into my life. You brought him to me. Why? After Jes etc., wasn't that enough for you? I did not want to give English classes. He asked to join me for coffee. He asked me to dinner and *he* asked me for the first kiss! He went to Paris for a weekend not a day like I had suggested. Then he made me pay for the hotel and never paid me back. The one who has it all! I don't have that kind of money and he pays her and looks for her and does her after being with me… Cocaine or not; "Fuckhead." I just want him to go to the right place and I want that ring back. Set me free from these men please – whatever. Then, when he does go, I will really be alone. Fuck again. I had only been here one week when he came into my life. Never even time to be with myself and get my thing going. Damn it! Damn it! The car? Is that why? All of the coincidences can they, should they be overlooked? The bear totem, the keys, the licence plates on Mitx' and Carles' car – similar to mine… Then I remembered what Elisabet (Belle) told me. Apparently while Carles was in Barcelona he'd told her that he would never go back to cocaine. That he wanted to return home, find a girl, buy her a Mini and take English classes from a native speaker!!? And go figure, one month later, *here I Am!*

> She'll only come out at night
> The lean and hungry type
> Watching and waiting
> She's sit'n with you, but her eyes are on the door
> Money's the matter
> If you're in it for love, you ain't gonna get too far
> She's deadly man, she could really rip your world apart
> Watch out she'll chew you up – Watch out she's a man eater.
> 'MANEATER' – HALL & OATES, LYRICS ADAPTED

The Black Widow

The Black Widow spider and the Praying Mantis are two very good examples of cold female power. The Black Widow is a black velvet coloured spider with a luring red hourglass figure on the underside of her abdomen. She uses it of course to lure her prey into her web. When she mates she is capable of killing and draining the male for her own self-preservation. Sometimes she does not even mate with it. She merely stings it and keeps it semi-conscious for a while until the male finally dies or she has no more need for it. At least the Praying Mantis kills and finishes the job in seconds. No suffering per se. The human female has in fact such capabilities hidden within her instincts, if she chooses to use them. The prostitute is very good at using them and any woman who carries an emotional vindictive weight with her. They are of course to be respected and in truth, in this world of business and other hidden evils, admirable for the woman who can wield them without scruples. Men do too. We all do it. It's always up to the individual's conscious that maybe from way back in time is influenced by its pre-natal evolution from nature. What are you really? A shark? A former rabbit? A cross breed? What? ...

..'The scripts are many,' I told him, 'two specific ones really.' Charlie and I were having a drink in C'an Chato which also happened to be, I noticed, Jes' childhood nickname. Anyway, I explained to Charlie that in the world of a prostitute, 'there are two clients: the first client is the one that she does purely for the money. There, while she dazzles him with a deceptive enchanting smile, she is secretly counting the time backwards, *twenty, eighteen, fifteen, ten minutes... Five, two, thirty seconds – done!* The Mantis has eaten. Delighted to be done and needing some quick down-time for physical and mental space in order to get ready for the next asshole. If she is good, she can do it well each time despite the emotional drain. She pretends to herself that she is in fact a very good actress and that the show must go on. This client was in fact the professional one. Then there is the other client who confuses everything. He's also the prostitute's best client and the client's own worst nightmare. The emotionally weak, kind and messed up ones. Black Widows feast on them. He is also attractive compared to the others; even maybe intelligent – a nice guy with a soft heart. The prostitutes are like cats among themselves; will look for him when he arrives. Actually eager to *work* for him – he's not difficult *to do*. Like a stupid rooster his awareness of this delights him and he enjoys the reaction that he provokes from them. He actually believes that he knows how to win the prostitute over by seemingly respecting her. She is softened, yes, and will deliver more sincerely, but he has only offered her more ways to manipulate him and get more from him. He is the one that the Black Widow prostitute will keep semi-conscious until he can't feed her anymore or until she kills him. So the exchange feels less like work and the client also gets wrapped up in this realisation. It makes the "pseudo-relationship" and the sexual encounter feel a little less hollow after it's done. Hence he returns more often because he actually feels liked and not just like *a job*. He spends more money and she makes more. Then there comes the danger – the emotional breakdown. Suddenly a prostitute will get possessive of him and even try to soften the financial rules if it will get him to be with her. She begins to like him and creates images of a life outside of her world. He could maybe save her? He too begins to think that she really likes him and the two of them cross the lines of being professional to being a prototype *underground couple*. Yet if the prostitute is smart, she is also aware of a constant lurking reality: the realisation that the client is there because something does not work in his real life. She is there for the same reason, and what if? What if they did try to live outside the dark world into the one of light? He would not want her to dance and she would comply, but only if he takes "care" of her. She could work a day job to keep herself busy, but she'd eventually crave more money from him or her work. Which is why most who stay with prostitution are where they are. They can't be bothered to work the crazy hours that we all do for peanuts, when they can just screw and get a month's worth of salary in a night. He will want sex whenever because deep down he owns a prostitute. She will want to be integrated into his family and friends while he might not. There will be jealousy and insecurity issues from him because she can be sentimentally detached, find someone else, while Possession and Obsession will survive on him. Eventually she will leave him and they will go back to their respective ways, but he will be worse off than before. So they are there, fucking or observing each other. Pretending to be something that they are not, in the meantime going deeper into their wells of no return. In the short term the prostitute always wins. She still goes home with the money. In the long term the client could win, but it would have to come from something greater than both of them...

Love,' I said coolly...

Charlie shifted his posture over the bar counter back to a semi upright position and contemplated me briefly. I'd obviously struck an inner cord with him. Then ever so purposely while he focused on my eyes, he placed his two middle fingers upon my brow, over my chakra's third eye, and with a quick but gentle swoop ran his fingers down the middle of my face and said: 'Aiii Michèle, sometimes being intelligent is not always good.' I agreed. In this case it actually sucked. Calvin and Hobbs came to mind: "*ignorance is bliss,*" I thought to myself, and we drove home.

> Now, you see, the world is full of temptation.
> JIMINY CRICKET, WALT DISNEY

Pinochos

One of the oldest businesses in the world is the sex trade and the most socially integrated business of that trade is the parlour and its women of the night; ironically often managed by women. Even if there is a male pimp behind them, that's only bad management on their part. At the end of the day it's a woman's manipulative business. When Charlie told me about the prostitutes I realised that I would handle anything with him except a personal desire for another woman. The ego here is bigger than jealousy. Feeling the indignation that he would give the privilege of his intimacy to another woman, and pay her for it. That he would satisfy her with a rewarding economy and a sense of privileged status over me. Thus depreciating me in exchange for nothing really: no love or genuine intimacy. Nothing. He spends all his time with me – has the privilege of having me by his side, while never paid for, nor charged for. One realises that sentimentality is quite possibly another Hollywood production. That in fact a prostitute is a very good business*man*. She knows the market and knows its demand and how to deliver it. Her A-typical clients are usually men with a sexual dysfunction in their relationships, who thereby gravitate to power and money, not sentimentality. Hence in love, these men spend their time trying to put-out their desire with quick fixes in order to relieve themselves of its need. Women on the other hand make love in order to live-out their desire by consenting to be *the* desired one, and in sexual failure of a relationship may gravitate to their maternal instincts for fulfilment. Hence a man says: 'No sex no love,' while the woman says: 'No love no sex,' and in the meantime, the prostitute says: 'Show me the money'...

.. 4:43a.m. O.K., let's see if I can remember the mental gymnastics that woke me up from my sleep: um, the image of me being there with him – some kind of therapy session... *They ask me if I want to keep going with Charlie once he returns to Mayürqa. I pause and realise that I can't. 'Why?' they ask... 'Well,' I say, 'I can handle just about everything; even the prostitutes but not pinochos.' 'What are they?' they ask. 'Well, it started out as a code word from me to Charlie describing a woman that had been and continues to contact him at unacceptable hours of the night. Naturally, he does not put a stop to it. She plays his buttons and he lets her. She creates negative energy by telling him gross untruths about people's comments about him or other people in order to get his attention. Anyway I discovered who she was and my defence mechanism kicked in and noticed that she has a long pointy nose like Pinocchio does when he lies. It's shallow, I know, but Charlie understood that "pinochos" were relationships with women outside the boundaries of the lifestyle he led at night, who could threaten or delay his intention to go to rehab. He was so emotionally weak. Not that prostitutes or junkies were any less of a threat, but I connected them with the illness, the addiction; or at least I'd told myself not to be affected as much by them. However with the pinochos, even if I had tried, eventually I would not have been able to avoid that emotional frustration. Nor should I try dealing with such frankly, but I probably would. Anyway, he crossed the boundaries with a prostitute* and played me by making it personal. Now she's a "pinocho" too. How can I compete with a 25 year old whose profession is prostitution? She's ready for him whenever he wants her. She knows how to satisfy him sexually, more than I do. She does coke with him and she survives on his income. She calls him, they exchange text messages and when he's having a craving his first instinct is to find her, not me. Plus prostitution itself, an attractive psychological dimension of competition for him to win her from other clients. Her profession keeps him unsure that he has her. So he keeps hunting until he wins kind of thing. While now there is no longer even the professional barrier between them because they go out beyond that parameter. When he walks into the club he enjoys the fact that other clients notice her openly looking for him. His ego is big. Immature and big. Moreover, because of the economic exchange he thinks it's all under control, which it is not. Like the cocaine, he lost control allowing himself to open up to her, and making himself vulnerable, thinking that the money would protect all that. He just goes deeper and deeper into that well; whatever. Though, more specifically to your question: he left the door wide open with enough hidden excuses to see her again. Never cut the ties or gave her any clear signals that he does not want her in his life. In order to see her again he'll use the ring that he never requested back from her. That he says she took from him – yea right, like he couldn't really get it back?... Bull shit, he never told her not to communicate with him beyond the professional limit. His subconscious sense of formality and propriety still wants to see her; maybe a need to help her in order to make things right for himself; an excuse to tell her that "even though she is a prostitute she is a good person" sort of thing. Be warm to her because he led her on too. He did like her and wouldn't even admit it to himself. In honesty, he might have lived with her if she had not been a prostitute. I am sure it crossed his mind. Whatever, it all kind of makes me sick. Yet, I don't think his psychological chip is unique here: works in the minds of all kinds of insecure people. Basically he never highlighted any borders *with her. Once, while we were having dinner, only a day after I had returned from being away for a week, she sent him a text message. He did not reply to it. If he had really been worried about me, or the frailty of us, he could have replied in various ways letting her know that her message was out of order. That he is with somebody or is with me, or simply "don't send me personal messages." When I asked him about it – out of "deference" to me, I said using one of his words, he answered that by not replying she would not know whether or not he'd got the message. Wrong of course. It just kept their door of communication open. Besides it was about me, not him or her. One who really cares about not losing something would do anything to safeguard the frailty of it. He seemed to protect her and that lifestyle more than this one. So in answer to your question, it would be hard to go back with him. I would have to see in person specific actions by him. How much does he really want to survive and get better? I wonder because Charlie gets bored with life easily. The mundane of relationships which I savour as just quality presence he fights because of his own personal feeling of lost time. His mind wanders and instead of being creative and impulsive with his real life, he takes the easy route backwards... No. I think Charlie's solution is always avoidance and that does not work. He allows himself to be manipulated into unwanted situations as a way to avoid the brunt of responsibility from a decision that could be ineffective or cause one to suffer if it failed to satisfy its purpose. Possibly by reason of the social environment he has been exposed to, Charlie himself has been made sensitive to its precedent for an unwarranted level of demoralising characteristics; be they verbal or insinuated. Tough. Constructive confrontation with people especially with himself, is a difficult tool for anyone to master. So he'll need to work on that before he can return home, because I think he'll need to do a lot of that when he gets back.'*

> Well the men come in these places, and the men are all the same
> You don't look at their faces, you don't ask their names
> You don't think of them as human, you don't think of them at all
> You keep your mind on the money, keeping your eyes on the wall
> I want to make a million dollars; I want to live out by the sea
> Have a husband and some children, yeah I guess I want a family
> I'm your private dancer, a dancer for money
> I'll do what you want me to do, any old music will do.
> 'PRIVATE DANCER' – TINA TURNER, LYRICS ADAPTED

Lady Veela

Found Lady Veela. Wasn't too hard. Down in C'an Colom. It was closed. I called around 6a.m. and a rather tired or stoned Andalusian voice said that it was closed. It opens at 11p.m. and closes at 6a.m. This is where Charlie goes to find "V" – Vanesa, the prostitute from Romania. Whatever. I will know who she is one day soon, and then what will be the point? The ring. Ha, an excuse I guess. I want the ring back. Not even mine to ask for. My imagination sees me talking to her and giving her money to get better and get a new life. She asks: 'Why?' and I tell her because she is screwing up her life and that of others. It's good for her, and it's good for me in a way although it does not solve the Charlie problem because he can do it again with another. Another thought: *if he is telling the truth that she actually took the ring from him, then the fact that he did not ask for it back can also play her. She will always have that lingering knowledge that he did not in fact give it to her and therefore disrupt her fantasy about them?* That's what I trumped up while I was driving my car. '*Thanks for the car.*' Then it occurred to me. Maybe, just maybe, Charlie does see more than I do? That perhaps he does not look for me when he is "buzzed", in order to avoid relating the coke to me; to in fact protect "us" and any future possibilities..? If he got better one day he would have to be with me without it – and he knows that? It would be important for him to enjoy me or relate to me without it? O.K. nice thought. However, I know that he sees her even before he does lines, or maybe even without them? Truth be told, I am not sure about the latter. Who cares anyway, and why do I?! Because like my horoscope actually said: "Like it or not, he does matter to you. Have faith." Great. ¡Una locura! (Crazy!) Really. 7:08a.m., am going to walk Dasha now...

.. Back. It would be nice to believe that Charlie in fact has control over all of this. That is to say the prostitute thing. He says that he does. However, the facts don't correlate with *his* truth. He has known her since before he met me. The cocaine won't let him go and now automatically relates his memory to her too. He sent her text messages even while he was with me. In fact they have developed a pseudo "underground relationship" with each other. Still he did casually say once, that she could be a bit "pesada" or a pain because whenever he enters Veela's she goes over to see him. I imagined ... *Charlie at a table with one or more dancers and she comes over like a Siamese cat wanting his attention. Instead of telling her to lay-off he enjoys the attention like a proud rooster. Is he so weak? I see myself asking him: '¿Tan debil? Un payaso disfrazado como un gallo feo... ¡Pero un gallo realmente feo! (Are you so weak? You're just a clown dressed up like a rooster and a real ugly one too!)' Then more Siamese cats surround him, causing her to hover more closely too, because her own kind are now a threat to her and her salary but more importantly, a threat of losing his desire for her; that false sense of emotional possession that she thought he felt for her. Indeed he does, but not the way that she would like. It's about the other clients watching, not about her as his true choice. He enjoys how she will react when he finally chooses her and frankly really just loves the emotional upper-hand in this...* That is until I come along and underline the fact that she is in fact the one in control of their relationship. She is insecure of course. Prostitution is all about that. Most likely due to some kind of a psychological stigma related to falling short of people's expectations, such as a father's or an influential person, which indirectly fuels a need to experiment but turns into a living... It's a theory, but back to the point. What if Charlie really was in control? What if someone could just shed some light on his heart? If in fact it was holding or reserving a love or feelings for me or maybe even buried ones for his wife, thus explaining the real need for prostitutes and the coke. His desire to avoid feelings because they are related to some level of emotional suffering? Wouldn't that alone alleviate so much, for all of us? Knowing the truth? Charlie told me one day after a coke binge, while going through one of his angry stages, that I really know nothing at all. That I really do not understand it all, at all. I thought, he is probably right to a great extent. Just like he manages to create the biggest *películas* that are exaggerations of the truth about me, I probably conjure up the same theatrics about him and my fears about him being with V… and I am not even influenced by cocaine. Who's really hallucinating? Then, my imagination goes wild again because I'm sure when he buys the stuff, he shares it with her. So who's the bad one then? Yuck. His conscious from that world would be a hard monkey to knock off in rehab, if he gets there. In the meantime that lifestyle seems to provoke feelings of sympathy and guilt from him, for her … just more ammunition for the vicious wheel to continue… Just can't win.

"Mothers are the factories of chauvinist ideology; we've raised them (men) to need us like a bunch of puppets on a string."
[*"Las madres son la fábrica de la ideología machista…*
Hemos criado una panda de comodones para que nos necesiten"]
'MUJER HOY' – EXCERPT SEPTEMBER 2005

Co-addiction or Love

Not sure where to begin now. I've been acting a little obsessive lately. Basically because Charlie has been ignoring me or just not getting in touch with me like he used to. I probably shouldn't take it personally and understand that it's about the heavy increase of coke that he has been taking in the last two weeks. I should just not think.

Wouldn't that be great? ... The prostitute has become a thing for me. Almost like I need to (hopefully) prove myself wrong and discover that he has been telling me the truth. That is it really. That thought of them being together disturbs me. I actually need to snuff-out this obsessive thinking by finding it. Seeing them together as a means to prove that I am right so that I can take the *drastic* measures needed without doubt. It's all about doubt. Usually my instincts are true even with the minimal amount of proof, but I hold on because I wonder how much of it is coke or how much of it is that he just doesn't care for me at all. Seriously though, he came on to me. He insisted on classes, and now that I am down and vulnerable? Sigh. He might see her tonight, but I have no gas in my car to get there. I was there last night. Went to Lady Veela's. Parked my car out of sight which made me laugh in spite of myself because unless Big Bird walked by I couldn't have hid the yellow car if I'd tried.

    I did not discover who V is nor did I see them together. Conjured up all sorts of mischievous ways to find out who she was, but in the end all that I could do, was call the club on behalf of a "friend" who wanted to know if she was working. Really, the easiest thing to do would be to call her directly after Charlie goes to rehab – if he goes. I would like to get his ring back from her. He says that by not asking for it back, makes it worthless. Whereas I think she feels that he gave it to her. Something tells me that he probably did, even though he says that she *took* it from him. Yea right. I want to catch them in the act and I think how stupid that I am. The thing is too – so what? So what if he has gone beyond the borders and now has a relationship that he desires with her because she is easier... so what? He can have her. I am just indignant that he never tried with me. Just want out. I want to make money and get out. Rub out any hint of hope or potential with him – stop seeing possibility. Just stop. WHY DID YOU LET HIM COME TO ME? Just for the car? So hard to believe. Help me. This sensation of rejection is horrible. When I think that I have the upper hand I never do. I've done everything that I can for him. Soon we will have to go to Seville – will he call me…What? He's waiting for me right? Spanish men? Spanish women! I read an article written by a male Spanish philosopher, who expressed that to him, "Spain is one of the least romantic countries" that he knew. That, "the Spanish strong sense of reality makes anything remotely romantic sound ridiculous. The stereotype that Spanish men are childish and robotic is true, while they maintain their adolescent behaviour and develop less. The woman relates more to joys and suffering. A man falls in love and gives up nothing, while a woman gives up everything: work, friends, family anything that limits her relationship with him."

After I'd read that, I reflected upon those traditional cultures that for a long time have appeared to be patriarchal societies, but in fact in a very discrete subtle way, like the way a cat walks without making a sound, are matriarchal in structure. Who in the end has played the key role in the man's life? Who, out of too much love and protection has inadvertently harmed the ability of men to think for themselves and act freely without a sense of guilt or being incorrect all the time? In essence rendered their boys ill-equipped and without the spiritual tools to handle and face the anxieties of adulthood because they were sheltered so much, as boys? The impending arrival of new economies and social dynamics are changing all that of course, and not necessarily for the better. In the meantime, I understood that Charlie was conditioned in such a way that taught him to expect the woman to initiate and maintain the guidelines of a relationship but too, he could ignore them like a boy who knows that he has the security of his mother's continued love and forgiveness… So, I sent him a sms while murmuring to myself: fuck, fuck, fuck.

> There's nothing you can do
> That can't be done
> No one you can save
> That can't be saved
> But you can learn how to be in time
> It's easy
> Nothing you can see
> That isn't shown
> Nowhere you can be
> That isn't where you're meant to be
> It's easy
> All you need is love
> Love is all you need.
> 'ALL YOU NEED IS LOVE' – BEATLES, LENNON/McCARTNEY
> LYRICS ADAPTED

The Plan

We arrived here in October. The idea at the time was to move into the new place. Get settled with Dasha. We'd just arrived from the long journey across the great puddle via planes and automobiles. Jes' death was almost a year old. It was hoped to have some introspective time while I waited for my things from Canada to arrive. Then find a car. I'd never owned a car before so if possible the one that I wanted or had literally envisioned was a Mini. Then back-asswards find the money to get it. Then unpack my things and go through all of that before focusing on getting a job. With Christmas in the middle I had hoped to get my stuff by February and be into a work related project by mid-February, early March. I just wanted an emotionally free mind-set to get going. Now my stuff won't arrive until tomorrow March 14th!? I am not working but seem to be onto something – I hope. So in retrospect I am about fifteen to twenty-one days behind my personal schedule and too, the foggy outline of how I wanted to live out here, seems to be coming into focus. That is to say that I'd had a lurking hope that Dasha my Golden Retriever, could be near or with me at work; something that maybe I could do at home? Live in a place, that would offer her a "terrace as nice as the one she used to know in Sichus, near the sea for her and the country for me; an arm's length from my past with Jes, and new enough to be a completely different beginning." There were a lot of requirements indeed. I'd listed several life plan possibilities before I'd decided on Mayürqa again or even got here. In one of my journals somewhere, I recall jotting down a silly wish to Life that was about a new home with my things finally unpacked. I even saw myself in a Mini with Dasha?! My work, money and then love. I realised that it would have to be in that order too. That I would need 2004 to close the door on my past and get ready for 2005's new beginning. Plant the seeds per se in 2005 in order to work the results in the years that followed from 2006 to 2008. Then possibly reap from them by 2009 and feel centered completely by 2010. It was a mock plan to give me direction. Heck, the Japanese sometimes make forecasts as far as ten years down the road. Anyway, all pretty good except maybe for Charlie's presence in my life. He literally walked into it only a week or two after having arrived here. He was looking for an English teacher and Elisabet, the owner of my flat, told him about me. Even though I did underline that "I was not interested in giving classes, at least not until my English stuff had arrived." Regardless, he came to me one late evening. I was already in my pyjamas, hair up in a knot and cream on my face when he saw me. He must have been amused. I just played it cool, although I did notice later that my heart was pounding. He was wearing a blue and white striped French polo. I hadn't really noticed his attractiveness then. In fact what had made my heart leap was the manner in which he'd found his stance once he'd left the final step to the porch. With a mini book-pad in his left hand, tucked tightly under his left armpit, he sort of clicked his heels together and with an eager but slightly nervous look, offered a crisp: 'Holà.' It was my dad in an art form. I'd even thought that he looked a bit like him when dad had shaved his head during his un-well days. Well, whatever the reasons were, bells went off in my head: I was attracted to him. He looked at me directly and intensely when we spoke. He has that talent. '*Oh God,*' I'd thought, '*not a cocaine addict? What test is this now? One of learn from the past and reject it? Or learn from past preparation with daddies, and Jes' cause he's meant to be yours?*' Then my heart leaped again. I remembered what I'd written in my journal just months before: "That after Jes' death I felt satiated. After travelling so far, maybe he would be the last beautiful experience..." and "having Dasha would keep it real."

If my other half was out there, then he would "have to find me now." I could not believe it. Once it was Jes and then I was getting a cocaine addict? Great. Instantly my thoughts went cosmic and all that came to me was a real hope that my presence in Charlie's life would help him make a change or get better? *'Please,'* I could hear my voice whispering, *'even if he can't be with me anymore because of it; please could I at least be a positive effect on him and not a bad one?'*... With just one encounter, *ALL* of that, came to me only *seconds* after Charlie had left! – Really. Soon after, things began from there. I'd quietly hoped that if or by the time he got to rehab, I would have introduced him to almost everything that he had talked about or said he desired in a life without cocaine. Once he was aware of the realities in both worlds, he could choose. Albeit he never seems to give enough time or effort for the new possibilities to have an existing effect. I remembered Jes, and I still don't know. Then again, Jes had a twin brother who died that also influenced the equation of his destiny. Still, I am not about to judge. As long as Charlie continues to respect me, I don't care. So following that first introduction, we did the English classes at my place, when he was attracted to the innocence and novelty of me. Now I guess that I know too much about him and am no longer a novelty because we don't do classes at my place anymore, if at all. Ironically my mother recently sent me an email in reply to one of my blurbs about Charlie, using her own words and a few famous quotes summing up well, what needed reminding: "Misery breeds misery. People with addictions, emotional troubles will try to bring you down with them. When they realise that they can't, then they become face to face with their issue and inadvertently withdraw from those they love or who love them. They can't be helped." That, "Confucius says to "seek out and learn from those who are equal or greater than you"." ...The five words, "they can't be helped", hit my ego and echoed in my head. It's true of course. Then again, this is true for all living creatures. One can only *save* oneself, but "man is not an island" per se and according to many philosophies, we are all connected by the ambiguities of life and energy. The virtue of trying enough to offer someone the tools needed in order to make it possible for that someone to help him or herself, is also what keeps this world upside up. Then I concluded with my own observations that some of the more courageous or best people are those with addictions. That is why they are addicts. It does not have to be under the guise of drugs or alcohol. It's about anxiety levels or an emotional blank that needs to be filled. Some do sports, some are workaholics, caretakers, others drink coffee... Whatever the quirk, my mind manages to find logic and then a level of comfort, primarily with men, from the unfeigned truth they live by. I don't trust women as often as men. Rarely do they tell it like it is. Men on the other hand are usually more direct. It can hurt, but you always know where you stand and they're often loyal friends. Hence my closest female friends, metaphorically speaking, tend to be male cats. Sigh. It was unfair of course because Life knows who I am and where I come from: Michèle Teresa Fang Short, born in Toronto and raised in Montreal Canada. A lot can be understood by the influence of my parents on my life, especially that of my dad's. My name alone if analysed, was enough to defend anyone's belief in destiny. The French name Michèle is derived from Latin's Michael as in archangel Michael, Teresa, is erroneously spelt in Spanish on my birth certificate – or isn't it? "Fang" was bestowed to me for the two that support my smile and is symbolic of the Wolf Totem. "Short" in Mayürqan is pronounced "Sort" and means "luck" or spelt "s'hort" means "an orchard". I even went as far as to include the fact that the name Michèle transcends directly into the foreign languages that I speak while my surname is an apostrophe away from being Catalan, the official language of where I currently live. Finally the letter "M" in my name stands strongly on two legs, is stoic and unmoving like two mountains or undulating and calm like hills. It's also versatile as the only letter with a *twin* that can assume a role upside down and become the open minded "W"... That was enough for me. Whether it was merely me manipulating me, or the desire not to let go, I decided to call Charlie.

If you want to be afraid, just be afraid
If you want to be alone, just be alone
If you want to watch the sea, just watch the sea
And If you want to give a kiss, just give a kiss
If you want to fall in love, just fall in love
If you want to throw a fit, just throw a fit
If you want to weoh, weoh! Just weoh, weoh!
But do it NOW! – Timing is the answer
If you don't know where to go, and if you don't know what to say
And if you don't know what to do
Just, do it now.
'TIMING' – KEVIN JOHANSEN, LYRICS ADAPTED

The Kiss

The ball started to bounce. Of course at the beginning, I still had the serve. He asked if he could join me for coffees. Later, I see now, that I was good therapy for him. I had enough perception to hold a conversation with him about his demons. Being fresh to the situation he shared a lot with me. Later on, I interpreted that as a privilege, and suffered from it when he took it away. Still, I remained cool. He would send me a message if he could not make the get-together, and I could reply "O.K." with indifference. A neutral response that even then, I'd anticipated losing, but decided to dismiss the concern. 'Fear is no object,' I told myself. Looking back maybe it was not fear rather my instincts trying to tell me to be cautious. Dunno. Just don't know. At the time I was a female friend and really that is the way it should have stayed. One day, I went to pick him up at his place and he was a mess. I had not realised then how badly he had returned to the coke. I still thought it was just a small relapse. Anyway, we took off in his car to his restaurant for lunch. While he drove frantically, I could not help but be impressed at how easily he could drive a family sports van between the narrow stone hedges that often line Mayürqa's country roads. Then he began telling me about the day before. He had been at a therapy session in Menorca, and the group had shunned him for being "active" again. This revelation caught my breath slightly. Then all at once he suddenly let out an anguished groan followed by a run of tears that escaped from behind his shades and streaked their way down his cheeks. I looked for tissue, took some from the passenger door and handed it to him. He wiped the tears and muck from his face – apologised for the reaction … I made him stop the car. Using "Spanglish", words in Spanish and in English, I asked him if he knew what a "hug" was. Even a question was too much for him. Confused, I just hugged him. I had not understood then, as he had, the impact of this relapse. It meant that he was not better and falling backwards again. Later on I discovered that it was probably better that he had been rejected from that group because the group leader actually allowed Charlie's wife to attend their sessions? '*Gees*,' I thought presumably, '*she doesn't even have an addiction; just lives off of Charlie's emotional instability as her main source of self-preservation.*' Anyway, within a short time these simple moments of coffees, car rides and classes evolved into him asking me out for Chinese. Bells again. Can I drink alcohol with him? Is it ok that he does? Not my issue? He knows if he should or shouldn't – no? So, I said, 'vale (okay).' Then that led to a Van Morrison concert in Palma, and the night when he asked me for the kiss. He'd driven me back to my place and I had just given him the customary two Spanish kisses to say good night, when he let out; 'I want to give you a kiss.' My hand froze on the door lever. Sitting in his car a million contradicting thoughts went through my head. What do I do? If I said no, then he would lose his confidence or feel ridiculous. Like: 'Why would a chick like her want to be with a cocaine addict?' If I allowed the kiss, then we would cross a line that would not only lose the natural dynamic of our friendship, but I would lose the serve. I had not expected the request. Had I not felt pressed, I would have formulated an answer that would have avoided the kiss and allowed him to keep his sense of dignity and our friendship. Simply, the question had caught me by surprise. He focused on me with his intense look and already it seemed that five seconds might have been too long. So, I replied: 'Okay.' It was a quick kiss because I too desired him, but my gut said: 'No, don't – too soon and too easy for him.' The gut was right. I should have said, 'not yet' or something. He even sent me a sms right after saying, "it was good but too quick." Plus too, had I known about V, it would have been easier to control my desire. Bla, bla, bla. Then Christmas and New Year's came. He made efforts to be with his family and partake in get-togethers, only if I was involved. He wanted to be near me like I was his. (*When did that feeling go away? Was it a natural ebb or was it the cocaine?*) He seemed comfortable and attentive only to me. Even Elisabet noted how concerned he seemed about me; cutting my food at meals and speaking on my behalf like he was the only one who really knew me. There was never any expression of his feelings, but there was a hint of something. Then because of our English conversations, I bought him a trip to Paris for a day. I made it a day because I really wanted it to be a birthday gift for him without other obligations, but he changed that to a weekend with the understanding that he would pay for the extra days that I could not afford. In the aftermath, I did end up paying for it on my Visa. I wondered if Charlie had done that to test me? Money was a delicate commodity in our friendship. People, wanted money from him and I wanted to be unique from this; it avoided sentimental accountability. As a result, he'd actually assumed that I had money and was not about to be *used* by me. So on our check-out from the hotel, he didn't have any cash on him; even though he knew that I hadn't wanted to put charges on my card. He of course, like many of his flock, does not own a Visa card. My reaction to the situation however, was enough to show him that his way of testing his suspicion about me was an erroneous assumption and inadvertently hurt me. My unconditional friendship would later provoke a level of confusion and guilt from within him, too difficult for him to grasp. A month later the cocaine would increase his concerns of hurting me and feelings of indebtedness towards me that he began looking for ways to pay me back. He remembered about the hotel and I told him not to worry about it. He had in essence, paid me back through the many meals and events we had attended together during the months that we were together. In hindsight, we had a great time in Paris. At least I did. He seemed so relaxed and well with me. Only upon returning to Mayūrqa did the "cocaine bells" go off. Basically a memory call to the brain about cocaine that is easily tripped by people and places such as his wife, son, work, anxiety from unresolved issues or anything that stimulates the senses that can provoke the emotional craving. After Paris we even tried having him stay at my place as a way to separate him from the "bells". Looking back his intention was probably just the effect from having been clean from the coke for over a week. Yes, he had some intelligibility and felt better after only a week but even then, cocaine addicts are not realistic neither with themselves nor others for that matter. Had I known this fact then, I would have been more cautious to translate his efforts as intentions only. Anyway, I was going to be his buddy for a month. He needed at least a month to detoxify in order to make further efforts feasible. Now of course I know more. It's not the cocaine. Charlie needs heart therapy. This is where the cocaine is hurting him. He can't think clearly or sort-out his feelings. He is very unsure – a life of emotional and physical turmoil. Funny, I feel the same sometimes and I don't even do drugs. We managed a month and barely ended the challenge well. I almost lost his regard for me completely. During my efforts to dissuade his need to satisfy his cravings, he began to lose his trust in me. 'Never has a woman spent so much time in this car,' he'd tossed dryly at me. Then he would tell me that distance was needed between us, in order to allow the possibility of trying to develop something further together to exist. He did not want to jeopardize that. That if it weren't for the "situation that surrounded" him, with time he said that we could get to know ourselves better – that we could probably "share a good lifestyle and sexual compatibility". He spoke about so much. I remember the cinema in Namacor, where I impulsively sat on his lap facing him and kissed him, the church road where nature heard our call, my couch, his bed and mine where we fooled around. Does he? Does it even matter? Does he confuse the physical intimacy with me and the prostitute, then get turned off by me? Does my appreciation for him make him feel worse because he does not like himself? Carles doesn't feel emotionally abused by a prostitute but does by one who wishes to be with him. Like paying a fee is the only kind of abuse that justifies why the prostitute is with him; or does the fee relieve the emotional obligation that he might feel, if the intimacy from a woman appeared to be real? Sigh. Truth be told, we were wrong to get physical. I was wrong to let it happen and even offer it. He needs a female friend for at least a year before anything physically intimate can evolve. The vicious trap, however, is that even if Charlie encounters a woman worthy of such a sacrifice there is still risk that her presence could evoke sexual frustration between them. Thus it would influence Charlie back to his comfort zone with prostitutes, and/or back to the coke, and therefore cause his partner despite herself, to find a need for another man because of Charlie's erroneous belief that he is unable to satisfy her the way *he feels* he should. It is a relationship that would require a lot of trust and communication. Hard. When the root of Charlie's addiction stems predominantly from an emotional and sexual void inherent from his relationship with his wife and a fear of falling under what I would call *the female spell*: something that could lead a man to homosexuality, but is vexed by his biochemical preference for women. Like a type of sexual stigma that never really allows him to find love. That, compounded by a difficulty to manage commitments and/or any sensation of obligation perceived by Charlie makes him retreat. In short, the addiction is a shrew. Then considering that people who seek regular therapy generally require a long period of time before managing results on their own, imagine how much harder it is for a drug addict? Multiply that with growing up on an island, in a village where coolly berating one another is an act of love and folkloric tales and stories consist of demons and saints while anything remotely romantic and/or sentimental borders on a sense of ridicule and weakness... Hmm. Anyone in the medical profession will tell you that the odds of a full recovery by a cocaine addict are very very low. A complete change of lifestyle is required. Therefore, even after a year there is no guarantee that a relationship can exist let alone survive... Then again, isn't that true for any relationship?

Life shrinks and expands in proportion to one's courage – ANAIS NIN.

A gift to Mi

My birthday is January 28th. Charlie and I had been doing the buddy thing since January 9th. On the 27th, Elisabet was kind enough to organise a surprise birthday dinner. Charlie and I had gone to a film and rather than have dinner there, we decided to just head home. I had not really suspected anything until we got into his car. He drove so slowly and so closely to the lane's outer white line that even the electrical tin cans that are presumably cars, were passing us; I thought he'd done a few lines for sure. He drove us to Alcudia from Maratxi which is a simple forty minute drive out of the way. Truth be told though, I really enjoyed the ride with him. Then once we got to C'an Colom, Charlie headed us home to Sa Ema. Before we got there Charlie had called Belle. It had been close to 10p.m. when he'd called to say that we had not eaten and were stopping by. I thought, '*Wow, talk about abusing family rights.*' When I discovered later, that it had been the call to let her know that we were arriving, I was reminded instantly of Socrates in his *Apology* where he says: "Is not this ignorance of a disgraceful sort, the ignorance which is the conceit that man knows what he does not know?" I remained humble for a few days after that. The surprise birthday dinner was very nice. Belle made a super meal and a determined effort to get me a cake and ice cream too; something very unlikely if at all common in Mayürqan culture. Notwithstanding, although Elisabet's actions were sincerely generous, events further along the way would redefine them as an instinctual interest to maintain Charlie's respect and affirmation by pleasing me, the woman towards whom he'd suddenly shifted all his interest. Some cats will openly hiss at a new feline when the males' attention shifts to her. While others will seek affirmation and attention by performing tricks and using the new feline as a means to regain the males' attention – especially the ones done with generosity. I don't doubt that the events during that time were sincere. Elisabet and Mitx simply acted in their altruism without recognising the full nature of its cause and effect. Mitx', was logically rooted in the interests of his brother's health and his family's alleviation from it, while Elisabet's was rooted in graceful social conduct, her affection for her brother in-law and her need as a caretaker to maintain Charlie's dependency on her. Such that months later the traditional root of the culture would rudely reveal its inability to maintain friendships well, by virtue of its traditional emphasis on the family clan. They in fact were and remained oblivious to it all, while I went through major character building trying to adapt to what I felt were the imbedded Arab whims of the culture. During those months, Garfield and Odie suddenly highlighted new undercurrents for me while I sided with the dog. In its simple form, it was the first time in a very long time, that I truly felt a sense of belonging that could be my own. It would be the first time ever, that I experienced all a once, to be next to a man that appeared to want me and whom I was very happy to be with, and whose family too, was an added gift. I felt located for the first time in my life which is probably why events down the road would affect me all the more. In hindsight, that night's dinner turned into a bigger blessing the next day, when it was my birthday. On that day I spent my night from 6p.m. until 3a.m. at Charlie's, wanting him to sleep so that he might get past the crucial hours of his craving without him heading out into the night to meet it. The buddy idea was to keep him off the cocaine for a month in order for him to detoxify and regain enough coherence to make decisions intended for proper rehab on his own. It included his willingness to give me his car keys when we were home, change his phone number, and even accompany him to pay for a "charly" (cocaine) debt of 300 euros to some gypsies who ran a coke house in a remote location of Namacor. Both the emotional and psychological stages that we went through were interesting to say the least. We only managed to stay clean for eleven days, but life through this was far from dull – that's for sure. My days with him were long. The mornings were the easiest: I'd get up for Dasha and do our walk and coffee thing. Then I would check my emails and such, then send a wake up message to Charlie by sms. I'd walk over to his place where he'd get up to let me in. He was usually in a T-shirt and boxer short underwear, then back to bed he would go. Always very patient and kind to me. Once he said that I was the "perturber of dreams", but I actually enjoyed his little comments. They contained affection. Finally when he would get up, we would head out for a coffee and then the gym. It was hard for him, but he managed to get up. A cocaine addict who intakes the quantities that Charlie has would find it impossible to get up at 10a.m. let alone to get up and open the door for someone. He and Jesy often made me think about me. The slightest discomfort in my body and I am just not a happy camper. At the gym he would exercise a bit and do the sauna. After our work-out we'd have a fresh orange juice and head to his restaurant for lunch. While he would over-see things there, I'd sit in one of the Mayürqan rocking chairs that are located at the front of the restaurant, enjoying the atmosphere, chatting with clients, or often just going over my agenda and things to do. By 3p.m. or so, he would pop up and give me the signal for lunch. We usually sat together at the same corner table from where Charlie could watch the activity in the restaurant and have lunch, which always consisted of at least one "paella" dish. Following that, we'd visit his mum at which time I never got out of the car. I'd made a decision to myself not to go into that territory yet. I would just wait for him. He was never too long; just enough to say hello, eat something and offer his mum some relief from the worries she had about him. At 5p.m. until 3a.m. was when my *work* with him would really kick in. If there weren't any chores to manage, like going to the cleaners etc., we'd head back to Sa Ema and hang out at his place with him on the couch and me in the chair. Sometimes he would sleep, or watch TV or go for a walk. The restlessness and craving would kick in around 7p.m. The cocaine house opened from 5p.m. until 3a.m. the following day, so that I had to find ways to keep him detained until 2a.m. at least.

So there I was on my birthday. He was antsy and moody. He would go from the couch to the bed in hourly intervals. Watch his porno videos. It was cold that night and I was very tired. By 11 p.m. we were still at his place, so I lay on the extra bed in the guest room while he battled between himself and his desire to go out. Then he went to bed and I listened for his deep breathing. It never came. After half an hour he got up and went back to the couch. The anxiety of this was beginning to get to me. A sinking feeling of déjà vu came to me. How many times had I done something like this before? Finally my thoughts were interrupted when he at last went to his room again, but this time he closed his door completely. I was alerted by this. Then I heard a bang! I was up like a lightning bolt, got to his door and knocked while quietly asking at the same time: 'Charlie are you there?' The control between getting there in a flash then trying to sound calm and soothing was not an easy one to manage; my heart was already at warp speed six. There was no reply. My heart sank at the same time as my adrenaline soared. I opened his bedroom door and saw that his window was open. '*Oh no!*' I thought. I did not know whether to quickly run out after him or to take the extra seconds to check the bathroom. I checked the bathroom and he wasn't there. So I headed like mad to the front door, acutely aware of the loud sound of my boots' heels against the linoleum floor and ran outside! I expected to see his car gone, but it was still parked!?! – It had been a trick. Anger mixed with fatigue and sheer bewilderment at myself for even having that moment just baffled me. I was so tired and still breathing fast from the adrenalin. When I got back to the front door I had to knock to get back in.

Charlie opened it and went to the couch. He was fully dressed, shoes on too. I did not know whether to laugh or to cry? He had such a cute smirk on his face. It really was a twelve year old boy smoking a cigarette in front of me. Still huffing and puffing from the run I asked: 'Charlie! What did you *do*?! – Why?!' The mere intonation of my voice and my choice of basic vocabulary was hysterical. I wasn't sure if I'd spoken that way because I was too baffled to think in Spanish or because I wanted him to sense that I was not mad by speaking at an English level that he could understand. He had not in fact left the house; he was just testing me and wanting to see my reaction. The rerun of it all in my head was in fact quite funny. However underneath it all I could see that this was way over my head. In retrospect he was the joker who played me. I turned on my heels, walked back to the guest room and laid down again. It was close to 1a.m. by the time he finally went to bed. The relief I felt from hearing him sleep released tears to pierce from my eyes. It was my birthday. Bells went off in my head again: '*A Jesy syndrome repeated? What am I doing here and why do I not go home? Charlie with or without the cocaine would always be better off than me. He has his roots, his business, his friends and family all around him, but, but, he is ill, and tonight's episode was the cocaine reaction...*' I felt the need to stay because I really wanted him to have a second chance. Charlie could do it. The life we talked about and the one he wanted were reachable for him. Again I reminded myself that he was ill; or was it more than that? To be steadfast and loyal were qualities inherited from the ancestors of my British and German background. I was not only conditioned by them, but circumstances during my childhood would develop them into a natural instinct that could be called upon instantly. In my mind's eye they are great warrior's tools. Psychiatry however would call it obsessive disorder or co-addiction. Maybe. It was not called that in the days that soldiers stood by their leaders, neither when Sancho followed Don Quixote into his travels, nor is it labelled this way when parents put all their energies into their children. In these examples it is called love: an urge so deep and so strong that keeps you where you are despite yourself, so selflessly and determinedly. Its essence becomes a stamina equal to the power of a hundred horses. Like a real warrior you just battle-on in the name of love. A kind of gratifying profession that is so powerful to make you live and want to get up every morning, because its purpose is for another and its virtue for oneself. While no one's effort is ever guaranteed a return of greater or equal value, if at all. If I had a degree in social services there would be no questions. It was the Mayürqan "tan mateix", the "laissez-faire" or "whatever" fatalistic sense of letting things go, which to me would not work this time. Charlie had already lived more than fourteen years as an addict and nobody, not even Charlie, was prompted to do anything about it until the one day when he couldn't get off his couch. The realisation of this astounded me. So many years of his life gone by and no one even tried to convince him otherwise? "Tan mateix, TAN mateix" did not work then. If permitted to repeat itself, Charlie, I told myself, would die before his twelve year old son's thirteenth birthday. But, if I could make a difference in one life, as asinine as it seemed, I would do it. My gut screamed it. Even at the very real risk of losing Charlie from my life, because if we were successful in getting him to rehab, then every day that I would be in his face until then, would make it more difficult for us to be together later. He could go back to his wife, find another, or simply relapse again. In any case I would be forgotten. My ego and all my hope had to digest that for a moment. Then in spite of it all, I stayed there until 3a.m., walked home to poor Dasha, who was alone and slightly stressed by my unusual schedule, then walked her through the cool morning air, faintly noting that on that same day I'd be up again at 7a.m., and one year older. At least things hadn't been boring. When

I finally put my head down on my pillow I realised then, that this entrance to my new year at 38 was a bell in itself: I was in for a roller coaster year. Followed by another truth: I like roller coasters. Their ride, albeit terrific, only lasts an instant in time before you have to get off with at least the wonderful reminder of how good it is to be alive!.. Happy Birthday to me!

La mujer que no te deja indiferente

In a book that Charlie gave me for Christmas he signed it. *"Para Michèle, mujer que no te deja indiferente (To Michèle, woman who doesn't leave you indifferent)."* The dedication pretty much sums up the relationship between Charlie and I from early November until late April: bitter-sweet. The events from the beginning and beyond April are numerous to write about. I have data, but it's all so overwhelming. I really enjoyed Charlie during that time even though he was increasingly *coked* (intoxicated) and debilitating more and more each month. March and April were the bleakest months for both of us. While his cocaine dependency increased so did my involvement in getting him to rehab sooner than later. They were probably the months that my passive attempts to encourage him shifted into active tactics that bordered if not entered the parameters of co-addiction. The initial idea to try the 24/7 buddy system was influenced by a bad relapse he'd had on his 44th birthday. It happened to be the same day that Elisabet and Mitx had organised a lunch for the family and Charlie was supposed to have met his brothers that early morning to go fishing but hadn't shown up. The latter was a bad blow to his brothers who'd allowed themselves to get enthusiastic about the event. Mitx especially deceived himself because he's normally very pragmatic about it all. However Charlie had said the night before that he would go and I too, had offered an unrealistic faith in him that he would. Then he called at six that morning on return from his night out, to say that he wasn't going. He could have gone straight to the boat after his night out but didn't. Up until that point I still had the privilege of being exempt from such disappointments – never letting me down nor failed to meet his commitments to me. At that point too, I was invited, rather expected to attend their lunch. Charlie and I were quite together and it seemed that everyone was quite pleased about it. Anyway, Charlie almost did not make it to the lunch. I went over to his place. He let me in, still showing deference to my text messages and knocks on the door. He was there on the sofa, bottle of whiskey on the floor under a ring of stagnant smoke just hanging in the room like suspended fog in a cemetery. I sat on his chair and we chatted. He still confided in me. Still appreciated my presence. It was not long after that when his mother also came by. At the time it bothered me. I felt that her presence was counterproductive. So I left. Soon after, she came back to the lunch, spoke to Elisabet and then cried. My last attempt was to send him a sms that said: "It's o.k. to come, your family wants you here." About twenty minutes later he came. I was very happy to see him and and when he'd entered the patio area, gave him a kiss on the cheek thinking that it would reassure him. However, the look he gave me was contrary to that hope. He sat at the opposite end of the table and ignored me the whole time. I felt quite embarrassed and hurt. He did not want people to see the affection, even though we had been seen together every day for four months. Either I was being used or he was unable to assimilate our relationship. I was just a friend. I managed to get my heart around it then by the mere fact that he really was coked-out. The psycho-physiological effort alone for him to even be at the table was both tremendous and impressive to me considering the night he had had, and the amount of cocaine he'd consumed. Later I would learn more about the local culture's subtleties in personal relationships. I was "una amiga con derecho a roce" – a friend with "benefits", to be polite. Initially I would feel indignant about this. Nonetheless, he was after all still married and because of that, the title was not really untrue. Anyway, that lunch on January 2nd, was just a hint of things to come. The real emotional adventure would not hit me until after we were parted in April. I was not prepared to be impeded by a third challenge that's own power carried the same motto as mine but with a different life source: blood. Until then, every challenge had just been about the cocaine and the power of addiction, against the power of Mi.

The whisper

It found her one night while she was lying down on his bed. The natural light that comes just before the break of dawn, had seeped into the bedroom through the window's closed shutters. Her face was down on the pillow facing his profile, and while the blue grey light softened the contours of his face her eyes were able to adjust their focus on him. Then in a whisper she asked him: 'Do you want to get better?' 'Of course I do,' he whispered back. 'Then you will.' She paused and then added: 'I'm excited for you and sad.' 'Why!?' he replied slightly higher than a whisper. This time almost inaudibly, she whispered again: 'Because once you are better, you will forget about me.' With that, he turned on his side to face her and with gentle precision, moved a fallen tousle of curls from her eyes and whispered back: 'Nahhhh.'

THE FIRST HALF

This ain't a *story* for the broken-hearted
No silent prayer for the faith-departed
I ain't gonna be just a face in the crowd
You're gonna hear my voice
When I shout it out loud

It's my life
It's now or never
I ain't gonna live forever
I just want to live while I'm alive
My heart is like an open highway
Like Frankie said
I did it *My*way
I just wanna live while I'm alive
It's my life

This is for the ones who stood their ground
For *Charlie* and *Carles* who never backed down
Tomorrow's getting harder make no mistake
Luck ain't even lucky
Got to make your own breaks
Better stand tall when they're calling you out
Don't bend, don't break, baby, don't back down
It's *your* life
And it's now or never
'Cause *You* ain't gonna live forever
I just want you to live while *you're* alive
Your heart is like an open highway
Like Frankie did
Do it *Your*way – I did it *My*way
I just want you to live while *I'm* alive
'Cause it's *My* life!

'IT'S MY LIFE – BON JOVI, LYRICS ADAPTED

PART I

MYSTRO MEDIATION

Maestro
Teacher, conductor
Mediation
Involving an intermediary without direct connection
Acting as go-between or peace maker
Coming between two in time, place and character.

POCKET OXFORD DICTIONARY

> One
> Doesn't
> Discover
> New lands
> Without
> Consenting
> To lose sight of the shore
> For a very long time
> ANDRÉ GIDE

The departure

Wednesday October 27th, 2004. 2:30p.m., Frankfurt airport. She started writing in her journal: "Planes, coffee shops and foreign beds". She was there in Frankfurt waiting to board her flight to Mayürqa at 3:15 p.m. Her life, since forever it seemed, had been about "planes, trains and automobiles". How often had she spent time in an airport or between points A and B, when neither A nor B were ever really her own home? Anyway, she was there alone. Like most often was the case. No one would greet her at the airport. Dasha was also travelling with her. They left Canada yesterday and were about to begin their new chapter. "Thank you" she wrote, while murmuring it to herself. It was a message to Life in general. Writing it down made it possible for them, or whatever was out there helping her, see it. She was anxious about returning to Mayürqa especially because she left Canada feeling good about it and the people. Certainly fell in line with the saying: "Go when the going's good". "Canadians are really the best!" she wrote. She'd seen enough of the world to know that it was true. The anxiety was enough to stir up doubt and made her wonder if she should have made a better effort to stay in Canada back in Montreal or somewhere in Ontario? However, they hadn't felt right, and her mum had not been crazy about her staying with her either. She was disappointed about that, but her mum was right. She needed to get back to work and establish her new self again. Plus, it would not have been right either to live at her mum's on free room and board, especially at the age of 37.

So once again, a place was needed to start from, and Mayürqa was going to be it. The area where she was heading to, was all pretty different from where she used to live but just happened to be where Dasha, Jesy and her, had shared their final summer together! Incredible but true. As she wrote in her journal her worries about getting settled began to feel lighter. Her personal things and an income still had to be established, as well as BUYING a car?! Gees. Her dad's birthday would be on November 10th, and she had been quietly asking if the lottery on November 9th, could bring her family enough money to pay their debts and a few needs. The request made her chuckle twice over. *'As if,'* she thought. Although the year before she'd won on a lottery ticket that she'd bought using Jesy's number 3 as a reference. It was 100 euros to be exact. It was obvious, that kind of luck was not going to make her rich. Still again, events since Jes up until the current moment had been very kind to her. It was as though she was being watched or protected even more so than before. That morning before heading to the airport, she and Dasha had taken a final walk along Bobby's Road; a long and narrow gravel stone way hidden off a main road that is tucked between Northern Ontario's deep woods and lakes. It's a place where trees still stand tall and majestic in multitudes. Where nature speaks freely, and where an infinite horizon between land and sky simply humbles man's existence down to being a mere hiccup in the scheme of it. Then her mum had to drive her to Pearson airport because Dasha was not permitted on the bus. Nonetheless the three hours it took to get there offered her a quality moment with her mum. Endorsed by the fact that her mum was going to be able to drive back home with a friend of hers who happened to be flying in from Halifax on the same day. Hence little synchronicities like that one, helped make the move feel right. Check-in, except for Dasha's flying fee of $300, went really smoothly. The new Terminal1 at Pearson airport had a wonderful animal handling for Dasha. There was a holding area for the animals and the owners at the check-in. Plus, if owners and their mascots were travelling through Canada the owners were permitted to see their pet and walk it! She and Dasha were flying with Air Canada via Luftansa which was not only a nice convenience for air miles, but the best way for Dasha to travel. If all went well, then the stop-over in Frankfurt was only going to be a few hours, before continuing on to Mayūrqa. Furthermore Frankfurt, like Toronto, also had a great handling area for the animals to run around in. Water was provided as well as an on-sight vet. Just great. Nothing like the trip from Mayūrqa to Canada the year before, when she had had to stop-over in France and spend the night in the airport hotel with Dasha at an absurd price to accommodate them both. Anyway, she'd find out if Dasha was okay once they got to Mayūrqa. Frankly though, as she sat there in Frankfurt writing, all had gone well up until then, and she was grateful. The flight from Toronto had been great too. After having travelled so much before she could honestly say that Air Canada International had been very pleasant. Even the man, who had sat next to her, and was travelling with a little dog, had been quiet and inoffensive. He had had the aisle seat while she had had the window. They had not chatted at all with only a few polite words exchanged. He'd reminded her of what her granddad would have looked like if he were still alive. Like him, the man had an English accent and didn't seem amused about travelling. The dog, a little Scottish terrier had been in a red sports bag at his feet and offered little leg room for the man. Once the plane had begun to prepare for take-off, she looked out the window thinking about the next few days that would still be unsettling for her and Dasha, but also, somehow, would be fine. The only thing left then, was to get to Mayūrqa and hope that she and Dasha would find each other at the luggage area, get the rental car without too many hassles, and be blessed with safe driving. In the five years that she had lived in Mayūrqa before, she had never driven a car there. It would be the first difference indicating their new beginnings in Mayūrqa. Then to sum up the writing in her journal: "Thank you dad, Jes and U. Thank you for the walk this morning, the breaking of a beautiful day and the safe and good arrival to Toronto. The ability to leave Dasha at mum's for the year I worked, the help with my tickets, my ideas, and my constant requests. I know it can all disappear in an instant. I promise to *let you go* more, once I am fully back on track. Jesy, we're going to Sa Ema de Farrutx. Pretty incredible. Are you still nearby? Let's see how all of this goes for us in January 2005 – Love you!"

Every departure has an arrival – ARAB PROVERB.

Mayūrqa

Lufthansa flight 4561, Frankfurt to Mayūrqa – '*Here we go!*' she thought. '*Goodbye to Canada for a few more years.*' She was starting anew. 2004 was about closure. 2005 would be about planting the seeds. 2006 was perhaps about work and 2007 a balance between love and work. It's a plan? We'll see, we'll see. '*The Japanese would be impressed,*' she thought and smiled to herself while also noticing that the same gentleman that had sat next to her on the flight from Canada to Frankfurt was still with her. He smiled at her. This time however, he had the window seat and she was on the aisle. The Scottish terrier was still at his feet. With a little more chat than the last time, she learned that he had been living in Mayūrqa for twenty years. He lived above Port Andratx and had originally arrived from England. His trip from Canada had begun in Chester, Nova Scotia, 'Lovely people,' he said, 'but the thing with Canada,' he continued, 'is that it has a problem with winters; too cold.' With that she laughed. The nuance of his British accent mixed with his matter of fact attempt at diplomacy was all too familiar to her. Her paternal grandparents had been British. Besides he was right. The chat expanded a bit more until she expressed her hesitation to him about leaving her family behind. The man did not take long to reply. 'Well,' he said, 'you have to live somewhere'. Her heart skipped a beat. Almost as if it were delivered on cue and their whole reason for meeting had been for her. Indeed her journal from a month before highlighted those very same thoughts that had helped her to decide on trying again from Mayūrqa. "I have to start somewhere. I have to live somewhere", she'd written ... She took a moment to take it all in, and then sent Life a mental note of 'Thanks'. Somehow that man next to her had told her that she was heading in the right direction...

Dasha came out on conveyer belt number 10. As the belt whirred around, she did not know whether or not to feel relieved at being off the plane or indignant at still being in her cage for almost fourteen hours. She was anxious. Much like her parents she could look calm and non-pulsed on the outside, while her insides danced with butterflies. *Where was she? Had she done something wrong? In all frankness what the hell was going on?!* Her memory recalled sleeping on warm tiles and her dad's deep voice talking to her with a lot of love, to suddenly finding herself in below zero temperatures, living with a woman who could have been her mum but wasn't, discovering insects and animals bigger than her, to being put back in cages and planes and moved around on conveyer belts again. Then, a sense of familiarity came to her. She knew the place...'Dasha!' she heard, and instantly recognised her mum's voice. Then there, coming towards her with very determined steps was Michèle and Dasha's cue to relax. The look of relief on Michèle's face at finding Dasha was enough to make Dasha want to leap from the cage. Door or no door she so wanted out. Michèle was so relieved to see Dasha's cage on the conveyer belt, that she sent out another note of 'thanks' to Jesy for watching over her because she really felt that he was near. How many times had she done this with Dasha and Jesy before? The thought kind of relaxed her a bit. She remembered the time that the three of them had gone to Galicia. They had a stop-over in Barcelona and Dasha was supposed to come out on conveyer belt number 4 and never did. Jes always played it cool, but his cigarette smoking always gave him away. That, and the fact that he would get to the baggage area before anyone else even seemed to have gotten off the plane. He loved his dog very much. Besides Michèle, Dasha was without a doubt the most important thing in his life. She was the only thing that he could honestly claim as his own, and was simply his first niña (girl). Trotting closer to Dasha on the conveyer belt, Michèle drifted back to that day, *recalling Jesy's very cool but anxious strut, getting him to the luggage conveyer belt in seconds, and making Michèle smile to herself. She was there, talking to the information desk about where the cage might have been, while Jesy was waiting expectantly at the conveyer belt without any sign of Dasha. Despite the calm perception he gave off, he was distressed and doing his best to show otherwise. He was such a sensitive man, affectionate and caring. Physically too, he was also a beautiful man to look at. Athletic and elegant in appearance, but it was the depth within him that moved Michèle the most. He was very good with Dasha too. At the time, Michèle's anxiety levels were less about Dasha and more about him. She could tell by the wrist action in his smoking that he was getting ready to do something regardless of whether or not it was allowed. If Dasha didn't appear soon, it was apparent with increasing intensity that he was getting ready to go through the conveyer belt entrance to find her. Besides too, the three of them still had to check into their connecting flight to Galicia. Finally, as Jesy stomped out his cigarette Dasha came out on the belt. Man and dog were very happy to see each other although neither one of them showed it. With a sudden macho air, Jes grabbed the cage, swiftly swooped it down to the floor from the conveyer belt and let Dasha out.*

He was more indignant about having her in that cage than she was. He was so protective of his girls. She could not hear of course, but she was sure that he was murmuring something to Dasha as he placed the leash around her neck. Then Dasha's merry trot and Jes' cool stride met up with Michèle in silence. It felt so good to be together... The image of the three of them ebbed away as soon as Michèle got to Dasha's cage. With the same swiftness as Jesy, she grabbed the cage, swooped it down to the floor from the conveyer belt, let Dasha out and woman and dog were relieved to be back together again.

When she and Dasha finally got through "Luggage" at Palma, things went well except for a few small details with the rent-a-car that she'd booked. The rental company charged her Visa for eleven days instead of seven. It would get resolved of course. "When?" was a question better avoided, if one did not want an ulcer. That was the way things worked in Mayürqa; always a thin thread of discrepancies to test one's patience. Having just come back from the world of "quick fix" the car trauma was probably a good way to ease back into the island's culture.

That is why this chorus is heard, "long live Spain!"
People sing with ardour, "long live Spain!"
They shall always remember her, "long live Spain!"
[.. Por eso se oye este refrán, que ¡Viva España!
La gente canta con fervor, que ¡Viva España!...
..Y siempre la recordarán que ¡Viva España!]
'Y VIVA ESPAÑA' – EXCERPT FROM ORIGINAL LYRICS

Fresh orange juice

Before heading out to her friends' place, she let Dasha run around on the same grassy spot at the airport where the two of them had been exactly a year earlier. The only difference she noticed was the area had been reduced to half its size by a new parking lot. It all coincided with their arrival. Things would be the same and not.

Fortunately the airport was still a pleasure for her to arrive at: modern, airy, waterfalls, grassy spots, less cement, fewer restrictions and naught advertising. The place promoted nothing less than serenity. She called Xisco and Maribel from her cell phone to let them know that she and Dasha were on their way to their place. Prior to getting there she stopped at the pizzeria next to her friends' place and ordered two pizzas to go. Dasha was greeted and allowed to sit with her in the bar area while they waited for the pizzas to be ready. The owner was Italian from Naples, great and congenial. The restaurant had had a few improvements made since she was there last, but its authentic personality still remained. She fell back into one of her favourite moments and asked for a glass of red wine. The lingering sense of fear that had been with her began to dissipate into a sensation of calmness. She was very happy to be back. Spain's news blared from the TV set that sat on top of a tall oak cabinet. The two young waiters behind the bar had dark hair and smiles that could not go unnoticed. They chatted about Naples, and football and she noted how little elements of her existence were brought together there: the European atmosphere, reminiscent of her childhood in Québec, was her in her element entirely. Her teenage years playing soccer for a city team, the Castilian Spanish she spoke from living in Spain and her experience with Italians from her work on ships all seemed conducive to where she was and where she should be. She missed Jes yet decided that he was there: they would have equally enjoyed the moment; wine, football talk and a dog under the table. Once she and Dasha got to Xisco and Maribel's place they were greeted with smiles and warmth. With the passing years Xisco and Maribel had become her best allies in Mayürqa. She needed that. She was not ready to be alone yet. Francisco was Michèle's friend from way back when she had first arrived to Mayürqa seven years earlier. His name in Catalan is Francesc or Xesc. Michèle met him as Francisco which is the same name in Castilian. However, between the two of them he was Xisco and that never seemed to change. That and the fact that he or Maribel always seemed to have an ailment whenever she met them. This time it was Xisco who had butterfly band-aids on his forehead from a motorbike accident the day before! So the evening began with Xisco's tale of the motorbike accident, then a dinner of genuine Italian pizzas and one of Maribel's great salads, wine, water and non-stop conversation. It all felt good and it was not long before she and Dasha were ready for bed. The next day they got up at 8:45a.m. She and Dasha had to be in Sa Ema de Farrutx by 1p.m. in order to meet Mitx the owner of their new place. She had not slept that well, but she felt good. Xisco was already up and had made her fresh orange juice for breakfast. According to Xisco fresh orange juice has to be drunk as soon as it is processed because its vitamins dissipated in seconds. He is seven years older than her. Attractive and a wholesome human being. One of the few Phys-Ed teachers that actually practices what he preaches. At the time he was Head of Studies for one of the main high schools in Palma. He was also one of the few Spanish men that she'd ever met who seemed truly secure with himself. They'd chatted a little over fresh orange juice before she said goodbye and headed out to the car with Dasha. The morning was cool and still quiet. Familiar sweet island scents came to their nostrils instantly. A vibrant blue and pink morning sky hovered above them while invisible partridges cooed nearby. As they drove out to the highway she pondered about her morning start. It was another thing that she loved about her life in Spain: fresh orange juice.

U and I motivate me – M.

Metaphysics

She enjoyed the drive from Palma: blue grey mountains, open fields dotted with sheep, fascinating open skies and two-lane highways lined with Mayūrqa's stone hedges. The interior of Mayūrqa was in her opinion prettier than its coast. It was raining by the time she and Dasha arrived. When she parked the car Mitx was there waiting for them. After a light greeting, he led Michèle to the flat which was a new addition above his family's home. Only three months finished, the outside of it was in whitewash stucco with a small private entrance up a half dozen widespread steps that led to a broad front patio and the main door. The inside of it, was a lightly furnished open-concept apartment with a brown loft stairwell to the roof. It was airy and spacious with high ceilings, white walls, two bedrooms and a smaller study with doors and full wooden closets varnished in dark brown, two bathrooms, two sky-windows with one located in the hall and another in the main bathroom, a new modern kitchen with marble counters, a new stainless stove and oven, a brand new dishwasher which was completely uncommon, and a full window over the sink! How many times had she told herself that the next place she'd live in would have a window from the kitchen? Well there it was and it had a sea view to top it off! The living room was a large open floor area that extended from the kitchen. It was defined on one side by tall glass sliding doors and a bay window that connected to a long balcony terrace and made the space in the room seem even larger and the view, despite the houses in front, bright and expansive. Even the house entrance had a wonderful covered porch set with traditional Mayūrqan rocking chairs that she looked forward to using on rainy days. If that were not enough, the modern stairwell was designed with wooden steps also varnished in dark brown, and held by black steel rod supports that went from the open living room space up to the roof offering both she and Dasha a huge terrace from which to stargaze at night or take in the sea view. It was in fact another secretly wished for detail for Dasha who had enjoyed a similar terrace in Sichus at Jesy's place. It was a flat very different from past ones but similar in location and privileges. In a nutshell, the place was simply her description on paper, gone real. A blury image from six months earlier had somehow come true two weeks earlier when she'd come to Mayürqa to look for a place.

Once Mitx opened the door to let them both in, the flat instantly materialised before them and caused a chill to run through Michèle as well as a dream she had had a few years earlier about a white house, to flash past her: *the house had been spacious and white with a sensation associated with freedom and lightness. However, that dream had come to her when her life with Jesy in Mayürqa had been feeling confined and unorganised. At that time, her interpretation of it had been that changes were needed in her life, and not as a projection of something that was to come...* Goose bumps followed as her mind ran through the way that it was all coming together. If anyone had asked her directly, she would have summed it up as divine intervention, however people did not enjoy that kind of talk. It was easier just to say that she merely followed her gut and Life's little hints. Only a year earlier, she, Jes and Dasha had been at Sa Ema de Farrutx' very beach with her mum. She had already been living in Mayürqa five years and ironically enough her mum had decided to visit in the same year that would be Jesy's last. Sa Ema de Farrutx was not a Jesy place to live in, but they used to enjoy the beach and coffees at the beach bar nearby. She remembered asking him on their drive into the area, what he'd thought about the idea of living there to which he'd felt that it lacked personality. *It had been the same day that her mum had taken a picture of the two of them and Dasha huddled together in the sea. She and Jes standing thigh deep in the waves, with Dasha propped up between the two of them on Jes' arm, their arms around each other, sun blown, wet and smiling. Almost laughing. Since then, it happens to be the only shot of the three of them as a family that holds them together indefinitely...*

.. Mitx left the rental contract with Michèle to look at and then finalise later with his wife, Elisabet. 'My wife is the owner of the house so she will have to sign the contract,' he said as he placed the contract on the table. 'She's been in hospital for a week but should be home tomorrow.'

'Oh,' replied Michèle, 'is she okay?'

'Yes. I spent the night with her yesterday and she was fine.' It seemed to her that Mitx was making light of his feelings, especially if he'd spent the night before in the clinic with Elisabet. 'Ooof,' she added, 'it must have been crazy for you trying to get this place ready, deal with your own place during her absence and then be here for the Canadian and her dog all in a week – vaya *(wow)*.' His eyes acknowledged her intuition but offered her no more and said, 'Well, if you have any questions or problems just let us know okay. Do you need any help with your things?' he asked. 'No, I'm fine,' she said. 'Plus the rain seems to have let up,' she added. 'Yes you're lucky,' he added. 'Well I don't know, maybe the date is good,' she continued, '28 is a significant number for me,' she said thinking of Jes but ended with, 'it's my day of birth.' 'Ah really,' he said with interest, 'well it's mine too,' he smiled. 'Really! What month?' she asked. 'Well today actually,' he added modestly. 'Today?! Today is your birthday!?' she asked surprised. 'Well, this is a memorable day for you then.' 'Well I suppose so,' he replied, 'but more because of your arrival. We don't remember birthdays here as often as our saint's name day,' he concluded. 'Hmm yes,' she confirmed. 'Well Happy Birthday anyway' she offered, 'and please give my regards to Elisabet.' 'Thank you,' he said. Then, 'Au! I'm off!' and he left. Both he and Elisabet lived downstairs with their two sons. The oldest at twenty while the youngest wasn't far behind at seventeen. The fact that she was also the oldest of two brothers back home, gave her a cozy sensation knowing that they were downstairs too. Funny too, was that the boys downstairs also had the same initials as her brothers'. The coincidences didn't end there either. Now there were three people in the same house with the same name. 'Mitx the father, his son, and Michèle .., *the holy ghost!*' she rhymed in amusement to herself. Then from her position next to the front door, she looked at the flat before her, still unable to take it all in. Outside the rain fell lightly through partly sunny cracks in the sky that added serenity to her moment. Eventually the car was unloaded. Things were unpacked and notes were made about food and things that were needed. Dasha seemed to be adapting but for the most part, still disoriented and ill-decided on where to lie. What with jet lag, the cage drama, different floors to sleep on, a rehash of old scents and places, it would take a while to adapt.

By late evening the two of them had been to the nearby village for groceries. When they drove back Michèle noticed that it would take her a while, too, to adapt to the area. In spite of the new place, Sa Ema was more like a retro coastal suburb with a village twist to it. It was definitely nothing like the old village of Sichus where she had lived with Jes and Dasha. Sa Ema had little charm to it except its proximity to the sea and the countryside. Its street light management was appalling as it was in most of the newly urbanised villages and developments in Mayürqa. Every fifty feet had a tall white pole with white light blaring from it that depreciated the ambiance and potential beauty of the place tremendously. House lights were almost unnecessary because of the brightness from the ones on the streets. In fact from a plane's view in the sky, Sa Ema looked like a giant "L" lit up in white. There had even been a newspaper article written about how poorly Mayürqa in general wasted its artificial light. '*They could have at least used soft yellow light instead of the white fluorescent stuff.*' she thought. Even if it the white lighting were a counter measure against vandalism there were better ways of doing it. Then again, back at the flat, once she'd unpacked and sorted the groceries, she went up to the roof terrace to have a look at – '*Oh!!*' The moment she stepped out to it, all concerns of not adapting melted away. It was another world up there! As she took it all in, her mind reviewed in awe, that secret list of requests that she had written out for a new place, before ever having found it...

..One request had included retaining the privilege of living near the sea as she'd done before even though much had changed since her first arrival to Mayürqa and higher prices made the idea seem less than hopeful; then pushing her luck, something near some country space so that she and Dasha could relive long walks through sweet field scents and remote open spaces like they had in Sichus; then the request for a terrace for Dasha similar to the one she'd enjoyed in Sichus and finally, somewhere with a bit of village mentality, near progressive commodities and if possible too, arm's length from Sichus. It was an over the top list, with little chance of having one or maybe two items on it materialise. She had not wanted Palma. 'Seen it, been there, done that,' she'd thought. 'What was left?' Her thought process had moved her bit by bit on a polar line from Palma south-west, to Sichus centre, and then it seemed, to Mayürqa's north-east. Any further and she and Dasha were into the water. Sa Ema de Farrutx had seemed like the only possible area on the island that wanted her. Even when she had been on the plane a few weeks earlier, just before landing in Mayürqa, it had seemed crazy. She had no money. Most of all Sa Ema was a place without transportation. There was a summer bus schedule of course, but nothing for the daily transit needs to Palma. There was the train from Juníper village or Sichus, but even they were a twenty minute car ride from Sa Ema. What about work? Palma was the place for work. Her salary? She would need something equal or better than the favourable one that she had had on ships and that already was a crazier notion because everyone knew that the privilege of living in Mayürqa was vexed by a salary scale less than its own standard of living. As the plane

had been landing she'd pressed her forehead against the plane's window watching the island come into focus. It was beautiful. It really was. Despite the fact that it was being plagued by a cancer called progress, the island still looked stoic and majestic from above. All the reasons not to head north had flooded her mind. Even her practical arguments were little use in shifting what was by then, somewhere deeper between a strong tug and blind faith. Her mind had already decided. She'd leaned back into her seat, yet despite the mind, still felt anxious? Had she been living in her head too much? Was she using her faith wisely or being a fool? Mum's voice had come to the rescue, 'Fear is no object,' to which she'd exhailed. She would take the rented car and drive north the following day to check out an area near sa Ema de Farrutx. She would buy a newspaper just to say that she had but in essence, knew that conventional methods had never panned out for her. Ever. It had always been her metaphysical understanding of how life evolved for her that had worked. That and her philosophical interpretation of what she sensed were Life's ways of directing her. She'd continued to think: in the winter the area was a ghost town. Surely there would be lots of places for rent? Maybe even cheaper. Her mind's eye had wanted to pay 500 euros a month for rent although she'd known that it probably would have been closer to six or seven hundred euros. Her budget for six months had been an even 3,000 euros. The coastal hamlet of Sa Ema de Farrutx was a second residential burrough for people on summer holidays, much like Yarmouth's version in Cape Cod used to be when she'd been a child, where homes came to life in the months of July and August. Rents tripled in the summer, families got together in clans, summer friendships were rekindled with a lot of get-togethers, but from September until then it was an empty suburb plotted amongst wind, sea, sand, and countryside, where few locals and foreigners lived all year round... Then, as the plane had started its decent her thoughts had recollected how well she'd always felt the moment she'd entered the airport's terminal. She'd loved being there, Mayürqa it had seemed, still had room for her. On the day of her arrivall to Sa Ema de farrutx, the weather had turned into an unexpected Indian summer in October. At 1pm there hadn't been anyone around, so she'd decided to go for a swim in her skivvies. Lying there on a mound of seaweed she could not get over how decided she was about being there. Back and forth her mind had gone on analysing the "absurdness" of it all. Once again, she had no money. At 37 she had never owned a car in her life. Buying one was an experience in itself so how was she going to buy one in Mayürqa? She would have to take the Spanish driver's course but thought, maybe it could be stalled with an international driver's licence. Worst of all, she'd always kind of hoped that her first car would be something special and not just a result of being financially depleted. Plus, it would also have to be an automatic. How many automatics were there in Mayürqa for a good price? Moreover she'd never wanted a car unless she could have a good one. Her brothers and mum had always had second hand cars. She just didn't want that. She'd laid there some more. It had been quiet and comfortable. The sea had been clear and splashed over her feet. Risk. She was waging her gut against risky ideas that had actually been fermenting as far back as June when the only reason she'd decided to go back to the ship was so that she could get another copy of her ship's contract that was post-dated until January 2006. If she needed help from a bank the contract would highlight a desirable income to support any loan ideas that she might have had. The mental gymnastics in her brain had been causing her distress. She had to make a decision in order to follow through with the rest. 'Arrgh!' Impulsively she'd sat up, looked out at the sea and had tried to work-out her thoughts, when ever so cleverly, her dad's song found her. It was so clear that she even began to murmur it to herself: 'By the sea, by the sea, by the beautiful sea!' Her vision had blurred momentarily from a salty liquid in her eyes. If that hadn't been enough, right about the same time a seagull feather had floated into her toes. Jes was also near. He'd always picked up feathers because he'd thought they were lucky. It was clear. Both Dad and Jes had complied. She would write by the sea and Jes was going to help her find the place from where it would all begin. She'd laughed out loud, then dried her eyes and whispered 'crazy, just crazy!' Still it had been that same day, she'd come across the Serra's place. It had happened after her swim when she'd taken the rented car and opted to drive it where she'd felt would be nice to live. Maybe nearer to where her mum had taken their picture the year before? She'd written down a few telephone numbers of houses advertising for rent and called a few. Some had answered and one had offered a showing for the following day. One more street and then she'd intended on heading back down to Palma. As a result she'd come across a place with a front terrace, for rent. It was gaudy but new looking. She'd called and they'd answered. The owners would be by in twenty minutes to show her the place. On the outside it had potential, but she had not been sure. Living in Sa Ema was definitely nothing like living in a quaint traditional village. It was a coastal residential area. Latent with houses of all shapes and sizes bonded by cement, oversized sidewalks, and too many street lights. Like an oil painting, its charm was unnoticeable unless you made an effort to stand back and really look at it. Each house when observed had personality or detail that was often overshadowed by the multitudes surrounding it. Still, between the cement and the houses, pockets of unprotected marine fauna and ecosystems were left undisturbed. It was a pretty place if you could ignore the housing.

 While she'd been waiting for the owners to arrive she'd moved her car slightly forward into the shade. Only then had she noticed the house. It was next to the one that she had just called but separated by a plot of land between them. Below, the house had appeared lived-in and about twenty years old; like a home for a year rather than a season. Then it changed. The top part was new. The face of the place had looked like a mix between a soft stucco yellow and beige colour. She hadn't been sure. It had a tall grey cement pillar in the middle of a balcony that supported what seemed to be a very large roof terrace on top. The pillar had *an unfinished look, because it was still in its natural colour. The balcony was accentuated by large bay windows with modern blinds pulled closed and a rental sign hanging from the right hand side of it. She'd noted down the number and called. A gruff, somewhat unsure voice had answered. It had been Mitx'. If she'd wanted to wait an hour, his wife would arrive home from work to show her the place. Her mind had raced: it would give her enough time to see the other place and then have something to compare with... She'd agreed to meet the wife at half past three. No sooner had she ended the call when a small red van pulled up with the owners of the other house behind her. They had been very congenial. The woman was short and feisty and the man was slightly taller and rounder. Their place was very large and quite new inside. Apparently they had renovated the place for their daughter who'd decided that she did not want the place. It was another of those cultural traditions that Michèle felt were ever so lacking in North America. The new world, as it were, required families to move a lot. Such that houses were hardly ever paid for in full. Never mind the fact that most families in general did not have the privilege of passing down their homes from generation to generation. North America was too young to ever establish such security for its generations because its very nemesis of constant innovation and progress also seemed to be the foe against tradition and stability... The house had a fireplace and had been very well furnished. Too much in fact. It would have been hard for her to add her own stuff. It had felt more like a summer place than a home. Nonetheless the owners had been friendly – maybe too much. It made her hesitate. They had no problems with Dasha, and even suggested that she could use their patio downstairs because they only ever came up in the summer. The rental price had been 600 euros all year or for as long as she'd wanted!? Normally a contract was made up for six months to a year before longer ones were agreed upon. It was also understood that if one rented all year then the rent would be lower than what it would be at high season. 600 euros was good. Up the road she had been quoted 700 euros for a much* smaller place that was much closer to a seaside cottage in Cape Cod than a home. With that in mind, the gaudy house had been good and if nothing else had come up over the following two days, she would have taken it. The thing was, that it hadn't been what she'd been looking for exactly, nor did she really have a clear vision of it either. Yet her thoughts on how she hadn't wanted to live were very clear, which in turn meant to her that the very opposite had to be out there somewhere, and it would become clear if and when she saw it. Anyone else might not have taken the chance to keep looking, especially when the fear of being so far up north was already beginning to cloud over faith. Still, it was a feeling, a foggy outline that she had had. Nothing to lose, she'd got back into her car and driven around a bit more before heading back to the other house where she had agreed to meet the man's wife...

Michèle had driven up to the house, just as a woman appeared to be unlocking the door to the home below. The car parked in front of Michèle's rental was a red Alfa Romeo. The woman, who Michèle presumed was the wife, had been dressed in black boots, casual professional clothes of black slacks and a mustard coloured blouse. Her hair had seemed thick, was dark and shoulder length. The first thing Michèle had noticed instantly about her was a friendly smile that really appeared to be sincere. She'd felt a little bad at arriving right when the woman had, so with a smile to meet the woman's, had offered an exasperated gesture from within the car to indicate empathy for the woman who had to have been feeling tired from her day. Once Michèle had gotten out of the car to meet the woman, her first impression had been made positive by the bourgeoisie image that projected from the red car and the woman's professional look. Despite being in the boonies, it had suggested to her, a middle class suburban family similar to the neighbours she'd had growing up, and recognised the comfort pattern instantly. They'd introduced themselves to each other. The woman's name was Elisabet. They had walked through Elisabet's house to the south side where the main entrance to the place upstairs faced another road. Proceeding through the small entrance door and up the stairs to the main door of the flat, Michèle's heart had begun to beat faster as her fog had started to clear. Just the entrance itself, had been very nice. So new. The front patio to the main door was an open area with two lovely old wooden Mayürqan rocking chairs. Elisabet had put them there thinking that it would be nice for winter evenings. They'd chatted a lot while they walked around. Elisabet had explained that they had only just put the for rental sign up a few days earlier. That in fact the place had yet to be finished. They had had some friends in it for the summer months and intended to add the final touches afterwards. When they'd got to the roof terrace Michèle had let out a "wow!" despite herself. It had been so unexpected. The fog had lifted. It was the place that she had requested in her journal. It really was. Had it been divine intervention or just the power of projection she had not been sure. Her stomach nerves had begun to tense. Something so right always worried her. What was the catch? Was it a gift or the devil's temptation? Plus she still had had to ask about Dasha and the rental fee. New place and all, they might not have liked the idea of a dog and the rent had been bound to be high. She'd already started wondering about "how much she could deviate from her budget if the place were to be true?" Timing and presentation of the questions were everything. On the roof they'd chatted some more. Apparently both Elisabet and her husband were also teachers. They, unlike everyone else, lived downstairs all year round. In the winter it was just their family and a few other cats from the neighbourhood. Elisabet even liked football!? Plus, during the football season she and her family often went to the local bar restaurant to watch it on TV! Michèle had been dumbfounded. One of her favourite rituals with Jes and Dasha had been watching the football from one of the bars in Sichus.. It had all sounded too good to be true. Then Elisabet had asked her if she would feel alone so far away from everything. The concept had amused Michèle, who had just arrived from her mum's place located in Northen Ontario. Sa Ema was not so isolated. Especially with Elisabet's *family downstairs, Sichus twenty minutes away and the local villages only ten minutes away. Elisabet's face had lit up. "Sichus?" Apparently a local authority from Sichus had asked her husband if he could offer a young girl from there, some personal therapy sessions because her father had died in May that year. Michèle's stomach had gone tight again and the goose bumps had come back. She had known the man that had died. It had been the same man, who a year earlier, had been driving her Jes to the hospital and somehow drove off the road. Jes had died instantly while the man had been completely unscathed. Elisabet had been embarrassed and surprised. Despite the unfortunate details the coincidence had been evident to both of them. The moment had arrived for Michèle to inquire about the rent to which Elisabet had replied, '500 euros.' Everything had suddenly seemed unreal. Surely someone had read her journal and casually whispered it into Elisabet's ear? It had been even cheaper than next door. Every muscle in Michèle's body had wanted to move with excitement! Thankfully her urge to do a tap dance had been quickly snuffed by caution: '500 euros?' she'd questioned. Elisabet had hesitated, 'It seems too high?' she'd asked. 'No, to the contrary, it is a very good price,' she'd replied, 'especially as this place is so new...' 'Well,' Elisabet had said slightly more relaxed, 'It's not quite finished yet.' 'How much more do you think you might raise the rent later?' Michèle had asked directly. 'I don't believe it will go up much more than the annual percentage of the cost of living...Three, maybe four percent,' Elisabet had concluded. Michèle had watched her body language and understood that she had been guesstimating. Nonetheless the answer had been fine. In light of the standard of living in Mayürqa her emergency budgeted plan had been prepared to pay up to 600 euros a month, and 650 euros if lack of time to even find a place had become an issue . 'Vale (Okay),' she'd said. Next was Dasha. With a slight inhalation of air, Michèle had managed to maintain a casual tone and ask Elisabet in such a way that she'd hoped would dissuade any discomfort from Elisabet, if she'd wanted to say no. 'The place is* lovely, but I would like you and your husband to know that I have a dog... Dasha,' she'd explained, 'is very quiet and well mannered, practically the village mascot in Sichus. The only real problem if at all is the constant ritual of picking up her fur.' Elisabet had hesitated a little. Michèle felt she had spoken too much. A small sense of fear had found her insides. Maybe they would disapprove of the idea. She hadn't had to tell them, but truth be known she could not have lived there comfortably if she'd felt that they didn't like Dasha's presence in the place. Then Elisabet had spoken. She would talk to her husband about it and get in touch with Michèle in a day or two. The reply had been enough to remind Michèle to exhale. Finally just as she had been about to get back into the car, Elisabet had asked her if she had wanted to teach? The question, like everything during that moment, had been unexpected. In essence Michèle hadn't but had yet to really formulate a decision. So that she'd replied to Elisabet that her priorities at that time were about getting settled first. That maybe in the New Year once she had her belongings and home figured out she might consider it. The answer had seemed to drift passed Elisabet as if she had not really been convinced or had already formulated an image or idea about Michèle teaching in the near future: 'It's too bad that you hadn't come in September. My school is one of the few that offers the English immersion programme with native speaking teachers. We needed a teacher for this term,' she'd said. As if on cue Michèle had replied: 'What a dummy I am for not coming sooner,' and they'd both laughed. By the time she'd driven out of the coastal village she could not help but feel overwhelmed by gratitude. The village next door has a school that hires native English teachers!? How improbable was that? Marooned up north and there had been the ideal job just next door. It would never have met Michèle's salary expectations, but still it was incredible. Elisabet's family was into football. They'd be a presence downstairs for her and Dasha all year round. The terrace was bigger than the one in Sichus. It was lofty and new. The rental sign had only just been put up. Even the furniture had been exactly right. The kitchen had a great window, and even the address' number 50 highlighted the 5 and new beginnings for her that year. Most of all the rent was 500 euros!! Tears of pure emotion or stress had become second nature. She had been so awed that even the butterflies in her stomach had stilled into a suspended freeze...

..She came back to her moment on the roof and realised that she hadn't done the tap dance yet. Faith and Reality were once more in conflict with each other. Dare she feel or even believe it, might turn it all into folly, but it was as though the place had been built for her and Dasha in mind. Even on that day of discovery.., *when she'd turned out of the private entrance from Sa Ema onto Artà's main road to Palma, still unsure of how or what to think, everything around her then, had just seemed to glow, while fields, mountains and sheep were held captive by a sleepy sun. Dusk had been on the horizon with everything else flushed in pink. She'd opened the car windows, letting hair and wind move wildly around her while a sense of freedom and wellbeing took her over...* Hmpft. One thing she did know for sure; the now that she was in, was beautiful.

The religion of the future will be a cosmic religion. It should transcend personal God and avoid dogma and theology. Covering both the natural and the spiritual, it should be based on a religious sense arising from the experience of all things natural and spiritual as a meaningful unity...
..If there is any religion that could cope with modern scientific needs it would be Buddhism.
ALBERT EINSTEIN

Cosmos

The white lit street lamps did not reach the roof top and finally provoked her long awaited tap dance. The midnight sky dotted with blue-white diamonds greeted her, while the full moon offered enough light for her to set up a little welcome ceremony to the new place: Dasha's old quilt blanket, local cheeses, Mayürqan olives, toasties and a mini bottle of Benjamin cava for her and Jes. It was still hard to take it all in. They had arrived. This was their place for at least the next six months. She sat next to Dasha and took in the beauty of the full moon. There was so much mystery in her. Unlike the sun it provoked from Michèle more questions and a calmer sense of being that enabled her to see things better. The contradiction made her smile, considering that one might see things better at night with the moon's mysterious light, than in the day blinded by the sun. She let out a slight hum of conjecture and then remembered Jesy who also loved full moons and always looked for her whenever he saw one. It was October 28th. In front of her mind's eye, the month and the number were bold and heavy in significance. Especially with the recent knowledge of it also being Mitx' birthday. In two months' time December 28th would be Jesy's one year anniversary since his death and in three months' time, January 28th would be her 38th birthday. She focused back at the 28 and began her play with numbers. The 8 was evident everywhere and just happened to be her dad's numerological number for life. She noticed too that he and Mitx were both Scorpio while it was exactly 10 years earlier in October on the 22nd of 1994, when her dad had died. She considered the 22. The sum of its digits was 4, her lucky number in astral terms, while the total sum of each number in the date 10.22.1994 was ironically 28 and summed up into a 1: the digit that suggested strength. Her heart fluttered slightly. She was having fun with her number game. In numerological science she was a 7 which correlated well with her Asian year in Horse that was the seventh cycle of the Chinese calendar. She raised her cup of cava to the lady that hung above bold and bright in white, and made a toast to the men. Then she lay down on the quilt next to Dasha whose spirits seemed to have improved. Alone together it was like being a part of the world above. The breeze was cool, the stars were out, and the moon was full. Off into the distance the tranquil sounds of breaking waves fell into a hypnotic sound. '*By the sea by the sea by the beautiful sea...*' She was connected again. Quietly yet audibly she began to speak. First she thanked her dad once more and then spoke to Jes for a bit. Ironically she felt that he was taking care of them then, in ways that he could not when he was alive. He would never have enjoyed living in Sa Ema, but he knew she and Dasha could. He had taken them to Sa Ema on their last beach day together. Had he known without knowing? There was so much terrace for Dasha. '*Incredible,*' she thought, '*just incredible. Did anybody care? Write a book.*' Again it came back to her. A secret notion, years old that sounded good and ridiculous at the same time. As if responding to the comment she went on: 'Actually do you know what the horoscopes said?' she asked aloud, '"to go into unknown areas". Maybe something "in publishing or that can be done from home," to "stop stalling because the stars are routing for me!" In other words if I want to write a book or at least decode my own M codes that I should get typing now! I could not believe it when I read it! Like it had been written for me!?! –' She caught herself. She was having a full conversation to *them* out there. Not sure if it was Dasha's presence that made it easy for her to do that, or if being on her own so much was making her find pathological refuge believing that she was not alone and actually being listened to. '*No,*' she thought. '*These kinds of conversations only happened when she really felt connected.*' There were times when she wanted to talk to someone and actually felt that there was no one there, and in such cases, just vented to herself. She took another sip of the cava and considered the numbers again. It seemed interesting to her that significant dates and events that past year were all about 2, 3, 4, 5, and 8; especially 3 and 8. 3 was Jes' favourite number while 33 she reasoned, was him complete because he had had a twin brother who'd died 6 years before him. Half of 6 was 3. Jesy died in 2003 at the age of 33. Finally 3 was the sum of the digits in his birth date. Her imagination put her in a court of law making her closing statement: *'Beyond a reasonable doubt, 3 is Jesy's number.'* She laughed softly to herself and stared back at the black canvas that surrounded her. '"Life is not a problem to solve"...,' she murmured to the night, '"but a mystery to experience".' She inhaled and exhaled with a feeling of tranquillity inside her. She loved the night world above her at once feeling calmer by it. Then slowly, the dampness of the night started to set into her bones giving her cue, to get up and collect her things. She gave a final look towards the full moon and waited for a moment while she sent out her mental notes: *'Thank you, for the food in my fridge, the hot water, the great shower, a super place, the rental car, Dasha by my side calm and safe. I know it's mine for at least six months and there is relief in that knowledge. Thank you dad, over all, for instilling in me the spirit that makes it possible for me to live my life in the standard that I wish it to be! Thank you Jes for helping us get here. You know I told you that once we did, that you could leave us, so if you go, don't forget us o.k.? If not, glad to have you nearby...'*

Somewhere over the rainbow – Way up high
There's a land that I heard of – Once in a lullaby
Somewhere over the rainbow – Skies are blue
And the dreams that you dare to dream
Really do come true.
'OVER THE RAINBOW' – JUDY GARLAND, LYRICS ADAPTED

The rainbow

While driving the rental she remembered the many times that she used to be the passenger while Jes had always been the driver. Once, they were driving along the Palma-Inca highway... *It was summer at dusk and somewhere into the distance it had been raining. Colours were vibrant and the air smelt fresh. As they passed the cemetery where* his grandma was buried, he honked the horn and gave a slight wave with his right hand. He often did that slight wave whenever he was thinking of someone past or passing a memorable spot. This time as they were almost past the cemetery they both noticed an incredible rainbow that literally looked as if it had come out of a fable. It seemed to start from Sta. Eugenia village on the south-west side and arc over to Algaida to the north-east. That if followed to its end, they would indeed find a pot of gold. It was so awesome that Michèle impulsively took the camera out of the glove compartment and took a photo of it. … That photo was now somewhere in Sa Ema de Farrutx among the zillion others that needed to be sorted, but she hadn't been ready to do yet. The reminder caused her some discomfort and suddenly made her mind move from Jesy to Mitx' brother. Musing over the fact that she'd agreed to give his brother English conversation classes even though she had not intended to think about such things for a while. However within only a few days of her arrival, Elisabet had popped by twice asking, then Mitx had made another valiant attempt following that… *She'd opened the front door to find Mitx and greeted him warmly, '¡Hola Mitx – entra, entra! (Hi Mitx – come in, come in!)', she'd said. He'd responded with a kind smile before his eyes and head's posture shifted slightly towards the plant that was down on his right. His body language made her think quickly of Dasha's humble approach when she wanted something by tilting her head down slightly and lifting her left paw up at the same time. His left hand was deep into his jean pocket and his right hand held the end of a cigarette butt that he drew from eagerly and intently before going into the flat. 'No pasa nada (no worries),' she said referring to the cigarette, 'puedes pasar (you can come inside),' she added honestly. 'Nah,' he said between drags, 'it smells up the house.' She said nothing, detecting that the conspicuous manner in which he drew from his cigarette was probably more about his wife's disapproval of him smoking, than about the flat. She kept her smile on while he put out the butt with is foot, then picked it up with his left hand that went back into his pocket thereafter and finally entered the flat. 'I have a brother who has just come back from being in Barcelona,' he began timidly, 'I dunno, a few weeks now. He was away at a rehab centre for drug addiction.' His eyes quickly searched hers for a reaction. 'Uh huh,' she smiled coolly. '.. And well now he's back, and the other night he was here and asked Elisabet to look out for a native English teacher because he wants to take English lessons.' He paused again leaving it up to Michèle to give a reply. Her stomach had tightened slightly because it was clear that he was there against his better desire and above all probably felt embarrassed asking his newly arrived tenant from Canada to give his drug addict brother English classes, especially after she'd already politely refused his wife ... 'What's the addiction?' she'd asked. He'd cleared his throat slightly and gave her a furtive glance, 'cocaina (cocaine).' Neurons in her head had fluttered slightly. The addiction didn't faze her, rather she'd simply never had any direct experience with a cocaine addict before and self-preserving instincts automatically kicked in ... 'Well, do I have to worry about aggressive behaviour or anything?' 'No no,' he contended sincerely, 'my brother is very correct and congenial. He's fun to be with. It's just that he's back from Barcelona and needs to follow a strict list of rehab rules while he's here that's all...'*

..The recollection faded and she sighed out loud. Teaching was positive of course, but it was all happening too quickly. Even though Sa Ema was nothing like the village where they used to live, it was unique and well-chosen for her own and Dasha's needs. She felt strongly that Jes had had a strong influence in their new beginnings and she missed him even more. Sometimes it was apparent to her that she was still waiting for him. Her subconscious still carried a sense of fear of losing him or letting him go completely. There was a sense of comfort in the thought of his presence being near her such that she suddenly honked the horn, glanced quickly to the passenger side of the car and waved at the window like he used to do; as if the action would catch his attention from way out there in case he were not nearby, and when she did that, she saw the rainbow. She couldn't believe it. The sky was a backdrop of an intense pink on fire! While the rainbow, so bold and wide plunged over and behind the mountains at Santa. María and Conseilles, and so similar to the one that she and Jes had seen over his grandma's cemetery. Then as if to add melodrama to the moment, Luz Casal's song, "No me importa nada (I don't care)", sung out from the car radio. It was one of the songs that Jes used to turn up every time he heard it. It had been for him the dichotomy of a song with beautiful lyrics and a sad memory of his cousin who died on his lap while trying to get her to hospital. His eyes always filled with a slight wet brim whenever he heard it. Michèle had always enjoyed the song too but only really heard the lyrics then, while she was driving past the rainbow and in turn, caused her eyes to see through that same wet blur. It really brought her close to him and she guessed that he knew that. Her eyes swelled wet. She let her feelings and instincts go despite concerns that much of what she felt or thought was nothing more than psychological rhetoric, but it did not matter. It was what gave her comfort. The rainbow was still there to remind her of its fables of good fortune and God's promise to Noah that it would never rain again for forty days and forty nights. She honked passionately a few more long ones and then sped off to Sa Ema de Farrutx with the rainbow's reflection beautifully arched big and bold across the car's rear view mirrors.

> For one human being to love another
> That is perhaps the most difficult of our tasks
> The ultimate, the last test and proof
> The work, for which all other work is but
> Preparation.
> RAINER MARIA RILKE

The Preparation

Michèle was slowly but surely getting into the new place and it seemed to her that Dasha was doing the same. The place was feeling cosier and both of them appeared to be finding their spots. An added bonus was that the owners who lived downstairs all year round were good people. A few days earlier Elisabet had sent her an unexpected sms giving Michèle thanks for her arrival. It actually embarrassed her because she felt more incline to thank them, and wasn't really sure why they should thank her and simply accepted it as a polite gesture to welcome her arrival. Dasha entered Michèle's room, and went strategically to the corner between two walls, and lay down on her new pillow that Michèle had given her. It was cozy and thick enough to keep her warm from the room's marble floor. She was calm. Michèle was there too, wearing a beige coloured pair of plaid flannel pyjama bottoms, a blue-grey long sleeved long-john shirt, lotion vaguely apparent on her face and her hair twined into a tiny bun that was propped directly on top of her head. Dasha looked up at her and seemed to thump her tail in laughter. '¿Que Dasha?' smiled Michèle, 'you like my look?' It was about eight o'clock and obvious to Dasha that Michèle was in for the night when unannounced to both of them, the front gate outside buzzed. Michèle was beside herself. Like a nervous cat she moved quickly to the door in the bedroom that led to the front terrace. There was Elisabet down at the front gate. '*Okay,*' she thought, '*it's just Belle*' and without much more than that, stepped out onto the terrace from the bedroom. Well, it wasn't just Belle. '*Dad!?!*' her mind blurted. A quick quasi nausea went through her. Right behind Elisabet, as if determined to be seen first or to do it alone a man walked up the stairs to the porch landing. Elisabet hardly had a chance to say hello. With a writing book pad in his left hand tightly tucked under his left arm he left the final step to the porch and with a slight click of his heels and an eager sort of nervous look, said: 'Hola. Soy Carles (Hi. I'm Carles).' Michèle's mind went into over-drive. Everything about the moment was an attack on her senses. While he must have been amused to see her dressed up like a clown before show time, the fact was momentarily overshadowed by the manner in which he'd introduced himself. What made her heart leap was his stance. It was her dad's in an art form. One that until that moment had been uniquely his. Then almost simultaneously she noticed that he was wearing a French blue and white striped polo. Her memory beamed her to Paris, then to her first love from Bordeaux, then to her childhood friend's mother wearing the same in a dress design for Vogue Montreal, to finally back at the moment. He stood in front of her. It might have been the image of her dad that kept her focused because she had not really noticed Carles' attractiveness then, and by pure instinct ignored the humour in her physical disposition and played it cool.

Mitx' brother was bald, taller than her, and as if to give herself strength, she spoke to him directly in English. His reaction was friendly and slightly embarrassed at not completely understanding her. Now, the terms of introduction were on even ground and suddenly, as if a spell had been broken or created, despite their own vulnerabilities they begun communicating easily and intently with each other. Their eye contact was direct and intense; especially his. She could not be sure if it was his look that held her or the mere fact that they both seemed to relax with the eye contact. After a brief exchange of words, they concluded their meeting on an agenda for classes, and then Carles stepped back and turned on his heels to follow Elisabet back down the stairs. 'See you on Wednesday,' he said. 'Yes, on Wednesday – bye,' she replied. 'Bye,' he returned. She stepped back into her room and felt the speed of her heart pounding. She looked over at Dasha lying upright against the wall. Her tail thumping against the floor seemed to be in sync with the beating of Michèle's heart rate against her chest. Dasha's body language stirred left-right with concerned expectation while her eyes, a clear velvet brown, were fixed on Michèle. '¿Que Dasha?' she spoke softly. The question was not hers. It was Jesy's. It had always been his way to calm Dasha down or show patience when she got too needy. Then the bells went off in Michèle's head: she was attracted to Carles. Suddenly like the thought itself had caught her heart, it skipped another beat at the realisation of what she had written in her journal the year before: *"… I shall not need to look for love anymore because I'd travelled so far and found Jes. If I am wrong, then I have journeyed the distance and my other half, if he be, will have to find me now."* She could not believe it. *'After Jesy, I'm getting a cocaine addict?!'* Her head spun into mental gymnastics while she unconsciously moved to an open bedroom closet and shut its doors. What was she supposed to do? She needed to be clear with herself before their next meeting. There was trepidation. Her experience with Jesy and the final outcome of it all made her feel uneasy and worried about the consequences. She sometimes felt that the depth of his problem had been increased by her attempts to help them both survive it. Nonetheless the relationship had been beautiful and intense. 'Sigh.' The debate was unfair because Life knew who she was. Carles wanted English classes, while she had a teaching certificate and time to do them. In which case, past experiences aside, might it also be viewed as unethical not to teach if she was capable? Then as if relieved of all responsibility she remembered that she had in fact said "no." She had told both Mitx and Elisabet that she did not want to do classes, at least not until the New Year. Still within two days they'd returned to her to enquire if she might reconsider or at least meet Carles. They'd insisted. So she'd agreed to meet him. It was meant to happen. Life, it seemed to her, wanted the classes to begin. She and Carles were meant to know each other in a way that only the drumming of her heart was foretelling the extent to which their encounter might grow. She heard her mum again: "Fear is no object." 'But he's a cocaine addict for Christ sake!?' she rebutted out loud. Still, it wasn't enough to convince her. Albeit an important consideration, it was not a factor to judge. Then there was also the imminent conflict with the family downstairs. If the attraction she felt actually blossomed then her relationship with the family below could be at risk. In the end she had a lot to lose, and him? Nothing, except English classes. All this information was wisdom from past experiences that should have been enough to focus on English classes and nothing else. Yet it was over-ridden by a nervous gut feeling vexed by the sensation of fear and attraction.

The former she thought, might have been more to do with her ignorance of the addiction and all the stereotypes attached to it, or maybe it was an alarm to protect her? If the latter was true, then it was out of her hands. In which case, her own guidelines were what were being tested? Not to be afraid of the unknown. Not to judge simply from past experiences, but to make second chances better than the last. That it occurred to her again that up until that moment her life's experiences might have been destined preparation for him. That she could honestly believe without a doubt the sincere truth that she had not asked for that situation. That it had entered into her life. Even before her arrival to Sa Ema, Carles had actually asked Elisabet to keep her eyes open for a native English teacher!? That was enough. She knew even before the mental gymnastics had ended. It was inevitable. The heart raced and her body felt held by goose bumps. As if she had just discovered a special truth from Life about her very own existence up until then. Carles, whoever he was going to be to her, had found her. They would be something and it was going to be something big.

At some point it was also going to hurt. Causing her to feel concern, and desire that her destined presence in his life should at least have a good ending for him … 'Please,' she whispered out, 'just tell me that I will make a difference, or at least have a positive effect on him. Not a bad one – okay?' To which her inner voice responded: *"'Great love and great achievements involve great risk…'"*

..'I know,' she sighed softly.., 'o.k. then,' and climbed into bed.

We are trav'ling in the footsteps
Of those who've gone before
And we'll all be reunited
On a new and sunlit shore
When the sun begins to shine
When the trumpet sounds its call
…When the saints, go marching in.
'WHEN THE SAINTS GO MARCHING IN'– LOUIS ARMSTRONG
LYRICS ADAPTED

The Day of Saints

Dasha watched Michèle for a bit. Despite Michèle's air of calmness Dasha sensed a level of sadness coming from her too. Then the flickering light from two candles on the side table next to the bed caught her attention. It was playing with a photo of the man who used to share the bedroom with them and whose smell and sounds were now gone. Next to the candles, sitting upright in bed, pillow table on her lap, brown pillow rest behind her back, was Michèle writing feverously: "Carles' arrival this night has been incredible. It's November 1st otherwise known in Spain as the "Day of Saints". The same day that Jes' twin, Jaime died 7 years earlier. It's a significant day twice over now. The two candles are lit for Jes and his brother. It's actually the first year since Jaime's death that the two of them can honour today together. Funny, Jes' death on December 28 – The "Day of the Innocent" in Spain, is the day that historically pays homage to all the children who died under Pharaoh Herods' rule at the time of baby Jesus' birth. Today it's a way for people to pay respect to those who have died. How quietly absurd that Jes should die on a day that honours baby Jesus. Still, in light of the day, I find relief in thinking that he sort of died and was literally reborn, and that he and his brother might now feel together as one. Perhaps that is why Jes was not afraid to die. There was comfort in knowing that his own twin would probably find him?" She paused her writing for a moment while she considered her thoughts on paper. Death was a topic that she and Jes had talked about. They'd shared its presence. There had been something about Jes and what had seemed to be a constant flow of accidents, near misses and hospitals combined with the fact that the death of his twin empowered the sensation of it. There are theories about twins. Some say that if one goes without the other, then the one who is left behind can suffer a sense of emotional purgatory between the halves of oneself and the deceased twin. Suggesting that even though Jes and Michèle fit perfectly well as a heterosexual couple neither Michèle nor Jaime's girlfriend at the time could have expected a life into old age with the brothers, if one of the twins should die early without the other. The yin yang of them, she reasoned, was too complete to survive apart. Then she looked at Dasha in the room with her. She seemed fine although her spirits had been a bit low lately. If possible Michèle would try to take her swimming the next day. Finally she looked at the photograph of Jes on the side table. After dinner that night she'd put on his old blue suede coat and had gone up to the roof with two tubs of ice cream. Lit a candle and placed the photo that her mother had taken the summer before of Jesy, Dasha and her in Sa Ema, next to it. She had not noticed until a few days earlier, when she'd unpacked and put the photo of the three of them on the fridge, that her future had been foretold in it, because in the distant background of that photo were houses including the very house where she and Dasha were now living...

So she'd sat on the roof "with" Jes and Jaime while Dasha had stayed downstairs avoiding the oncoming of a storm that had been brewing up over the sea. Still it was cool on the roof top, yet the night sky had stayed clear long enough to offer her time to eat the ice cream. The sky had been crisp with stars and a bright moon. The brisk air felt imported from a Canadian Fall and the moon in its splendour highlighted a sea that raged from a storm somewhere below it. Then out there to the left of her view, by Formentor's lighthouse, her eye had caught the stark contrast of one very large white cotton batt cloud that extended in a horizontal dimension across the black canvas of the night. As Michèle ate her ice cream she'd watched the cloud entertain incredible flashes of light. Including some spectacular lightning bolts that had zapped out of it like vertical rods, shocking the water below. Watching it was like witnessing a light show that had been placed inside the cloud. Everywhere else was clear...The very tip of Formentor Mountain that jutted out to sea, remained protected by the lighthouse that seemed to flash its becon in a synchronised kind of way with the light show in the cloud. It had reminded her then, *of Jes, and the day they had had sex somewhere out there, leaving behind his effort and her womanhood to mark their territory. They had walked from the look-out point at Formentor's lighthouse down into the mountain under its ledge. There the mountain's walls framed a narrow and very steep gully that had grooved itself a very deep way between rock and stone down yonder into the sea that was nothing more than a Deep Blue crashing on a rocky coastal border. Without a word Jes had begun his way down the steep gully of loose rock and gravel in order to swim with a few other guys who had already made the descent. She'd watched from above how he sometimes lost his footing on the loose stone and rubble that encouraged his way down – afraid to try with him and in awe of the beautiful man who went leaving Dasha, his puppy and her, to stay above and sit waiting for him. The sun was hot yet she had felt no need to challenge his wordless move to leave them. In fact why should she? He soon became a dot bobbing in the deep sea. He'd made it. How he would come back up was another question but she watched him intently with the same attention that Dasha gave when left behind on the beach to watch the two of them swim off into the sea. He had been out there bobbing so far away from them and then he had eventually returned to them without much more to say. There had been nothing to say. He'd gone for a swim and they'd waited.* ..Her mind had drifted away from the memory and back to her moment on the roof and that of the white cloud that hung over the sea where Jesy had swum. It was in clear view from where she sat yet seemingly so far away. It was almost possible to imagine him still bobbing out there... Had he known then without knowing that she'd have the view to recall him back? The lighthouse continued to flash where once upon a time her man had been and because of it, still was...

Michèle came back to her spot in bed and looked over at Dasha that was by then sleeping on her mat. Michèle's senses were acutely alive and the sea that could be heard outside instantly beamed her back to her childhood memory of Cape Cod. '*By the sea by the sea by the beautiful sea...,*' hummed in her head, '*November 1, 2004 the Da–,*' Floating thoughts suddenly froze momentarily at the realisation that the déjà vu she'd had of her dad via her encounter with Charlie was precisely ten years since her dad's passing and, just happened to be on the Day of Saints. She exhaled lightly. She'd been doing her thing on her own for a long time, so why the current sensation of her dad and Jes' presence? The candles for the twins had almost burnt-out, so she wrapped-up in her journal: "Love you dad. Thank you sincerely for everything. Happy anniversary guys. Together at last."

A coincidence
Every precision, every approximation, every scene
Under supervision
Every failure, every imperfection, every detail
All under control.
*[La casualidad.../ Cada acierto, cada aproximación, cada escena/ Bajo supervisión
Cada fallo, cada imprecisión, cada detalle/ Todo bajo control.]*
'MARIPOSA' (BUTTERFLY) – OREJA DE VAN GOGH, LYRICS ADAPTED

La mujer de casualidades

The woman of coincidences

I met Carles on November 1, on the "Day of Saints" while November 3, Jesy's Life number, happened to be the first English class with Carles from 8:30a.m., until 10a.m. Ironically too, the date 03.11.2005, when broken down into numerology happens to be 3, 2 and 7: Jesy's, Charlie's, and my Life numbers totalling 3 and making my Love number the main influence for that day. Charlie was on time for his first English class with me. He came with the writing pad clutched in his right hand and an aura of excitement and nerves. It was at this first class that I began calling Carles, Charlie. It's the English nickname for Charles and at the time, suited him. He said that he liked it because friends of his used to call him that too. It would not be until much later that I would be told that "charly" is also street slang for cocaine. It was the first subliminal message to catch my attention that suggested to me in more ways than one, that the charly was not only Charlie's addiction, but an essential part of his greater destiny. After the class I accompanied him to Namacor where he'd scheduled a maintenance appointment for his sports van which is a Lancia Phedra. Once again I was surprised to discover that Lancia is ventured with Alfa Romeo. Mitx and Elisabet also own an Alfa Romeo. I have always been attracted to the Alfa Romeo. The first time that I'd ever seen one was parked on Main Street in Burlington Ontario, in Canada. I must have been about thirteen or fourteen. It was a classic baby blue and silver coloured 1966 Duetto Spider model. Very pretty. After that, if I was ever asked what my favourite looking car was, I always answered the Alfa first. Not the Ferrari, nor the Lamborghini nor the Porsche but an Alfa. To which I was always told that the Alfa Romeo was pretty but little reliable. Plus I'd actually seen the same model as theirs for the first time a few years earlier. It was in a smooth chocolate brown on display at the mall in Palma. Both Jes and I had liked its look. I'd enjoyed the "what if" question. He reminded me that the Italian made car never escaped the reputation of being unreliable. Sexy but not practical. So there I was four years later with Carles in Alfa Romeo's dealership in Namacor. While he did his thing I walked around in the show room. The new models for 2005 were already out with an attractive price tagged from 25 to 27,000 euros. Despite coincidences it didn't meet my budget. Not that I have one. I need a car and find myself focusing on only a few models when I don't even have any money let alone an income to support a personal loan. I just seem to think I will get something because it's what I believe or know? That my subliminal list of innumerable hints since my conjunction with the Serras, who are also Alfa Romeo car owners, is enough to keep this feeling steadfast, regardless of how foolhardy and back-arse-wards it is. Just this June after being away for a year I went to Sichus for a coffee. Once I sat down I quickly thought of Jes' friend Pepa. Well, no sooner had the thought left me when I saw her coming up to the coffee shop. 'Hey,' I said, 'I was just thinking about you!' '¿Aaa si!? (Really!?)' said Pepa, 'eres realmente la mujer de casualidades, ee (you're really the woman of coincidences, ehh).'

Really, I took her comment to heart. What were the chances of meeting the Serra family in one of the remotest areas of Mayürqa, who own an Alfa Romeo let alone the same one that I had seen with Jesy a few years earlier? What were the chances of finding a family whose patriarch bears the same initials MS, as I do? Whose sons could be surrogate brothers for mine back home in Canada and whose initials are the same as theirs too? Who inadvertently put their place up for rent only weeks before my arrival and whose white washed house puts into focus a dream of mine that I'd had years back? What were the chances of Elisabet giving me the keys to the house with a bear key chain on it? Did she know that the bear had been my totem for 2004? What were the chances of the owners being teachers, and that the school where Elisabet works is not only one of an exclusive few that offers a bi-lingual English immersion programme using native English teachers? What were the chances of Mitx' younger brother Carles making a casual request to find a native speaking English teacher in the remote area that they live in, only months before I moved into his brother's place!? Finally what were the chances of my new address in 2005, being reserved for Dasha and I with number 50 while the house facing right across from mine appears erroneous with number 33. Or is it?? Jes and Jaime would not think so. There is more but really, I ask again: what were the chances? There was a time too, that I liked the image of me driving a white automatic HRV Honda. It came-out three or four years ago. I'd test driven one with Xisco. Well, actually, he test drove it while I sat in the back seat because it was a manual. It was priced at 25,000 euros with a five year warranty, but I remember thinking that it was too bare on the inside for the price it was asking, regardless of its Honda name. Notwithstanding Xisco ended up buying a Honda Civic hatchback! Well on the day with Charlie, I noticed that there happened to be a Honda dealership next to the Alfa Romeo one. While Charlie continued to do his thing I walked over to have a look. Apparently there is no HRV automatic model on the island let alone a white standard one anywhere in Spain? Plus, I was told that the HRV was going to be phased out in 2005. There was however a second hand mustard model on display in the parking lot with a five year renewal on the warranty, but, but, if they are being phased-out maybe not a good idea to buy? Especially at 25,000 euros? Truth be told, I am hoping to get a new car. As my first car, I don't want to worry about what I am driving. Renting has probably spoiled me there at some level. Plus I am secretly wishing for it to be an automatic even though a standard widens my options and therefore makes it easier to find, and of course, makes it less pricey than an automatic. Sigh. My head says to go for a standard and just learn to drive it. I used to drive Jes' Ford Fiesta around the village area, but I really do not have the confidence or the skill. I would have to take Drivers Ed and that is another issue of contention; six months for 500 euros when I already have a driver's licence. Then again, regardless of what car I might get, I'll still have to get a Spanish driver's licence at some point. My international one won't get me by forever. At any rate, all logic aside, I prefer an automatic car especially out here with narrow streets, poor parking areas, etc. Just easier. Besides, like all things here, with time it will become just as popular as it is in America. Gawd. How or where am I going to find a new automatic car of my choice? Without a Spanish driver's licence, and above all, the more important detail: no income or funds. Crazy. Just hysterically crazy. Why doesn't any of this intimidate me or how is it that I feel that it will happen? Other choices: The Citroën C3? Ford Focus? Dream car? A Mini... Hysterical, absolutely hysterical!

> Neither a lofty degree of intelligence
> Nor imagination
> Nor both together
> Go to the making of genius.
> Love, love, love
> That is the soul of genius.
> WOLFGANG AMADEUS MOZART

Mspace

We didn't go home right after the car dealership. Instead we drove to Charlie's restaurant in order to pick-up lunch for us and his brother Mitx' family. I couldn't believe it when Charlie turned off the Inca-Namacor road into a restaurant's parking lot. Only a few days earlier I had coincidentally driven into the very same parking lot in order to turn around from where I had come. In doing so, I was impressed by the large number of cars in the parking lot and thought: '*Wow, these people must be doing really well with so many people already here.*' It was only 1:30 in the afternoon, in the northeast of Mayürqa and in the middle of a work week!? Well, the business happens to be Charlie's, and when we drove in, it was still looking pretty healthy. As he parked the car I glanced at the restaurant's name: Sa Croix. I was slightly surprised by its religious content. It reminded me that Charlie with his apparent unconventional ways was still a product from pragmatic generation values deeply rooted in the catholic tradition. To which I furtively felt was reason enough for a cocaine addiction. Anyway, I read-into the name some more. "Sa" in Mayürqan is the equivalent to the Catalan use of "La" or "The" in English. It can also be used as a possessive pronoun in the third person singular to highlight aristocratic or hierarchical possession, or as an adjective meaning "healthy" when placed before its noun. "Croix" means cross in French. One could suggest therefore that Sa Croix – The Cross, is both "One's Cross" and "Healthy Cross" subliminally evident within the name. Either way the name is a subtle paradox to Charlie's current situation as well as a subliminal juxtaposition of terms. *One's* Cross could be subliminal for *Charlie's* Cross or in pseudo terms, even slang for *Cocaine's* Cross. "Healthy" can become ill, just like a "Cross" can be something to bear. '*How ironic,*' I mused, 'that Sa Croix, with reference to the idea of Charlie's Cross, covets a contradiction much like Charlie who is mostly at battle against himself. As if there had existed an unconscious dual between good and bad, whereby the polarity of the two words were kept in balance by yin-yang elements in disguise. Should one side gain in weight then the balance would lean in favour of that weight.' …I paused in my thoughts. I was obviously reading way too much into a simple restaurant name. The name was probably thought-up during a "why not?" moment void of any reason. Precisely why, I just could not stop noticing the camouflaged relationship between Charlie, the restaurant and his destiny. Something so complex yet simple was Life's work. Not a conscious effort. Sa Croix from what I had been told is very well known in the area and has made a lot of money for Charlie. That result however also encouraged Charlie's increased use of cocaine to the point of neglecting his work at the restaurant. So that, in light of what I saw that day, Sa Croix' business is not doing as well as it used to. A time that must have been a golden moment, because the parking lot on both days that I was there was packed! Metaphorically speaking, it's as though Carles' "charly" or "cocaine" gained in power, removed the polar balance and thus weakened Sa Croix by literally draining its *health* from the Cross.

Such that Sa Croix is no longer able to counter balance the "charly" in Carles. Instead it has become a "charly cross" to bear. In simpler terms bad gained on good. As I sat there waiting for him, I was both delighted and fascinated by my name game. In my mind's eye I had touched on something. Charlie was destined with cocaine and Sa Croix only made it clearer. It also offered me a hypothetical perspective of his future. If Charlie got better then he would have to change the name of the restaurant, because while the nickname

Charlie and its pseudo meaning could be forgotten, it would not disappear as long as his name was Carles. Even if the weight from regaining his health eradicated the "charly" within Carles, and restored the balance back to Sa Croix as "The *healthy* Cross" per se, the weight of the good in this balance would have to be indefinitely heavier in order to avoid the risk of the *charly* coming back. Of course the odds of a cocaine addict remaining in an indefinite stage of recovery are very slim. Then again, the power of a cross when rejuvenated is insurmountable by virtue of its own pseudo nickname: love. …'*Maybe*,' I thought, '*just maybe, he wouldn't have to change the name after all.*'

Cars

I am drawn to the C3 because of a few trips made with Jesy. In Ibiza, Menorca and Galicia the rented car was a C3: a small but mighty thing. When we went to Galicia, we had Dasha with us and her cage. Both of them actually fit in the back with our luggage. Anyway, it drove quite well, Jesy liked it, gutsy and not ostentatious looking. As a new car it might also be within budget. It's one of those cars that's middle of the road in quality, safety and price. I'm thinking no more than 15 or 16,000 euros. The Ford Focus is a better car and definitely has an automatic version, drives well and way back in 2001 Jesy and I actually looked at one when it had just entered the European market. At that time Ford carried the American stigma of being poorly made cars. Now it's quite a popular car. The Focus we looked at was a navy blue, fully equipped hatch back. I liked it very much. At the time it was priced at 20,000 pesetas., about 13,000 euros. Today the new Ford Focus hatch back is still quite nice and now priced at 18,000 euros! Higher than my suggested budget. However I can't wave away how often that car seems to pop up into my life. Aside from rentals, even Jes' company car was a green Ford Focus wagon and the same green colour as dad's first two cars. I know, absolutely ridiculous considerations when looking for a car or are they? Everybody has their way of doing things. People's methods are rational to others only when they can relate or understand them. I am not alone in my ways. This I know is true. However, the very nature of my way is a solitary one because it does not breed attention nor does it seek it. An intimate relationship with Life is what it is. Like that with a partner, it's not usually shared with others. Anyway, I also checked-out the more exclusive brands like Audi, Golf etc., and they all felt unpleasant. Automatic cars were available but would have to be ordered from the mainland and even then with basic equipment they started at 22,000 euros. In all honesty these cars are not me. Then when I went to look at the Minis the representative who attended me was frankly a male prat. Without even taking the time to sit down with me and discuss possibilities, he simply told me that there were no Minis anywhere on the island, that there would not be any until spring 2005 and even those were already all sold out!? So I suggested that maybe we could enquire on-line between Mini dealerships, if anything was available. He wouldn't even try and suggested that I could do that myself on the internet. He was your typical looking sales rep prat; dark shoulder length hair greased back and an attractive face that instantly disappeared when he spoke. Arrogant and presumptuous, he was dressed in the required tie and jacket that was severely creased at the buttocks. His body language towards me suggested that my casual-look was fashionably inadequate and failed to meet BMW's potential client perspective. In hindsight I'm sure they were insecurities on my part because I'm not in fact economically well-off enough to even buy, let alone shop for a Mini. Notwithstanding, his pompous behaviour which could have won him first prize as the best ass in sales representation provoked the stubborn roots within, and a fiery self-righteous desire to challenge his arrogance. His "Spanglish" continued to whirr past my ears, 'Not one Mini is available on the island, and for sure not an automatic one either. Sorry, I can't help you.'

'But are you *sure*?' I asked.

'Sure,' he said. Then as if content that Life was my witness, I left. '*First prize*,' I thought, '*he really deserves first prize.*'

The unexamined life is not worth living – SOCRATES.

The walk

The front view from Michèle's house offered a glimpse into thick pine woods that appeared to go on for miles. The back road into these woods was located about fifty meters in front of her place. Made up of dry brown dirt, the path was sediment with loose stone rubble, wide enough for cars to drive along, but not recommended for anyone who cared about their car's suspension problems. At around 9a.m. Michèle and Dasha headed out for their morning walk. She was going to call Carles but decided that she preferred to go alone with Dasha. Today was the first day that she and Dasha were going to try-out the back road and visit the pine woods. Their way into the woods began as soon as the paved road disappeared into the dirt path that led into an enchanted green and brown coloured backdrop. As their gradual pace into the woods increased, the view and the constant sound of the sea behind them faded lighter and lighter until the distance between there and them was petered out. She walked on watching Dasha lead the way, darting in and out of pine tree trails at the same time. It reminded Michèle of another time when they'd done a similar walk with Jes. He'd mentioned that Dasha had probably done an extra five kilometres from having run around so much. That memory was at least three years old and Dasha still seemed to have the same energy. The woods were quiet except for the odd muffled sounds of hidden partridges and Michèle's awkward footing over the loose rubble. Eventually a physical adjustment was made and the new environment began to sit well with her. There she was with Dasha suddenly walking deeper into a perennial view of sprawling pine trees that happened to exist just outside their front door. The geographical setting of their place directly centred between the sea and the woods hinted at an epitome of equilibrium. Again, how incredible it was that this very back road be in front of her place and behind the house with number 33 on it. She wasn't looking for ways to justify their destiny there, but divine intervention was not excluded from her thoughts or the sensation of well-being she was feeling from its presence. The sensation grew into amazement because she recalled again the mock wish list in her journal that basically brain stormed quiet ideas and blurry visuals of a lifestyle she was currently discovering, without having had any idea if they or it even existed. She'd known about Sa Ema, but she had not been aware of the back road until after their arrival. The path continued in a gradual ascension until the pine woods thinned out into nothing. She stopped for a moment in order to assess the distance behind her: trails blanketed with pine needles extended from the main path deeper into the woods like branches from a tree trunk, while pine trees loomed thickly overhead creating an optical illusion of a green blue sky. Finally, far off to the east were the mountains, stoic and patient above a lively sea below them. Her senses were overwhelmed by her sense of gratitude. 'Thank-you,' she whispered and veered back to her walk. Then as if someone only inches in front of her had suddenly stopped dead in his tracks Michèle stumbled to a halt: 'Oh. My. Gawd,' she voiced. The path, without even a hint from Dasha, who had already covered the ten yards ahead of her, had ever so subtly but swiftly given way to vast open farm land. She was so surprised. The scene before her was nothing like the one behind them. She loved the countryside and Mayürqa's was particularly attractive to her. It was tamed land that went on for miles. The colour of vibrant green fields was slightly smeared with a rusty coloured mud typically seen in the island's country side. There were medium sized trees that dotted areas of the open landscape; goats that meshed with the colour of the earth were made visible by the soft clatter noise of a jug-bell around their necks; man made trails led to rolled stacks of hay or distant farm houses. Then farther into the east, more mountains met the land with an equally stoic image as the ones by the sea. The vast area of farmland was equal in size to the open sky and flanked both sides of the path with well-maintained stone hedges. It was the yellow brick road without the yellow and without the brick. With the view thus made clearer, their destination point appeared to be an old church that could be seen into the distance. She continued along the path with Dasha and marvelled at the surroundings. At some interval points of the stone hedges, gates, made with thick wooden beams, offered access to the open farmland. Deeper along the path they came across a small closed-in section reserved for a family of chatty black pigs. One was a sow to which Dasha gave a nervous but confident bark of hello. The path continued to extend parallel with the stone hedges which sometimes impeded a clear view of the farmland, because of dense red thorn bushes entangled along the top of them. Then there was another sound, but Michèle could not make it out right away. It was not until the bushes had thinned out that the sound was heard more clearly. A hundred horses or more were romping and grazing within an open pasture. It was such a sight to see so many horses in different shades of brown, fill what was only minutes earlier a void space. There were even a few "Pinto" horses. As if saturated by the gifts, she stared at the moving picture unable to assimilate the mental sensations of what was going on in her head. She had often identified herself with the Pinto. It was to her, an animal of unique attraction and its very nature as a wild horse was something she felt close too. The more interesting part had come earlier that same year when she'd learned that her Chinese horoscope was under the year of the horse and that the Pinto's origins were none other than Spanish. '*Funny,*' she thought. The relationship between those subtleties and her inner image of herself as a Pinto provoked questions about destiny and fate... *Was she closer to home than she'd realised? Was it a mere coincidence or a sense of personal projection? Canada was her home, and like the Canada goose, was "strong" and "free" and had made her flight across the big puddle. Although Canada was a young country it still conserved the roots and the very origins of her existence from Anglo Europe. Maybe in a life before, she had been in Europe and sometime way before that, she had been a wild Pinto roaming a land that is now defined as Spain?* she smiled, intrigued by her own imagination. *Had she been born with such knowledge which had to be discovered by her from within her? Kind of like Dorothy in the Wizard of Oz who made a long quest to find the answer to her way home, only to discover that the answer had been with her the whole time in the red shoes that she wore. What if Life was about that? A plan, or set of destinies for one to discover and use to help achieve the right dénouement of one's life? Some people call theses destinies exams or scripts. Where only one of the many, is the actual one written for each individual before birth and made attainable by noticing subliminal messages in nature, coincidences, and images people call wishes or dreams. Her imagination was not so outlandish. Many traditional cultures offered different theories on the same questions, but they all shared the same bottom line: a simple recognition of another dimension from the world they breathed in. The same could be suggested about the different types of religions because they all shared the purpose of being an exemplary human being. Religion was about respecting Life on earth while spiritually it was about respecting its dimension beyond it. Key to both however was honesty to oneself. If one was strictly truthful to his or herself then the balance between the two could be found and one could live the life that was desired and therefore "meant" for that one. The analogy was simple enough but tough to do. Figuring out one's truth on a daily basis could be a lifetime task with no guarantee of success. One might even have to die and try all over again the next time round if there was a next time. Her conclusions she felt were not on target but not far off either. There was Ontology, and Asian philosophies that supported them, albeit theirs were down to a science while hers were mere gut feelings constantly battling against influences to confuse her truth. Hence Life it seemed, had a different exam for everyone before it granted or not, the pre-written script to its owner. Abstract thoughts continued to deluge her mind from one sensation to another. It was good Feng Shui living in equilibrium among earth, sea, and air; it was a shift from bear totems in 2004 to horse totems in 2005; there was the presence of farm animals, wild rabbits and a dog that underlined strength, sensitivity, independence, intuition, loyalty, abundance and intelligence. She was living between the patient pragmatic realism of nature and the passion, the movement and the ingenuity of the sea. In Chinese symbolism she was a horse and now she had a hundred in front of her. The country was Jes, and the sea was her dad nearby. There was another presence or angel she felt, but her spiritual memory had yet to remember its name. All three were involved in her arrival and in that she was sure. She and Dasha were exactly where they were meant to be. How long she did not know, but for the first time in her life it was neither a hypothetical question nor a mere sensation of faith. She knew. The information granted to her was just that. Life for some reason did not hold back in letting her know. Why? What challenges were ahead to disquiet the balance of the current moment which was so incredible? Metaphorically thinking she wondered if she had unintentionally made a deal with the devil? It was her habit to look for the polar side of her wellbeing, but the sensation of both Jes and her dad's presence discarded the notion. Many people had a life in plenitude without feeling guilty, nor the need to justify it. However Michèle could not. Her life's experience albeit beautiful was also deeply marked by loss and separation. Survival tactics included a provisional state of mind that anticipated change and its challenges before they materialised. It was about living the now intensely and watching the future almost simultaneously* ... Her walking pace had picked up with the velocity of her thoughts. Even Dasha was now trailing behind her.. *Perhaps this insight about her lines was meant to help her with impending challenges? A kind of reminder when things got tough and foggy that in spite of pragmatic solutions, Life wanted her there?* 'Wow, what's on the horizon?' she asked out loud. She did not know. She tried not to rationalise so much. Yet everything had a purpose and since the day she and Dasha had landed back in Mayürqa, this enlightenment about her script, had practically been handed to her on a daily basis. Or so she felt. She veered around a bend that ended the path through the farm pastures and led her and Dasha into the back area of a beautiful old farm house. It was possibly part and parcel with the farm land behind them, but Michèle was not sure. There were chickens, geese, ducks, dogs, and sheep in another annexed pasture, more pigs and to add fable to reality even a rooster with an intense red crown of the kind Disney portrays in its animation films. At another hundred meters or so the path turned back into a paved road that brought them face to face with the old church. It was a lovely area. The church was all closed up and its colour was a light brown that the passing of centuries had turned almost beige. Its structure was traditionally indicative of Arab and Christian influences yet maintained a tower with an old bell ironically the size of Liberty's. Facing the church was an extended view of a large estate home that looked reminiscent of Wuthering Heights from the eighteenth century. Then within a stone's throw away, as if to bring the walk into full perfection, was a local restaurant built in Mayürqan stone. Not only did the place offer patio tables outside, and a tremendous view of the farmland they had just walked through but coffee and croissants too! Michèle could not have designed her favourite morning moment any better. It was just too much. Someone or thing had intervened for her. Tears of happy frustration wet the eyes. She wanted to love or hug someone. Where was Jes? He was there. He knew about the country walks and coffee moments. Her dad was there too; much of how she'd lived her life had been by way of him. Her sense of emotion was frustrated by the inability to see them or touch them. So much energy without a means to feed it physically except for the light shiver and goose bumps that she did feel. It was a connection that might have been tangible enough for them but not for her. Dasha had treaded closer to the bar and found her spot in the shade. It occurred to Michèle in a funny way that she had knowledge about Dasha's future, thereby her destiny simply because she was human and had a hand in her life. That while Michèle was able to observe Dasha's life without her knowledge, protect or anticipate Dasha's immediate future slightly before Dasha could, the same might be true about Michèle's life. That someone or something was doing the same with hers.

Seek and ye shall find – MATTHEW 7:7:8.

C3

She wondered, "*Is it an XTR-C3?*" After discovering that the Honda was less than likely and that there were no Minis available on the island, it would seem that the only two possibilities were the Ford Focus and the Citroën C3. She could consider a Golf Volkswagon because they're pretty well recommended and friends of hers owned Golfs, but she just wasn't drawn to it. So, on her way back to Sa Ema from Namacor she was feeling pretty down trying to fish out other possibilities. Her memory went back to the C3 that she and Jes had rented a few times during their travels. They'd both enjoyed the car and it was economically practical too. Right about that thought, she'd already entered the roundabout from Namacor to Sa Ema and in the midst of the turn simultaneously wondered about where she might find a Citroen dealership and with that feeling, realised that she was not ready to head home yet. So within a millisecond of her thoughts she passed the exit to Sa Ema and decided to take the one for Juníper village instead. "*Why not?*" flashed passed her mind. Even though it was lunch time and things were bound to be closed, the exit to the village was one that she'd often wondered about. '*Might as well check it out then,*' she flashed back to herself while veering into the village. As soon as she drove in, she instantly felt well. It was pretty and retained a lot of the traditional flavour that Sichus also had. When she got to the second intersection she hesitated: 'G*o straight on to San Joan road or turn right towards Sichus road?*' Thinking of Jes, she turned right, and as soon as she finished her right turn she and the Focus found themselves right in front of a C3 dealership – and, it was open! 'Wow,' she uttered to herself, and didn't waste a moment in letting "*them*" know how impressed she was by the coincidence. When she entered the place a friendly man of about fifty years plus greeted her and gave her his full attention. Unlike the prat from the Mini dealership, this man from the village made her feel well. It was almost enough to justify getting the C3. The man took his time all the way through lunch. There was more than one model. One in particular was called the XTR-C3, a semi-automatic shift, fully equipped, ivory coloured like Dasha, and nicely priced at 14,000 euros. Plus the very same man had sold a car to Carles and knew Mitx and Elisabet quite well. In light of the fact that the Serra family was from Juníper reduced the coincidence only slightly but not completely, considering that only moments earlier, Michèle had no idea about Citröen in Juníper let alone the fact that Carles had bought a Citröen from that man? – '*No way!?*' The vision of Carles in a Citröen made her chuckle audibly enough for the man to explain that Charlie had needed a little van for work and bought a Citroën Jumper. *'So even Charlie liked Citroën,'* flashed through her head and then froze when the thought recognised a subliminal coincidence in C3: Charlie-Jesy codes. *'Gawd!'* her mind was amused, *'when does it stop?'*

The visit went well and she felt lighter in spirit to say the least. There appeared to be a slight push from above. She would check-out Ford the next day and see which dealership would process the paperwork easier without a Spanish driver's licence and which in the end was better priced. Something however was telling her that her connection with Charlie was the key. That night she wrote in her journal: "I just hoped my first car was a bit better? I dunno. Bla, bla, bla. We'll see. You could have a Golf. The Mini? None left. Yea, yea, I know."

Connected

Journal: November 10 today, and dad's 64th. birthday. The walk this morning, like several in the past, was through the pine woods and then via the vast area of open land beyond them. As far as the eye could see the land was a plush green, accentuated by strong earth tones lightly dotted by tree clusters here and there. The rain from the night before had intensified nature's colours, left the dirt road wet and pasty, pot holes full of water and puddles as wide as the diameter of the road. Then by the final bend, the freshness of the country air was lost to the foul smell of the farm animals nearby. Dasha and I held our breath until we got past the church. Then, with a sense of delighted relief, stopped at the bar-restaurant for the morning coffee and croissant. I sat at the patio table outside, Dasha found her spot nearby and I took in my surroundings. Tomorrow, torrential rain and thunder mixture are forecasted. The colours and the effects from the lightning over the wet green pastures; jagged mountains with mossy patches; the sea and a sky with flashing clouds – it is all so beautiful and I am here to see it!? I apparently live here right now …It scares me when it's all so good - for how long? I think of the black and white photo of daddy and I in Cape Cod Massachusetts. We are sitting on the beach by the sea on a windy day. I must have been about two or three while daddy was not quite thirty yet. It dawned on me tonight that the photo was probably taken by mum. Just like the photo of Jesy, Dasha and I in the sea at Sa Ema, was also taken by her. They are possibly two of the most foretelling photos that I own by virtue of the fact that my dad always used to sing, "By the sea". That the photo with Jesy Dasha and I was taken in May 2003 and not only happens to include the home where Dasha and I are now living but too, I've discovered, Charlie's place "by the sea" is in the photo as well?!! ... There is a sensation that both men are routing for me from heaven. Connected, as the year 2005 approaches, I am feeling connected. In light of today's weather it would appear that I will get an automatic Ford Focus in a blackboard grey colour. Funny the same colour as the floors in the new place. Seems like whatever I focus on, the energy from my imagination finds an added outlet to my life. Some would call it self-projecting although I did not have my floors in mind when I chose the car colour. Even the C3 highlighted subliminal messages that in the end were nothing more than offering me insight to options and the fact that the Serras are somehow important for me right now. I am anxious about money. Secretly hoping or believing that something will happen by the 18th. Vladimir will visit me from Lithuania that week, and I actually have a lottery ticket for an early-bird Christmas draw that week. Although we all know that I have never had that kind of luck. Although, thinking of dad up there yea never know! Heh, heh. Thankful to him for impressing upon me the lesson of life and patience; of how to make a life and not a living. Relieved by me for listening and respecting his guidance. At thirty-seven, I shall hope to purchase my very first car! Thank you for the angels in disguise – Happy birthday dad!

Let's see if I can buy me a Mini in Mayürqa – M. 9.10.04.

The Mini tease

Michèle looked at the date at the top of the daily newspaper: *'November 11– Remembrance Day,'* she thought. It was raining once again. Michèle and Dasha had walked to a bar that was by no means the closest but had an open terrace with a great landing over it. She loved those moments when it was possible to enjoy a rainy day. With her coffee and a local "pa amb oli", bread with oil, she and Dasha sat outside under the landing enjoying the sounds and the view before them. The sea in front of them roared in a grey rage with white foamcaps. Like those blustery days at Cape Cod, the Mediterranean Sea that day could have easily been mistaken for her ocean cousin on the Atlantic. Huge waves crashed on shore nonstop and the smell of wet salt and seaweed powdered the air via a wet mist. Memories of childhood days in Cape Cod with family and relatives swelled inside her like the waves in front. Then after coffee, Michèle found a sms in her telephone from Charlie. He wanted to know if she would drive him to the dealership, so that he could pick up his car. When they got to the dealership, there on display in full glamour was a yellow blacktop Mini Cooper! It was 15,000 euros, fully equipped with 17000km on it. A new Mini would cost about 20,000 euros, and an automatic was about 22,000 euros. So the price was good albeit a second hand. Notwithstanding, a new Ford Focus was the same price. Then again, as her first car, a second hand Mini was permissible just on resale value alone. Plus it was yellow! The colour that identified itself to her. Even her dad once surprised her with a high school ring in which its stone was fiery yellow. Heck even Dasha was a soft gold colour. She took a closer look. It was a standard of course, but she could learn. She sighed. How Life teased her. There was always something. In spite of her excitement it was still more logical to buy the Ford. It would be new, same price, under the dealership's guarantee and automatic. '*Keep it simple,*' she thought. It was already tough enough that she did not have the income or the proper paperwork in the first place. Better not push her luck getting a standard from a private sale. Once Charlie was ready to leave with his Phedra, Michèle got back into the rental and also headed out. As she drove home her mind whirred with frustrated thoughts until she couldn't keep them inside any longer: 'So WHY?! Show me the Mini!?' she retorted-out loudly. Her vocal action distracted her enough to make her take the wrong exit from the roundabout she'd come upon and drive until the first opportunity arrived for her to turn back. She was less than fifty meters away when she saw the little sign for Ariany. A tiny and reclusive village that she had never visited before and thought to check it out while she was there. However the road to Ariany from the main road was so bleak and the village seemed so remote that she changed her mind and slated the adventure for another day. Instead she slowed the car to a stop just within the entranceway to the village and sat there for a few minutes to take in the surroundings. Into the distance beyond sprawling fields, the rear view mirror reflected the little village propped on top of a hill like something out of an enchanted fable. It provoked wonderment about the place and a greater interest to return. Slightly calmer, she turned the car around and merged into traffic heading back the right way. The afternoon was grey but of the shade that soothes, so that the Mini tease was forgiven and a wrong turn became a pleasant introduction to a neat little hamlet called Ariany. She was in fact having a great day. A sense of quiet reservation and self- embarrassment flooded her cheeks, 'Sorry for my outburst,' she whispered, 'happy Remembrance Day everyone,' and drove home.

Luck, is when preparation and opportunity meet – ELMER LETERMAN.

Devil or Angel

Journal: The Ford company needs someone to co-sign their financing to me because it's full financing and the documentation that I gave them from work was not enough because the company is not Spanish. I'm feeling conflicting messages here. On one hand the sales rep willing to assist me is excellent. His name is Joan and he has been so good at trying to locate a car for me and finding ways to finance it too. I know that it's not all altruistic but heck, if we got the car I would be very happy if he earned a good commission on it. I've pretty much decided on the Ford Focus 2004. There are no automatics on the island, but Joan literally sat me down and spent a good while on intranet trying to locate one on the mainland and he did! He actually found a few and asked me to choose a colour among blackboard black, cherry red or navy blue. Not exactly the best choices so I went for the blue. It's not the car of my dreams, but it will be new with a three year guarantee. I won't have to worry about insurance and Traffic's red tape because the dealership takes care of all that, and the fact that it's from a dealership relieves anxiety about maintenance issues or being swindled. The catch however, is that I don't have any evidence of an income therefore I need a co-signer. The fact that I don't have any evidence of an income is a slight misdemeanour. I can take a loan from the bank with slightly better interest rates, however the banks won't give me a loan without a guarantor. Not even my own bank, even though I have a good credit rating and a loan precedence with them that was completely paid back even before it had matured! Hence both possibilities want a co-signer and it has to be someone Spanish and with convincing assets. Sigh. So on our walk for coffee today, I shared my concerns with Charlie. He was wearing jeans, a red and white ski jacket and frankly awful faded red dress shoes. He wasn't exactly dressed for an early morning walk for coffee as early as 8:30a.m., which for Charlie, was really impressive considering the fact that he'd probably been out doing lines the night before, until early this morning. Anyway, Charlie listened to me while I calmly shared my situation with him. He walked along beside me while sucking on the zipper of his jacket that he'd done-up to his neck. When I had finished, he simply said: 'I can lend you the money.' 'Why would you do that?' I replied, 'you don't even know me.' I could not believe how quickly he offered the money and how equally quick I shot it down. In fact I had not even thought about him as a possibility precisely because of his addiction, his brother being my landlord and the simple fact that we had only met less than three weeks earlier?! Then again, had I been a bit more astute I probably should have, by reason of the fact that a cocaine addict probably had the money. Duuuh. He was silent as if almost embarrassed and then said, 'Well I know where you live.' It was a good way to alleviate the moment. Money is never easy to talk about especially 20,000 euros. I thought maybe he was offering to help because I hadn't been charging him for the English lessons. Then in that same instant it also dawned on me that he had made a misconception about me. When I'd arrived in October I'd paid his brother six months in advance. It was money from a bonus that I'd received from work. I hadn't been sure about future employment so I'd wanted to guarantee rent for at least six months. It was obvious that his brother had told him. Charlie thought that I had money. 'Thank you for your trust Charlie. I won't borrow from you, but if I can't find a co-signer maybe you could help me with that?' He seemed relieved at the possibility of helping me. It must run part and parcel with the addiction: feeling a sense of worth. It is true. I am the new chick on the block and he is giving me his attention until the day will come when I will probably know too much or until he finds someone else who knows nothing about his past. Yes, in spite of my own warning bells I still hang out with him. Truth be known I just like him. Gawd awful shoes and all. Plus, Sa Ema's own local pink press has already notified neighbouring villages that Charlie has been hanging out with a blond chic. Apparently the day after our first coffee together, someone from the bar we were in, mentioned it to somebody in Juníper village which is twenty minutes away, who in turn told his wife who lives twenty minutes further from Juníper. The speed at which it reached his wife was even faster than the gossip that gets around on cruise ships. When Charlie told me my first reaction was concern for him. However he simply shook it away and said not to worry. Then later this afternoon we went to Sa Croix to pick up some *paella* to have lunch with Elisabet and Mitx at their place. Once we got to Sa Croix he did his rounds and showed me the restaurant entirely, including the kitchen and storage areas. I was impressed to say the least and also enjoyed the authenticity of the kitchen, where the U.S. Public Health commission would probably have a field day re-standardising it with sterile utensils, produce, and poultry! I was also taken by Charlie. Everything about him was attractive to me. He was very observant of the restaurant's activity, yet subtle about it. He dressed casually in jeans but wore sharp expensive men shirts. His charismatic skills were obvious ingredients to his success as well as his attention to detail. One of the first things I looked for was the washrooms, where my expectations on cleanliness and freshness are probably higher than the United States' Public Health's and influence how I feel about the food and atmosphere. Well they were impeccable. I watched him with his staff and did notice then, an abrasive streak that was less attractive and said to me that Charlie is the ingenuity, the organiser and the hard working owner, without the latest in management skills. It bordered the traditional top down of, "do as I say and not as I do" format. A point that I have registered and saved for myself because I think Charlie is somebody one would rather have as a friend than a foe. We had a coffee there and then took off for lunch at Sa Ema de Farrutx which was really great. It's becoming a nice routine having lunch downstairs with everyone. We sit in the kitchen, Elisabet, Mitx, their two sons, then Charlie and I; a quasi-surrogate family for me per se. Then after lunch, an English hour with Charlie upstairs at my place. After that, a pleasant walk with Dasha and my moment on the roof terrace with dad and Jesy dressed in his blue suede overcoat. It's raining torrentially right now. Dasha is under the bathroom sink anxious from the storm, while the car issue is challenging my anxiety levels. Charlie is willing to go to his bank and see if anything can be done, however the possible ramifications from his potential help dissuade me. I have yet to get my head around it. Would it be a deal with the devil or a gift opportunity from an angel? I'm not sure yet.

Déjà vu?

She and Dasha were on the roof terrace watching the arrival of an electrical storm. Evidence of the impending torrential rain about to hit their home was apparent. It was like a moving light show that vividly lit up what appeared to be an incredibly indignant sea! Dasha was in fact not impressed and already on standby at the stare-well that lead down to her safety spot under the bathroom sink. Michèle on the other hand wanted to stay as long as she could: *Where was she? How did she get there? Began a lucid voice... Moving back in time, she reviewed the moments of her life. Then, when she'd zoomed them down to the existential second, it struck her as overwhelming that every detail of them was contained within a mere thirty-eight years. Every chapter from the time that she was conceived until the moment where she was then, was connected. She could see that. Every episode had a message or a clue for her Way that she only then noticed. How far back does destiny begin? Even the birth of her parents belongs to hers and theirs before them. Her animated mind saw time flash back through centuries of relatives until a screened-like image just got sucked up into a black dot and poof! Disappeared! Her name, where she was born, her language skills, her features, her childhood in Canada, even the sports that stuck-out most in her life, her academic path, her life in Japan and other parts of the globe, her professional endeavours so neatly divided between vacation industries and teaching; the men she'd loved, the places where she'd lived, the people who are her family, their names. They all had indicative hints that foretold her arrival to Sa Ema de Farrutx ...* She paused from her mental kaleidoscope and took-in the view of the storm out at sea. It was like being out on a ship without having to be away from home. She had worked for prominent vacation industry companies, but understood much later that cruise ships had been a firm part of the plan... *She was thirteen when the first clue found her. She was in Jamaica with her dad and two brothers. While they swam at Dr. Caves Beach, a very large Cruise ship docked nearby. In water up to her waist she pondered the ship and unconsciously wondered what it would be like to work on one, unaware that exactly fifteen years later she would find out and even return to the very same port as an Assistant Cruise Director...* The smell of the sea came to her by a salted wind and changed the focus of her memory to Dubai, a place where she had lived for a year on her own. The memory recalled an image of her at Chicago Beach Village which had been an exclusive residential area in Dubai. ... *She was jogging on the spot in the middle of a pier that extended into the Persian Gulf. Friends of hers from Québec had a home there and she was staying at their place for the weekend. She remembered how the rhythm of her jog fell into pace with the ocean. She so wanted to stay in a place like that: a modest looking residential area with privileged amenities such as living next door to the sea. A place culturally distinct from her own, with a comfortable standard of living, and where time was still somewhat in the past and far away from excessive progress. It offered plenty of professional and economic possibilities, an international flavour of expatriates, and above all great weather and natural beauty. Its artificial fabric however was like living in Disney World gone surreal.* She had lived in Dubai a bit more than a year, then the experience was enough to let her know that there was somewhere else to go. She'd focused on her rhythmic jog and the way dusk in the Middle East fell before her; like a call from gravity the sun went down like an orange planet into the mouth of the Gulf. There were different pastel shades of blue, pink, and orange colours that hued the horizon, while the sea miraculously enough did swallow – Snap! She came out of her memory quickly as if she'd just been hit with something. Mayürqa, she realised, matched her mock description. Dubai had been close but not the place. Had it been a foretelling or simply mental projection again? She did not know or cared for an answer, but her memory suddenly widened and hooked on to something else. The mere coincidence that began as far back as 1990, *while studying in San Diego California, she had visited the San Diego de Acala Mission which had been founded by no other than Friar Miquel Jose Junipero Serra, who unknown to her at the time, was born in Petra Mayürqa!* There was even a street in Sa Ema named after him and even more absurd was the fact that Friar Junipero died on the 28th, in August of 1784... 28 again? Charlie and Christopher's Life numbers summing it up to 1: strength. Intellectually, she noticed two spirits that esoterically appeared to be one and all so connected to her. It was just an interesting observation and enough to highlight a pale yet ever so noticeable connection among them all. Her imagination considered a past life when they might have known each other and maybe she and Charlie had been in love and fated to lose each other causing them a life after life trying to break the spell? "Many lives and many Masters" was a book that she'd read and that offered her nonsense some probability and allowed her to imagine a further suggestion that it was not entirely about Charlie, but maybe about her dad too, whose mannerisms and way of being often surfaced in Charlie? She smiled at her mind's absurdities... 'Crazy, so crazy,' she muttered to herself, feeling that something was linked to her father and her attraction to Charlie and the Serra family... Rain drops began to mark the terrace. She looked up quickly into the dark wet and whispered ever so slowly: 'How long may I stay here? Keep this? Longer I hope? Maybe a place to grow old in; *my* family will come?' she asked. 'Thank you for everything,' and then went to look for Dasha, more than likely under the bathroom sink.

> The darker the night the nearer the dawn.
> HENRY WADSWORTH LONGFELLOW

Stress

Journal: O.K., car trouble. I need someone to co-sign a loan. I would ask Francisco, but I'm too shy or uncomfortable with that. The bank will lend me 6,000 euros which I could use as a finance payment towards the Ford Focus. I might still need a guarantor, but even if the car dealership waves that requirement then I will be stuck with two payments; one to the car company and the other to the bank. I would really prefer to have one significant bank loan in order to buy the car and consolidate my other payments into one statement a month. It just feels tidier. The difficulty is that I don't have a job. Should I be looking for a job while I have the rented car? I'm not in the mood to start that yet. Go figure. Like I am going to buy a car without any money or an income, then get my stuff delivered to me from Canada, sort that out, do Christmas and then in January begin my new year looking for a job. I love the agenda, but how unreal is that? Major unrealistic and stubborn. Then again there is no point in looking for work if my heart isn't there yet. If I don't make a financial deposit then I need to find a guarantor or co-signer. My girlfriend offered to help, but unfortunately her paperwork was not adequate; neither for the bank nor for the dealership. Then the Ford dealership offered to reconsider her paperwork with another lending company, but it was feeling too messy and dodgy so I turned the offer down. It meant that she had to photocopy and submit all her financial details to the dealership, never mind the fact that she was unveiling her financial status in front of me too. More importantly she is a friend with the least amount of economic support trying to help me. The experience of it all was quite humbling for both of us. It also made me sad. I have so many other "people" options in my life with strong economic lifestyles, yet not one of them would have been able to help me. Either because they are not Spanish nationals, or because they're already tied up with loans and obligations to family and friends. Sigh. It's already November 16th. Dasha and I have been here three weeks and it feels longer. Feeling a bit worried about things now. Of course it feels wrong suddenly – as if it's been the devil setting me up rather than the good energy that I have believed it to be. Fear is seeping in I think. I must not be afraid. I left behind cruise ships and a great job to try life on land again. Afraid of the boredom that can exist without having one's own family or a specific purpose to work for. The hunting and gathering days are gone or so transformed in the "new world" that people actually have too much time on their hands. We have really overshadowed the memories and left ourselves with no clue on how to enjoy life. How the "new world" has distorted the definition of enjoyment by suggesting that it may only be captured with fun or something money can buy. The irony of trying to create inventions that will give humans more time away from work and labour only to be reminded that we are a product of nature and all living creatures need to work in order to live life well. Instead we fill it up with more activities and unwanted stress. How much of society's lifestyle in the "new world" has been off-kilter because of places called Hollywood, Walt Disney World and a beast called television? Where human relationships are designed with needs and expectations that are sincerely impractical for Life's natural canvas, to the point of redesigning one that leaves us discontent and unsatisfied. It is so easy to second guess when you are afraid. Don't know. In spite of my minimalist attitude, I am already back into the social system of debts and material need. The "free" internet has not worked since we arrived. The purchase of the car has been delayed with Ford and I am paying through the nose on the rental. The windows and roof terrace of the flat leak immensely when it rains and there are terrible air currents from the roof terrace and balcony doors that it's too difficult and expensive to heat when all the warm air gets lost with the air currents. Even Dasha is unsettled by all the howling sounds that the wind currents make. My savings and my stuff from Canada have not arrived yet while the financial delay is costing me a mint too. Money, what am I going to do for money? Sigh. ..Saw lots of ants by the front gate. I'll interpret that as a totem reminder that perseverance and hard work eventually build something. Good grief. This can't be all wrong! Three weeks is not a lot of time, don't panic. Vladimir arrives on the 18th, so I should try to just relax. Things will work-out. Remember the bear key chain that Elisabet gave you and all the other incredible coincidences? Jes? Dad? Hello? Are you all there – what's going on?

Success, is less about getting there and
More about having the will to try.
CMS

Under the Mayürqan Sun

Many years ago I saw a film called "Shirley Valentine". I must have been in my early twenties.

It was about a bored English housewife who suddenly decides one day to leave her mundane life, fried eggs and all, to accept an invitation from a friend to go on vacation in Greece. The film did a very good job of highlighting the contrast between the life she had been living and the one where she'd rediscovered her self-respect and enthusiasm for life. After seeing the film I remember feeling good and proud of myself. Post my parents' separation, the years growing up with my father instilled in me a need to live my life first, before giving it to another. I am using my words carefully because from a very early age, I intuitively felt, that the man of my life would be someone like my father: intense and difficult to live with. So, by the time that I was twenty, I had already nurtured an independent ability to travel and be on my own. Aside from soft experiences within Canada and the United States, I'd also gone to Japan for nine months when I was only nineteen. In hindsight it is a wonder how I did it. Certainly innocence and my father's incredible enthusiasm kept fear at bay. More impressive to me now, is the courage that my father held sending his young blooming daughter to Japan at a time when the country and its culture were only making ripples in North American culture. At that time the only real reference that we had about Japan besides Pearl Harbour, was its advancement in computer chip technology and the television series "Shogun". It impresses me now, how he was able to let me go despite his own emotional turmoil. Not only was he letting his daughter go, but his life line too. I was a young nineteen year old about to graduate high school, who was not prepared to spend money at University, when she was not clear about what it was that she wanted to do. My suggestion at the time was to go to Germany because I had been studying it for five years at High School. My father's lines however, at the time of my disclosure, were nothing compared to the ones that I had pre-conceived and rehearsed in my head. That moment is a vision of him... *Standing over the stove, frying up an English breakfast with Marks & Spencer ham and egg scones in the oven; natural grey light was coming into the kitchen through yellow painted windows, that outlined his attractive silhouette as though he were a one-dimensional paper cut-out. His physical dexterity seemed to dance within the backdrop of the kitchen cupboards, the windows, and the trees branched-out in the backyard. I was standing in the hall entrance that was just outside the kitchen. 'Dad,' I said, 'I don't want to go to University yet. What do you think if I travel for a bit and then go to University after that?' He was watching the frying pan on the stove and coolly said, 'How do you know that you will go to University after that?' 'Well,' I said, 'I'd have a better understanding of what I want to do, I'd be motivated after being away for a while, and not waste money.' The truth was I never really wanted to go. It was a "should" situation that I am glad that I followed through on, but they were never my golden years. I waited for his reaction while I watched his left hand gently add bacon to the frying pan and then snap back with quick wrist action to avoid the spitting oil while his left leg had bent up behind him and made a light ballet hop simultaneously with the wrist snap.*

'Where are you thinking of travelling to?' he continued.

'Germany,' I said. 'Becau –,' he cut me off.

'Germany? Why do you want to go to Germany,' he said coolly.

'Well,' I tried again, 'because I have been studying the language for five years and I've never been to Europe, and–,' he cut me off again.

'You can always go to Germany Michèle, it's just across the ocean. You'll get there one day anyway. Why don't you go to Japan?'

I was silent. I was trying to figure out if he was serious. Japan? It was neither South America nor Europe. It was Asia. In all my mental gymnastics about where I could go that would earn my dad's approval without conflict, Asia had not been among them. I had a fascination about Asia this was true. One year my parents had given me a junior encyclopaedia set for my birthday. I'd loved the text on China. So much that I'd even done a class project about Mao Tse Tung and China's Cultural Revolution. Japan however was only familiar to me by that week's television series "Shogun".

'Dad,' I answered calmly, but my heart was already beating fast. He wasn't saying no. HE was suggesting Japan!? 'I don't know anything

about Japan.'

'*All the more reason to go,*' he said. '*If you're not ready for an education at University well make your time off worthwhile. Learn about the Japanese. Everybody goes to Europe. Why don't you do something different? Exotic? Maybe come back speaking Japanese – wouldn't that be a hoot. Your life would be set Michèle and you'd be way ahead of the rest of us when the Japanese start to dominate our economies. You can always go to Germany after that. With your Japanese experience people will send you to Europe so many times it will make your head spin...*'

It was my father's gift to me and my brothers – always: his clairvoyant mind. His intelligence. His experiences, and a philosophy about life that his spirit shared with great writers and thinkers of literature and science. He was a man with incredible susceptibility and sensitivity to life and the human psyche. His ability to predict the behaviour of individuals with unwavering assertion always captivated me. He spoke with such confidence that to disregard his advice would have kept me second guessing long afterwards. Even if my own path worked out, my father would find a way to demonstrate that his suggestion would have given more gratifying results. If I was willing to listen and heed his words I was admittedly never disappointed. Never.

That conversation that day was the precursor to the way my life was going to unfold. I went to Japan at the age of nineteen and my life as a result is where I am now. I returned to Canada with an impressive grasp of the language and I followed up with Asian Studies at University. I would never master the language enough to qualify interpreting or translation, but it was the backup key to every door that I went through. Years later when I had arrived to Mayürqa for the first time, I'd actually doubted my fathers' wisdom. Although I had an intuition that the Japanese market would find Mayürqa sooner than later, the island was and still is largely influenced by the German economy. '*Had I gone to Germany,*' I thought,

'I'd be fluent here and making great money.' The thought lasted about as long as I was panicking about being unemployed. The truth is that the German language might have helped me better in Mayürqa in the short term, but in the long term it would have made no difference. Most German citizens who live in Mayürqa are European with a good handle on foreign languages comparable to mine. Speaking German here is like speaking Japanese in British Columbia: the professional competition at this end is in favour of the language's native speaker.

In Mayürqa few if any, can speak Japanese. Since 1998 until now, there are now a hundred Japanese families on the island. The Mayürqa football team has recently contracted a Japanese football player from Osaka Japan and Japanese restaurants have sprung up all over the island. My father and I were right. I am in the right place at the right time. Withstanding, ever since that first trip to Japan I continued to travel extensively and referred to the experiences as doing my "Shirley Valentine". I carried this attitude and zest for extensive travel until about seven years ago when I decided to settle in Mayürqa. Then when Jesy left us in December of 2003, I relocated Dasha to my mum's in Canada and went back to my career on ships. It was something to do when I no longer had a clue what to do. It was a way to reduce the guilt and the emotional upheaval that inflicted me about Jesy. It was also another privilege that both my parents had afforded me: a spiritual confidence and the personal tools that would always give me an option to live the life that I chose or needed to live in that moment. Beyond that, it was Life's gift first, for having given me the ultimate privilege of being born to and raised by two exemplary definitions of what the human spirit is all about, in a socially privileged place like Canada and then being able to grow old with different privileges in a place like Mayürqa – if I chose to. The key being, the order in which these privileges were granted. An added bonus was having a father whose own trials and tribulations would be my bitter-sweet rewards and a mother who's intuitive and independent tendencies would also be my own. I am without a doubt a product of what democracy is supposed to be about: a healthy human being fully equipped to aspire to the life that I might wish to live. It has nothing to do with the freedom of rights nor divide and conquer. It's about the root of Canadian culture and its people that are completely unique from any other in the world. In spite of its youth, its traditional ties kilter the country's balance with depth and maturity far beyond its neighbours. Where the concept of democracy is the closest any one will get to. It is a place where its society can be so well prepared without an obligation to stay. Many of us are in fact Canadian Geese. Many of us don't even stay in our own country once the tools are afforded to us. It is understood that once the child is well prepared for life, it can leave its parent country without emotional repression or obligation. Defining freedom as the ability to live out the definition of ones desired life to the fullest.

During my *flight* last year, I saw the film "Under the Tuscan Sun" just before ending my career on ships. I was in my cabin when I came across it on the crew channel. It found me at a very vulnerable time of my life much like a book that comes into one's life right when it's needed. I'd simultaneously enjoyed and disliked the film very much. It was me. It was a marvellous portrayal of a woman who goes to Italy in order to start a new life. The circumstances that led her to her new chapter were lightly similar to my own, but what impressed me most was how well the emotional aspect reminded me of my own sorrow that still seemed to linger despite Jes' passing almost nine months earlier. Perhaps one of the good things about a wounded spirit is that it allows the other dimension of Life, a way to be closer to you and comfort you. In sorrow there is love albeit self-righteous, but enough to feel so lonely that the quiet energy around you is finely heard. I was wallowing in my sadness at the same time as I was reprimanding myself for being that way. Although Jes' departure was enough to justify my bereavement I knew that I was being looked after. I had the best job, the best ship, the best privileges on-board, the best itinerary in Europe, with the best people and the best company. On one occasion I was permitted to take an excursion in Italy that took us to a winery that happened to be called "Michi Factory" which I interpreted at the time, as a tiny morsel, letting me know that I was where I was supposed to be in spite of my sadness. Then the night of Jes' birthday, I looked out my port hole and whispered to him 'Happy birthday', and low and behold instantly from the dark of the night a shooting star soared and fell into the waves at my eye level. No word of a lie. I pressed my face against the cool of my port hole. The waves shot up and down against the glass as night sped by unveiled by white foam. I cried. Quietly, from the gut. I was living another privileged moment. I slowly felt calmed, warmed and loved in its hug. I missed him very much and thanked him for the message. So in my quasi foggy state I was being reminded by subtle hints that I was not alone... What I did not enjoy about the film was the truth. I knew that I was okay, but I was indignant that I had to start all over again from scratch. I had no clue where to begin anymore. My flight to Mayürqa in 1998 had been a very carefully assessed decision. I had spent six months in Canada fully reflecting on my life and feeling-out how I wanted to live it, and Life willing, how I wanted to grow old. I was thirty-one at the time, in couple with a great guy, living in Canada at my girlfriend's place and well satiated from my "Shirley Valentine" experiences. Yet my spirit would not let me stay. I had to go. As Hollywoodish as it may seem, it was just that. There was a pull to go. So I did. I went to Mayürqa and I found what I was searching for: an island, a man, a dog, work, and a place for old age. It had all been a part of my plan and appeared to be Life's plan too, however there is an adage that says: "Be careful for what you wish for" because Life will grant it to you. It just won't materialise exactly the way you'd imagined it. In some cases the painting on Life's canvas comes out better than the snapshot in the mind. Either way it's never a carbon copy. I had no problem understanding my loss. When the jug is empty then there is room to fill it with fresh water, but I was gun shy. It is also said that, "if you want to make the gods laugh, tell them what your plans are." I did not want to make the gods laugh again; at least not at my expense. So I leaned on Joseph Campbell instead: "We must be willing to get rid of the life we've planned so as to have the life that is waiting for us."

The woman in the film finds an old country house in Tuscany and quietly hopes to find a soul mate, celebrate a wedding in her home, hear the sounds of a child and friends and live a simple but wholesome life in Italy. As the film unfolds, her wishes come true with a slight variation from her original image. At some point, the woman requires a loan from a bank in order to finalise the purchase of the house. Despite all her attempts to follow protocol and convince the banks of her altruistic intention, not one bank is willing to accommodate her. Rather they outline to her all of the necessary formalities required from her before she may even be considered. Above all, she needs a co-signer: one who is preferably Italian to guarantee any potential loan. Naturally having just arrived she is in a dilemma. That is until a bird dropping falls on her head and both the elderly woman to whom the house belongs, and the Italian real estate man, who witness the embarrassment, are delighted by her stroke of luck. Such that, the real estate man suggests to her that they go to the local bank to enquire about her loan. The scene, in a modest Italian bank office, is wonderful because she has no clue to what is going on around her. The whole Italian experience between the real estate man and the female bank manager lasts about a moment until she is asked to sign on the bottom line. The loan is granted just like that. Once the shock passes her by, she asks the man: 'Why?' to which he replies: 'I told the manager that a bird shit on your head.' The subtleties of course in that reply, coupled with the clandestine ones in banking in small villages are classic to the point of becoming miracles for people like that woman in the film, and me.

Financing a car became a real lip biter. I had tried on my own to manage a loan with several different banks to no avail. It was true that I was not working at that time however the shooting star experience on the ship led me to reflect on my potential return to Mayürqa and the conviction that I should move forward from where I'd left off. The banks therefore had already been calculated into my mock ideas even before I'd left ships. My ship contract at the time was good until January of the following year. If I left on holiday early to set up my new life, the paperwork would still indicate my potentially high salary until January of the following year. Whether or not I went back to work on ships after the holiday was my concern. I also had been a loyal client to the bank since 1998, and had managed a ten thousand dollar loan that had been completely paid off within the term that it was allotted. At that time, Jesy had been my co-signer. Hence, after seven years I thought the bank would use my loan's precedence with them and accommodate me. Instead, like the woman in the film, I was reminded of the formalities, and the need for a guarantor. My girlfriend's attempts were denied even though she and her Spanish husband have been living in the bank's village twenty three years. It is true that her credit was not strong, but I also wondered if she had been Mayürqan, wealthy or male, if her weak credit would have mattered at all? In fairness, the bank was willing to give me six thousand euros; enough for a deposit on financing with the Ford company, but it would have meant two loans from two different areas that I really did not want to have. As silly as it was, I wanted the money from one place, in one lump sum, one payment, and preferably from the bank that I was familiar with: mine. In a nutshell, I hoped for twenty thousand euros and content if I received fifteen. How idealistic was that? It was my-stro at my best.

When I'd finally exhausted all efforts within my reach, I accepted Charlie's suggestion to try his bank. So the following day, he picked me up in his car and drove us to the bank. While we flew between narrow stone hedged roads I said little. I looked out the passenger window delighted by the ride and watched the scenery whiz by in blurred brown and green tones. Despite the speed, the curves and the many blind spots Charlie manoeuvred and drove like a true European. It's my opinion that while North America has done everything to make the driving infrastructure safer it has ultimately made drivers inept of driving skills. Even parking spaces wide enough for two tractor trailers, can still be too narrow for a North American who drives a Mini. In Europe the complete opposite is true. Limited space and challenging infrastructures may be hazardous, but the driver is usually better experienced and skilled to handle them. It goes without saying that too much control, too much protection and too much easy is not safe at all. I marvelled in India at how the roads could be full of cars without traffic controls, fully grown grey oxen sitting or standing in their centre, children playing blindly nearby, babies entertaining themselves with knives and not one accident. It was to me an example of a pure oxymoron in organised chaos. When Charlie turned off the main road and drove deeper into the interior of the island, it became clear that we were not going to his village in Juníper. I finally spoke: 'Where is your bank?' I asked slightly raising my voice over the sound of the drive. 'In Marisa,' he replied back over the noise. It was not a village that I knew well if at all. When we turned into the village centre I asked: 'What is the name of the bank?' 'Nostro Banco,' he said. My earlobes heated slightly as Charlie began to slow down and park next to the main square of the village. "Nostro Banco" means "Our bank", and in this case it really was. I couldn't believe it. Charlie and I used the same bank but different offices.

As soon as we opened the door and walked-in I was instantly launched into a reverie of deep Mayürqan culture. I felt as though I was a spectator attending a surreal moment. I floated next to Charlie as he walked up to the cashier sitting at her modest desk. The office was new but humble next to the ones that are often seen in big cities. At the cashier's desk there were two chairs opposite the cashier, a computer, a printer, a telephone and behind her a large and very open portable safe, displaying all its money and bank notes inside. Charlie sat down and I followed his example in the chair next to his. The preliminary guidelines between him and the cashier involved the family, health, and enough small talk to get us to the end of our visit. The language had changed of course into thick Mayürqan that hardly, if at all needs the mouth to speak. The real protocol exists in the body language and the evasive eye contact. Still to the foreign observer it can seem loud, gregarious and informal. Suddenly from behind the cashier a short, stout and kind looking bearded man appeared. Once again the preliminary protocol between Charlie and the man took place where somewhere in between I was introduced as Charlie's English teacher and the man was introduced as the director of that office. Then our attention was reverted once again to the cashier who suddenly asked me in a rather raised voice if I was going to use their office? 'Use your office?' I said in a perplexed tone. I looked at Charlie. I love his face. His forty-four years appear youthful with his dark eyebrows, hazel eyes, a predominant nose and beautiful lips that suggest a past life in ancient Greece. The fact that he is bald simply intensifies their attractiveness. As I looked at him he said nothing for a moment while he kept his eyes on the cashier. Then he spoke in a light gregarious tone while the cashier typed and printed paperwork from her computer system. Following that, the cashier repeated her question to me with the same volume but slower, 'Wiill you Uuuse this Offfiiice?!' My heart had started to pump blood to my cheeks. I was not sure what to say because the question seemed redundant to me. All the same it was not the time or place to act intelligent. Like a puppet I replied hypnotically: 'Of course...' to which she asked: 'How much do you want?' I lost all power. Nothing was on or working right. My upbringing had trained me to be modest when offered a goody. I looked at Charlie again unable to answer. This time with a charming smile and a gregarious tone he spoke to the cashier and this time she specified: 'Twenty or twenty-five?' My mind was not cooperating with me. I was trying to assess the moment. I was thinking a mile a minute. *Are we having a preliminary meeting to assess my possibility for a loan? Is this a test of my character? Don't you want to see my paperwork?* Instead my mouth uttered something like twenty, to which Charlie quickly seemed to holler, 'ODeumeuu! (Oh my God!) – Twenty or twenty-five!?'

'You can have twenty-five, if you want,' said the cashier … In all my life I had never imagined myself in that moment as I found myself. 'O.K.,' I said. 'If it's really no problem twenty-five is good.' Then the cashier's right hand seemed to soar from the printer down to the desk in front. With a slight slap sound from the paper, she asked me to sign the bottom line. My face was on fire by this time. My head pounded with the rhythm of my heart. Feeling overwhelmed by the pressure of the velocity and vexed by the action of signing something that I had not even been able to review. I was without a doubt under the spell of blind faith. Then it was over. She and Charlie began to converse heartily together, and I just sat there watching, expecting the pounding in my head to shoot blood from my nose at any minute. Finally the cashier looked at me and asked if I was happy. 'If I am happy?' I said softly trying not to offend, 'is the loan possible then?' The cashier eyed me directly and asked: 'Don't you look when you sign?!' With a hesitant glance I looked. I'd signed a loan for twenty-five thousand euros. The pressure from unconsciously holding my breath exhaled in controlled gasps and unplugged three weeks of stress to leak into my eyes. I looked at Charlie and then at the cashier. I had nothing original to say: 'Thank you,' I whispered, 'Moltes Gràcies.'

That day became my "Tuscan under the Mayürqan Sun". Yet when we got back into the car I tried very hard not to be melodramatic about it. That was the culture and what Charlie was used to. Dorothy and the red shoes she'd had on her feet the whole time flashed passed my imagination. I decided the moment was too incredible for it to be evil or a deal with the devil. I still felt a little uneasy about taking twenty-five instead of twenty as if the latter would have helped my karmic cause. As far as Charlie was concerned his intentions were good. It was in fact an opportunistic window in time that closed the moment that I signed the bottom line. I could not have been granted a loan in any other way. I had no money. No income. Nothing to even reason an effort to try except for the precedence of luck behind me thus far: the brother of my landlord, a man influenced by a drug addiction, comfortable in assets, local to the island, and taking English lessons from me, introduced me to a bank manager who made my wish come true – would never be repeated in a million years. 'Thank goodness I took the twenty-five,' I murmured to myself trying to vanquish all residual doubt. Beyond that, if all my quiet hopes about my encounter with Charlie were mistaken then it would all come down to the loan for the car. The date was Wednesday November 17th. 2004. The day would prove to be an important one related to Charlie while the date itself sums up to seven which is my numerological number for life. "Under the Tuscan Sun" is a film that ends well. I often wonder about the timing of when I saw it. As if the film was a small elusive hint about my own destiny and the loan experience was a morsel to keep me going ... Charlie and I swerved onto the main road back home. The music was loud and the moment was real. Charlie seemed pleased with himself and gave me a great smile when he caught my glance at him. I grabbed the safety handle over the passenger window, set my weight comfortably in the seat and let myself fly with the speed of Charlie's Lancia Phedra. 'I was in Spain,' I ruminated to myself, 'in time for the four-hundredth anniversary celebration of Cervantes classic tale of Don Quixote de la Mancha; nothing was impossible.'

CS' suggestion

They were cooking rice soup at Michèle's place. Charlie was leaning his backside against the stove module while Michèle stood next to him chopping up vegetables. It was the extent of her contribution to making dinner because it was really Charlie who was doing the cooking that night. She was not a cook. She could make the regular pasta and salad dishes, but she was better as the assistant who did the cleanup rather than the meal. The lighting in the kitchen was soft coming from the stove's overhead light and the wall light adjacent to the marble counter. It was enough to catch the steam lifting up from the pot of boiling water that was heating on the front burner behind Charlie's back. Once in a while he would turn his weight towards the stove and methodically stir the rice that was boiling inside the pot. They were both wearing jeans. Charlie wore a red casual men's shirt with cuffs unrolled and loosely opened over his hands, while Michèle was wearing a similar red shirt for women, cuffs buttoned and folded back. The fact that they both happened to be wearing the same colour shirt had not gone by Michèle unnoticed. She had become more astute to their dress code and observed with frequency how the two of them wore the same colour of clothing unannounced to each other. All just a coincidence of course, which she tried hard not to think about in order to keep the natural flow of the phenomena real. The last thing that she wanted was to start second guessing herself on what to wear, in order to coincide with Charlie. Unfortunately, her need to make a conscious effort suggested that she had probably already begun to, and she didn't like the signs of that. Their conversation was gentle with few words. It was apparent to her how the mere presence of each other seemed to calm them. She could not speak for Charlie, but he did feel more centred in her presence. She was probably projecting from her own tranquil sensation of having him next to her. Still words between them weren't always needed nor wasted, and that calmed her. Now they were chatting about Michèle's use of the car loan: 'Now you can buy a new car. Any one of your choice,' said Charlie. The casual tone in his words caused her to imagine them as drops of water falling into sand and leaving their impression momentarily before disappearing. 'I know,' she said. She really did. However, she couldn't explain nor express the magnitude of her disbelief and gratitude to him because it wasn't what he wanted to know. 'I think I'm going to go for the Focus. I know the model and the rep gave me a good feeling when I was at the dealership. It's not really the car of my original intension, but it's still a good car. Just the fact that I can even buy a car, let alone that my first car can be a new one is incredible Charlie. Plus it's available in automatic and the dealership will take care of all the paperwork. Nice and simple. Really, it's incredible.' The words fell out of her mouth sincerely but with effort. She continued to chop with a sense of guilt that she hoped Life listening had not detected. Despite all the luck, it wasn't the car of her dreams. She couldn't believe the hint of what she was feeling: unsatisfied. *'Holy cow!'* she reprimanded herself. *'Get real. It's all so good and you're still not happy!?'* What astounded her even more was her truth… *As her first* car, she wouldn't even have considered buying the Ford, if the location where she was living had not required the need for one. It was Michèle's personality to be somewhat sybaritic with anything where its significance to her or its consequential presence highlighted an important change in her life. It was also strongly idealistic, and although she could agonise through the process of making a decision she almost always experienced pure emotional freedom once it was made. The how and the when were minor details. It was also a detriment to herself, because she would rather not have nor do anything if it didn't meet the bill of what she was looking for. Patience was a virtue, but it also had a price. The more time and experience one had to consider and appreciate one's choices in life, also meant a clearer sketch of one's way all the more difficult to deviate from. It placed a greater magnitude upon the meaning of "the first time", when "the first time" happened later in life, to such a level, that certain things just became all or nothing. In relationships, it gave possibility to the undesired thought of growing old and alone. A possibility that Michèle quietly hoped might be made improbable by virtue of being honest with herself and keeping her spiritual child within alive–

'Why don't you get a Mini?' Her thoughts interrupted, froze and her body shivered instantly to Charlie's unexpected comment. The chopping ceased and her face turned towards the man that had spoken. Everything about its delivery, the collected nonchalant tone, Charlie's posture and more importantly his location next to the stove was the flashback with her dad when she was nineteen: *'Why don't you go to Japan?'* had been her dad's question while he too was next to the stove. She stared at Charlie on the verge of testing her reaction to the sensation, by saying 'hello' to her father. Instead she delivered it mentally and smiled at Charlie when she did. Charlie had not known about her secret Mini thoughts. It was true that the Mini had become quite popular that year, nonetheless he could have mentioned any other car first. His question provoked a flood of thoughts. *Who was she talking to? Was there any hint of truth to her ideas that Charlie's addiction made him an easier medium than others for divine communication to her, or was she just psychologically looking for her dad's support through him? Still, how did he know to mention the Mini?* 'Wow,' she exhaled, 'it's incredible that you should mention the Mini. I actually checked the dealership out in Palma and it said that there weren't any left on the island. Price wise too, a new automatic is about 22,000 euros, so it's over my budget,' she explained. 'What about the mainland?' added Charlie, 'and you can learn to drive a standard.' Everything about the moment with Charlie was too much. Perhaps it was the lighting behind him that played her senses, but he was not only attractive to her, she thought she saw a semblance of her dad in his dark eyebrows, the round face and the way he carried himself. Most of all his approach to her was the same as the one her dad had used when she tried to defend reasons on why going to Japan seemed unrealistic.

'Yes, I asked about that too,' she answered, 'but according to the salesman, who was a bit of a prat, next year's models are already all sold out.'

'I see you more in a Mini,' he continued, 'and it's a good car.'

That was it. He did not know her well enough to know that his casual comment was enough to awaken a challenge in her, unsettle her decision about the Focus and reconsider Possibility for a Mini. Her dad however, did. 'Yea,' she said knowingly, 'my aunt, my *dad's sister,*' she emphasised, 'used to have a brown Mini way back when, and she loved it.'

If tomorrow never comes...I love you moja malishka – VLADIMIR. 1.2.05.

With love from Russia

Michèle drove up to the arrival section of the airport in Palma, parked the rental and waited for her friend Vladimir to come out.

She kept her focus on the Arrivals exit and thought how nice it was to pick someone up at the airport in Mayürqa. She had known so many airports in her life that it was impossible not to have an opinion about them. Everything about Mayürqa's pleased her. Her initial arrival to the island in 1998 was exactly when the final touches to the remodelling of the airport had more or less been completed. Although it was new, its architectural work from the outside was in direct harmony with the island's size and charm: exotic, privileged, and simple. The planning of its infrastructure inside was modern and thought out well enough to accommodate it during the summer as one of the busiest airports in Europe. She could not remember ever feeling anything less than a calm and airy spirit whenever she arrived at the airport, and it made her feel good to know that her friend who was arriving from cold Lithuania was going to have a similar experience. She knew that the moment Vladimir's plane began its decent, the tranquil experience would last until he'd come out of the Arrivals gate and discover the warmer day that awaited him. "Thank you," she whispered just audibly enough for herself to hear. She watched the people swarm out of the airport but concentrated little on them. Her mind was making a review of all the events and challenges that had brought her to sitting in the car waiting for Vladimir. It had almost become a habit. As if it were her mantra for keeping the threat of audacity at bay by not forgetting anything that she needed to give thanks for. She suddenly had enough money to buy a new car in full. The realisation of that sank into her like the slow movement of thick honey down her throat. It was sweet, but not easy to swallow. She could not understand why her reaction left her feeling apprehensive and happy at the same time. She compared herself to a rabbit eating a carrot under floodlights. She was nervous bordering on fear. If she were a rabbit it meant caution. It meant to trust her instincts but remain alert. The loan was okay, but it was a lot of money and she had never in her thirty-seven years bought a car or negotiated one. Plus she was in a foreign country. It was fear mixed with the anticipation of something big. Something that she had quietly requested and so far been allowed to experience significant morsels of personal success without following the protocol of conventional ways. It was something that would undoubtedly require an equally unconventional quid pro quo with Life. Somewhere too, her father, Jes, a special other and even her grandmother were all involved in its dénouement. Life was setting her up and she could feel it. "May I stay on track and not screw up your plans for me," she mouthed inaudibly, "please help me to do what I am supposed to do for you." she finished. Vladimir was still not in sight. Her thoughts shifted slightly and began to recall how she and Vladimir had met … *She had been finishing up the first part of her contract just before heading off on an eight week holiday when Vladimir had literally introduced himself to her on the eve of when she was supposed to sign off. He had been a room service attendant and had apparently noticed Michèle on one of his deliveries to her cabin. At the time, Michèle was neither aware of him nor anyone for that matter. She was still too possessive and deeply close to Jesy to be good company for anyone. Undaunted however, Vladimir acted gallantly drawing for her an incredible pencil sketch of a rose in a hand and leaving it in her door for her to find on the day that she signed-off for her holidays. Then he waited the eight weeks for her return and spent the rest of her final contract being a good friend to her. The subtleties of this relationship were of course fragile. Vladimir wanted more and she didn't. Letting him visit her in Mayurca was a decision that she had not taken lightly. Her rule of thumb was sincerity even if it was painful, and Vladimir seemed to abide by it. Being from Eastern Europe the concept of being straightforward, concise and intense was all too familiar to him. They were regional noble qualities that to Michèle, lacked experience and were frighteningly innocent in their understanding of democracy and capitalism, especially under the guise of the European community. It was a world undergoing a metamorphism both in its economies as well as its relationships. Vladimir had grown up at a time when women from Eastern Europe could not even earn enough to purchase simple cosmetics for themselves if they were even available. The logistics of its economy fermented the custom of men saving women while women accepted their role as beautiful trophies as long as they were guaranteed a privileged standard of living. Many relationships therefore existed with the pragmatic understanding of "I'll look pretty and make you look good, while you ensure that I live like a princess". Those cases were far from females being subordinate because it was essentially the woman who'd designed it that way. Survival tactics by definition are what they are: a means to stay alive. Hence relationships and matrimonies in the East still stereotyped young attractive women with older economically capable men that often appeared physically incompatible. Such that arranged marriages had been a lucrative business and the idea of love came with a question mark on whether or not it even existed. To the Western culture it might be interpreted as a rosy form of legal prostitution. In Michèle's mind the pragmatic approach east of Europe was a favourable one compared to its evolution in the West where prostitution is singularly illegal by reason of the nature of its purpose: female subordination first, survival motives second. More disconcerting are the women who choose prostitution as an economic means but are rarely the managers of it. The business in the West therefore exists with little, if any scruples, unlike some cases of prostitution in Eastern Europe, where the women and men seem to have a clearer understanding of their roles. The bilateral rule of give and take is official and from a woman's perspective she is both the manager and employee of her choices. The man is given the right to feed his basic provider and sexual instincts under the guidelines of meeting his responsibilities to the woman. If managed otherwise, prostitution void of scruples provokes women to rediscover their male instinct to hurt, and put it to use via the female instinct to seduce in such a way equal to that of a self-preserving Black Widow spider. They attract their prey, tap him out, and then move to the next one in hopes of finally finding one that will save them from the destructive instincts. Ever since countries in the East joined the European community, prostitution by western definition seems to have increased alarmingly. The occurrence of women from Eastern Europe looking for men in the West to save them by way of their cultural guidelines think they have found El Dorado in the West and have become an added ingredient as to why prostitution in the West has risen. Eastern European women have become a subtle threat to the western prostitute because their naivety and alarming looks are more attractive to men. Notwithstanding, it becomes an interesting dynamic when the eastern woman soon realises that the men in El Dorado lack the noble qualities, ability or intention to formalise a commitment to them like their eastern male counterparts. In fact, right before Vladimir had signed off from his contract, a young Polish boy, who'd just signed-on the ship as a first contract, committed suicide. Apparently the boy had gallantly left his country in order to be with his girlfriend on the ship, only to discover that the young girl had found another. His response was to jump overboard within forty eight hours of signing-on. Naturally the drastic decision was labelled as acute insanity by the boy. However Vladimir was able to defend the boy's decision. Suicide under the guise of love was what the boy had to do in order to prove that his commitment to take care of that young girl had been real. In Vladimir's mind the boy was deceived by the wicked attractive girl and the boy's death was going to punish her through guilt. 'Michèle don't you understand?,' he'd said emphatically, as if his own love for Michèle was being threaten by her point of view, 'he loved her. When you love you'll do anything. Even die for it!' Vladimir's passion was beautiful and real. Influenced by Russian folkloric music about heroism and heightened by Enrique Iglesias, Brian Adams and most of Western pop culture. He was another example of how the West had become wiser about its pop culture, thus provoking pop culture's need to expand and influence the unsuspecting ones to the East. It reminded Michèle of her American history class in high school that included a lesson on America's need to divide and conquer under the pretence of expansion. Vladimir's vision from Michèle's perspective seemed short sighted, melodramatic, and immature. It did not offer any consideration of what lines the girl and boy had shared. Perhaps the girl had tried to tell the boy? Neither did it consider that the boy was going to be remembered as insane rather than a heroic martyr. It did not highlight the tangible fact that he would be dead and the girl would still have a life to live. The girl might live with residual guilt for her actions, or lack of but also relief, she had not remained with a "crazy" boy capable of committing suicide. Most importantly if he really loved her, he would have bared the emotional turmoil without letting it hurt her. Love was giving, synonymous with sacrifice and belonged to the giver not the receiver. Suicide might have been the boy's ultimate sacrifice, but it risked hurting and emotionally scarring the one he loved. It was therefore not the solution. 'What's the saying?' she tried to remember while Vladimir also searched for his defence. '"When you love something let it go. If it was yours it will come back to you",' or, she was on a roll, 'have you ever read Sun Tzu's book "The Art of War"?' she asked Vladimir in exasperation. 'Sometimes in order to win a war you need to join, or at least know the enemy and its rules,' she tried to conclude. 'If the boy really felt the need to get back at the girl, it might have been a better strategy to demonstrate indifference to her promiscuity. That, or maybe deference to another girl might have been enough to play her psychologically,' she stopped, satisfied with her defence. That was the life on ships and pretty much in the new world. Suicide in the name of love was beautiful in literature but no longer cool. Vladimir had stayed quiet for a moment, aware of his own fear. He knew ship life and had already been aware of his own loss of innocence. When he went home on holidays he no longer saw his country or his people with the same love. Now he feared for the ones who still had to learn. Some would survive and others would end up like the boy on the ship. In the end they agreed that the boy from Eastern Europe had been at a greater disadvantage because he was a new hire who had no clue about ship culture. He had been a young man who'd come from a more tangible experience: war and relationships were physical and pragmatic terms not subliminal or intellectual ones. Anyway, to say the least, the boy's suicide had spurred an intense conversation between the two of them. Both defending their cultural points of view, it was to Michèle an indication of how innocent Eastern Europe was next to the New World, where war was better won by substituting it with reformed and glossy terminology like protection, peace missions, or by way of financial institutions and candy coated promises. While Eastern Europe in spite of its natural beauty, cultural depth and historical wisdom, was joining the new world economy and legislation without being taught the rules and consequences of the game. It had not been Michèle's intention to hurt or to appear condescending, but she wanted Vladimir to understand that anyone who committed suicide in the name of love would not earn her respect. He seemed to understand her message and so she agreed to let him visit...* She saw Vladimir before he saw her. He was not difficult to notice. It went without saying that he was an A-typical looking Russian male. Although he was born Lithuanian his maternal roots were from Bella-Russia while his paternal ones were from St. Petersburg. When the world map was different, the pure Russian was said to come from Bella-Russia. He was a very attractive young man at thirty. Healthy, tall, blond, blue eyes with a very defined chiselled face that defied his age by at least five years. According to Vladimir, his looks, as for most young eastern Europeans, were a short lived privilege that dissipated early due to the post-effects of that region's stark standard of living. Michèle of course did not agree. She could imagine Vladimir in his late thirties, early forties in a way that was much more attractive to her. Unfortunately it was not enough to hook her: chemistry was missing. Vladimir was a gallant suitor for her until being physical got in the way. Although he had the energy, the sensitivity and the know-how, try as she might there was nothing in Vladimir's physical smell or touch that moved her. It was another matter of contention. Honesty. As shallow as it was she needed to be attracted to her partner in a way that was less about his physical appearance as it was about his scent and his charisma when he walked, or talked or did nothing. Other fundamental qualities were important too, but in the end physical chemistry was needed. That same primitive instinct that makes a lion discern one lioness to mate with, from all the equally attractive looking ones in line with her, was the same constant lure that Michèle required. Charlie was her best example. He was by no means a head turner. However he was charismatic, had attractive masculine features that sometimes whispered a bald Marlon Brando and he smelt good. She got out of the car and waved in Vladimir's direction. He saw her immediately and greeted her with a wide smile. When he finally reached her, he gave her a kiss on the mouth and hugged her. Michèle let the kiss go by without a rebuttal and hugged him back. It was good to see him and good to be with someone who really wanted to be with her. They loaded his things in the car and drove off to Sa Ema.

Small but Mighty

The next day Michèle and Vladimir got up early and headed out in the rental for a drive along the west coast of Mayürqa. Their first twenty-four hours together had gone well but not lightly. It became apparent to Michèle that Vladimir was expecting more from her than she was capable of offering. Their conversations had already become heavy and every time she tried to move into a lighter direction he felt the need to intensify it. It was hard to be honest when dealing with affairs of the heart. In Michèle's experience the one with the bleeding heart suffered regardless of how gently and respectfully the other one tried to let that person down. One could be truthful, straightforward, even talk it out with words of encouragement, but the wounded heart would still try ways to keep it alive. The more intense the individual was, or the greater that person's experience had been about surviving in life the more difficult it was to let go of anything that was not desirable to lose. The wounded heart will keep trying to manage the relationship the way it wants it to be, until all attempts have been measured. Inadvertently it causes respectful intentions by the sober heart to resort to aggressive terminology or tactics that were initially hoped to be avoided. Vladimir was making this predicament clear to Michèle. While they drove in the car the conversation between them was becoming so intense that Michèle began wondering why she was even tolerating the moment. She didn't need that crap. She had told Vladimir from day one about her emotional limitations and he insisted that he understood. Why then was she all of a sudden in a car with a young man delivering to her melodramatic lines about how she can't love if she won't let people in. That her lack of chemistry was against them so *why*, had she agreed to let him visit!? The answers were all in her head with little opportunity to express them. Vladimir was heated in his conversation. '*Because,*' she reviewed in her mind, '*he had been a friend to her on the ship.*' It was a concept that still lacked credibility in many parts of the world east of the Atlantic Ocean. Men and women could not be platonic friends without sex or after sex. He was expressing disappointment and her intuition felt that the source was about sexual frustration because it had not been a part of their agenda. She was not angry; rejection was no fun. She was frustrated too. Once again a man had sought her out, made attempts to enter her world, even when she made attempts to refuse him politely. The man insists, so she permits his presence under the understanding that she has been altruistic and that she won't discriminate against his friendship unless there is cause to. Basically the primitive ritual of the male hunt and the female resistance still had residual life even in the twenty first century. In nature many animals experience the ritual of the male species tolerating endless hours of the female's resistance, until she offers a hint of resignation. The male then jumps to mate the female who might still put up with some aggressive resistance until the act is over and she is subdued. Literature and film had done well to evolve these instincts into storylines where the man tries and tries and the woman denies and denies until the end, when the man finally ends up with woman. The only real evolution in the twenty first century has been unveiling that it's not just exclusively a male behaviour. The female species, as in nature, does it too. The new world had progressed a lot with regards to male and female relationships, but the young man next to her was still exempt from that experience; at least until then. It bothered her that he entered her life when she was emotionally wounded and wanted to be left alone. People in general created human relationships without any real consideration of its responsibility. Regardless of its definition, the moment one decides to be in the life of another then the responsibility begins. The Japanese, the North American Indian culture and many other homogenous cultures had this understanding. When they worked on ships, her sorrow at the time attracted in him the need to save her without her request, or any considerations to its responsibility or ramifications to her. His efforts regardless of how sincere he believed them to be were not purely for her, they had been for his interests too. At the time she knew this but gave his innocence a chance, by deferring her wisdom as being closed minded or fearful. Yet there in the car, she was stuck with the responsibility of taking care of his wounded spirit. Vladimir's intensity was tough for her. All her attempts at being empathetic or gently honest were attacked or perceived as being guised attempts at manipulating him. Her mind was beginning to burn out from all the emotional gymnastics and the car's motion from too many winding roads only added magnitude to her discomfort. Her mind was beginning to formulate counteractive thoughts. Once again she had over-ruled her instincts and gave the benefit of the doubt to Vladimir that he really understood. Hence he'd insisted on seeing her, but allowing him to visit was obviously an over extended time together. *'What's it all about!?'* she shot-out mentally. Everything had its purpose. She believed this. Maybe the only reason he came into her life was about that short time on the ship in order to help her get through the contract. In return she'd given Vladimir new found energy and a deference to his life that motivated him to go home on his holidays, renovate his flat and initiate mock plans about the "hows" and "wheres" he wanted to be in his future. Unfortunately he'd placed Michèle among them in a way that Michèle had to redefine her role for him. There was no doubt in her mind that he was going places. A part from his looks and introspective mind he was a doer, disciplined and spoke Russian and English aside from Lithuanian. With Lithuania on the verge of entering the European community, his work on the ships would give him a cultural advantage that could be lucrative for him in his own country. In addition to that, his name was Vladimir; a Russian name that meant "Great Ruler". She sighed within. Whatever the reason to their encounter, Michèle decided that it had been completed. What they were experiencing then was drawn out energy together...

.. He was nonstop and more disconcerting was his intensity. *'Just shut-up,'* he told himself. He was frustrated at the thought of losing his sense of manhood and the strategy that he felt had allowed him to be at par level with her. Now he was trying to overcome his feelings of immaturity next to her, but the more he tried to convince Michèle of his ideas all the more power he seemed to give her. If he could just shut-up and wait for a weakness from her...

They finally descended the last slope, left the curvy narrow road and hit the highway. They were still in bad spirits when Vladimir requested a pit stop to go to the bathroom. By then Michèle was already heading away from the coast inland and did not hesitate to show her frustration at Vladimir for not having mentioned it sooner. She regrouped her thoughts, aggressively clicked-on the car's right-turn traffic signal and rapidly crossed two lanes of traffic in a successful attempt to make what would have been the final off ramp exit before heading inland. When they drove off the highway, Michèle took the roundabout into the nearest town.

No sooner had they left the circle and driven into the community's strip of fancy shops and restaurants when they both saw a yellow Mini parked by a curve with a "For Sale" sign in the window. At this point Michèle drove past it resigned to her decision on the Ford but mostly too tired from her episode with Vladimir, and not in the mood to check out another unattainable Mini that was probably a standard. 'That Mini had a For Sale sign,' said Vladimir casually, 'don't you want to look at it?' His question was enough to unsettle the relentless beast in her and the need to check the possibility. Once again the right turn signal went on and she slowed the car to a halt. 'Go have a look at it Vlad – I'll wait here,' she said feeling relieved from his absence in the car. She watched him through the rear view mirror. As he surveyed the car, he looked through the windows and evidently admired its attractive features. He came back to the car, closed the door and said, 'Nice car. It has incredible technology for its size.' 'Hmm,' said Michèle as she waited for the traffic to pass them by, 'was it a standard,' she added dubiously as a means to finish the swing. 'No, it's an automatic,' replied Vladimir completely unaware of the ramifications to his non-pulsed reply. Michèle braked instantly causing the car to stop nose deep into traffic: 'The Mini is an automatic?! – 'Are you *SURE*?!' 'Well I think so, yea,' said Vladimir now stressed by her unconventional driving patterns. She couldn't even bother with the car; instead she switched off the left turning signal and switched on the warning lights and jumped out to have a look at the Mini for sale. There was a high volume of cars. Vladimir jumped out after her. She approached the driver's side of the small yellow car and looked into the driver's window with her hands next to her face to block out infiltrating light. The Mini was an automatic. She couldn't believe it. There was no way in the world that she would ever have found the car other than the way it had happened. A man all the way from Lithuania was the link to her discovery. It was yellow. The same yellow as the stone in the high school ring that her dad had surprised her with; and again, it was an automatic and for sale! Her reaction was effortless and without concern of on-lookers. She placed her arms along the extremity of the little yellow car and gave it a simulated hug. She knew it, beyond a reasonable doubt that the car was meant for her. There was no mistaking what she was feeling. After her joyful dance next to the car, she ran back to the delinquently parked rental car, grabbed her cell and proceeded to dial the telephone number indicated on the For Sale sign. Vladimir watched in amazement at Michèle's dramatic display in front of the Mini. She had to call the number more than once due to her excitement and the nervous inability to remember her own telephone number for the voice mail that answered her calls. The little girl in her was completely unplugged. After several incredible attempts she wrote her telephone number down and then proceeded to try her message again. By the time they finally returned to the car and headed in direction of the nearest bathroom, Michèle had left enough messages on the voice mail that risked classifying her as a loony bin. It was enough to convince Vladimir that the small but mighty woman next to him, was not only beautiful, but also a part of another world that he wanted to be a part of too.

> Only those who risk going too far
> Can possibly find out how far they can go.
> T.S. ELIOT

The art of Charlie

The next few days were everything but relaxing. First the Ford dealership had called on the Friday to say that it had located an automatic Focus on the mainland but not in the colour she had hoped for, and that her choices were limited to a cherry red or grey colour. Neither impressed by the choices nor the delay it would cause, she went for the Cherry red. Every glitch in her attempts to get a car made her anxious and wonder if she was doing the right thing. Worse was her need to get psyched about the luck in even being able to get a car even though it was not going to be *the* car. Then Vladimir's love for Michèle and her anxiety about the unanswered voice mail messages she'd left about the Mini created tension between them that only experienced relief when they were in the company of others: one day on a fishing excursion with Elisabet and Mitx and the next day having coffee with Charlie at the local bar-restaurant. The day they met Charlie for coffee, the two men found a common point in the world of prostitution. It came as no surprise to Michèle seeing as Vladimir came from the original land of Rasputin and Charlie's clandestine lifestyle dwelled in it. She sat back and observed them. Vladimir flipped through the want ads astounded by the amount of promiscuous advertising and by how much of it was in Russian. In light of his culture the eastern woman who resorted to prostitution in the West was ill fated and earned little respect from him. His views delighted Charlie who listened from a different perspective. In his experience, the women from the East were kinder, less complicated and very attractive. Plus too he was a cocaine addict. Sex was less of an issue, compared with a simple desire to observe the women, be entertained by them, have light conversation, or physical petting. He conformed completely to the eastern prostitute's male prototype.

The result was that he was a favourite client among them. Many often hoping that he would be the one to save them and offer them a better life. Naturally the ego enjoyed the attention and he fell into the trap of helping some of them with their housing and costs. In return, they favoured him and sometimes even waved their fee, which he would have no part of. Charlie did not like to be indebted to anyone especially women. The rule of thumb earned him more points, and his reputation in that world by night was described as respectful and kind. Troubles only occasionally surfaced when a less experienced girl became intensively attached to him much like Vladimir had become with Michèle. In a way that her mental gymnastics with Vladimir, caused her to feel envious of Charlie's mindless world of superficial love. It was not until they'd returned to the house that Vladimir suggested that his presence made Charlie jealous. The notion was so oblivious to her that she asked why he felt that. 'I am a man,' he said with great emphasis 'and I know a jealous man when I see one.' She was not about to enter into territory that was foreign to her biochemistry. She knew that Charlie could be possessive and immature at times, however jealous over a man seven years her youth, while there had been nothing formal between herself and Charlie seemed unlikely. On the other hand, maybe it was Vladimir projecting his own sensations of jealousy. She was not sure. That night the owner of the Mini called. It was Sunday evening and the owner called to see if Michèle was still interested in the car. He and his wife had been away all weekend and had only heard her many messages just before calling. After an informal exchange of words and apologies about the messages the owner quoted his price for the Mini: 18,000 euros. Michèle's heart sank slightly but still enquired, if it were possible to see the car the next day. The owner agreed and they met the next day at the same spot where she and Vladimir had originally seen the car. She was nervous to say the least. On her own albeit with Vladimir, she went through the actions of checking out the car when in fact she really didn't have a clue or care. The owner's name was José but referred to himself as Pepe: tall, dark hair and a new father. According to him, he had bought the car for his wife. However despite the car's ability to accommodate a baby seat his wife wanted to sell it for something larger and less cumbersome to manoeuvre the baby in. They walked around the car sizing it up including its engine. Michèle went through the motions, but it meant little to her. Certainly there must be something wrong with it, but in her mind's eye it would not have mattered how careful she was about buying any car. It was her first time and only the trials and tribulations of the experience would teach her what she needed to know. Beyond that she wanted the car and further that she was so sure that the car was meant for her that she would have signed the bottom line with her eyes closed. When they took a spin in the car she asked Pepe to drive. Both he and Vladimir were surprised at her request. A test drive was customarily done by the potential buyer. Again, it all seemed irrelevant to her. If anything was going to feel wrong or go wrong it would happen after the car was sold. Instead she preferred to experience the drive from the passenger side. It allowed her a better ability to focus on questions about the car rather than traffic. Besides, thirty-seven years without a car had made her an expert in the passenger seat. They drove around while Pepe offered information about the car. She had no clue what kind of person he really was but at the time, she liked him. He seemed genuinely concerned that she understood the mechanics and history of the car. Vladimir was sitting in the back and listened intently to the information sometimes inquiring about specific electronic gadgets that were unknown to her. It was, for lack of a better word, an incredible car: yellow with a black top and two sunroofs. One of which was automatic. It had a black leather interior, fully loaded with CD player, halogen lights with an automatic headlight water gun, automatic transmission and windows plus five star alloyed hub caps. It was all great. The meeting came to a close and the price was 18,000 euros. She looked at the owner and asked if his price was negotiable and his answer was no. He explained that a new Mini automatic was valued at 22,000 euros, that he'd added a lot of extras to it and that the car was only ten months old with 9,450 kilometres on it. She looked at Pepe. 'My budget is 15,000 euros,' she said to him shyly, '*maybe* 16,000 euros,' she stressed. Pepe was at a loss for words. The price was not negotiable and they came to a standstill. Michèle by her own analysis closed her own deal without success. She thanked him very much and they left. Back in the car Vladimir said nothing while Michèle remained pensive. Maybe she should have tried harder. It was not possible that the car deal was over. She really felt the car was for her. She must have been thinking out loud because Vladimir offered an answer: 'The Focus is a good car, new and within your budget. I think you did the right thing. That man doesn't really want to sell the car. Otherwise he would have negotiated more.' She appreciated his support, but she was not convinced. What bothered her more was her sincere belief that the car's make up was meant for her. It was crazy of course, but everything about the assembly of the car was as if it had been made to order for her. During her teenage years her dad used to say that if he won the lottery, he'd buy her a car and her mother a cabriolet convertible. His desire to have that possibility made Michèle hope that he would win, not because of the promises, but because his desire to be able to offer such gifts was like a small ache in his heart. Although he was a tremendous man in his role as a single dad, doing his best to set up the ideal infrastructure for his family, the departure of her mother from his life made all of his commendable virtues feel insignificant to him. Such that she really felt that if her father had been alive and capable of buying her a car it would have been that Mini. It just seemed to her that ever since her dad and Jesy had died miracles were occurring for and around her and her brothers, in a way that suggested that they could deliver better from where they were then, than when they were alive. When they arrived back at the flat, Vladimir took Dasha for a walk while Michèle hooked up with Charlie for his English hour. During the course of the lesson the Mini came up and Charlie listened intently while Michèle explained in careful English the details of the meeting to him. Once she finished he looked at her in a way that suggested that she had not been clever. Then in his casual approach, as if not to offend her, said in proper English, 'Why don't you make him an offer?' Michèle's face rose in temperature from the obvious mistake that she had made. She wanted to reply that Pepe had made it clear that he did not want to negotiate even when she lightly suggested that she might adjust her budget to 16,000 euros. However she did not reiterate any of that to Charlie because the truth was she'd never made Pepe an official offer. She looked at Charlie embarrassed. 'I suggested that I might pay 16,000 euros, but he didn't make any sign of being interested,' she explained dully. 'Naaw, it wasn't an offer,' he replied assertively in Spanish. 'Don't speak Spanish to me,' she prompted. 'Well Carles,' she said now wanting to play the devil's advocate, 'I don't want to pay more than 16,000 euros for a second hand car when I can have a new one for 15,000 euros.' He smiled lightly at her words. They were trite of course, but he went along with his defence: '16,000 euros is a good price for a Mini. 15,000 euros is an acceptable price for a new Ford...,' he paused as if challenged by a lack of English vocabulary, 'you have the money,' he finally finished in English. She did. She had twenty five thousand euros, but had not intended on using it all on a car. He was right of course. The Mini was a much better car, had a greater resale value, and it was only ten months old with 9,450 kilometres on it. It could well have been a new car. Above all, it was an automatic car.

The Ford dealership had not even confirmed finding one yet and she was still convinced that some kind of divine intervention was involved. '*You just don't find an almost new, tailored made automatic Mini on an island like Mayürqa by simple virtue of luck. No way!*' she was saying to herself. '*Everything had been premeditated so that the right time, the right place and the right person all fell into the discovery of that car on that day. If Vladimir had not visited…*' The dynamics of it all boggled her mind to no end. It said to her that every day up until that moment had been a slight thread leading her to that car. The way of her arrival might have deviated from a better intended direction, but in the end Vlad was meant to find her in order to bring her to that car. She came back to Earth and Charlie in front of her. She felt embarrassed and anxious. 'How much?' she asked. His eyes darted to his hands and the tissue that he was holding. She was asking him for specific advice and understood his wariness. Mayürqan culture often reminded her of the Arab one. The fact that Mayürqa had not been exempt from the eight hundred centuries of Arab imperialism in Spain, probably had a lot to do with it. Such that neither one enjoyed responsibilities nor commitments that might be formalised in a way that they could be accounted for, especially Charlie. He looked up and replied: 'I dunno, 16,500 euros,' she liked his answer. It's what she would have suggested too. 'Yea,' she offered, 'I was thinking the same,' and then Charlie relaxed. That Monday night, she called Pepe and got his voice mail: 'Hi Pepe it is Michèle calling. The Canadian you met this morning regarding the Mini. If the car is still for sale, I would like to make an offer for it. If you are interested please return my call, thank you.' She put the phone down and exhaled, suddenly relieved that Ford had been delayed by not finding the colour that she had originally requested. Now it was a matter of who would get back to her first; Pepe with an answer, or the dealership with a cherry-red Focus. Logically Pepe needed to get back to her first. If he declined then the cherry red Focus would be her car. If he accepted then she could call the dealership and decline their search.

> Nothing important was ever achieved
> Without someone taking a chance.
> H. JACKSON BROWN, JR.

Fear is no object

By Wednesday Pepe had not called back nor replied to Michèle's second voice mail attempt highlighting an offer of 16,500 euros. Ford on the other hand had called her on Tuesday. They confirmed finding a cherry red automatic Focus and required a deposit from her, in order to guarantee the cars arrival to the island. Apparently there were no more automatics available in that model for that price and of course, the cherry-red one was on request by more than one client. The pressure was on. They gave her until Wednesday to decide, but she convinced the representative to hold it for her until Thursday. If Pepe did not get back to her by then, four days would have gone by without his reply and enough to make a logical choice. Besides that, her rental was due on the Saturday and she really could not afford to keep it any longer. Three weeks was enough. She held off until Thursday afternoon and finally felt no choice but to call Ford and confirm the transfer of 15,000 euros to their account. Then, that very evening, Pepe called her back to accept her offer on the Mini! Michèle marvelled at her stupidity that seemed to increase with the car experience. Gone were her younger days when she used to save her money scrupulously or examine every text before she signed it. Either age or travel had mellowed her too much or she was simply digressing into a dits. The fact that Pepe called her right after she'd made her decision to send the money to Ford was Murphy's Law at its best. Everything about timing in her life was always crucial. When it rained it poured and it was never about a lack of choices that plagued her but about too many. Pepe's acceptance of the offer did nothing less than put her insides back into their well-known position upside down. Still, she did not waver. Without the slightest reservation she explained to Pepe the truth about her predicament with the money. That she would call the dealership the next day and then call him back to confirm her offer to him, provided he could hold on until then? He accepted. The phone call ended and Michèle exhaled quietly. In this case "honesty is the best policy" actually worked. Vladimir on the other hand was shocked. He could not believe that she would even try back stepping her decision for the Ford after she'd made her choice and sent the money. 'You never cease to surprise me Michèle,' he said in a frustrated tone, 'I just can't figure you out. On one hand you are so organised and logical and now you are completely idealistic and complicating things,' he added almost angrily. She detected that his anxiety came from a deeper feeling of hopelessness to help her. However she had no room for psychological empathy when she was already quite aware of her "faux pas." The next twelve hours were sleepless. She agonised over how she was going to ask for her money back from the dealership and then from the fear that they would not return it to her. When she saw Charlie for English hour the next morning his comment was clear, 'Wow, you're awfully quick with your money.' He was right. She was one of those profiles with the potential to make millions, but would probably end up with just enough to live through retirement. In essence money wasn't what raised her emotional temperature as much as the number of personal tools she had to survive without it. Having them was like having survival keys that enabled her the privilege of being able to access just about any door to living the life she aspired to.

> Cherish the life you live – It's yours.
> It's probably the only thing that you will ever own
> That is exclusively you and yours
> From birth to death.
> Most precious!
> CMS

Courage

After Charlie left, she paced back and forth on the roof terrace getting ready for her call. What was really stressing her? Ego and embarrassment at her impetuousness. The shameful realisation about her immaturity with money and her ego that had wanted to impress the dealership and appear non-pulsed about the money at the same time. In short, she'd given them a false impression that she actually had money. 'Gawd, where had that psychological crap come from?' she wondered out loud. She also felt sorry for the representative who had been all out professional in finding her the car and who'd probably celebrated the anticipation of his commission the night before. She sighed. Business was business and even though her circumstances were sincere, she did not want him to be professionally bitter after his experience with her. Then, technically she had not signed anything nor had she seen the car. The latter being another point which increased her embarrassment and self-chastisement. Albeit was a car, she thought it was a product with no point of sale that supported her right to receiving the money back. She anticipated a penalty fee, but considering her folly, it was minor. She grabbed her phone ignored the geyser in her stomach and dialled. The representative she wanted to speak to was in a meeting and would call her back. She hung up feeling worse by the delay. She wanted to inform them as soon as possible or, was it a sign not to be so quick about changing her mind? There was assurance and simplicity of paperwork with the dealership, while the Mini would be a private sale and would require treading in territory that she had been happy to avoid with the dealership. What if Pepe changed his mind? The dealership might gripe, but in the end they wanted to sell cars. She could go back with her head between her legs. The Mini was a more expensive car any way one looked at it. However she reminded herself of its resale value and the services it would offer just by being a BMW brand. Once more the value of the car worried her. More money more problems in life? Did she deserve the car? Yes. It was her first car in thirty seven years. There was no doubt that it was meant for her by virtue of how she found it and how tailored it was to her private wishes. If the Mini got out of hand she could sell it. *'Don't be afraid – "fear is no object",'* repeated the inner voice. In an impulse she called a friend in Germany. She'd known him for years and always admired is rational ability to make decisions. Once again practicality was ignored as she called Germany from her cell phone and wasted more money on the long distant call. Luckily it turned out to be worthwhile because her friend told her that he'd been thinking about buying a Mini for his girlfriend. So it was thumbs up for the Mini enough to keep her motivated about the dreaded call she'd have with the dealership. She spent little time pondering on it and called her brothers, but they were not home. She was on an impulsive nervous streak. Then suddenly the phone summoned and startled her in the process. It was the Ford representative. As calmly and confidently as she could she explained her desire to cancel the order of the car. It wasn't really the car of her expectations and she preferred to wait. The representative was silent. He stalled in his answer: 'The order has already been made and I don't know if they can send us back the money order..,' he said matter of fact.

'Hmm, yes… Could you inquire please and get back to me? I don't mind paying a penalty fee for the charges they might incur from transferring the funds back,' she asked kindly.

'Well it's already Friday afternoon. There probably won't be anyone at the office now. I will try to get back to you on Monday,' he said timidly. 'Thank you,' she said slightly relieved and still stressed,

'I would appreciate that,' and their conversation ended. The call had been made, although without any real solution. Now she had to call Pepe and ask for more time. A whole weekend had to go by and the chances of him getting calls for the Mini were inevitable. She would have to give him a deposit. Another risk. If Ford said no then she would lose her deposit with Pepe. What if all her intuition and subliminal crap was just that? Crap! 'Ohhh! Blind faith how you test me!' she voiced into fresh air. Fear was a horrible thing. Believing in one's self was a virtue only when one was right. It was so much easier not to. She pulled on her resource of words: '"There were two paths and the easy one was all that it was".' She kept on, '"the easy way is not necessarily the right way".' Contradicted by, '"Stop while you are ahead"' and '"One bird in the hand is better than two in the bush!"' – 'Aarrgh!' She growled out loud. She sat on the ledge of the terrace window, giving her a spectacular view of the sea and surrounding area. Her situation was the epitome of her life: trying to make the best decision. Surely it came from her dad's influence that nothing was impossible as long as one tried while her mother's supported the Zen ability to let go and not always have to follow through at once. Metaphorically Michèle saw her parents as the best balance between yin and yang for their kids, however as a couple, a night and day that could not meet at dawn. As a result Michèle accepted both philosophies as long as they both served an evolutionary move or a change distinct from the past. In the end life had to go forward and meet into a full circle before a renovation of one's life began again. It was just a matter of applying the knowledge correctly. Still as easy as it was to preach, she still experienced doubt that largely got in the way and either saved or sank her. She thought about all the pinnacle moments in her life. They had all suffered and evolved similarly. It got down to fear, self-doubt and impatience. The antecedents to boldness, self-confidence and wisdom. It was the complete gamut of someone who has lived a life mostly on his or her own. It annoyed her that she had not mastered the latter traits in spite of her knowledge and experience. Japan reminded her that there was always space. Scuba diving showed her that there was always air, and Life had taught her that there was always time. Always. It was one of Michèle's challenges to tame her visionary qualities within the scope of real time. Many cultures had sayings about time, and while she sat there pondering, she remembered an African one that says: "The West has watches, but Africa has the time." She smiled. It spurred a juxtaposition with a memory she had from when she was twelve … *She had been the anchor runner for her grade eight class' one hundred meter race on the same Saturday that her soccer team had had to play a finals game in a city two hours away from the school's competition. She'd gone to the soccer game first, and as soon as the whistle blew its end, her dad had called her from the side lines to which she'd shot off, and jumped into their car already in motion for the school race. Her dad squealed the car out of the parking lot and swerved between traffic in order to get her to the race in time. In fact the more important of the two activities had been the soccer game because she played on a formal city team. Her school however was a small French institution where the teachers and students were almost like family. In light of the competition her school was the underdog and neither she nor her dad wanted to let them down. She remembered the song, "Heart of Glass" had been sounding from the car radio, and the image of her dad turning up the volume as he concentrated on his driving mission. Within an hour and a half's time their light blue station wagon had veered into the school parking lot on two wheels. Her dad pulled up to the field, at the same time as she'd opened the door and heard the announcement for the one hundred meter race. Her dad had been elated with his role in getting her there. As she ran out to find her team mates, she shot a glance back at her father, whose smile transmitted nothing less than success and inspiration! 'Thanks dad!' she yelled into the air, to which she heard her dad's reply, 'Go get 'em!' and she* did. It must have been all the adrenalin cooped up from their race against time, but she ran like the wind and her team finished in first place... It was one of many similar moments with her dad that supported her spirit to survive. Then it gripped her in the throat that her experience with the Mini was another déjà vu in a slightly different colour. She'd done exactly the same thing seven years earlier when she'd arrived to Mayürqa looking for an apartment. *It had been that big move in 1998 when she'd arrived to the island on her own, knowing no one or anything. It was one a.m. in the morning when she took a taxi from the airport to the unknown hostel in an unknown location that she later learned was the cultural centre of Palma. The taxi drove her along the seaside boulevard lined with soft yellow street lights and gallantly protected by Palma's majestic cathedral. When the taxi dropped her off she walked hesitantly up a shady lit cobble stone lane. The resounding noise from the wheels of her very heavy duffle bag vexed her insides and the need to locate her hostel. Upon arrival she rang the bell and waited a few moments until a man in his pyjamas and wearing glasses opened a pair of window shutters above her and enquired: '¿Si?' Hesitantly in broken Spanish, she explained that she had a reservation and apologised for the late arrival. He came down, growled lightly about the time and then proceeded to help haul her heavy bag up two flights of nineteenth century stairs. Once arrived, her quasi blurry image of the flat she'd hoped to find was preferably on the Mediterranean Sea, had affordable rent, clean and near to transportation. 'Otherwise,' she'd said to herself, 'what was the point of being in the Med?' As always she arrived with less than enough funds to get her through two weeks of apartment hunting. The strategy was to find a place first then get a job, contradicted by the fact that she'd arrived with little if any Spanish language skill, no clue about the locations of the places she would see for rent and without a car, limited her choices within walking distance. She spent the first week maintaining composure with the odd sleepless nights drenched in tears and panicked thoughts about the dénouement of her life. Doubt and confidence were at a constant battle until the eighth day, after having seen so many places, she was shown a new studio apartment located in the nucleus of Palma's cultural centre overlooking Palma's cathedral and the sea in front of it. It was modern and owned by a German woman who wanted seven hundred pesetas a month. Needless to say she decided on it and on that same day gave the agent first and last month's rent before hauling her stuff from the hostel she'd been staying in, to the new place. Similar to the Ford, she experienced little time between her decision and the sense of regret. When she finally got into the studio, dropped her bags, opened the new wooden shutters that overlooked the city's cathedral she was overtaken by a surge of noise from outside that she had not noticed before. Her heart suddenly began to beat at an unbearable rate. She sat on the sofa bed and wanted to cry. It was a very nice place and she could stay there until she found something better. How she wanted to just unpack and get settled. Yet she couldn't. It wasn't what she had gone to Mayürqa for. She did not want to move into a place only to move so soon again. It was better to look longer for the right place, but money and time were an issue. She'd already paid and moved in…No? 'No!' Her dad's voice resounded in her head clearly and sharply. Again it was the embarrassment of going back to the hostel and then having to ask the agency for her money back! Would the real estate agent even do it? Still, the point was to stay true to herself. In a light panic she ran out of the studio and down to the nearest telephone booth to call the agent. The telephone card that she had was out of time. Frustrated she went to the local bar and asked a waiter for change who only managed to help her after he'd served a few tables first. Almost beside herself, she dialled the call. When the agent answered she was less altruistic and gave him a cock and bull story about needing to go back to work on ships. The agent was annoyed but agreed to see her at the office. She took a taxi despite her budget and when she finally got there he returned* both months' rent to her! Apparently if she had waited five minutes more, he would have stamped the contract and made it an irreversible transaction!? She got back to the hostel feeling drained from the stress of that experience. Then in her room, she found a message from another agent asking her to return his call. That evening she did. The next day he drove her to an apartment building located on a quiet road. At first she was disappointed at its frontal view that was at least fourteen storeys high. She was not a fan of apartment buildings and would use the stairs first before taking any elevator. However the apartment the agent showed her was right on the sea, on the southern rim with natural light from the east and the west coast, directly accessible without the elevator and for seven hundred pesetas a month. It was nicely furnished in reminiscent Côte d'Azur summer blue and brown colours, quiet, full outdoor pool with private access to the sea, café, central to a handy shopping district that was evidently home to several diplomats and well established people. The fact that it was a building was quickly dismissed and on the tenth day she moved into the place and stayed there for five years. Her first night in bed she stared at the ceiling and whispered, 'Thanks daddy,' and in her heart he replied, 'Way to go Michèle!'... She came out of the memory and back to real time. Enough was enough. She preferred the Mini and that was certain. She followed up with Pepe and explained the circumstances of her call with the dealership. Although her story bordered on crazy, he still agreed to keep the car for her in exchange for a 500 euros deposit. She agreed instantly and they decided to meet in Palma the following week. When she hung up, that same drained sensation from stress relief came over her. She recognised the fact that she was currently 15,500 euros in the hole, with no car in sight, but it did not matter to her. As unconventional as it all was, things were still flowing in the right direction, and that's what mattered most.

The gift of Charlie and C'an Bon Jesús

Journal: O.K. Vladimir went home on the 28th, and on the first of December, I asked Charlie if he would go with me to Palma when I gave Pepe the deposit for the car. I thought his presence would probably support my credibility a bit with Pepe, especially as Charlie's presence was what had helped me with the loan. That, and the fact that I was going to feel more comfortable knowing that Charlie had experience and like Pepe, is Mayürqan. I agreed to meet Pepe at his restaurant in the industrial sector of Palma. We went in Charlie's car and arrived into town after having had a great lunch at Sa Croix. I love those moments with him. We usually sit at the same corner table from which he can watch the restaurant's activity while we eat a meal from the daily menu. Usually freshly prepared hot paella, Mayürqan homemade malt bread, the olives, water and coffee. Charlie usually has all three entrées to the menu while I am content with one full serving of paella. The food at Sa Croix is prepared daily with a special of the day for 7 euros. It's just basic good food at a very reasonable price. His clientele are truck drivers, and locals from surrounding villages, and even a few regulars from Palma. It has the same charm as the local highway diner with all the traditional cultural trimmings to it. Anyway, I give thanks every day for the experience. Outside of home cooking, you just can't eat any better. When we arrived at Palma we entered Pepe's restaurant and without even a chance to make introductions Pepe says, 'Wep! I know you!' to which Charlie replies, 'My goodness, how are you?' I couldn't believe it. I'd just gained or lost a hundred brownie points. People who know Charlie also probably know about his drug addiction and possibly more. Still, they shook hands and began their music in Mayürqan. Then suddenly, as if realising that I was there, Pepe said to me: 'I know him from Sa Croix because I am originally from Ariany,' he said pronouncing it "Arian", the tiny village next door.' I think I let out a small gasp when he said that because he and Charlie gave me a surprised look at the same time. 'Ariany?' I half whispered and squealed at the same time. It was just too much. I suddenly lost my capacity to speak fluently or correctly. I think Charlie was embarrassed and Pepe probably just thought I had a very bad accent. 'I actually turned-in there by mistake a few months ago, wondering about that place…' I paused. I was sounding silly. As if he cared to know about the logistics to the coincidence that I was seeing then of the "Mini tease" that had caused me to stop there in the first place – indeed! We sat down at one of the restaurant's tables and only began talking about the car after the two gentlemen ceased catching up with each other. I gave Pepe the deposit and in return he gave me a receipt for the amount. Then he explained the process needed to make the private sale official and legal. Naturally, it was an area that I could have avoided if I had gone for the Ford, but Charlie's presence and the coincidence of Pepe's village being Ariany, never mind its proximity to Sa Croix… It was simply incredible and only made me feel better about the whole deal. Best of all, he asked to take care of the transfer of documents when it is normally the buyer who incurs the responsibilities and charges. Once again I could have felt uneasy about that, but there were too many morsels of luck for it to be shady. He seemed genuinely concerned that the paperwork be done correctly because he did not want to get dinged by any legal infractions, such as parking tickets that I might incur, while I had the car and the documentation was still being processed. He has his own notary who can do it all for us quickly and efficiently. He'll use the five hundred euros that I gave him towards the fees of the paperwork and deduct the difference from the total price of the car. The only thing that I needed to do was send Pepe copies of my particular details as soon as possible. At which point Charlie suggested that I use the fax machine from his accounting office in Juníper. We agreed that I would send them off the next day, chatted a bit more and then said goodbye. When Charlie and I got back into his car he did not hesitate to say to me, 'Vaya suerte que tienes (What luck you have).' I looked at him and said matter of fact, 'Yea, really incredible,' all the while thinking, *'thank you for Charlie.'*

The next day I called Charlie at 11a.m. and he did not answer. I had the sinking feeling that he had taken coke the night before and was probably drugged-out somewhere on his couch or his bed. It was frustrating because I had no clue where the accounting office was located and if he had been out all night, he would not get up until late evening, if at all. I resisted the urge to wake him up directly and drove to Sa Croix on the off chance that I was wrong and he was already there. No such luck. Rather it came in a different shade. His father was there and was kind enough to tell me where the accounting office was located. I took down the number from Charlie's dad and called. Once I got through, I explained that I was Charlie's friend and wanted to know if I could go by to send a fax. The reply was positive although a bit uncertain by the mere fact that Charlie had not said anything to them yet. I was so anxious. Charlie was not responding to calls. I needed to get the information to Pepe and most of all a week had almost gone by without an update from the Ford dealership about my request to have my money returned. My thought had been to call the day after the fax was sent to Pepe because it would have been exactly one week since I'd spoken to the representative. I drove into Juniper village with my stomach in knots and my head feeling a slight headache coming on. *'What was I thinking!?'* I asked myself feeling a sense of panic within. *'Not only have I given Pepe my deposit, but I gave him all indication that the deal was going through when I really hadn't and still don't have a clue! I mean shit, I can't believe that I sent the entire 15,000 euros to the dealership! I don't even want to tell people, it's so embarrassing! I mean okay, they can't really keep my money, but they might charge a penalty fee enough to diminish my ability to buy the Mini. Plus, I don't want Pepe to wait too long or he might get antsy and want to change his mind too. Uuugh, Crap!'* were all the thoughts that went through my system as I came up to the address of the accounting office. I instantly recognised the corner as the one next to where I had visited the Citroen dealership a few weeks earlier. *'Amazing,'* I thought, *'so close, yet so far.'* I buzzed the main door and they let me in. I climbed the dark stairwell all the while thinking that it's all too incredible for something not to go wrong somewhere or somehow. Funny though, I never doubted that I would get the car. Simply that my indecisiveness and push to get it would result in bad news later on. *'What if Pepe was not so altruistic and the car gives me nothing but troubles? The financial maintenance might be well out of my reach, and then what?'* were the kind of thoughts I had that day. Apart from my stupid mistakes, I was simply nervous about whether or not Life would really allow me to have such a great car so easily? I introduced myself to the accountant, gave her the paperwork, the phone number to dial and headed back to the rental car. When I got back into the car, I looked up at the office from where I had just come, and noticed a signboard for an office next door: "C'an Bon Jesús 42." (House of the Good Jesus 42.) It was Jes, my confident number 4 and Charlie's life number 2 all in one; another morsel for all of my doubts. My eyes cried of course. Probably from built up fear and the shame of being so worried, but there he was again. It is true that Jesús is a commonly used and referred to name. It's also true that people's perception of things heightens in relation to the mind-set that they are tuned into. However, I was not thinking about anyone in particular at that moment. The shop's name and address could have been anything else, while there will never be any proof that what I'd felt, were small hints of encouragement by a life beyond the one that I breathe, or just a product of projected self-energy. Then Charlie called me right in the middle of my tear drama to enquire if I had the paperwork for the fax. 'Yes, yes,' I said, 'it's already been sent.'

'How did you find the place,' he asked.

'Oh, I was just lucky I guess, and found your father at Sa Croix,' I replied still staring at the sign. 'How are you?' I asked.

'O.K., I went out last night and I'm going to sleep some more.'

'Vale,' I replied.

'O.K.,' he returned and we hung up.

I dried my eyes, sniffed audibly and spoke to Jesy: 'Hi bebé,' my throat felt so dry, 'is it you…? Thank you very much,' and then I drove away.

Paradise

The following day Pepe called to let Michèle know that the fax had not arrived. Perplexed and slightly anxious, she called Charlie to verify if the fax had gone through from the office. Within a few minutes he called her back to let her know that the number she'd given had been busy, and that the accountant would try again that day. The information perturbed her, but she said nothing, thanked Charlie and called Pepe back in order to inform him of the incoming fax. They were little things like those, which made her edgy about the chances of everything falling into place. Had she not seen the morsel of reassurance in C'an Bon Jesús, her nerves might have had the best of her already. The waiting game was a character builder to say the least. It was Friday and still no word from the dealership about the money. On Monday, Pepe was supposed to send her a fax outlining the car details so that she could go to the bank and get the car insured. When Monday morning came around, the fax still hadn't arrived. Vexed by this she decided to wait until the afternoon before calling Pepe to inquire about it. In the meantime she went to the bank and got a quote for the car insurance. When she arrived at the bank, another obstacle was brought to her attention. She did not have a Spanish driver's licence, and the international one that she had, was not convincing enough for most insurance companies. Despite the European Community, it still made no sense to her. If the English could change their driver's licence for a Spanish one, why wouldn't the Canadian one supported by an international driver's licence be enough? Withstanding, Canada still recognised the Queen as their monarchy and unlike England, drove on the same side of the road as the Spanish. '*Pfft, such baloney.*' Again, all companies want their money and there had to be one out there that would have an international product to offer. She just had to find it. Then if she did, she'd probably have to expect a higher premium than most, as a result of the licence issue. She sighed within and made a mental note to herself, 'S*o be it.*' She left the bank on the premises of returning the next day both with Pepe's fax and a solution to the insurance and hopefully by then too, an answer from the dealership. She got into the car and headed to Sa Croix to have lunch with Charlie. The fear of added costs was beginning to fester on her already quiet stream of anxiety. Had she gone with the Ford all of that nonsense would have been taken care of. The thoughts found her but had little impact against her redeeming spirit, '*No pain no gain,*' she defended. Maybe it was her personality to seek out conflict in order to justify any reward. Certainly it was an ingredient from her culture that defined the degree of hard work or tenacity in relation to the value of the cause or thing one wanted. It was not the first time that she had ploughed through obstacles in order to attain something. Sometimes the challenges were so many that the desire itself, to overcome them, became a greater need than the one being sought. University for her had been a constant challenge. The bureaucracy and administrative tape was so thick that it often undermined many students to excel, or be recognised. She remembered a particular time at the end of her second year at University... *She had been working too much in order to make the salary she needed to pay her living costs. The Canadian* winter had made it less bearable to get to classes and overall she just wasn't enjoying university life. Her only solution was to keep up with the classes but change the atmosphere. So she decided to apply to an exchange programme between her university and another one in the Unites States. When she requested the paperwork from the Registrar's office she noticed a sign that said: "Students wishing to do a student exchange are recommended to apply with a minimum 3.0 GPA" She remembered feeling low at that moment because her GPA was a mere 2.4.; satisfactory but not outstanding. Nonetheless, there had been no thoughts about not trying. In her mind's eye her GPA was not well reflected due to the part time work that took her away from her academic focus. Her summer courses in July had proven her theory because she had not worked that month and achieved some very good marks. She was also multilingual, had lived abroad, adopted, she'd felt, good diplomatic skills, and was determined to study better in a different environment. It was a surprise to her when the woman at the desk nearly refused to give her the forms by referring to the sign. The mere denial provoked Michèle's goat. Had the woman just given her the forms and allowed her to apply and probably be denied, would have sufficed the attempt. However, she was being told that she could not even try. Indignant and then steadfast, Michèle referred to the wording of the sign: "Recommended" was not the same as "required". It gave students like her an honest understanding of their possibility, but it did not suggest that they could not apply. The line up behind her was becoming edgy and the woman remained annoyed but gave her the forms. 'There is really no point,' said the woman. Michèle looked at her. 'How?' she thought, 'did this person get her job? She's apathetic, bored and over paid.' Michèle gave the woman a smile and replied: 'Thank you for your concern. I'm willing to do all the work towards this. It's my risk, no worries,' and walked away thinking, 'Ya dits.'

Indeed the paperwork had been extensive and probably a subtle test to weed out the tough ones from the weaker ones. It required a lot of signatures, letters of reference, photocopies and an essay of purpose. It was time consuming and bureaucratic. Some students from a good family or a wealthy standing had it easier by virtue of connections or their parents' secretary. It almost made Michèle give up except for the fact that her lack of tools compared to the other students made her feel like the black horse with potential. It took her two weeks to finally get all the paperwork together. When she presented her documents to the Dean's office the secretary sifted through them to ensure that all the items needed for presentation conformed to her paperwork. 'I'm afraid I can't submit this. Your GPA is below the recommended 3.0.' 'Yes, I know,' replied Michèle already tensed, 'it's a recommendation that does not disqualify my right to apply,' she said coolly. 'If the Dean sees the paperwork and decides to trash it, then so be it. All the required items are there for his perusal,' she added. 'I'm sorry,' said the secretary narrowing her eyes, 'we have to be selective,' and returned the envelope to Michèle. Feeling at once very angry, bordering with the frustration of a child, who has been denied something without logic, Michèle coolly tagged back, 'Perhaps the sign should be changed to reflect that?'… On her way out of the building she wanted justice. Need had turned Challenge into Obsession. The line between, "let it go" and "don't give up" was very thin. The matter was no longer about whether or not she should apply. There were most certainly other students with very good GPAs and qualifications that made them more deserving of consideration than her but at University, discrimination against one's rights was not acceptable. She tried to talk with a guidance counsellor to no avail. Her final attempt was to present her envelope to the Dean directly. It was mad, but at least it would get to him and at that stage it was all that she'd wanted. She called the Deans' office and made an appointment to see the Dean. When she approached the secretary the woman looked at her suspiciously and enquired about the nature of her visit. 'Information about my programme of study and programmes abroad,' she replied. The woman sighed and informed the Dean of her presence. When she was finally allowed into the office, the Dean greeted her with a smile and they sat down. Finally there, she felt *guilty and slightly panicked for taking up his time. 'What can I do for you?' he asked. He was slim built, had a moustache and wore a striped tie. Those were the things that she remembered about that visit. In one endless breath she pulled out the envelope from her bag and placed it on his desk:'I want to apologise for taking up your time. I am here under false pretences. I just wanted to hand into you my application towards an exchange programme to California or North Carolina. I am not usually so aggressive, but the requirements highlight a list of items needed for submission while the sign out front only highlights a recommended GPA. I am below the GPA, but I felt that if I was willing to try, do the work and risk the chance that the department won't even look at it, then that is my problem, not the department's. You may trash it now if you like.' She paused rather embarrassed at being a rambling rebel with a justifiable cause, that wasn't as tangible as a strong G.P.A. – or was it? So much fight had almost lost its reasoning. The Dean looked at her rather sternly then lightened it with a smile and thanked her for her sincerity and mentioned that he was impressed by her courage and tenacity. She was suddenly shy by his diplomacy and apologised again for doing it deviously. Then they both stood up from their seats and Michèle escorted herself out of the office. As unconceiveable as it vwould have been to her at the time however, the outcome of that meeting and a hint of chance would award her another visit with the Dean.*

A few days had had to go by before Michèle could regain a sense of self-composure and stopped by the Dean's department to check-out other possibilities. She was dressed in the fashionable undergraduate style of holy jeans, untidy hair and a baggy shirt. Within a few minutes of her arrival a blond woman approached her and said that the Dean wanted to see her!? She looked around and caught a glimpse of the man heading into his office. He must have seen her walk in. At that meeting he had her paperwork a strewn across his desk. Apparently her marks from a French summer programme showed promise including the fact that she'd been to Japan on her own at the age of nineteen. He continued to tell her that it was important for her to understand that there were many students with better marks and similar experiences to hers however if she could convince him why the University would rather have her, than another student, then he would consider her furthermore. ... And so she did. The result awarded her half a term as an exchange student in San Diego. Following that, her marks were so good that they granted her a second term. Not only did she excel in her programme, but she received several letters of reference from the foreign university requesting that she finish her programme with them. The experience was still made difficult by financial conflicts, but the value it added to her inner strength became one of her most important survival tools in years to come ... She drove into Sa Croix' parking lot and finished her thoughts about that special Dean. Where was he and how was he? Contrary to the woman at the Registrar's desk he was one of the few people that she'd met in her life who really set an esteemed example of the work he was required to perform. It was also the last time that Michèle went to such an extreme to be heard. She got out of the car feeling good about where she was and the lunch that she was about to enjoy with Charlie. Everything was about timing and the codes of conduct towards success were nothing like those from home. Her childhood experiences, years of travel, professional lessons, eastern studies, were all being drawn upon and testing her now. How well she had learned to tame her shrew would demonstrate itself in her ability to manage her life with tranquillity and patience. As she entered the restaurant for lunch, she smiled back at the synchronization of it all.

My most beautiful, small and unshakable woman – why?
Why do people create the problems in order to solve them after?
Why are fears and mistrust a basis for any relationship?
Why is destroying anything easier than to create?
Why when somebody's trying to create the colours
the other is trying to delete them without having any right?
Why is it easier to separate than to get together?
Why? Why? What is the point of our life to do this useless work?
So tasteless this world. I would like to stay with you together in real life not in a spiritual one, but I know that it's not going to happen, as you do not love me. It is too hard to be friends when you love a person so much without any response.
VLADIMIR

Mway

The next day the dealership called to inform Michèle that the money would be transferred back to her account for a 60euro charge. The answer was so positive that all emotion just felt flatter than what she was really feeling inside. She thanked the representative and apologised again for causing him so much trouble. His reply to her was polite but not warm. He was obviously displeased. On that same day she picked up Pepe's fax from Charlie's office and took all the information to the bank. This time the meeting was more productive because an international insurance company was willing to take her on as a client. Better still was the fee: five hundred euros for third party collision for a year. Documents were exchanged, photocopied and signed. All that was pending now was to receive the transfer from the dealership and pick up the car from Pepe. She sauntered pensively to the parked car. It was Tuesday and the date was December 7. Pearl Harbour sixty three years earlier yet one of her best days since she'd begun her drama with the car quest. The paradox amused her. Seven was her Life number. It had also been seven years since she'd first stepped onto Mayürqa and exactly ten years since her father's departure in 1994 had closed a circle of life and launched her into 1995 with a completely new one. In her life, the theories of time and recycled energy had not been insignificant to her. In the third phase of 1995, she found herself alone and in financial dire straits without a professional solution in sight until on October 23, when exactly a year and a day from her father's death, she received a call from a cruise line that she had applied to. Not only did it offer her a post in Asia and a healthy income, but it sent her to foreign places that her father had always wanted to see. Hence she wondered intuitively, if it would be precisely at the end of the upcoming year in 2005 when a full circle of time and events would come to closure and begin a renewed one similar to what she'd experienced in 1995? Silly as it was, the thought of it made her feel better and apprehensive. It meant that she might also find herself in dire straits again. She sighed and decided to relax a bit, and think about other things ... *So many things were still pending: her stuff from Canada still had not arrived, Christmas was already upon them, she needed to think about work, her relationship with Charlie and his family below were so wonderful that it worried her. Dasha was still adapting, the car would be hers soon but at what sacrifice, and above all it was happening all so fast. Really. The year? The people, the luck, the fear, the energy. The entire trip in getting there, all the events leading up to that moment, they all gave her an unrealistic sensation of being so close to Jes and her dad. Now that the quest for the car seemed to be coming to an end she was feeling distance, separation and a very large void all at once? – Emptiness by its true definition? Nonsense of course, but she still felt it. That, or perhaps the feeling was confused with fear. She still had a lot of that. Living out and away from it all could do that – intensify the sense of mortality. Especially when living on one's own. The intensity could be so real that it was hard for her to speak about things until they felt "safe" to talk about, that provisional strategies were a way of life. She was well, but also recognised a major loss within her. It was like an emotional no man's land. Jes alive had been dying alongside her, while Jes gone and spiritually alive made her feel lost and distorted. As if she were being drifted out to sea, farther and farther away from shore. Positive sensations and moments came fleetingly and without continuity, like a caffeine hit from coffee or a nice night with friends. Direction appeared foggy or bland. Her reality understood that marriage, family and that "kind" of familiar fulfilment which supports old age was lost from her plans and possibly never to be found. The consolation prize? The second chance offered to her from Life looked well, but her comfort zones would have to come from another idealism, something else to fulfil her and that was where she was stuck. A human soul mate was required for her particular void. She wondered if she had been deceiving her mind by relating to "everyone" spiritually. It exemplified a spirit that loved from a distance. One that tended to choose relationships which were in some way elusive. Either settled some place far away from her, committed elsewhere emotionally or challenged by something in between. A spirit that could be deeply thoughtful and responsible, but could also block her way when she got close to people, by filling her system with anxiety and worry to a degree that was neither healthy for her nor the others. She knew that there was a severe problem on the horizon that had yet to materialise but would; money. Her last attempts to hold her final dimes were coming to an end. She could see another déjà vu from when she had first moved to the island in 1998. The same situation seemed to be on the verge of playing itself out again. Back then, a loan from the bank to help Jes and to pay off of her Visa had been secured. However, despite a full-time teaching job, the Visa still had to be used to supplement the salary, until she finally dipped into her Canadian savings to "fill the water bucket with the hole in it". Crazy. She even allowed herself to believe that after all the years that her dad wanted to win a lottery that maybe she or her brothers would reap from their dad's virtue of hope. He'd always said that his numbers would win but maybe not in his lifetime. In her current moment, she wanted a year, after Jes and so much upheaval, to just not worry about an income. Maybe unpack her boxes, meditate on life for a while and focus on what work could be created or started-up that would not require a supplement income? Living alone in spite of her conservative attempts was still too expensive. Writing a book remained a constant suggestion in her mind that she negated as ridiculous, crazy and pathetic. It was just a dramatic display of getting by on her idealism. Yet she felt she had something to do and like the rest of the world was unclear about what it was. She'd considered the writing because her dad had been a writer, who would have done but never could... Thoughts that she automatically dismissed to "Never Never Land". Yet, yet, she'd also seen images of her with Dasha in a small car pulling up in Sichus, and by reason of the possible Mini, maybe her blurb of thought was not so far from a focused image? It said to her that her visions were close but not accurate. Mayürqa seemed to be the right place to be. The first time she'd come to the island, it took her the first year to get her bearings and the second year to settle into home, work, friends and love. Her renewed arrival to Mayürqa the second time, gave hints of a similar pattern that she would have preferred to have avoided. How much of her new experience would be another flash in the pan like so many other experiences, before she would finally feel settled? She wanted continuity from a sedentary perspective not a nomadic one and that was difficult to create without one's own family or lifetime friends nearby. Time and circumstance were seeds that needed cultivating if one didn't want their season to pass by indefinitely. She worried about abusing the privileges that she was being afforded, because they increased the courage to continue with her unconventional ways of managing her life in a way that could eventually deceive her. There was also the awareness that once she found her space in work and in love her connection with Life would diminish in such a way that she would see and notice less of its hidden messages. It seemed like such an ungrateful reality, to slowly forget and not say goodbye to an imaginary friend that had always been there for her. Naturally, Life understood. In return she simply needed to remember to appreciate her luck as much as possible and not to be afraid of the good things that came to her. She felt particularly grateful and the notion of luck did not seem to give credit where it was really due. Miracles? Moments of chance? Divine protection? There had been so many, almost as if fluorescent paint had been splashed on her life line from birth until then and her destiny so clearly highlighted. She felt the same would be true if it were splashed out ahead of her – she'd see her life's plan. She could see it now but too vaguely to know how, when or where exactly. Now the second time back in Mayürqa was a second phase and consolation prize where she was being tested again as another opportunity to do it right or better than the last time. She was being watched financially and romantically because these were always her challenges. She compared Vladimir to another relationship she had known from ships exactly ten years earlier. In both experiences the men were intelligent, real, attractive, blond, blue eyed, younger and loved her. The pattern with Vladimir of his professed love, her denial of it, and then her attempt to alleviate the hurt by offering her compassion ran parallel with the man she had met ten years earlier. The experience taught her to expect Vladimir to return hoping and her unfortunate need to be painfully clear with him. Her relationship with the other man ended and she wondered if Vladimir was a test on integrity or another chance at love? Doubt and insecurity seemed to be feasting better on her veil of years. Did Vlad move her? Did he really want her? He was young with the potential to be the man he wanted to be; kind, thoughtful, and he had entered her life. Yet despite his attractive looks, she felt no chemistry towards him; only affection. Not desire or contentedness. Perhaps it was too soon, and his maturity in time would bring her closer to him? She doubted it. She decided that if they were lucky, and she remained real, Vladimir would meet another woman who would reciprocate the beauty of his love and then maybe she and Vladimir could maintain a friendship. It seemed clearer to her that her presence in his life was the energy he needed to regain his morale while his presence in her life had rejuvenated her vanity and unintentionally helped her to find the Mini. She did not know, but at least it was a proven theory. In fact it occurred to her that mediation between her and divine intervention had begun its incubation in 2003 via her mother's visit to Mayūrqa. In the five years that she had been living there, her mother finally managed to visit and take the photo of Michèle, Jesy and Dasha just before he died that year. She marvelled again, at the coincidence of it being the only photo of the three of them that she had. Withstanding, how it included the houses where both she and Carles were currently living. Certain dates, and numbers had become predominant too. Especially 28, as "the Day of the Innocent" when Jes died, the date of her birthday in January which was also indicative of the Chinese year of the Rat in Charlie's birth sign, the year of the Rooster in 2005, the day when she moved to Sa Ema, as well as being Mitx' birthday. That Mitx' initials were hers too, while Charlie coincidentally had the same initials as her father's. Michèle was in all of them and them in her.* She exhaled softly. *The subtleties she read into were countless, and difficult to grasp or hold. She knew… It was all abstract just like time, yet people accepted time's existence. It was respected albeit invisible too, because it could be identified by the passing of day and night. Numbers, dates and coincidences on the other hand, could be pure crap or maybe, just maybe, the next level for those who had advanced in their self-development towards finding Life's answers to the many questions about its meaning?* She halted her stroll. Pondered on that thought briefly then resumed walking towards the car. In any case, she decided, it was a personal feeling, to be shared discretely and used with a grain of salt. She got into the car. 2004 was coming to a close and Jes will have been gone for a year. Dasha will have been from Mayūrqa to Canada and back, and Michèle will have crossed the Atlantic at least six times! Been to the Panama Canal, Caribbean, the Middle East, Europe, and finally seen Venice with Jes the only way that they could have. Then she saw her name Michèle, Mitx', her dad's middle name Michael, the Mini, and fundamental places in her life like Mayūrqa and Montreal just to name a few. "M" was everywhere! She laughed out loud in spite of herself. Her imagination needed to be dashed with a huge grain of salt. Still her thoughts were alive now and she recalled the coincidence of having seen a few bears in Canada before she'd arrived to Sa Ema only to receive the bear key chain that was attached to the house keys that Elisabet gave her. Bear suggested solitude, inner strength and 2004 had definitely been all about those. She started the car. The list of her evidence was long, and crap or not, it was perceived by way of how she was feeling at the time. As she drove home the notion put a smug smile on her face, while she reminded herself not to let such things go to her head. If in fact it did all fall well into place and she was allowed to enjoy that Mini, how absurdly close to everything it would be, to every possible childish detail that she might have wished for. It really was, incredible. ... She pulled up next to her place, turned off the car and gathered her things from the passenger seat that she knew so well. She liked driving but mostly preferred being a passenger. It reminded her of her best friend's mother who'd spent her life as a passenger in taxis, limos and her husband's car because she'd never learnt to drive. She told Michèle that being a passenger had allowed her to watch others, reflect and see things that as a driver she never would have. Michèle mentally agreed with the memory, but as she got out of the car she hoped that thirty seven years as a passenger meant that she would not miss out on too much as a driver. Now it was time for her to drive and really focus on the road ahead of her.

He who asks is a fool for five minutes.
He who does not ask remains a fool forever.
CHINESE PROVERB

Question

Journal: What more? Pay the bills, get by, write a book...? Things are good but not right? Right but not good? Dasha will be seven in February. Her role in my life has been so significant in keeping everything with Jesy and Mayürqa past, real. Otherwise I'd feel completely detached like a boat lost in the middle of the ocean without any markers at all. She is what gives me the reminder that he was here. Yet, yet, the mind still waits for him to find me. Come to me. Hug me. Talk to me. Text message me... fill me. I go to bed in a mixture of confused tranquillity with Dasha on my right and Jesy's pillow between my arms as if the three of us are still together. Healthy? Unhealthy? Very wrong? Unreal? The inner voice pipes up and says, 'Jes is dead and feels nothing, knows nothing, or sees nothing related to me or Dasha. Just accept it and be realistic. Life and death. Black and white,' sigh. Again is this my purgatory to be stuck between two worlds? Or am I found and balanced by mediating between them...? Thoughts about '*Just write a frick'n book!*' then, '*Why and what for!?*' I see the years 1998 to 2003 summed up by difficult love, a man and his dog. While 2003 to 2008 is about independence, money and success in attaining quiet aspirations? There was Jes, Dasha and that entire experience in order to be prepared for this one? Perhaps to fulfil or do something that my own "guardian angel" from day one, wants to ensure that I get to? Dunno. He, she, it, is out there; the special one. I have felt that one's presence since I was old enough to potty on my own. Then again, perhaps it is the mind that conjures up the ambiguous presence when one is born first and on one's own for a few years? It is true that I had at least six years before my older brother arrived, so I'd been on my own a lot of the time. Perhaps that is what it's all about. I motivate *Mi* and without me, I would not have survived my journey on my own? If in fact I am simply talking to me out loud, or relating thoughts to a spiritual dimension in order to comfort myself, find my own reason and face the unwanted realities of the life I breathe, what is wrong with that? Why do people accept those people who do the same thing via their partners or via a professional service, but label those who don't, as unglued or eccentric? Socrates wrote that "an examined life was the only one that deserved living". The answers we want are always within... Not with one's relationship, on the moon, or in the well of another country – no? ... And why am I writing or expressing this? Because I have become my own best friend, who needs defending or support, and have unconsciously made me comparable to no one? Shall I never truly be calm by virtue of my respect and loyalty to *Mi*, even when our bond is not always a healthy one? Hmm, questions, questions. In either case of esoteric or psychological reasoning, I should learn to be able to impede personal relationships from interfering with my focus, without depending on me or the spiritual world as my back up? Yet I talk freely with Life and ask how to write "a book?" How do I begin? Is it a book or something else? Some kind of profession? You will let me know? I just don't want to abuse or use this "free" time unwisely. Am I delaying? Am I on track? Are you just giving me this time now because I will soon be crazy busy again with events? Work? What? It's all been done. At this stage of my life my chosen profession and income must be equal, or greater to what I have achieved so far. I know what I should like to do: I see the years of training and preparation pointing me finally, in a direction, but how practical is it? Am I wrong? Close but no cigar? The "men" in my life are gone now, so I am waiting, trying to go with "your" flow. Trying. I am here now. I have the bear key-chain. I am in the house that is in the photo with Jesy, Dasha and I without ever having known. I know the man named Carles whose house is also quite visible in the photo – whose features, "guidance" and emotional challenges are confused with dad's and whose addiction sometimes feels like it's being used as a spiritual channel for my father to assist me. I believe the yellow Mini is dad's gift to me. The loan to manage it, the thought to find it, was his via Carles who said, "why don't you get a Mini? I see you with a Mini". The "by the sea" mantra that lightly sings in my head when I least expect it, yet seems to help me make decisions right when I need one when all logical and practical purposes are a "locura", ludicrous to even consider: no money, no job, no car, and no Spanish driver's licence. Forgive the false intention I gave the bank about returning to ships. In truth, if things change, I might very well go back to work on ships. In which case it won't be a fib. I have to make money now and how will I do that? Trepidation is muffled by the evidence that I am here. I am in a house that loves football, demonstrates kindness and generosity. I must find a way to give back or at least give value to the hopes and white lies. I am here because of my time alone at mum's where a black bear crossed my path more than once, rabbits ran ahead of me, a seagull's feather floated into my foot right on cue with dad's song! It was all so crazy, but I *am* here. I hope that this is not a temporary image. I love U, and am in awe of you at the same time.

Memories
Light the corners of my mind
They may be beautiful and yet
What's too painful to remember
I simply choose to forget
Misty water-coloured memories and scattered pictures
Shall be my memory, of the way they were.
'MEMORIES' – BARBARA STREISAND, LYRICS ADAPTED

Visions

Journal: Those of daddy driving. His hands on the steering wheel, sometimes firm at ten and two or moderately cradling five and seven. Still very clear after ten years! The same is true for Jes. His image in so many places is so vivid to me, especially too, from the car. There is the vision of the confident look when he drove. His beautiful profile sometimes in a James Dean shot with the cigarette balanced at the edge of his mouth, smoke slithering up to his eyes, while hands simultaneously handled the steering wheel and stick shift. I see his clothes and most of all I see his right hand on the stick shift and follow with my eyes the way he changes gears. Then I focus on his silver Rolex that accentuated the masculinity of his forearm until the folded cuff of his sky-blue shirt veils it from my sight. I loved his looks. I opened a photo of him from my email and traced his profile with the mouse. I could still remember, almost feigned feeling his touch, the smell behind his ear, the texture of his lobe between my teeth and slightly on my tongue, the warmth of his body. Tears wet the keyboard from the intensity of my passion with him on screen. There is the recollection of him in bed; lying on his side with his back to me. I see his head with thick soft black hair. The sensation of his skin was smooth and I would reach my face between the naked lull between his shoulder blade and his spine and place my nose ever so lightly against his body and breathe in deeply. I loved his smell. Even when he passed out drunk, exuding the alcohol toxins from his body into the bedroom and snored wildly, I loved his presence. There was the vision of him in a dream too. I could actually see him and we were talking in Castilian. Then we are talking on the phone and I am asking him if we can meet for dinner. He says: 'Why not, maybe we'll even get back together again.' At which time my "character" feels very happy as well as indignant and muffles something back to him like: 'We were never broken-up', but as I am saying this to him I am feeling guilty because I know that I had once suggested that we should, even though I didn't want to. The contradiction caused me to feel shame for manipulating or being so unclear with my words. Anyway I woke up with the words "reunirnos", get back together, still drifting in my mental state. Confused feelings of elatedness that maybe Jes was going to come back to me in this life flanked with depression at the reality of such a stupid notion. Then a slight feeling of apprehension that maybe I should die soon attacked with the better notion that he was simply close by. Anyway I got out of bed and walked Dasha. Then Charlie picked me up at noon so that I could go to the bank to retrieve the money for the car. Following that we drove to a village called Selva. Charlie was really low when he picked me up because his group therapy had ousted him out for relapsing back to the coke. He was so upset that he wore dark shades to cover his eyes, but they were little use to hide his tears. At one point I asked him to stop the car and I gave him a hug. They don't do hugs out here and frankly it is a real shame. I am convinced that if I got at least two hugs a week I would feel and be so much better emotionally. Anyway, once we were finally having lunch and Charlie slipped off to the men's room, I asked "God" what I was supposed to do with Charlie? Help him how? I need to work and I need an income. I paid for lunch not because Charlie wouldn't have, but I wanted to thank him for all his help with the car. I mean there he was feeling emotionally and physically like shit and still managed to pick me up and take me to the bank when I could have gone myself with the rental car. Although truth be known too, that even though I enjoyed the drive with him and the bits from our talks, most of the day from the time that he had picked me up until he dropped me off was about him. Sitting there at the table waiting for Charlie, I found myself missing Jes, only to have the feelings heightened instantly from a song that began playng through the restaurant's internal sound system. It was Luz Casal's song again, "No me importa nada". My body shivered slightly. I turned my head towards a window next to the table, allowing my eyes to turn moist with the sensation of his presence. The terrace outside was empty at that time and the mountains beyond were distant. I got lost in memories about him and I with Dasha on a day that the three of us had been at the very same restaurant where Charlie and I were then sitting ... *It was called Café Parc at the time and the three of us had gone there to have a coffee outside on the terrace.*

*The place had a lot of charm with Poplar trees surrounding a typical bar-restaurant and an open air music stage. The café was quaintly located high above the village from where a spectacular view of deep Mayürqa could be seen. Dasha at the time could not have been more than two and a half years old. It was a memorable day because upon leaving the place, Dasha had come across cat and was led into bushes that bordered along a hidden ledge that fell at least three and a half meters onto a flat stone stairwell that out-stretched down in front of us into the main village below. Jesy and I had not been aware of the impending predicament until we heard the cat wail and Dasha give a slight grunt as she attempted to avoid the ledge but ended up in mid-air above us. It was like watching Dasha fly in slow motion. She just came soaring out of the bushes above us, head and tail up, paws flapping slightly, then instantly dropped straight down into the stairwell ahead of us, rolled a few stairs, and sprung back up on her paws. She stood still for an instant not moving. I was beside myself. I only had time to squeak something like 'Jesy!' to which Jes in his cool and collected way proceeded to saunter down the steps to meet Dasha. 'Traanquiila,(Eaasy)' he said to me softly while swirls of cigarette smoke suddenly grew into a miniature cloud over his head. '¿Que Dasha?' his deep voice asked her casually. He ran his hands across and around her little body with gentle precision. Then seemingly satisfied that she was fine, gave her a light but firm pat on her rump's right side, "¡Bien Dasha!(Good Dasha)" he prompted her. She evidently still had some of her puppy malleability in her and never once squeaked or complained. Nothing. Just picked up from Jes' signal, tail waving back and forth and down to the car we all went...*When Charlie came back to our table, we had our lunch and went back home. The Café Parc area was still the same except the restaurant where we had lunch was no longer the typical local place. It's been renovated into a generic nouveau riche place. In fact many places and parts of Mayürqa have changed that way since my chapter with Jes. Sigh. Time is all about change, but I thank Life for the intensity of the memories, and moments, I shared with him.

If you can dream it, you can do it – WALT DISNEY.

CJ

Charlie drove Michèle to the train station in Juníper village. The ford rental had been returned to the dealership the day before and the money for the Mini was now in an envelope in Michèle's briefcase. She got down from Charlie's Phedra, said goodbye and he sped out of the parking lot like a man trying to drive away from his thoughts. She enjoyed that man she knew and "why?" was a question that she did not want to analyse too much. However, an attraction definitely existed whether she liked it or not, and cocaine or not, he had been good to her. The day he'd get better would be a different story of course, so she tried hard to remember that. Now was the time to enjoy him. Without a doubt she had been the privileged one to receive the fruit of his personality and abilities. Apparently from what she had been told by him and his family, no woman had ever spent so much time next to him, or received so much of his attention before. Not even his wife. Although she suspected the latter was untrue by reason that few people in his family really seemed to know him. Still, it made her feel good and sad at the same time. The men in her life always came and left. Always. Even the ones her mother might have chosen. She walked up the ramp to the train's platform. She loved taking the train. It was her favourite source of transportation. When she was a girl growing up in Canada she had used the train constantly to get from the suburbs to the city or for longer treks between provinces. Time on a train was like no-man's land between the departure and the arrival, a quasi-nirvana. She would write or transcend to other levels in her mind and heart, sometimes using her Walkman and the moving scenery to guide her... It was always her down time. As she waited on the platform, Michèle focused on her current location and loved were she was; in Juníper waiting for the local train to Palma. Her surroundings were nothing more than a few Mayürqan stone buildings from the eighteenth and nineteenth century. Misty blue grey mountains in the back drop similar to any of those seen in Eastern Europe, Turkey or even places in California. Palm trees, sheep and the clanking sounds of a bell around their necks resounding from within miles of open farmed land and fields that seemed to vacillate between green and gold hues. Behind her was the main road and Sa Croix tucked at the top left corner of her view. It was quiet with a few local people from the village also waiting next to her. When the train finally came into sight the warning lights came-on and the traffic barrier descended to stop cars from crossing the tracks. The train sounded a deep lazy yawn from its horn at the same time as the conductor waved to her as the train passed by and stopped. She depressed a release button before the doors slid open, then a few whistles from the ticket agent, doors slid back together and the train chugged on its way jerking from side to side to the next stop in Sichus. She slipped into her seat next to a wide scenic window and followed with heart and soul the moving show of traditional time and more fields. She noticed with irony a similarity to the experiences she had had as a young girl living in a little suburb just outside of Saint Dorothée Laval. At that time the train system and the quaint surroundings of her home were very similar to where she was in Mayürqa. In a funny way she had found a way to go back in time and extend the lifestyle that she'd loved so much as a child. Despite all its national fervour, it had been a gift growing up in "La Belle Province." The French twist, was in Michèle's mind one of the many cultural privileges that made Canada even more unique from the rest of the world. Without a doubt North America was the child of the world, but Canada was a child with an old spirit that made it uniquely different from its neighbours and closer to its Scandinavian and European relatives. She loved her country very much and only wished it protected itself more. Sharing in life was good, but "keep the farm!" Places like Mayürqa would eventually get sucked into the economic vacuum. The cracks in the foundation were already visible. The generation of Nouveau Riche Mayürqans was giving the mortar a different consistency with little if any understanding of globalisation's hidden evils. Notwithstanding, the cultural root of a traditional society tends to fasten itself deeper when threatened. The villages of Mayürqa were thus far, the pillars to its identity, beauty and survival. Hopefully astute enough to recognise the worth of their values system, and stubborn enough to instill in following generations, not to forget the smell of their own traditional coffee... She could only hope. The train ride lasted about forty five minutes making several stops at local villages and suburbs of Palma. When she got to the city she hopped on a bus to Pepe's bar-restaurant in order to pick up the Mini. In light of the moment she was far from really feeling anything except nervous. It was her first car and never would she have guessed way back when she was a girl in Canada that it would be found and bought in Mayürqa Spain. She remembered again the film "Under the Tuscan Sun" and the woman who concluded that "Life always has surprises," so one shouldn't try to figure it out too much. Michèle met Pepe by the Mini. He had done a wonderful job making it look like a squeaky clean brand new car! Then again, it was only ten months old with 9,450 kilometres, so in many ways it was. He sat next to her in the passenger side of the car going over as much information as he could about its mechanics and maintenance agenda. It was another point that Michèle had thought about but neglected to do. She had not requested a mechanic to look at the car before she'd bought it. In all terms and purposes it was a dumb thing to disregard. However, it also remained in her mind that regardless of what he might have said it would not have been enough to deter her from getting it. Besides, she had done her own little test with Pepe by asking him directly for the problems and concerns, to which his replies appeared to conform sincerely with his eyes and his body language. After all he had bought the car for his wife and his ten month old baby. It couldn't have been all that unsafe to drive. Plus he was from Ariany village and that was enough for her. Furthermore, he'd even called BMW and made an appointment for the car's annual inspection that was included in the first year of its guarantee. All that she had to do was take it to the shop for its review. After about fifteen minutes they finalised the paperwork, shook hands and parted ways. Pepe had even left her his CD mix of music that he had been listening to when he brought her the car. The only pending detail was the official traffic certificate with her name on it, which was going to take a few months to process.

In the meantime she had a temporary one that she could renew every month until the authentic one was available. They agreed to keep in touch until it was ready. Needless to say the car was magic and Michèle spent her first few months treating the Mini like it was a baby. The slightest evidence of dirt, dust or scratch received severe action and attention. Every sound and speed bump caused her heart to freeze momentarily until she was sure that the car was alright. It was so hard for her to really accept the fact that she was the owner of a yellow black top Mini Cooper! She drove and thanked Life at least a hundred times a ride. Every day seemed to highlight another wonderful fact about the car and her privilege to have it. Night driving in the Mini was heaven. Beautiful orange interior lighting, great CD sound system, stars above its glass roof top and most importantly, she could drive without any qualms about safety. It had been one of her main points of interest when considering her choice of car. Most cars within little time absorbed a film in the windshield that made night driving unclear against oncoming car headlights. Not the Mini. It was the cat's ass! Its headlights gave her vision for miles before even using its high beams. Wind shield wipers cleaned so effectively even when one of them lost some of its rubber, they never let her down. She felt so protected. It was definitely a gift from the men who loved her. With time the dread of ominous energy finding her dissipated. In fact for quite a few months following its purchase, she felt her spiritual companions were still with her and even gave her a few extra coincidental morsels to keep her fear at bay. The first one had arrived on the very day that she took the car home and parked the yellow Mini in front of Mitx and Elisabet's red Alfa Romeo. Everyone including Charlie was anxious to see the car. It went without saying that the sight of the two cars in front of the house was already eye catching, but it was Charlie who noticed that both the Mini and the Alfa had the same licence plate registration: CMR. The second morsel came right after Charlie's observation. Michèle had not taken the time to look at the Mini's plates until then, and when she did her heart stopped momentarily. 8384CMR was the Mini's full licence plate I.D. Both Charlie's name and her Dad's initials – C.M.S. looked at her. The "S" was left up to the imagination as a pseudo for the writer Robert Shaw, while 8384 were digits that belonged to her dad in 8, Jesy in 3 and hers in 4. Summed up in pairs they either summed up as Charlie and Jes' numerological numbers 2 and 3, or hers as 7. Either way the plates totalled 5 and her new beginning into the year 2005. The day was Saturday, the same day on which her dad had died. The month was December, the same month that Jes had died. Finally, the date was the 11th, the numerological number for mastery, and as a whole: 11-12-2004 summed up as 2, Charlie's Life number. Then about a month later Pepe called to give her an update about the certificate. In their conversation he let her know that because he and his wife had ordered the Mini through a department store's agency, he in fact was supposed to have returned the Mini to them in return for a line of credit or an exchange for another car. That in hindsight he said that she was lucky because he really missed the Mini and would not have sold it if he had to do it over again. However a little time later, the biggest and most significant morsel of all would become her beacon when fear would blind her, doubt would vex her truth, or when loneliness would try to overcome her. It was the backup morsel to remind her of her personal connection with Life. Only a few days after getting the car a good friend of her mother's in Canada sent her an email wishing her luck on buying the Ford. That even though "the Mini is a popular car, the Ford is also good and much more practical economically." The message had made her laugh. With all the excitement Michèle had yet to inform her family of her last-minute dramas before finally acquiring the Mini. Further in the message, the friend advised her that she had sent Michèle a Christmas package that she had hoped Michèle would get before Christmas. Indeed, CJ did arrive in time and it was an incredible gift! A miniature black top yellow Mini Cooper windup car EXACTLY like the one she owned!?! She could not help but ask: 'When do people stop denying the presence of divine intervention?! How much proof is required?!' Her mother's friend had purchased the little car way before Michèle had finalised the Mini; before the friend had even known about the Mini; why was it identical? Why not black with a white top? Or solid yellow or, or...No. It was identical! Upon the unfolding of Christmas paper it had arrived in, the moment of its discovery had caught her throat. She looked up to the air, to the left and to the right, frustrated at only being able to say "Thank you." Who would understand her? What could she touch to feel them? Then she looked at her hand and kissed the high school graduation ring from her dad that held a yellow Sapphire stone in its centre and the engagement ring from Jesy. Together she had JC, the presence of Jesus Christopher on her hand. She rolled her eyes at the imagination before her, but it was not totally untrue. She had been a well-protected woman thus far, and any way she wanted to look at it, that small but mighty yellow powered Mini Cooper, was meant to be hers. She decided to call the miniature Mini CJ, because the "C" was first on the plate and it recognised the men who helped her, Charlie and her dad, while "J" was for Jes. … Later on, she placed the miniature Mini strategically in sight from where she sometimes sat on the sofa. In moments of great doubt and confusion about her unconventional ways, she would look at that miniature Mini and remember the improbability that became a probability and then a reality. So many things could intimidate a person from creating his masterpiece entirely – half assed per se, but that Mini was a personified reflection of her and there was nothing half assed about it.

Saint Teresa
Saint who believes in doing little things in life well and with great love
May you be content knowing that you are an angel of the universe
May you trust life that you are exactly where you are meant to be
May you not forget the infinite possibilities that are born of faith
May you use those gifts that you have received
And pass on the love that has been given to you.
SAINT TERESA'S PRAYER – ADAPTED

Love

Journal: I've really been enjoying the gift of the Mini. On my way home from Palma the other day, I took it through Sichus and along the St. Joan and Juníper back roads to Sa Ema. At 3:30 p.m. dusk had already begun to urge out the country colours. Hence the earth tones, the many shades of olive greens were out playing with sun golds and a sleepy blue cotton-batt sky. I parked the car on a muddy farm trail and went snap crazy taking photos of the Mini centered within the beauty of it all. In light of everything I am still feeling somewhat low from Jes' void. Christmas came and went and so did his one year anniversary. Ironically the date December 28, was even more accentuated by the fact that the Mini had its revision check-up on the same day. Anyway, they say that the bereavement of a person dissipates within half the time of the total time spent with the deceased person. Jes and I were together for five years so I guess that means I'm normal to feel something like this for the next year and a half – At least until June 2006? It certainly makes sense about daddy because October of this year was exactly ten years since his departure and I still manage to think that only four or five years have gone by. He was in my life for twenty seven years! So by April 2007! I should have my life figured out in a way that his presence can feel freer to go? I don't think he ever really left. Ever. I think he has been very close by, watching and helping his family, particularly my brothers and I, and won't truly relax until he sees us arrive at our determined destinations, because it would be unlike him to do otherwise. Smile. In any case, the drive through the back country roads was a great lifter and I thanked Life for the ability to get away in a Mini. Christmas went by very nicely. Even though I was stressed about where and how to spend it and I really did not want the Serras to feel obliged to invite me. I would have been just fine to get through it on my own. However in hindsight, there was so much family activity around me that to suddenly have been without it, might have somehow left me feeling emotionally disoriented? Like suddenly being alone after a personal relationship ends. I think the presence of the social vibe while on my own might have caused me to notice my solitude negatively and then really feel lonely. I see Charlie dysfunctional, married with a son yet his presence settles me, conflicted by frustration that there isn't more – can't be more. So I think there is no hope. His affection towards me will not flourish into something stronger and maybe even stop. Yet, yet, I recognise a high level of sexuality towards him from me and I don't like it or really understand it. Is it desire or just loneliness? We had dinner at Pinxets in Namacor the other night and he'd said that he wanted to tell me about his life. So naturally, I wondered if there was another woman somewhere or if he had committed a crime or something, but in the end he shared very little with me. Instead he suggested that I was ill because I offer too much kindness to him and others and to strengthen his point quoted: '"You can't help others if you don't help yourself".' Naturally, I offered a counter attack and asked: 'Have you ever heard of the butterfly effect? The migrating pattern of a zillion butterflies to South America each year actually affects the hemisphere worldwide! It's a scientific fact. Blind faith is not required. We're all connected Charlie, so that helping others does help oneself. It's just finding the balance. Besides,' I continued without inhaling enough, 'does your point of view hold true for Mother Teresa or Ghandi too? I don't know Charlie, maybe you're just not comfortable with kindness? After all, it's in your culture to be suspicious of it.' He looked at me for a moment with a twinkle in his eye. He enjoyed my fervour and catching my goat dazzled him even more. 'You consider yourself to be a Mother Teresa?' he said with a smug smile along his lips. How was I supposed to answer that? He'd deviated from my point entirely by challenging my integrity and ego at the same time. 'Charlie!' I said in a childlike cackle, 'okay touché. However I do share something with her.'

'Ah, yes,' he said flirtatiously.

'Yes,' I said. 'With respect to *your* tradition,' I teased, 'she and I have the same Saint: Teresa de Jesús. B*ut*!' I continued just a pitch short of cocky, 'unlike Mother Teresa Charlie, my full name on my birth certificate *is* Michèle Teresa.' I was smiling wide by then; couth or not it felt good.

On the 23rd of December, I invited Charlie to a Van Morrison concert in Palma. In fact I gave theatre tickets to the bank director and his assistant for their assistance with the loan and the Ford representative for being so professional with me despite his loss. I really hope he doesn't go sour after his experience with me. In hindsight I am not so sure what my need was for the bank. Frankly they did nothing more than add a new client to their loot of interest rates, but having been a part of that memorable day, I guess that was reason enough. On that same night Charlie asked me for a kiss. It threw me for a loop because it was the first time and we were parked just outside my place when he'd asked for it. I was both apprehensive from Mitx and Elisabet possibly being nearby and impressed that he did not seem to mind. I wanted to kiss him so much. Yet I was afraid of where it might take us. I also did not want to let him down on his first request, so without further ado, I agreed and kissed him on the mouth firmly but quickly. I loved it and wanted more. Of course I played it cool, opened the door to his Phedra and said, 'See you tomorrow.' He looked a bit disappointed or unsure but said 'See you,' and drove off. Within minutes of his departure I received a text from him saying that it was nice but too fast. I laughed because I'd been thinking the same and replied with my own sms: "Igualmente. Poc a poc (Ditto. Little by little)." Following that night he became quite attentive to me. One of the more romantic moments that I remember is a simple one on a simple afternoon. We were all downstairs at Elisabet and Mitx' place chatting when I decided to leave to walk Dasha. 'You going?' said Charlie. 'Yup,' I said, 'I'm going to walk Dasha,' and walked out the back way. I was wearing a black dress shirt, blue jeans flared over black bike boots, walking with my arms folded against a cool breeze while my hair was being tussled about. I guess my leaving first was a good move because within minutes of starting the walk with Dasha I suddenly saw Charlie's Phedra appear and drive around the corner of a street towards us. He had literally left from the front end of Mitx and Elisabet's place to overtly find and catch up with me. It was so unlike him to do that, so it was entirely romantic for me. He pulled up beside me with the window down and with a shy smile said: '¿Que?' I smiled back calmly, '¿Que?' I replied, 'are you heading out now?' 'Yes, I am going to see my son now,' he replied. 'O.K.,' I said, 'I'll see you then,' and with that, I darted my eyes sheepishly to the left and then to the right before I leaned into his window and we both kissed without fear. 'Bye,' he said. 'Bye,' I replied, and then he sped away.

> Your family in Sa Ema de Farrutx, wish you a Merry Christmas.
> Filled with love, happiness and a prosperous New Year in 2005.
> Wishing you lots of luck in your life.
> BELLE. 12. 2004

Navidades

Then came Christmas, made official by my first card from Elisabet. A post card with a big bold and beautiful multicolored heart on it. On the back was a very warm message that kept me pondering for a moment. It was awfully nice for only having known me for two months. I assumed it was about a mixture of empathy towards being on my own after Jes and just her sheer desire to reach out. I placed the card within a plastic frame and once more let my eyes feed my spirit with the vibrant layers of changing colours on the card. Then on Christmas Eve we all met downstairs at Mitx and Elisabet's for dinner. Charlie was there too. Apparently it was the first time in twelve years, that he'd spent Christmas with his family let alone buy a few gifts for people! Everything about the evening was wonderfully memorable. The dinner was meat ball soup, seafood dishes prepared by Elisabet, and lots of Spanish Cava. The atmosphere was happy and all in Mayürqan. I'd added a little Canadian tradition from home of the British toy crackers and was surprised to see them all wearing their paper hats including Charlie! I'd put a big Santa bag together and left it on their front door. Then while we were having dessert, mentioned that I'd heard a noise. Elisabet reacted well and went to the window, but did not actually see the bag! So I had to insist as casually as possible until Charlie's eye twinkled and he told his nephew to check outside more closely. Finally! The big red Santa bag was discovered and a real hit! Charlie acted as Santa and handed out the presents to everyone. I really felt happy that I could give back that way. Then from Belle, I received some wonderful items and Charlie actually gave me two gifts that included a black Ferenze bag and a book with his dedication inside that said: "To Michèle, woman who doesn't leave you indifferent." Considering that he's not a man of words that dedication means a lot to me. Following that, the four of us jumped into Charlie's Phedra and we flew to Juniper village to spend the last of Christmas Eve with Mitx and Charlie's parents at their other brother's' house. Elisabet and I sat in the back with the guys at the front. The music was loud and traditional and my imagination had a bird's eye view of the Phedra zipping up, down and along Juniper highway with the sounds of three very bad singers chanting in Pop Mayürqan! We arrived at the house in time for the very traditional *ensaimada* pastries made for dipping into a purely thick warm chocolate liquid with lots more cava, whiskies and cigars! The brother's house was renovated with modern touches yet clearly a traditional and reminiscent of the old seigniorial homes in Québec; lovely to say the least. There was even a well right inside the kitchen that they still use to drink from. I was among the Serra clan which was a privilege indeed. I sat within the smoke, the loud conversation, the laughter with Charlie and Elisabet at my side. I also noticed that Charlie and I were both wearing red shirts. Seeing as it was Christmas it really was no big deal, but no one else was in red that night.

I have no idea if the moment would have been the same with or without our presence. Nor if it was any better in years past, but that night I truly felt that the barometer of happiness and relief from everyone including Charlie was the highest in a very long time. We drove back to Sa Ema at the speed of light along Juniper road the way Jes used to do along Sichus road. The night was cold, clear and made very bright by a moon on its way to being full. The music was good while Charlie's Phedra suddenly felt like an oversized vehicle bopping along the narrow moon-lit stone hedged road ahead of us. I held the safety grip over my head while I watched silver blue scenery whiz by me. I missed Jesy very much and at the same time loved and worried about the people who'd made me happy that night.

> In spirit they have been here for generations
> Some of the oak and elm for over five thousand years
> Leave a good tree alone and it is a far more worthy
> a far more valuable asset to this Mother Nature
> Than any human being could ever be
> It carries more dignity, more class, more pride
> It feeds and nourishes both the soil and the air
> Provides homes to generations after generations of living creatures
> Be they scaled, winged or furred
> Human beings destroy trees with less compunction
> That they would do a bug
> Myriads of forests are being destroyed all over this globe
> Each and every minute
> Perhaps this will be read some time in the future
> When a tree has become an endangered species, or even worse,
> A tree?
> What's a "tree"?
> I hope they will be here long after I have gone.
> CMS

Hug a tree

On Christmas day Dasha and I got up early and opened our gifts from home. I'd made a cup of tea in my Canadian tradition, plopped some butter cookies on a plate and headed out to the front patio where Elisabet's artificial Christmas tree was located. The lights were still on from the night before and together with the little parcels under it kept me transfixed until I finally decided to open the gifts. At night too, the tree is quite pretty and adds a nice feeling to the entire house. Charlie and I had actually gone to the beach in his

Phedra a week earlier to collect sand for the vase that the tree is now standing in. We'd gone after lunch at Sa Croix. On our way home he took me to an industrial area where a friend of his is holding an olive tree for him. The tale is that several years ago Charlie was owed funds for a business deal that went dry. Instead he and his partner were given Mayürqan olive trees as payment. They sold the trees to local businesses, Charlie kept one, and had it moved to a friend's industrial plot near Sa Croix. … The drive into the back area of the plot was nothing more attractive than machinery, scattered construction equipment and blowing garbage. Once we got out of the car and walked about fifty meters, there was the olive tree. It's tall, majestic and wise in years. The opportunity of seeing an olive tree of that size and age – roughly a thousand years old or more, was another privilege. I contemplated the tree. Then I noticed that no one had given it much respect with all the rubber tubes and electrical wires that were literally wound and caught around the tree's trunk. In fact the tree is situated right among warehouse garbage and tall field grass; a beautiful tree living in squalor.

I looked at Charlie, dismissed my images and turned my attention back to the tree. While we spoke, I tried to remove the debris from around it. 'What are your hopes with this tree?' I asked coolly. 'Don't know – I was thinking maybe putting it in front of my house,' he answered admiring it from a few feet away. 'A house? You have a house?' I asked slightly annoyed by a wire that would not move from the tree. 'Nah, I have a plot you know. Open space. I was thinking maybe I could build one and put this tree out front ..,' he said through a few draws of his tobacco. I gave up on the wire, frustrated but not undaunted – '*I'll come back with wire cutters,*' I thought quickly. Instead, I pressed my hand against the tree. My dad would have loved this tree. He really enjoyed trees and if he could have, he would have saved them all. Funny that Charlie should own one and not just any one: a priceless olive tree, a thousand years old or more, classic looking from Abraham bible stories, the one in Vincent van Gogh's paintings, Greek mythology, children's books and Mayürqa's history. 'You know Charlie, one day soon people will pay to see a tree like this...' 'You think?' he said putting out his cigarette and folding his arms while sizing it up closer, 'I don't know.., it is a beauty.' He started on his way back to the car and I followed. On our drive to the beach he explained the delicate ramifications of moving the tree if ever that day should come. Without even trying, my mind assimilated Charlie and the tree as one: 'The day will come,' I said assertively. 'You'll see.' … A month later, while helping Charlie organise his place, I would come across a few things that Charlie had brought back from his last rehab attempt in August. Among them was a drawing of a big tree, and under it was his writing: "I am tree …"

After I'd opened my gifts and drank my tea, Dasha and I did our walk up the back trail. I guess I was feeling rather sensitive to everything and found myself in a tearful moment when we came across a fallen tree. 'Hug a tree hug a tree,' I whispered inaudibly. There are many fallen trees in those pine woods yet that particular one across our path just seemed to pull-out all sadness from within me. It was a big tree, long in length, and wide in diameter. I touched it lightly where the bulk of its pain appeared knee high into its trunk. It wasn't a clean break and I wished that I had had a saw to end its suffering. The pine needles were still quite green and fresh, its bark was weathered but strong, and I wondered what natural life had joined us in exchange for its departure? I thought about Jes, my dad and a poem called "Tree" that my dad once wrote, and a zillion other thoughts that only the thoughtful, pensive and eccentric dare to plunge into. It was Christmas day and I was crying over a fallen tree. I gave it a hug and laid my head close to its bark as if my energy would relieve its grief when in reality it was the tree relieving mine. … Sometimes the absurdity of how we humans continue to inflict so much pain into nature can overwhelm the senses in a way that the concept of becoming an extinct race seems almost divine to me. The power of love comes from nature and its polarity is hate. Therefore we destroy nature. In my deepest moments of sadness I manage to find ease and fear in knowing that the universe has it all under control. I ask myself: 'When will people understand that everything requires a balance? That everything has an opposite?' The greater the infliction on nature the greater shall be its defence and the greater humans' suffering shall be. Natural disasters and a plague of unknown disease will not only kill us, but they will provoke a longer time line of suffering before dying and that is the worst; the suffering. I looked at the tree and apologised to Life for the indifference we often show it. I wiped my face and kept walking with Dasha along the lane instantly feeling comforted by the natural surroundings. That night we all watched a comedy film at Elisabet's and Mitx' that made the emotion of my morning walk seem far away. Charlie was also there and I delighted in the fact that he could watch it, because films in general are too disturbing for a person with an addiction like his. Jes too, when he was alive, had also really enjoyed the same film that we were watching: "Mortadelo and Filemón's Great Adventure", a mindless laughing cure for everyone.

Twin polarity

Journal: Monday December 27th 2004? ... A year ago today Jes picked up my Christmas package from the local post office in Sichus. I'd sent one to him and one to his father in Barcelona, on the 22nd. He was supposed to pick up his package sooner, but had not got to the Post office in time and needed to wait until after the 26th, to collect it. When he opened his package he discovered Christmas goodies, candy, chocolates, a mug, some photos and a letter from me. That evening he stopped to visit a friend of ours and commented on the package he'd received. Apparently he seemed well that night. The next day he would trip and hurt himself from construction materials that he'd been using to renovate his home; call his mother who wouldn't take him seriously, receive no answer from his brother's phone and end up taking a ride to the hospital with a kind friend whose driving left someone else's to be desired. Thus fate was allowed a way to take Jesy's life that day on a clear morning, in a fluky car accident, at kilometer 12 on Sichus road. Sigh. Six months later that same friend would also die in a fated bicycle accident on the same road? Unreal. The beginning of this journal started about six months after Jes' death never anticipating a year to go by. Tomorrow will be the day that marks a year since he left and the day that Dasha saw him last. It will end a year and begin a second one where Dasha and I will have been alone together without him. This moves me to an emotion that is still waiting for him. A silhouette in the fog, blue jeans, his walk. I can even see him in the shower. I think how a year ago he'd received my Christmas package to him, so it felt good to plant flowers for him today near the area where he died, and where only a year before his death, we had just driven past kilometer 13 heading towards kilometer 12 and I'd felt his loss.., even then. Anyway today, flowers and a mini shovel in hand, I chose a bare area in the field that is next to the road and protected behind a barbed wire fence to put together a small marker. I left him a note, a colour photocopy of the three of us, talked to him, made a toast and then drank and poured cava over the marked area for him. Then I dug a hole for the little cava bottle and placed it halfway inside so that I can put fresh flowers in the bottle when Dasha and I return on visits. I had initially wanted to do the ceremony tomorrow on the 28th. However, funny enough, the Mini has its check up on the same day. Hmpft. It's been a whirlwind of a year. Moments that hit you like a tidal wave: he's not coming back. Then a sudden empty feeling of foreverness makes you feel weaker. Right now trying not to think, but letting myself ride those waves when they do come rather than stifle them. In any case, I choose to feel that all the events that led to his departure suggest it was a destined moment. Jesy was a twin. His twin brother Jaime died under very similar circumstances in 1997. There are several observations about twins when one of them moves on to the next life and the other one is left behind. I know that Jes had a difficult time "finding his Way" after his twin left. Almost as if caught between two worlds or callings. He was a very connected individual and many said that he was the more sensitive of the two. Hmm…They are nice theories to help accept it all. He died on the same highway as Jaime did six years earlier. Like his twin, in a car accident, unprovoked by anything specific, just a distraction by the driver who also survived without a scratch!? Jaime, died on "The Day of Saints" while Jes died on "The Day of the Innocent" at the age of 33, just like Jesus had. In numeric terms kilometre 12 highlights the month in which he died, while the sum of 12 is 3, also Jes' favourite number. Withstanding a Spanish paradox that the same day is lightly used synonymously with April fool's day in North America. Now I hear Alanis Morissette signing, 'isn't that ironic, don't ya know…' He was just one month short of his 34th birthday. Apparently there is often a small psychological challenge getting to the 34th year for some whose name is "Jesús"? Hmm, I dunno. Anyhow, several other little details help make his absence feel easier to accept. I remember, I had been in Canada at the time *… and the phone call that came to me on the night of the 28th happened to be the only one to get through to mum's place because of bad weather! Right after that call, telephone lines were completely down from December 27th until December 31st, the same day that Jesy was cremated! I'd flown back to Mayürqa within two days of the call, spent a sombre week with his family and attended the cremation ceremony. The flight back to Canada from Mayürqa included Dasha and in spite of the long journey went very well. Dasha and I arrived up north at mum's* *at about 11 p.m. on January 5th. A day that I noticed later, as being the same one when Spain celebrates the arrival of the Three Kings, as well as being the same date of our anniversary in June. There was also a full moon lighting up our way to mum's while snow had started to fall lightly. Then as to add magic to the fairytale, there ahead of us, surrounded by the aura of white snow, were two healthy young bucks in the middle of the road. One had the beginnings of small antlers while the other did not. Dasha almost jumped out of the car when she noticed the latter one. When we'd got close enough they both darted into the bush. As we drove past them, I chose to believe that Jamie and Jes were being represented by those two bucks. As totems they represented to me peace and tranquillity, and suggested positive new beginnings. I understood then, that he was fine and that Dasha and I would be fine too ...* It was, esoteric medicine to help swallow. Finally, grateful, that Jes and I had had good closure. We'd spoken just before the accident and he'd received my Christmas package from Canada the day before he died. That in itself was a miracle. Especially when I'd also sent the packages to him and his dad on the same day. Packages to Barcelona arrive before those in Mayürqa. However, Jesy's dad had not received his until the 5th, the day that Dasha and I arrived safely to Canada. ... I took a picture of the little marked area that I'd created for him today, called for Dasha and returned to the car. When we drove away, the Mini spun around the curved road just enough for us to see the marker in the distance, and give it a honk before saying goodbye.

A frog in a well knows nothing of oceans – JAPANESE PROVERB.

Back to charly

It was New Year's Eve and she had been blessed with more than one social option for that evening. As always she'd waited until the last minute to figure out her heart and in the end shared a pleasant dinner with Elisabet and Mitx at their place. Then gently refused their invitation to enter the New Year with them at Juniper village and left with the preferred intention of finding Charlie and taking him to a girlfriend's bar in Sichus for the Spanish tradition of grapes and cava. Truth be known, she would have been fine to have stayed in Sa Ema or gone to Sa Croix with Charlie. She had not initially wanted to enter the New Year in Sichus, but her girlfriend who had been a good friend to Jes, was on her own at the bar and it was a good way to combine a bit of the old and the new into the next year. As a result Michèle had tried to juggle it all. She swerved the Mini into Charlie's place with enough time to get them to Sichus before midnight. However, Charlie was late getting himself together so that they were still driving to Sichus when the night hit midnight into the New Year of 2005. They were just outside the village when the black canvas sky above it lit up with bold oranges and red colours, falling palm tree shapes in white light and more! It was very pretty and despite inner twinges of guilt for not having arrived on time, she was very happy to have entered the New Year that way: racing through country night in her yellow Mini, with a full frontal view of a New Year's light show over an enchanted village and Charlie at her side. It was for her the best New Year's entrance in a very long time. It was also another bell foretelling her relationship with Charlie. She was late trying to be somewhere for a friend because Charlie was late getting himself together. Yet in sincerity it had been in her favour because deep down she'd wanted to enter the New Year alone with him. It was also a sign of caution not to repeat the same mistake that she had made with Jes. She was a binger by nature in direct polarity with her discipline. In everything: love, food, money, friendships, and experiences were all intense for her. She was a romantic, yet she tended to choose partners who were terrific individuals with a personal challenge that could make her choice to be with them risky or unwise. It became apparent to her then that Charlie and she were going to grow a lot being near each other. Whether or not they would reap the benefits together depended on how much they grew and matured in the upcoming year. Charlie had his cocaine addiction and the challenges of recuperation to face, if he wanted to meet any of his personal goals. Michèle had to train herself not to put all her eggs into the same basket as her partner's or she would damage herself and the world that she had managed to create without him. Otherwise, her relationships wouldn't survive anyway. The fact was, being with elusive men provoked her need to get too involved. Some would say to change her choice of men, but to her that was like taking an aspirin for a headache which merely relieved the problem briefly. It did not solve the reason for the headache. No, her challenge was greater than that. Where Charlie's addiction inhibited him to give or work at any kind of relationship her challenge was ironically its complete opposite. To what extent was unknown to her, but it was her belief that she and Charlie were in some universal way, each other's half. They had both spent their whole lives in a similar pattern of unsettled experiences and unexplainable anxieties, yet when they were within the presence of each other there was a remarkable sense of balance that unfolded itself from within all the layers of false airs. In a funny way they were like an individual yin and an individual yang at risk of going through life eternally off kilter unless they could mature enough in time for their halves to join and finally feel balanced inside. She sighed. It was heavy, and the stage of their current lives made the odds of success pretty slim. A lot of time and inner renovation by both of them was needed. Notwithstanding the amount of trust and independence they'd have to establish in order to get there. 'Hmm, we'll see,' she said through an exhale so as not to be heard. They arrived at her girlfriend's bar by 12:05a.m.! The place was empty except for her and her husband Paco, such that Gabi was obviously pleased to see them. Then within a few minutes of their arrival, more people stopped by the bar. She and Charlie stayed until 1 a.m. and then headed to Palma to check-out a few "parties" that Michèle had been told about. On their way down Charlie was good enough to mention that he was carrying coke on him. He wanted her to know and she really appreciated him telling her. Of course his attempt to quit before the New Year was a goner, so while they zipped along Juniper road, they talked about it, or rather Michèle asked him a bunch of questions so that she could have a better understanding of her situation. In truth, until Charlie, she had never been around that scene or really befriended anyone who was a serious cocaine addict.

'Umm are you sure you want to?' she asked calmly while her eyes followed the pavement and the stone hedge walls that lit up under the Mini's headlights. No reply. '? .. Do you want me to hold it for you until you really think you need it?' she offered in disbelief at herself. She really did not want that stuff in the car let alone on her person. '*Gawd, New Year's Eve is swarming with police and there you are offering to hold it for him – HelllooO!!!?*' berated her inner voice. She'd really put her brain on a tray completely and she wasn't even the one doing drugs. Charlie on the other hand was beautiful. He sat in the car semi watching the road in front of him and the moving darkness outside the passenger window while he listened to her yatter on. 'Naw, it's o.k.,' he said, 'I'll hold on to it.' 'What if you just throw it out the window?' she added, again impressed by her stupidity and another voice saying, '*Yea, just throw it outside for some kid to find it or an animal to eat it.*' … Charlie seemed sensitive to her embarrassment and said quite matter of fact: 'I'd only go back for it tomorrow.' She looked at him, in an attempt to take in what he was saying to her. The drug was that powerful. It wasn't just an expensive addiction where one went great lengths to purchase and feed the craving, but it was an obsessive attraction. Like a sexy woman he never got to fuck, he wouldn't entertain another one until he'd had the one he'd chosen and paid bucks for. The drug's power was astounding. More disconcerting to her was her parallel of its power to that of a female's sexuality. If abused it could be just as unhealthy ... Carefully she asked, 'Anything I need to know about you when you've taken? Are you aggressive or anything like that?' He gave her an amused smile. Although she thought that she was being responsible and smart, she got the impression that her questions were interpreted as being sweet and innocent. 'Naaw,' he replied, 'cocaine doesn't have that kind of effect on me. Alcohol and marijuana can but not cocaine, which is why it is more popular. The real problem with cocaine is what it does to the brain cells and one's health. It depreciates them at an alarmingly faster rate than other drugs. It's an addiction that increases in dosage because there is a moment when the drug no longer satisfies the cravings. The need remains but not the experience. So the addict experiences frustration and therefore more need to fill that void. Plus cocaine stays in the blood system for years even while one is in recuperation. Therefore the brain is always at risk of deceiving the mind into wanting the drug again.' There was silence in the car. She could hear the sound of the Mini hum along the pavement and felt warmed by the orange lighting coming from the dashboard controls. They remained silent for a while so she used the moment to reflect quickly on her current situation. She was in a car with a serious cocaine addict and she liked him. If she even whispered that to anyone she'd be labelled as a masochistic or simply dumb. '*Why?*' she interrogated herself, '*people who spend their lives working in social services are considered courageous professionals because they get paid poor salaries for what they do and individuals who stand by loved ones who suffer from an illness such as cancer or aids are virtuous. Yet those who attempt to love individuals lost in drugs are perceived as being ill themselves? Isn't drug addiction also an illness?*' She wanted to clarify with Charlie, but he seemed to be enjoying the silence... '*Granted,*' she continued on her own, '*the drug addict is the one who must initiate the decision to get well. However,*' she thought more precisely, '*the decision is often made, but if the addict is not well to focus on his or her will to try, how is he or she expected to initiate without the presence of someone to act as a beacon for the addict's focus?*' Her imagination envisioned the example of a silhouette of an angel exuding an intense white light as an alluring distraction towards the addict's decision to focus on getting better, rather than the drug that's light was dimmer and keeping the addict in his or her well. Charlie had made it clear to Michèle that he wanted to get out of his well and for reasons still unclear to her, she felt compelled to reflect herself in his sight; much like an irritating white light until the vision of her bothered him so much, he'd feel compelled to climb out of the well just to move himself away from it. Besides, she could. She had the time and the stamina then to do it. '*How many friends and families,*' she thought again, '*wanted to invest more time in such challenges and couldn't for lack of time and economy? Plus up until then, Charlie had been straight forward and forthright with her. That was reason enough no? Some would argue that he needed to be left alone until he hit bottom and saw the eyes of death. If Charlie had been younger or had had less time with his addiction she might agree. However he was a man of forty three who had been an addict for more than fourteen years of his life. He had already been to the bottom, seen death, jumped out of his well, seen the light, then lost his sight and fallen back into the well twice already; an indication to her that somewhere between light and death he loses sight of his focus. Like the aspirin, Charlie's remissions were only temporary relief for his problem and therefore short lived. Why..? If she was suffering and someone told her that the only way she could relieve her agony was to die and be reborn back to the life she was leaving in order to try again, why would she want to do that if it meant returning to the same point of suffering where she'd left off? Getting into remission was one thing but maintaining it, and getting past it, into a normal lifestyle felt to her like an overwhelming step across a chasm. Especially if there was no greater reason in sight and no motivation behind her. She certainly wouldn't be motivated or have the confidence to try either.'* The notion of motivation flashed at her. *'It seemed true to her that many people who appeared well balanced seemed to have had at least one positive individual influence their life. She didn't think Charlie had that, albeit his family were good people, the influences from Charlie's days growing up would have come from regimented practical philosophies, and staunch Catholic traditions unlike the ones used today...'* Her mind seemed to process at the same velocity as the Mini, retracing what she thought she knew about Charlie and his background. Then out of no-where it stopped to consider a butterfly and imagined a parallel between the concepts of re-incarnation and drug addiction? *'... In re-incarnation it was suggested that before one died it was good to understand one's karma so that one might return to life in an improved way than before. Hence there was a catch-22 among suffering individuals who hung on to the life they were hurting-in for fear that death would bring them back to the same suffering that had inadvertently caused their inability to recognise their karma before dying. A return to a life unique from the last one could only exist if the departure from that first life had also been unique from its last attempted departure. So that the only way she could see Charlie's remission having any hope of success, was if the reason he got there was different from the last times he'd tried, and at that particular moment, the new ingredient was her...'* The thought was bold but not vain. Up until Charlie had found her, he was like the frog in a Japanese proverb, which was similarly in a well and had thought nothing about oceans. *'As presumptuous as it was, maybe her presence could add a unique perspective on things and offer his spirit a different philosophy about how to live before he finally decided to try again. Naturally he'd want to try again, especially when his cocaine intake would increase and his instincts for survival kicked in. She'd just rather he, do it sooner and before that point was reached because that in itself would be all the difference from the last few times.'* She sighed quietly. She didn't know. What she did know, was that Charlie aside, she was learning about a world that was often judged unfairly by ignorance. Jes' way with life and his own challenges with alcohol had also taught her so much. Maybe Charlie was her ultimate test to see if she had actually learned anything from her past experiences? Again, as if they'd been preparation for her and Charlie? She recognised that thought from the first day he'd popped into her life at the top of the patio stairs. Either way she hoped she could use the precedence of her past to help them.

When they arrived at Palma she started calling people, but no one either answered or was already passed out that they decided to park the car and just walk around the old town. They entered a noisy pub, ordered a few drinks and chatted loudly for a bit over the noise. At one point Charlie went upstairs to the men's room and while he was gone she started to feel Jes' absence again. Then once Charlie was back, an attractive German speaking man on his way out of the bar approached their table leaned over a bit and spoke very politely to Michèle: 'Pardon, but you're a beautiful woman – very natural looking.' She looked at the man shyly and replied lightly, 'That's very kind - thank you.' It would have been a lie to suggest that she had not enjoyed the compliment, but it had also embarrassed her a little in front of Charlie whose female experiences were all about the young foreign sinuously attractive tit and ass girls. She was also surprised that the gentleman said it so boldly in front of Charlie. Then again it was New Year's Eve and every one was pretty drunk. Although Charlie could not have cared less about the compliment, she wondered if it had been Jes' way of saying 'hi' to her. She had just been thinking about him and it was certainly his style to make other men jealous. Still, Charlie's reaction was nothing more than a simple demure smile at the man who then looked at him and apologised again before going on his way. Once they headed out into the crowded cobblestone street she casually asked him if he'd taken any coke. His eyes darted a bit of self-consciousness, but he replied just as casually, 'in the men's room.' They checked out a dance bar and then left within five minutes of getting there. As the morning progressed with just the two of them, she started to feel uncomfortable that he'd have preferred to have been with his friends up north. Mostly she wondered if he felt trapped or unable to cruise the women, as he might have, if they had not been together. Finally they returned to the car and drove to the other side of Palma near where she used to live. There they found a bar that was familiar to both of them. In her case it was the very first bar in Mayürqa where she had sat and had a coffee in 1997. At that time she worked on cruise ships and her ship had docked in Palma for the first time. She'd gone a shore to write in her journal and have a coffee unaware that one year later she'd find a place to live only ten minutes nearby. In Charlie's case he knew the owner of the place quite well. Plus his cousin and a few friends were also there. They ended up staying there until 6a.m. and got home by 7a.m. Charlie of course could have stayed longer – the cocaine helped in that area. Michèle on the other hand was getting tired of the drunken conversations and superficial people and started thinking about Dasha alone at the house. It wasn't long before Charlie understood her mood and without much ado they finally left the place. As she turned the car on she said: 'Sorry for not staying longer.' Charlie was sitting on the passenger side with his body turned towards her while resting against the seat. His eyes had a twinkle in them that she supposed was the cocaine. He looked at her while he replied, 'I could have stayed until late afternoon. I really enjoy just hanging out like that and talking…' It wasn't the "no worries" reply she was accustomed to hearing and it only made her like him more. Nonetheless it still provoked some feelings of guilt and defensiveness. She too enjoyed staying out until the sun rose and then eating breakfast before finally going to bed, but those were the days among her friends and without a dog waiting to be let out at home. He must have caught her vibe because he suddenly leaned in on her and they started to exchange tongues while he pressed his hand up and down the inside of her right thigh. She was wearing trousers and Charlie's hand moving up and down within her inner thigh seemed accentuated by their smooth cotton fabric and turned her on more. Charlie too whose sensations were magnified by the coke became equally excited. During the drive home, Charlie kept his hand between her thighs. It was in fact one of her favourite hot spots and she wasn't sure if she had told him that or not, but she didn't think so. In any case, the drive home started to feel long. Michèle just wanted to get home and fool around! They got back to Sa Ema, she stopped-in on Dasha, let her out, and then went to Charlie's place. His place was cold, although it helped accentuate the feminine parts of her body when they got physical. He was good with his mouth and hands. She was okay, noticing that she felt more attracted to him than Vladimir. Neither one was Jes and no-one would ever be. Anyway, sex with Charlie was not feasible then, which was better and safer for them. The attraction to Charlie in bed was in his face, the foreplay, bed talk and his aroma. Sex was desired but not essential, and that's how she preferred it. She left his place by 8:30a.m. It was a bright, cool morning, with sea, mountains and skies all looking clear. 'January 1, 2005 and a beautiful day,' she murmured to herself, 'let's see how we do for the next 364!'

PART II

CHARLIE VERSUS CHARLY PLAY BY PLAY

Fed up – Yea I'm fed up!
I'm tired of sitting – Half on my butt, half on my side
Of talking a lot and doing nothing
I'm fed up!
I was born tired – Half standing, half lying
As much as it sings and sings, I'm dragging my voice tired
It was hoping for so so much from me
I want to live!
I have taken so so much from you that I can't even feel a piece of me
I'm tired of my past and the future that I never get to
By my unwillingness, I'm raising haemorrhoids
I'm tired of looking for someone to blame for my tears
It's the blind loving in the now, if one doesn't feel the heart beat
So now I want life to follow me to where I say
I'm really *Fed* up!

[Estoy harto – ¡Si estoy harto!/ Cansado de estar sentado, de media nalga de medio lado/ De decir tanto y no hacer nada/ ¡Estoy harto!/ Nací cansado – Medio de pie medio tumbado/ Por tanto que canta y canta, voy arrastrando mi voz cansada/ Se esperaba ta-ta tanto de mí/ ¡Quiero vivir!/ He tirado ta-ta tanto de ti que no siento ni un pedazo de mí/ Estoy cansado de mi pasado y del futuro que nunca alcanzo/ Por mi desgana estoy criando almorranas / Estoy harto de andar buscando algún culpable para mi llanto/ Es amar a ciegas en el presente, si no se siente el corazón latir/ Así que ahora quiero que la vida me siga donde yo diga/ ¡Estoy realmente Harto!]

'ESTOY HARTO' (I'M FED UP) – GUILLERMO, LYRICS ADAPTED

> Walker there is no way; the way is made by walking.
> *Caminante, no hay camino, se hace camino al andar.*
> ANTONIO MACHADO

"Aii si caos!"

January 1 2005

We were driving in Charlie's Phedra, along Juniper road when I noticed that the sheep were lying down. Back home in Canada when the cows are down it usually means that rain is on its way. So I said audibly enough for him to hear me, 'Sheep are down!' His face contorted into, 'I don't understand you,' expression to which I continued in a sing-song tone: 'I see sheep!! ..The sheep are down!' He looked at me again. The state of pure static in his head was apparent. I could see that he was feeling ill-confident at not understanding the English I was expressing to him. So I quickly interjected his confusion and told him not to worry that he did not understand me because what I was saying was in fact unusual even in English. 'So what are you saying?' he asked in Spanish. 'Well,' I said, 'it's not quite right because it's really about cows and not sheep.' Charlie kept his eyes on the road, as if waiting for more clarification. He was right. Even in Spanish my explanation left something to be desired. My problem was Charlie's attention deficiency. I suddenly felt like the pilot in the Little Prince when he was trying to draw a sheep in a box. I wanted to keep my explanation short and simple and ended up giving Charlie a digressed version of my explanation instead. I started again: 'At home when the cows are lying down it means that it is going to rain…' A controlled smirk found his lips. 'Really!' I said in English like an indignant child, 'at home or even in Asturias, I would have said, 'I see cows!' And if they were down I would have said, 'The cows are down! I see cows!' His eyes were completely alert with laughter so much that it provoked my goat: 'It's true Charlie!' I resounded in high pitched English. I thought maybe he did not really understand what I was saying. 'Charlie, listen,' I tried more calmly: ' "I" is "Yo" in Spanish; "see" is "ver" in Spanish and pronounced in English like the letter "C" or "Si" in Spanish, and "cows" are "vacas".' He was obviously delighted. 'Aii si caos!!!' he suddenly broke out with a big smile and a wave of his right arm as if he were singing at an opera. 'Well, that's very good,' I said a little unsure, 'but it's cows not "caos".'

'Que nooooo,' he replied in exaggeration. 'It's "aiii si caos"!'

'Charlie! Cowwws not caooos!' I enunciated as carefully as possible.

Well Charlie was beside himself. Now I was the one who did not understand and he loved it.

'What *are* you saying!?' I asked him in Mayürqan. He took a moment to savour the fact that he was about to offer me a revelation. I looked out the passenger window trying to dissimulate my enjoyment and anticipation for the information. The sheep outside, were then half up and half down and I smiled at myself at the absurdity of it all. Then Charlie, as if to mimic me began chanting, 'Aiii si caos!'

'Where?' I added. I was enjoying the nonsense, 'I only see sheep.'

'Aii si caos,' he began rather officially, 'is "A*iii*" such as "Watch out!" in Mayürqan; "*si*" is "if" in conditional, and "*caos*" is the verb "to fall" in Mayürqan: 'Aiii si caos! – Watch-out if you fall!' he exclaimed triumphantly. 'Cha*rli*e!!' I cackled. I watched him change gears, glance quickly at the scenery through the driver's window and focus back on the road before him. I enjoyed him so much. He is well read in Catalan grammar and could be just as sybaritic with language as me and got great pleasure in displaying it. 'I see cows, aiii si caos!' I rhymed in the car. 'What a coincidence,' I told him, 'because if the cows are down it should rain, so in theory it's better if the cows are up. Hence we could say, "I see cows, and aii si caos!!"' I chanted, 'because we don't want it to rain!' I laughed out loud at my own word game. 'Wow! Charlie,' I was delighted, 'that is soo good!' I was beside myself with the discovery while Charlie was already back on Earth. The radio was on, scenery flew by us and Charlie's eyes glimmered an air of amusement within, 'menos mal,' he conjectured, 'que son ovejas (lucky they're sheep).' My delight at the moment came out in a broad smile. As I began to calm down from our language play I wondered if Mayürqa's sheep were as accurate as Canada's cows? The Phedra got us to Palma in time for a movie and dinner before heading back home. Once Dasha and I had settled into our beds the tap dancing of rain could be heard lightly against the window panes from the terrace above. In the darkness of the room I whispered to the man who'd made me laugh and was probably still out and not yet asleep: 'I see cows Charlie.., aii si caos.. Be careful,' and fell asleep vindicated by Mayürqa's sheep.

That which is the easiest is all that it is.
No easy way will lead you to something that is worthwhile.
CHINESE PROVERB

Alcanada

January 2 2005

Charlie turned 44 today and dived deep into his well to celebrate it. I hung a birthday package on his door late last night and am wondering if he even saw it or understood it. I'm offering him a day in Paris. He'd mentioned to me during an English hour that he liked travelling and living spontaneously but not on his own. So I decided why not a day in Paris together? Such that last week at dinner I asked him to draw the area where he used to go in Paris and saved it as a part of his birthday gift. It's just for a day because he has been there before and I can't afford a full weekend. My hope is to fly early, do lunch and fly back. A cool way to enter 44. Besides the tickets from here to Paris are not too pricey and a day will avoid hotel room and intimacy issues. Anyway, he should have opened it and seen his drawing with a few added details by me asking him to guess where he's going for his birthday? Then again, in light of his night out, I'm guessing he hasn't really looked at it yet. He was supposed to meet his brothers to go fishing this morning too, but hadn't. Apparently, he'd called Mitx at 6a.m to let him know. On the one hand there was no harm done because he did call and it is his birthday today, so frankly he was able to do whatever he wanted. On the other hand his brothers were really looking forward to it because it's not something Charlie has ever done with them and it would have been a good time for the three of them to hang out together. The middle brother had brought cava and cigars while Elisabet had prepared sandwiches and everything for them. I felt badly because I was confident that Charlie would show up and even got Mitx' hopes up for it. So far I am still privileged at being exempt from such disappointments. He hasn't let me down nor failed to meet his commitments to me – yet. Then this afternoon after the two brothers returned from their day at sea, the Serra clan had lunch downstairs. I thought the lunch was about Charlie's birthday, but in fact the only one who had remembered it was his mother! I casually mentioned it to the brothers who were still unimpressed by Charlie's no-show, but they did call him. They're details like those where our cultures are noticeably different. Traditionally Mayürqa still celebrates one's name or saint day instead of one's birthday. In deep Québec this tradition is a subtlety kept in vigor by the second name which is often shared with a Saint's. However these days, the birthday has priority. Naturally it is related to religion and also the practical notion that it is easier to remember someone whose name corresponds to one particular date than to remember the individual dates of when people are born. "Practical" and "Easy" are almost synonymous words in this case. What I don't understand is why people would celebrate the name of a saint or person who might have lived a zillion years ago and that they never knew? Most of the world recognises the birth of Jesus and the kings who brought him gifts by celebrating Christmas. Well, if people actually pay respect to Him by saying, "thank you for coming to this world?" then someone celebrating a birthday should be content in understanding that the same idea holds true for him or her too –no? At the far end of the spectrum, if Christmas is all about Jesus, love, and giving then the birthday is neither arrogant nor presumptuous, but a tribute to love. It might be difficult to remember people's birthdays, but sometimes the easy way is not necessarily the right way. Besides, who said love was easy? ...

I was expected to attend the lunch even though in my heart's heart I really wasn't in the mood. I have been having some anxiety thoughts about the proximity of the Serras in my personal life. Naturally it's related to Charlie. Sigh. I had the same concerns with Jes and really the problem is the family unit in general. If I want to be with Charlie I have to accept his family in the back seat, sometimes even in the front. Very difficult and another hurdle even for the healthiest of relationships. One's partner never really gives a relationship his or her full trust and intimacy until years have evolved or unless many miles divide the couple from the family. It's even worse if the one without family is a foreigner, like me. Anyway, Charlie almost did not make it to the lunch, so I went over to his place, knocked on his door and waited. No reply. Then, I sent him an sms that it was me. The door opened and he let me in. He had been on the sofa. A bottle of whiskey stood on the floor next to it while a ring of dead smoke just hung in the room like fog does in a cemetery. I sat in a chair next to him and we chatted. He still seemed to open up with me and appreciate my presence, which frankly, really appears to lighten up his mood. He's capable of expressing and demonstrating his vulnerabilities with me without any feeling of discomfort between us. However, not long after I'd arrived, his mother came by. At the time it bothered me. I felt that her presence agitated him rather than alleviated him. She opened a quiet inquisition with him, while her soft elderly presence stood there in the room like another witness to the state of squalor that he was in. So, I thought, '*Too many chefs in the kitchen,*' and left. She returned to the house a little after me, found Elisabet and cried. My empathy extended to her as a mother who really did not deserve to be worrying about her 44 year old son whose life has sincerely been a spoiled one. However I have no patience for melodramatic notions, when it is the very same people who spoil him. It's a tough call, but that is why I feel that my objectivity might be useful at this point. He's not family to me so there is less emotional confusion; at least for now…

After a short while Charlie behind his dark shades actually drove up to the house. Incredible. The effort for him to even be at lunch was both impressive and tremendous to me, considering the night he had had, and the level of coke he'd taken. I was very happy to see him and let my romantic notions lose sight of discretion and made the mistake of giving him a kiss on the cheek. I thought it would calm him down, but now I think I did it for me more than for him. I don't really enjoy the family scene without his presence and recognising his attempt at being there, wanted to transmit that to him. 'Duugh.' Wrong timing, wrong place. The look that glared at me from behind the shades was enough to put me back into my place. He sat at the opposite end of the table and ignored me the whole time. I felt quite foolish and hurt. I'd embarrassed him. He was not prepared to let his family know about our affection, even though we had been seen together practically every day. I thought: 'W*ell, I'm either being used or he's not able to assimilate our relationship.*' I think I've managed to get my heart around the fact that I am just a friend. The "amiga con derecho a roce", a friend with the right to affection. I was a little indignant about this and his inability to be more sincere in the eyes of his family, but upon further reflection; it's exactly what we are. Plus he is married and truth be known, it is wiser not to inform the family of too much because there are undertones that he is obviously aware of that I cannot recognise. It occurred to me later that even in his coked-out state of mind his behaviour was in regard to the theatrics necessary for the undertones. Sigh. My ego took a beating for not being on the same wave length as him. Besides too, in some perverse way, my title as his friend is in fact quite respectable.

He did not stay past the main course and went back to his place. He probably just wanted to crawl under a rock. It was not until much later in the evening close to 11p.m. that I decided to go over to his place again. I parked the Mini in the drive way, walked through the entrance gate and knocked on his door. The address, I'd noticed, happens to be number 4 and directly facing the sea. The night was also very dark and I realised that unlike the rest of Sa Ema, there are no street lights there to hide its beauty. The sea then, was alive although the only things that I could see were the white caps of foam that sort of rolled up and disappeared into the dark. Charlie finally opened the door, gave me a quick glance before heading directly back to his room. He was wearing a black t-shirt and grey boxer underwear. The cloud of smoke from his day's afternoon session on the sofa was still hanging in the living room. The long table next to the kitchen and the TV were laden with porno CDs while the little table next to the sofa displayed evidence of white residue imbedded into the wood lining of the table where he probably scraped-up his lines using the plastic miniature calendar that was lying on top of it. Next to the plastic calendar was a lime green ashtray overflowing with cigarette butts. The white linoleum floor was dusted with cold grey cigarette ashes, the bottle of whisky was empty but standing, and the couch was dishevelled with a fleecy blanket and a few multicolored Ikea pillows on it. The whole front end of the place was heavy in tobacco smell and dampness. The only relief to the scene was the view of the sea through the large sliding glass doors which shutters happened to be open. Normally Charlie had the doors covered and closed, shutters and all. I turned and headed through the hall following his steps back to his room where a little table lamp softly lit-up the room. He was on his back lying deep under his fleecy blankets. The only thing visible about him was his nose and his right hand flopped over top of the blanket still wearing a few of his heavy silver rings. Standing next to his bed I looked at him. He was like a big boy who didn't feel well and didn't want to go school. Yet I felt great empathy for his own feelings of self-disgust that were probably relentless in his mind's eye. I thought: '*He's the cocaine addict that a conservative society has no patience or empathy for, the liberal society abuses and makes a living from, and I'm in the middle with love.*' There was no need to talk about the day gone by or the stupidity of his actions the night before.

'¿Que?' he prompted.

'Nothing,' I replied nonchalantly, 'just stopped by to see if you'd like to go for a car ride somewhere...'

'I don't feel well you know..,' he offered politely.

'Yea that's why. Why not feel gross somewhere else? Maybe get a bite to eat? I thought you could just sit in the car, sleep if you want, just something light and easy. That's all.' I couldn't say more for fear of pushing my luck with him and having him reject me completely. However to my surprise and relief he replied: 'O.K.'

'O.K.,' I said coolly under great control. Turned on my heels and said in the same tone, 'I'll wait for you out here,' and headed to the front room. I heard him get up, the clanking of his belt's clip against the buckle, the shuffle of his shoes as he slid them on, a few more moments to blow his nose, then the aperture of the fridge door in the kitchen, the sounds of drinking juice directly from the bottle and then he appeared: 'Vale (O.k.),' he said passively with his hands in his pockets and a quick check round for anything that he might have forgotten. Once we were in the Mini he placed his shades on his eyes reclined the seat and said nothing. I turned the music on, but he asked me to turn it off. So I did. I was happy in his company and glad that he took my advice. Once in a while he looked up from his glasses to see where we were going until he finally asked me. I wasn't really sure myself. I'd somehow gone in direction of where there might still have been a fast food outlet open. Sure enough we came across a chicken place. I stopped the car, picked up a few boxes of fried chicken and fries and kept driving until something matched my mind's visual of water, isolation and stars. Then I remembered a place with Jes, but couldn't remember how to get there or what it was called. I kept driving along with my mind on that place. *'Where, where, where was it!?'* I scolded my brain. We came to a roundabout and just as I was heading full left I saw the directional sign for Alcanada. *'Oh my gawd,'* I thought, *'that IS incredible!'* I made an abrupt turn change to the right that perturbed Charlie's mental state: 'Where are you going?' he groaned. 'To Canada,' I laughed. He was getting annoyed and I wanted to find a place to stop soon before he got past his passive mood. Then there it was; the place where Jes and I had been before. I recognised it as the one from the memory with a few changed exceptions. I had not realised that Alcanada, which is pronounced like "Ocanada" and that memory with Jes, were one and the same place. *'Wow Jesy,'* I whispered to myself. Charlie and I got out of the car. Found a rocky patch to settle the food on and hung-out there facing the water. It was damp and chilly so that I was not prepared to stay out of the car for too long. Charlie took his chicken and fries pack and devoured the food in large bites. I don't think he even recognised or cared about what he was eating. After a few moments while he crumpled up his napkins into a ball and wiped down his hands, I spoke: 'Umm did you notice a package on your door this morning?' He gave me a slight nod of recognition: 'Siii, but I haven't looked at it yet.' 'Oh, okay, as long as you got it though. Open it when you're ready…' I added relieved. We stared into the black before us, 'So, how come you went out, I thought you wanted to do the fishing thing?' My question was sent light and uncritical. Still looking out at the water he answered sort of scolding himself, 'Yea, I did want to go, but I don't know – just stupid,' he finished while banging his forehead with his hand. 'Well,' I said, 'it's not about them it's about you. I thought how disappointed you must have felt with yourself. Yea know… granted, your brothers too, but you called to let Mitx know and the amazing thing was that you went to lunch today, despite the fact that you really didn't want to. Your mum was relieved a bit too. Anyway, my point is that the only one you really hurt was you… so try to feel better now. No worries Charlie, happy birthday.' With that I patted his right thigh, got up and turned around to collect the garbage. Then out of the blue Charlie hugged me from behind. It was a little awkward because we were both slightly off balance and I wanted to move a bit so that I could get the full effect of his embrace, but there wasn't time. His movement reminded me of a twelve year old boy overwhelmed by good-boy bad-boy feelings, followed by an indebted love to the mother who forgives him. Unsure how to fill his need for affection or how to reach me, it felt like he'd gone through a millisecond of hesitation and then lunged into a hug before second guessing himself. He held me tightly with his head nestled sideways at the back of my neck, and affectionately whispered, 'Thank you Michèle,' then before I could respond, he let me go. Despite my own feelings of want, I tried not to make too little or too much about it. Smiled at him and said, 'Thanks. Ready?' We walked to the car without any discomfort between us, at least not apparent to me. We got home said goodnight and that was that. The day hadn't been easy, although the hug from Charlie made it all feel right. I turned the Mini back towards my place humming: 'O Canada! Hum, hum, hum! …We stand on guaard-forr- theee!!' … I parked the car, amused by the paradox of the evening: I live in Mayürqa and had just got back from Alcanada defending a man I care about. A sense of silly pride came over me. Any one from Canada would say that living there is not easy, but the beauty of its people and its natural wealth make it one of the best and most beautiful places to be. I got to the front door where Dasha was eagerly waiting to greet me. I crouched down gave her a hug and said to her: 'No pain no gain D.' To which I quickly thought that depending on his learning curve, if Charlie could get through his addiction into remission then his gain after his pain could be equal or greater to what he might have suffered. '*Wow,*' I thought impressed, '*that's fair,*' and then mouthed across my lips: 'No pain, no gain,' as if it were some kind of new revelation. Stood up, found the leash and went for a walk with Dasha.

Ships in harbour are safe but were made to sail – JOHN A. SHEDD.

Risk

A few days ago, Charlie and I decided to try an intensive month together in which he refrains from taking cocaine. It was the day after his birthday. I had already had a full morning to myself walking with Dasha, doing my coffee thing, brushing Dasha, driving into town to manage errands and returning home in time to vacuum and receive Charlie's invite for lunch. We always go to Sa Croix so that he can be present during the lunch hour. In the meantime I usually stay by the bar conversing with the rush of people that come and go, watch Charlie work and overall enjoy doing a little P.R. without a sense of obligation. By 3 or 3:30p.m., once the rush is over he gives me a sign and we sit down together at a corner table for lunch. The daily lunch menu at Sa Croix always includes three plates, dessert and coffee for seven euros. The price for the quantity and the quality of the food is incredibly good. In my case, I usually go for the paella dish, and that's enough for me. The food, the colloquial atmosphere that feels so much like the one from my childhood days in Québec, being with him and the sheer truth that I am granted a free healthy lunch almost every day keeps my appreciation in check for when it could all end. It's all such a pleasure to me and a total indifference to everyone else who was born with it. After lunch he stopped in at his parents' place to say hello to his mum while I stayed in the car. I've made my own rule not to get any closer to his family than needed, unless things between us are recognised formally. Such that I'll probably never see more than the front door of his parents' place. We went to town, the cleaners and even picked up a movie.

The intention of seeing a movie was courageous to say the least. Few people with a similar case as him will watch films or read books. It is less about attention deficiency and more about a film's ability to cause them anxiety by stimulating unwanted emotions and or a craving for the drug. However, the real highlight of the afternoon was cleaning the inside of his car! Up until that day his car was a completely disorganised pig sty and according to him it had been that way forever. We had time to kill so we went to a service station and organised his car. In reality he did most of the work. My role was the suggestion. I did not want to do things for him. I merely wanted him to see other possibilities and maybe feel satisfaction or motivation by them. He parked the car next to the automatic vacuum cleaner and we got started. He was the delegate of garbage and placing things in their spot while I was the voice of reason: 'Okay, so do you want this Caribbean straw hat with a hole in it?' I asked casually hoping that my tone was enough to suggest a negative reply from him.

'Nahh, throw it,' he said.

'*Thank gawd* – What about these elastic bands and pens without ink?' I continued. A pause.

'Keep the bands,' he decided.

'Is this your tennis racket!?'

'Yea,' he said.

'It's exactly like mine – cover and all!?'

'Really?' he added with a smirk, 'what a coincidence – no?'

'Well yea,' I replied, 'you own the same Pro-Kennex racket as I do? Charlie what are the chances of that considering we come from two different parts of the world while the brand is at least ten years old? Come to think of it, even your bicycle at Mitx' is like mine!? Wow no?' I added with a tone of awe. Charlie contemplated the racket and responded with an audible sound of intrigue about the matter, then continued to go through the stuff at the back of the car. The radio was on loud and we frankly had a really good time going through and organising his stuff. Charlie in particular seemed to marvel at all the things he was finding that according to him must have been there for at least five years!? The dead spider fossil into the back carpet of the car suggested to me that he wasn't exaggerating. There were CDs without cases, jackets without CDs, empty cans and bottles, an array of used Kleenex tissues under the car seats, everywhere in the doors' side pockets. Cables of all sorts with no connection to them, an overflowing ashtray, food crumbs and cigarette ashes imbedded in the floor and seats, loose papers, a ripped map book, fast food bags of garbage, clothes at the back, etc, etc. It was one of the best indications of how deep he was into that snowy well. A cocaine addict by nature is usually very tidy and organised with his or her personal belongings. The degree of disorder in their personal surroundings is a good benchmark for how far into their well they've gone. Even more intriguing to me was after we put the car through the automatic washer, he told me that he'd never washed his own car in his life. It was something that he'd automatically delegated to the dealership. His comment reminded me of Dubai and its issues of exploitation and cheap labour. When I used to live there, people would say that the nice difference between Bahrain and Dubai was that in Bahrain Arabs washed their own cars. Charlie is not Arab and literally pays through the nose to have it done, but I am sure that in a past life he was a ruler in ancient culture and has retained his ability to be taken care of or have things done for him. The problem with the addiction is that he lost control of both powers, which now command him.

It took us about an hour to get the car in spick and span order. My final touch was placing a small plastic bag between the front seats for garbage and so far I am delighted to see that he's using it. We got back into the car and started to head home. I was possibly more delighted about the *fait accomplit* than he was and blurted out: '"Ships in harbour are safe but were made to sail".' He smiled at my comment but said nothing. 'It means that you can spend your life in a state of secured comfort, however miss-out on never discovering what you are made of or what it can bring to you...,' I offered. The brightness in his eyes showed evidence of an oncoming challenge. 'So cars are safe in park*ing* but *made* for driving!' he declared in his prophetic opera like voice. I laughed. It was so relevant to our moment and so much more adequate to people's lives in general. I was trying to convey the message that if one never tries one will never know. At least life to me is about living. Not about being safe. In fact, a ship in harbour goes out to sea during a storm. Charlie is a cocaine addict, which in itself, is one of the highest perverse forms of living because of its risk and its approximation to death. He did not need to be reminded about discovering life's trials and tribulations. It's the story of his life. He has sailed so far away from his port that all he needs to do now, is consider taking an uncharted way back. 'Yea,' I said, '"Cars in parking are safe but were made for driving".' His analogy was better than mine. People drive and disregard its risk every day, because it's identifiable. However, anything that may seem intangible or unknown inhibits ambition and sustains a false sense of security until it hits home and there is no choice but to react. People forget that it's possible to leave the parking lot or the harbour to at least get an idea of their options and still choose to go back to the lot or port if they want. Even the risk of getting lost invites knowledge that would not been found otherwise. In so many words, the only risk in trying is not trying at all.

Dismiss me from the shadows that were in me
Your soul's twin, you shall find – always at your side
Let me come to you on tiptoe
Make me live every verse that I gave you
We're going to erase and start anew
Remind me not to remember again
And make me forget if I can't forget
There is little to lose and so much to gain
There is so much left for us to live for and say
Erase and start anew you'll see
Wake me in California ...next to you.

[...Despídeme de las sombras que hubo en mi/ Tu alma gemela, la encontrarás – siempre a tu lado/ Déjame entrar de puntillas por ti – Hazme vivir cada verso que te di/Vamos a hacer borrón y cuenta nueva/ Recuérdame que no vuelva a recordar y hazme olvidar si no puedo olvidar/ Hay poco que perder pero mucho que ganar nos queda tanto por vivir y decir/ Borrón y cuenta nueva ya verás/ Despiértame en California...junto a ti]
'CALIFORNIA'– MIKEL ERENTXUN, LYRICS ADAPTED

Nothing to lose

When we got back to his place we sat on the sofa, both slightly slouched against each other, with his feet extended out upon the little table, while I'd crossed my right leg over my left one. The proximity of our bodies while we examined the contents of his birthday gift lasted about fifteen minutes before he became self-conscious and moved. I said nothing, but the affection was another novelty for him. During that interlude, he looked at the drawing of the Champs de Elysée that he'd roughly sketched one night we'd had dinner together. I had added extra blurbs and stickers of the Lido and the Eiffel Tower to it, in order to give him hints about what his gift was all about. His face looked perplexed as he turned the design around as if to see it differently or understand it better. 'Do you understand the hints?' I asked. To my surprise he questioned: 'Are these circles and triangles supposed to represent my wife and I?' His tone was almost uneasy. Somehow in the game of discovery his mind went dark and his sketch of Paris was likened to those obscure images on flash-cards that doctors use in therapy. His comment swiped me from left field. 'Your wife?' I said confused. 'Charlie, don't go there,' I said calmly, 'it's a birthday gift from me to you. I don't even know or think about her. There is no subliminal message here. 'Why? Is there something in the drawing that reminds you of her?' I added fearfully. The last thing I wanted was to stir up those emotions. He continued to observe the drawing more closely. 'Well,' he said more relaxed, 'I dunno. What is it?' he asked sounding tired of the game. 'It's your sketch of the Champs de Elysée,' I counselled, 'remember? I asked you to draw it for me the night we had dinner in Cap de Pera, so that I could use it for my surprise to you. What does the card say?' He read the contents of the card, looked at the photo of the Lido and suddenly found peace within. 'Paris!?' he questioned. 'Ding ding ding,' I chanted lightly and added, 'a day in the life of Paris.' 'You mentioned in English class that you liked Paris and travel so, happy birthday Charlie!' 'Well.., never had a gift like that before. Thank you very much.' He said it coolly, but it felt warm. I was relieved but astonished by the difficulty of the moment. We continued to talk about the trip to Paris. He liked it very much and had no qualms about it. In fact he suggested that we go for the weekend and not just a day. 'Paris for a day is hardly worthwhile,' he said. 'Well,' I replied, 'the idea was just to wet our whistles, have lunch and come back. Besides I can't afford a weekend.' 'Don't worry about that,' he replied. 'Charlie, it sounds great to me however you would have to consider taking care of the hotel and most of the meals,' I said matter of fact. My budget already included the plane tickets, a lunch cabaret at the Lido and the taxi fares. If he wanted to manage the hotel and meals it would have been a fair deal. Still it placed a small shadow on my desire to relieve him from giving or paying for anything. It was my gift to him to spend an expense free day in Paris. In hindsight, I should not have expected any other kind of reaction. In the first place he is Mayürqan, from a village upbringing. Its culture still perceives altruism or the mere act of giving with scepticism. Receiving for the sake of it is complicated by a sense of indebtedness or the cultural habit of removing the beauty from the deed by almost immediately giving something back in return. It's quid pro quo abusive and evidence to me, that Arab influences in Spain have incubated longer on the island than on mainland. Then of course the addiction intensifies Charlie's inability to receive without guilt, or a need to give back. People attend seminars on how to receive and give and I thought I could give a gift to a Mayürqan man who has been a cocaine addict for fourteen years without further ado? 'Duuuh...'

Once he moved, I stood up and went over to the glass doors to enjoy a closer look at the sea. He chose a lying position on the sofa that also faced the sliding glass doors. I stood there motionless looking at the lethargic toss and tumble of blue-grey waves. I heard the click of his lighter followed by the sound of his inhale and then the scent of smoke once he exhaled.

'¿Que?' He asked.

'Nothing,' I said. I was feeling very content by the consistent movement of the sea... 'So, do you have any thoughts about stopping the habit?' I asked casually.

'Yea, I suppose I will have to go back to the centre in Barcelona.'

'.. But that did not work for you,' I added casually.

'Well, I didn't really follow all their rules you know.'

'Hmm,' I offered, 'what other options have you looked at?' I turned my look towards him. His head shook. 'It's the best centre in Europe,' he said. The lack of expression on my face was over shadowed by his own admission that he had done little to really get better.

'Oh,' I said, as if that was reason enough, 'before you go back might you consider trying other possibilities?'

'Maybe,' he replied in English.

'If they don't work out,' I continued, 'then at least you can feel satisfied that you tried all else and it might even make you appreciate the centre in Barcelona enough to follow their programme more attentively. Besides, why would you want to spend so much money on something that you don't fully respect?' I paused. 'You surprise me Charlie because your personality is professional and attentive to detail yet you don't apply it to yourself?' I smiled.

He was listening to me. ... 'It's true,' he added. 'You know what it is,' he continued, 'it's that I've never been clear enough to think about other options.' I kept silent for a moment. I knew that the centre in Barcelona was the result of a consensus from his family's own attempt at researching on the internet and feedback from other addicts that Charlie knew. The problem was that Charlie had no example to compare it with. 'How much time do you need to be able to think clearly?' My question was candid, but he did not seem to mind. 'About a month,' he said. 'Normally it takes about two weeks to get past the withdrawal effects then another two weeks for the body to feel some relief from the amount of drug in the blood stream.' In a nutshell, he explained to me that the programme was a process of therapy sessions, the gym and above all, isolation from people and influences that diverted him from his ability to focus on himself. I turned my look back to the sea thinking that rehab centres were a glorified crash course on self-reflection that humans normally acquired in a lifetime through their personal stages of human development. That Charlie could just as easily be left alone for a month in the middle of some remote field and that would suffice. 'So you need to avoid cocaine for a month in order to consider your options better?' I asked.

'I guess so,' he replied.

'The thing is Charlie,' I began my speech, 'what is the point of getting better somewhere else when your problem lies where you live? I mean do you plan on living somewhere else? What if you tried reaching some exactitude about it from within your well? I mean, if you meet the task then you'll save a lot of money and feel good about doing it differently. If the task is too unattainable then you'll be more open to a centre 'cause you would have tried it at home and maybe even have a better understanding of what you'll need to do when you return from wherever you go for rehab?' I paused to let my words settle for a moment, and then concluded: 'It's not like you don't have the time Charlie. Time is always on your side if the objective is right.'

'What would you suggest?' he asked with interest.

'What risk is there if we set up a buddy system that includes the gym, a temporary telephone number that you only share with your family, we ask your wife to communicate with your brother if there are any real emergencies, and at night when you are most vulnerable you hand me your car keys and phone?' He considered what I'd said and then added: 'None for me really, but a lot for you.'

His answer touched me because he had taken me into consideration. He was right. It was a win-win situation for him. Not for me. At the time I had no answer for him. There was a drive and a desire in me that just wanted to try. Possibly somewhere I was hoping for things to work out between us, but my nature leans more towards motivating the underdog. I believed in the challenge and I believed in him. I had the time and it gave me purpose. 'Well Charlie,' I answered, 'maybe that is true. Yet to deny the coincidences of our arrival and meeting, would be a lie for me and I think we should follow through with the swing. Regardless of how you and I end, if we make it, then our reward would be every day you manage to avoid the coke. If we don't get there, we can at last say we exhausted all possibilities first. That's it. No big deal,' I tried to sound as casual as possible. 'What's the biggest challenge if we do this?' I asked him.

'I can't be left alone.' He said soberly. 'There are too many cocaine bells here. I can't trust myself.'

I said nothing to that for a moment. He wasn't flirting with me. It was true. An active cocaine addict can't rely on his own good intentions. When the cravings came, their means towards their end was supported by a zillion excuses that blinded all rational. 'Would you consider staying the month in the guest room at my place?'

'It's not a bad suggestion,' he answered casually.

'Well, you have to remember that your family lives downstairs. I'd stay here, but it already has too many cocaine alarms for you. In either case it means that we will be with each other 24/7 for a month Charlie.'

'O.K.,' he said.

I turned to face him again: 'Charlie think about what you're telling me, because if it doesn't work-out it could hurt our friendship.'

He puffed out smoke, 'Don't worry,' he replied.

'Okay then. Let me know when you want to start.'

'Vale,' he said, and snubbed out the end of his cigarette butt.

That night Charlie prepared a wonderful dinner for us. We never watched the movie that I'd rented because we caught a hilarious Spanish movie called "Torrente II" on TV instead. It was a memorable moment for me because he was so attentive to the moment too. We watched the film from the same slouched position on the sofa under a flannel blanket with my left leg swung over and dangling from his right thigh. The cosy position lasted only until the commercial period began, but the quality of it was enough. He got up to do the dishes and refused my help. I made no efforts to insist. His place was not as disorganised as his car, but it required attention to say the least. He was aware of it and I felt that his refusal came from a level of embarrassed pride that preferred that he deal with it himself. The evening ended with the film. Charlie had by then, kept sentimental acts in check and positioned himself in the chair that I normally sit in. Without much ado about anything, I got up from the sofa, threw my wool sweater over my head, leaned into him for the Spanish kisses and bid him goodnight. Then returned home, walked Dasha, showered and found my bed by 1:30a.m. By early evening the next day the news about our trip to Paris and Charlie's possible move to my guest room was already hot off the press and delivered to Mitx and Elisabet. Apparently Charlie had told them that morning. I was pleased that he seemed serious about it, however I still wanted to talk with Mitx and Elisabet personally. There were a lot of things to take into consideration and I wanted to be sure that we were all on the same page. Hence that evening they came up to my place and we talked. I was equipped with pen and paper and a slew of notes and questions: 'O.K., so I guess Charlie mentioned to you the idea of spending a month together? The hope is that the experience gives him enough reason to move out of his well and into rehab sooner than later.' I said. 'However, I wanted to know how you feel because your support would be important. Things could get difficult between Charlie and I and as you are his family and my landlords ... it's risky. Hence regardless of how Charlie and I do, I am more concerned about maintaining a good relationship with you. What do you think?' I paused. 'Well,' Mitx spoke, 'Elisabet and I are completely supportive. You don't have to worry about our relationship with you. However, as much as I would love to see my brother get well, God willing,' he smiled lightly, 'but he's been a cocaine addict for fourteen years or more! It's not the first time that he has tried and as much as I would like to believe... you know? A cocaine addict is a complicated person. Even if he gets through one month or a year, it takes at least three to five years more before an addict can even feel a level or normalcy in life!' he said flapping his arms slightly. 'The thing with cocaine is that physically, it stays in the fat cells even after being inactive for a year. That's why it is good to exercise and sweat. With time they dissipate but before they do, they have to loosen up and travel through the blood stream and tease the brain cells. Then, psychologically! Uf! At least a year or more of therapy and support groups! You need to understand that Charlie is a 44 year old man with the maturity level of a twelve year old.' When he said that, I was reminded of Charlie's hug at Alcanada. 'When he went to Barcelona he didn't follow the centre's programme...'

'Hmm,' I interjected, 'he told me.'

'The centre in Barcelona is rated as the best in Europe,' he continued, 'it's a five star hotel where Charlie must have paid about 7,000 euros a month to be there, so don't think that his recuperation was anything less than comfortable. He went for three months, felt better and then decided to come home against the centre's recommendation. He gets impatient, doesn't want to spend his money on rehab and wants to get back to Sa Croix, then stresses and falls active again.' Then Elisabet casually added, 'It's that he doesn't want to leave it. If he really wanted to, he would.' Then Mitx added, 'A part of it is that too. If a cocaine addict really wants to get better, a complete change of lifestyle is required and in Mayürqa that is very hard to do. My brother's life is Mayürqa. I understand that cocaine is an illness, but my brother does what he wants. He's been an addict for fourteen years, that's a long time – why change now?'

'Because he'll die,' added Elisabet evasively.'

'Well that too,' said Mitx. 'You haven't seen Carles when he goes deep and starts taking every day. Eventually he'll stop coming over. He'll sleep all day and then go out at night. He'll lose a lot of weight and become more and more despondent, until my other brother and I will have to head over to his place. We never know if we're going to find him alive or not. My mother is almost eighty years old and has suffered a lot because of Carles. In addition to that, Carles is married.'

'Well, it's a very unusual relationship,' added Elisabet, 'it's always been that way.'

Then Mitx added: 'Yes, in fact she called me this afternoon because she couldn't get hold of Carles. So I told her about your plans and do you know what she said? To tell my brother to "stop being a fool and talking about such foolishness", I didn't of course... My brother got married when he was 30 or 31 and none of us really know why. Well, he was using cocaine then so who knows how he really felt. They've known each other since they were eighteen or so and have never been fine since. They've had a lot of conflicts and their twelve year old son has suffered a lot from it. You should know too, that Carles watches a lot of porno. He goes out and buys them, takes them home and spends hours watching them. He has tons of CDs and magazines stashed away at his place. Sometimes he sees his wife in them, or thinks that she leads a second life, I don't know. Carles has been no prince and Cat his wife insists that she has never been with anyone else, although there is a lot of reason to believe the contrary – Ack! it's all pretty messy. I personally can't bear to see her or her family. They are all kind of strange and unwell.' I listened intently to Mitx and Elisabet impressed by the volume of information they were sharing with me. Like talking to a stranger on a journey, sometimes it just feels alright to let it flow. Despite their airs of calm resignation they craved a solution. My concern was their realistic perspective on life. It was so pragmatic, that it risked stifling the very energy from the faith that was needed to get us there. They wanted to help and hoped Charlie would get better much like he did, but how much had everyone really tried or got involved? Charlie had been an addict for more than a decade and only signed up for serious help a year ago?! I respected the fact that they were tired and after so many years they continued to put up with it, survive, and live their lives well beyond other families touched by the same problem. They were in so many ways respecting the medical prescription for co-addict families and frankly deserved a medal. The sadness is that it requires a choice between protecting oneself first or the addict. It gave me a better understanding of why it took Charlie so long to go to rehab and why a third party was needed. Mitx has a diploma in psychology that seemed to me like a destined blessing in disguise. It must have been his staff of emotional strength when he was faced with doubt in remaining steadfast with his family first and then his brother. Then, there I was, like a bright eyed bushy tailed rabbit, optimistic and still without the scars or the damage to myself. The worry was if my observations were right, then how long would the energy of their good intentions and efforts support me once I hit troubled waters? I was vexed by what I felt and knew about the Serra family as being genuinely wholesome people, versus a stereotype about deep Mayürqa's reputation for being a self-interested society known for walking up to the plate with the wrong team colours if opportunities changed or even "selling their mother" if the financial reward was enough; "La pela es la pela" – "A dime is a dime", was a Castilian saying often used in Catalan. Bottom line: I was undoubtedly going to be on my own and that was my risk. Not Charlie but them …

'Would you be comfortable with Cat communicating with

Charlie through you?' I asked Mitx. 'If Charlie can let her know of his intentions and if she really cares about him and their son...It's only for a month.'

'Sure, I have no problems with it,' replied Mitx, 'but we'll have to see if she wants to or not.'

'Okay. Is there anything else you think I ought to know? – Anything about Charlie's behaviour that I should be aware of?' I questioned. 'Naw, naw, Carles wouldn't hurt a fly. He can be self-righteous, but he's fun to be with, and he's intelligent. Don't underestimate him because of his addiction. He made a lot of money with his ideas and his way with people, then got carried away and fell into that *damn* drug. At the centre in Barcelona he had little respect or patience for the therapists and would just tell them what they wanted to hear. We have an expression here that says: "I'm dumb but not stupid". Carles isn't clever with how he conducts his impulses. Otherwise he's very respectful and polite..; at least to the best of my knowledge anyway.'

'Ookay,' I spoke, 'we'll see what happens. I understand that the possibility of Charlie getting well let alone past one month is a long shot, but he has expressed to me that he wants to get better–'

'Oh really,' Mitx interjected, 'he's never said that to us but never eh?' We looked at each other.

The facial similarities between him and his younger brother Charlie were evident. Both men have predominant facial features that are softened by a great smile however Mitx' power lies within the crystal sky-blue colour of his eyes that expresses nothing less than cool kindness. Try as he might it would be difficult for him to intimidate people with his look. Rather the strength of his presence is felt by his sturdy athletic physic that stands at a meter seventy-two, and is mellowed slightly by a cuddly overtone that has adapted kindly to him at 48. Like Charlie, he also keeps his head shaved and somehow looks his best with a day or two of facial stubble. He is the oldest of four siblings with two brothers and a younger sister. There is little about Mitx that does not match the definition of what it meant to be the oldest, let alone the first son in a traditional Mayürqan family which entitled him to what was then considered the best opportunities: a rudimentary education of Catholic boarding schools run by nuns and monks when it was rarely if ever granted the right to visit family on weekends, military service during Franco years, and the torch of responsibility to set the exemplary way for his siblings that followed. Even Charlie went to boarding school, but by the time he got there visiting rights had changed and he spent most of his weekends at home. Mitx also received the love of a caring mother and a working father, but the sensitivity that lives in his voice, or the spot of loneliness that beats lightly under the sturdiness of his presence, the periodic evasive coolness of his mood, the single roar in his temper, the skill in his diplomatic approach, and the fierce love for his roots and family can only come from a man who has had to pioneer the trials and tribulations of his generation on his own. Any scruples that he might have about his life would come from the conservative influences of that time. In generic terms he is a good man, whose human acts of improbity may be relieved by all his inherent qualities of propriety...

'Oh,' I said a bit surprised. Already the fine line between sharing with the family and being their personal yellow press had become visible. I took on a matter of fact tone. 'Frankly Mitx, I've told Charlie that if he prefers the life that he leads now then I'm sorry, he should keep it. It's his life.' Then I spoke softly and tried to make my gestures sympathetic towards them: 'He might die sooner than later, but it would have been his choice.' Elisabet listened and Mitx gave me a nod of understanding. 'At home,' I continued, 'my perspective might be called as a kind of tough love. However, I also told him that he should then tell his family so that they can get on with their lives and not worry about him.' They were attentive so I continued: 'I don't know enough. I only know what I have been allowed to hear and experience which frankly needs to be taken with a grain of salt. My suggestions or perspective about Charlie and how to help him are subjective from my own life's experience and background. I don't want to presume anything more than the fact that you know more about this. However, perhaps my presence can inspire ideas that have not been considered before? I have a problem with an acclaimed rehab centre that allows its patients to leave after three months when it is precisely then when they need to be deterred otherwise. I know that Charlie was not cooperative, but the fee he paid expects the centre's efforts to be at par with it, which in my opinion wasn't. Although, like I said, I really don't know. Then, Charlie's unwillingness to respect the centre's rules frankly conforms to his personality. You said so yourself Mitx that Charlie is naturally an animal of habit. Barcelona was too new for him, and he hadn't even looked at other examples to really appreciate where he was. Plus he is somewhat spoiled, and not by his right to do what he wants. Rather by, the assurance of his family's cradle care whenever he wants or needs it. My other question is how does the centre apply what appears to be a generic programme for everyone, when each individual has his or her own identity? You know the Chinese don't hand out aspirin to people who have headaches. They take a full personal and physical report of each individual and prescribe medicine that is specific to the individual's needs.' I paused aware that I'd side tracked. Plus my voice had become dogmatic and I suddenly worried if it carried a tone of arrogance. 'Yea,' answered Mitx, 'the thing is that cocaine addicts all have very similar, if not almost identical symptoms in their behaviour. Although, it's true, the centre could have adapted a few areas with Carles before he returned. When he returned home he was supposed to follow a prescribed agenda that included, taking his medicine, maintaining a journal, exercising, avoiding stressful influences such as Sa Croix or his wife, having his money allowance monitored. Basically doing nothing when Carles can't be idle for more than two minutes. So he just goes to Sa Croix when he wants more money and goes out. The staff isn't going to stop him...' At the time, it did sound pretty lame considering the calibre of the centre's reputation. 'Well, again I don't know,' I softened, 'I have to assume that the centre knows more than I do. Neither one of them did each other justice. Such that my point of reference is that, that time at the centre for Charlie really didn't count. It's like he went there much like making a decision on a dish without having tasted all the samples from the buffet first. May I ask what happened to Sa Croix when Charlie left?' 'My other brother has power of attorney while Carles undergoes his treatment,' replied Mitx. 'My father takes care of the till, keys and the opening and closing of the restaurant while my sister helps on the floor with tables and staff issues. My brother has done a nice job cleaning up a lot of Carles' administrative mess. Carles is great with people and worked a lot but a lot, to get where he got economically. Only the organisation of the accounting and administration were really off kilter. So my other brother improved that area, a few human resource areas, and placed a head girl on the floor to manage the staff schedules and the restaurant's catering.' 'Would it help to hire a manager to oversee Sa Croix that could report to your brother and Charlie? Maybe take away a server from the staff and make up a manager's salary from that? It might even relieve Charlie some stress if he gets better or at least give him room to stick with PR and not have to deal with staff and on-sight issues?' I ventured. I did not want to sound pretentious, but I needed to know what had been considered thus far. 'Yes, yes. It's not so easy to find someone to work and live up here that is prepared to stay more than a year. It would be important to find someone who can manage the floor, work long late hours, and can get along well with the clients and staff,' confirmed

Mitx. My mind did not hesitate to consider myself for the job, but I rubbed it out quickly: '*One challenge at a time missy,*' I told myself. 'What else?' I said casually skimming my notes, 'hmm, more or less that's it. Anything you want to tell me? Are you sure you are okay with my involvement? I really am more worried about our relationship than mine with Charlie." I expressed with a hint of affection in the tone. 'Naaw, don't you worry about us,' confirmed Elisabet, 'but you know that you don't' have to do any of this just because were your landlords, or because Carles is Mitx' brother,' she ended. 'Over all,' said Mitx, 'I don't want you to get hurt. If my brother hurts you, I'm gonna take care of him myself,' he said earnestly behind an affectionate smile. I was touched by their warmth and trust and cackled almost like a young girl at Mitx' heroic attention. It was hard if not impossible for me not to be drawn to them. I was living on my own after a lifetime journey of trying to find my own sense of home. Mitx and Elisabet and their two sons are like the middle class family from the fifties, who just seemed to exude warmth, love, stability and that false sense of security that I've yet managed to find. In light of my recent past it was hard not to adopt them as my surrogate family. If not for the truth of my emotional need then for the mere destiny of finding them.

'Well likewise, please don't worry about my decision to help. It's my choice and no one is responsible for it except me,' I said calmly. 'As I mentioned before, I'm doing it because I can. Right now I have the privilege of time, and it gives me purpose Belle. I don't have Jes, or a child of my own, so... Charlie has been very straightforward with me thus far and if it doesn't work then it doesn't work out... It's o.k. to lose a football game if you tried every play and did your best, you know..? Charlie might focus better if he's had to eliminate options on his own... Again like the effort a football player puts into a finals match versus a league match. It's all or nothing.' The football analogy seemed to work well with them. 'I intend to give it the full month. I say this because my personality is such that when the going gets tough then the tough get tougher. Difficult communication does not intimidate me the way it should that's all.' Mitx and Elisabet watched me. My words were bold especially for a culture that avoids, at all costs, public displays of conflict. I wasn't trying to sound courageous, but I really felt that my life up until that moment had been for something. Maybe this was it.

Your reward is in the effort and not in the result.
A total effort is a victory in itself.
MAHATMA GHANDI

La démarche

January 14

Observations, Day 1, January 11:

First full day inactive. Day 2 until day 4, his sleep and lows are deeper adding greater difficulty in waking up in the mornings. He would easily sleep until 5p.m. or later if left undisturbed. Siesta mood kicks in heavy by 2:30–3:00p.m., though today he had a siesta on the couch between 3:00p.m. and 4:00p.m. He is also restless and easily irritated. Displays whimsical and impulsive qualities. Is insecure. 7:00p.m. – 8:30 p.m. a noticeable mood shift into tranquillity. 8:30 p.m.–9:00 p.m., childish hyperactivity and touchy. 10:30p.m.–11:00p.m., craving for cocaine kicked in and then levelled out after thirty minutes.

Air France flight 4899 from Palma to Paris. Friday, 8p.m. Twelve days later, Charlie's birthday gift is coming to life. So far so good. I feel good and would like this feeling to last. I can't help but notice that our seat assignment is 21E/F. The sum of its digits is Jes' number 3... Charlie has the window seat and seems okay and I think that he is fine with Paris. Maybe he will enjoy himself. I hope so. We began our intense month together on the 9th, by taking the bull by the horns and dealing first with a cocaine debt that he owed. Mid-afternoon on the day before going, he'd called some woman named Maria from the car phone completely uninhibited by my presence in the car. The girl spoke Spanish and greeted his call with a notable tone of pleasure. After a few exchanged words of informal salutations, he advised her of his intention to pay and she promised to pass on his message. When they hung up I mentioned about the affection she seemed to have for him to which he quickly snickered through a quasi-laugh and said, 'Of course, they want my money.' In light of the positive exchange he'd projected to her during the call, he was evidently clear about the nature of the business. He was an addict and they were his suppliers. His congenial rapport with the woman was his insurance as a regular client to receive a high quality of snow. The latter being a lovelier way of referring to cocaine. Still there was contempt in his tone. 'These people are scum – you know,' he'd said, as if equally disgusted with himself. 'Well okay then, tonight you pay them and that's that.' I said directly. We drove out to Namacor in his car a little after 1a.m. on the 9th. Apparently the "shop" opens at 5p.m. and closes at 3a.m. the next morning. It was remarkable to me that their hours of operation were so much more accommodating than those of businesses that cater to sobriety. Anyway, the whole event to me was like a scene from the movies. Namacor already has a poor reputation for drugs, crime and gypsy-styled neighbourhoods. The streets were empty and lit with yellow street lamps. Charlie drove quickly but was evidently accustomed to the drive hitting every round-about precisely on the turns without much concern about velocity. Eventually we drove past the city core and headed into the outskirts of the city that by day was nothing less than beautiful farmed fields and open spaces. In the night, however, once we left the shelter of street lights and entered the pitch black of the country roads the only sign of beauty was in the stars above. I held onto the safety grip above the passenger side window while I watched the headlights' narrow vision of the road ahead of us smoke from the damp night air outside. I was impressed by my imagination that began filling my head with the fear and anticipation often found in mystery books or conjured up by campfire tales, which led me to chastise myself mentally for not having been more attentive to the road signs and roundabouts we'd already passed, in case I'd need to return on my own one day. Perhaps to save Charlie from the evil manipulation of those who sold it and fed on him like vampires, or worse, to help his family find him if he should suddenly disappear because of mafia and a missed cocaine payment. Then I looked at my cell phone and felt a pit drop in my stomach; the battery's logo was a line away from empty. Thoughts of a cell phone commercial likened to those hysterical ones made in the fifties with the exaggerated deep voice of a man saying: *'In danger and your cell phone battery is out? Next time get da, da phone with infinite battery power. The phone that'll keep you out of danger!'* The vision brought some humorous relief to the all-so-crazy yet real predicament that I was in. I tried hard to stay focused on the moment. We were merely going to pay what he owed. Three hundred euros. He finally slowed down and turned into what looked like a large land possession. At the end of the long entrance, the driveway circled wide enough for several cars to park. When we parked, there were two old Ford Fiesta hatchback cars stationed in front in complete contrast to a large house that could have given the Beverly Hillbillies a run for their money. We got down from the car and approached the house. Charlie walked up the wide stair veranda to the front door while I stayed behind on the steps. I would have stayed in the car, but I wanted my presence to intimidate Charlie and anyone that might have considered exchanging more than money with him. The large estate door opened and a tiny woman with a few front teeth missing greeted Charlie warmly: 'Hey man, Carles, long time since we've seen you – how are you?' He was an obvious preferred client. It intrigued me how casual yet professional they acted towards him. Standing next to her was a slim man only a few centimetres taller than her wearing a tuque with tufts of unruly hair sticking out beneath it. The loose Indian pants that she was wearing and the cotton muscle pants that were a fad from the early nineties that he was wearing, were a clear give away of the local farmers market. Nothing about their cheesy clothing conformed to the size or wealth of the house let alone the tacky decorum of odds and ends that appeared in the background of the hall they were standing in. '*Gitanos (Gypsies),*' flashed passed the mind's eye. Charlie was brief and counted the bills in front of them, then handed them the payment. I stood in the background arms crossed and an inoffensive smile on my face. Each of them at one point sent me a glance but said nothing to Charlie. 'Do you want to come in,' they invited. 'Nah, thanks,' replied Charlie. 'Okay well take it easy then Carles – goodnight,' they said. 'Goodbye, goodbye,' he said as he proceeded back down the veranda stairs. Everything about Charlie was respectful and polite towards them. Despite his earlier comment about scum it was evident that his brain was not so supportive because the door of negotiation with them was kept wide open. We headed back home. He was visibly relieved to distance me from the place of transaction while I remained amused by the residual voice of my mind's phone commercial: *'Is your battery low again..?'* Once we hit the main streets and found light again the rerun of the commercial in my head was interrupted by Charlie: 'Gracias Michèle. I wouldn't have done it..,' he said candidly. 'Thank yourself for letting me go with you,' I offered back in the same way.

The next day on the 10th, Charlie went full out and snorted every four hours until he'd finished off the 500 grams of coke he'd paid off the day before. If it weren't for the fact that he also deleted a lot of unhealthy telephone numbers from his phone I would have doubted strongly that his intentions with the 500grams of coke was a final binge to get rid of it all before starting our "detox" plan the next day. Nonetheless we're on Day 4 now, since we'd initiated the tactic of changing his telephone number with one of my extra phone chips, of giving me his phone and car keys whenever we're out or at home, going to the gym in the morning, and avoiding people and music that may induce unwanted anxiety and anything else that might inspire the cocaine bells to sound louder in his head. Sigh. The reality is nothing less than trying to fill a bucket with no bottom: completely asinine. Then again, Rome wasn't built in a day either. Maybe Paris can help us gain a few extra days away from it all and closer to our objective? He'd picked me up at my place at 5:30p.m., this afternoon before we headed to the airport from Sa Ema. He was noticeably overwhelmed by anxiety from the task of having to get ready, pick me up and get us to the airport on time. As we flew onto the main road I said as casually as possible, 'We're doing good for time – no worries.' The anxiety seemed to dissipate slightly from his face even though the velocity of the car did not. I positioned my butt firmly in my seat, placed my left elbow strategically against its arm rest, kept my right hand firmly holding the safety grip above my head and enjoyed the thrill of the ride. As we drove away like fugitives I sat back and allowed my thoughts to pass through me at the same speed of light and that of the scenery outside blurring by me. *Fear like everything else I suppose, is such a personal thing. Charlie is not afraid to snort cocaine yet says I'm crazy for eating raw fish? I sit in a car with a man who is driving like a bat out of hell and I am not afraid? My adrenaline is alive, but I am confident that I will be okay? Why? There is no reason whatsoever that my mortality will not be used up today? Is it arrogance or a quiet knowledge that my time won't come for a while yet? I've noticed that so much has entered my life this year without my request that makes me feel like I am working a plan right now. Is that possible? Still, I shouldn't be so sure as to abuse my protection...* 'Charlie,' I said suddenly in an inoffensive tone. He gave me a facial expression of recognition, '"Don't drive faster than your guardian angel can fly",' I finished with a smile. The saying wasn't mine. It belongs to a pewter angel that I have clipped to the sun visor over the driver's seat of the Mini. Funnily enough, it was given to me last year by a passenger just before I left ships. In the ten years that I worked on ships, I happened to receive a trinket for a car in the same year that I actually bought my first one. Had I known then more clearly about how things were going to pan out until now I would have said that the gift was a subtle foretelling of my journey thus far. Charlie smiled and asked: 'Are you afraid?' 'No,' I answered, 'but if our angels pass out from flight exhaustion they won't make the plane,' I replied dryly ... Sa Croix came into sight and answered my request without challenging Charlie's ego. He turned into the parking lot jumped out of the car and walked energetically into the restaurant to pick up some money for the trip. He was back in a jiffy and we were off again to the airport. Within seconds of leaving Sa Croix we came to our first roundabout and Charlie proceeded to clip his seat belt into place. No sooner did I hear the clip sound from the buckle when Charlie suddenly swore and proceeded to pull out of the roundabout circle. I didn't clue-in right away until I saw the official motorbike and the official man dressed in an olive green uniform giving a ticket to another car stopped ahead of us. Charlie spewed-out a few more indignant words as he let his seat belt fly back to where it hung only seconds before. The window on Charlie's side went down and the national police guard, now standing by Charlie's door began his spiel: 'Good day sir, your driver's licence and I.D. please,' said the officer un-affably. There is nothing remotely pleasant about the

National Guard in Spain. They immediately remind me of the highway patrol in the United States. Depending on which State one is driving through, the degree of intimidation by the officer varies with that of the State's level of discrimination or unrest. Stereotypically it exudes an arrogant posture of militancy often blown out of proportion to the task at hand. However, it was my experience too that once the US officer ascertained the situation sufficiently enough, he or she would adapt slightly to the driver on hand. Not in Spain. At least not in my experience. A child could have been responding to the officer's requests to Charlie and it would not have wavered the intimidating tone in the slightest. My only margin of understanding extends to their obvious plight with ETA, Euskadi Ta Askatasuna, the Basque terrorist group in northern Spain, which undoubtedly, has left a deep wound in Spanish security. Still we were in Mayūrqa north, being ticketed because Charlie was seen putting his seat belt on! The timing of this encounter was priceless. It was then just after 6p.m. and we had forty minutes left on our trip to the airport and needed to arrive there no later than 6:45p.m. Trepidation began to find its way to my nervous system. '*We were doing so well,*' I thought in dismay. Charlie, I could see, was in no proper state for the officer's delivery and made no attempt to hide it. 'What? You're going to give me a ticket for putting my seat belt on?' he responded offensively. His aggressive reaction surprised me for the simple reason of never having seen him address people without the best level of professionalism or diplomatic courtesy that a situation expected from him. Even the drug suppliers received better treatment. My intuition suggested that the cocaine withdrawal wasn't the only contributing factor at that time. Something about the National Guard provoked him: 'Pardon?' reacted the officer. That was it. 'Please step out of the car.' Besides the one interrogating Charlie, there were two more at other intersections of the roundabout and from the rear view mirror on my side, three more could be seen standing around their motorbikes behind us. It was either a meeting point for them or they were getting ready for a shift change. I waited in the car while my stomach entertained agitated butterflies. Suddenly the officer walked over to the three behind us while Charlie made a noticeable scene of cursing and kicking the back left tire of the car at the same time. I followed the young officer from my side view mirror and observed how none of his colleagues paid the slightest attention to Charlie or even recognised his belligerent behaviour towards the officer. Charlie finally got back into the car, mumbled a few words to himself in Mayürqan and waited for the young officer to return. When he did, Charlie took the ticket from him and immediately tossed it at the glove box: 'Would you like another one sir?' simmered the officer.

'Why not?' said Charlie quick to the bite.

I really thought we were going to be hauled to the brink and miss our plane. I even began to wonder if Charlie was subconsciously doing it on purpose to avoid the trip to Paris. There was so much incongruity to the moment that I was suspicious about everything. The officer wrote up another ticket and handed it to Charlie. This time I interjected before more could be said and announced, 'O.K., let's go.' The officer stepped away from the car and we pulled out of the roundabout in a fury that was deserving of another ticket. I was speechless. On one hand the officer was doing his job. Charlie did not actually have his seat belt on at the time the officer saw him. Charlie's reaction did not embrace his personable skills and I dreaded what it might be like in two or three days without the cocaine. I wondered too, why we had not been detained longer. Charlie's behaviour was blatantly aggressive. I was once detained for almost an hour because I ran a red light at 6a.m. in the morning in Palma on my bicycle! Such that I knew that my perception of what had just gone on was awry. We got to the airport just before 7p.m. I hopped out of the Phedra at the Arrivals entrance to check us in, while Charlie went and parked ...

It's now just about nine o'clock and we should be landing into Orly Paris fairly soon. Charlie is acting slightly hyperactive and touchy right now, but I enjoy it when he responds to me or shows me his affection. There is chemistry with Charlie that I did not feel with Vladimir. I dunno, maybe I did not try enough. Maybe a relationship with him might have been easier, but I doubt it; too intense and no chemistry. With Charlie there is a feeling of synergism and simplicity added to my life in Mayürqa, the proximity of our age, the rapport with his family and the fact that he is older and owns his own business is also a welcomed change. He also does not match any of the physical attributes of any of my past relationships – not at all. He has physical beauty but not like Jes, who was a head turner. However, I am attracted to the way Charlie dresses. His personality is witty, intelligent and free-spirited enough to challenge me. We share an independent and stubborn character too. His most beautiful moments seem to come out when he's having a serene moment and his face and whole upper body look soft but strong. His body is well proportioned with his height that is slightly taller than his brother Mitx'. I like his legs and his butt especially after he's exercised. His arms have less definition to them, but I like his hands. Aside from the obvious size difference between us, sometimes the wariness of his hands' skin and the malleability of his arms remind me of my own that seem to betray us by defining our age more accurately than our faces do. His sex is attractive, he has a bit of a stomach with a slight predominant chest cave, but it's in proportion to him. I don't know. I miss Jes, but I feel well with Charlie. Truth be known I am beginning to appreciate him a lot and this worries me. There is no guarantee with him let alone an "us". It would be such a rock'n roll relationship and I don't know if I am up to, or even able to handle that. He seems willing to try and hang in there, but it's so intense. I need to find work... '*One year?*' Something's telling me that I have to be with him for at least one year.

> Fire in the fire are your eyes through me
> When I see you I know that I know everything about you
> What is it that you want from me?
> Leave your print on my heart, we're looking for love and it doesn't wait
> It's the most direct emotion there is and it won't last forever
> Because we're already on fire – this passion, yours and mine
> The story is this … We're fire in the fire today.
> *[Fuego en el fuego son tus ojos dentro de mí/ cuando te veo sé que entiendo todo de ti/ ¿qué es lo que quieres tú de mí?/ Dejas tu huella en mi corazón, estamos buscando amor y el no espera/ Es la emoción más directa que hay, no será infinita/ Porque ya somos fuego en el fuego, esta pasión, la tuya y la mía/ La historia es esta… Somos fuego en el fuego hoy]*
> 'FUEGO EN EL FUEGO' (FIRE IN THE FIRE) – EROS RAMAZZOTTI
> LYRICS ADAPTED

Paris

January 15

Day 5: *Not well at all. Tough to get up. Mood state down, even though we are in Paris. Lifeless. Did not sleep at all last night – lots of gas and belching. 2p.m., deep siesta. Very low and tired.*

Concord Lafayette Hotel. Room 2624, 2:40p.m. Charlie is in a coma state sleep. He's on Day 5 without the cocaine and the effects on him are apparent: restless, irritable, and lifeless. I only wanted to come here for a day. Fly in, maybe do the Louvre or the Lido then fly out. Instead we are here from Friday until the Sunday. I'm tired. Last night our arrival went very well. I had a really nice time with him especially at dinner. Great dinner – just great! We went across the street from the hotel to a tiny bistro that seriously reminded me of Montreal or something out of the movie "Cabaret". Once we walked in, the small dimension of the place encroached upon us instantly making it impossible to avoid being in the way of the waiters' bustling activity. Little square tables were set next to each other with only a hand's diameter between them. Still people were undaunted by the tables' proximity to one another and simply leaned into their conversations as if the space around them were cropped away from them. Over the noise and through the maze of narrow spaces, Charlie and I were directed to a super corner table right next to the window. He ordered for us wine, pâté, seafood, and a Chateaubriand for two. I thought he'd ordered way too much, but he was right on the ball. The presentation and variety of each dish was as impressive to look at as it was to the palette. It was almost eleven o'clock by the time we started eating and Charlie was really on by then. So was I. Our eye contact with each other was intense. Charlie does not have a problem with eye contact, which always arouses me slightly, but last night it surpassed the wine's effect. We ate, we talked, we laughed and I allowed my femininity to go loose. I wanted him. My sexuality wanted him. In the midst of our animated conversation between seafood and the Chateaubriand I'd slipped my left boot off under the table and gently found his masculinity with my foot. I loved his reaction which didn't waiver and offered nothing less than a sign of gusto in his eyes and a permissive smile on his face. We kept talking, eating and drinking feverishly. At dessert he was still all attentive to me and observant. He never actually offered or displayed any physical gestures of affection, rather it was in the complete focus of his eyes or in the way he ordered or placed the food on my plate that lured me into him. I enjoyed Charlie's style which did not attempt at prematurely taking my hand over the table or whispering sweet nothings into my ear, which would have felt exaggerated and unnatural to me. He paid the bill and we headed back to the hotel's bar lounge. It was just after 12:30a.m. by then, when Charlie called Mitx and Elisabet at home. I watched and listened to Charlie in an animated conversation about our dinner. In light of Elisabet's culinary proficiency and Mitx' supportive appetite the call lasted a good ten minutes. I stood next to him at the bar wondering when the last time had been, if any, when Charlie was able to share a good time with his family or even let it be known that he was out with a woman? Certainly Mitx and Elisabet enjoyed the novelty of it. I could hear their voices full of energy over Charlie's. It was all so good until we got back to the room. We both wanted each other, but apprehension was there too. Mine was sensitive to his possible fear of impotence, while his was probably all about that, compounded by his misguided instinct that felt required to respond to my arousal. Mental gymnastics started doing their thing in my brain and I wasn't sure what to do. I'd had such a good time that I was frankly fine to take a hot shower and just hang out with him and TV in bed. I almost told him that, but we didn't know each other enough then to trust each other and believe a contradiction like that; especially after such a heated dinner. I was concerned he might misunderstand me and actually think that I'd been a tease all night or that he wasn't good enough for me. It was the crux of the trip that I had wanted to avoid when I'd suggested a day trip only. He finally came close to me and we started making out. He did not initiate as much as I was, so that it provoked my brain to do the unwanted process of thinking. 'Tell me what you want,' I whispered between the exchange of our mouths' hot air. I noticed that his eyes were slightly closed like a person without sight might do, when really taking in a sensual moment. 'I have a skirt, do you want a skirt?' I continued to whisper while we fumbled with jean buttons and leather belt buckles. 'Yess, get the skirt,' he whispered back. My suggestion for the skirt had been an impulsive response to my untimely memory of Elisabet casually telling me once that the Serra men liked women in skirts. So Charlie and I broke our connection and took a moment to get better prepared for each other.

 I wanted to shoot myself for being so stupid. I hadn't packed a mini skirt. Rather the truth of my intentions shot back at me from a long classic black skirt that was meant for professional business meetings and not a provocative interlude. I was no longer relaxed trying to think up ways to make the skirt a sexy thing. Charlie by this time was already on the bed. It was sad really because if I were a prostitute it would have been easy for him to say, 'No thank you' or 'Lets just talk.' Both of us were nervous and really neither one of us would have minded to have just gone to sleep. I was intimidated by the fear of being misunderstood to say anything, while he was intimidated by being with a woman who wasn't a prostitute or on drugs. Holding the skirt gathered in my hands I moved across the bed to him on my knees, propped myself over his legs facing him and leaned into his face to kiss him. The television was on by then without volume and while I kissed the contour of his face he zapped the remote for adult movies. Like clockwork the passive mode took him over and he turned into an observer. The effects of cocaine, too many porno videos and prostitutes had rendered him incapable of feeling or wanting any real passion. Passion eventually leads to feelings, which lead to sentimentality, then to responsibility and finally stages of guilt. Porno films and prostitutes on the other hand, covet passion temporarily with short lived excitement, kinky sex and a fee. It's cold turkey to the emotions that logically turn into one empty and unsatisfied void. All that, or he quite simply, wanted to find a way to get it up... First, I tried to ignore the TV thinking that maybe he would see something to bring his attention back to me. Then I even turned my attention to the television to see if I might get some ideas or feel excited by what I saw. I turned back to him and eventually felt nothing more than empty and frustrated; a "ménage à trois" with the television might have been tolerable had I known or got some sign of what he'd wanted from me. I slid off of him and went to the washroom and had a shower. When I came out, the TV was off, and he was lying in bed on his back, eyes closed with the covers all the way up under his nose. Once I slipped into bed, he took his turn in the bathroom, returned to bed and then with a quick instinct, turned his back to me. At his place he usually lays his hand on my buttocks or puts his leg over top of me. Not last night. The moment of his euphoria lasted as long as a cocaine high or a sex fix. 'Charlie..,' I whispered, 'dinner was great...' I paused a bit not sure if I should go on... 'The first time with someone is never the best yea know.., my favourite is the time learning about your partner.' There I spoke. No reply. I'd made the damp experience even damper, but I had nothing to lose. As I laid there staring at the broad frame of his upper back, I just wanted to hold or slightly press my body against his, but his body language and silence warned me off. I'd said and done enough already. The rigid position of his body reminded me of my dad. Suddenly I was unable to remove from my mind, the unsettling vision of my dad who often slept on the couch or in his bed lying on his back or side like a tense soldier with a thin blanket pulled up just under his nose much like Charlie often does ... *It always made me sad to see my father sleeping that way because it was to me a reflection of my dad's personal defence against affection. He was a highly sensitive individual who had been hurt by love and dismayed by the knowledge of his own inability to ever find it again. A sybaritic personality is often persecuted by Desire and Perfection. Once their objectives have been met by a decision nothing else can ever take their place. If the objectives are lost or misdirected, then there is an eternal sense of dissatisfaction within the personality that can only be filled from a completely unique point of reference or experience. In my father's case, my mother was the decision that did not work out and neither time nor circumstance would ever give him or his ego the freedom to lose sight of her or to let her go, by virtue of his kids. Everything about my mother to him was like an internal deep wound that never had the chance for enough air or time to even develop a scar. It was hard to hug or touch him, even in his warmest moments. He turned into a minimalist with just enough to get by. The venues of pure pleasure or comforts risked emotional ease that he learned to avoid. His soul's hunger was so great that there would never have been enough to fill his void unless it was an indefinite life source. It was better to become physically hardened against love than to taste it a bit and then die from want of it ...* I looked at Charlie's back and felt angry. He didn't have to be so withdrawn like a hermit crab. Even when he siestas it would be enough if he held me for a bit – but he doesn't. Like last night, he just turns away and rolls up into a ball. Sigh, complicated men. Even Vladimir in a covert way was too intense. At least Charlie's reasons are more obvious. He simply doesn't know how or can't after so long. Maybe his sense of correctness makes him feel guilty about his matrimony? Or maybe he's gay? He likes to draw crayon under his eyes, sometimes he demonstrates gay tendencies in his mannerisms or in his platonic behaviour towards women. He's a mama's boy, and really appreciates Elisabet, I think, because she is not a threat to him. When his twelve year old son visits him they sleep in the same bed and Charlie has no inhibitions at all to cuddle him like I would like him to cuddle me. Then again, it's not unusual in Europe for parents and their kids to extend that bond for as long as twelve to thirteen years, and in Charlie's case it's safe because it's not being unfaithful to his marriage. Rather it's his only other means of bonding with his son, besides car rides in the Phedra. It's just another key difference between the breeding of co-dependency and independency of cultures. I don't know. I lean on the mother syndrome again. Many Spanish men seem to experience a dichotomy of fear and inhibition with their female partners from the heavy influences of their mothers. They go to bed with their partners and their mothers' voice buried somewhere within. It is not until they feel secure enough with their partner that they cut the umbilical cord and cast the mother shadow away. Unfortunately, the test of time can exhaust the patience of their women who, especially today, are becoming more liberated and choosing not to put up with these influences anymore. As a result many of them don't learn to trust any other than the one responsible for their plight: the mother. I see articles about the evolution and trends between men and women in Spain today, which existed in North America five years ago, or more. Anyway, homosexuality in Charlie's case is not an impossibility. It would be taboo in any village let alone in a culture that is still severely proud and chauvinistic. So that the best way to hide or avoid it is exactly Charlie's way. Surrounded by women without any real relationships, a love affair with cocaine and a wife and son on the side for the sake of appearances … Gawd, I love and hate my imagination. The man is a cocaine addict and by virtue of my ego and ignorance I am prepared to label him as gay? Not.

We went to Lafayette shopping centre this morning. I was up first. Got dressed, gave him a kiss on the cheek, which I don't think he even noticed and left to do my own thing before returning to get Charlie at about 10a.m. I stood in the room for a few minutes contemplating whether or not I should wake him up. He had not slept well all night and he seemed tranquil under the covers. I could, I thought, just take a cab and do my own thing or wake him up and give him the option to stay or go. However, he was in Paris and may not feel so good about himself later if he spent the whole time in bed. So I moved to the window of the room and started off by opening the curtains. The extra light made a big difference to the dimly lit room and Charlie reacted slightly to its intensity against his face. When he moved I made a quiet attempt to get his attention: 'Charlie?' I whispered. 'Charlie?' I tried again. Finally a voice from beneath the covers answered mine: '¿Que?' His tone was perturbed much like someone's initial reaction at having their dreams interrupted or simply being brought back to reality. 'Umm,' I hesitated. I was going to speak in English and decided that would have been too much for him. 'Umm, it's about 10:30a.m. now, do you want to get up or would you rather sleep?' I asked softly. Waited. Then watched the wave movement of the blankets as Charlie manoeuvred his arms from beneath them and pulled out his right arm where his wrist watch was fastened and abruptly used his left hand to adjust it to face him, focused his eyes on the time, then while he dug his arms back under the warmth of the blankets said: '10:30? It's still so early!' I said nothing for a moment. It wasn't an answer. Did he want more time to sleep and have me wait or should I just take the initiative and go out on my own? Then truth found me. I knew that Charlie would not initiate any resistance towards me if I made my own choices. If I'd said that I wanted to walk around Paris then he'd have said O.K. and let me go on my own. His mind was in a sluggish state and, despite being in Paris, he felt better under the covers. Furthermore, it was too cold to just walk around and enjoy the sights, withstanding that Paris coffee shops are too expensive and the waiters are hardly congenial enough for a romantic moment in Paris on one's own, to even feel worthwhile anymore. Especially, when one lives on an island where remote little villages offer all the romantic charm and nostalgia for half the price. I felt stuck by the cold weather that intimidated my desire to just walk around on my own, coupled with the fact that I preferred to save my limited funds for activities with Charlie, and consequently frustrated by my inability to just hang out in the hotel room because we were in Paris after all! There it was. It wasn't about him, it was me who wanted to wait for Charlie to get up and I wanted him to do it sooner than later. The analysis of my truth only took me a moment to figure out. It would not have been wise to have tested Charlie with a fake suggestion that I was prepared to go out on my own and leave him there if he did not get up, because I really wasn't. Being a "bocazas" or a gas-bag with idle threats is something I try to avoid falling into. Besides, Charlie would not have felt provoked by it. Which in turn also vexed me. I knew that he probably wanted me to go and relieve him of the need to get up, while I was the insistent little girl who wanted attention. My silent musing must have unsettled him because he suddenly asked: 'Have you had breakfast?' 'Yes,' I replied hopeful. The whole scene reminded me of Dasha and me. Where I was like Dasha when she's lying on the floor, body in a tensed ready position, waiting and listening anxiously for my "okay" signal that we're off for our walk, and Charlie was me, slightly irritated at my waiting presence obliging him to get up when he wasn't ready yet. 'Aiii! ..., my God, I'm getting up,' he muffled under the covers in Mayürqan. I was delighted and felt tremendously guilty at the same time. Charlie, who was battling with his own demons, was still sensitive and able to sense my real desire and whether or not I was right to try, the sense of obligation he might have felt to entertain me did not make me feel that much better. I tried to remove the latter feeling by blaming his decision to spend more than a day there, but really my guilt was about my quiet persistence for him to get up and enjoy Paris together. I was uncomfortable because it irritated my own code of conduct of live and let live and therefore was only about to feel totally relaxed if it got his approval. Until then I'd managed to find some relief from myself, with a conversation we had had together about him and how the cocaine abuse has affected him. He didn't use to have a problem getting up early. So that his need to sleep this Saturday morning was less about the Spanish stereotype of sleeping-in late and more about the cocaine. Similarly, I thought about people in physical rehab who experience a lot of pain when they initially start working their wounded areas. Charlie needed to override his mental state's desire to stay in bed. Once he got going he might possibly feel better and grateful later on. Besides that, he could sleep all he wanted once he was back in Mayürqa. Within a few moments of his comment, he got up. I gave him space by leaving the room to walk around the lobby area before heading back. When I re-entered the room, he was dressed and standing at the window looking out at Paris while he rolled up the cuffs of his shirt with rapid and accurate hand movements. I noticed too that the few days that we had started at the gym had already begun to define his buttocks and his upper body. He turned and saw me, went to the little fridge and pulled out a bottle of juice. I watched his body language and said nothing, imagining about almost everything that might possibly be going on inside him and the boy within: *the incessant distraction at the front of his mind's eye from an unsettling clutter of unorganised thoughts that remain in his view similar to the irritation felt when one's field of vision is too dark or impeded by a constant shadow; the constant waves of anxiety brought on by an overwhelming number of unsolved issues, the uncomfortable sensation of fog that engulfs his brain and won't lift; the ears that hear but can't listen, the eyes that focus but won't stay open, the barometer of emotion and guilt that rises and falls with every reminder about those he loves, can't help, or worse who suffer by his illness. The boy who wants and needs a hug but doesn't know how to get one... All of it alive at the same time of every minute that he is awake compounded by his body that is strong but weakened by the cocaine, in the same way that kryptonite affects Superman. So that his will remains lethargic and practically impotent while he puts all of his efforts into overriding the daily call of the coma that comforts him. I think this or feel this by virtue of what I see in his face. Especially when the simplest of tasks such as fastening his watch, rolling the cuff of his sleeve, narrowing into a moment or a conversation without missing it, or resisting the lethargic urge to nod off into a deep sleep often require an exaggerated level of concentration by him to focus. When he does, his face simultaneously provokes three to four horizontal lines to appear predominantly across his forehead then causing his dark brow to pinch slightly and cast a slight shadow over the beauty of his eyes, while at the same time his mouth will sometimes jut-out slightly in order to breathe better because his nose is full from the endless accumulation of mucus inside* ... While I sat on a corner of the bed, he was in that state of concentration and resistance. Then as though to divert from his thoughts and relieve the stillness in the room, he casually asked, 'Is it cold out?' My posture was upright and cool. 'Yup, it's about the same as last night,' I replied calmly. 'It looks cold,' he acknowledged. His attempt at making me feel comfortable touched me. So far there is nothing about Charlie that bothers me. Neither his silence nor the intimidation that I might feel from his irritated mood brought on by my presence. It surprises me, but I think maybe I just wave-off or ignore his moods as being related to the illness. Nurses put up with crabby patients all the time. I dunno. In layman's terms because I have no official reason like a nurse or a soldier, it's called being masochistic. Yet when Jesus died on the cross it was in the name of love. Charlie moved to the bathroom to finish off the ceremony he often needs to do before he goes out of blowing his nose several times, attending it gently with Qtips and then cleaning away the slow tooth decay in his teeth. In the meantime I sat there allowing the tension of the brief mental gymnastics I'd just put myself through to wash away and wondered about myself. *Should I be worried? I am no Mother Teresa nor do I wish to be. However I recognise in me a constant childish passion to love and to be loved. I see it in my elementary style drawings of flowers, suns and rainbows and the colours that I give them, synonymous with the variation of sketched character renditions of me? Then I see maturity in the black and white sketches of my thoughts or visions. I feel okay yet I am obviously not always convinced if I need to express it visually? Almost like I need to be seen or known for who I think I am by way of my actions or visual aids. A personal debate between the need to be heard or communicate, with the insecurity of that very same need not being clear enough so that it could in fact result in me being misunderstood and unwanted? I don't always feel understood, but who does? I am loved and my worth to others is often confirmed by them. So do I care* when I am not wanted or appreciated? Might it be better to be appreciated more than wanted? The latter can be superfluous... Or maybe that's it? Needing to be wanted rather than appreciated? In spite of my independent streak I am still true to the human instinct or vocation to belong to someone and in my case it is a man because I'm not gay? Hmm, daddy comes to mind and all of that which is related to being a baby from the sixties to young parents whose marriage was a result of my arrival. One parent reacted with the tide of that era, while the other assumed the reality of its responsibility like an unwanted collar around the neck. It was not the child of me that was unwanted, but the responsibility that I brought with me. Without a doubt I was sensitive to that undercurrent of being an undesired problem. I remember that I was the one trying to comfort my mother when she had to go. Telling her that it was okay and apologising to her for not vacuuming more often. How old was I? Eleven, twelve? It makes my psychological understanding of being appreciated versus a greater attraction to being wanted more understandable. In hindsight, all of that at an early age was a blessing in disguise, when I apply my philosophy of life that what you suffer as a child you make up as an adult and vice versa. I think I would prefer to go through it as a child and excel as an adult by it. Maybe I am too conscious of change, the trends of love and separation, but the acute awareness of its volatility is what makes me able to really appreciate and know what I want and need and above all, the gift of a relentless will to get there. By result of my parents' courage to have me, I think I just try to excel and become a better person in order to be a good decision or choice rather than a bad one for others and myself. Certainly in my relationships with men, my father's initial resistance within himself and the intermittent drops of affirmation that he managed to give me as a child, coupled with my mother's healthy need for independence, probably influenced my preference to be with intellectually challenged but loyal men. I'm rarely able to accept a relationship with a man who wants to be with me so willingly. I doubt the value of his love as being *more about appreciation rather than want, because my bench marker for love and loyalty with men comes from having experienced very candid communication and friendship with a man who knew me inside and out, called me a pain in the ass and told me to "go get 'em" all at the same time. A man whose emotional challenges wanted love but kept sentimentality in check and thereby made his children's life his personal agenda and reason for being. While I followed his guidelines with an emotional and present devotion that was often appreciated yet forbidden by his wandering desire for my mother's love instead. My father was simply always there. Never left us. Whether my brothers and I always liked it or not. Such that I am drawn to men who are intellectually sensitive and self-righteous by nature yet emotionally loyal regardless of how far or how long we are away from each other. As a result, my affirmation is loyal while my spirit is not a co-dependent one. Hence I can want and be wanted by elusive love because it's what I trust most... It's ironic but impulsive love, from a man without the experience of Michèle is too risky for me. In my case, the need for emotional loyalty and the desire to be wanted by one, is required, because these ingredients ferment freedom and independence by virtue of the lucidity of one's choice. When someone really knows what one wants that is neither fanciful nor impulsive and gets it, he or she usually keeps it. Hence when I really choose someone it's for keeps, allowing me an emotional sense of freedom that allows me to be in elusive or in long distant relationships without the fear of deception by Me, not my man. Such that I would expect the same result from a man who loves me the same way. Tough. That state of mind that wants someone and also wants to be wanted by that someone in the same way, is a bilateral balance difficult to find in a couple. Like the quest for the Holy Grail, finding one's other half can be a lifetime search especially when I don't think it's about the one who is like me as much as the one who shares the same core of what I am made of, but in different quantities. Like divine proportion or yin-yang theories where elements share everything about each other, but in different volumes of equal parts. One who carries the polarity of one's strength and one's weaknesses: where the joining of each other's half makes one a complete being. Hence the yin-yang symbol seems less elusive in my mind when I think about Charlie and I as being in complete balance together. I am the white with the black dot while he is the black with the white dot; imperfect but whole. I believe we both need proof of a suitor's love before we accept it as real by reason of our mistrust of people's fickle emotional ways, especially when our own independent and spiritually elusive streaks can unsettle them and eventually jeopardize the relationship. We are also aware of our imperfections and can only trust another's love once we are convinced of his or her loyalty to us, in spite of them— doesn't everyone? So that we need to feel assured of being truly wanted more than appreciate. Only the former would survive by our often detached personality. Gawd. Charlie? Maybe, dunno. If Charlie decided to get better then we'd both be at ground level in our lives and to one another. Sigh. I think I know myself well enough to understand that a complicated man can have the privilege of my love and loyalty. My life's experience has shown me that it is usually the other type of man that charms and deceives me while it is this complicated man who tends to have a sincere spirit and a warrior's loyalty by virtue of his own sensitivity brought on by his own challenges. Hmm, necessary to keep up at my side – I'm a handful. I will invest more in an emotionally complicated man by virtue of the intelligence and wisdom that comes from personal suffering. It certainly does not coincide with those cultures where men, whose mothers dote on them so much, have no emotional tools to know how to be in love or to give to their couple. It's as warm as their experience with their mums. Likewise the women of these cultures are unsure of how to be loved or communicate it. Who needs the security of feeling "wanted" when their families remove that need and their ability to appreciate it or even notice it? Unless a man has cut the emotional need to his mother and family, it usually takes him a long time before he desires a need to be wanted by his partner and thus begin the process of giving and therefore loving. Until then, or until the "new woman" arrives to these cultures, love remains easily managed this way. When a real crisis arises it is still easier to break off the emotional link with their partners, than to persevere because their internal need to belong or be wanted already exists from somewhere else. The loss of emotional and physical security from their partner is less of an issue to them. Hence, these men might say they want me, but my instinct resists under the pretext that they have no clue and though they may mean what they say, they are to me confusing love with the romantic instinct of hunting. The paradox in nature to want what is unattainable, assisted by the philosophy of the easy way won't get you to anything worthwhile, impressed by the belief that easy love is not really love. Sigh. I don't consider myself to be fanciful or impulsive about matters of the heart. I can be obsessive because I am passionate. It is difficult to have one without the other. Yet, like a good sportsman I think that I am a good loser if I've given my all and still finish short of attaining what I'd hoped for. Love to me, like everything, needs to be proportioned as evenly as possible or it can also run the risk of being harmful. It seems only logical to me because its opposite is hate. Those people who are capable of death or terrorism for example, in the name of something they care about passionately, have in my mind abused their love's power and gone too far across the balance and landed the weight of their love into hate. They too, are obsessive and passionate people unable to see that their love as altruistic as it may be, has been misguided or managed incorrectly. I don't know... What I do know is that there is little difference between myself and Charlie where obsessive compulsive behaviour is concerned. We are both addicts, who need to learn how to manage the behaviour better. It's such a wonderful productive tool if used wisely and correctly. It is often wondered how people can possibly even consider doing drugs or frankly anything that might harm them, when the notion of "harm" to me is relative to each individual. We all harm ourselves in some shape or form. Some abuse is less obvious than others and some are tolerated by society better than others. I imagine any drug or alcohol abuser. They are normally creative, imaginative and intelligent people. They have a gift for success and tend to excel in whatever they put their mind to. Famous people are the more susceptible to such avenues. When you have a passion for something you just want to get there. You want to finish it. Nothing else really entertains or seems worthwhile and you become obsessive to get it done. Stubbornness grows into a dogmatic state of mind and persistence becomes stronger each time people try to deviate you from it. Then with time, the excessive focus starts to burn you out and diminish in intensity making you strive to find it again. So you might have a glass of wine, a small sniff of cocaine, maybe half a roll of weed, a cigarette to pause and think, or two chocolate cookies with the tea that used to be enough on its own, to keep you going. The routine from the obsession is suddenly less stimulating yet the desire to finish the swing is still there. Maybe you try to take a break, and tidy the living spaces you've left unattended, face pending chores, and rejuvenate social lines of communication. Yet, try as you might, you can't, because anxiety and attention deficiency find you for every moment that you could be working on your swing. Insomuch that even sleep can impede tranquillity if you feel that the day went by without enough effort on your part towards your task. This is where Charlie and I differ. Charlie's addiction depletes his organisational skills while my discipline to keep things organised is often my "drug" or main obsession against dealing with unwanted thoughts or circumstances. As a result I am good at preparing for things: always on provisional guard, another tool against anxiety afforded to me by my childhood experience. Charlie on the other hand just worked his passion blindly until he fell into his well completely. His home and his car are nothing more than a direct reflection of what goes on is his mind as an active addict; chaos. People who enjoy sports are prone to such obsessiveness too, because competition breeds an inner strength that if left unobserved can side with the ego that won't let go. In sports, if* the effort is full then in spite of the result there is no personal loss. However, if the feeling is contrary to that, then an athlete might carry the frustrated ego for days or weeks until it finally subdues and allows the mind to override the obsession, let it go and focus again on the next opportunity. Hence "a healthy mind a healthy life" is a direct result from individuals who can manage this balance the best and who tend to excel consistently beyond their peers. Otherwise, you keep at it until the mind is distracted and wants the perks first; another glass of wine, another snort in the washroom, or more cookies, until the project on hand is second after the reward becomes first. If the individual is not careful a perk becomes the habit that takes over the focus. Some are lucky to notice it and make a conscious effort to take a break or make a slight change of scene in order to start over again without the cravings. In basic terms: recharge passion's battery enough without the perks, to continue feverishly on its natural flow. The cycle of cravings always comes back, but those who manage that discipline of recharging the battery without the perks have a better chance at escaping the worst of the addiction. Otherwise those addicts like Charlie steam through until their desired goal is met, but not without the bitter sweet glory from a severe addiction that remains and eventually destroys the very success they've achieved ... 'O.K. Let's go,' said Charlie. I was relieved. Thankfully he came out of the washroom and interrupted my world. I was tired by fault of my own head space; left my brain in the room and off we went.

Eyes that make mine shy and look away
His mouth lost in a laugh
There's the portrait untouched of the man to whom I belong
When he takes me in his arms and speaks to me so quietly
I see life in pink
He is in my heart, a kind of bliss, of which I know why
He's for me and I'm for him
And whenever I see him, I then feel within
The beating of my heart.
[Des yeux qui font baiser les miens, Un rire qui se perd sur sa bouche/ Voilà le portrait sans retouche. De l'homme auquel j'appartiens/ Quand il me prend dans ses bras, il me parle tout bas, je vois la vie en rose/ Il me dit des mots d'amour/ Des mots de tous les jours, et ça me fait quelque chose/ Il est dans mon cœur ; une part de bonheur, dont je connais la cause/ C'est lui pour moi. Moi pour lui, dans la vie. Il me l'a dit, l'a juré pour la vie/ Et dès que je l'aperçois/ Alors je sens en moi mon cœur qui bat]
'LA VIE EN ROSE' (LIFE IN PINK) – PATRICIA KAAS
(ORIGINAL ÉDITH PIAF)
LYRICS ADAPTED

La vie en rose

January 16

Day 6: *Better. Up quickly at 9:30a.m. All day mood was a bit "high"? Some moments quite "on". Then a levelling out. Pretty much "up" all day though. Seemed to sleep better last night. By 5:45p.m., still "up" and O.K. Possibly because he snoozed a little during the Lido show at 3:45p.m.*

Orly de Roissy Airport, waiting for the plane back to Mayürqa; best time over the weekend was the first dinner we had and today. We've had a full agenda this morning up until now and almost didn't make it here on time because of it. Charlie's time management reminds me of India: organised chaos. When I was there, I remember being impressed by the amount of people and car chaos that moved within and around the streets with oxen sitting lethargically in their midst, or children literally playing in traffic without the slightest accident. The dichotomy of the energy was the epitome of balance. It only strengthened my belief system that fear breeds fear, so to avoid it don't be intimidated by it. If you want something let it go, if you're in a hurry go slow, wanna lose weight eat more …The secret ingredient is finding that fine line between polar thinking; that line that abides nature's way guided by one's sixth sense. Oddly, Charlie seems to have that fine line with time intrinsically, because despite the often unfavourable odds of circumstance he somehow manages to get to wherever he needs to go right on time. It's stressful for the one who enjoys provisional room for unexpected delays, such as the one we experienced on our way to the airport for Paris, but it's definitely never boring. Anyhow, Charlie was up by 9:30a.m. We did the croissant, coffee, juice thing at a café across the road, followed by a cab to the Louvre. The Louvre was great. Just before we headed inside a man with a Polaroid camera suddenly popped up from nowhere and asked to take our photo. He was a small French man, silver haired, slight in frame, overly charming and gregarious with us. He insisted on taking our picture together, while I think both Charlie and I were quietly embarrassed about the idea. At least I was, because it unsettled a quiet understanding that had not been discussed, nor confirmed between us. Then the man made me feel over the top self-conscious, telling Charlie that he was a "lucky man" to have such a "positive and supportive woman next to him". That we made such a "wonderful pair". I was strangely taken by his choice of words that were so relevant to us and our circumstance. He never suggested that we were married or even a couple. I suppose he'd taken so many photos of people that we were easy to read. Yet, I cannot deny that I briefly wondered if that encounter hadn't been a morsel for me, just to affirm my role in Charlie's life? So just in case, I transmitted a note of "thanks" to Life for sending me an angel in disguise to keep me going. Needless to say that the Polaroid shot of Charlie and I together with my arms clasped around him, hair flying, shades on, with Charlie in his typical stoic stance of hands in his brown suede jacket and a slight smirk across the face behind his dark shades; did nothing less than demonstrate beyond a reasonable doubt that neither Charlie nor myself is photogenic on cue. Once we were in the Louvre, we split up to do our own thing and met up an hour later. Had a light snack and started for the Lido where we had tickets for an afternoon Champagne show. Charlie was wonderfully attentive. I know his mood swings are related to the illness, but I'll take his good ones whenever I can. I asked only once just before heading into the show if he'd taken any and he'd said no. In hindsight, I can't think of any time at home when he might have been able to get any, because for the past ten days until now, I have been with him practically 24/7. Only since we arrived here, has he had room to find it, but he explained to me that he would have to really look for it and there hasn't been time or room for that. I dunno. There is no reason for him to lie or to tell me the truth. So it's up to me to decide how I want to go about it all, and frankly I've really enjoyed myself today. The Lido was not what I had expected, but I liked the novelty of having seen it. It used some great stage sets and costumes that are traditional to the Parisian nostalgic style of the early twentieth century, however the show as it was, did not impress me. Charlie and I were located in an upper balcony at a quaint little booth with a miniature lamp in the centre of the tables reminiscent of those cabaret clubs when Al Capone would have been the owner. We had a bird's eye view of the show area down to the main floor where fifty tables of what appeared to be five busloads of elderly tourists were sitting. I guess the matinées are reserved for large tourist packages. Unfortunately, it reflected at me a generic and cheap tone that momentarily removed some of the glamour from the moment. I suppose too, having worked so closely behind the scenes with some of the best in entertainment, has taught my eye to involuntarily see more, thus it's more difficult to please. I find myself seeing through the fantasy and glamour straight to the face behind the make-up, the routine in the dancers' methodical smile, the crane behind the flying car or the bored man within the charming waiter of our table. What I did appreciate was the skilled attention to detail in the costumes and the techniqal work involved in the production. Dunno. Charlie actually slept during most of it and we left about twenty minutes before it ended, on the basis that we had to catch the plane, although I think we were just ready to go. As a result, luck brought us sun and warmth to the tail end of our visit in Paris and we used the extra time out from the show to take a memorable walk back to the hotel along the Champs de Elysée. Charlie seemed sincerely relaxed and enjoying himself and even went with Paris' romantic nuance and held my hand for the last leg of the walk. I allowed Patricia Kaas to sing in my head the verses of "La vie en rose" while I let the girl in me enjoy the fantasy through a sun-coloured moment with Charlie. Everything about our steps had a bounce and a "joie de vivre" in them. I acted silly pirouetting under his arm a few times while he gave me a shy smile of amusement similar to the one Richard Geer is famous for: the one that softly pervades his face when he is self-conscious of an unexpected warmth of blitheness inside him that is simultaneously intimidated by the possibility of happiness without pain, at once inhibited by the realisation of this and then, kept on guard behind his lips. We both agreed that all we'd missed was an evening of Paris night life. Charlie likes Paris. When I asked him why we were so relaxed he replied, 'I dunno. I suppose the change of scenery, people; it's fresh you know…' I was pleased to hear that. It meant to me that he was understanding something about his life. Maybe the freedom he felt would not be enough for him to make a total scenery change, but the experience we were having then would allow him to go back to his life in Mayürqa content that he had had a romantic moment in Paris with a Canadian "rubia". Although I'm not blond. Charlie insists that I am, but my hair is dark with light strawberry blond highlights that only come out when the sun catches them. Anyway, for all Latin terms and the sake of the memory, I accept being the "rubia."

> Garfield: 'Democracy is freedom.'
> Odie: 'God forbid if everybody did what they wanted.'
> Garfield: 'Uh Huston? We have a problem…'

Auld to Odie

On the plane. The only damper today thus far, has been the Visa. Charlie was supposed to pay for the hotel and didn't. He doesn't own a Visa card. Funny, many wealthy people don't. It's the nemesis of freedom; no record or trail of expenses, no fear of debt or assuming interests, no restrictions to clandestine activity and no jurisdiction for Uncle Sam, just point of sale cash. Good old fashion cash. So that when we'd checked-in, the hotel used my card as a security payment, but only after I'd underlined the fact that we intended to pay cash on the check-out and not to charge my card. I seriously didn't want to use it, especially after having paid most of it off. Plus Charlie had agreed to take care of the hotel in light of the weekend stay. Yet, when it came time to pay, the hotel had already charged my card. I couldn't believe it. The five star hotel was at the point of knowing my wrath when Charlie saw it coming and interjected with, 'No pasa nada (no worries). I'll pay you back.' His lack of deference to me in front of the receptionist stabbed and infuriated me at the same time. My thoughts went into warp speed … *Protecting the ineptness of the hotel to avoid a scene. That kind of passivity to my mind is nothing less than a completely banal mentality, void of self-esteem and the farthest thing from being diplomatic or classy. On the other hand, my right to communicate discrepancies is likely to be perceived as overbearing, defiant and finally labelled as a tight ass. Once more fault is rarely claimed by the owner of it, who simply deflects his or her own sense of embarrassment and guilt by finding unrelated discrepancies in another. In simpler terms the childish practice of passing blame and the immature result from actually looking for it, rather than just solving it without provocation or need to fester another. Then when the muck is on your face from having reneged on your own truth, by following the mediocre attitude of others of letting the matter go by, people are quick to underline your error in bad judgement as incompetent or irresponsible without ever so much as admitting that they were the ones who influenced your decision in the first place! Possibly the years under Franco have made Mayürqans gun shy. Maybe it is another geographical point too. Look at the Japanese when they first made waves in the eighties. At that time they were a very self conscious culture. To them, everything about the West was great while everything about them was shameful. Somewhere, too much isolation seems to lead to a level of personal retardedness. That, or the Arab tendency to deflect blame is still inculcated into the culture. It irks me to no end the culture's continued ingenuous approach to being responsible and intelligent for the sake of social graces and avoiding public scrutiny; not excluding the intimidation that social pressure can permeate into those who try otherwise. While it has done well to assimilate the speed of economic development it has not assimilated as well, personal or spiritual development. No one is a victim and I choose to live in Mayürqa. I am happy to live in Rome and do as the Romans do. However these days, cities like Rome are being reformed in a day without consideration to its traditions or its culture. There is confusion similar to a soul without a way. You can cut down a tree, but its roots will continue to breathe uneasily until they are either stumped out, or a new tree takes over. Sigh. I thank Life for being a product of Canada where the advent and timing of its inception enables Canadians with an understanding and respect for the natural laws of tradition and time in balance with the new world. It has in my opinion, afforded Canadians the gift and privilege of a mature and coherent respect for human rights and social understanding. The experience is without a doubt one of the best avenues towards personal and human* *development, which is the most important tool and greatest weapon needed today in order to survive the invasion of indefinite economic development and materialism. While discovery can evolve humanity's potential good, its side effect is a venom that spreads faster than the rate of human development. I wonder how much farther humanity's "civilised" rubber band will stretch before it begins to recede backwards and digress completely; not from overextension, rather from having being abated by the venom of discovery. Without a doubt it is harder on these newly developed economies that have excelled too quickly and been made aware of their own weaknesses in social development, which is ironically more difficult to manage than the economic success. À-propos, mature countries like Spain where populations are double that of Canada's that were conditioned to fight with arms against oppression have been working hard to learn other ways and have progressed extremely well in light of their challenges. Spain for example has faced the issues of ETA* in such a valiant and respectable way that one might even suggest that it has evolved better as an exemplary country for the world than the United States, the spokesman for peace talks, which has never been faced with a similar domestic issue and still manages many of its policies by force. Caught in the crossfire are mature child countries like Canada that try to remain steadfast to its example of bi-lateral communication against the incessant aggravation of socially immature countries to bear arms. The young and the old can learn from each other. Canada and Spain are in many ways a yin yang of east and west, while the United States is the new world and may never live in harmony with the past or tradition, by simple virtue of its history; cutting roots, conquer, divide and reform. Hence its balance can only be found in those countries that are in direct polarity to its nature: the purely under developed ones represent the yin of the US' yang. Furthermore, there is no comparison between*

---

*ETA is "officially a disarmed organization" since April 8 2017.

Canada and the United States except for the English language and the generic customs of consumerism. Otherwise Canada has more in common with its northern neighbours by virtue of its climate, its modest population and traditional ties with Europe. While dogs and cats are compared to men and women, I liken the relationship between Canada and the United States to Odie and Garfield. Canadian DNA is pure and friendly and nothing less than Odie's altruism.., the cold country with a warm heart...

My mind returned to the current situation at reception. There is a time and a place for everything, but putting my brain on a tray for lack of professional services for which I was paying for called upon a solution, not "no pasa nada", not a big deal. I requested that they cancel the transaction then and there. However, Charlie then hummed in that he didn't have any cash on hand anyway. I just stared at him. 'How did you expect to pay?' I asked quietly tho' the strain in my voice was evident. My direct question to him in front of the receptionist did not amuse him either. 'I don't know,' he said with a cocky smile, 'your card?' I felt deceived. Like the whole weekend for him was a big joke on me. As if he was testing me. He still believed that I had money and wanted to see my reaction. His moods not only swing between up and down, they also alternated from the cocaine that I address as his jealous possessive girlfriend and Charlie, the one who wants a new life and lover. Again, my imagination draws up a visual of an ugly woman that is the cocaine girlfriend with me trying to reach him through the boy that may still have enough innocence in him to recognise good and bad, and respect the voice of truth. In the meantime my mind remains on guard against volatile behaviour from both of us. Well, the bill was paid. My doubts about his motives might have festered, if he hadn't apologised in the taxi. 'I didn't realise it mattered to you so much,' he said with a matter of fact tone, 'I'll pay you back at home.' His words were welcomed but counter-productive on me: had I over reacted? He had after all paid out much more than we'd expected in cabs and in food. 'No worries,' I said, and added: 'Happy Birthday.' That was it. In one motion I'd stood my ground and lost it in a blink of an eye. Even Odie would have found a classier way to dismiss Garfield's insolence better than I had with Charlie. Who's really the dumb one? … Certainly not the dog.

La vie en bleu
Life in blue

Then on our last day yesterday, after Charlie got up early to have breakfast with me, we went to the shops. Had it been warmer outside, Charlie and I might have enjoyed another memorable walk to Lafayette centre, but the sun came and went between grey clouds in such rapid intervals that it was not possible to soak up the warmth of its rays. So we took a taxi from the hotel instead. Being Saturday afternoon, the streets and the shops were inundated with people making the taxi fare to get there nothing less than exorbitant. Hmm, despite the costs that I have incurred for the plane tickets and hotel, Charlie has without a doubt contributed the most in expenses. I rationalise that it had been his choice to stay more than a day but then again, if it had been the cocaine talking then maybe it should have been my extended responsibility not to agree? Anyway, we did the shops and frankly, I could have done without them. I hate shopping centres. Except for the nostalgia of holiday decorations, music and great window displays, everything related to commercial abundance in cold linoleum tiled buildings disturbs me. We gave each other an hour. Charlie went his way and I went mine. Needless to say that I wondered if he'd look for a junkie to get some. I even had to resist the urge to follow him, reminding myself that the trip was for Charlie's birthday.

Despite the intensive task at hand to detoxify, Paris had been a gift before we'd made the agreement and he could do whatever he wanted. After the shops we headed back to the hotel. Charlie bought a few shirts for himself and I bought some famous French soap for gifts. His mood was tired and irritable. I'd made arrangements from Mayürqa to meet a girlfriend for coffee for that afternoon in the lobby of the hotel which gave Charlie room to be alone and have a siesta before dinner. We settled in the room quietly, hardly saying much to each other. Charlie put the TV on and I used the hour before heading down to the lobby to chill out. I sat at a little writing desk by the television set to read the room service menu, while Charlie sat at the top of the bed, smoking and reading the hotel TV guide. Everything felt pretty copacetic as we chatted lightly about this and that. We agreed that being in Paris while it's cold is not better than being on the sofa in Mayürqa, especially for someone who has "been there, seen it and done that" sort of thing. In truth, there is little reason to travel beyond the Balearic Islands other than to visit friends and family, or to feed a craving for big city bustle, art and culture; and of course, the sheer purpose of expanding one's horizons. The latter being my strongest reply whenever a local suggests to me that there is no need to travel when Mayürqa is the best place to live. I then try to underline the fact that my contentedness at staying within the boundaries of the island is precisely because I had travelled so much before getting there. At which point, I begin to lose my argument because the local will tell me that there is no need to see farther, if the view is already appreciated as the best. I'll try to make a last stand by word selection and suggest that the view maybe "considered" the best but not "appreciated", until one has experienced something else to compare it with. The conversation then ends rapidly by way of evasive eye shifting and or silence until I finally put in some diplomacy and give deference to the local by admitting that Mayürqa had been my choice after having seen other views. Specifically, Mayūrqa is simply spoiled by abundance, while there is no excuse for ignorance. I often see similarities between Mayūrqans and Arabs who appear to be lucky by virtue of their land's wealth and the privileges it gives them. However, the abundant ease drawn from these privileges seems to have handicapped slightly, their ability to appreciate their destiny wisely. Mayūrqa has been stung by the "Nouveau Riche" lifestyle, without the education or the memory of it. Such that there is an interest in the new but only, if it does not require an upheaval or change from their life in Mayūrqa. This in turn reduces the desire to know more if it's not instantly gratifying. Thus personal development and wisdom appear delayed from a lack of comparative and personal experiences. Although true, the same cannot be said about its next generation. The iGeneration, the one born after 1981, appears to be coming along at the same rate as the rest of the world's "iGen", and offers a potential possibility of reverting the reigns to Mayūrqa's indigenous beauty and culture – largely its language, back to itself simply by virtue of that broader view of experience its predecessor didn't have. It's not really a Mayūrqa thing anyway, as much as it is a geographical one related to islands or largely homogenous cultures. In any case, it saddens me a bit because these places are precious, but the result will be that oil runs itself out, while Mayūrqa from lack of vision and careful planning will lose its view as the best place to live. I shared a bit of this with Charlie, who appeared to be serene somewhere else and not really listening to me, but then he said: 'My son has been to Euro Disney…We went together with my wife.' His comment caught me by surprise. I knew that he had worked in Paris and even stayed in the hotel that we were at, but I had not known about his family. I was also not sure what the relationship of what he'd said had to do with what I had been saying to him. Was he trying to say that his family had travelled and compared other places? Had I somehow insulted him? I answered his comment with, 'Oh really, you took your son to Euro Disney... Did he like it?'

'Oh yea,' he answered, 'until we got back to the hotel,' he said in a rather dark tone.

'Oh.' I waited.

'We were just getting back from a good day and my son began to play or something on the floor; then my wife wanted his attention and then suddenly hit him.' I said nothing. 'You know, he was only about five or six,' he added.

'Was she upset at something?' I asked with a calm interest.

'I have no clue, but there was no need to hit him. It was so sudden. I really began to wonder after that – you know?' His words were clearly filled with contempt. His eyes moved scornfully between me and his cigarette while he spoke. I said nothing, but my mind raced with thoughts.

I know that Charlie does not tolerate physical or verbal abuse to the point that he is laissez-faire when the call for disciplining a child might be needed. Still, in light of the volatile relationship that has apparently always existed between he and his wife, I couldn't avoid giving the mother some benefit of the doubt. I wondered if her outburst was related to pent-up tension that she'd accumulated from her day with Charlie? Maybe Charlie knew that, and felt guilty that his son had paid the price for it? I questioned if the story he was telling me was even accurate or true, yet the current moment that we were in, was an emotional low from the effects of the cocaine withdrawal. I am realising that Charlie only ever speaks his truth when he's wallowing in the depressive stage that arrives as the cocaine high begins to dissipate and a level of transparency and unwanted realities begin to storm the mind. Maybe the hit was not how Charlie perceived it to be? If the boy was five or six then Charlie was already active. Either way, Charlie's truth will always be challenged unless he can control his addiction. I stayed in the chair and continued to listen to him: 'That night we did it three times...She doesn't remember, but I do. I remember everything, you know...' The disdain in his tone was disconcerting and his eyes had narrowed on me in a way that made me feel like the object of his resentment. Suddenly our moment on his couch in Mayürqa, when he associated his Paris sketch to his wife became clear. Murphy's Law had allowed me to give him a gift to the last place where he remembers making love with his wife. I was horrified by the possible ramifications of this knowledge and I froze a bit inside. Then almost as if he'd heard my thoughts: 'Why did you bring me to Paris,' he asked. My insides grew tighter. 'Why did I invite you to Paris?' I repeated his question more for me than for him. My instincts were alarmed and I was apprehensive to say anything. Rather than be a new experience, Paris was unsettling unwanted memories. I was in a no-win situation. 'Charlie, I invited you for a day in Paris because of our conversations during English classes, *remember*?... I understood that you loved to travel and that you enjoyed Paris. My intention was a gift for a day in Paris not a weekend...' I ended. I could have told him bluntly that it had been his choice, but I did not want to ruffle more feathers. I remained sitting where I was, watching him without trying to stare. His thoughts were black and my presence became a side effect that fed into it. Being there in the hotel room, I wondered if his emotional memory had brought up to surface his prostitute experiences making him think that I expected sex and therefore making him feel obliged in a grudgingly way to do something but couldn't? Or maybe he was feeling sexual frustration from the night before, or even at that moment and wanted me to know about his ability with his wife as a way to remove his own sense of emotional and physical impotency at not having been able to show or perform for me? Or possibly he was thinking that I had invited him to Paris as a trick to remind him of his wife and highlight his unfaithfulness to her. Gawd, despite the fact that he has been clean for six days, guilt still managed to find me as the problem and the source of his current suffering. Altruism had gone out like a light and made me wish twice over that I had played it cool and platonic the whole time. There was a bit of silence. As I watched him take a final concentrated puff from his cigarette butt, I got up to go to the bathroom and got ready for my meeting in the lobby. 'Listen Charlie, I'm sorry if I offended you, it was not my intention, okay', I said softly. Once I got out of the bathroom he was already in bed. I reminded him where I was going to be and headed to the door. I wanted to add that he could join us if he wanted to, but enough had been said already. Instead he surprised me again and said: 'Have a good time.' 'Thanks,' I replied and heard the door shut behind me.

A few hours later Charlie came down to the lobby and met with my girlfriend and I. We chatted for a while more and then she left. He was a bit better, but mostly volatile between being irritated and negative. Still, we decided to hit Paris by night and took a cab to Montmartre. It was much colder than when we'd gone to the shops and even though I was wearing mitts and a scarf, I still wasn't warm enough. Charlie only had his brown suede leather jacket on, but didn't complain half as much as I did; when he did, it wasn't even a complaint, more like a comment. 'Oof its cold,' was about as much venom he put into it. His modest approach to the discomfort made me appreciate him more. Jes was similar. Often acting restrained and unassuming towards the physical pain he often experienced in his ligaments. If I had not witnessed their ability to cry, I might have defined them as brave soldiers. However the added element of sensitivity and humility made them, by my definition, beautiful men. We got out of the taxi at the bottom of Montmartre village and walked up. The quaint area of narrow streets, tiny shops and restaurants was all dolled up in a wonderful holiday theme, reminiscent of Disney winter scenes. The night was clear and cold; hailed on by a wind that practically made it impossible to appreciate the wonder illuminating from it all. We walked and walked looking for a place to buy a few t-shirts and then have dinner. It was brutal and I got to a point when I was willing to stop anywhere, but nothing seemed right for supper nor open long enough to offer it. Charlie was patient and I was getting irritated. In my heart I just wanted him to choose a place, but he never did. Almost as if he wanted me to decide or possibly he was testing my stamina? There were a few times when I really wondered. Was it him or the side effects of the withdrawal again? Then again, maybe I was just reacting to the effects of the cold: impatient, irritable bordering on miserable. I was really cold and my body was one blue popsicle. The only good thing about it was that it gave me another peek into what Charlie must deal with almost every day while he's an addict: complete physical and emotional discomfort. Anyway, we finally got up to the very centre of the village and found a shop where in fact, we bought some great t-shirts for everyone. Not much following that; a lot more walking, a wonderful view of "Le Sacré Coeur Basilica", the occasional stop into an open concept souvenir shop to look at rings and gadgets – Charlie likes rings. A few of them are nice, but most of them are simply gaudy or gypsy in style. At one shop, he finally gave in and bought himself a tuque to cover his bare head. I looked at him with a smirk on my face. Somehow his sense of practicality surpassed his normally stronger sense of ridicule with a less than charming oversized hip hop ski hat on his bald head: 'Which one?' he asked while he decided on the red one. 'What? Is it ok?' he checked as he proceeded to the cashier. 'Yea... It's fine,' I replied as nonchalantly as possible, while my insides shivered from a double time reaction to the cold and pent up laughter. It certainly made me enjoy him and our walk even more, because he honestly looked silly and didn't give a damn. I don't know how many kilometres we walked, but it must have been many. We eventually walked out of Montmartre along main streets and even past "The Moulin Rouge" which was a nice surprise for me, albeit quickly overshadowed by cold and hunger pains. Charlie was subdued but unfriendly. Reflecting irritation at my presence with a slight or derogatory comment about something I would have said or done; sometimes more than a day old. The style was not verbal abuse rather obstreperous. Much like putting up with Garfield or a twelve year old boy's insubordination and whining when he's irritated by something. Although he has been clean for several days, it was apparent over the weekend that his mind still played delusional or neurotic scenes in his head. We were both getting crabby and tired when we finally came upon a tiny Italian restaurant. '*Thank gawd,*' I thought. The place only had room for five or six tables and we received a window table again. Dinner was nice, cosy and simple. The warmth did us good and when we left we were both calmer. We walked until we were able to hail a cab and returned to the hotel: a night cap in the bar and off to the room. I took a shower, watched the blue fade from my toes and gave thanks for the hot water. Charlie to my surprise had a bath. Ever since Elisabet and I gave him bath salts for Christmas, he's been taking advantage of the tub. I slipped into sheets and allowed my muscles and mind to melt into the bed with me. '*What a day,*' I'd thought, '*what a fuck'n wonderful day...*'

> Give a little bit
> I'll give a little bit of my life for you
> Just give a little bit of your time to me
> I see you man with the lonely eyes
> So take my hand, you'll be surprised to find yourself
> We're on our way back home – Don't you need to feel at home?
> 'GIVE A LITTLE BIT' – SUPERTRAMP, LYRICS ADAPTED

The warrior's belt

January 17

Day 7: Mayürqa – *sms Mc: "Hi C. I am coming to meet u now. Get up ok. M." Up by 11:30a.m., quiet, pensive, and closed off. Worked at Sa Croix. Irritated by my presence.*

Paris with Charlie came and went very nicely. The return flight on our way back home had been the icing on the cake before we landed in Mayürqa and headed back to what I perceive as Charlie's well. This time, I was the one with the window seat and after I'd stopped writing in my journal, I took in some of the tranquillity from the darkness and the inanimate blue-white dots that hung outside the window. I pressed my face against the cool Playtex glass and used my hands as shades against the cabin lights. The sky was like a deep black to which I drew a mental parallel with scuba diving in the deep blue where all perspective is lost, if the eye doesn't have a point of reference to follow; while one moves weightless through the tranquillity of vast blue water, there is an initial hint of distortion and uncertainty until the body's mass finally adjusts and becomes one with the space. When I looked out to the night, my vision felt distorted until my eyes were able to focus on the stars that looked like glowing dots sporadically placed throughout the sky. There was a soft white light from the moon that I could not see, which directed my eyes to the warrior's belt of three bright stars that shone steadfast in Orion's constellation. My mind roamed and I remembered a movie with a dragon named Drac which was interpreted by Sean Connery. It was a warm film with a greatly courageous ending, because the dragon had to die by the sword of his friend, a dragon slayer, in order to fulfil the dragon's prophecy. When the deed is done the dragon slayer is mortified by his act, but the dragon reminds him that every star in the sky is a soul from earth after death, while every constellation is a group of comrades, one of which the dragon finally joins, and completes the circumpolar constellation of "Drac the Dragon". 'Drac the *Dragon*,' I uttered to myself with a stronger lean on the word. It recalled my memory of the song *Puff the Magic Dragon* "that lived by the sea" and a visual of my dad singing and playing it on the piano. I love the magic of that song despite its sad ending which contrary to belief, has never been about drugs or marijuana rather about the innocence of childhood lost. Ironically to me the utter notion of the former only justified the song's truth.

My eyes scanned lightly through the pale blue night that had come more into focus, and then rested back on Orion's belt. My thoughts about courage, warriors, magic and the three bright stars invited thoughts about some that I knew and before I pulled my face out of the sky, I whispered hello to my dad, grandma and Jesy who were all that in their own way. Charlie next to me was quiet and responsive. Sometimes letting me rest my hand on his lap, or slipping his fingers in between mine, or in a boyish way leaning across me to look at some "unseeable" object outside the window. He smelt good. His addiction might have made his senses more receptive to touch and smell, but mine were actively receptive naturally. Then he pulled out two plastic cases and showed me their contents. The first case he opened, held two black leather bracelets with flat silver heads and a black leather pinkie ring next to them. He pulled out one of the black bracelets from the inserts of the case and asked: 'Which one should I keep for myself?' 'Which one do you prefer,' I asked back. He tried them both on. 'This one,' referring to the one that came with the ring, 'I'll stick with this one.' 'The baby ring looks a bit small for your finger,' I added, 'maybe your son would like it?' No reply. 'Or maybe give him the other bracelet. Might be kind of neat for him to have one like his dad.' 'I dunno. We'll see,' he said, while his eyes contemplated them both. Then with the second case he added unexpectedly, 'This is for you.' I was really surprised and like Charlie, when he'd discovered his gift for Paris, quickly felt self-conscious. 'For me?' I hesitated awkwardly. His look was intent on me, and he seemed delighted by my embarrassment. I didn't want to say or do too much to make us both "go there" so I quickly changed my posture and opened the case. Inside was a very unique and attractive looking silver Swatch ring original in design, with jagged mesh links. It's one of a kind and I like it very much. I am without a doubt a difficult person to buy for, and Charlie had done very well. It would seem that while I was weighing the chances of his possible search for dope, he was shopping and bought me a cool ring from the Louvre. A better souvenir and memento of our trip could not have been chosen. I placed it on my index finger and also tried it on my thumb. 'It looks good there,' he said admiringly. It did. Although, the texture from the mesh inside the ring irritated my finger a bit, I loved the novelty and uniqueness of it. It was a gift from Charlie. How rare was that? I gave him a focused kiss on the cheek, 'Thank you,' I whispered next to his ear, 'I really like it.' More was not required. We sat pensively for the most part of the flight after that; Charlie clearing his nose once in a while, or reading the flight magazine. Only when the plane began its descent to Palma did Charlie speak: 'Aiii the bells,' he sighed out loud while pulling out some tissue from his jean pocket and fumbling to blow his nose again. 'I almost don't want to go back,' he said with a weak smile and folded the tissue neatly into a square, lifted his butt slightly off the seat and pushed it neatly back into his pocket. I directed my eyes to his face. He looked uneasy, which made me feel uneasy, 'Do you feel nervous?' I asked as plainly as possible. 'It's that I don't trust myself you know...' I felt my heart miss a beat. I looked at him more carefully and saw no evidence of foul play. He had just confided in me and managed to tell me something that he'd probably regret later on. It was the boy in him who'd got away from the lure of the girlfriend, just enough to let me know that he wanted help. He can't trust himself and he was letting me know. The bushi, or warrioress in me was instantly alerted and activated; I was Frodo's loyal friend Sam, faced with the evil prowess of cocaine in Charlie like the ring's evil spell over Frodo. I wore the crest of my loyalty on my finger and in my heart, prepared to go into Charlie's well after him; even if it meant fulfilling my pledge beyond our month. Most unusual of all, was that my instinct was completely natural. As if it were an innate instinct passed down to me from generations and generations before them. Maybe it was my paternal family's influence from valiant British war songs and its relentless motto to defend until the end, which was revived. My memory found my dad again, when we were having an argument ignited by my critic about his being too tolerant and obsessively involved with people, to which he shot back: 'Because I *Care*!' I'd remained silent for a moment in an attempt to counter fire, but words came to my lips and dissipated. The power of his three words had silenced me. There was nothing that I could retaliate that wouldn't have reduced my integrity down to the mediocre of society. Even though my father's ways could be compulsive, overbearing or indifferent to self-preservation, his point was clear: does anybody care? There is no way to win an argument against someone whose effort and altruism stems from kindness and love. The moment that happens, then reason is automatically given to apathy, war and indifference to life. Even if the effort quietly simmers for some reciprocation for its virtue, it will never be for anything more than the deeper reason that desires to be understood, with a little bit of love and respect in return. Some hearts go void and kill. Other hearts try to fill others' and reap from the spill ... I focused my thoughts back to me and the man sitting at my side. There was, without a doubt, an incessant tug or unexplainable gravity pull towards Charlie and a need to see him triumph. Almost as if my survival in life was gauged or dependent on his too. Who cares? The factor of all factors was that I did. *'Bells bells bells,'* I thought as we started to land, *'neither Charlie nor the girlfriend's damn fuck'n bells, have a clue about the power of love.'*

> Imagine all the people, living life in peace
> A brotherhood of man
> Imagine all the people, sharing all the world
> You may say I'm a dreamer, but I'm not the only one
> I hope someday you'll join us and the world will live as one.
> 'IMAGINE' – JOHN LENNON, LYRICS ADAPTED

Imagine

We landed in Mayürqa, hopped into Charlie's Phedra and headed back to Sa Ema de Farrutx, stopping in on Mitx and Elisabet's to give them the overall update of our weekend. The fact that I live upstairs is kind of a mixed blessing. On one hand, it offers me little sense of privacy. On the other hand, they are there if I need them. It's the love and hate paradox of family. Still, the Serra family could not have been a better gift to me in light of our cultural differences. When I am reminded of the challenges with Jes' family there is no room for my mental gymnastics to get into the way, even if and when I feel justified: none. Charlie, flies in and out of his older brother's home like a cool autumn wind. He stirs up the mood, eats the mandarins, talks to Elisabet, winds up Mitx and then flies away leaving the high of his presence to settle on them all and dissipate until his next visit. Back home this kind of "Hi-ya and see-ya later alligator" ritual, might be interpreted as abusing one's family rights because the house is not the family house, rather Mitx and Elisabet's. Instead, I sense an unspoken expectation between them, *where Charlie is to his brother and sister in-law, the unsung angel whose enigmatic and combustive presence validates their existence beyond the trials of their own couplehood and keeps them alive and together. The advent of his arrival regardless of its purpose, always resuscitates a simmering anticipation in them all, back to life. In exchange, they are his family with a surrogate twist. There is a quiet sense of stability in the knowledge of their routine; tranquillity felt at the visual of their car parked out front, or a light that's on, or in the comfort of their wholesome non-pulsed ways. Whether Charlie calls them or bounds down the street to their place he is assured of their presence. One of the few that he has subconsciously grown to rely-on despite himself, because the dependency should have grown with a partner, his child or himself. Families by nature, will always protect each other under the pretence of unconditional love, trust and loyalty towards each other. Yet the epitome of such virtues, can only ever be applied to a friend, by reason of no blood lineage to influence them. Hence couplehood can be understood as one of the more difficult, yet rewarding challenges to human nature. Charlie by his own independent nature might never have been married nor may he ever wish to be in a couple relationship. However the cocaine addiction has disrupted that self confidence and gradually reduced his emotional level to that of a boy grown co-dependent on his brother's family. The ramifications make recuperation even tougher. Not only does he have to stay away from the coke, but he needs to relocate his emotional maturity level, redefine his trust and loyalties and in whom he places them. Worse, the family unit despite itself, cannot let go enough to give him room for that self-discovery. Indeed blood is thicker than water, but which is clearer? Each family member has a perspective experience with one another, so that when a member begins to wean away from the confidence of its family and place its intimacy with a third individual without lineage to the family, egos and jealousy tend to surface. In the meantime the rigmarole between Charlie and his brother's family continues to work as a veil over all that and at least keep the pace of recuperation stable, while the passing of time manages with the rest of the merits found in the family unit's continued support system, to ensure each other's survival by its free-exchange of basic needs. The value of this privilege is all second nature to these cultures where traditions have not been fully uprooted yet by the new world. In retrospect, the privilege is really just a natural instinct that shouldn't require much ado about anything. Yet I am a product from another world where this instinct has been choked or mutated. 'Ojalá,' God willing I think, 'if only man could appreciate things before they were lost.' In North America the family unit has evolved into communities of people living together without necessarily blood lineage involved. On one hand, it does not have the inherent stamina that the instincts of blood lineage have and therefore risks dissolving at some point in time. However on the other, it induces greater self-development and requires a consistent level of respect among members of the community that is often taken for granted, or abused by blood lineages. If both models could find a way to fuse together as one, Utopia would not be just a figure of speech. I remember my own childhood and my dad's relentless attempt to maintain the family unit in our home. It was a small case of the haves and the "have nots". My mother, from the baby-boomer generation grew up in the fifties and had the "Leave it to Beaver" experience and never noticed. My dad on the contrary was from the World War II baby era in England who, post his own parents' break up, emigrated to Canada with his mum and younger sister, thus placing a heavier need for the family unit's survival, regardless of its size. My parents' upbringing were polar in nature but passed down to the children in perfect balance. By the late seventies their childhood experiences collided with the "Me generation". The "haves" from the fifties rebelled against the confinements and responsibilities of family, which somehow found its way into our home and made the movie "Kramer versus Kramer" a respected interpreter of the unsung heroes of broken families. My father had some strong and persuasive opinions on present day society, and once wrote how, "Its ills all stemmed from the break-up of the family unit..." that he would have liked "the reader to agree" with his "summations" ... "We cannot reshape the nature of humanity, and all the analysis in the world, correct or otherwise, regarding the condition of things, means Diddley Squat if it's incompatible with some of the factors governing it." That with reference to the Me generation: "It's the experience, "the action", "the sensation" people want, not the person. People are in love with "being in love..." Camaraderie and friendship; companionship, sharing life's trip with others. That's the key." The balance he summed up as: "Never promoting marriage but the family unit." In light of North America's evolution since then, his views have not been entirely elusive. The family unit in North America has been redefining itself in society where the fundamental purpose to support its members and maintain their survival is offset by an emotional distance among the unit's members that albeit matures self-development and independence, is all generated by the intrinsic burden of economy: there is none. It is not a better model, but better to exist than not at all against the volatility of the new world. I often marvel at how the inherent Mayürqan manages to live so well when the salary scale is the lowest in Spain and the standard of living is the highest? In Spain it is called "enchufe" and it is like North America's modern label for networking, but with a thicker and better quality weave that has been developed over time. Unlike North America where families tend to move house every two years, the dentist in Mayürqa knows the banker, who knows the restaurant owner and whose children will also know their children precisely because they don't move. They have had until now, an economy in goods not in plastic. Again the free exchange of basic needs is shared among them. "Scratch my back and I'll scratch yours." The clan model that only a few places in the world can still use. Hence I live in Spain where the Me generation has only just begun, and where the pillars of traditional support and free exchange are still entrenched in some parts of the country where the effects of capitalism are slightly delayed. Almost as if I took a time machine and went back in time, where I might lightly relive in Mayūrqa, the traditions from my childhood era in Canada. I am at once benefited by the ability to assess and appreciate the good and dismiss the ills from both traditions. In fact it is the timing of my generation, the baby-busters, the x-generation, flower babies, Expo babies, anyone born between 1965–1969, who have been afforded this advantage of knowing about both worlds before they began to mutate. We are in fact the hub from when the process began to diverge indefinitely. As a result no other generation shall know or receive a better experience or balanced exposure between the traditions of the old and the new, than ours. When I look at Mayūrqa and its family system in 2005, I think they are an example of a modern family unit that no longer exists in North America. A small clan of blood lineage that will most likely be passed down from one generation to another in the same house that has been theirs for more than twenty years, where the basic needs of shelter, food and economic support are supplied by the heads of the household in exchange for their children's continued survival and ability to maintain the lineage in the future. At a glance they might be compared to North America's version of "Leave it to Beaver." However, that family of the fifties was white middle class America reflecting the times and the political bodies that governed them, rather than the basic clan instinct to protect and survive as a culture. In addition to the fact that solidarity and security of the American family was challenged by a younger version of the new world that has since grown more rapidly out of proportion with time and barely leaves room in today's families to manage a household with confidence. In a global sense, the Mayürqan example may be shared with many other traditional cultures where clan values are respected and maintained. Canada alone, is a platform of indigenous and multicultural families living between both worlds, challenged by the nemesis of progress' insatiable appetite, yet attempting to preserve their existence from one generation to the next. It is here that families such as Mitx and Elisabet's still maintain a slight advantage because the new traditions have not yet penetrated entirely into the pillars of their culture. It is often said about Mayürqa that it is a closed-off society. Even Mayürqans will tell you this. The tone is similar to what might be whispered in Québec. The need to protect one's own species is without a doubt important against the ills of the new world. However, it must not lose sight of its purpose and erroneously work against social integration, language or culture, but rather against the beast of consumption. Indeed the English language is a scapegoat for capitalism because it is the native tongue of the powers that control it; a subtle hegemony of the new world. Spain's history for example, and the Franco years left a wound that spurred several regions of the country to react belligerently against the new government. While their anger is justified, it is fired at the wrong generation. Franco and traditional governments no longer exist, but left those who suffered under their tyranny without an apology and bearing a grudge. So the new generation has had to pay the price for its history as the brunt of cooped up resentment and the target of spiteful attacks from the wounded generation before it. Thus placing it sadly at risk of also becoming marked with remorse and vindictive thought from the onslaught of misguided anger towards it. The parody of it all is that while some regions in Spain such as Cataluña, fight hard for their language and cultural rights as a way to bereave their loss and impede its repetition, they fail to see that their energies are misdirected at the wrong beast. Crimes of the past were executed by souls of the past. Québec for example has managed to move with the times and has done* well to let the next generation of Canadians be aware of its history with licence plates that say: "*Je me souviens*" (I remember). The message is straight to the point and when it first came out in the late sixties, the bile in Québec's purpose was evident and most of Canada felt slighted by it. Yet today the message has matured with a different purpose for Canadians. It is in fact a subtle but clever reminder to everyone, to keep the balance between the old and the new and respect history. Time and space do invade the memory and can leave the next generation without a marker of history from which to learn. Especially as the new generations can barely focus or read a book, a licence plate is a good subliminal way to reach them. Today all language cultures that are not English speaking still have a chance to implement legislation to protect themselves better against the eventual encroachment of capitalist interests. In "the Art of War" by Sun Tzu the best way to win a fight is to know the enemy but not enough to befriend them, or else the understanding of each other would prevent the war. Hence one child, one world, in my opinion is contradicted by the quest for one common language, because it removes understanding and respect among cultures. It resembles more Hegemonic than Utopia. Rather the ability to communicate with more than one language broadens understanding and "befriends" cultures' mentality, such that it can eventually define that child as "one with the world". Canada right now, is the prototype of that world. I say, 'Chapeau!' to Québec for protecting its language rights, 'Kudos!' to the indigenous North American cultures who have sought education and the skills of communication to preserve their traditions, 'Bravo!' to the rest of the Canadian salad bowl for its class act in putting up with the challenges of discourse, 'Hats off!' to Canada, for being the closest thing to "Imagine..."

Anyway, our routine of bounding into Elisabet and Mitx' place regardless of the late hour has begun to rejuvenate parts of my wilted spirit and I am at once delighted and distrusting of it. The little girl in me is melodramatic and wants to enjoy the experience of wellbeing this rare family entity instils in me; my romantic nature refuses to listen to reason and plunges into the warmth of others' stability. I hear Dido's lyrics in "Life for rent" and I know the risks because none of it is mine, yet I permit myself these short lived moments because they are also a part of a quiet search to find my place. So I soak up the sensation of feeling secure and protected, wanted and respected. The insecurities of economy, old age and loneliness are vanquished. My spirit impetuously feels reassured and complete as if I have suddenly, finally, been found.

Elisabet – "God's promise."

The gift of Belle

After a few minutes of boastful conversation between Charlie and them, we all hopped into Mitx and Elisabet's car and drove to Juniper village to celebrate the festive night of Mayürqa's "Sant. Antoni" and its "foguerons". It's quite impressive really, as every street corner or section of streets, is lit up with bold and healthy bonfires. Residents come out and sit around talking, drinking and eating local festive food. Designated houses keep their doors open for neighbours and friends to help themselves to cold meats, bread and cheese plates much like neighbourhood Bar-B-Qs in America. Tho', what impresses me are the bonfires that are left unattended or rarely supervised. Little concern or caution is given to the location of many that are less than a few feet away from trees, homes, electrical wires, or held by the wind's direction that blows sparks and hot sprigs all over the place, whilst people get more and more inebriated: yet never once a hazard or a scene is recorded.

We stayed in Juniper for a while. I found a chair and sat there quietly trying to enjoy the experience while watching Charlie like a hawk. I was tense and really felt unfairly challenged in an environment that was not mine or empathetic to my task. Then to make matters worse, Elisabet went along with Charlie's suggestion to go to Sa Pobla which is one of the hubs of Sant. Antoni tradition and made Juniper's experience a walk in the park. Anxiety to watch Charlie felt like déjà vu with Jes when we'd gone to the same village four years earlier under similar circumstances – drinking and unpredictability. I was relieved slightly to see that Mitx was not impressed either, by Elisabet's lack of foresight. Charlie could do whatever the hell he wanted, but I felt that Elisabet's decision to go along with it was to win favour with Charlie. That her feminine instinct has defined me as an intruder in Charlie's exclusive attention to her friendship with him, coupled with her self-interest to go out that night. In light of what Charlie and I were trying to accomplish, her flippant attitude was indifferent to me and reflected little concern for Charlie. Now, had I done the same by offering her husband Mitx, who has a heart murmur, cigarettes because he wanted to smoke, she would have felt the stab of indifference by me to her wishes and concerns for Mitx' health, equally well. Mitx can also do whatever the hell he wants – it's his life too no? Yet because I respect Elisabet's personal battle with him, I would have found a way to avoid taking sides. She thought nothing of that with regards to me and her husband, and indicated to me then, that her interests in Charlie are unconsciously self-motivated. She would rather preserve his misguided respect and trust in her, than to cross the line and risk diminishing it. Besides she doesn't have to when Mitx and others are doing all the dirty work. She feeds and receives Charlie in her home never openly contradicting him. A well intentioned politician whose comments about Charlie in his absence are often incongruent with the ones she uses in his presence... And yes, I am angry that Charlie prefers and considers this kind of friendship. I felt deceived especially as she wastes no time in joining me on my walks with Dasha, or coming up to my front patio for a chat, or inviting me to lunch and dinners downstairs while she coolly siphons information from me about him. Sceptical, I still permitted her the privilege of that knowledge on the basis that they are his family and that Charlie's own example of delivery to them, suggested to me that I should. However, that night at the bonfires my sixth sense interpreted something else from her that delivered anger and caution to my senses. I realised it was her feminine way, albeit unconsciously subtle, to part from me what she feels has been robbed. What? Insecurity? Jealousy? That I receive Charlie's deference in a way that neither she nor his wife ever have? Fuck, I can't deal with these types of women. My mind went dark … *Are all women so disloyal to their own kind? Men do it too, but they're more obvious about it and less often with their friends. Rarely a guy will screw around with a friend's wife and when he does he's considered to be a big asshole. While many women play around with their girlfriends' men and when noticed, it's the victim who's over reacting. In women it's an instinct not a purpose. I find it hypocritical that women blame men for not being more civilised about their natural instinct to fornicate while women rarely respect their sorority and allow their seductive instincts to prowl rather than keep them in check. It takes two to tango, but women are more calculating than most men and can disarm them before they realise what's going on. I wonder about my views, because I am one of them. I have no doubts about the woman and her virtues: we are beautiful creatures born with an extremely potent and powerful instinct we call love. Life chose to give the burden of responsibility to manage its power to the female first, via her role in procreation. Ironically enough, Life also designated the man as the one to enable it to her. Still, power in the hands of one is never good; the hump and the woman who grunts submissively to the man who trails off with her by her hair has disappeared, we hope. It's hard to define our roles while we are bombarded by new ways and the challenges of being "civilised". We are who we are. Humans by nature are good. I believe this because love is nature in its purest form. Nature incubates from within the human being before it sees the light of day and is passed on to all humans at the time of conception. That, and a psychological nuance in humans to romanticize the good from their past, yet rarely recall the bad if it's not dug up on purpose. However, many traditional societies have narrowed the definition of "good" down to the woman only. Insomuch the cliché can turn into a combustive fuel where a society's tradition of the woman's role is still about her responsibility in caring and defining the men and women of its society; the definition does not mean that she is perfect or an exemplary human being. Thereby this juxtaposition turns into women's nemesis: guilt. As a result, it is hard to be angry at a woman because she's protected by a transparent veil of good intention. In North America men and women's roles have evolved or changed in a way that the role of the caretaker may be performed by either one and the sponsor for guilt no longer belongs to just the women. The caretaker role automatically unsettles those instincts within an individual, which that require all the compassion and patience that love has to offer. There is vulnerability with this giving if it is not kept in check because the code of conduct of a caretaker doesn't request or altruistically expect a return for the virtue of the work and worry. There is rarely a bilateral exchange of the love. Yet the demise of the caretaker is that it's human and will eventually need a sign of respect or appreciation for having binged so long without. Despite itself, it will give-in to promoting some harmless deception, or create a tiny guise for good intention that turns into a claim ticket for emotional blackmail in order to feel some attention and inadvertently hurt the ones being cared for. Indeed the caretaker is not perfect and yet tries to be and can cause more damage than good. The receiver thereby feels restricted and confused about his or her right to feel unforgiving or even justified in anger, which then creates a level of turmoil between love and hate at the caretaker. Such that, in most countries where the woman's traditional role as a caretaker still predominates, many of its men remain emotionally distant in their relationships with her. Ironically, women have lived with the caretaker's emotional limbo forever by reason of her natural instinct to care and nurture, vexed by her imperfection as a human being. If she is constantly challenged to find balance in this dilemma, how can she expect men to trust her if she still can not trust herself? The same applies to men and their innate search for balance between love and abuse. The point being that men and women should stop judging each other and work on self-reflection in managing their natural instincts. Otherwise they are useless to each other and the progress of this world, if they can't understand their own nature first. In the meantime, compassion is needed between them until their innate balance is found within and finally on kilter with the other's. As an example, there are now countries like those in North America where men can stay home defining the next generation of society while women can work defining the next generation of the workforce. Yet, I still worry about this. Although the steps are in the right direction little has been done on the self-reflection to do it well. So that I hope women don't reduce the potential of a new world that may for once glimmer with equilibrium between men and women. We have been oppressed as caretakers and this anger may cause us to return the same oppression onto men if we do not keep our natural instincts in check. There was once a time when the caveman hit the woman over the head for the last time when the lioness in her finally lashed back so unexpectedly that she herself was surprised. The reaction resulted in giving her a new understanding of her prowl instincts in life, which created a matriarch society that learned to govern and oppress men's "uncivilised" nature. Except, she was not quite civilised yet herself and then for the last time, men got tired of making love under the feminine spell and broke away with other men to rise and become a patriarchal society. This time with armour and a code of conduct that would never forget the power of the female spell. Then in the late twentieth century came hope, from men who slowly regained their confidence, faced their fear, and offered the woman the benefit of the doubt by allowing a few women to rise. They are the men who were willing to work side by side with her and give the notion of teamwork a renewed chance. Despite her trials in getting to that point you'd think she would have kept her virtues alive and respected the anthropological and the sociological reasons that made it so hard for her to get there in the first place. Now in the twenty-first century she is tasting the same power of success as men did and frankly men are losing their confidence again. In simple terms he no longer knows which instincts to follow: to open the car door for the woman or not? More importantly he has become lethargic and passive about the virtues in his instincts as a man and provider. Sigh. The woman has done well to regain equilibrium, but if she is not careful, she will abuse again her potential to govern and botch up a century's work based on trust between men and women. Yet, yet, Life seems to be hopeful about the task, giving countries such as Spain and Japan, the torch to lead the way with the birth of baby princesses, whose royal parents have defied their country's traditions on the basis of education. Not on equal rights or on the ills of sexism. It's about individual capacity gained from guidance, self-reflection and solid education. They have in fact assumed the greatest challenge of all: the responsibility of defining a woman leader whose example might be from a woman who maintains a balance between "the him and the her" within. In the meantime, may the woman use the power of her potent spell for the good of her family and friends and may the man remove his armour against sensitivity and just keep his instinct to fuck between himself and anyone he doesn't love. I mean, men and women, dogs and cats, who's really the caretaker? Really, side by side there would be no room for hegemony of the sexes ...*

My mind came out of the dark when Elisabet started to introduce me to some of her friends. I looked at her and felt instant shame while the immediate flood of my own emotional guilt removed my right to be angry. Suddenly all the good that she had brought to me since my arrival, simply slapped me hard in the face... *Elisabet, is-a-belle person, with a beautiful disarming smile that softens her strong features and automatically melts away the forty-eight years from her face. Her hair is thick dark brown and in the latest wispy cut just above shoulder length. Physically she is an attractive woman by way of the aura of her innocence. There is kindness in her approach equal to her intention. Life made sure I saw this when she handed me my bear totem on a keychain attached to the keys to the new flat. I'd understood from that day that she is a gift to many but particularly to me. How I manage her gift is my test on personal growth, while my only reference for truth, when confused by her actions, is life's reminder on my key-chain. That when my mind leaves its serenity and reads into her intentions with a negative light, it is best not to read at all and appreciate the moment for what it is: innocent. Sigh, it all comes back to the individual which in this case is me. Whether or not it was a way to welcome a new tenant, or an expression of empathy for my loss of Jes guided by her own experience with loss, a self-preserving need for a sympathetic ear void of bias, or a subliminal way to protect Charlie and her interests in him, it has been Elisabet who has made the attempts to make me feel welcomed and adjusted to my new place – even as soon as her first recuperating day home after having spent a week enduring her own trials from an operation in hospital. It has been Elisabet, often bringing up the stairs to my door wonderful plates of her home made cooking that frankly is an exclusive privilege in the midst of microwaves, frozen dinners and my staple diet of pasta "Al dente". How often has Elisabet buzzed my doorbell and invited me downstairs for lunch or dinner when I was secretly craving the warmth of their company? How did I feel while I shared the festive days of Christmas wrapped in the warmth of her family's traditions and stuffed to the gills with homemade traditional dishes? How often have I stood looking through my kitchen window while sipping the broth of Elisabet's hot soup, grateful that beyond the glass window to Charlie's place, he too is being warmed by her care? While at once intuitively aware that Elisabet's unassuming efforts are the joining links in helping two lost souls find themselves, while they try to recognise each other again. How many times have I sat for dinner with my personal tray given to me from Belle? Worn the white summer house coat or the furry red winter one after a shower that are both from Belle? When have I seen the plastic frame on my table where I placed a beautiful post card from her of a big bold colourful heart that is signed "with affection from your Sa Ema family" and not felt better by it? What does it mean when a household entertains friends and strangers with a meal or just an open door? Above all, I have the memory of a December morning after Christmas day when I was not well, joined with the visual of Elisabet standing at the bottom of the steps to my door, wrapped only in her housecoat, clutching a belligerent umbrella that wanted to fly with the wind and rain that assaulted them. Even after I had sent her a sms not to worry she came. Even after she might have been told to let me be, she tried. I had been disturbed at having to respond to the call of the doorbell, but when I saw her I saw the epitome of good intention. Like the innocence of a child that calls you away from your deeply needed sleep just to say that it loves you – how to remain perturbed at that? Then there is the presence of my physical femininity that often threatens the creatures of my kind. Yet Elisabet in this area has been the rare lioness to adopt another feline into her den when there are already three males there that she cares for. In return, I have kept my feminine instinct to prowl at bay. I thought of my mother who is a beautiful woman with a gentle free spirit and whose own lifetime experience growing up within the comfort parameters of a conservative era and social protocol did not offer her the wisdom of this discipline that comes from self-reflection and solitude until much later in her years after fifty. I see this in Elisabet too. Both women are young spirits, sensitive to their environment and the ones around them, yet their lack of self-esteem can involuntarily arm their feline instincts to roam unchecked and heighten a level of male interest completely oblivious to them. Elisabet's generosity therefore, like most of us, is like a double-edged sword because Elisabet doesn't have an evil bone in her, but she carries the residue of insecurity that most people have, from some moment in her lifetime when her self-esteem was hurt, and therefore dismisses it. Hence I have been the receptor of her kindness faced with guilt at feeling angry at a woman's imperfections despite her overwhelming nature of good intention. I might have been justified in my anger at Elisabet, by the rational that she is a woman of mature years and not dumb, or simply at the feline in Elisabet that was unaware of her indifference to her husband and me, in order to reclaim her sense of self-worth via Charlie. However that would be like justifying one's anger at a child's innocence. No the problem was mine. Should Charlie have found the snow or not, was beside the matter that it was still my decision to be involved in all this. That Elisabet could have expressed some deference to the task at hand is forgiven by reason of innocence. In the end both the problem and the responsibility are mine because I am the one who recognises the weakness or at least suffers by it. Indignant that age in years is irrelevant to that of one's spirit or intellect. Like with my mother, I must weigh how important Elisabet's human imperfections are against me, against the sincere beauty of her heart. I cannot discipline an adult of fifty, but I can work on myself on letting these things go. Hence at thirty-seven with my trial in emotional purgatory, I found a way out, and saw that it was not too late, and whispered to life: 'Thank you for the gift of Belle.'*

> To abandon might be justifiable.
> To abandon oneself, never.
> RALPH WALDO EMERSON

Blind faith

'Michèle pleased to me you,' I shot my attention back to Elisabet and the friend who spoke to me while simultaneously making a mental note to do something kind for Elisabet. Then I realised that Charlie had disappeared into a bar. I was abruptly rude and dismissed myself from the round of introductions in order to get to Charlie's side again. There were so many people and so much noise. When I joined Charlie his shifting eye movement suggested to me that the coke he was looking for wasn't the drink. 'What? You following me like a "perro faldero", a lap dog?' he said to me with an annoyed casual tone. I looked at him without a response, still feeling the uncomfortable residue from the way that I had left the introductions and by his indifference to our task at hand. In the eyes of all, I must have looked like an unwanted lap dog, even though it was all of them, who handed me the role. Did they not expect me to fulfil it? What is their definition of try? I felt like the lone agent again. 'I shouldn't have told you that on the plane,' he continued then swallowing the last of his coke-cola and letting the ice cubes fall back to the bottom of the tube glass with a loud double clank. I guessed that he was referring to his confession of self-distrust. I calculated quickly and looked at the wall clock for help. It was approaching half past twelve and Charlie's girlfriend was on time. I had thirty minutes to deal with her ravage attempts to lure him back to her. If I could stay with him for the following thirty minutes his craving would subside to normal levels and at least give us breathing space until we got home. In fact, the thirty minute bracket of time when Charlie's craving is at its strongest influence, became apparent to me from the week and a half of being together, but it was actually Charlie who'd managed to inform me about it before we'd even got started. I liken him to Doctor Jekyll when Charlie is being seduced by the sensual lure of the cocaine, and then to Mr. Hyde when Charlie is allied with the boy in him. So far Charlie has been good at telling me these things before the "girlfriend" increasingly tries to take him over. After Elisabet, I found it ironic that my battle with Charlie was about a drug, which is likened to an unhealthy love affair with a possessively insecure woman. In our talks Charlie has often defined his inability to let the cocaine go, like a man who can't let go of a bad relationship because of the attraction and intense sex. It's another reason why I think he needs to divorce his wife, because the "fait accomplit" would remove an emotional safety net and force him to make decisive choices. Anyway, when he doesn't have the coke, his mind romanticises the memory of its effect on him and confuses his compulsive need with missing it; much like a man who misses a woman. Yet after taking "her" he feels like shit and regrets deeply for having looked for her. Such that his own vicious circle of emotional turmoil brought my mind's eye back to the irony of Sa Croix being something of a healthy cross to bear for Charlie, while his fear to love the wrong woman is cause and effect for his erroneous love affair with cocaine. I thought, *fuck'n women, and I am one of them. Do I threaten other women or just myself? Like Charlie, I might have gay tendencies because the women with whom I get along the best, have a no-bullshit attitude similar to men's. Plus the men that I am best friends with are precisely those who have adopted a mature appreciation for the female's positive traits and try to keep the less attractive male traits at bay. Charlie's male friends have sensitive or disarming qualities usually evident in women first. Likewise the women he feels unthreatened by, are those who exude masculine or a neutral aura of sexuality and don't stimulate his "shameful" instincts which he finds difficult to keep at bay. However, I prefer men by a long shot especially as I recognise that my feminine persona depends on their attention in order to feel stimulated. I don't get any of that being around women. I admire women's inner stamina and often appreciate their bodies. However that is more about insecurity not desire. I hypothesise that Charlie on the other hand, respects the power of a woman's natural instinct but not necessarily the creature because he has been made confused by her maternal nature while he deals with his own natural instinct to fuck with personal contempt; compounded by the fact that he's "married". It is a hypothesis that could attract a gay tendency, but Charlie has been a cocaine addict for more than a decade, thereby stunted at a maturity level of a twelve year old therefore giving him little room to dismiss his ego, define himself clearly and respect the instinct of his manhood, without feeling ashamed of it...* Charlie moved and I came out of my thoughts. We headed back outside to join the others who had also begun their walk through the festive crowd. Elisabet was in her world of clouds and kittens while Mitx shared my tension and desire to leave. Charlie of course looked for Elisabet and instantly revived my ego! *'Why do I care about this stupid man?'* I asked myself. I was tired, stressed and lonely in the middle of a crowd of over-the-top inebriated people while Charlie almost seemed to make it difficult to follow him through it all, on purpose. At one point he decided to go to the john, so I asked Mitx to go with him. With all the bullshit I had to stay lucid about my purpose which was about getting Charlie through a month inactive, so that he could be clear enough to get professional help. I had to remind myself that his actions were not by him but by his fear of letting the coke go, or by the psychological metaphor of a *girlfriend's* fear of being left behind for another; *she'd* helped him do anything that would find her and keep him away from the other feline, in this case, me.

They finally came out of the bathroom and we pushed our way through the rowdy crowd. Elisabet had gone ahead with some of her friends while Mitx, Charlie and I trailed behind. I followed Charlie with my eyes while he gradually became one with the fire crackers, the music, the laughter and the sea of coloured bodies around us. Why do I choose to help a man who has clearly stated that he fears me for my intelligence and femininity? What does that mean exactly? If he hadn't selected the word "fear" then I would understand that my personality makes his natural instinct for sex feel shameful and perturbs or intimidates the desire to the point of not getting it up? ... *Except, Charlie is also intelligent, and much of the synergy between us comes from that knowledge of each other. In light of his intelligent mind, perhaps he feels more comfortable by the uncomplicated, happy go lucky air of ignorance because it doesn't stimulate his manhood and allows him to sustain a false sense of discipline over himself because he's not drawn to screw ignorance? So he goes to the prostitute who is not ignorant, but whose trade is. Rather than try to discipline the nature of his manhood he goes to the prostitute, pays her and relieves his 'shameful' instinct without guilt? Okay maybe the addiction is responsible for having stunted his emotional development, but in Charlie's case, I am not a prostitute, not entirely ignorant, and somewhat attractive. I think Charlie fears me because I am potentially someone he could love. He worries that my intelligent mind could manipulate his love and hurt him? Relationships breed manipulation regardless of their virtue. However, it is the original motive behind the manipulation that matters: my manipulative instinct is a personal desire for love fuelled by love, not a survival instinct to survive by him first then maybe feel love, like a prostitute might do. I don't need him to survive, such that my choice is real. I dunno. That his intelligent mind and his cocaine experiences have offered him an insight about women that most men do not have: her natural prowl instinct and fears it. He's an independent spirit that still wears the armour and remembers his code of conduct from having been disarmed by other women before me. It gets back to the woman's role from traditional cultures that influence her boys so much, she practically removes their ability to survive without her as adults – the caretaker's unconscious means of always being needed. In Charlie's case it's about his wife or his mother or women in general who are not aware of their instinct and let it roam and dominate their men, much like some men who still fuck around. Should he love a prototype like me there is risk of losing his independence and a sense of self? He has never known a woman who knows when and how to keep her prowl at bay. Therefore he has never known a woman who could and only would, share a life with a man at her side rather than above or below him. It's not about an aversion to responsibility, fidelity or sex. Charlie is all that, rather it is an aversion to the power of love that if not shared by way of equal parts may be used and abused like kryptonite to the souls and damage or weaken them to suffer. Charlie doesn't wish to suffer from loving a woman. It would kill him from inside, yet, yet, using cocaine as a scapegoat for his sentimentality, is like a love affair doing that to him anyway. The sensation to me is interpreted from a boy's heart but as a man of forty-four, such fear would be diminished albeit not vanquished to the facts of life and just another hurdle within the greater value of sharing love. Ok, so I might understand why he fears me or maybe he just doesn't like to be next to someone who can think like him? Certainly reduces the ability to hide clandestine thoughts or the truth about them. Regardless of Charlie's reasons I still perceived them as rejection. Like so many before him who insisted on their presence in my world even after I tried to politely resist them, and then succumbed to their plea only to be rejected after their self-pity, curiosity, sympathy or whatever it was they felt to satisfy by me, was achieved. People want to choose their warrior, not be chosen by one and I felt Charlie had chosen me. Above all, in his few moments of lucidity his instincts trusted me enough to decide on me for help. That if we are successful it will be because he'd decided to receive my involvement with him. Then I recognised a pattern reminiscent to my dad. In the wake of my parents' separation, my dad wanted and needed support and accepted mine. Yet at the time I was only twelve and similarly perhaps to Charlie, despite his need, the ego felt guilt for receiving my help not solely on the grounds of my age, but his greater love was still for my mother, the one who'd hurt him. Charlie's love might still be for his wife or more than likely for the image of what he would like them to be, in order to remove the sense of failure from the marriage and the portfolio of his life. It's a love reserved as a way of trying to deny the death of an ideal, rather than retaining the good from that vision and applying that reserved love to a similarly desired one but better selected. As a result I notice a stigma in me about the ones I love, that often feels appreciated but never wanted. Rather like a surrogate wife, mother and friend. So while Charlie still thinks about his wife or his "girlfriend", I remain something like a surrogate unsung girl-friend. Gawd intelligence kills, ignorance is bliss so where is my medium? I'm not always smart. I look at Charlie and I know that I am attracted to him. Hence chemistry is important to me because I have other complicated male friends who do not receive this level of attention from me. Being with an elusive sensitive man, who feels humbled by his emotional challenges, draws attention to my equally elusive nature and invites my insecurities about myself to unveil my weaknesses. My outer packaging as a person exudes a perception about me that is not a complete picture. Likewise I am aware of my product in its entirety and it's not perfect. The only men that I feel capable of unveiling this to, are those who have similar packaging on the outside by reason of attraction and chemistry, but more importantly to me is his personal product that might have weaknesses that are at par with mine, and a personal depth of sensitivity that can only come from a life tested by solitude. A kind of spiritual suffering that in turn generates a level of stamina and courage to weather the trials that are commonly present in a lifetime and strengthen a reciprocal need for complete emotional loyalty. It's "birds of a feather flock together." That and the natural need to feel wanted, to be "allowed in" because I can feel what's going on inside them and want their deference so that I can exchange my intimate needs too. Such that only the intensely healthy or emotionally complicated man will choose me, albeit for a limited time only, while the other man is intimidated by a woman who seems so well equipped that she doesn't appear to need him or fit the caretaker's role. Sigh. The modern woman is a product of circumstance it doesn't mean that she has lost her nature to nurture. "Men want to marry their mothers"* — *Hello? All women are mothers. Plus, these days, the fact that a woman doesn't cook can actually give a man room to feel needed by cooking for me, because he can manage physical concepts of providing better than the emotional ones. Hence, I think of Charlie who cooks for me; I want him to get out of his well. I want to know if we have a chance, or if he may know love with someone before he dies. Maybe without the cocaine the rest of his qualities will still refuse the need for love, but at least he will have known the beautiful side of its power ...* We finally sifted out of the wave of bodies and into a quiet solitary street. Garbage was strewed along the way or blowing lightly above the pavement like miniature typhoons. Elisabet and Mitx had fallen into step with each other and to my surprise Charlie had fallen back into mine. 'Charlie,' I asked, 'do you trust me?' My question was sent out while I kept my eyes focused on the street before me and noticed its black asphalt glistening slightly from the damp night air. 'I don't know,' he replied. My heart sank a bit, but I welcomed the candid answer. After everything I'd done, what did he or a man need to trust a woman? Most of all what did she need to trust herself? 'Charlie,' I continued.

'What?' he said lightly.

'Close your eyes.'

'What?' He repeated.

'Close your eyes,' I insisted gently. We stopped in our tracks briefly while he contemplated me for a moment and then closed his eyes.

'Now what?' he said. 'Now, I just want you to follow my instructions to the car. Don't open your eyes ok. Trust me,' I said hopefully. A beautiful smirk went across his face. I was not guaranteed that he'd keep his eyes closed until we got to the car, but his effort to humour me was appreciated. So we started to walk again side by side while I prompted him on where to step. I didn't touch him so that he could adapt the distortion from his blind perspective to the space around him and my voice. 'I don't like not knowing where I'm going,' he said.

'But you know that we're going to the car?' I queried.

'Yea, but I don't like being mandated you know.'

'Hmm,' I listened, 'but if you can't see and choose your help, then you are still directing your destiny – no?' I offered.

'I suppose,' he contemplated.

'I guess the risk, like in anything – go left, O.K., is whether or not your choice was a good one..,' I said.

We were coming up to a puddle in the middle of the street. The obvious way around it was via the sidewalk, but it meant initiating a few complicated moves to the curve, up onto the sidewalk, and down again which I did not think Charlie had the patience for. Then again, going through it wasn't going to please him either. I was suddenly faced with a decision to make a choice for him or end the experiment. 'Charlie stop for a moment and please don't open your eyes yet ok?' I pleaded slightly. 'Whaaat now?' he stopped. I felt his impatience and could tell that he was going to open his eyes any minute, if not already. 'Listen, there's a puddle ahead –,' he opened his eyes. 'Charlie!' I said like an exasperated child, 'listen to my instructions carefully...' I emphasized... He closed them again after having taken a look at the puddle, smiled and said: 'Okay.' This time as we approached the curve, I found myself struggling against taking his arm and physically directing him, because I wanted to see how well I could communicate his way past the puddle. We managed to get to the sidewalk, although I'm sure he peeked a few times. Then we were just about to complete our mission when Mitx and Elisabet asked from a far, 'What are you doing?' simultaneously with the passing of a noisy motorbike that involuntarily splashed the puddle over to us. That was enough for Charlie whose eyes flew open at the same time as he sent out a few sacrilegious words at the motorbike. I actually felt frustrated. Like I had been impeded from fulfilling my task with Charlie and unable to show him the merit of his trust. Even if his choice in me might have been a good one, there was no guarantee that I could help him and above all, that he was going to hang in there with me. I could follow through with the swing, but the simple example of the interruption said to me that factors beyond my control were going to challenge me more that Charlie and his relationship with the cocaine.

'What?' he said as we walked on to catch up with Mitx and Elisabet.

'Nothing,' I said, 'you didn't like it huh?' I added casually.

'Well not much, and you – what? Is it that you like directing people?' It was a candid stab, but I turned to face him and gave him a polite smile: 'Okay. You direct me now.'

He didn't reply, but I knew he liked the idea, so I closed my eyes. I was instantly filled with trepidation. Charlie wasn't about to play nursemaid with me and that was unsettling. I told myself to walk boldly and just give him the opportunity to see my trust in him. I walked as straight as I could while he said nothing.

'Charlie? – How am I doing?'

'Fine,' he answered nonchalantly. The apathy in his tone was disconcerting.

'What Charlie? You have to indicate if I'm going wrong!' As if he needed to be reminded. I put my hands out front of me and kept going until I began to feel silly and alone in the game. I opened my eyes still feeling slightly distorted from my attempts at blind faith. We were almost at the car and Charlie was over a bit to my right. I wasn't heading into anything, but I was straying off the wrong way.

'What? Were you just going to let me walk off?' I asked as I joined his side again.

'I knew you'd open your eyes,' he replied.

'Anyway, to answer your question,' I dismissed his answer, 'some businesses send their staff on retreats to do these kinds of team building activities. They're supposed to promote group trust and self-confidence,' I added calmly. 'I don't trust myself or anyone – you know. So why would anyone trust me?' he said directly.

'True,' I contended.

I waited a split minute wondering on whether or not I should go on with my ideas. I mean, I really don't know shit about shit, then again, he only knew shit about shit, so I turned my glance over to him: 'But Charlie?..,' I began, 'I'm sorry, but you do trust yourself because you still prefer to make your own decisions, while you chose your help and we're on Day 6, okay. Plus you haven't deceived yourself at all nor me for that matter. Rather you're just having a hard time in being sincere with yourself because the cocaine, a.k.a., your "girlfriend", doesn't make it easy for you and I'm not trying to kiss your ass, but it's just a fact that's all,' I said candidly. 'Besides Charlie,' I continued, 'I wanted you to get the sensation of trusting a woman whose only motive was to get you past the puddle, while I wanted to know what I needed to trust *myself* with you,' I finished rather passionately.

'Shall we go?' said Mitx as we caught up to them by the car. Once we got into the car and headed home. I stared out the car window at the stars. It occurred to me then, that my game had taught me a lesson and not Charlie. He knew that I would open my eyes. He had enough faith in my self-preservation to let me wander off from him and trust myself before trusting him. He had been right. Was it that his childhood experience nurtured him too much and fed his need to live and let live to the point of total detachment? Guide someone too much and it reduces that one's self confidence. Guide not at all and that one's self confidence grows to the point of finding oneself alone. I realised too, or maybe again that what I needed in order to trust my commitment to Charlie was his trust in me, to keep the faith in me, alive.

Only change is constant – HERACLITUS.

Home

January 18

Day 8: *Upbeat in the morning and waiting for me when I went to meet him at his place.*

Gym, then we cleaned his place together: several months of laundry, three to four boxes of juice and whisky bottles, three garbage bags from the kitchen, floors washed, sheets changed and added to wash; clean bedding with new flannel sheets from his mother, shirts sent to the cleaners, fridge laden with open containers, overripe fruit and vegetables, food with fur on it, cleaned out! A zillion un-rinsed dishes, several pots and pans with baked bottoms caked-in rice and noodle sauces, cups, utensils, dirty stagnant water in the sink from weeks gone by all cleaned and rinsed by Charlie. Stove top, oven, wall area and counter surface smeared and sticky from fried oil – cleaned. Dining table cleared from porno films, CD cases matched with CDs, books and language supplies organised, cigarette ashes, food crumbs and dust balls swept and mopped in TV area. Large sliding bay windows to the sea view, lightly cleaned. Bathrooms with vomit and urine residue around the bowl and toilet seat cleaned and sterilized. Bathtub covered in dust – wiped clean, dust balls on linoleum floor swept-up, dank towels changed, empty sundry products thrown away and purchased a few mini floor heaters in Can Colom. His place is now a warm and cosy place to be. Charlie told me it was the first time he'd ever done that? Other times waitresses from

Sa Croix, or his seventy-six year old mum did the cleaning for him? Gawd.

Day 9: Sms Mc – *"Hi C. Please get up for Palma now. Mxx."* Up-beat. Craving very strong, though humour was good then at night, had our first confrontation.

Had Indian dinner in Palma. First time for Charlie, and I was impressed that he tried. Food didn't sit well with him though, or the whisky that he drank at a friend of mine's house that we briefly visited afterwards. It caused him to get anxious and unpleasant towards me. Said a whole bunch of bullshit to me in the car especially when he was getting ready to drop me off at my place. He wanted his keys and things and I said it might not be a good idea. We only have twelve days to go. Then he tried to change his tone to a sweet plea and I had to deny it just as quietly. Then he revved and drove the car abruptly from my front door, to the first street, turned right on two wheels, then again aggressively but miscalculated, and went right over a curve causing us both to ricochet within the car's interior and damaging the transmission to the extent that it's now hanging under the car near the front left tire. I'd grabbed the safety handle over my head and said nothing. Then when he'd parked the car outside of his place, it was like nothing had happened between us that I wondered if we had just experienced that thirty-minute crave rage? Needless to say the he didn't feel good about himself after that. I was going to walk home, but he was okay for me to stay over. So I did. Put his car keys and phone on the dining room table, praying that he wouldn't run off with them and went to his bedroom to sleep. The TV's light flickering off the glass door in the hall kept me aware of him on the sofa with the porno films he watched in mute mode all night. Then, I heard the TV, him walking back and forth between the fridge door and the sofa, the click sound of his gas lighter on and off for a cigarette, the belching from the heart burn in his stomach or the nose blowing in the bathroom. Finally at seven a.m., he joined me in bed and tried to hold me from behind in a heavy blundering sort of way. Like he'd forgotten the comfort zone and left the twelve year old in him to try, but whose action was nothing less than what a young boy might experience with an older woman: awkwardness. Either that, or a thought of impropriety, despite the amount of infidelity in his marriage, badgers his sense of propriety. Still, I was happy for the affection even though he hadn't felt comforted by it. So many options for him and he chooses none.

Day10: Sms Mc – *"Hi. Am having a coffee next door. Go slow. Mx."* 10 days clean! Gym. Sa Croix for lunch.

Hung out at his place in the afternoon – him on the sofa me in the Ikea chair. I like these moments. We don't do much. I read or write and he watches TV, naps, smokes a cigarette, gazes out at the sea and occasionally offers the odd commentary. I just sit there enjoying the solitude of my moment with a man I somehow enjoy having next to me. Verbal communication is not important and I consciously relish this synergy without words. Like an aged relationship that has mellowed with time and that's trials and tribulations have rendered two people synonymous with each other. We have hardly had the trials or the tribulations to merit such a feeling of comfort, yet it is there. Perhaps it is not about each other but about loneliness? Maybe we just feed from each other's presence to fill that quiet void within us? I often hear the Beatles' song: "... So many lonely people, where do they all come from?" Charlie feels alone because of his addiction and I feel alone because I am. It's a sin to feel this way when I am loved by my family and those who call my name. There is something to be said about having one's own family. The sense of ownership seems to promote a false sense of worth and added value to the already fading ones because there is a power of self-esteem that enjoys being the important individual in the eyes of those that the individual is permitted to control. Like running one's own company and having the privileges of being one's own boss and the example to others who look to the boss for guidance. It lasts as long as the business goes well or until one gets tired of the responsibility and perpetual maintenance of it, or until the employees begin to think for themselves and also leave to start off on their own. Funny, I have ambition, but no desire to open up my own business and manage a staff. Wonder if that coincides with my being single? Professionally I have managed large teams. I usually try to hire the best employees with the understanding that they will eventually leave by virtue of their free and professional spirits. So my work area often runs on adapting to change. However as a caretaker I am involved and domineering to an excessive ability that intimidates my desire to be a mother or companion to someone. If I could instil within me, the emotional detachment that I exercise with my staff I would not burden my loved ones so much. Both areas of my life receive the freedom of being, but my loved ones get too much of me. Ironically to care for them with the same emotional detachment that I apply in my professional work would handicap my demonstrative ability to love and feel loved. Should a loved one and the family unit therefore be treated and managed like a professional economic community? Seems to work in Mayürqa, in Britain with a stiff upper lip, military families, Japan's traditional honour system, countries where war, and oppression have been felt. Love is not talked about, it's just there. Canada would be the young country with the innocence of a child that loves openly because it has been blessed with a childhood without war or oppression? A place where its multicultural personality has enabled older traditional cultures within it to influence its upbringing congruent with how grandparents enrich a family unit's character to being sensitive and pensive with life's volatility? In all cases, balance between sentimentality and impartiality is maintained with a heavier kilter on displaying indifference. Charlie and I sit next to each other in this way, playing with a greater air of emotional neutrality. Should I change the rules and let the child in me express something stronger our balance would fall completely off-kilter. When I looked out of the large bay windows from his place, the sea was thick and heavy in grey and white foamy waves, and I was reminded again of "Puff the magic dragon". Being an adult is only supposed to be about attaining maturity in order to express and receive love, not about how to deny it. Philosophies tell adults to grow old with a young heart yet when they do they're told to grow up? No wonder the world is not yet "a better place to be". Charlie spoke: 'What?' He said to me as he looked up from his extended lying position on the sofa and tapped the ashes of his cigarette into an ashtray. I smiled, happy for the break in silence: 'Noth'n … what?' I returned. '"¡Se hace camino al andar!"', '"The way is made walking!",' he suddenly declared while he swooped his right hand to his mouth and puffed from his cigarette.

'Who said that?' I asked.

'Antonio Machado.'

'Hmm,' I said. We'd have these moments when he would suddenly show signs of intellectual lucidity. I was attracted to them. They stimulated my own capability to reciprocate them. They often came just before he got negative and headed down from the sudden buzz. 'What's your interpretation of that?' I asked. He puffed from his tobacco and crossed his right arm over his left one, still staring out at the sea. 'I don't know... It makes sense. What do you think?' He then turned his weight onto his left side, looked over to me with a smile, put out his butt and began to cover himself with the flannel blanket. 'Just do it, I suppose. The rest will fall into place. If you don't move or try the Way won't expand or improve,' I pondered.

'And if you don't walk —What?' he asked delighted with our mental match.

'Things will walk without you and leave you behind. It's the law of nature. Everything changes,' I said with a matter of fact tone, 'so why not be the guide of your own tour?'

'Maybe I like the tour that I have now,' he answered, 'and don't want to change it.'

'Yea, true, but you answered your own question. Everything changes. Whether or not one goes ahead of the rest, or behind the rest, or along with the rest is based on the individual's circumstance. Eventually, you will walk and your Way will appear,' I summed up: 'I think one just needs to decide on which Way one wants to walk.' Pause. 'Why do you prefer being in a well than in a garden?' I asked, 'it's like you're more comfortable with dark and cold than light and warm?'

'I don't know,' he replied, 'it's more sincere – I suppose.'

I quickly remembered a scene from the movie "Pretty Woman" when Julia Roberts tells Richard Gere that it's easier to believe negative criticism from people than compliments because people use the truth as a tool to hurt. 'The truth only scars when it comes from anger not compassion,' I said, 'and just because something is said to be negative or positive doesn't mean that it is. I mean sincerity depends on the source of its intension – no?'

'The thing is…,' he added, 'you for example are the best thing to come into my life… Yet I don't work to keep you .., or want you, you know? … I have a scar on my head from an ashtray my wife threw at my head, but I still think about her. I'm in this shit when I don't have to be. It's like good doesn't attract me or grab my attention … I don't know – I'm fucked up here yea know.' He tapped his forehead with the palm of his right hand while he balanced a new cigarette between his fingers. 'You don't want me because you think that you have me. Possibly you think of your wife because she has ignored and verbally abused you – it's like you're conditioned to negative responses and your obsessive ego is attracted to the hunt of getting her attention, like you were when you'd first met me. What you don't understand is that my presence in your life is more sincere than that of your family or your wife's Charlie. I don't believe in you in order to kiss your ass and I don't have a family obligation to be here with you. It's friendship Charlie. That's all. My feelings towards you are my problem and to your benefit. I tell you what I see based on my experience with you and what you have delivered to me. Maybe in time this will change when you start to challenge my sense of integrity or when I am fed up with your indifference. Who knows! However, the only difference between being with me in a garden and being with the rest in your well, is that I know how to criticise constructively without hurting you and you are not used to that nor do you know how to recognise it, let alone trust it. I am the first to tell you to piss off, but only when you really deserve it, and not because I am interested in stimulating your hunting instincts in order to provoke your attention towards me or anyone else for that matter. Your addiction makes you an easier target to manipulate, Charlie. The ones who do are not sincere with you. They are taking advantage of your insecurities, including your "girlfriend" that will do anything to avoid your ability to live in a garden with me. Anyway Charlie, I think you refuse me because it's too much work for you. It's a great place, but it needs care by your hidden qualities as a man. It's like the boy in you actually doesn't want the garden for that reason. He prefers the well where it's easier to live, but wishes you'd leave the cocaine out of it. If you can live in the well without your relationship with cocaine then you're set. That's all. Get through this month with me, get rehab and go from there. Yea know.' I ended my speech. Charlie was standing by the glass windows by then and said nothing … 'Shall we go?' he asked. Our session between the sofa and chair was over. I might have said too much or maybe just enough, but it did something to his insides. 'I'm used to being alone, yea know. I've never even had a woman spend so much time in my car. Your presence irritates me, or I don't know – I feel tied by your presence.' 'I know,' I said, 'plus the feeling is magnified with the task of being together 24/7. That and my presence perturbs your cravings for the cocaine. You want to do something bad or unethical and can't under my vigilance. It frustrates and provokes you more. Any other situation I'd let you be, because it makes my task harder being with you so much, but you said that the cocaine deceives you even when you don't want to be. The crux to the addiction is that you need to be reminded or inhibited from following the craving. The point to this month was about that – remember? Sigh. Your presence isn't always enjoyed either yea know. We knew this would happen Charlie. Listen, I don't need to continue if you don't think that we should try anymore.'

'It's that I don't want to hurt you or vice versa you know…,' he said.

'I don't want us to lose our friendship over this either,' I agreed. Pause. I was sitting up, at the edge of the couch, in a matter-of-fact position with my legs apart and my hands clasped and set between them, looked at him directly and said: 'If you want, I'll just give you the English classes and that's it. I'll go home now. No big deal. We tried, did ten days and fine.' He was standing in front of me with his hands in his pockets. He wasn't sure about anything. Emotions probably debated with fear. I felt a twinge of guilt too, because even my words manipulated in some shape or form. I did not want to say so much. I just wanted to be by his side and let him do the rest. 'Shall we go?' he said again, and we went on our way. While we walked to his car, Charlie came up behind me and hugged-walked with me for a few yards. I reciprocated by squeezing back until he let go and walked beside me. I kept my left hand hooked to his back right pocket for a bit longer until we were in view of the Phedra, and then I let go.

Later: He has arranged to meet a good friend for lunch in Palma tomorrow. The friend has a wife and kids and no drug history at all. – I can't go with him. They haven't seen each other in a while and my presence would be like that of a wet-nursemaid. Charlie told me about him one day when we somehow got into a talk about his relationship with his wife. He's been out of their house for a bit over a year now. Apparently the friend was one of his partners from when Sa Croix first opened and was around when things between Charlie and his wife got ugly. Then when Charlie left their house, he took a few bags with him that for reasons still unclear to him contained a few of his wife's belongings, and asked his friend to keep them because Charlie didn't think his place was safe enough. Apparently things have gone missing or been moved around at his place in his absence? He seems to have an incredible hang up about the bags. Contempt mixed with guilt. So I suggested that we at least pick them up. He doesn't have to look at them, but at least getting them would be a start in his new direction –no? The friend has had the bags for almost two years and Charlie doesn't have a clue anymore about what's in them. Anyway, much like the cocaine debt we paid off and the organising of his car and home, the bags are on the same To Do List. Sigh. Tomorrow, he'll get some and I won't try to stop him. Frankly while he lives in Mayūrqa he can't get past it and nor does he want to. I will have to re-locate myself again emotionally and physically. He's not focused, does what he wants, and it's too frustrating for me physically. He's not affectionate enough although he alludes to it. Miss Jes of course and wonder if there was ever a man? Wonder *what* am I doing here? Then like Jes used to, Charlie gets rebellious, closed-up and non-communicative. Since the confrontation last night he's not the same with me. Whatever. W*hy* bring him into my life? All the potential is there for him, like Jes, but they don't and won't. Again, whatever. Carles is going to fade away soon, I think. Unless there is hope, and we make it to rehab? My savings and things from Canada have yet to arrive. Internet now works, but my computer doesn't. Murphy's Law? To learn a lesson? To change my patterns? Or to help? I need to work now… Or Life knows better and is stalling things for me because of a bigger picture that I can not see yet? *Be* with Charlie is what I *feel* – why? What? I don't know. TBA.

Day 11: Friday January 21– Damn it, damn it, damn it!
I saw it coming at the gym when he went outside for a smoke instead of just doing it inside the building like he normally does. The no-smoking laws here are not official yet.

I wondered then but said nothing, so as not to infringe on our code of trust. Instead I watched his body language and it seemed to me that he was contemplating on whether or not to do something erroneous. He made a phone call and I suspected it was to his friend. He came back inside and I said nothing. My gut reaction was kept at bay with chains, while I tried to edit my lines from so much paranoia. Charlie's car was in the shop and wasn't going to be ready until that night, so we'd gone to the gym in the Mini. When we got into the car I asked him for his friend's telephone number. 'What you don't trust me?' he accused while he searched his cell for the number. 'Charlie, respect my motives please,' I said in Spanglish. 'Besides, I don't trust "her",' I said coolly. We headed to Sa Croix where I understood that he was meant to meet his friend for lunch, but Charlie corrected that assumption and said that he was going to be picked up at the office in Juniper. I said nothing while my internal alarms rang high. I dropped him off at the office and saw no sign of another car, or his friend. 'I'll wait for him inside,' he said. 'Oh, ok,' I said, 'I guess you'll call me when you guys are back?' 'I'll call you,' he replied, gave me a kiss and left. The kiss should have been enough to convince me to follow my fear and secretly spy on him from behind a tree or something. At least wait until I saw him get picked up by his friend. 'Hard to hide a yellow Mini behind a tree,' I said to myself followed by a stunted laugh. I drove away from the office and back around to the street parallel with the office and stopped. I wasn't decided what to do. Just drive away and let it all follow its course or make an effort to avoid a breakdown? I was seriously vexed. '*What was my hard line of conduct and involvement?*' I asked myself. My role was to help him get through a month clean. Our effort up until then had completed a tough 24 hours on 7, for a solid ten days clean. Plus it was only going to get tougher and to the point when my presence would be needed most. '"When the going gets tough, the tough get going",' I mused to myself. Then I thought, *fourteen years or more that his friends and family let him run his own course and look where it got him? If I don't intervene then in essence I will have failed the warrior duty that I've assigned to myself. All this time will have been for nada. Yet, if I drive around to check up on him, then I am invading our code of trust and if I am wrong maybe harming further trust between us down the road. If he sees me? – Wouldn't he understand my predicament and empathise with my concern? He didn't when I asked him for his friend's number – why? Was he reacting to something he's going to do and shouldn't...? It's not about Charlie's effort. It's about the addiction, the "girlfriend" that overpowers him. If I am wrong he'll be mad at me for not trusting him. If I don't follow my gut and he falls off the bike, then I will have failed his need for me to think for both of us. However, if I drive around that corner because I know he'll take otherwise, then I will also stimulate co-addictive behaviour in me and evidently end up in the well with him...* Charlie said he was going for lunch and would call me. He didn't wait with me in the car and kissed me before he left. Jes used to do that, when he knew that he was going to do something against our better wishes. Like a son trying to find peace with himself by being in his mother's good graces just before he did something erroneous and premeditated. Charlie can do whatever he wants. Likewise so can I. There are no rules of conduct when we are talking about drug abuse. Ethical behaviour adapts to the circumstance. Whether it be considered dubious or a result of situational ethics the fact of the matter is the cocaine is bad for him. It will kill him if something isn't tried or done. I choose to be here for that reason. In this case, I'm the voice telling him to "eat your vegetables" sort of thing. Everyone else has told him including his mother. If I get into his face too much my voice of reason will fall onto deaf ears like that of his family's, but if I say nothing then what the hell is the point to all this in the first place? When the child resists and says "no", the parent remains steadfast and says "yes": no idle threats. If Charlie wants this small and mighty machine to stop then he needs to tell me that he wants me too. That he prefers to stay in the well and I'll turn off automatically. Until then? Face *Charly*! In deference to myself and my own sense of peace of mind, I have to do something without over-reacting... '*Meet him half way then.*' So I sent his friend and him a sms: "Hey guys – 10 days! – Charlie, don't let it beat you." I sent the message in a way that Charlie would understand and his friend might get the gist to protect our interests. I started the car again and drove to Palma using the exit by the office and gave a quick look down the road behind me. Nothing except Poplar trees. I left the Mini in Palma for a check-up and took the train back to Sichus where a girlfriend was waiting to pick me up. Then after we hung out for a bit I asked her to drop me off at the Lancia dealership. I knew that Charlie was meant to pick up his car by six o'clock closing time. He hadn't called me yet, so I took a chance in getting there before or by the time he got there. Once we got there, I saw his car in the garage and told my friend not to wait for me. As I walked into the building I saw Charlie in the process of dialling a number which turned out to be mine. So far he was following a reasonable code of conduct towards me. 'Hi,' I said, 'I'm right behind you.'

'What are you doing here?' he asked coolly.

'Gabi dropped me off – I saw your car.' He had a right to be angry or suspicious, but he wasn't, all to the contrary. I felt guilty for not having given him the full hundred yards. We went to Sa Croix, had a nice dinner out and headed home. I took his keys and phone and decided to sleep at my place. Don't ask why. I probably wanted to give him back some of the yardage I'd denied him earlier that day. Duuuh.

Day 1: Saturday January 22 – Getting back on the bike.
He was at a low. Even the date 22 suggests his number twice over and stronger than its sum of my confident number 4.

What does that mean? That this is a hopeless cause – the weight of my success with him is undermined by the strength of his addiction? He did the porn videos, whisky and five grams of coke last night. He bought the coke yesterday with the help from one rep supplier for Sa Croix!? Apparently his friend had rescheduled yesterday's lunch to Monday. That was the phone call from the gym. I suppose he decided not to tell me and took advantage of the chance. I failed his test. He knows he can trick me at any time. Thing is, I knew and I was feeling bad for not having given him enough yards!?! After I left him at the office in Juniper he called someone from Sa Croix to pick him up. Took money from the till and had the rep drive him to a bar-restaurant in Campos village to buy the stuff. The rep ought to be reported to the supply company for being an accomplice to the purchase! Needless to say, I felt sincerely discouraged when he told me. It was 11:30a.m., when I'd gone over to his place today, to go to the gym. I knocked on the front door a few times without any response from inside. I knew where the extra key was hidden, but I had reserved the right to use it for emergencies only. I waited a bit more. He was probably out cold or just ignoring me or maybe not? What if I went home when he could have had a brain clot? What was worse? Guilt of entering his home uninvited – literally trespassing, or him dead because I was worried about respecting his privacy? '*This is no regular situation,*' I thought. So I went for the key and opened the door ever so slightly and said: 'Charlie? Are you here?' I heard the quick movement of a loose belt buckle, and the couch squeak then saw erotic images quickly disappear into a blue screen and Charlie's voice: 'Whaat?' 'It's me – I used your key. You didn't answer my messages, so I wasn't sure..,' I said nervously and edged in a bit further. The room carried the scent of his manhood and the permanently stale tobacco one in the air, while he was on the sofa where he'd been all night. Half dressed in his clothes from the day before, jeans below his mid-section, naked butt to the air, shirt hanging out, TV on standby blue mode, cigarette ashes all over the linoleum floor with a whisky glass next to the foot of the couch where he laid and the sea view had been removed by closed shutters against the bay windows. When I saw the evidence of a white powder caked into the wood of the little table next to him, my whole being inside, dropped like an iron weight in water. I truly felt ashamed and embarrassed. Yet I did not feel wrong. Had he just sent a quick "O.K." to my sms I would have gone home knowing that he was alive. 'Carles – I'm *really* sorry... I didn't mean to invade your intimacy,' my voice was hardly audible. I felt sick from the embarrassment that I'd caused him. It was his place – what the hell was I doing there!? His eyes were bloodshot with an intense perturbed look yet he said nothing to me. I was so annoyed with myself and disappointed and tormented for not having been over the top and parked my Mini behind a tree in Juniper. I just wanted to go back in time. Another chance to make day eleven clean. It was like being on a team where one member really wanted to try hard to win and the other wasn't trying hard enough. In spite of the fact that it's Charlie's addiction, getting him through a month of detox, or far enough towards some coherence to receive proper help, has also become my mission. I can't worry or include weak players in our game – just do my best. Until he tells me otherwise, I will assume that he still wants to get better and that my methods to help him get there, don't have to include his blessing. If there are consequences contrary to our friendship or my health, it will have been my choice. However I intend to win or lose, feeling satisfied. I watched him as he pulled his jeans up to his mid-section while he remained lying flat on his stomach. Then let his right leg hang from the couch onto the floor with his head buried deep into a malleable cushion. 'What happened,' I asked calmly. No reply. 'At least tell me how I failed you,' I asked plainly. 'When you left me alone in Juniper, I thought you were testing me, you know,' he droned accusingly into the pillow. 'At the gym, you accused me of not trusting you and told me that your friend was coming,' I said soberly. 'Yea, that's why I thought you left me on purpose; to see if you were right,' he replied. The tone in my voice remained quiet and level: 'Why would I want you to relapse Charlie? Please don't throw your guilt from your own sensation of disgust at me – I am already mad at myself for trusting you with your devious "girlfriend" and not my gut feeling to watch you like a hawk. Now I know better. This was a good trial run. Do we keep trying?' No reply. My approach was intended to avoid direct conflict with him by making the culprit the cocaine. 'Charlie?' I insisted lightly. He moved his head out from the pillow in an attempt to wipe his face on it, but was not entirely successful in removing the evidence of tears and snot that had slightly been smeared to the left of his nose. He sat up with a dishevelled look, found his tissue and blew his nose into it. Then stood up and went to the kitchen. Drank juice, instigated belches from his abdomen, went to pee and came back to the TV room: 'I'm going to bed. Let's talk later.' His tone was cordial. In hindsight, he had been incredibly patient with me. 'Ok,' I said, 'I'm taking the car keys and phone, and will come back later.' I was no longer asking, simply informing him. He closed the bedroom door behind him and let me leave without further comment. I went back to his place by 12:30p.m., and sent him a sms before I got there, asking if I could let myself into his place. Waited at his door a few minutes and finally got a reply, "O.K." His room was dark with the curtains to the bedroom window closed and a blanket tucked over top of them. He was on his back buried under the covers up to chest level, with the same black t-shirt he'd been wearing for the past 24hrs, his left arm was out and draped across his forehead with his watch and a few rings still on his left hand. The room entertained a light body odour from Charlie's warm body temperature soaked slightly into the flannel blankets. He had obviously been sleeping heavily and I marvelled again at his ability to even answer my sms. I stood in the doorway.

'Hey, can you get up?' I asked.

'For what?' he muffled past his left arm that had moved down to the mid-section of his face.

'It's a beautiful day; maybe sweat a bit on the tennis court – found a good place in Ca'n Colom,' I said optimistically. He exhaled deeply through his mouth, moved side to side a bit with great effort and no desire. 'I'm tired,' he said. It was like watching a man under kryptonite or under the influence of a very heavy magnet; all he had to do was make a clean break from the bed. 'What time is it?' he asked.

'One o'clock,' I guesstimated.

'Michèle I don't feel like it okay.'

'C'mon Charlie...,' I whispered to him, 'I know you can do it. Just for a bit. Get some fresh air, we don't even have to do anything. At least go outside a little.' I wasn't asking, rather suggesting, because I didn't want to feel like his decisions were to please me. Pause. I stood there waiting. Then I moved in and sat on the edge of the bed next to him… 'Charlie?' I whispered again. I felt like Dasha when she comes up to my bed and pokes her nose at my feet, then moves up to my head level and rests her brown muzzle on the bed; her brown eyes completely intent on me, while she sits there and just waits with controlled anticipation for a sign of life from me... I waited. Then, 'Okay, I'll get up in five minutes alright...'

'Great,' I replied and went to the TV room to give him space. He actually got up and we drove to C'an Colom. We even managed to hit a few tennis balls together. He stood at the middle of the base line, racket in hand, wearing black shades, long track pants and the same black t-shirt. He reminded me of Dan Akroid in the Blues Brothers. I simply hit the tennis balls as close to him as possible so that he wouldn't have to run too much. I didn't want to push my luck. I had already been insistent in persuading him to get up, then get outside, followed by a suggestion to drive to C'an Colom and then finally, to try the rackets that were at the back of the car. He was really low, irritable and sluggish from the drug abuse and in no mood for anything. I think his willingness to humour me was to get me off his back so that he could sleep later. While we managed to hit a few balls I felt pangs of guilt. The man was feeling like shit and I'd managed to coerce him to get some fresh air and sweat for a bit. Had it been me with the slightest ache in my head there would have been no approaching me. I am a real suck. Even Jes was formidable in getting up to do morning coffee with me after a full night out of drinking! I could have left Charlie in bed, but the fact that we were there, said to me that Charlie was a fighter too. He just needed help.

Later: Sweating was good for him. He felt calmer and sleepy. Slept, up and down from bed, between 4p.m. and 6:30p.m. Evening though very irritable, shared some dark conversation with him on the sofa and me in the chair: 'I'm tired of them watching me you know..,' he said with a dark look across his face. 'Who?' I asked while nonchalantly watching the TV commercials.

'I don't like being made a fool, and I'm tired of being alone – you know.'

'Are we talking about the people around here or the night clubs?' I asked more interested.

'I like watching their reactions you know – the *reactions*..,' he emphasised as he turned over onto his left side to put out his butt and looked me in the eyes, letting the 'r' in reactions roll off his tongue. 'Charlie,' I said, 'I'm not sure who we're talking about, but that's why you want to get out of the well and take control of your life again. It doesn't matter what people think as long as you are clear about what you are doing.' There was no point in rationalising with a man on the verge of another major craving, but it made for conversation. At 9:30p.m., he actually made an appearance at the Saint Antoni bonfires in our town and lit up like a peacock when three women from Juniper village approached him. One of them is recently divorced and has been sending him a lot of suggestive sms to his cell phone. She has short red hair and is rather butch looking, but Charlie enjoys the attention. Apparently she told him that word had been going around the village that he took 2,000 euros from Sa Croix and that his brother was really pissed off at him. It's the same woman who'd asked him who the blond was only a day after our first coffee together. I'm not sure what troubles me most? Her attempt at taking advantage of his ego and addiction in order to get his attention, or the fact that he is gullible and actually listens to her obvious attempts to provoke everything except positive energy? Where are his parameters? Loyalties? I was not enough. I was not even in a different category from the rest, in spite of my actions and motives. Unbelievable. After an hour, we drove the youngest of Belle's boys to the village next door then returned home to his place. I took his keys and things and went home to get Dasha. Then walked her back over to his place where I stayed up until 2a.m., which is when the need to go out usually subsides. When I arrived, Charlie was already in bed. I checked in on him from behind his bedroom door. Cold pockets of air found my body while I stood there feeling calm by the sounds of his snoring and the rattle of the floor heaters. He was somewhere in a deep sleep and I wondered where? 'Gooo Charlie, go,' I exhaled, '... good night.' I left his car keys and phone on the table, then returned home with Dasha.

Day 2: *Charlie slept until 11:30am.*

Day 3: *Palma – lunch with his friend. Got the bags. Drank wine, irritable. Slept ok, night ok.*

6:45p.m. Charlie's place: cold, wet and windy outside. The rain hits the wide bay windows with anger. The sea is out there. I can't see it from where I am sitting, but I can hear its roar. It moves with anxiety in rhythm with my own. I also hear the rattle of the small floor heaters, three in total in the TV room, yet it is still cool in here. I am not badly off; the writing helps. Charlie is on the sofa, now awake. How long I don't know. Maybe the TV will go on, maybe we'll have another challenge of spirits for and against his desire to get some "snow". I am already fed-up or tired of this. I don't see hope for Charlie to make it with only my time and spirit involved. He needs to live outside of Mayürqa for a while which he won't do. He drank with his friend at lunch today and retrieved the bags he was supposed to get the other day. When I picked him up in Palma he was very negative towards me. I suppose the act of meeting him and his friend in a service lane off the highway in order to drive him home was patronizing for him. Still, it's one more thing to check off the list of small accomplishments. He hasn't seen those bags in two years! He has a real emotional hang up about them so now it is just a matter of going through them and returning them to his wife. The unravelling of that past will hopefully close it and allow him to discover his future at the same time. The real battles have yet to begin. I don't know. So what now? – let him go. Yes. I just thought that if he tried to do a month here before deciding back on Barcelona he'd feel better about his choices. Barcelona is very expensive and things did not work the first time. Besides his problems are here: wife, son, money, misguided relationships and the bells – bells everywhere. Though, he's not well and does need to be clearer before he can reflect on things. Go out and come back? Even without the coke he's not entirely well. Who is? In or out of the well he won't be happy. Then again will I? Funny how life is. He has it all and will never be alone even with cocaine, yet has little ability to feel satiated. Why? Because he did not choose the gifts. His loving someone and the sharing of his gifts have to be his choice. Such that, his wedding, the arrival of his son, as well as the presence of his family by right of blood lineage were to a large degree in his life in a tacit manner. Only his work, his relationships with people and even me, are by his choice. While cocaine, prostitutes and life by night is where he goes in order to escape the influences and vigilance of those who care about him. Where he can do what he wants without someone judging him and because it runs polar from that conservative presence which tends to restrict and coddle him at the same time. Sigh. It is hard not to be taken by the tide of its influence: the currents of social imposition, family guilt issues and naive sentimentality can inhibit one's self confidence and delay one's truth. Factors that genuinely insist to exist through a method of imposition by being self-appointed protagonists of an individual's life but yet, can, at the same time also deflect and or impede that life's desired way. Trying to avoid them or even politely resist them therefore often causes the individual to manifest an inner sensation of emotional blackmail and or guilt. Still, "no one is a victim" and there is integrity in selecting the people we want in our lives. Such that the blunder is neither Charlie's behaviour nor the level of immaturity in his relationships, rather the way he manages them. Too much *tan mateix, laissez-faire*, letting it be, go unchecked. Balance. All he needs to do is respect the man between Carles and Charlie ... Then again, don't we all?

Day 4: Tuesday January 25 – *Snow in Mayūrqa. He was up by 11a.m., down and depressed. Allowing stories in his head to affect him. Did the gym. The divorced woman from Juniper provoking him with inflated gossip about his brother and Sa Croix. I call her Pinocho. Evening, mood up but not well with me. Gave me a speech out front of his place about not wanting me around anymore. "O.K." Slept at my place; still had his car keys and phone with me, but he has a second set at home anyway.*

One month from the 10th would have taken us to February 11th. Oh well. At least he got his divorce thing started. Sigh. Charlie is over my head. I slept at my place against the greater pull to stay at his place. It's becoming more about me than him. I want to get him to "safety" in order to relieve me of the responsibility that I have taken on. If he went to rehab tomorrow I would breathe easier. I want him to avoid taking the drug so that he can get to safety. This time his body and soul are not guaranteed to take the same beating as he gave them just before he went to Barcelona the first time. That's all. The impending presence of death is magnified and again would not bother me if he said that it was the way that he wanted to go. Ironically, however, in his darkest moments of depression when the fog lifts slightly after the high, is when he expresses to me from a reflective mental state that he does not want to die like a rat on a sofa. He's ill. I can only trust what he tells me during these sensitive moments not during those angry ones fuelled by the cravings. Remember that. So how much can I resist his moods without him feeling provoked by me or otherwise? It's not worth it? Guess I give up? Dasha is too much on her own. I need to work. I've had a few interviews for work, but there is always some little obstacle in getting hired? Why…? *'Don't give up on Charlie just yet.'* – Okay.

Day 5: Wednesday January 26 – Snow on snow.
Charlie literally went out of his way last night to get some cocaine. Just after I went home at 11p.m., after his speech about not wanting me around. No wonder. The "call of the snow" deceived us again. It was a stormy and snowy night too, but he still walked undaunted to the local bar. Called a taxi, gambled with money the club owed him. Then borrowed a car from there and got some. Went to the clubs, got a ride home – arrived at 6:30a.m. At 2p.m., still sleeping.

Day 1: Thursday, January 27 – *"Our true identity is to love without fear and insecurity. Our higher potential finds us when we set our course in that direction. The power of love and compassion transforms insecurity. Love fulfilled sees where we could have gone the way of love before, if we'd known how and how insecurities limited many of our choices. Love fulfilled perceives new meaning and higher reasons behind many of the mysteries of why things happened as they did. Living from the heart is business; the business of caring for self and others. Understanding this will take us past the age of information into the age of intuitive living."*
DOC CHILDRE.

He slept over 24hrs, from 6:30a.m., on the 26th until 1:30p.m., today. Looks run down. Nervous breathing but calm. Difficulty focusing his mind and eyes on things – feels physical discomfort. Slept some more. Movie and dinner later helped. I slept next to him all last night. Not sure why. If I were a dog, I'd be called faithful. As a person, I'm a co-addict; not a caretaker or a defender of the underdog, human rights or anything valiant because it sounds corny? Why do I have to be a parent, a wife, or a nun, or need a diploma in sociology to justify the intensity of my desire to see Charlie achieve a second opportunity to know the potential of his dreams? Why isn't the word love enough? Why does its intensity have to be gauged against the quality of its purpose rather than the quality of its potential? Just bull shit – love is power. A state of mind distributed in many ways, while each way has the same potential for intensity, regardless of the value of its intention. Whatever. We're both pretty down now. I think we are still trying, but even I have somehow become a little foggy about what we're trying to accomplish. I know it's the addiction but to what extent, is it him or *her* talking to me? I guess it began to go downhill when he lied to me and went to Campos village instead of lunch with his friend. He really needs someone 24/7 which isn't healthy for anyone. So, trying to stay focused on the focus: he shouldn't take for at least a month. With that, maybe getting away would help? He can't stay here because the bells are too loud to avoid. Attend Dubai's Franchise Show…? A cocaine addict in a Muslim country? – Not. No real reason to try anymore. Sad that it feeds people's gossip about us when in fact we're on track. Now it's a matter of finding a rehab for him to go to, because he can't do it here: tested and proven. We needed to know by doing. He should hire me as his assistant. I need work and he needs help managing things? Angry at Life for bringing these men into my life; the moment I return an interest in them they reject it. Vladimir said that I am dangerous to myself and Charlie. A truth blemished by the heartache he was feeling from my inability to reciprocate his passion. I think, who isn't? Everyone carries all that to everything in life, but not everyone unfolds it. Charlie said that I have a violent temperament. Another truth expressed in frustration at me, when I challenged his craving to get some coke. "Pain in the ass" were my dad's words once, when I managed the roles of surrogate mother and friend. Why am I here? Mother Teresa died a long time ago.

Day 2: Friday, January 28 – The Great Escape.
Up at 10a.m., gym and regular sauna for him. Fresh OJ afterwards together, then off to Sa Croix for lunch and a bit of work. He's okay but still struggling from the other night out. Nose not good. Very anxious, despondent and unable to stay still. Suppose to see his son tomorrow. My birthday today.

7:30a.m. – Still dark outside. Just got back from being at Charlie's. Quite a night. He put me through the wringer with a great escape that ran along the lines of a premature April fool's prank. The juxtaposition of his behaviour next to the one he had prior to arriving at his place last night is remarkable. A complete good boy – bad boy experience. We got to his place around 11p.m. I was zonked and went to lie down in the extra bedroom. Charlie was nervous, up and down and all around between the sofa, his bedroom and the bathroom. I kept myself there like a mummy, lying flat on my back arms crossed and fully dressed with my boots on, waiting for him to settle down and go to sleep. In hindsight I think it was my presence that perturbed him. Had I gone home right away I don't think he would have gone out anywhere. He'd bought some on the 25th, taken it all through the morning of the 26th and slept all the way through until yesterday afternoon. Maybe he had extra charly at home and wanted me to leave so that he could finish it off? Dunno. His reaction was possibly a second high from what's left over in him from Wednesday, plus he's supposed to see his son tomorrow. His cycle of intake is shrinking down to every four to three days. Sigh. The good news is that his prank was actually quite funny. While I was lying there stretching an ear for the sound of his snoring, I heard his bedroom window bang instead. I literally ran to his bedroom door, then clamped down on my impulse to invade his room directly and politely called his name: 'Charlie?' No answer. '*Crap,*' I thought. Opened the door and the room was empty. I ran back down the hall acutely aware of the sound of my boots' heels hitting the linoleum floor, while I threw open the front door certain that I was too late, only to be left totally beside myself in seeing that his car was still parked in the driveway! Never mind the fact that it was seriously cold outside and that my nerves had been shot to hell from the back-pressure of having kept them cooped up all night in anticipation of his sleep. I walked back to a closed front door. Knocked and little Charlie let me in and disappeared back to the sofa. When I veered into the TV room and saw him lying on the couch he had one of the biggest childish smirks on his face that I had yet seen. 'Charlie!' I chanted in an exasperated tone, 'what did you *do* – Why!?' My condescending tone was hysterical and despite myself, provoked an unavoidable smile on my face. He was truly amused by his little prank. 'I wanted to see your reaction,' he answered with a mischievous smile. His behaviour reminded me of Dasha when she gets mischievous from being cooped up in the house all day and chews up a few of her toys. Plus, it was then officially past midnight and my birthday of course never occurred to him. I was amused by his prank, but it completely spent the last of my energy. I was truly emotionally and physically tired. I went back to my mummy position in the guest room and waited. A sensation of released pressure evaporated from my body causing a few tears to clean their way down my cheeks. It didn't last long and then I finally heard the sound that I'd been waiting for. Charlie started snoring by half past two. I walked home just after six this morning to take Dasha out and now I am about to eat my frozen birthday cappuccino tart that Elisabet arranged to get for me last night. She and Charlie gave me a surprise birthday dinner at her and Mitx' place. Charlie and I had gone to a movie, which is another feat in itself for Charlie because most films are too hard on his senses to watch. They unsettle all sorts of undesirable memories or feelings. Anyway, after the film, he took forever to drive home and I thought it was because he'd sniffed in the men's room or somewhere and was really looped. Instead he was waiting for Belle to get the dinner ready. It was like a family dinner with Mitx, Elisabet, their two sons and Charlie next to me. He was very attentive. The complete antecedent to this morning's fiasco. Even Elisabet had noticed how he cut the food on my plate for me, talked on my behalf, let me sit tightly next to him and place my hand on his lap. He even patted my butt in their presence. I was emotionally high all night. I was overwhelmed and still am. All the elements to a wish were there: a man of my intention beside me, a family that accepted my presence as if they were my own, a warm house and a sense of location and future in my life that I have only ever felt once before. I am 38 now. I like the number. Apart from Charlie, next on my agenda for this year: I want to begin a new career. Something that reflects an equal if not greater return on who and what I might already be.

Day 3: *That woman is killing me – thorned my heart. As much as I try to forget about her my soul won't let me. My heart has been squashed wounded and abandoned. Hey, hey my love please you know, what pain is there left? How it aches, how the heart aches when it arrests us. Tho' don't forget woman that one day you will say: 'Hey, ya, ya, how love hurts me, how to be the forgotten one hurts me. How the heart aches, how it hurts to be alive without still having your love at my side.'* [*Esa mujer me está matando – Me ha espinado el corazón. Por más que trato de olvidarla mi alma no da razón. Mi corazón aplastado, herido y abandonado; Oye, oye tu sabes dime mi amor por favor; ¿Que dolor nos queda? Como duele como duele el corazón. Cuando nos tiene entregados pero no olvides mujer que algún día dirás* – *'Oye, oye ya, ya como me duele el amor* – *Como me duele el olvido. Como duele el corazón. Como me duele estar vivo. Sin tener tu amor aun a mi lado'.]* – *'CORAZON ESPINADO' (THORNED HEART), SANTANA/MANÁ, LYRICS ADAPTED.*

He saw his son in the morning, tho' it was too soon after his relapse three days ago. It got to him and he went on a binge at 4p.m. Got home by 5p.m. and clammed up with the cocaine, whisky and pornography. Shutters closed. I went over to see him at night. Knocked on his door a few times before he let me in: 'What happened?!' I asked. No reply. He was lying in his regular frontal position on the sofa. The TV area was a strewn with videos, a whisky bottle on the floor with an ounce of drink left inside, a glass on the table, and a bit of snow left over on the table next to him. 'You know I put up with my wife's abuse because I don't want my son to suffer – you know..,' he said to me while he turned onto his back. His son's football game was in the village where he and his mother live, which is like Charlie going into the queens' hive every time. 'Charlie – I'm not sure I understand. You were there weren't you? Why do you let these people get to you? Is there no way to see your son via your parents or somewhere neutral?' I asked.

'She told me to thank-you,' he said.

'Thank me? Who?'

'My wife. What, are you in cohorts with her too?' he asked defiantly.

'Charlie, I've never seen nor met your wife. However I'm sure she has gone out of her way to find out about me. Her thanks are kind, but I don't think it's wholesome. She doesn't know what to make of me and probably feels threatened by me. After everything that she feels that she has endured by you, it would feel like it was all in vain if no one appreciated her efforts; namely you. She's probably conflicted by vindictive mood swings and a desire to rise above them by trying to appreciate our attempts at controlling the addiction. It's also an effective way to manipulate your weaknesses. Her gratitude to me disturbs you because it suggests that she has risen above your separation before you have, and that your efforts in this are secondary. Besides Charlie, she's definitely not above it – if she were, then she should have thanked you. You're the one who decided to try and get help. Plus, if she really wanted to let you go and improve all of your lives, why aren't you divorced yet?' Silence. 'It's like your egos have taken over Charlie. Kind of like who will move on before the other, or neither one of you wants the other to feel well before the other. If she found a new love, would you feel relieved or jealous? Find a way to make her feel guilty instead of well and vice versa from her to you? You can't be together, but you won't allow each other the emotional freedom to be free from each other? The very thing that might improve your affection with each other... You know?'

'She told me that I was a bad father,' he said tears welling from his eyes. He got up, and blew his nose. I felt anger surge inside. These people were either really cruel or just simply stagnant in their communication skills. Everything is about blame and finding a guilty party. About humiliating one's self confidence to covet another's envy. Franco years or not; it's definitely not progressive. 'Charlie,' I said calmly from my spot in the chair next to him, 'I don't know enough. I only know what I have experienced with you. You have an addiction which needs to be treated. You are not perfect and neither am I, and I'm not a cocaine addict. However you maintain your economic obligations to your son, you're not abusive, you're patient and have enough sense not to see your son when you are active from the cocaine. Somewhere in your conscious you are able to control that. It says to me that you have the will not to take the drug; that your turmoil is caught up with emotional blackmail issues from your wife, because you love your son very very much. So by definition this doesn't make you a bad father. You can be better at it if you want, but you're doing pretty well considering your circumstances. Let's look at those who don't even have an addiction or illness! Plus Charlie, your son chose to be a goalie just like you. He admires you. Doesn't matter what your wife feels about you, it will only fuel his love for you even more. I'm sorry, but playing the victim does eventually boomerang back to the owner – you know? Above all, your experience in this, if and when you get past it, may possibly save your son's life one day. There is a reason for everything Charlie. Maybe this is about helping your son when he finds the same well? You'll be the one to perceive, before anyone else, whether or not he has. Most of all, you'll know how to deal with it...' Charlie sat up, blew his nose and sighed an air of relief: 'Thank you Michèle.'

'Nah Charlie. It's just what it is.'

He got up somewhat refreshed looking, went to the kitchen and boiled some rice soup for both of us. We had dinner together in the kitchen and chatted lightly about the cold weather and the merits of a warm bowl of soup. After that, he did the dishes and then found me while I was watching the television: 'I'm going to bed now. See you tomorrow okay?' he said to me in English. 'O.K,' I replied.

Day 1: *Cold. He slept until 6pm. Calm and unable to focus. Came to the second half of a football game on Pay per View at the local bar next door. Lots of stories in his head; paranoia. Went home alone, tired and sad.*

In ten days he knew a lifetime; in twenty-two he saw it was possible.

February Blues

February 1: *Paris, moments with his family – Christmas, gift giving and reunions, kind words of thanks from his wife, divorce process started, the bags, new people, new sensations like Limon Cello and pizza in Palma. Conversations in English, time in the gym, an organised home, a car wash, movies and dinners too…Friendship, laughter, affection, vulnerabilities and strengths shared with a woman…All for the first time in almost a lifetime…*

February 2: *She's a juvenile scam, never was a quitter, tasty like a raindrop – She's got the look… Heavenly bound cause heaven's got a number when she's swaying to the band spinning him around. Kissing is a colour, her loving is a wild dog – She's got the look…Fire in the ice, naked to the T-bone, it's a lover's disguise. What in the world can make a brown-eyed girl turn blue? …Everything he'll ever do, he'll do for her… And I say la la la la, she's got the look!* – 'THE LOOK', ROKETTE, LYRICS ADAPTED.

Tough Love – say goodbye. I lost Charlie. Lost him. In fact, my fault. I did not stay focused on my "mission" with him. The bitch of his addiction played me very well. I asked him for dinner with Xisco and Maribel in Palma and he drank like a fish. I should not be going to dinners or movies with him if we want to keep him clean for a month or at least attain a level of clarity towards obtaining real help. We're supposed to try and simulate a balance between life here and rehab in Barcelona. He can do what he wants, but I should not have organised the supper. Not good. On our return home, he left me at home and firmly did not want me to stay with him at his place: 'Charlie – I'll just go into the guest room and let you be,' I said softly when he stopped the car in front of my place. 'Nah. Michèle – I want to be alone. I had a good time, now let me be,

O.K.' His body language was tense and being tried and tested by me …'Charlie – we can go for a drive. Let's do Namacor together then, if you need to go out – Ok? Let's go together,' I tried.

The intensity of the thirty minute craving had begun to set in him, but I had no back-up.

'Nahh. I'm going home,' he said.

'Really?' I asked.

'C'mon Michèle – good night.'

He did not give me a direct answer. I knew what that meant. Jes used that tactic too, when he did not want to lie before doing something undesirable for both of us. 'We'll see each other tomorrow!' he said in an exasperated tone while I sat there, head against the passenger window, contemplating him in silence, trying to use up as much of the thirty minutes as possible. How or why, should I believe him or care? … 'Okaay,' I said slowly. Gave him the Spanish kisses and got out of his car.

He went directly to Namacor. Binged again, on cocaine, gambling, prostitutes, porno videos the whisky etc. He was home by 9:30 this morning, just before I went by to pick him up for the gym. I knocked on his door and then had to send him a sms from my cell letting him know that it was me, before he let me in. Again from his position on the sofa and mine in the chair, he was willing to tell me what happened. I'm grateful for that. At least he still opens the door and talks to me. His bowler glass on the floor next to the sofa shimmered a gold colour from a narrow beam of daylight that had managed to find its way through the closed shutters, to the whisky in the glass. That's how I knew that he'd just arrived. He drinks the whisky to level out the high from the cocaine. The problem of course is that the mixture is lethal to his health. Many deaths in cocaine addiction occur from brain haemorrhaging or a clot caused from the mixture of the two.

'Where did you go?' I asked.

'C'an Colom,' he droned into the cushion.

'Oh,' … 'the prostitutes?' I concluded.

'I go to talk and hang out, that's all,' he mumbled back.

'You pay only to talk to them?' I nudged. No reply. 'Charlie?' I poked a bit more.

'That's all! Can't do much else! – you know!' he groaned into the cushion. He lifted his face slightly out from the cushion and added: 'I'm sorry Michèle.'

I sat there, stuck. He'd crossed all the lines with me and now I had to make a choice and was mad that I had to make one. I looked at the man on the sofa. He wasn't going to get up. There was nothing more to say or do; no more parameters. He'd do it again, and again. I just needed to get up and leave him alone. Had he even really tried? When did my love and hope in our endeavour get lost in a crossfire? I sat there in silence with my gut glued to the chair while my dignity was already pulling me from the front door, unsure how to let go or to give up. I sat there in a swim of silent thoughts … *He pays women for their time to be with him. Funny how that hurts me the most: not just the ego but me directly. Sigh. I did it to myself. All the time and shit I shared with him – he never paid me? The point of sale is what hurts, not the activity. It directly devalues me as a person. Not as a woman, but as a person. While strip clubs simply poison everyone's self-esteem; including the friends and families of those who interact with the clubs. It's a plague per se. People don't see it that way, of course. Men respect their women so much that they would never think of paying them for the love and attention they receive from them because likewise, in the men's eyes, that point of purchase would degrade the value of that affection to them, as well as themselves. I think how little we have evolved, when all tangible things are still given artificial value and attention by way of currency's lure, while all intangibles of authentic value, that which cannot be seen nor touched, are ironically made priceless, yet often mistreated because its very nature is often too difficult to trust for many humans, who still need the tangible in order to feel secure. Besides, prostitutes are for fun and carry little of men's respect – nope, try again. Charlie won't pay me because he understands that I'm not "that kind of woman". That by not paying me for my time with him, he's respecting me or the woman of me? What bull shit is that? Many men respect the role of the prostitute, it's the business that they give shit about. They're not paying the women; they're paying into the business and the service that they ask for. I wonder if that's one of the reasons why women who go to male strip bars don't get the same satisfaction from it as men, who go to female strip bars. Men don't care if their partners go to male strip bars because men treat it as a business – not an emotion like women do. Frankly, the business does not infringe on a woman's rights either – the prostitute is in her right; it does not degrade women's role in society – the prostitute is working to survive her way; it does not enforce men's control over women – the business drains the men dry. Prostitution simply hurts people. The men who pay, the prostitutes who charge and most of their own entire world that surrounds them. Similar to tobacco, alcohol, drug abuse, consumerism, capitalism etc. It's all about economy. The world can't move without economy so really what's left? Solve the absurdity in salary distribution and prostitution would no longer have a purpose? Why work forty to fifty hours a week making peanuts when one can work in a sex bar for five hours and make a minimum of fifty bucks a night or a few thousand? Even on the worst night, a prostitute can make the same money as any other doing a different job and maybe meet a few new people, dance with good music, have a few free drinks, and if one is a student or a mother then the day is free to manage that part of her life. So why not? – The price. Everything has a price equal to the value of its polarity. There is nothing degrading about being paid for sex when it's about a business that is far away from matters of the heart; both the men and the prostitutes suffer the emotional repercussions similar to anyone in any clandestine business transaction. Everything has a price.*

Society tries to control the sex trade by designating the women and men involved as indecent or messed up. Something to give mainstream society some level of dignity. Duuh. How does Charlie's example of maintaining a woman's emancipation by giving her the income she depends on classify as "indecent" or "messed up"? I need an income too – pay me! Besides the fact that I am with him 24/7 for something that he'll pay up to 7,000 euros a month for, if he goes back to rehab in Barcelona, where the only difference is that he's there and not here. Notwithstanding that he also pays-out close to 2,000 euros a month on cocaine and its related activities. That's what's twisted: the disequilibrium in Charlie's financial management and me doing this for free! Gawd, I epitomise one of the oldest trades in the world that is controlled by women, and yet run by men when it ought to be women making all the bucks as the pimp and the prostitute! Hell, just place me on his pay roll! Why not? Because it takes away from the altruism of my endeavour? Because it places me in the category of indecent women – the prostitute? Bull shit. Who's the prize idiot? The woman who makes a living with her body or the man who pays for it? Neither. The prize idiot is the one who chooses to judge them. Why do people pay for someone to clean and take care of their homes, yet never consider paying the homemaker? The extra income that household might be making is lost on the hired help anyway – no? Is it a philanthropic attempt to give someone work? Or is it for the right to work outside of home? The need to demonstrate one's independence and status, when being a parent at home is possibly one of the biggest and most valiant professions in the world? Family education? Why have kids if you won't be home? Won't and can't are two different things. The whole self-righteous: "I have a right" thing. Yes you have a right. So don't have kids? On one hand, people have children without proper economic planning and then wonder why their kids fall into shady areas of economic survival? While the absence of economic privilege in a home, can develop character and independence, it can also fuel an independent spirit to survive on personal means separate from the family unit. Contrary to the newly developed economies, the traditional family system still raises its children like string puppets in a way that breeds co-dependency. While these families can maintain economic support systems likewise they also handicap self-development. Then on the other hand, it neither helps that developed countries and the newly established ones, place so much status on artificial commodities as "the good life". Even individuals with more than adequate survival skills to maintain an adequate lifestyle have been influenced to live beyond their means. Such that, families with modest economic status are defeated in teaching their children the virtues of living a good life modestly by reason of a materialistic economic culture called Capitalism. So back to the same: "Don't have kids!?" It is ironic how the developed countries with the best resources to educate and nurture societies towards being a better human race, are precisely the lowest in birth demographics, which contradicts the ability to extend the education to new generations of children by defeat of its own information and economic intelligence. How messed up is that? While the less progressive countries are having all the kids without access to advanced education and therefore counteracting the new world's attempts at humanity's progress. Geesus! It all pisses me off! ... Sigh, have children. Romantic vision or no, they are the future and the ambassadors of our success or failure as intelligent human beings. In all the absurdity the key once again is balance... The new world should continue its way towards maturing mankind – much has been achieved. Withstanding the next phase ought to be about assimilating some of the traditional virtues from the old country's experience. That's the beauty and secret to the past– Learn from it! Take the good from it and apply it to the Now. It's not cheating, it's wise. That's what grandparents and old age are for! Apply the wisdom to the new world philosophy. Anyway, Charlie would gladly lend me the money until death do us part, but that infuriates me more. I can't earn it from him I have to borrow it. It's like making big bucks has to

be related to some kind of definition of sin. Then the most absurd of it all, is that if Charlie offered to pay me for my time without some kind of label like assistant or operations manager, I'd still be hurt. The psychology of my mind would automatically define the point of sale for the purpose as a business transaction that would remove the value of his affection for me and above all, reject mine towards him. Uuuugh! ...
He was still lying there not moving. I sensed that he was waiting for me to leave. I sat there wondering if I was anything like those people who suffer abuse from their partners yet never leave them. '*You stay with it because you don't know how much of it is him or the illness,*' I thought to myself, '*one month clean? Very hard to achieve. He's ill. Daddy had cancer and we did not abandon him, but we got help. I'd have to control areas of Charlie's life without his permission like he was a child and that would be counterproductive. He went to rehab for the first time in fourteen years because his mother was on the verge of a breakdown. Not because he'd really decided. How do we get Charlie to decide on his own, to go to rehab sooner than later? ... My presence. The continuity of my presence next to him might provoke his need to get away? Or would guilt make him resist more? (Sigh). I don't want to give up right now, but I have to. I can't help him. It's over my head. I have to get out,*' and I left.

Later: I left his side. If he was testing my tenacity I failed. He won't call. Then my horoscope says: "Fight for that love" hmpf, great timing. Do horoscopes take into account drug abusers, assassins, and cultures in third world countries? Is Charlie my love or a private purpose? It's supposed to be the latter, but I seem to be leaning into the former for the wrong reasons. I want to achieve the latter first with a quiet aspiration to get to the former later. Tho' can't have love until time and space make it feasible. However, my ego and obsessive nature have begun to sprout prematurely from the love in my purpose, rather than just from the purpose itself. That kind of love that I might quietly aspire to is not ripe enough for such feelings to grow healthy. Gotta keep an eye on them. Sigh. I'm not working and should be. Fact: Charlie found me. His wish for a native English speaker, the Mini and his desire to live his life differently by making tough choices is the same as mine. Our arrival at the island only a month apart, my presence in Barcelona while he was there too, while Mitx and Elisabet are not a coincidence either. There are so many to list: our names, the cars, the address, the photo, our professions, birthdates, the timing of my arrival etc.; no way a coincidence. Even Xisco and Maribel went on their first date at Sa Croix, four years ago and they live in Palma!? All connected to me in some way. You confuse me. Don't know clearly what it's all about, but it's about something. Maybe Charlie goes back to Barcelona and returns? Finds me again? Maybe just about the car and helping me get started on my projects, or about me helping him assimilate his love for someone? Naaah. *They* all doubted. The odds have been against me since before we even began. Nobody has ever really believed in the attempt, not even Charlie. Feeling used. Hard to win a battle when the soldiers go AWOL.

February 4: Haze.
Found some coke packed in plastic about the size of my thumb in his jean pockets while doing our laundry. When I gave it back to him he said it was about five grams. He's confused for lack of a better word. Wants help and doesn't at the same time. Inability to commit to things. Indecisive until the last moment, mixed with such lucidity and perception at another moment. Doesn't want me around and then pops up at my door.

I wonder about myself too. When do dedication, passion and intensity lose their dignity and turn into their polar evils of obsession, deadly and crazy? Charlie is a constant presence. On my walks or keeping busy with mindless chores my mind is eternally having thoughts and conversations with myself. Some crisp and others bleak and sad. I wish they would drop on paper every time they appeared because writing them down never equals the original state of mind. Wonder how Dumbledore's "Think Bowl" would fare with my thoughts? At 8:30a.m. Charlie was still out. My mind goes where it should not. He has found a new lady interest that gets paid for her time with him. Maybe he will keep her for a few months, avoid all emotional obligations, with no responsibility attached to it, just money. Sigh. I think how stupid we are to place so much pressure on sentimentality and love. It makes it a rather unwanted commodity in the end. I'm reminded again at how the new world seems to have allowed superficial commodities to create unreasonable expectations from love that are not natural to its nature. It's like making a cat bark. Not impossible, but there will be complaints and imperfections; after a while, maintenance issues will probably leave the cat stranded in an alley sort of thing. In general, people want quality without the responsibility and patience needed to attain it. I call them the "wannabes". People might say that I live in the clouds, but that's where aspirations and dreams come from before they are made tangible. Going to Disney, watching films, living in places like Dubai or paying money for a relationship in order to simulate one's hopes is a quick fix just like any drug or emotional impulse: they don't last or satisfy. Whose lifestyle is really the fake one? A cocaine addict paying a prostitute is merely living a wannabe situation with no long-term reward or goal. At least the prostitute makes an income and in many cases hopes to use the client in order to turn secret hopes into tangible realities. Plus, depending on the class level, the negotiable benefits in prostitution are baffling; men pay to watch, to be seen with a good looking woman, to be listened to, or make their porno videos interactive. A lot of times there is no sex because they can't. Impotent. No intimacy. Their possessive relationship with drugs and alcohol won't let them be with any other. They're excellent clients and can cloud a prostitute's focus right when she's ready to leave the business. What about me? Has Charlie's haze veiled my mind? He found me right after he'd returned from Barcelona the first time, when he was clearer, and expressed a desire to try something "real" with me. Now I feel lost in the smoke. Even if Charlie went back to Barcelona, beyond and after all that, there is no guarantee that he could attain the life he thinks he wants in Mayürqa where everyone and everything will have remained the same. All expectation will be on him to make it happen, when the very same people involved in his illness and recuperation will have done nothing to change their patterns with him, in order to benefit his new Way. His purpose already appears defeated before he even gets started because the people in his well, will remain as they are and that is a bigger challenge in recuperation: how to move on, when those people are your family and friends? Especially at 44 years of age? So, I think of me. I am the new ingredient. Yet upon his return he might not even be interested in me. The focus of getting him into a state of detox long enough for him to "see" the options rather than imagine them, seems to have been smudged quite a bit already. There is a feeling of resistance coming from somewhere and its source is not coming from Charlie. As if others are surreptitiously encouraging his low self-esteem to believing that anything beyond the reality of his illness is foolish and above all, he can't possibly be the owner of my heart: that I too am confused. Sigh. Well, feelings put aside, he's stopped confiding in me. He takes every four to three days, impeding even a moment of transparency let alone time to exist, for me to reach him. How far does one go? When I left his place on Wednesday, I actually considered leaving one of the glass doors unlocked so that I might have continued access to him because now is the most crucial time. While he's going deeper and farther away, it's harder to "reach the bull by the horns". Anyway, I didn't do it. Despite my reasoning, my instincts won't justify it. In the meantime he's increasing his consumption and drifting farther into the well and letting prostitutes condition him against his natural need for intimacy. I saw it when we were in bed - as if the inability to perform an economic transaction with me removed his surrogate way of performing sexually and feel confident as a provider. Like my lingering presence in the room unsettled him because he felt unprotected against the power of sentimentality; unable to receive it without feeling indebted because he couldn't give something back. When a prostitute probably just gets dressed, takes the money and leaves him feeling falsely satisfied by a successfully completed transaction, without much more. No lingering emotional thoughts or second guesses to deal with, just a tidy organised moment without further ado. Suddenly he wants to be alone, and I can see how intensely cocaine and prostitution feel threatened by the presence of Love. Like evil versus good. Should their host like Charlie, notice it, these evils risk being abandoned by him. So their grip on the minds of their hosts intensifies fiercely for their own survival... When I think this way, I can't give up on Charlie.

February 5: Sms Mc – *"Hi would you still like to do coffee? M." He sent me a sms on Friday, the night of the 4th to have coffee with him on the Saturday morning.*

We did later that afternoon. We had not communicated since Wednesday the 2nd, 10a.m. I missed him. He was insecure and noticeably thinner. That night went okay; Chinese together for dinner and then his place just hanging out with him while we chatted and watched TV. He went to bed early. I stayed until midnight and went home. Left his phone and car keys at his place. That effort no longer has meaning to it.

February 6: *Perfect love is rare indeed – for to be a lover will require that you continually have the subtlety of the very wise, the flexibility of the child, the sensitivity of the artist, the understanding of the philosopher, the acceptance of the saint, the tolerance of the scholar and the fortitude of the certain.– LEO BUSCAGLIA.*

Great night. Football at the local bar and "pa amb oli" with Charlie, Mitx and Elisabet were there too. I drove over to his place in the middle of the first half, knocked on his door. He sent me an sms to let myself in. So I found the extra key in its hidden spot, opened the front door and went in. He was in bed. 'Wanna come to football?' I asked. I was standing in the doorway.

'I don't know – whose there?' he asked. 'Just Belle, Mitx – the regulars,' I replied.

'I don't know. My eyes are red you know...' He was self-conscious and a little paranoid.

'Charlie – people perceive what you give them. If you're cool they're cool. Who knows, maybe your eyes are red because of a hang-over or allergies – you know?' Silence. 'C'mon Charlie, people are interested in the football game, not you. I'll walk over with you.'

He got up. He was wearing his red ski jacket and sucking on its zipper while we sauntered casually to the bar. Then he suddenly stopped. 'I don't feel like it,' he said. It was cold and windy. I looked at him momentarily before answering him. 'Why?' I asked. He looked around nervously, hands in his coat pockets and chin pressed against his chest in order to keep his mouth within reach of the zipper below it. I felt like I was walking Dasha when she was a puppy. She would often stop in mid walk for no apparent reason and then after some soft coaxing continue the walk. 'Charlie,' I said calmly, 'let's go – stay until the end of the first half and then we can leave. At least say hi to Elisabet – when was the last time you spoke to her?' We ended up watching the full match and having dinner. He loosened up while we were there. His eyes shifted around a lot and he made more than one trip to the men's room, but I was relaxed because for that time being, he was being entertained in a safe area; possibly long enough to make him want to sleep later rather than go out.

February 7: Miss Perfect.
Sms Mc –"R U UP YET?"… Nope. After football, I went home and he'd basically gone out at 2a.m. and got back at 5:30a.m.?! Gym together at noon.

Incredible. I really didn't think that he'd go out. He'd surprised me because we both had a dentist appointment that day at 10a.m. The night before he was *doing o.k.* I could have stayed overnight at his place; after some serious resistance from him he was going to let me stay. Still, even if I had, he probably would have gone out anyway and I might have thought my presence provoked it. Sigh. I just thought the dentist appointment would have been a deterrent, but at 2a.m., V and the coke found him and took him away. I am of course over my head. He actually went out and had "a" line before 9a.m.; the time we had agreed to meet. He of course felt like shit and when I went over to his place, he almost didn't answer the door. I had to ask him to open it for the sake of relieving my concerns about him. He projected a lot of tension and anxiety towards me. My presence really annoyed him. He'd been on the sofa smoking. Everything was closed up, but nothing was visible. TV off, shutters closed, no whiskey. Despite the coke, he's usually very good at meeting his engagements; at least the ones with me. Plus he hates "failing" to meet obligations, that's why he avoids them. So at 9:30a.m., in spite of the friction between us, he stayed true to his word and drove to the dentist's.

The dentist is Charlie's. I'd never been there so that's why we're going together. Once we arrived however, he stayed in the car making it clear to me that the only reason he'd gotten up was for *my* appointment. In reality he had come through with the obligation of getting me there. In fact to him, I had been the obligation not the dentist appointment, which could be re-scheduled and was. Indeed, it had been more important to me that he complete the swing and manage the consequences of having gone out the night before. Also, he'd gotten up when he must have really felt awful; even did the morning coffee with me first – a small but evident sign of my importance to him that I feigned to overlook, simply because he went out of his way to make this very fact an issue. Then too, I thought, '*I could have gone in my own car.*' Still, I remained undaunted. I sat there in the car next to him, narrowed in on him and tried to convince him to enter the dentist's office. Nothing. As I got down from his car and closed the door, I watched him slump further into his seat and feign repos behind his shades. Unfortunately, once I'd stepped down from the car, I was still so wound up from my battle to get him there that midway between the car and the dentist's door my ego suddenly got away from me and all at once found myself looking back, then veering on my heels, already offering a prelude to a given theatrical scene in the street, and pronounced at him in a loud and patronizing tone: '¡Mal – muy mal! (Bad – very bad!)'. The result of that move was more dramatic than effective. I didn't like myself for doing it. It showed a shift from patient tactics. Needless to say, on the way back home he didn't hesitate to lay into me, about how "arrogant" and "over-bearing" I was: 'How dare you shout at me from the street! (People may have seen or heard.) No one, not even my mother, has ever yelled at me!'

'*There's your problem,*' I thought dryly. He is so spoiled. Then he growled at me that no one has ever yelled at him before?!

'*Right,*' I thought, '*instead they have thrown ashtrays at your head, called you son of a bitch and then cried about having wasted their lives over you. .. Cocaine,*' I concluded to myself, '*she's quite the beast.*' The ranting did not stop there …

'Who do you think you are? Miss *Perfect* above everyone!?'

'Char-'

'Yelling at me trying to coerce me like I was your *dog* Dasha? Well I'm *not* your *dog* and I'm *not* Jesús either!!'

To which I thought: '*Where or how did Jes get into the picture?*'

'Jesús!? What does Jes have to do with this? Charl-'

'I don't know *how* Jesús put up with you but I *won't*! … And I'm tired of you always comparing me to him – I'm not Jesús!'

'I don-'

'That out of deference to me! Out of *deference* to me, you wouldn't have his photo in your telephone. I feel bad enough as it is, you know…' he defended.

When we turned into Sa Ema de Farrutx I asked him to stop the car, so that I could get down and walk home the rest of the way. He stopped without flinching. 'Thank you,' I said calmly, 'umm, your dentist appointment is for Wednesday 11:30a.m.,' I said while I opened the door. He nodded. I stepped down after which he instantly revved-off like a bat out of hell, and unlike Jes, or Jesy as I call him affectionately, did not come back. It was a bit chilly that morning. I had about a kilometre or two to go, wearing a light blouse and high heel boots that were completely wrong for the walk. Nonetheless, the trek did me good and had revealed to me that I too, had committed mistakes. Somewhere between the dentist and home, I'd allowed myself to be provoked by his anger and had attempted to rationalise and defend myself. It would have been better to have just let it run over me. It was like having an argument with a very inebriated person. There was no rationale or point. In retrospect too, he had not thought about his lack of deference to me with regard to Vanesa. Another tiny indication that I'd overlooked: she was not important to him. Again I noticed the incongruities between men's and women's behaviour. A man will admit to an affair, if she or it matters. A woman on the other hand does the opposite. If it matters to her, she won't mention it because of the guilt brought on by how women are supposed to be virtuously correct. On the other hand, if the affair does not matter, we mention it: which of course, gets misinterpreted by the men. We are so challenged by "female perfection" issues that we deny our own guilt and avoid these kinds of truths. So if an affair becomes something, we tend to cover it. In many ways women can be more dishonest than men.

Once I got home, I took a hot bath and reflected further on the moment we'd just had. Charlie's ability to leave me behind prompted thoughts about the fine line between tough love and indifference. In replay mode, I too had gone over the top. My push to get him to the dentist hadn't been necessary, and he was truly hung over from the night before. 'He was the ill one, while I was the psychologically obsessive one,' I mused. '"Miss Perfect…",' I rewound. That hurt. 'I am far from perfect. Nobody's perfect,' I sighed-out. '*Had I done the same with Jes?*' I wondered. '"Out of deference" to him?' I muttered. I didn't think he cared. 'Besides, Jesy's *DEAD!*' my voice echoed defensively from the bathtub. 'And *DASHA!?*' it echoed again, 'doesn't even *HAVE* a collar around her neck!' … Charlie's delivery hadn't been appropriate either. We'd both been wrong. So I dried my hands and grabbed my phone right there and sent a text apology to him for my imperfections: "… sometimes they get in the way of my simple intentions," I sent. Within moments he replied with an equally sincere apology: "Sometimes I don't even recognise myself. Sorry." That night, after I'd been out, I sent another text asking him if I could stay at his place. "Ok" lit up my phone. I arrived there at 2a.m., and the front door had been left ajar for me to enter. When I reached his room, he woke easily and responded warmly to my silhouette. We exchanged light questions and answers about my night, while I coolly undressed by his bed. He even suggested that I might be his assistant, if he opened up a new business. Leaving me to swing between the duality of feeling reaffirmed by his desire to have me stay in his life without feeling guilty about it, and the truth about the addiction's precariousness, which contradicts all the above. Then I got between his soft flannel sheets, and we continued to chat quietly, buried under the warmth of the covers: the events of the day had made us closer. Albeit, it had been a hard day, the peaceful outcome had made it all worthwhile. Following that, I did change the photo in my cell. Right or wrong, it was time to start moving on from Jes too.

February 8: Dasha's Duck.
"Don't walk in front of me, I may not follow. Don't walk behind me, I may not lead. Walk beside me and be my friend" – ALBERT CAMUS.

Dasha's duck used to be daddy's duck. Today is her birthday, making her seven this year. I bought her a few stuffed toys, but she's partial to the duck which she found a few months ago, among a grouped plethora of other stuffed animals that I have set up on a chair in the office. I'm also partial to the duck because it belonged to my dad more than fifteen years ago. I tried to dissuade her from it, by placing it out of reach (or so I thought) and offering her a new sea-blue stuffed mouse but within a day, she somehow had the duck back in her mouth. It's a simple duck. Small, white and malleable with an orange bill and orange duck feet. It's interesting how she goes for the duck because her breed as a Golden Retriever holds an instinct to retrieve ducks from the water. Beyond that, it's incredible that it's still completely intact. Regardless of how hard she plays with it, tosses it, growls at it, or even chews on it. Except for the plastic eyes that popped off, it's completely intact. No other stuffed toy has survived so long without being un-stuffed. If she has anxiety or whenever there is a thunder storm she carries the duck around in her mouth as though it were a pacifier. So it's official. Dasha's surrogate companion is dad's duck while mine are Jes and dad in a long distant kind of way. On our walks, Dasha is my companion, without a collar, not even a leash. We head out sometimes as early as half past six in the morning. I lead first while she trails behind me. Once in a while I'll turn on my heels and motivate her to keep up. Then mid-way, she will pick up her walk and turn it into a trot and pass me, so that I may follow her lead. Sometimes she pauses as if to make sure that her way is correct, but I get the impression that she is waiting for me to catch up. So I give her a sign that all is fine and we continue our walk. We go in tandem like this until we reach the highway. She often stops before I've even called her name. Once I catch up, I place a wannabe leash made out of a soft leather strap over her head. It's not about the cars or the trucks, rather the birds that fly high and tease her to try, that prompt me to care, so I sit the leash around her neck like a loose tie. When we get to the next side road the strap is removed and we somehow finish our walk side by side. During the day while I work from my computer, she finds a spot on the floor and waits for me to finish. In the winter because it's colder I close the study door in order to keep the heat with me. So as not to keep her out, I've shown her how to push the door open which has become a mixed blessing of periodical wet-nosed visits and open air drafts that detract me from my work because she has yet to learn how to close the door behind her. At night she is free to sleep wherever she likes but always ends up in my room on her mat, by my bed. Just this year, I found something my dad wrote: "The best for writing: Mozart and a good dog." Funny, I don't have any Mozart at home, but his 250th anniversary is next year so maybe then I shall find out if it's true. In the meantime I think about all the chain of events and circumstances that brought Dasha to me. She was and will always be Jes' dog. Her presence is his gift as I think his presence is in her. There are days when I quite honestly feel that he is looking at me through her eyes. I chuckle because many times it is when I am getting undressed, or when I'm in bed that I wonder if he's also there, by my side. I think of Charlie and of what he said: "... I'm not your dog and I'm not Jesús either" and I think he might never be so lucky; to be with a woman who chooses him unconditionally, who trusts him enough to respect the space he needs, who believes in him enough to let him lead, confident enough to support and follow, patient enough to wait and motivate, valiant enough to defend him, mature and independent enough to sleep in his bed without him. He might never be so lucky as to have the privilege of a woman, whose only wish is to grow old in tandem with her companion, long enough to die at his side, having only been by his side.

February 9: Dogmatic. *Helped a dog get back home.*

We went to the dentist's. Charlie made up the appointment that he'd missed on Monday. I sat in the waiting room playing with a manual brain teaser that I picked up from the reception. Charlie's check-up must have taken about an hour. The effects of the cocaine prompted him to make a few trips to the bathroom to blow his nose and to clear his system. Then while I could hear him gurgling a conversation with the dentist, I tried to focus my attention on three solid metal rings that I was holding in my hands. The object of the tease, was to separate the two outer rings from the middle one. I've never been good at such things. I've never even figured our Rubik's cube, because I gave up trying. This time, however, I had nothing to do, but wait patiently for Charlie. I sat there for an hour tugging, pulling, refocusing my eyes and berating the call to just give up. It was not until I literally heard him end the check-up that the two rings literally slipped apart in my hands!?! I was beside myself! '*Did any one see?*' I thought wishfully. 'Charlie,' I stammered as he walked into the waiting room. 'Look! – I did it!?'

'What did you *do*?' he asked with a slight grin. I smiled.

'These – they were together and I pulled them apart,' I showed him.

'Nahh,' he contested while he approached me and took them into his own hands. He looked at the evidence, clanked them back together and asked: 'How did you do it?' then returned them to me.

'Aaah!' I exhaled audibly, 'I don't know – something like this? Or like this?' Try as I might, I could not remember the moves that it had taken to separate them.

'Yea,' he said, 'they were already apart – shall we go?'

'Charlie! – But I did!' I was truly upset that he did not believe me. I was so shocked at having done it, and there was nobody there to have seen it! I hoped he was teasing me, but it didn't *feel* like he was. I was really indignant and annoyed that he could be so unsupportive and sceptical. He did not believe me. It was the epitome of our relationship and my constant challenge that he'd trust the intention of my actions. How else could I have separated those rings if my intention had not been focused and natural?

After the dentist, we fulfilled our routine of going to the gym, drinking the fresh orange juice, spending the lunch hour at Sa Croix and stopping in at his parents' house, in order for him to greet his mother. When we got back to Sa Ema, Charlie was willing to join Dasha and me on a walk. I'd asked him casually in the car if he wanted to come, thinking that he wouldn't and was pleasantly surprised when he said, 'Yes.' We actually took the dirt path that leads from home to the church. It was all so improvised especially for him, who had never walked the twenty minute distance before. He was a basketball player, football goalie or car driver but not a walker. This was another first. My understanding of this unsettled a small level of anxiety in me, because I wanted the experience to be a positive one for him. Plus he wasn't wearing the proper sport shoes, but the red dress shoes that I'm not crazy about. It reminded me of the time we took a train to Palma. Again, a first for him and of course it happened to be the one day when everyone and his brother had decided to take the train too! Needless to say he swore never to repeat that experience again. Anyway we walked the entire way to the church, talking about new experiences and why he'd never had that one before. Once we got to the end of the path a black dog crossed our path. It was a male cross breed about the same size as Dasha. I recognised it as the one that is usually chained to a dog house and barks maliciously at Dasha and I when we walk by on our morning routine. This time it was still barking, but the chain around its neck was no longer attached to the dog house. The moment was a delicate one. The dog was barking furiously and made no signs of getting out of our way. I kept walking with Dasha and Charlie followed, while my peripheral vision saw him sending a few doubtful side glances at me. I don't know why I wasn't worried. My adrenalin was up, but I kept walking and started up a friendly tone of introductions to the dog. The dog continued to bark and remained steadfast in our path. Somehow, I felt that it was just scared. Having been tied to a dog chain no more than a metre long the sudden impact of being free must have disoriented him completely. At least that is what I allowed myself to believe at the time. 'Don't stare at him okay Charlie,' I said nonchalantly to him. 'No no,' he said with a quick side glance. Bold as the dog was, we kept on walking and passed it. No sooner had we done that, when the dog charged us from behind. I turned to face it and shouted: 'No!' The dog stopped in its tracks just long enough for Dasha to pick up the lead and greet it. The sudden change in the dog's behaviour was remarkable. Tail wagging and whining with excitement, the dog couldn't exhaust its pent up energy fast enough. Of course on our way back the dog followed us. The trek was so new to the dog that it was completely overwhelmed by the discovery of new scents and space that it was hardly able to walk straight. Finally almost mid-way, I tried to send it back. If the dog followed us any further it probably wouldn't know how to head back on its own. Sa Ema de Farrutx has a lot of stray dogs and it would not have taken it long to meet at least one and really get disoriented. His street sense was nil and I feared he might find the highway before the path. There was no deterring him. We came out of the wooded area black dog and all. Charlie and I sat on the front patio of my place for a while watching the black dog come and go from the front gate. He was truly vexed and unsure. 'Charlie,' I said, 'he needs to be taken back home – at least halfway, so he can pick up a scent,' I said as a matter of fact. 'He's a dog – he'll find it on his own,' he replied. Under normal circumstances this would have been true, but the dog had never been as far as a square meter away from its dog house. It was hyper, nervous and young. I tried to ignore it, but then Elisabet came out from downstairs and almost panicked at the sight of the black animal. I quickly headed down the steps and grabbed its collar so that she could get by to the car. 'Where did that come from?!' she asked. Charlie gave her a quick synopsis from the patio to which she added: 'Aiii be careful you never know it might turn on you.' It was true that the dog's hyper behaviour and black colour were not in its favour. However, it was still an immature puppy and very much in need of affection. Once Elisabet left, I let him go. 'The poor dog seems really lost,' said Charlie sympathetically. I stared at him for a moment. Charlie's personal debate with himself sometimes leaked past the armour and into my heart. 'Okay.' I pretended to be unaffected, 'so can we put him in your car and take him up the path? – What do you think? Do you mind putting him in your car?' I ended politely. 'No,' he said casually. So we did. Dusk was turning into night and there we were in Charlie's super Phedra, the dog and I, at the back of the car, gassing along loose rubble and dirt, into the woods on a mission to save the dog. In that moment I loved Charlie. He didn't care about his car, but he empathised with the dog even though he tried to pass it off as a favour to me. Upon our arrival I guided the dog back into the parameters of his home and left him there. This time he did not follow. I got back into the Phedra feeling good about our efforts. Even Charlie seemed pleased, but as he turned onto the highway to head back home the sensation of relief was replaced by worry. The dog was home and safe but certainly the next day, the owner would place the chain back around its neck. Would it have been better to have left it alone to meet its fate or was he better off in his world from a chain? I looked out the car window at the night. Our paths had crossed outside of its home. Had we not shown up, he might never have left the area. In a way we were responsible for showing him more. Then again, like Charlie said, he was bound to head back anyway. The concern was whether or not he'd make it. I relaxed at that. He'd seen a bit and got home safely. We were finally back at Charlie's place by half past six. He was tired and found his spot on the sofa while I found mine in the chair. 'That was good – no?' I asked him. He drew on his cigarette and pondered the ceiling from his position on the sofa. 'What do you think if we don't see each other for a few days?' he asked. The question surprised me. 'You want to stop trying?' I asked. 'It's just that I feel bothered by you and I think it's a good idea to have some space – you know.' I quickly wondered if we were heading into another thirty minute craving. 'Is this you talking or your girlfriend?' I replied. No answer. 'Charlie – how long is a few days?' 'I don't know – give me fifteen.' My stomach went into a knot. I'd decided to go to Dubai on the

17th, to visit a cousin and hoped that we'd have reached a decision about rehab by then. 'So you've decided not to go to Dubai with me? Charlie if I give you fifteen days you will go deeper into your well without little chance of getting out this time…' 'My father told me once that he almost wished I were dead rather than see me like this.' His tone had shifted into the dark. 'I'm tired of being in this squalor – you know. People are waiting for me to die.' 'Well Charlie, I don't know – I think your dad loves you. It's easier for him not to see you suffer when he feels impotent to help you. Besides, what about your son – do you think he feels the same way? Didn't you tell me that he was the only one who respected you and let you live your life?' 'My wife told me that I'm useless – you know?'

I've tried to remain objective about his wife. I'm sure she has her side of the story too, unfortunately however, I had yet to see or hear anything to help maintain an intended healthy level of objectivity. 'Hmm. Charlie, there is a purpose for everything. You know… People's suffering also tests some of the one's who aren't suffering by bringing out the good in them. Like the dog. Possibly the act of getting it back home saved its life… Or like your friend you told me about, who died in a car accident right after he dropped you off at home; maybe Charlie, it's because you have more to do? Maybe Life is willing to get you out of the well because it wants you to help in something else? Maybe it's your son? When he hits the teens his father will be needed, if not more than his mother. I'm sorry Charlie, but your experience in this might be for a bigger picture. You just don't know, but as long as you are in the well you can't know. That was the point to all this, no? Just get out sooner than later – lift the fog. You can always go back to this life, if you don't like the other one… So?' He had turned on his side to face my chair and said nothing. Stubbed out his cigarette and sat up. He looked out the glass doors and drifted far away. He was wearing a black short sleeved T-shirt and blue jeans. My heart felt as though it had paused. 'I'm sorry Michèle, I think it's better for both of us.' My insides went numb. I did not want to challenge him because his decision seemed hard for him to make. He was also being sincere with me and I did not want to vex that. Yet, I was truly afraid to let go. I thought: '*Who is facing me now?*' Was it him? Was it the cocaine? It was probably the both of them talking to me. 'Charlie... are you sure?' I asked quietly. He gave me a slight motion of a nod.

The space around us suddenly felt so silent. I moved to the sofa and sat next to him; looked at him in the eyes and said: 'o.k.' The two syllables removed my sobriety and water leaked into my eyes. 'I'm sorry I didn't help Charlie, but I *know* you *can*.' I gave him a hug, and noticed that he was very good at it and held on until I shifted to kiss his cheek. Then selfishly, I gave him another one on his mouth and paused a fraction of a second before pulling away. 'Take care o.k., go Charlie go,' I whispered. My words provoked a mist across his eyes and then he nodded without a sound. I got up, grabbed my stuff and left. …

The intensity of that moment peaked when I got home. I cried a lot. Then in lieu of tears, got mad. Got my journal and laid into Life: "My question to You is WHY after everything I went through and got past with Jes?! WHY did you bring me Charlie?! I KNOW it was my destiny but WHY? Did I do it wrong the first time, so that I have to relive it again? If it's not about him or about us then WHY? I hadn't even got started here when HE came DIRECTLY into MY life! I HATE you! I'm sorry, but I DO! I don't want anyone in my life anymore – especially if they don't want me! He fuck'n wants fifteen days on his own!? To do what?! *Overtake* Don Juan?!" My head went on some more... '*You know why he didn't erase those missed calls from his phone the other night at football? Because he wanted the phone numbers that we'd erased from his phone chip when we'd first started this idea! Damn it!*' … I paused in my fury. Something hit me. He wasn't giving up. He never said that he wanted to give up. Only that he wanted a few days apart. There it was. Like the metal rings it just happened. Charlie wanted to binge madly before going into rehab; one final good time before giving it up, sort of thing. Relief and panic lapped over me like tired waves. My tears had stopped and turned into dry salt marks on my face. The concept was ludicrous, of course, because the binge would last longer than he thinks and then nobody would have a chance. It had been the cocaine talking to me, not Charlie. The hug? It was all in the hug. Like the dog that needed... My emotional state shifted to wretchedness. I just wanted to go back and hug him again: 'Okay, *what* to do?! Tactics? One: don't let this happen again. It doesn't matter what he tells you, don't give up until he's there. Two: get to know your enemy. Three: patience is a Fuck'n virtue. Four: use the power of words! Five: "careful what you wish for".' I closed my journal, went directly to my computer and began pulling up as much information as possible on rehab centres for cocaine addiction. As I typed my request in GOOGLE my memory recalled an observation that my dad had once made about me: *'You're dogmatic Michèle.'* 'Is that good or bad?' I asked him. *'Great for your friends, not so great for your enemies but definitely good for you – you'll go places my dear, you'll see.'* I remembered smiling shyly and feeling a great sense of fear and excitement from the unequivocal tone of confidence in his words... GOOGLE then gave me a list of options to choose from and as I opened the first one, I whispered to myself: '*Go* Michèle, Go!'

February 10: Tan Mateix.
He took lots of money from Sa Croix last night. And? It's his money, his business. Guess I was right about his intentions. So what? It's not him and you have to deal with charly first, before you can get back to Charlie.

Sent an email to Charlie's brother Mitx letting him know about our decision to stop the challenge. Didn't like his reply, even if it was under the guise of protecting my better interest, it was just typical *tan mateix* (laissez-faire) bull shit! "The addict deceives and misleads people. Let him go and don't follow him on his path. (El adicto embauca y engaña a la gente – déjalo y no lo sigues en su camino)." Hmpft.., couldn't have him on my team. Gives up too quickly. Pragmatic approach curtails possibility. Makes me wonder whose really deceiving who? No wonder Charlie spent so much time in the well; fourteen years trying to call him out of it, without ever trying a rope.

February 11: *Met the owner of the black dog and told him about the other night. He gave thanks. Also mentioned that the dog's chain probably broke loose from the dog house because the dog is so hyperactive. Even when it runs around for a few hours off the chain, 'It's just that it's still a big puppy with a lot of energy, yea know,' said the owner. Mental note to Life: 'Thanks for the reply.'*

February 13: *The hooker seduces and deceives in her professional way. The more she masters her work the more money she lures from the client. In knowing her client, he is almost arrested as her prey, just like the male that enters the web of the Black Widow dame – M NOTES.*

I am privileged to have been the only woman to have spent so much time in his car? The only one, to have been *allowed* to know Carles and Charlie inside and out? Charlie or no Charlie, he's a beautiful man to me; am very attracted to him. Enjoy him very much. It was great. If he wants me – bring him to me. Elisabet and Mitx are at football; will have lunch with them. This is good. They gave me the bear key chain – must not feel betrayed or insecure. Now having a glass of wine, simmering ideas to write, feel like they're on the verge of a boil. I see things but really, what's the point? Yet something pulls? Gawd, please don't let this be just the wine moving me!

February 14: Valentine's.
Walked Dasha this morning after giving a silly home-made Valentine's card to Belle and Mitx. During the walk realised that I don't write about the brief moments of intimacy that Dasha and I sometimes share. Yesterday on the roof terrace when I lay out to get some sun, she came over to me and practically sat on top of me. For about ten minutes she lay there next to me, taking in the sun when, ever so lightly she kissed my exposed breast with a light lick equal to the way of caring for a puppy. We stayed there like that for a bit longer until the heat was too much for her and she moved away. My intuition breezed *Jesy* past my mind... I have had many moments like that with her. She is my world and lucky star – Jes' gift to me. Again, his way of being with me? Walks in the morning and at night, me in bed with her next to me on the floor. The sound of her breathing when we sleep, sometimes she even snores! She is always there to greet me even when I've left her alone for so long. She's calm, gentle without an attitude, beautiful and Aquarius, so much like her dad was... And I love her very much.

February 15: Be my valentine.
Sms Cm:"Gracias Michèle, por todo. Un beso fuerte (Thank you Michèle, for everything. A big kiss)." Charlie hadn't known. He'd just done "it" right, without even trying!

An intuition that called him and told him? Whatever, he followed it. I think Jes was there – I don't know, but late morning on the 14th, I received a surprise sms from Charlie, asking me if I'd like to go to Dexia village with him in order to check out a hotel for his parents' fiftieth anniversary that is going to be celebrated on the 19th. He hadn't realised that it was Valentine's until we made a pit stop into Sa Croix and his employees teased him because he happened to be wearing red! I'd actually made him a card at the same time as I'd made Mitx and Belle's, but had yet to give it to him; I hadn't wanted him to feel any unnecessary pressure about it. So there I was with Charlie. The one *I love*. We drove to the west coast through Juníper, Bunyola and arrived at Deixa by early afternoon. So great. There was rain, sun and wind to conduct a spectacular coastal view of a blue and emerald sea, with foamy white caps that entertained our ride along its rim; moving so elegantly in a deep, anxious, beautiful way. It was really a gorgeous day. After we checked-out the hotel in Dexia Charlie wanted to eat in Estrenc, but the restaurants were closed, so we ended up discovering a nice place in Banyalbufar. There secluded in a village etched into mountains that drop to the sea, Charlie ordered a great lunch: cod salad, paella, wine, water café – really nice. He was ok. He paid for lunch. He even drank, 'To Valentines' and held our eye contact while we clinked and sipped from our glasses. We talked and touched on many things – it went well. On our way back, we stopped at Maribel and Xisco's place. There is a good chance that I'll be in Dubai, so I wanted to know if Maribel wanted to use my car while I'm away. She said yes and Charlie actually offered to drive me to, and pick me up from the airport as a result!? Wow, all so unexpected. In all my years, I have never enjoyed the romance in Valentine's. Ever. Even with Jes that day never really fell into place for us. Close to the final stretch of the way home, Charlie had to make a pit stop into a no-name gas station that was off the opposite side of the main road. While I was waiting in the car, my eyes drifted around at the surroundings and got caught by the name of the side road that intersected ours "Cami de Jesús" (Jesus' Road). Tears filled my eyes instantly. My throat went tight and my body shivered lightly. It was him. 'Holà,' I whispered. I don't know why, but whenever I feel his presence my reaction is instantly emotional between laughter and tears? Anyway, when Charlie and I got home he popped in to see Elisabet and I used that interlude to leave his Valentine card on the passenger seat of his car. He would have found it and known that I had been thinking about him even before his message came. In hindsight, I choose to believe that yesterday was Jes' Valentine gift to me... Perhaps Charlie is a subtle alternate way for another dimension to reach me? It is no secret that being under the influence of stimulant substances increases the human spirit's receptiveness to Life near and far. Different cultures and tribes use them in medicine, spiritual events, the art world uses it for creativity etc. Maybe? ... And maybe, just maybe, Jes and his challenges were my preparation for Charlie's arrival into my life? I cared for him alive in a way that he is now able to reciprocate from Heaven? That maybe a piece of Charlie's greater purpose is about me and helping me to get where I'm supposed to go? Whatever the case, I was the chosen one and spent the best Valentine's ever, with the men of *my* desire.

February 16: *"Unchain my Heart" – Carles singing with Ray Charles in the Phedra.*

"The addict deceives and misleads others"– well everybody's capable of that. Which is worse? One that does it "on" addiction or one that does it on purpose? In fact it is the addict, who is easily deceived and victimized by others: there is the Praying Mantis that hangs around him and to which the addict goes to for a false sense of comfort that is ended within a moment's notice; there are the ones that sell him the drug – the very best in quality of course; the place that gambles and wants him back for more – always makes him feel welcome and cared for while he loses his money more and more, but the worst of them all is the Black Widow dame. The clever one that manages her work with such a fine web of seduction and compassion, to fool her prey into feeling like he is her special one. The price is higher because the addict will return again and again until there is no time between now and then. Like the male sedated in the Black Widow's web, it cannot reason or see beyond her red hourglass bed. Finally, still semi-unconscious when it no longer serves her purpose of maintaining her web, she might choose to feed it to others or simply let it suffer until it's dead. Sigh.

Notwithstanding, being a victim is also a convenient way to nurture one's denial of one's responsibilities. In the film about Ray Charles, his mother says to him: "Ray Charles Jr. promise me that you'll never be a victim by reason of your blindness!" and he promises. So that by reason of the era when he grew up in the United States, his bigger handicap turns out being his skin colour and not his lack of sight. However, when he begins his affair with heroin his handicap turns into a drug addiction. After years of dependency, circumstances finally push him into rehab. Once he has suffered through the worst of the physical detox, he feels ready to return home. At which time his doctor tells him that he must stay in order to continue his psychological therapy. Ray denies the need under the pretence of feeling better. The doctor then continues to explain his understanding of the addict's tricks and lies such that he does not wish to deal with him, if Ray Charles does not wish to follow the rules. Out of frustration, Ray Charles gets up aggressively and as a result trips and falls. Suddenly his mind is flooded by a string of guilt-filled images that have been pursuing him for years since he'd succumbed to the heroin, not his blindness: his wife, his baby brother and his mother. This time however something happens and the images in Ray's memory actually talk to him and forgive him. Including the one with his mother: "Promise me that you will never be a victim again! Not any kind in any colour!" Soon after that, he continues to live his life with the fact that he's blind and threatened only by the heroin. Unfortunately Charlie and I saw the film, without a clue about Ray Charles' heroin addiction and, of course, it hit rather closely to Charlie. There were scenes in the film that he literally lip synced as if it were his own script. Needless to say, I was horrified at myself for having even suggested seeing a movie. Then when I went to bed that night, I pondered the parallels between the men and even managed to find a subliminal absurdity in their names: Carles, Charles, Charlie, charly – Ray? Ray Charles, "Raya de charly (line of coke)" and then I thought, '*what works for the blind, must work for the even blinder*' and so I proclaimed in a louder thought: '*Carles Charlie Serra! Quit being a victim! Get out of that fuck'n well, leave your turmoil in Hell and show them what you're made of!*'

February 17: A better man.

8:50a.m., Barcelona airport to Dubai. Dasha and Mini with Maribel and Xisco. Ironic considering that last year when the three of us drove past a Mini I jokingly said to Maribel: 'How about I buy one of those and lend it to you when I'm away, in exchange for taking care of Dasha?' ...Glad I'm not *all* talk and no action. I'm anxious, but the distance from home will do me good. I went straight to bed at Charlie's place last night. He never joined me and that sucked. He came into the bedroom, sat on top of the bedcovers next to me, leaned over me and while gently moving the hair from my eyes asked quietly: 'Do you mind if I go out for a bit?' 'No,' I answered in a whisper, but my insides tensed up. Would he get back in time to take me to the airport? Even if he did – would he be able to drive? 'Do you want me to party with you?' I said, totally dismissing the former effort to hide my concerns. He contemplated my face in an attempt to read between my lines. All I could see was the amber colour that the hall light brought out from his eyes. He seemed to understand something, smiled slightly and slowly shook his head against my suggestion. 'I'm not going out for that,' he answered and

I didn't say more. I slept little if at all. I was left behind with a plethora of scenes made wilder by my imagination. Was he with the prostitutes? Particularly the Romanian one? I know she has his number and vice versa. According to him, she has a short blond hair cut, which rings bells about his wife who has the same hair style. My mind escaped to the wife. Everything about their perpetual relationship was correlated with his addiction. According to Charlie, they met when he was only 18. His professional success began much before he'd even started doing charly at the age of 28; a detail that I sometimes remind him of, when he is feeling ill confident about his personal capabilities. By the age of 30 Charlie was consuming on a regular basis, his world by night became bigger, while prostitutes and pornography became another way of life. Yet during those years, according to him and everyone else, he and his wife still maintained a turbulent relationship until they were finally married by city hall in a village that was familiar to neither one of them. Such that Charlie's commitment was most likely not made in complete sobriety. A fact that only fuels my doubts about his wife's own sobriety. One year later his wife became pregnant and Charlie was faced with fatherhood most likely by reason of tradition rather than desire. Everyone knows including his wife, that Charlie's views on marriage and parenthood are more realistic than traditional, such that he probably would not have ever been married or had a child until much later in his life, if ever at all. At 31 his son was born. In hindsight, there had been love between them and their son a gift from that. Charlie acknowledges this; to which I suggested that the marriage is not their demise, rather, their inability to mature by it. Anyway, the trials of their relationship deepened and underlined nothing more than two people incompatible for each other, flanked by the social restraints of their time, their families' shadow, baser emotional skills and psychological challenges with both of them: his addiction and her inherent negativity. So that during his dark moments, once the cocaine's high begins to subside, his thoughts often border on paranoia and anger about her. During these moments he sometimes suggests that his wife has been a prostitute behind his back. Once he showed me a photograph of a prostitute and associated her to being his wife. In between those lines, there had been hearsay unrelated to Charlie, from people including Charlie's family, who speculated that his wife had not been entirely faithful to him either. However in light of Charlie's own catatonic lifestyle, it would seem logical that neither one could be. It is quite possible too, that his insecurities about his wife were trumped up from a mere reflection of his own scruples trying to find imperfections in others in order to relieve his own. That a man who loves a woman and works obsessively away from home is bound to inherit insecurity issues about his wife, especially if she is not able to understand his devotion to her, through his work. Communication between someone like Charlie and his partner would have to be forth coming and real; in light of his cultural background tough to imagine. Hence his suffering is not about imagining infidelity but about her denial of it. He just wants the truth. Few people understand that there is compassion in undesired truth. It's not the information that matters so much as how it's delivered. Once, when he was having one of those dark moments, I went with his flow and suggested that if his assumptions were true, maybe his wife went to prostitution in order to be closer to him and his world? He remained pensive after that ... Sigh. By 3a.m., I was lying awake in bed. He hadn't called and wasn't answering his phone either. Then I was baited by the fact that he has no qualms sharing a bed with his son or a prostitute, but he does with me? Okay, so there is no attraction or desire. It's platonic with the security of my friendship. I felt queasy thinking about the times he's patted my forehead like I were his daughter, rather than a mature woman of 38. Then my anxiety shifted briefly to Dasha and a fear of losing her, over to my need to establish an income and position a new career. Then the thoughts bobbed and floated back to Charlie – he lies to me? Uses his predicament to his advantage? I know that, but dismiss it as a part of the addiction… Mental gymnastics kept me alert until he arrived home at 5a.m. I heard the front door open, bang closed and the sound of the couch objecting to his weight. I had already been up and waiting to go. My flight left at 7:30a.m., so we had to leave by 6a.m. latest. Incredibly, he got back into his car and drove 45 minutes to get me to the airport. I never could have done that. We talked on the way. Apparently there were no women involved in his late night out, just a few buddies, his girlfriends: Cocaine and Whisky. I shared my vexation about the prostitutes and he offered more details about his night out, ending with the fact that he'd left his phone in the car. It explained my unanswered calls, as well as an intention to avoid them and not have to lie about it. … 'Sorry Michèle – for not getting back sooner,' he said.

'Nah, it's okay Charlie – you're still driving me to the airport like you said,' I replied sincerely. He nodded slightly to my words. 'I wanted another moment to share the bed with you before Dubai that's all, melodramatic stuff you know…'

'No no me too, that's why I'm sorry.' His words made me feel better; lies or not. I placed my hand in its reserved spot upon his right thigh while he drove and we stayed content like that for a little until I removed my hand, shifted my posture slightly and spoke again: 'Charlie, I have a difficult time understanding the prostitutes..,' I said casually. A pause. He looked serene behind his shades and seemed to be thinking. 'I don't care about the prostitutes you know. I never went to them before. They're a part of the squalor I live in,' he said with a slight reproach.

'Hmm,' I said while looking through the passenger window. 'You know Carles,' I looked at him and continued calmly, 'if you told me that I was great, but you're not attracted to me, I'd be hurt, but better off you know?' I added soberly. He turned his look towards me then back at the road. 'It's not that. I find myself content and satisfied with you,' he said. 'It's just that I can't. Plus I don't think that I meet your needs...'

'What do you think I need from a relationship?' I asked.

'I suppose fidelity, sexual compatibility, a best friend, responsibility, emotional support, trust...' he trailed off. I noticed that he hadn't mentioned economic security or independence as possibilities. Some things in Spain are evolving faster than others. Self-awareness for each gender and relationships between men and women however, are not one of them. There are still men who meet an economically capable woman and think there's no room to provide for her, rather than enjoy sharing the responsibility and the economic benefit that comes with it. Such that I'm often perceived as neither needing nor wanting their help because I'm often too forthright about carrying my own weight and pay or go Dutch on things. The truth of the matter is, I've never had the privilege of having my livelihood paid for. Ever. My parents equipped my brothers and me with the tools, not the money. Hence the very tool that allows me to be self-sufficient simultaneously contradicts my sincere appreciation for chivalrous and gallant protocol by men. In truth my needs require a love sowed with economic sharing, personal independence and emotional fidelity. Charlie by virtue of his accepted role as a provider could and would handle the economic issue well, by economically supplementing and/or supporting my own. His suggestions therefore were good, but not unique to me or anyone for that matter. I was quiet for a moment ... 'Hmm. Pretty much what everyone needs no? You didn't mention money or independence – two factors where you score well with me Charlie. I am almost 40 years old and have a pretty good idea of my needs. In light of what you have said there isn't one that you don't do well. You are all of that. O.K., so you seek out porn and prostitutes but not because you love them. Maybe because your ego still feeds on Obsession and Possession? Maybe you don't race out at night for the coke, rather you can't handle losing ownership of your prostitutes to other clients. Like Vanesa. Maybe you really do want to try something with her and don't know how? It's your way of life now which is all connected to the addiction and a proud misinterpreted love between you and your wife. You said so yourself, that in health, you don't need any of them. That you and I could "probably enjoy a compatible relationship with a satisfying sex life," were your words I believe. I tend to agree Carles. Until now, you have been quite forthright with me. In spite of the addiction and your catatonic lifestyle you've been painfully sincere and told me like it is – you know? ...You still get to me on time, you're not a talker-no-action guy. Say it and you do it! You've proven to be sensitive and affectionate, you can maintain a conversation with me, which says a lot about you, you offset my weaknesses, you have passion and adventure in you, we share languages, you respond and communicate to me directly and I don't think you have overtly lied to me – yet.'

'No I haven't,' he confirmed quickly. 'Well then, you pretty much give me what I need Charlie. You've been great,' I responded as nonchalantly as possible. He gave me an appreciative look before it seemed to scurry back behind his fear of not being able to maintain the beauty that I see in him. 'Well,' he said, 'when I'm better, I *give* more!' he added emphatically. 'That might be too much for me,' I replied and laughed. When we got to the airport I gave him thanks for following through with the ride, hugged him and kissed him. He then folded his arms and said: 'I wish I was going with you.' I didn't reply. It was another emotional whim that he was feeling, but it did feel good. 'Good luck with your parents' anniversary and go get 'em Charlie!' I tooted. 'Take care!,' he shot back and I disappeared behind airport doors.

Dubai, February 18
Sms Cm – *"M sabes donde esta mi americano negro no lo encuentro (M do you know where my black jacket is, I can't find it)?"*
Sms Mc – *"En tu armuario. Sinon mira en el mio. Tal vez debajo los mios de la lavandaria (In your closet. If not look in mine under my suits from the cleaners)."*
Sms Cm – *"Thanks."*

Dubai, February 19: Parents' 50th anniversary, sms Mc – *"Hi C. U o.k."*

Dubai, February 21 – Friend or foe?
Sms Cm: "Have nice dreams. Cuidate. Saluda de mi parte a quien quieras – un beso para ti. (Take care. Regards from me to anyone you like – a kiss for you)."

No income. My Visa card is maxed-out. This trip to Dubai is about something but nothing soon, is what I feel. Glad I was here ten years ago – now it's such a silly place. I'm sad and very alone. Depressed and sincerely worried about my life, love, age and money. I suddenly feel my age. I have no money, no idea or real desire to *get there*, confused by my feelings and hopes for Carles when there are none... Dunno. My concern is that I'm losing stamina from so much rejection and uncertainty. Maybe my "love" will be infectious and dissuade Charlie from the prostitutes? The more involved he gets with them the longer it will take, to get him out of the well, if at all. Then there is his "wife" who actually told him, 'Be careful, I heard that Mitx is sniffing for the rubia too...' The comment was not only insensitive to Elisabet and Mitx, but simply provoked nothing more than bad energy and Charlie's insecurities. 'What?' I said to Charlie when he told me, 'is she trying to show her deference and loyalty to you by manipulating you with gross untruths? Somebody in the village probably asked Mitx about me and he probably replied with a few kind adjectives, that's all. Every time you get close to emotional freedom she finds a way to arrest you! Why don't you just ask him instead of enjoying the attention? She's toying with *you*, yea know! You hate being the object of ridicule and deceit, but you don't do anything to avoid it! Fuuck Charlie!' I'd pronounced to him emphatically, "that pisses me off! Even my reaction plays into the game – yuck!!' … Really, Cat and Carles are meant for each other in squalor. Her name written with a small *c* means "human excrement" in Castilian Spanish while the diminutive *charly* is slang for the dirty snow. They can't be together in happiness, but they can wallow in each other's misery very well. He's a cocaine addict and she borders manic depressive. He's possessive, with a large ego, while she plays the victim with dramatic self-interested lines directed by an immature spirit. Both are emotionally obsessed with each other's lives – one can't allow the other to be happy before the other. Prostitutes and wives how can any woman who wants to be with Charlie compete with that? Then again, w*hy* would she? Is a better question. *Why*, do I want him out of the well? What are my quiet expectations…? Success; to win. To defy the ones who say he can't when I say he Can; to let Charlie know that he *can* and for him to feel good about himself and me about me. Arrogance; to sentence artificial reality that manipulates the truth. I want to know the truth. I want to know which one wins my debate. My head or my heart? They work together, but which one is my warrior? I want to know which one is friend and which one is foe? Which one will clearly define my idealism into reality? Emily Brontë would understand, if I used her words from "Wuthering Heights" that my "most powerful emotions" seem to "lie with" Charlie. In which case, we don't actually hook up until after death. Still, I will expect head and heart to do everything in their power trying. Then whatever the final verdict, I shall be satisfied.

February 23: s*ms Mc* – *"Hi. At airport. Would you like to see me when*

I return?"
Sms Cm – "Claro. Claro que si *(Of course).* Have a good trip. xo."

Trip back to Mayürqa fine, until I arrived at the airport and discovered that my luggage was lost. Got home with Dasha and the car and saw Elisabet before everyone else. We gave each other a small update about the week gone by including the Serra's anniversary. Apparently Charlie's wife attended too. After the update Charlie picked me up around 8:30p.m., and we went for dinner in C'an Colom: 'You're very pretty,' he said looking at me as though it were for the first time. I wasn't wearing anything great. Just blue jeans and a blouse, tho my hair was a bit different because I'd pulled it back a bit. I smiled: 'Thank you. I should go away more often,' I relayed theatrically and climbed into the Phedra. Our first intention had been to have dinner at the restaurant next to the church. Once the Phedra turned onto the main road and got ready to enter the side road Charlie impulsively ran his left hand over my breasts. His impulse surprised me and my body responded instantly. He was still driving and glanced between me and the road while I responded to his caress by meeting his hand with my lips. As he tried to go beyond the restriction of my blouse, I tried to help by undoing it. The Phedra turned into the dark side road and stopped. Our reaction was impetuous. Seat belts went flying, belt clips clattered and zippers went down and mouths met letting tongues intertwine. Charlie's good with his mouth. I really like his mouth. Then despite the Phedra's physical restrictions we managed a sort of 69 position within complete darkness of the car, with only the stars to witness and hear the sounds of our breathing and physical fury. I listened for him and when I heard my name whispered, followed by his groan, I then gave-in too and from a stone hedged road the Phedra echoed passion into the night. The flurry of the moment ended as quickly as it started. 'I liked it,' he said, giving me a final quick kiss on the mouth and looking overwhelmed by the moment. I don't know who was more needy, he or I, but this time it was me who wanted more. I was delighted by the moment and Charlie seemed both delighted and unsure about what his next code of conduct was: I was not a prostitute, nor his wife nor some hitch-hiker he'd picked up. It was me. I tried to alleviate his insecurity and said: 'The Phedra's definitely not the best for fool'n around in.' I grinned. 'Nope,' he smiled back. Started the car and we drove off. Most restaurants happened to be closed so we headed for C'an Colom. Once we sat for dinner, I gave him his gift from Dubai. A very unique silver ring with a moveable centre and an Arabic script etched inside of it. It fit his wedding finger perfectly. I was pleased with myself because he is not easy to buy for and his hand size was difficult to imagine without him. 'Molt guapo, (very nice),' he said while he admired it on his left hand and shifted the centre piece back and forth with his other hand, 'me gusta mucho. Gracias (I like it very much. Thank you).'

I sensed from his body language that he really did like it. 'Now we both have cool rings from cool places,' I said referring to the one he'd given me from Paris. After dinner we stopped-in at Mitx and Elisabet's and gave them their gifts from Dubai. It was a nice time…

Now it's 12:30a.m., he's probably gone out again. I know Charlie's impulse tonight was less about missing me and more about his invented obligation to please. Wish I was wrong, but he's been with the other. He saw the prostitute the same night I flew to Dubai and then after. Basically he had an emotional debt with me, like he has with gambling, his wife and intimacy, plus the fact that my presence unlike the prostitutes, does highlight his infidelity to his wife because he does care about me. All cocaine aside, I could find myself victimized from loving a married man who won't divorce himself from his wife because he uses his marriage licence as a surrogate truth and emotional scapegoat to fend off sentimentality from prostitutes and off-road flings. Unfortunately this transmits to me and makes me feel like a mistress or a young chick that doesn't convince a man to take me seriously enough to want to grow old with me. I'm almost forty, content to do it on my own with my dog, and yet I can still feel like a has-been when an almost-been rejects me? I might be attractive to him but don't fit the wife, or mother stereotypes that he's used to. I'm thinking that the addiction is used as an excuse for his evasive behaviour when his yo-yo ways probably existed before it started. That his relationship with his wife just fuelled the addiction more? '...*Hmm.., thank you Dr. M. for your opinionated assessment.*' 'Any time.'

February 24: *Sometimes I feel I've got to – run away, I've got to – get away...From the pain that you drive into the heart of me, the love we share seems to go nowhere and I've lost my light for I toss and turn I can't sleep at night. Once I ran to you, now I'll run from you. This tainted love you've given me I gave you all a boy could give you. Take my tears and that's not nearly all. You don't really want any more from me to make things right... you think love is to pray. Well, I'm sorry I don't pray that way! Don't touch me please. I cannot stand the way you tease I love you though you hurt me so. Now I'm going to pack my things and go, Tainted love.[Me haces sentir que tengo, que huir; Que tengo, que salir del dolor inmenso que está causando en mí. Tu amor ya no tiene solución y si pierdo la razón es de darle vueltas sin poder dormir. Una vez fui hacia ti - ahora me voy de ti. Este amor envenenado es todo lo que tú me has dado – Ni una lagrima vales de amor. Nunca has hecho nada bueno por mí. Sabrás que el amor no es aguantar si es tu forma de pensar de esta forma no quiero jugar...Ohhh Falso amor"]* 'TAINTED LOVE', SOFT CELL / 'FALSO AMOR', LA UNION, LYRICS ADAPTED.

Psychology. It exhausts me when I try to sort it out. I can do it quickly with my mind's eye but to dissect it, or "solidify" it on paper or with words is tiresome. This time it's about the wife. That will never go away, even with a divorce she will always be in the picture by reason of their son; a convenient tool to get Charlie's attention using their son's rights. I thought that I was dealing with a guy in love with cocaine when in fact I am emotionally arrested by a man fucked up by his wife! Really, a marriage that fuels the cravings, black widows that nurture them and a cold hearted addiction, offer little room for possibility when there was little room to begin with. The wife attended his parents' 50th because the parents had invited her. According to local protocol, social graces prompted Charlie's parents to extend an invitation to her because of their friendship with her parents. With the same token I think the wife's protocol should have been to kindly refuse the invite, especially as it is well understood that she and Carles are not together anymore and especially because the emotional dynamics between them are so unhealthy. It would have been correct and enough to have sent the parents a gift on her behalf with Charlie's son who also attended. Instead she attended, dressed in a mini skirt, just the way he likes it and maintained airs by sitting next to him at the table and displaying physical attention to him, even in the family photos. It would seem that after a few drinks she stung him well and they agreed to meet each other after dinner. Charlie's rendition was that she'd invited him home after the dinner to talk about things and I'm thinking why couldn't it have been somewhere neutral like a coffee shop? So she left the event first and he caught up with her later at her place, which used to be their place. Like high school lovers who share a secret plan for intimacy unbeknown to others because they're not *suppose*d to be together. Once Charlie arrived the Black Widow simply lured him into the home, spun her web, teased him and then left him in emotional turmoil again. In simpler words he felt a desire and she refused him. He left more messed up from the humility of rejection by his wife than by being with a prostitute. Like a Black Widow she won't kill him or let go of him, just exhaust the emotional turmoil until he's his own demise not hers. In this case too, the prostitute wins because he'll look for her afterwards. In all fairness to the wife her drama is no less difficult. Charlie's lifestyle invites insecurity, emotional confusion and when love is rejected it metamorphoses through the stages of hate. Notwithstanding it is assumed that she has had more than ten years to at least file and complete a divorce. That she is still healthier than Charlie and out of respect to her son's rights would act more maturely about her pain, while Charlie has said to me more than once that his marriage needs ending: 'Esto tiene que acabar YA! (This has to finish NOW!)'

February 25 – Avoiding the way to perdition.
"Take care of the end as you do the beginning and you won't reap failure"– LAOZI.

As early as January we actually drove to the village where Charlie and Cat were married in order to pick up a copy of their marriage certificate. Again it was the first step towards solving something between them, ever! Such that it came to a climactic moment for Charlie just outside city hall doors. He wouldn't go inside. Instead he wanted to sit on a bench and smoke another cigarette. It was close to 2p.m. right when the place closes. I stood out front refusing to go in for him. It had to come from Charlie. The role was not new to me. I became "Attila of the Hun" when faced with turmoil. It recalled my memory about my own father and his own struggle to follow through with the separation from my mother. Like shooting a horse with a bad leg it had to be done. Truth can only be stretched so much until it snaps back like a rubber band and hurts you twice as much. Likewise, it's always easier to see things from the outside of someone's dilemma but in reality, I was not. I was my father's daughter and in Charlie's case, I was the one with the memory. All time and effort has been exhausted between Charlie and his wife. Still he was sceptical and hesitant. The scepticism was about me; a female so insistent that he get a divorce, so insistent that he get better sooner than later – why? If I were a male friend to Charlie my actions would be defined as an altruistic good friend. However as a female friend my energies are constantly challenged and never accepted for their logical reasons. Not excluding the fact that my presence shows him another road that in his heart he'd never wanted to take. In all fairness what does it matter what my desired end is, if it means nothing less than a win-win situation for him and his family? The latter reason was deeper. Charlie is by definition an ethical man who works hard and believes in family. A step towards divorce highlights an unwanted truth. A feeling of insecurity that one's choices might have been wrong. Indignant that one's sketch of the future was not good enough to be a painting or maybe in Charlie's case anger at himself for having vacillated for so long that a lifestyle chose him before he did. Even more difficult is the option of finally being the owner of his destiny, that is overwhelmed by a starting position at the mature age of 44, affected by an addiction that will require psychological time to heal even beyond the physical remission, while a sybaritic spirit denies him the ability to try the experience again even if it may be attained differently. Without a doubt, it makes the option of holding on to the past seem more attractive than building anew… Sigh, "Join the club". If he could, Charlie would, like most, go back to his wife. Ironically though, the perfect goals are only fulfilled after knowing the defects from a previous experience. 'But life doesn't have to be so drastic,' I told him when we were in the Phedra, 'try to change the chip Charlie. The choice to get married was not wrong because you have a son. Now there is an opportunity to end things well and move on. Learn by doing is a lifetime experience you know?'

It is also true that sometimes things are better left as they are. Especially when Charlie and his wife have been attached to each other in a stagnant position for more than twenty years – why bother? ... Because they're all needlessly suffering greatly from it. ... It was five minutes to two: '¿Que Charlie? – what's wrong?' I asked him. He shook his head left to right as if to shoo his thoughts away: 'I don't know..,' he replied. 'Poc a poc, little by little. Charlie, you can always reconcile with your wife if there are regrets, but if you don't try this option you'll never know or have the chance to get back to it, you know..? It's not about me Charlie. Really. The sooner you listen to yourself, the sooner you'll get there. Venga (C'mon).' ... At a minute to two he walked in and walked out with the certificate. Following that, the idea was to get the divorce process rolling, while the steps toward it were as straightforward as handing the copy to his brother, who has power of attorney over his affairs until further notice. Then allow his brother to manage the paperwork between the lawyers and the wife. That was in January and suddenly the process has been delayed. Naturally, it is not in Charlie's best interest to file for a divorce while he is active, with the same token such rhetoric would not exist if the wife's interest were invested in her husband's health, her son's needs and her own freedom. Had she initiated a divorce sooner, Charlie's reaction might have been to plunge deeper into the drug or run to rehab. Either way fifteen years would not have gone by, did anyone think of that? Why hasn't she followed through if Charlie won't? Black Widow? Co-dependent syndrome? Ignorance? What are people waiting for!? ...A life lived in purgatory is a life not lived!

February 26: "*Aw baby... Now you found the secret code, I use to wash away my lonely blues well I can't deny or lie 'cause you're the only one who can make me fly. You know what you're doing to me don't you... You can turn me upside down inside out and I must react to claims of those who say that you are not all that, because you can make me feel the real deal - I can give it to you any time because you're mine! Sexbomb, you're my sexbomb and baby you can turn me on...*" – 'SEX BOMB', TOM JONES, LYRICS ADAPTED.

Vanesa. Charlie's favourite prostitute and cocaine buddy; Romanian, brunette about 24. He wasn't sure. He thinks that she might be older while I bet she is. According to him, she's only been in Mayürqa for eight months and does cocaine already. He enjoys her when he's with her in a way that I will never know. I don't do drugs. He'd met her before he'd met me, kissed her way before he asked me. Found her on nights after he'd already found me. Took her places where he was going to take me. With all that, I'm actually okay with her presence and the others, except now he gets tired of me quickly. Sigh. I think that the more he falls for me, the more his obsession for her resists me and re-calls him back to her. We had some good bed chat before the crack of dawn this morning about her and a few other areas. It was like a good therapy session that wouldn't be repeated because Charlie's behaviour changes constantly. The adage that "the same river can't be crossed twice." is a good metaphor for anyone living with an addiction. Today he made a reference to us as a couple, but how long his mind's eye retains that thought is anybody's guess. Still, these moments save us, rather energise us. He seems calmer and I am definitely more focused on getting him away from here. 'What do you talk about?' I asked.

'Nothing really. Mostly about her,' he answered... 'Sometimes about you,' he suddenly added.

'Me??' I was both surprised and sadly pleased by this. 'You talk about me?'

'She knows that you're my English teacher; since then she'll say "how's your teacher?"'

My mind zoomed into sick happy land. If he talked about me

that could either mean that he has feelings for me or none at all. 'She's jealous Charlie,' I said softly, 'she's possessive of you.' I saw him smile and realised that telling him that only fed his ego more, but they were words of caution to him. 'I know what you're thinking Charlie, but I don't deny my affection for you. Nor do I charge for it. Does she know you're married and have a son?'

'Probably.'

'You don't talk about them then?' I asked fearfully.

'Nooo,' he cooed.

'Well, I think that's wise, not that my opinion matters.' I added. 'Why?' He asked interested.

'No reason really, but you have become intimate with her Charlie. The repercussions of a prostitute rejected by a man she falls for are greater than one who leads a different kind of profession.'

'Meaning?' he asked.

I sat myself up, 'Profession aside, you don't know the culture that she's from. Her experience with men from her country is not the same experience here and life or death in the name of love is not unusual to her. She's from a country in Eastern Europe; a country that is economically challenged and where the young woman's best tool for survival is still her looks. A place where the Cinderella theme is twisted because love is not even a priority until she finds a mature man who can give her economic security first, then work on the love part. Hence arranged marriages there are common. Some do well and others are unhappy and dissatisfied because they can't keep the love rhetoric alive forever; especially when they're unable to find the chemistry, you know? In the meantime, she remains as the calendar type housemaid stimulating her man's lost sense of vitality as long as he takes care of her like a princess. It's actually to their advantage, because the lack of initial love makes it easier to focus on their egocentric needs first, much like prostitution, but glorified Charlie. It's one way of living, that's all. Then my imagination goes wild and I think of the film "Fatal Attraction" you know?' He smiled …'Where's your pinkie ring from Paris?' I noticed it was missing from his hand and then realised that I had not seen it since my return from Dubai. He was a bit self-conscious and answered: 'I dunno. She was around me and being a bit of a nuisance, asked to look at it and didn't give it back to me.'

'Took it from you? Did you ask for it back?'

'Yea, but she played hard to get.'

'Charlie you gave it to her the same way *you* gave her your number – she's your girl right? You're like a pseudo underground couple,' I trailed off.

'Nahhh. She took the ring from me while I was playing cards. I didn't ask for it back to avoid playing into her game and she got my number from there.'

'Cards? You said you would take me out to those places and never have. Yet you take Vanesa. If you didn't ask for the ring back she will think that you gave it to her; she'll add sentimental value to it. I think you like that Charlie.'

'Nah. I don't think so,' he added.

'Really Charlie it's no big deal, but look at your actions. Vanesa gets the ring instead of your son. Okay, but at least admit it. If you like that world so much then just let us all know so that we can stop trying to help you when you don't need it. Do you have feelings for her?'

'No,' he replied quickly, 'she does coke you know – It's all here,' he said tapping his forehead.

'Is she addicted to it like you?'

'No, I don't think so. Though she's been taking more lately – I don't know,' he said shunning his words.

'Maybe it's an insecure reaction to your deference to me?' I offered. 'Charlie? Your memory's connection between coke and her will take you down faster; you've already crossed the professional lines with her into personal ones. You open up to her, you're vulnerable to her and worse than that, your cravings now associate her with the taking. I worry Charlie. Pretty soon you won't open the door for me you know. Then how do I reach you?'

'Nah Michèle,' he said rubbing his eyes. 'Don't worry so much. I will get the ring back,' he sounded through an evasive yawn, 'it's cocaine, nothing else – all under control.'

February 27: Intellectual Love.
She studied something hardly known; something to do with arts and philosophy. She was smart and enchanting in such a provocative way and her catlike eyes would pierce right through me: Jung, Freud, Simone de Beauvoir, Goethe, Beckett, Cosmos, Gershwin, Shakespeare William, Guggenheim.. I don't want you to think so much, "cumbiera" intellectual. I'm gonna pray to your Saint for yea, so that you can be more normal and set yourself free ... [Estudiaba una carrera poco conocida; algo con ver con letra y filosofía Era linda y hechicera su contoneada; sus ojos de lince me atravesaban.. Jung, Freud, Simone de Beauvoir, Goethe, Beckett; Cosmos, Gershwin, Shakespeare William, Guggenheim... ¡Yo no quiero que pienses tanto, cumbiera intelectual! Yo voy a rezarle a tu santo para que te puedas soltar...Para que seas más normal.] – 'CUMBIERA INTELECTUAL', KEVIN JOHANSEN, LYRICS ADAPTED.

'Hi Vanesa – I'm Michèle. May I ask you out of deference to me and with respect to Carles to keep your professional life at work ... Don't call him anymore. Thank you.' How I wish. My ego didn't want to accept that I was wrong. With deference to avoid making idle threats I wasn't going to call him or see him, but I let Id convince me to do something, left Ego at home and went over to Charlie's, content with Super Ego's case that I ought to give Charlie a new telephone chip in exchange for taking mine back from him last night. Hence at eleven this morning I was at his door and he let me in. When he saw me, I think I detected some happy gloating in his expression; the one pleased for not having given in first. As he might have been thinking about me, but his ego or dubious state of mind made it easier for him not to call. My arrival therefore alleviated both of them. I went straight to his room and laid beside him, suddenly feeling a flush of relief through my system. I think he felt it too because we were at once calm, comfortable and able to chat again about the night before.

We'd gone for dinner and within minutes of sitting down, his phone on the table received a sms: "Hola guapo. ¿Que haces? (Hey good looking what's up?)" He calmly looked at it but made no attempts to reply. 'It's her isn't it?' I said as casually as possible.

'I suppose,' he said.

'You can answer her back you know – it's no big deal,' I said as if I had it all under control.

'Nah– leave it.' I was irked. I wanted him to reply. His words from that day we'd gone to the dentist's, "Out of deference to me..." flashed passed me. 'If you don't reply she'll know that you're with someone, most likely me...'

'Nah. If I don't reply, she doesn't know if I've seen the message or not.' His answer was rhetoric. If she knows Charlie like I do, she would have guessed correctly that he was not alone. Charlie turns his phone off when he does not want any calls, otherwise, it's always on and mostly with him. 'Um, Charlie? Not replying suggests to me that you share a code of conduct between each other; you're allowing the lines of communication to stay open because you want her. O.K., so it's personal between you two.'

'Nah,' he denied again.

'O.k., so can I send her a message? Just a simple "Hello V, this is M how are you?", so that she knows that you're with me? She already knows who I am; just your English teacher. Its not like I'm a threat to your relationship you know?' My words had been easy going, but my adrenalin was rising. I picked up his phone. He watched and said nothing. Who was going to react first? Without a doubt, Charlie was enjoying my reaction to the little cat game he'd provoked. As soon as I picked up on that, my instincts suddenly allied with V and a need to send her an sms reply in defence to our sorority. We were both being manipulated while both of us were also allowing for it, as a means to our desired ends. Charlie too was being manipulated and this is where I got caught: who was the joker? Who was playing who? She wanted money, he wanted coke and I wanted to organise chaos in the name of love. As if my *beautiful* motives would protect me like a warrior's shield against evil. My memory recalled my mother: "Michèle come down to earth!" Indeed, I was the fool being played. The two of them could use and abuse each other, but I was the one being hurt trying to defend the underdog when the underdog was me. 'O.K.? Can I send her a hello?' I said once more before taking myself seriously. I caught a flicker in his eye that told me that he was no longer having fun. 'Venga,' he said as he reached for his phone, 'dejalo (let it go) – okay.'

We ordered and then he went to the men's room. My brain whizzed and whirred. *'Was he replying to her from the men's room? Was he taking a hit? Do I really care?– No.'* Relief found me. I really didn't care. It was the child, my Id in me that did. It didn't like them getting away with the truth and suggesting that I was the fool. Id wanted to prove itself right with the same craving as one who investigates a crime until one's assumptions are satisfied. Charlie and I are not so different; we have dogmatic and sybaritic qualities meaning our behaviour can be excessive as friend or as foe to ourselves. I was sitting at the table in the restaurant suffering mental gymnastics for the same reason that he does about his wife's unwillingness to satisfy his truth about her presumed infidelity: I needed self-justifying. Like those individuals who search for the Holy Grail, whose quest will always be a courageous and singular one because it is lived without the masses' voice of confidence. "I motivate Me" then becomes the other voice you learn to trust, regardless of whether or not logic and emotion are temporarily blind, self-justification becomes a pinnacle tool for one's own personal survival. When he drove me home the final drop that overflowed the cup was either me or the one glass of white wine that I'd had at dinner: 'Charlie,' I explained once we were back in the Phedra, 'your deference to her confuses me. I would like to think that my presence in your life means more to you than hers, tha –'

'Of course,' he said cutting me off in mid-sentence.

'Okay, but you could make that clear to the "enemies",' I ended in a puff. He said nothing which provoked my need to say more. 'What *do* you clearly understand about me with you?' Pause.

'I don't know,' he answered.

'You *don't* know? Charlie! We've been hanging out since November, and you don't know!?'

My tone was childish and I sooo wanted to list *every*thing that we'd achieved since then, but it wasn't up to me to remind him just because I was feeling rejected. Under copacetic circumstances such things really *don't* matter to anyone. Not even to me, you just thank Life for having been there, seen it, and done it...

'I don't *know* – I *don't* know!' he replied anxiously. He stopped the car at my place. Pause. I looked at him, on the verge of making a dramatic exit, I said almost inaudibly: 'Charlie please return my telephone chip to me.' He hesitated. 'Really,' I said, 'you gave your number to everyone including V and your wife. There is no reason why you can't go back to using your own telephone number.' He listened to me with a sad face, then moved slowly, almost meticulously in returning the chip to me, followed directly by a swift movement of his arms back into the defensive folded position.

'Thank you...' I paused a moment then followed through: 'Charlie?' I began with an assertive but soft tone, 'I love you very much, but please don't call me until you're clear and not before.' Without a word he gave a light nod and I kissed him good night on his cheek. Got down from his car and he drove away; so much for avoiding drama. My heart was going a mile a minute, my head was exhausted yet the debate between the two continued. Logic was angry with my statement to him because my words left it up to him to contact me, removing therefore any likelihood of us getting in touch again! Uuugh. I was finally challenged by my own golden rule not to say anything that I did not intend to stick to. Up until last night I'd made that task easy to do: 'NOW W*HAT*?!!' I ranted and raved throughout the house, 'Charlie isn't clear because he can't be, *stupid*! His cocaine buddy is a prostitute, he's practically doing every two days on and two days off and he's losing weight as we speak! You got mad at him when the culprit is you! It's going to get worse and you're giving him ultimatums!?! When did Jealousy knock out my objectivity? Where was *I*?!!' Insane malicious hope wanted him to blame our little conflict on V and the cocaine because I wanted him to see how it damages the good things around him, but then my heart piped in: 'He doesn't want to hurt you and he doesn't want to lie to you so stop lecturing him! – don't pressure him! *You* led him to believe that you're O.K. with everything, only to patronize him when he least expected it! – Y*ou're* the fogged up one!' I scolded. 'Women!' I continued in full soliloquy, 'beautiful creatures put on Earth to substitute for guilt while trying to find a balance between their nurturing instinct for others and that for themselves. In the meantime, until we get it right we're forever confusing things by over-riding our truth that we're NOT Perfect! While Men!!' I continued feverishly, 'are the sensitive creatures put on Earth to substitute for guilt while they try to find a balance between their natural instinct to hurt the things they love and their natural instinct to protect them! .. Intimidated by the fact that they KNOW that they're not perfect! ... *Who* the fuck IS Perfect!? – I wanna smack him! And don't give me any of that God rhetoric! We all know that Jesus died because His dad wasn't perfect either! Men hide the truth from women because they don't want to be reminded that they're not perfect, while women deny the truth from men because they can't admit they're not perfect! NOBODY – nothing is perfect so that makes us all PERFECT!?! Who's WE - The Universe!? Got it all under *control* have you!?!... fuuck,' I paused. Realising that my only audience was Dasha on her mat, sending me a mild look of shock and concern from her velvet eyes, at the same time as she offered me nervous tail batting on the floor for my performance...

I stood there, with the bedroom closet doors opened in front of me, but I couldn't remember why or how I got there. I chuckled slightly, closed the closet doors and rubbed my forehead lightly. 'Gawd .. and Who *am I* talking to?!' I laughed despite myself and went to the bathroom. Sitting there, I spoke quietly: 'God? ... It's wrong. Why give us a heart when we seem to survive best without it? Charlie came into my life. Still, I can only allow for so much disrespect and humiliation before they team up against my ego. "Don't be with those who vex you?" So never be with men? Avoid love? Forgo the fundamental experiences needed to mature the man-woman species? It's wrong God. I am the one who needs the help yet the prostitute wins – makes money by it too!? You have a contradiction I think – Emily Bröntes, Martin Luther Kings, John Lennons, Terry Foxes, dads, and Jes recall Billy Joel's song: "Only the good die young." Well here's my song: "Sex and money are power and I have none, but maybe if I'm good – I'll die young?" Like it? ...What about Mother Teresa, Ghandi, the Dalai Lama, Pope John Paul II, U2 and the people over ninety? ... Intelligent love. Okay. That's a good answer too.'

After coming to terms with myself last night I'd picked up a new telephone chip for Charlie this morning before heading over to his place. Naturally, it was a deceptive means to suffice my need to see him, highlight my imperfection and apologise to him. In the end the time together chatting in his bedroom turned out more therapeutic than harmful. Somewhere in between the chit chat and the serious chat he tried to assure me that he felt fine despite the fact that he goes out almost every second night, no longer follows our rules about going to the gym, avoiding calls to and from the well, or hanging with Vanesa. My reaction to that, was reminding him that he had probably been feeling better because he had been following the rules, particularly the gym, 'Or maybe you haven't had a dark hour because you haven't come down from the high yet Charlie – no?'

'Maybe, you think too much,' he said ...

'.. Sometimes,' I said.

'Alllways,' he muffled through a hand covered face. I smiled, 'Intelligence is a difficult power you know... It's the positive balance with love while truth is synonymous with one's perfection and kind of like the lost parent both intelligence and love wish to find.' He peeked at me through his fingers and I looked at him more intently. He seemed to be listening so I went on, 'According to Buddha, "The gift of truth excels all other gifts" Charlie, but when you have too much of one it tends to do more harm than good, especially intelligence. At an immature stage it's only about discovery – *seeing* something that hasn't been tested or tried, which means that its infant stage will have to kill something away before its genuine purpose is perfected. At a macro level, we've got today's information societies, abortion rights, new economies, war, medical discoveries, science, mass media etc., all removing life in some shape or form in order to offer a better reach at something that may or may not enrich humanity. At an individual level I don't think being intelligent is about being smart as much as the ability to reflect and see into the future Charlie.'

I turned my look from the ceiling to him, 'I mean that figuratively. It's not about foretelling it's about prognosis. Like a doctor telling a heavy smoker that he or she will likely die of cancer. Intelligence is like an intuitive language with the part of life that the naked eye can't see; a view through a small window that not everyone uses albeit it's available to all – you know?' I asked lightly. 'What's the point in thinking about a prognosis that hasn't developed yet, except to stress you out and miss a day doing it?' he asked. I loved Charlie when he was in a lucid mood. He can follow me through my maze of thought and bring me back when I go too far: 'Precisely,' I answered. 'It's lonely "at the top" when one is getting there before the others. However that's the mature stage of intelligence. At the macro level, it's knowing how to use its virtues of anticipation, planning, creation, protection and responsibility in conjunction with the virtue in the power of love; patience. While the micro or individual level is about growing from within closer to oneself and the life that shares the intuitive language; nature. The problem is that the Earth is evolving and changing as well as nature's patterns. The news talks about beached whales committing suicide or dolphins getting lost in the Thames and I think, they're not lost they're just moving with the changes while man-made obstacles are in their way. Like: 'Where did that London Bridge come from? It wasn't here a million years ago!' which is probably as far back as their memory goes. You know? That nature is being removed faster than humans can mature. Then, the more one learns about this, the lonelier that person becomes because few people speak or understand the language. It's like a spiritual move away from this life towards the other dimension before actually getting there via death. That's why intelligent individuals are perceived as slightly eccentric and usually only have themselves to depend on; few people will help something that they can not understand or translate. Then to complicate matters, many intelligent individuals tend to exude an aura of strength that intimidates others into believing that these individuals don't need help. I speak four foreign languages Charlie, which means that I am four times more sensitive and perceptive to life around me, because I can feel the passion and understand the behaviour of those languages. It makes me a unique breed of person that separates me from the rest. My personal development is learning how to assimilate my uniqueness with the mainstream because few can assimilate mine. "Ignorance is bliss" and frankly, I sometimes, wish for it. However, it's a lateral move not a forward one. 'What's wrong with that?' he suddenly asked. 'Nothing. It just delays the evolution process that's all. Nature is a constant change forward; not a lateral one. People wonder why animals don't talk even though they are considered intelligent. There are questions about why apes don't talk if they evolved from man? Perhaps intelligence *is* the ability to live without words. Look at the information age we now live in? It's only at the child stage yet already people are communicating more comfortably by screen than face to face. Perhaps we are heading into an era that does wipe out man's means to communicate by words? Have you ever seen the film called "Cocoon?" in which intelligent sources from another planet are able to communicate with each other by moving out of their human shell and simply blending their spiritual energy, like two light sources into one?' No reply. 'Maybe intelligence will simply *progress* back to body language and the sixth sense that nature uses? They're labelled as primitive or archaic only because our memory doesn't go back that far. There is something to be said about music and sign language as two possible sources of universal communication. Perhaps this stage of humanity is just another metamorphism towards its perfection as a pure intelligent being? It would mean suffering a lot of loss and inflicting a lot of pain before achieving human truth. If love and intelligence are the pure forms of truth, then hate and ignorance are their challenges in achieving humanity's perfection sooner than later. The exam lies with the fact that the human spirit matures and evolves at a different rate than others – we're not all getting there at the same time, so that the grandfather clause might take centuries before humanity is perfected – if ever. I don't consider intelligence a fortunate gift. I consider it a responsibility that requires me to tolerate and educate those near me while I am constantly asking love to humble the immature side of my intelligence by keeping arrogance at bay so that I can evolve better .We are so close to turning the child of intelligence into a rebel against its own ally love. Truth might never be achieved for the masses, only for the few. Einstein had a theory that energy recycles itself. That life is a recycled energy that constantly stretches out and snaps back like a rubber band. So I imagine that every time life snaps back it brings with it the changes or mutations from the future it came from, so that the next extended era evolves from that. Maybe we are the weaker species because frankly speaking, it is a heck of a lot easier than using body language, or the sixth sense and not necessarily as accurate either. Did you know Charlie, Ganesh, India's God of intelligence is an Elephant?'

'Elephants have good memories,' he replied with a slight sardonic smile.

'Yes but, maybe there was a time when Elephants really were the leaders of their tribes? When only animals or intelligent life existed without words? Eastern philosophies certainly consider it and they have a better recognition of their ancestry than we do. Maybe Charlie, the caveman began communicating with words because we, as the future, snapped back from perdition with a residue of language from that time causing man to start all over again from that residue. People talk about reincarnation, well, maybe humanity as a whole is doing it again and we're all supposed to remember from humanity's past mistakes. The glitch is that our memory won't take us back far enough to know what happened that made us snap back to the caveman era in the first place. Maybe we had really screwed up and maybe that's why we've been experiencing a flood of esoteric thinking, because this extended era is recycling better than the last – it's hard to tell.'

'Aiii Michèle!' he yawned out loudly, 'I don't know – you're exhausting me,' he said with a polite smile. 'Sorry Charlie,' I answered quietly. Then with a light exasperation.., 'All theory aside, I think intelligence works hand in hand with love. If one is really true to them then I think they are the secrets to fulfilling the life one wants. You know, you can be on a train heading for your destination when it suddenly gets diverted somewhere else. You can choose to go with the new direction or you can choose not to. That is where intelligence comes in. It's like a map of life with a lot of ways to get where you want to go and intelligence lets you visualise them all and pick the right one for you. Animals don't need a visual map. They already know their truth through their sixth sense. They just follow it until they get to where they have to go. Their direction might take longer, but the point to intelligence is perceiving a destination before it's a reality. Hence truth and perfection remain synonymous with each other. You can see your truth before it's real. Achieving it is your perfection. It's the transfer from "there to here" that's hard to do.'

'What if you don't have a clue where you want to go?' He asked.

'You always have a clue Charlie. Always. You just have to open your senses. It's like Dorothy from the Wizard of Oz. It took her an entire journey through a dream to discover that her way home had been with her the whole time in the shoes that she wore. Buddha says that if "your question comes from you, then so does your answer." Once you find it, then things tend to fall into place naturally and make your here and now where you want to be.' He turned his look at me and I could see that he could not humour my flight any longer. 'Come here,' he said. The tenderness in his voice caught me off guard and I landed instantly. So that when I lay in nearer beside him, my body felt a thousand weights lighter and I fell asleep right away.

February 28: *"If you have made mistakes, even serious ones, there is always another chance for you. What we call failure is not the falling down, but the staying down"* – MARY PICKFORD.

PART III

MICHÈLE VERSUS CHARLY INTO THE WELL

I shall pass through this way but once
Any good therefore that I can do
Or any kindness that I can show to any human being
Let me do it now
Let me not defer or neglect it
For I shall not pass this way
Again.

ÉTIENNE DE GRELLET

Quiero vivir (I want to live) – CHARLIE 3.05.

The Report

It was about eight o'clock at night by the time she'd finally finished typing and printed out Charlie's report. It had taken her a while to put it together. About a month since February 9th when they'd stopped trying to get through a month without the coke. Actually, it was really only three weeks, but her trip to Dubai had taken up a week in the middle. He'd said that he wanted fifteen days well he'd had them and more. So much had happened since then that it occurred to her that the silence between them for the past three days had been the longest they'd gone without being in touch since they met in November. '*Wow,*' she thought. The final page printed out and she collected the report, tucked it neatly into a manila envelope and added a sticky note to it: "Pa ti. Un poco de claridad cuando necesitas recordar..x (For you. A little bit of clarity when you need to remember...x)." This was her new strategy: words. When Charlie told her that he wanted to stop with the 24/7 buddy system, she figured that it was his way of binging big before possibly going into rehab. It also meant that their chats together would diminish slowly but surely, and she would not have any way of reaching him directly; however words might. Most of their communication up until then had been about their use of words. He respected them as much as she did, to the point of being very well read in the Catalan language. When they talked or sent sms' there was always a stimulating exchange between them. Either in their attempt to master the other's mother tongue or to play-off one another the correct use of rich vocabulary. Above all, Charlie enjoyed interpreting the exact meaning of something with the exact word to express it. The problem was that there were few people if any in his personal circle with whom to stimulate such activity. It just underlined for her that Charlie was just another intelligent individual who fell into mental boredom, didn't watch where he was going and then inadvertently fell into the well; that whether or not he admitted it to himself, she knew without a doubt that he could be just as sensitive and romantic as she could be. Hopefully the report would get his attention. Despite the level of cocaine he'd been consuming until then, he still seemed willing to read because the last time she'd seen him, he'd actually finished a book and read the different astrological forecasts she'd given him for the New Year ..."Bum bum bum," her telephone suddenly sounded the arrival of an sms: "Hi. No hemos hablado últimamente y me sabe mal. ¿Quieres comer mañana? (Hi. We haven't spoken lately and I feel bad about that. Want lunch tomorrow?)." She contemplated the message in disbelief at the timing of its arrival. They hadn't been in touch and just before she is about to deliver the report he sends her an sms. Incredible. It was little morsels like that one that kept her going with whatever it was that continued to tug her along. She didn't reply right away. Instead she grabbed the report drove over to Charlie's and placed the manila envelope on the Phedra's front window. The night was cold and windy especially down by the sea where Charlie lives. Once she got back into the Mini she sent her reply to him: "Hi. Timing incredible. Go to your car. What time for lunch?" Then drove back home. Five minutes later: "Bum bum bum," another message: "Thank you. One o'clock." She looked at the message and a smile ran across her mouth; his English was correct. "O.k.," she sent. So they were going to go for lunch at Sa Croix and he was going to pick her up.

It was the window that she needed in order to talk to him about the report. She wanted him to understand that it was about making an educated choice or at least making sure to keep him on track towards rehab. "Bum bum bum," another sms: "Do you want to come here?" it asked. She hesitated. It was all so simultaneous. She wasn't sure, but she honestly felt that she was allied with something or someone who wanted to keep the contact between her and Charlie alive. All his horoscopes for the New Year highlighted nothing less that the need for Capricorn to "fight for the new life" that it wanted. That 2005 was "the year to make it or break it ..." 'Okay,' she said to herself, 'as long as we are *all* in this together, then there's still a chance.' ..."Ok," went the sms back to him and she spent the night at his side.

Love is the triumph of imagination over intelligence.
H. L. MENCKEN

Timing

Journal, March 1, 9:30a.m.

Sitting at my kitchen table for the first time really. I can see the sea in the far distance. Grey skies give the sea a deep dark emerald green colour – one of my favourite looks for her. Went for coffee but my heart, or my system didn't really want it. Now I am *waiting* to make sure that Charlie gets off alright to see his son. Then I think that will be it for me. I am tired right now – that is, I did not sleep at all last night, so now even though I am awake by nervous energy my mind does not focus or see things quietly enough. Thoughts; I have many but right now, they won't flow onto paper. Dasha – a great puppy, but she's bugging me. Sleeps on the couch and my bed when I am out, even though she has three great pillow-mats for herself to choose from. She wants my attention. The sofa and the bed have my scent; must be her way of being close to me. I suppose that I should have realised that the way that Charlie manages his love with his son or his marriage would be the same for any woman in his life? Cautious. Dunno. He shares himself more with the prostitutes – hmm; easier but sad. More a reflection about me. Ironically I am the one without a life and for that reason I think too, that I have lost Charlie's respect. Growing old alone seems to be my destiny. Anyway, I began to get too involved again with Carles instead of the purpose. Not good, especially if my involvement is not wanted nor used. I could go on like this, but my initial hope for Charlie is being threatened by my quiet aspiration of growing old with him: no way. I want money, love and a place of my own with someone. In that order, because if the latter two don't happen then at least I'm okay on my own. I wanted it to be with Charlie because we've got all the ingredients and I really thought Life was showing me that way in spite of *all* the impossibilities; for every impossibility there is a possibility. Don't know. Kept that "heart" open. Most people don't even try. I see daddy in Charlie while I am a slight reflection of mum. I see it and *feel* it and fear my own thoughts – they are so crazy. Yet I *see* it. Dad loved mum very much. Even though the years that passed often fluctuated that barometer of love for her. So I wonder, if Charlie and I are like a surrogate ideal of what daddy wanted with mum. Maybe mum was an image of me from a past life that dad had shared with me, hence the confusion and failure of their love because she was not me. Maybe dad was my Charlie in a past life? One doesn't know, but I don't remove the possibilities. Who knows, if dad via Charlie's addiction has not found a karmic path through Charlie in order to feel the love he wanted with mum by helping Charlie and I find each other? Some philosophies believe that souls come back to Earth after several years of death. Charlie is still Charlie but, but... I think that if Charlie did get well and stayed well long enough for us to evolve together from that, maybe just maybe there could be a consolidation between us not only because I see it, but because it would be daddy's way of really being at peace before his channel to me is closed by Charlie's sobriety. So that in the end I am with Charlie whose karmic spirit is one and the same as my father's? Even Jes, I feel is near me by way of Dasha... And I wonder way out there, if Charlie and I did consolidate something, then Jes would go too and would he take Dasha with him? I hope not, but in gaining a new love and a new life I would have to lose something

… I confess that I truly feel that Carles is my man by virtue of the fact that daddy and I were so close to each other. I also believe this because of all the evident circumstances and coincidences Charlie and I have experienced in the past months withstanding the parallels between our past. Both Charlie and I met at a pinnacle moment of our lives. Before getting here I had made severe choices that changed the direction of my life radically. Choices that I believe had to be done in order to meet my truth. I was late in deciding and things were almost too far gone to make the window – but I did. Just like Charlie with his wife and the cocaine – the window is still open. The delay of our encounter coincides with our personality. Never until now have I actually felt like I was in the right situation to have a home or even a family!? How little people understand. It is not that I have not thought about it rather to the contrary; place and circumstance had to be right. I don't necessarily need children or a conventional way to live, but should they come along into my life, it would be because I found my perfect circumstance to have them. I might have been the woman of Jes' life, however I don't know if he was the man of mine? We had problems and while Charlie's are so much greater I feel more assured by him? There is my memory. I was only thirteen sitting at the bottom of the green steps in our home in Canada. I was emotionally vexed by a conversation that I had had with my dad and somehow plopped myself on the stairs to think more clearly. At such a young age my head was already aware that the man of my life would be a man like him; someone that I loved and understood so well but couldn't live with, by reason of his complicated nature. Love at a distance; freedom and independence. That in fact the affection and intensity I shared with Jes was not right for me? That in fact I do understand that the better man for me is the one who loves me from a distance because I do function better without an excess of emotional dependency testing me? That much of *my* power is being alone. In light of the parallels that I see between Charlie and dad my battle remains the same: other women erroneously received Charlie and dad's dedicated love and then rejected them. Thus both men by their sybaritic nature feel unable to love again. My loyalty and dedication towards my father were appreciated by him, but never satisfied him. If anything my younger image of my mother was a constant unsettling reminder of her to him. I know that he often said that my brothers were. My challenge with Charlie is the same vis-à-vis his wife. However something tells me that I could be vindicated this time. That if in some far mysterious way dad has helped me to find him again through Carles such that our love would honestly be reciprocated in a way that we could not as father and daughter. That my father through Charlie could finally love my mother through her image in me and receive the love he wanted from her from me: perversely deep but not impossible. Even films like "Birth", have been made to suggest that such an absurdity is not necessarily untrue... (Sigh). There is still room for Carles to try and trust again. There is still purpose in my drive. Perhaps too, that clairvoyant thought while sitting on those stairs in Canada was not misdirected by reason of my father's destiny. He died when I was 27, so that yes, I could be with a man like him because his spirit would have had in fact, enough time to be a part of another. Maybe Carles' addiction in some universal way is also an esoteric parallel to my dad's illness and their destiny in my life. While the influence of the drug makes transcendence between there and here easier for my dad to reach me by way of Charlie? It convinces my mind that a life with Carles is probable and if achieved would be positive. Withstanding too, that at 27, the 2 and 7 hint at Charlie and I while their sum of 9 stares back at me as our truth number. I'm also reminded that with all my analytical prognosis that's all that it is. I tend to get very close to my images, but the circumstances around them never really come into focus exactly the way I'd idealised them to be. It is the part of me that belongs to the Universe I guess. Then the fear – so much fear. What is it? Discovering that I have been so wrong about all this? No. I can choose to fall out of love, but I choose to be in love until further notice. The fear is ridicule and losing my confidence. I was so disillusioned about the outcome between Jes and I that I truly lost all reason to plan, to think or even move into my life. I wanted to be a pure Taoist floating along letting Life decide for me much like Charlie has let the cocaine decide for him. However truth be known – I knew. I knew with Jes that it was not flowing as well as it should have. I was so indignant to let us go. We seemed so close to the mental snapshot, but I knew. We both did. We both noticed and felt the resistance. We'd tried so hard. Even secretly asked Life why? Then, quietly looked to each other and asked why? One morning while we held each other in bed he told me to take care of Dasha and I told him to tell his brother. We knew. Jesy was going to leave us and we both knew... So with this knowledge I know about Charlie. I know that I am the best thing in his life and that a life by him would satisfy me. I know too, that I can say that "I love him" and that the words just roll off my tongue even when I am suddenly so pragmatic and want nothing more to do with him – I don't know why. Finally, despite all my mental imagery, I really don't know how exactly we shall end, but I do know that together or not, our story was meant to happen...

Three hours later and I am back from Charlie's place. I'd sent him a text message to see if he had time for a coffee to which he replied that he was not going to meet his son!? Fuck. I could *not* believe it. I went to his place. He managed to open the door and talk to me, but he was heading down into his thoughtful well. After fifteen minutes of a hard pep talk, he managed to shave and get dressed, only to go back to his couch. Then his wife called and he told her that he wouldn't make it, after having confirmed with her and his son a week earlier and again last night, that he would. She hung up on him. I was so enraged too! He was so close. All he had to do was get up! He finally did and we went for a ten minute spin in his car to get some fresh air. In the car we discussed whether or not he should go to his son's football game. I suggested that he call his wife back and "ask" her: 'It's not the damage that matters Charlie so much as how it's repaired. Just because she lacks communicative protocol doesn't mean you have to as well. Besides Charlie, her reaction albeit childish is understandable.' Right then, she called back. Amazing. Lately I've been wondering if Life is listening to me. Is it just coincidence and energy, or am I also being used to pass on messages just before they're needed? Anyway, Charlie picked up the call on the car speaker and managed to "ask" her for her opinion about the game which appeared to throw her for a loop because the tone in her voice changed instantly to a purr. Charlie then switched the car phone to his cell and continued his conversation with her that way. In the end he relayed to me that she told him not to show, but she would call him afterwards. His son must have been really disappointed. I was. Still am. Charlie was too. It's just incredible. He said that he hadn't gone out since that night he went out after our dinner on the 26th, but he went out this morning!? Perversed, literally – what *was* that!? Pressure before seeing his son? His wife? Cocaine paranoia for sure. He is so full of the product. Said that he was thinking about trying another seven days with me of 24/7? I don't know what to think. Even if he goes to rehab in Barcelona, so what? Would he give his wife a divorce? Could he come back to Mayürqa? Would I go there? Visit or just forget about him? It's too hard. I realise now that he must have taken more charly this morning just before I went over. God: *How can* we *help* him *help himself!?* And me? Money? Job? Self-something? Business cards? – *What?*"

Journal, March 2: Jesy's heart.
Absence sharpens love, presence strengthens it – ENGLISH PROVERB.

Noon. At Charlie's. No real reason to be here. "It's gone" I think. The need. I come here now to think and be calm by being in proximity to Charlie. I am sitting in the Ikea chair that faces the large glass doors that face the open sea. I could throw a stone from here to the sea, it is that close. He's sleeping in bed; too late to go to the gym. I have prostitute and porno visions in my head. Frustrated that he doesn't come to find me. He goes for the "puta" the hooker instead. She knows him better "sexually" than I do. It's all so so sad. He's really handicapped himself. Me? I'm stopped. Still no light on the professional front. My savings for twelve thousand dollars is somewhere but not here, because the asshole bank manager did not send it when I asked for it. Mum had to send me rent money that she doesn't have either. Over three months have gone by since I requested the transfer. It's all of my savings, so maybe Life is trying to delay its arrival? I don't care – my anger just wants to sue! ...

My office. 7:40p.m.. Went for a very long walk with Dasha this evening and ended up by the city hall building. An area of open land, with a pine tree forest behind it and a few hills made from gravel. I stood at the top of one of the hills and stared out at the view of sea, mountains and homes. The sun was bright before it got ready for dusk. The music from my ear-phones woke up my emotions and uncovered my feelings. I thought of Jes and missed him terribly. Watched Dasha and missed him more. After what must have been a few songs later, I came out of my mystical melodramatic spell with him and walked towards Dasha, when I came upon a heart-shaped clay stone. I saw it and actually continued to walk past it, but then I paused and went back to look at it more closely. It was indeed a close replica to the one Jes and I used to have on our steps in Sichus; not as well defined, but the very same sandstone texture with the same shape. Then Dasha came over and just sat *right* on *top* of it and stared at me!? I thought: '*What is going on? Why did she suddenly come over and do that?!*' I crouched down to her level and looked into her eyes. I wondered if he was there? I don't know… Nice thinking. So I spoke to her, to him in a direct way, moved by the possibility of his message: '¿Eres tu Jesy? (Is it you Jesy?) …The stone is now propped up on one of the steps to the front door.

Journal, March 3: 1:40p.m., am in my office. Plugged into my MP3 or else my mind won't let go of Charlie thoughts. Crazy. All crazy. I am prepared to work on-line and *now* the internet does not work. Mum's thousand arrived for my rent and only gave me 600 euros. Now, I'll have to ask Gabi if she has the 300 euros I lent her last month. Meanwhile my $12,000 from Canada, nobody seems to know!? Want *my* twelve thousand – damn it! Now I have to pay both mum and Visa back when the twelve thousand was supposed to avoid all that! Plus my stuff from Canada; also not here yet. It's been over four months already! I'm looking for something to do and all indications send me to Charlie? Go figure. I have time on my hands and not necessarily by choice. Ideas: articles and excerpts. My stories. Start small. Money? Eventually Oprah-like stuff? The answers are with me in these pages, like Dorothy in Oz? Sort and do. Need to sort and divide. Begin with the things that I *do* have now: journals, my printer. Kind of story? Just a matter of getting started? It will come to me later? What do *you* think?

Journal, March 4: Hegemony of the sexes.
…*We shall require a substantially new manner of thinking, if mankind is to survive* – ALBERT EINSTEIN.

Charlie conversations, do I really want to go there? Kind of have to or else it won't go away.

A few days ago he showed me this building that belongs to him – very nice. Antiquated, Mayürqan and located where the old train station used to be in his village. When he showed it to me I felt close to it instantly. There is also a wide open field in front of it, with only a few local homes next door. He started, but didn't finish a project to renovate it; story of his cocaine life because he did build and finish Sa Croix with his own hands when he wasn't doing coke. Again I was reminded that despite his illness, his life is much more "complete" than mine will ever be. He has money, possessions, family, and friends all within a twenty minute radius of him. Plus a son, a quasi-marriage, drugs, a Romanian woman who knows his sexual whims and grants them to him whenever he wants. Frankly he has it all and I feel stupid for being used by *me*. Think that even before his marriage or the addiction he might have been similarly moody such that his wife after twelve years, got themselves married just to get on with her life and have a child – smart woman. The cocaine would have been a result of his sense of entrapment? Why didn't he end their relationship or at least go for another woman? Then getting married and not getting divorced? She trapped him with a son? Is she another Black Widow or a woman in love? Charlie was naive? Daddy never wanted a divorce either. He and mum were just officially separated. He wasn't ready for kids either – mum just had me. Gawd, the similarities. See a photo of Charlie at 26 or shave dad's hair when he was 44 and I swear there is a resemblance between the two men; sensitive, shy, gentle, moody, intelligent and extremely private about their lives. That although Charlie's motto is to be in charge, under it all he is not a dominant figure. Just like my dad. Temper yes, but only out of anxiety. My mind whizzes and whirs about this. Charlie has an independent spirit that was largely shaped by a strong influence of women in his life, much like my father's. Particularly Charlie's mother, whose dry and pessimistic personality makes me think of his wife. Men are there too, but only as secondary figures. Women have basically predominated in his life to the point that as a man he no longer wishes to be under that emotional control and chooses to be the one in charge. Similar to many men who have begun to widen their search for love into Eastern Europe and Asia in order to find a woman who by reason of her standard of living will offer her caretaking instincts demurely without questions in exchange for the men's economic care. Even North American men have begun to lose their self-confidence and are also searching for another type of woman because she has become all too domineering again. Both the demise and strength of a woman is her natural instinct to care and take charge. Much like Mother Nature that can offer a great day or devastate a country with a natural disaster. She is a powerful creature and unfortunately can go too far with it. As a result, centuries went by when men took action and placed women under submissive control in order to avoid her domineering effect over them again. The solution was primitive and underestimated the natural instinct of the female. Again, much like the way nature resuscitates in the darkest and bleakest of conditions, women adapted to being restricted to the home and simply empowered their natural instinct and inadvertently began raising men to adhere to their control. Hence men too are also largely responsible for their own demise. Notwithstanding, examples of new generations in places like Canada have already begun to promote the sharing of power by assimilating the ability for both sexes to manage the caretaking at home and or be a part of the workforce. The domineering instincts of both sexes are finding their balance with one another via a stronger ability to communicate directly with one another. It's not about equality. It's about a tremendous level of communication and spiritual respect necessary in order to eliminate what I see as the hegemony of the sexes. Otherwise men will increase their search for uneducated women and thereby weaken their manhood in doing so, while the new woman will forget the lessons from the past and impose her dominance on society all over again and probably snuff men out for good. Sigh. We need men. We need each other and we need to control our instinct to conquer and divide ... Then, I think of my mother. Like Dasha, her Life number is a 1 and thereby my Strength number. An ephemeral, stellar creature who is the epitome of nature's alchemy and simply is *all that*. She does not impose her ability to dominate and therefore people gravitate to her almost unconsciously, often placing her high on a pedestal that she often refuses to stand on. She matches what I feel all women can aspire to: balance between their caretaking instincts and the need for individual self-preservation. Buddha calls it "Intelligent Love". A quality so pure, that I hope has been my mother's gift to me, when I think of Charlie's instinct to protect himself from me. He does not want to be dominated by the aura in me. He does not trust my intention to share our powers and above all to draw out from him his better qualities as a man and therefore my own as a woman. Finally, with all my parallels between him and dad, I realise that I am Charlie's antecedent because my years growing up were strictly influenced by men. I am a product of a male experience that is at once undaunted in the face of conflict and slightly weary of women's alluring nature. Hence it is only logical that both Charlie and I tend to empathise more with our sexual counterpart than our own and that most of our lives have been challenged by the ones we tend to worry about and defend most often: the opposite sex. If the polarity of our family upbringing, emotional development, our personal and social experiences, financial status, as well as how we manage our weaknesses and strengths, were joined together; I imagine that our core would appear to be one and the same – a perfect fit. Without a doubt, Charlie and I could grow a lot from being with each other. I recall a walk with my mother, when I was in my mid-twenties.

We'd slipped into a conversation about life, our future and our fears; the when, the who, and somewhere I mentioned that I would prefer to grow old by someone but if not, I could also see myself alone with a dog. In either case, I would have made the choices that would have taken me that way and therefore would be fine with it. She agreed, but added that she did not see me alone rather she'd imagined me with an older man who had already been married and had kids of his own. I wondered. I have never clearly advocated that I would like to have children of my own but yes, to grow old by a man whose emotional loyalty is to me as mine is to him would be divine. GOT to finish the report!

Journal, March 5: *Baby take off your coat real slow. Take off your shoes - I'll take off your shoes girl. Take off your dress – yes, yes, go over there and turn on the lights. Suspicious minds are talking there trying to tear us apart. They don't believe this love of mine, but they don't know what love is. You give me reason to live...* – 'LEAVE YOUR HAT ON', RANDY NEWMAN, LYRICS ADAPTED.

The prostitute sends him short text messages daily now. He thinks about her more and more, while she's making good money on him. It vexes me. It's a jealousy generated by the fact that he never gave me a chance. So I say: '*Charlie your explanations don't match the truth. You said that you only take coke at home, but you go out looking for "her" and her. Like you don't want me to please you; what are you afraid of?*' So my problem is two-fold. One is a semi-rational projection, teased by fear of what she does to him indirectly. So, I imagine myself as a *protective feline wanting to pull him away from the source of evil that is taking Charlie for granted and hurting him. I want to save him. I want to pay off the prostitute in such a way that she can leave him alone or find herself another lifestyle...* Vexed by my other self that plays and provokes me emotionally *with slighted immature feelings about being rejected for a prostitute that does coke with him* – All that! She took his baby ring that he got in Paris as a means to see him again? They both let the game go on. I imagine she gets dressed and gets ready for him every time he sees her. Dress in kinky, girlie, or in a mini skirt; whatever he wants. How they take coke together, how he does not need me because he's been with her. She might dance for him, gyrate in front of him – alone or with a few… Whatever the case I can't compete. NOR should I. Plus he still wants his marriage to survive and tries to get back to that life he projected with his wife because he doesn't feel capable of keeping that projection with somebody new. In the end the prostitute suffices his void appetite while he does nothing to protect the frail line that holds us together. He just doesn't care about it enough – so why should I? I'm asking: '¿¡Que coño hago aqui!? (What the *fuck* am I doing here!?)' May I remind you that *you* walked into my life. You wanted English classes. You asked me to call you for the coffees on *my* walks. You requested dinner and the first kiss. You wanted a weekend in Paris, when I only offered you a day. Then you made me pay for it!? You achieved it all and not alone. The love, the words, the intimacy – you drove back to find me so that *you* could give me a kiss. *You* wondered how I was in Dubai. You did drive me "there" when you "couldn't". You enjoyed the fool'n by the church. You liked the ring – very much. And now do you still have it? I wonder, did I lose your love?' – '*You never had it*' … 'But you *chose* me and you were *not* wrong!!… Ah, I think I understand now. Do your thing, I am still here.'

Journal, March 6: *Love doesn't make the world go round. Love is what makes the ride worthwhile* – FRANKLIN P. JONES.

Moments to remember: football nights with Real Madrid or

Barcelona at the local bar, only two small blocks away from our front door with all five of us: Mitx, Elisabet, Carles, his nephew, and I together watching it on the big TV screen. Drinks, a ham and cheese "pa amb oli" and Charlie next to me. We are well. It feels good and somehow familiar to me. Dasha also there, like when Jes and I used to do it in Sichus. Then there are lunches downstairs with Elisabet and the Serra family: a home cooked menu, then a coffee down by the local beach bar. Charlie doesn't always attend, but I am still invited. Last Sunday he met us at the bar. When I see him, I am in fact so attracted to him; even after a glass of water. He was not feeling one hundred percent because he'd been out until 6a.m. that morning. Hence it also meant that he went out after I'd left his place that afternoon on the 27th, when we'd chatted about Ganesh and the quest for truth. Hmpft. Anyway when he joined us, he did not sit next to me nor pay much attention to me and also acted overly polite with me. He did however light up for the blonde waitress. Yadi yadi. I wonder if he is so different without cocaine. He suggested yes, but I'm beginning to doubt it. My feelings obviously outweigh his (if he has any at all) towards me. Then I feel out of place, self-conscious and ridiculous. How easy it is to fall into someone's well rather than climb someone's stairs. The relationship dynamic in Spain still leaves a lot to be desired, particularly in Mayürqa where communication skills between people are weaker than what I'm used to. In simple terms it's the boy who hits the girl he likes, while the girl flirts with the one she doesn't like and communication between them is all about mindless suggestive word games between the dog and the cat; seriously below and over me. In this social culture I have a choice. Reduce my tennis game in order to be able to play with this dynamic in hopes that maybe we can learn something from each other. Such that the entry level into this cultural dynamic could actually win me over from lack of concentration which would be fine until it says "nice game" and tells me how clever it was. Or, I can simply play at my level and finish the exchange 6-Love, 6-Love. Accentuate whose got more experience, shake its hand like a good sportsmen and leave it up to the culture to learn from the game or not. The thing is, "when in Rome do as the Romans do" … to what extent? Again patience and tolerance come into play. Understanding the perceived foes at play and then deciding whether or not the time and the effort are worth further exchange? I think only if the parties involved want to learn from one another. Deep Mayürqa does not seem to want to, possibly because it does not know how to, or does not recognise the need to, yet. The problem with tradition is that it endures time without change and therefore sustains a degree of ignorance into maturity that is greatly more harmful than a mature level of intelligence. Such that the opposite is true when intelligence is at its infant stage of discovery and places like Mayürqa turn opportunistic and nouveau riche without the education or the experience to manage it wisely…

Well, besides feeling out of place that day, I also felt a fleeting moment of sadness, knowing that the real gift at that time was Belle and her family. Not Charlie; whose attention to me was light and superficial. Again the irony of life. Jes loved me very much but there was no family support, especially when his troubles got worse. I perceive Charlie as a relatively cultured man from a village trying to find his medium between that experience and the new one beyond it, while I am from the new one trying to find my balance with the old world. We can make it if he tries, and if I can pace myself with patience. Balance, just does not come together at once. Rather it is measured through a space of time between then and now equal to the rate of learning and adhering to one's truth; the sooner one listens, the sooner one will get there. Our experiences of the past seem to have already satiated certain individual needs in order to bring us the possibility of culminating the third phase of our lives together into one satisfying balance. Best of all, we seem to have arrived on time for each other. It's all good, and I secretly and silently give thanks to "Life" for listening and watching. Whatever happens we will have at least found each other momentarily.

Heaven doesn't understand – Who made sense of my love?
It wasn't me but my heart that won't accept an apology
I don't care anymore what they'll say
I don't give what I have, to know which way my heart beats
It's enough to be your other half –Who has answers? Not me
My shield is only the truth – Talking of rights is to dream
Here what I ask for, is too much and I'm only looking for freedom
One day heaven will understand – To be the other half
Is not enough, I also need his forgiveness
Who made sense of our love? Not me but our hearts.
[...El cielo no entiende de este amor, y no nos conocerá el perdón, ya no me importa que dirán/ No doy lo que tengo por saber de qué lado late el corazón, me basta con ser su otra mitad/¿Quién tiene respuestas? No soy yo/ Mi escudo es tan sólo la verdad/ Hablar de derechos es soñar, aquí lo que pido está de más, y yo sólo busco libertad/ El cielo algún día entenderá, que ser su mitad no basta, también necesito su perdón/ ¿Quién le dio sentido a nuestro amor? No fui yo, fue nuestro corazón. ...]
'EL CIELO NO ENTIENDE' (HEAVEN DOESN'T UNDERSTAND) – OBK
LYRICS ADAPTED

Into the well

Well, if this wasn't crazy focused it was crazy obsessive behaviour. She was sitting in the Mini parked out front of Lady Veela's. It was about 10p.m. Finding the place wasn't that difficult. It was actually a fluke, because the battery on her personal phone went dead and required her to use a backup phone she has, with the old chip she'd given to and taken back from Charlie the month before. It had never occurred to her to check it at the time. So when it activated, it beeped in a whole bunch of text messages and voice mail messages for Charlie. There were several text messages between him and the pinocho woman from his village while one third of them were between Charlie and "V". A few were dated back as far as before she'd gone to Dubai. One on December 25th and another on the night she'd flown to Dubai – the same day he'd flippantly said to her at the airport that he'd wanted to go with her. They were affectionate messages and many. Mostly sent between 11p.m. and one in the afternoon:

Cv – "¿Que haces? Un beso (What are you doing? A kiss)."
Cv– "Hola. ¿Supongo que ya has olvidado de mi? (Hi – guess you've already forgotten about me?)"
Vc – "Hola. Claro que no. ¿Quedamos?" (Hi. Of course not. Shall we meet?)"
Vc – "Hola. ¿A que hora quedamos? (Hi. What time are we meeting?)"
Cv – "Te recogo después de trabajar – en frente (pick you up after work – out front)."
Vc – "Vale. Besos (O.K. kisses)."
Vc – "Hola. ¿Duermes? (Hi are you sleeping?)"
Cv – "Si. Te llamo después (Yes. Call you later)."

Despite herself the messages flipped-on a reaction inside her. It annoyed her to no end how this young woman was taking advantage of him. He was being a fool without question, but V was poison for him. He was taking so much cocaine – did she do as much too? Plus he was spending so much money with her, never mind the others that prowled around him. It explained why Charlie was calling and seeing less of Michèle. A need to put an end to this began to swell into a slight panic. She grabbed a paper and pen and began to register all the numbers in the phone's agenda. All of them! Made a short list of the most frequent ones and then matched them with another short list from the sms agenda. Then the voice mail; most of the messages there were from people asking him to call them back. One of them however happen to be Vanesa! Michèle figured out it was her by matching up a sms from Charlie to a cell number that was sent shortly after the voice message had been received. The cell number came up as "V" in the agenda. V had obviously broken a code of conduct because it was the only voice message she'd left. All the rest were sms. Her Spanish on voice mail was weak and highlighted her Eastern Europe accent enough to delight any man for sure. The voice sounded like a young woman of 24 or 25 years of age. It was soft and carried that slightly annoyed tone that indignant girls use when things don't go their way. There was music and bar noise in the background that suggested that she'd called from the club: 'Carlos ¿Dónde estás? Me llamas para quedar ¿y no vienes? Una hora más y me voy— ¡¿Vale?! (Carlos where are you? You called to meet and you don't come? One more hour and I'm leaving— O.K.?!)'

She had been so surprised to hear the message that she listened to it twice more. The disappointment in V's voice was more like a girlfriend's that had been stood up rather than a pissed off prostitute who'd wasted time waiting for him when she could have been making cash from someone else. The call was made at 4:30a.m., on March 6th. The telephone number was from a land line rather than a cell. When Michèle called the number a husky Andalusian or stoned sounding voice answered the call: 'Si,' said the voice in a bored drawl.

'Hi – A friend of mine is having a birthday. What time does the club open?' she asked abruptly.

'11p.m.,' replied the man hesitantly.

'O.K., where's the club located?' she asked dryly.

'C'an Colom,' said the man cautiously. 'Great thanks. Could you – ' the man hung up before she could inquire more. It took time, but it wasn't difficult. She merely looked up all the clubs in C'an Colom on the internet. None of them matched the number that she had. So she short listed all the ones that came with a number and called information for help. 'Hello. I require a few telephone numbers for a few dance clubs I'd like to call in C'an Colom please.' 'The name?' requested the operator. She gave the names and the operator assisted. None of them matched. It would seem that V called from a staff phone or one that protects the club's identity. It was not until she called the penultimate number that she found her match. The same Andalusia stoned voice came over the phone: 'Veela,' the voice slurred unclear. If it hadn't been for the guttural sound in the G she wouldn't have been sure, but the number she'd called was listed as "Lady Veela." This time she hung up and called information again and got the address. Went to the Mini, checked her road map and found Lady Veela's location in C'an Colom. It was all crazy and probably would have stopped when the man hung up on her, but her insides were already into a knot. Albeit, one third of the messages were from V, the rest were not. Charlie had not deleted any of the ones from Michèle to him. In fact the only sms in the phone were V's, hers and one more. It was the epitome of all of them and as far as she was concerned it was a divine intention that she saw it: "Fill t'estim (Son I love you)." – The first and only time she had ever known Charlie to express the word love. It caught something in her throat, sunk deep into her veins and pumped kerosene into her tired flame! She just wanted him out! She had to get him out! God damn fucking drugs! How do parents and families deal with the constant daily threat at home and in schools? Michèle had the time. She could move her ass and be in his face 24/7 if she wanted to. How did parents and families who worked and were detained by other responsibilities survive? Michèle could and she did. She got into the Mini and drove to C'an Colom looking for a lost "dancer" named V" and a boy named Charlie!

No idea when nor how. There are certain powers that she hides. Don't ask me – don't even be amazed, she's called Daisy, the man-eater ("No sé ni cómo ni sé de dónde. Ciertos poderes ella se esconde. No me preguntes ni te asombres – se llama Daisy, la comehombres.") – 'DAISY', KEVIN JOHANSEN, LYRICS ADAPTED

It was 10:15p.m. Now that she was there she really did not know what she expected. The club opened at 11p.m. for clients so she figured she might catch the staff and dancers heading over just before then. She sat there in the warmth and comfort of her car watching the night life come awake. The club was on a side street close to the beach and tourist area. In the summer the place would have a lot of business. However in March it probably ran on local regulars and generated more social activity between the staff and clients than money. The street was quiet, dimly lit with a few street lamps and closed off at the bottom because of road work. A few people walked by unaware of her presence in the car and it struck her as interesting to watch people, who think they're alone and can't be seen, simply because there was a pending element of surprise for the watcher. It was like "Candid Camera" from the Mini. She saw a few young men walk to the club and walk away. They were obviously too early. Then a light lit up in an apartment over the club and bodies started to come out from a side door that led down stairs to the street. A young girl dressed in a white raincoat with white stiletto heeled boots came down the stairs followed by two young guys. She had dark hair and walked with a confident stride that was simultaneously reduced to maladroit steps because of the heels she wore. Then one by one a few cars came by and parked. Both of them driven by men and loaded with three or four girls. Half of them went into the club the other half went down the road to the left. Michèle figured there was a bar or coffee shop around the corner where they met before starting work. Another girl came up the road on her own. She was tall, dressed in seventies attire with a pom-pom scarf around her neck, a long wool jacket left unbuttoned that flopped behind her with the wind, jeans tucked into mid-calf suede boots and rounded off at the top with fur. She had a definite eastern look to her. Her walking stride was also assertive but not alluring. Her hair was dark, thin and shoulder length. She did not seem to be what Michèle considered as Charlie's type; her energy was too offensive, but mostly did not seem to suit the voice on the voice message. Then another car stopped in from of the club. She saw a girl kiss a male driver and get out; thin, short hair, dressed in a jean jacket and jeans. The guy then parked the dirty white hatchback and also proceeded into the club. '*A couple,*' she thought, '*interesting dynamic.*' He didn't care, she wasn't jealous, they both did it for the money while he probably hung close by just to make sure she didn't run into any real pricks. They shared a plan – probably kept themselves separate from the rest in hopes of making enough cash to one day leave it all behind for a healthier lifestyle. 'Good luck,' she whispered and meant it, but didn't believe in the ending. *It would more than likely end up with her breaking up and going for another guy because the boyfriend would get tired of waiting and want to start their new life before she was ready; thus showing her true colours – money. If the guy had money they would have left ages ago because in prostitution, love remained on standby until personal needs were fully met and only once it developed a conscious from having starved the heart for too long ...* Her mind shifted out of thought and noticed three girls coming down the street behind the Mini, and walked right past its passenger door. They were roughly the same height as Michèle at about 1 metre 67cm: two brunettes and one blonde. The one who walked closest to the car wore black leather boots with her jeans also tucked inside them. She spoke in an eastern language and walked with a slight scraping of the boots' heels over the pavement. '*Cheap-sexy void of any class,*' thought Michèle to herself. These girls were not calendar types; pretty and definitely attractive with their young slight eastern bodies but not sophisticated. Michèle's shallow side came up to her defence... *She was twice their age and looked pretty good, maybe even younger. She also gloated with the knowledge that most of those European girls plumped up like turkeys after thirty. Still, truth be known, even Michèle preferred these girls over the ones that came from America because most of them still appeared natural looking; attractive with real breasts, real butts and real bodies. The East European man was at least getting a realistic physical understanding of women. Though it wasn't going to last long because the silicon and touch-up fad had already begun to infiltrate Europe's market and frankly it was a shame. One of the most beautiful things about European women was their natural beauty. The Sophia Lorens, Brigitte Bardots, and Juliette Binoches: simple, sexy, sophisticated developed figures – natural. Even the men were being affected. Charlie often scowls about his body being too soft or too hairy when he's talking about three strands on his chest. Things that make him masculine he wants to shave or even wax away! While nouveau riche moms getting their boys to wax their legs for aesthetic purposes, not athletic ones? 'Gees, I want a healthy man not a Ken doll!' she voiced to herself. She remembered how the touch-up fad in America sparked a small catty stand-off between the women who did and the ones who promoted their bodies as "real not plastic". Such that, the tide in America seems to have changed back to the all "natural" look, while Europe, which usually sets the trends in style and fashion, has gone Hollywood by allowing America's media power to undermine it...* She focused back on the girls. The girl with the scraping heels had thick, wavy, long dark hair. The other two were not so easy to see, but Michèle's instincts reacted to the one that walked passed so closely. *'Now what?'* she thought to herself, *'get out of the car and ask: 'Hi, anyone here called Vanesa?'* Her mind whizzed. If she did that – then what? *'Hi, I'm a friend of Carles' can we go for a coffee? How much do you get paid for an hour without tricks? Can I pay you for an hour of your time?* or *'Here's some money for you to start a new life, because you're messing up yours and that of others; it's good for you and better for me sort of ...'* Then again, paying her off would not solve Charlie's problem because he'd go to another one. *'Better to keep the devil you know than the one you don't,'* she thought, *'and pay her off? With What!? Free rides in the Mini!?'* Fuck'n imagination sometimes even surprised her. So she did nothing. Just sat there like a lump on a log and watched the girls go into the club. Maybe she could just go into the club, say hello and get to know them? At least understand them or the place, in order to get a better idea? Then what? Charlie was a regular and well liked. Although their relationship ended in a business transaction most of the time, Michèle did not doubt that he probably got away with not paying in exchange for sharing his cocaine or some other perk like lending them money when they needed it. She exhaled. Knowing him the way she thought she did, Charlie's heart might have been involved in all that, but grossly misguided. *His style, she knew, wasn't abusive, so that his dynamic attracted the girls and made it seem more like a need for him to be appreciated by them, where his wife might not have. On the outside one might call him a soft pimp because of his attempt to help the girls with their problems in return for their affection and deference to him. In fact his lack of sexual expression reflects something closer to a surrogate father-daughter dynamic instead. Something that probably started off innocently, but turned into a way of life especially with the cocaine, because Charlie was sensitive to helping the underdog and felt a stronger empathy for the opposite sex or people he really has no obligation to: the emotional roller coaster from that would hurt less than the same from someone he might have chosen to love or care for, such as his wife or family. That and a need to gain affirmation, which is briefly achieved from the dynamic with these women who perfidiously stimulate his self-confidence for as long as he meets their needs: a kind of perverse Cinderella theme again; while he is trying to "help" them, he temporarily responds to their need to be saved and cared for. The dilemma arises the moment a girl incubates feelings for him and these turn into an exclusive desire: she's human, and regardless of the professional experience, cannot fully accept the fact of his shared intimacy with other girls, without some evidence of psychological suffering. Hence Charlie becomes the very problem that he's trying to help them to avoid. He probably ran into a few emotional conflicts with them too, albeit not as much as he would if their profession wasn't prostitution, and resents it when he feels that he has been clear about the formality of their relationship. Maybe there were some instances, where he might have helped a few, by his cordial and respectful manner, which could offer the girls a bench marker against other men who may not be? His "friendship" with Vanesa also made her wonder that maybe his obsession with her harboured feelings for her and he simply did not know how to get past it, if at all. Trying to maintain a relationship with someone whose profession and instinct is about prostitution simply gives Obsession and Possession a host to survive on because their capricious ability to change partners without a sense of accountability manipulates a man psychologically even more, because it's a direct reflection of his own primitive instinct. While the very nature of prostitution for many girls is a long-term definition about using and abusing until the host is no longer useful to one's self-righteous needs. It's a princess syndrome trying to feed from men, the same way some of them learned how to manipulate their own fathers who fell into materialistic expressions of love more often than the verbally communicated ones. Hence love with these girls rarely makes the cut. Notwithstanding that a traditional society is little supportive of a 44 year old man walking down the street with a stunning 26 year old girl and still makes unkind judgement calls even when such a couple might actually be very happy together. Vexed more by the man's concern about growing old that thinks that being with a young and less complicated mind are the ingredients to feeling and looking younger. When in fact their physical juxtaposition is probably what highlights his age the most; like a mouse next to an elephant. Naturally, the solution was to* be with an equally attractive woman that is closer to his age and shares the same fundamental spark for life. "Pick me" she mused to herself with a wry smile. However truth be known, if Charlie really wanted to be a saint he simply needed to keep things platonic which wasn't likely to happen, or offer them ways to have a life without prostitution. 'Maybe he just does it all without any sensitivity at all, plays their vulnerabilities against them like they do to him?' she tried. However, in light of his cocaine plight that argument didn't convince her. She just didn't think so. In fact she thought his real problem was the psychological abuse that comes from an unhealthy marriage and his relationship with the prostitutes, which confuses all professional protocol between them and basically gets him wrapped up with his own insecurities by the "Black Widow" syndrome. She wasn't sure… She came out of her head space, awed at her capacity to presume so much with so little information. 'Stop it 'Chèle,' she whispered to herself … 11:05p.m., the girls that had gone down to the left had returned and went into the club. There were two entrances. The main one and a side one next to the stairs of the place upstairs. She sat there some more. If Charlie was going to show up it would not be until much later. After the card games in Namacor or the coke-house or wherever it was he went first. Her guess was that he went to Veela's just before closing. When there were fewer men or people to recognise him from the village and when those men would go home to their wives by 3a.m. She stared some more at the club. She knew that he went there at least three times a week. The telephone agenda and his sleeping rhythm at home suggested that he went out late Wednesday nights into Thursday morning, Sunday nights into Monday morning while Thursday and Saturdays seemed to be V's days off by reason of the text messages they exchanged around 1p.m. She hadn't a clue – it was more self-abuse really. Maybe the challenge to find out who V was and where she lived was more about jealousy and less about knowing where to find him in case of an emergency? If something happened to him or a member of his family – who would know where to find him? She closed her eyes, shunned the latter and gave Jealousy priority. There had to be some, or else her feelings for Charlie would seem more superficial than the prostitutes. She sighed and glanced once more at the club. Everything around it was like a ghost town while inside, that place was booming with music, drinks and sex. Even she was enticed to go in. Charlie probably went there late, hung out and then drove V and whoever else home. Most of these girls wouldn't own cars and the transportation system out this way was little if any at all. It would explain the carpooling she'd observed earlier. Maybe Charlie even stayed at her place somewhere around the club. Her imagination was on automatic pilot and envisioned them doing it all at V's place and for some reason Michèle wanted to know – had to see it. Like seeing it would satisfy her emotional doubt? He maintained that he never brought the club home with him. That he usually did the coke alone at his place while the social aspect of his night life stayed at the club or other people's places. Not his. Yet she doubted that he was still following that protocol and wanted to prove her suspicions right. As if knowing would arm her to find him and really lay into him about rehab. Without proof beyond a reasonable doubt she couldn't demonstrate to him how deep he was going. She looked quickly at the car clock. 11:30p.m.. She started up the Mini and headed home. When she got back, Charlie's car was still outside his place. A mild sense of relief found her. He might be taking lines, but more than likely he was sleeping or on the couch. *'What to do next?'* she thought, and went home.

4:30a.m., Saturday. She made herself get up and try again. Drove back to Veela's thinking maybe she'd see Charlie there, or possibly see him and V leave the place. Maybe even follow the Phedra and find out where she lives or where they go together ... Find out, why? Again she was at a loss for reason. She pulled up in front of the club and parked. Then felt too obvious. A yellow Mini was hard to ignore and she suddenly thought she should be more cautious. So she moved the car and parked higher up on the road away from the street lamps. It meant that she had to sit on the passenger side of the car, so that she could see the activity if any, moving from the club. Life between the midnight hour and 7 a.m. was such a different world. It used to be a major part of hers when both her university years in Montreal and then her professional years abroad required many all-nighters into daybreak. She recalled a chat with Charlie in the Phedra about why he liked to go out so late at night... *'I like seeing the day break,'* he'd told her. *'I like it when there's nobody on the road. The air smells of wet fields, the sky is just waking up and it's quiet. I used to sometimes work at Sa Croix from midnight until 6a.m. – you know. It was better for me.'* She did understand. *'Hmm I know what you mean, I like hearing the birds wake up,'* she replied. *He nodded in affirmation, while he looked on at the road and the two of them flew along Juniper road. She remembered feeling a sense of envy then, because she wanted to see the daybreak with him and do the club thing that he was enjoying. They'd only seen the daybreak together once and that was New Year's Day coming back from Palma ...* She looked at the time in her phone. It was close to 5 a.m. The air was damp and the streets were moist. Except for the birds that had begun to wake up making their light chirping sounds, everything else was still motionless. The Phedra was not there. People, she assumed clients, began to mill out of the club from the side door suggesting to her that the club had already closed the main door and was now shutting down. A few young guys came out, followed by an attractive dark haired man carrying a whiskey glass. Then a few minutes later another man of middle class composure and a hefty weight, sauntered heavily to his four-by-four all-terrain jeep. Then nothing. Then a bunch of guys with two girls approached the club and turned away when they realised that it was closed. She sat there. 5:30a.m ... 'What are you doing here Michèle?' she whispered earnestly to herself, 'this is ridiculous. Like I don't have anything better to do at 4:30a.m.? This really borders obsessive compulsive behaviour – you know!' she said a little louder as if to make it sink in. She grabbed her phone. 'Si,' answered a husky voice. 'May I speak to Vanesa please,' she asked. She didn't know what she was doing, but her heart was pounding a mile a minute. 'She didn't work tonight,' replied the voice. 'I've got some buddies who are asking for her. Does she work tomorrow?' The voice wasn't comfortable with the conversation but finally answered: 'Probably,' and hung up. Great she thought. The first time she tries "Get Smart" and her objective isn't even there. She was probably somewhere else with Charlie; maybe dinner or the gambling house – 'WHO CARES!?!' she yelled into the car, '*Get* a life Michèle! – I *Will* GET a life once we get *Fuck– Head* into rehab!!' she counter attacked. 'Maybe he really doesn't want to stop this lifestyle?! Maybe he's taking you for a ride?! Cocaine, club music, hard tits and ass, promiscuity of night into day! He's already got a wife, a son, done the business thing, made the money, been out of Mayürqa, has the family and friends – why not die on a high!?! It's certainly more INTERESTING than 9–5!!' she bellowed back at herself. '*But* he said: '"Quiero Vivir! (I Want to Live!),*" that's* why!!' she shot back, 'and I *BELIEVE him*!!' She hollered at the top of her lungs ... The strain she felt in her throat caught her attention and she was suddenly self-conscious and instantly silent. The car remained quiet as she looked around wondering if anyone had seen or heard her, because she wasn't exempt of that possibility either... It felt good to scream. She felt drained but better. She sat there a moment in quiet, safe and alone in her Mini. She took in a deep breath and emitted a 'Thank you for the car.' It really was a wonderful gift. Next to Dasha it was her world, her dad, her Jesy, her yellow power – small but mighty. She owned a Mini? '*Mi–ni,*' she smiled at her word play. It just came to her, but she saw it: "ni" meant "to" in Japanese. 'A Mini *to Mi*–chèle.' She amused herself and was calmer by it. 5:45a.m., the girls started coming out of the club. The tall girl in the seventies jacket came out first and headed back down the street from where she had come the night before. Then a guy with four more girls came out and they all pooled into his white car. About five minutes later the boyfriend with the white hatchback came out and started the car. Right after that, the girl in the jean jacket and jeans came out and got in. Then she saw the girl lean into the driver and kiss him and then they drove off. Following that, they all seemed to come out at once. Then another car pool and two girls with one guy climbed into a four-by-four all-terrain. Within minutes the street went from motionless too busy to motionless once again. Only Michèle and the Mini were left behind. She shifted back over to the driver's seat and started up the car. 'Mission incomplete,' she murmured to herself, although slightly relieved because she really had no idea what she would have done, if she had run into them. Then incredibly enough, when she neared Sa Ema's main entrance, Charlie's Phedra was just turning into it from the opposite direction. It was just after 6a.m. and he was alone. The morning sky was coming alive with pale shades of yellow and pink. The sea was still asleep and the mountain peaks were just coming into view through the morning mist. She was not sure if he'd seen her or not, so when he pulled into his place she came up behind and stopped in time to see him open his car door, collect empty bags of fast food and shut the door behind him: 'Hi,' she said through the car window when he saw her. His initial facial reaction was not pleased, but he still approached the car: 'What are you doing here?' he asked with a quizzical look on his face. He was having difficulty keeping his eyes open. 'Out late,' she replied. 'You'd turned in before me. Did you not see me?'

'No,' he said with a seemingly concentrated effort to focus .....

'You o.k.?' she asked.

'O.K.,' he replied with a polite nod.

'O.k., sleep well,' she said. He nodded again and she drove off.

So you're with her – Not with me
Oh how lucky one man can be
When she lays in your warm arms – Don't think of me
In fact your best friend I heard, he spent last night with her
Don't think of me.
'DON'T THINK OF ME' – DIDO, LYRICS ADAPTED

Focus

At 9p.m., Carles was picking her up to go for Chinese. While she waited for him at her place she wondered what the point was. He'd only drop her off later and look for V afterwards. Then she wasn't really sure why she was so bothered by that? She really didn't care, yet 'gawd,' she thought, how the feline in her reacted, such a powerful instinct. In retrospect, if she could keep it at bay, all was going well. Charlie was still in touch with her, while he'd actually read through the report she'd given him and had called Narconon the day before, after lunch. *'He's got the info. That's all I can do.'* She thought. She had to get busy with herself. Not with him or the squalor around him. She understood that the prostitute was nothing more than the addiction. By day he was with Michèle before anyone else and that had to be worth something, especially as he'd never openly done that in public before. 'Using me?' she mused: 'Yes. Best of both worlds for him right now and you're allowing for it.' She kept trying to remind herself that they we're just meant to be friends on a mission to get him to rehab as soon as possible. She was dealing with a 44 year old with an ego of a twelve year old, who was making her work frankly unbearable. It was like fighting for and against the same person. Meanwhile, Vanesa had become an obsession to her even though Charlie was just as responsible for his actions. However like his wife, the prostitute understood his illness and was sucking everything she could from him and that was her anxiety: Charlie blindly putting his trust and affection into people who were hurting him, deceiving him and who didn't respect him. '*Shit!*' she thought again, '*how did sentimentality get to the battle field and fog up my objectivity and focus?*' Then it occurred to her that V, Vladimir, Venice and Valentine's all represented illusive romances that began with "V" and which happened to sit comfortably between "M's" shoulders. '*Great,*' she thought melodramatically, '*I'm the bearer of peace and vexed love at the same time – Geees!*' She understood that the addiction promoted low self-esteem. Yet what was really bothering her, was that Charlie did not trust her. As if Michèle were the one deceiving him! '*Too kind, she's not for real – what does she want from me?*' Her mind processed: '*Maybe all "she wants," is for him to show the world the potential "she" recognises in him and then maybe evolve a future from that.*' Was that so bad? Perhaps he was feeling guilty from her help because if he did get better, he probably wouldn't want her, or he simply didn't want the responsibility of someone waiting for him? Okay. That wasn't his problem. Besides, once he was in rehab she would do her own thing. She needed to get productive for herself. She'd thought briefly about making money as Charlie's assistant, but that wasn't going to happen. She wanted to make 2,500 euros a month. She could see it and somehow knew something was there, but she had to figure it out first, then follow through with it. She was 38 but she saw 40 as an important year for her. What was in 2007? 2004 into 2005 was Dasha, the move, Charlie's family, the car, the bear totem, the licence plates and a string of other coincidences: the delays, money problems, all felt like subliminal hints towards something she hoped was more positive. 'Gotta focus!' she whispered: 'Don't lose sight of me or him just yet! Just stay focused!'

... Because Charlie, the future is synonymous with now. Everything you do *now* influences the "now" of later and before – M.

Seville

Phase one from the report Michèle had given Charlie was coming into effect. It was incredible but a girlfriend of hers, whom she had not seen in years, called and invited her to her wedding in Cadiz on March 19th. Ironically one of the rehab centres Michèle had mentioned in Charlie's report was in Seville. Only forty-five minutes from Cadiz.

He was sitting on the couch and she was in the Ikea chair: 'What do you think if we go to Seville and check out the Narconon centre there?' she asked. 'I could attend the wedding, you could help me with the driving and we could check out the centre at the same time. At least give you another perspective you know?' she sent out in one breath. He was stretched out along the couch on his side with his upper body propped up with the aid of his left arm, cigarette butt balanced between his lips, its smoke irritating his eyes as he tried to focus on the report and flip through it. She sat there watching him. The ash from his butt was about to drop when Charlie consciously removed it from his mouth, tapped it off into a small ashtray that was on the small table in front of the sofa, and placed the butt back into his mouth. He flipped through the pages quickly with sporadic glances back and forth between pages as if to clarify or check the information. She could not tell if he was impressed or amused by its amateur level of research. 'It's not extensive,' she said modestly, 'just enough to give you some ideas you know..,' she trailed off. He removed the butt from his mouth with the four fingers of his right hand, exhaled and stubbed it out into the tray; dropped the report on the table, lay back down onto the sofa then bunched up the Ikea cushions under his head: 'When is the wedding?' he asked. '*He's thinking about it,*' she thought. This was the difference between Charlie and her experience with Jes. Charlie's illness was clearly defined and he in whatever capacity he could, was trying. Jes had developed a drinking problem that no one wanted to acknowledge; not even himself. It finally caught up to him when he seemed to be held between the world he wanted with her and the one his twin called him from, until she finally understood to let him go: two weeks later he died ... 'On the 19th,' she replied. Charlie said nothing. 'Charlie it's straight forward. My intentions are selfish too you know. I'd like to attend the wedding, but I don't want to drive out there on my own. Narconon is just outside of Seville. We can fly in, visit the centre in the morning, spend a night in a hotel and the next day you drive me to Cadiz. You don't have to attend the wedding if you don't want to. You can just sleep in the hotel. It'll give you some space from here and help me too.' Nothing. 'I'll pay for the car and my plane ticket if you can pay your ticket and share the hotel with me. Separate beds too, no worries.' She ended. She really wanted him to say yes. 'Vale (O.K.),' he said. A sense of bated breath was released inside her. 'Okay. Shall I reserve the plane tickets while you call Narconon?' she added coolly. He nodded. 'What time is it now, is it a bad time to call there now?' She was pushing her luck, but there was no telling when this moment of lucid conversation was going to end or come back. '11:30,' he said looking at his watch. Then automatically grabbed his phone and called. A man at the other end received Charlie's call: 'Hola. I understand you are a centre for addiction, could you give me some information?' he began. The conversation between Charlie and the man was about ten minutes. Charlie reviewed his case with the man in a way that sounded like two guys having a chat over a few beers. It was casual and very frank. The end of the call concluded that he and Michèle could visit on the morning of the

18th or 19th. Therapy sessions started from 10a.m. so that they should call to confirm they're arrival. The fee was only 2,000 euros a month and quite a bit cheaper than the other centres, which raised some doubt about the quality of the place. However that was the point. She wanted Charlie to *see* his options. The cocaine was rendering him unable to think clearly. However, his senses were to the contrary, very sharp and alive. Sight and touch were particularly receptive too and influential on his decision making process. Plus they both had the time and enough funds to do it. Charlie was wasting his time between the couch and doing coke while Michèle was living on her savings and in spite of her desire to organise her personal and professional life, was being held back by a series of unwanted delays. The internet was down, then when it was up, her computer stopped working. Her things and savings from Canada were lost between continents, while the companies she'd applied to for work, had yet to reply. It was as though she couldn't start the things she wanted, even if she tried. Maybe it was an excuse, but she took the Zen way and went with the flow. The truth of the matter was, she was not ready to go back to work until she could figure out a way to make the salary she wanted per month. Teaching was there, but it would still require her to supplement funds from somewhere else. Timing. It was all in the timing of things and she and Charlie were using it. So it was decided. She went home and started calling about plane tickets to Seville. Confirmed her attendance at the wedding and checked out affordable hotel options. It wasn't going to be anything like Paris. She didn't have a lot of money and she didn't want Charlie to think that she was trying to take advantage of him. She checked out the hotel options for the wedding guests in Cadiz and wasn't too impressed by their generic style. Instead, she felt that if she could find a Parador for the weekend, it would meet Charlie's need for modern comfort and her need for the traditionally renovated. She remembered the last time she'd stayed in a Parador and loved it. It had been in fact in Andalusia in a castle renovated by the ministry of tourism. Most Paradors are old relic structures, or stoic old castles kept alive by restoration and tourism. They used to be economically approachable until recent years when their popularity turned them into a money venue, more than a cultural one for all to enjoy. So much so, that many tourists from abroad never have the full Spanish experience and herd to the ugly generic hotels instead. Anyway, the Paradors that she did find in Cadiz were fully booked. Then she came across one in the village of Los Arcos de la Frontera. Her memory was triggered back exactly ten years earlier when she had been there with a boyfriend and stayed in a local Bed and Breakfast. It had had high beamed ceilings, white Spanish tiles with hand painted designs, Andalusia music and fresh orange juice for breakfast. Overall her recollection of the village was good. Unfortunately the Parador there was also fully booked. So she decided that they could either spend two nights in the same hotel in Cadiz, or one night in Los Arcos and one night in Cadiz for roughly the same price ... Might as well take advantage of the trip and stay in Los Arcos one night? Besides it was on the way to Cadiz. They could get to Seville on the Friday. Visit Narconon that morning, break up the drive and stay in Los Arcos that night, then head to Cadiz the following morning, attend the wedding and finally drive straight back to the airport on the Sunday– done.

Needless to say that getting to the airport with Charlie that morning on the 18th was no less exciting than the last two times she'd gone with him. They needed to be at the airport by 8a.m. At least leave home by 7a.m. She was up and ready to go by 5:30a.m. Her nerves were already into action. He'd make it, she knew, but it would all go down to the seconds. At 6:15a.m., sure enough Charlie called. At least he called. 'Hey,' she said. She could tell that he was driving. 'I'm going to be late,' he said, 'maybe you should go ahead in the Mini and I'll meet you at the airport,' he offered. Her gut sunk, he was resisting ... 'Charlie no worries. We have time. I'll wait. We'll go together and if we miss the plane no big deal; get here when you get here ok,' she said calmly despite fluttering butterflies in her stomach. 'Vale,' he said and hung up. She intuitively collected her things, grabbed her carry-on and went over to Charlie's place just in time to see him swing into his driveway at 6:45a.m. He was flustered and anxious. 'Hey no worries Charlie, we have time,' she tried, as she watched him rush to the front door and enter. He hadn't put anything together. It was a crazy moment of throwing things into his carry-on: maybe a dress jacket for the wedding, an extra pair of shoes, dress shirt? What colour? Passport? Telephone? Sundries bag? Check, check? O.K., let's go! They climbed into the Phedra and revved out to the highway by 7a.m. on the dot! That was the art of Charlie; organised chaos that was always right on time. It was truly impressive. Once they got to the airport, she trotted to check-in and he went to park the Phedra. Big mistake. He usually parked on level four where departures left from. She was already there by the automatic staircase searching for him. It was 8:05a.m. and their flight was boarding. No signs of him. 'Ding, ding, ding, Iberia flight 1–7–0–7 to Seville is now boarding at gate A20. Ding, ding, ding, Iberia 1–7–0–7 para Seville embarque inmediatamente en la puerta A20.' The P.A. system was causing her to feel an ulcer more than Charlie's absence. 'C'mon Carles where are you,' she hummed to herself. They still had to get through security and then down to the gate. Then there he was; sauntering coolly towards her as if time was not an issue. His air was so cool that she felt a slight sense of anger, almost as if he was testing her reactions again. The funny thing was she cared less about the wedding and more about Charlie seeing Narconon. If they missed the flight, she was not sure when the chance would come again, if at all. He finally caught up to her while she held her composure and said nothing. They walked to security when all she wanted to do was run. He secured through one while she secured through another. He was being evasive and distant from her. Once they got past all the rigmarole of stripping down for security's sake, she decided to leave him behind and head to the gate on her own. She knew that the plane would only wait five minutes beyond the last call before closing the gate; they had no luggage on board. 'Last call for Iberia 1–7–0–7 to Seville gate A20.' '*All right already!*' she heard her thoughts lash out. She trotted quickly along the linoleum white floor thinking that if they couldn't see her they would certainly hear her. Once she veered into the gate area she was instantly annoyed at the fact that there were quite a few people still boarding. She already disliked Iberia intensely, now she frankly hated it. It monopolised Spain's air service industry while its Passenger Relations staff from ticketing to flight service were frankly secured paper pushers, unpleasant zits waiting for their pensions to kick in. She knew the tricks of flight control, but most companies did not send the last call until it was really last call – no wonder people didn't rush. It was all cry wolf. Charlie walked into the gate area behind her like a cool cat. It instantly made her realise that although Charlie might have been lucky to receive a new perspective from the Canadian woman, she in turn, was learning just as much from the art of Charlie.

They got to Seville. The car was too small for Charlie's liking but they adapted. Then the ride through Seville was nothing like the positive recollection she'd had from ten years earlier. Maybe they were driving through an unfavourable area, but Seville centre looked drab and felt tired. The weather was grey and traffic was heavy. They drove forty-five minutes to the nearest town to Narconon called Alcalá de Guadaira; from there Charlie still had to call and confirm directions to the centre. His mood swings were severe and leaned heavily on the negative side. He was defensive and suspicious of Michèle from the time he'd parked the car in Palma, until the time they'd finally parked the rental and went inside a local bar for a coffee. What intrigued Michèle the most was that she was still having a good time. She loved trips, especially with her chosen one. Somewhere however, it was unhealthy and she'd spent most of the car ride trying to understand it … *It was true that she got a lot out of small pleasures, yet she was willing to put up with a lot of emotional crap in exchange for the moment or the brief sensation of happiness she felt, much like an addict, but with a different influence. Best moments were when she and her partner were on the same emotional wave length, while the perfect ones were all that and the ability to reciprocate their love at the same time. Naturally, her self-analysis fell back on her father again. They spent a lot of car rides together while much of it was to suffice her father's void of loneliness and not so much because of his love for his daughter. At least that is how she saw it thirty years later. She had been a surrogate companion adapting to his mood swings to the point of just understanding one another so well that they might have been better to die and be born again as a couple. Her dad had wanted to move on in life much like Charlie wanted to live. Hence Michèle recognised in herself, a little warrior whose steadfast commitment could on occasion end up taking over other people's fights, coupled with an independent streak once the fight was over; at once becoming the warrior "en repos" capable of living her own life completely detached from those she'd avenged.*

Sitting in the local bar however with Charlie, she could see that no level of repos was in sight yet, and dialogue with him was not going to help either; not even the Universe's. He was drinking beer and eating olives at 11a.m., while she sipped her coffee with milk. His behaviour told her that his body was still a drench of cocaine and whiskey from his night out and that within the next hour or so his mood would dive severely into the dark side of his mind. He was already noticeably annoyed at her presence, as if she had done something deceptive to him. She tried to take it with a grain of salt understanding that he had not slept in 24hrs. Regardless of his night out, he was simply saturated by the effects of the cocaine which he'd been doing in heavy dosages just about every day. It was frankly impressive that he even managed to get them to the airport, let alone *be* in Seville; the sofa and Ikea chair suddenly felt so far away. 'What exactly happened to your luggage?' he asked with a bit of a snarl. It took her a moment to trace what he was saying before she could see where he was going: 'I don't know Charlie. It got lost from Dubai to Mayürqa,' she replied. 'Why did Elisabet think you lost it in Dubai?' he followed. 'I don't know. We don't always understand each other very well,' she said carefully, but her thoughts offered more … *Anything related to Elisabet with Charlie had to be handled with kid gloves. He was fiercely deferent to her in her absence, which would not have bothered Michèle, if she felt the dedication was reciprocated by Elisabet. However in her experience, the latter had not been true. There is something very unattractive about Mayürqan culture and that is mendacity. As much as Michèle could appreciate Elisabet and Mitx, they were still a product of their generation and the teachings from their social traditions, in which to be altruistic was in direct conflict with the superficial ability to change one's colours faster than the wind changed direction, for the simple matter of avoiding an immature understanding of ridicule or confrontation. Such that when the tough got going one often found him or herself the only voice of reason. One might say that hypocrisy is not limited to culture, it breeds everywhere, but that did not make it acceptable. Michèle was not comfortable with the level of criticism that existed among family members in the absence of the one being depreciated. Especially when airs of solidarity and trust were being promoted when that individual was present, or offering them something in exchange. Mitx applied it consistently, as if it were a crutch to keep him up from his own insecurities, while Elisabet applied it eloquently under* the guise of diplomacy. Charlie, as far as Michèle was concerned, was the only one who did his best to avoid it and likewise suffered from the turmoil of emotional confusion between love and mistrust that the culture can easily provoke. Mitx would say that "the addict" or "those people, deceive and disarm people" when the only one who had not been evasive with her thus far, was the addict. The worst part was that she too, was falling into that habit of pessimistic thinking. On one hand Mitx would say that he would like to see his brother get better while on the other hand he seemed to be waiting for Charlie to fall. Perhaps it was his pragmatic defence mechanism to avoid disappointment on the off chance that Charlie did not get well. However it felt more like a level of envy from him towards his younger brother, who "gets away with it all" and could still end up at the same retirees' card game as would his older brother, who had not necessarily lived as many lives as Charlie. Above all, Michèle felt that her affection for Charlie provoked silent envy. Mitx asked for Michèle's help when he was unaware of her stamina, then tells her that it's in her best interest to leave his brother alone. When that tactic did not work, she sensed that there had been dialogue between him and Charlie that must have highlighted her motives as being unrealistic and unhealthy. Simply because during a mild conversation with Charlie over "pa amb oli", he referred to her father as an example as to why it was felt, not necessarily that he believed it, she seemed too ready to help people. She could not remember ever having mentioned her father to him or anyone except once, when she'd had lunch with the Serras and they'd inquired a little about her life in Canada. Mitx, she assumed, probably arrived to an analysis about her from his books on psychology and shared it with Charlie. Sigh. Reading into things too much or not, it just seemed to her that in spite of Mitx' affection for Charlie, his male instinct of conquer and divide was stronger than himself. Elisabet was another perspective. Michèle was not sure if her less than supportive lines during Charlie's absence were about protecting her interests with Charlie by *trying to dissuade Michèle away from him, hypocritical, or simply an act of solidarity with her husband. However unlike Mitx, Elisabet's actions were more naive than intentional; a dual personality who simply fit the bill as a well-intentioned politician for non-governmental organisations. Probably too, Charlie's affection for Michèle was not validated by him. He would have denied any interest thus fuelling their belief that she was more a pain in the ass than a friend. Above all, like a puppy that poops on a carpet, they were completely oblivious to their actions and in the end, it did not matter what the reasons were, if any. Michèle was a pain in the ass; being otherwise wasn't going to get the job done. More than likely too, she was having conversations with herself. However her intuition was rarely so wrong, and –*

'I don't know,' he interrupted her thoughts with a sceptical tone, 'you had your MP3 and camera with you when you got back..,' he said. She came back to him. '?? Charlie I carry those items in my carry-on.' He looked away and said nothing. She was bothered. She began to feel self-conscious. Had she deceived him? Why were they really in Seville? His fog was becoming her fog. The trip was a chance to be with him that was understood. She told him the trip was just as much for her as it was for him, but her answers did little to ease the undercurrent of guilt she was feeling. Charlie got up and went to the men's room. His absence relieved a level of pressure she was feeling by him and allowed her to focus on her location. She immediately enjoyed its authenticity: the bar was bare, with a few modest tables and chairs, quite spacious with high ceilings. It had a row of Spanish tiles that ran along the walls, with a TV set high in a corner over the bar. The bar was long with a "tapas" oven at the far end set on top of it, a rack of potato chips, peanut shells scattered all over the floor and voices echoing loudly within. Charlie came back from the men's room looking tired and nervous. He went over to the bar, leaned into it and asked for the total. She got up and asked if he wanted some money to which he quickly said no. They left and headed back to the car.

> Ooh, now let's get down tonight
> When I get this feeling – I want Sexual Healing
> Helps to relieve my mind – Whenever blue teardrops are falling
> And my emotional stability is leaving me I want Sexual Healing.
> 'SEXUAL HEALING' – MARVIN GAYE
> LYRICS ADAPTED

La Palomar

It was horrible. Really horrible. Anxiety levels were even killing the butterflies in her stomach. Neither she nor Charlie was having fun. They were lost in Los Arcos de la Frontera. After they'd left the local town Charlie called Narconon and postponed their visit until the Sunday morning. He was in no shape to see or talk to anyone especially since he'd taken another line of coke in the men's room in Guadaira. The village was busy and jammed with cars. It would seem that the wedding had fallen on the weekend before Easter. An important detail that had not occurred to her and explained why all the Paradors were booked. The place had changed a lot since the last time she'd been there ten years earlier. The old town was basically untouched, but everything else had been upgraded or touched by modern generic buildings and commercial outlets. The place where she'd booked was the Casa Grande which of course just had to be tucked away at the very top of the old town. It meant that Charlie had to drive through narrow winding roads, tolerate a sea of tourists, wait patiently for locals and their animals to get out of their way and most irritating was the fact that Michèle had no clue where exactly the bed and breakfast was located. She had to call more than once for proper instructions which always seemed to come a street too late and required them to start their trek from the bottom of the village all over again. As much as she tried to enjoy the action surrounding them, the tension in the car was horrible.

At one point, while the car was at a 75 degree angle waiting for local painters to move their car, she feared Charlie was going to start thinking that she had chosen the remote and tucked away place on purpose. His state of mind was so insecure that he was bound to feel trapped and deceived by her, while all that she wanted was to get to the bed and breakfast and sleep. After the third round from the bottom, they figured out their destination point and parked the car in the square opposite the village's Parador. Memories flooded her while they unloaded the car. She had been to that very same place exactly ten years earlier with another man. *'It had also been Easter weekend then too? Wow,'* she thought, *'what a coincadink.' At that time she was new to Spain and its ways. Her boyfriend then had decided to take her away for the weekend and Los Arcos de la Frontera had been his choice. While he was driving she'd suddenly noticed from the highway into the distance a majestic looking village in brown and white colours with what seemed to be a castle perched high above the village. 'Ohhh!' She'd instantly sounded loudly, 'look at THAT over there!' she'd exclaimed to him. Her friend was thrilled by her enthusiasm. 'Yes, that's where we're going, Los Arcos de la Frontera and THAT is the church of San Pedro!' he added proudly* ... As she dragged her carry-on from the car over the square's deeply set cobble stones she admired the church of San Pedro before her. Charlie was already making his way out of sight, so that her moment to reflect was curtailed by her need to catch up with him. She still liked the old village and gave a quiet thanks that her first time had been the other time. "La Casa Grande" from Michèle's point of view was simply wonderful. Charlie of course did not share that view. It was definitely a typical Andalusia bed and breakfast well restored with high ceilings, wood floors, white washed walls, an exotic library of incredible books, magazines, and travel encyclopaedias, green plants everywhere, old memorabilia, narrow spiral wooden stairs lacquered in white paint, a small maze of different halls, while the rooms were fully equipped in traditional style but modern comfort. Their room happened to be the suite room at the very top of the house with a patio terrace view of the entire village and the valley below. The name of their room was "The Palomar" and Michèle loved it. Charlie however did not. He took a brief look around and said nothing. Meanwhile Michèle unpacked her sundries bag and put it in the bathroom. When she came out he was standing over an empty book shelf, separating two lines of coke and sniffed both of them in front of her. *'Ouch,'* she thought, *'how can people do that?'* 'Is that the end of it,' she asked. 'Yea, I wanted to finish it all off! That's it, no more!' he said with a determined voice. Her guess was that the intention was sincere. He was going to check-out Narconon and that had to mean something somewhere. Besides, if they were going to visit Narconon on the Sunday it was logical to take it all then. He'd have 48hrs to sleep and regain a false sense of sobriety. He sat on the bed looking slightly calmer which is exactly when it hit her: she really wanted him. How long had it been since he'd paid any physical attention to her? Three weeks? Then the undercurrent of guilt she'd detected at the bar came back and this time she knew what it was. The purpose to their trip was clear enough. Narconon for him and the wedding for her. Los Arcos de la Frontera was a nice way to break up the trip and take advantage of the sights. She really thought the little village would have been a nice place to hang out. Paris went well, why not there? It was two months later and Charlie was hardly Charlie anymore. She had been competing with cocaine, wives and a prostitute. Whether or not she liked to admit it, she somewhere at some time had hoped to seduce him back into wanting her over the *girlfriends* and somehow find a way to get his sights back on rehab. She caught her reflection in the front door window; she'd straightened her hair two days earlier, was wearing black mascara, her black Marcel Marceau top with big buttons, black pants with outside cuffs that fell at the knees just slightly above a pair of black leather boots that hinted to the black garter tights and the belly chain underneath. Everything about the way she had dressed revealed a subconscious desire to be with Charlie that its image was about as subtle as "Roxanne's" red light. It was hardly the proper attire for a cobble-stoned village in remote hills to say the least and in light of their location, made her look trampy and out of place. Naturally, Charlie had noticed instantly that morning and his reaction had been fear and a sense of entrapment. Worse, was that her craving for attention was so strong that it dismissed her guilt and let vanity take over from her reflection in the mirror, making her feel even sexier. She was straightforward horny and wanted him. Sexual frustration had been culminating with every day that had passed with Charlie giving V exclusive physical attention and none to her. In light of their dynamics up until then, she saw nothing wrong. After all, if she was going to tolerate a prostitute, the least he could do was humour her a bit – no? Desperation. She took advantage of the moment and sat on top of a mini bench and feigned getting undressed in the hope that he would get the hint and give her a sign to go for it. He did. He turned onto his side and watched. She kept her boots on and removed her pants first so that her top flared lightly over her buttocks like a mini dress leaving the thigh stockings visible under the black boots. At which point Charlie asked her to wait for him and he got up to take a shower. Within minutes he came out fully dressed? Something was wrong, yet it seemed unwise to change direction. He moved in behind her, placed his hands firmly around her waist and rubbed up against her lightly. Although Charlie was not having any luck with himself she enjoyed the sensation of his hold on her. It was not aggressive but it was firm. He suddenly stopped and laid on his back on top of the bed while Michèle took over the seduction. He allowed her to explore his body while she helped him get undressed. There was a mirror on the far side of the bed that made the moment all the more enjoyable because Michèle was really feeling erotic by her look. Her mini top came off as well as her panties, but the boots and the thigh stockings stayed on. Finally, at one point she sat up over him and began to touch herself while getting a fuller enjoyment watching her feline in the mirror. Once in a while Charlie would whisper a 'Si' or that he liked her "look" before she quietly made it known that she was satisfied. Then she leaned in to him, kissed him and rolled over to the other side of the bed. Charlie got up and found his cigarettes. After about a moment, she sat up and asked him to help her remove her boots. Then they both got back into bed and laid there next to each other without saying much. She had her left leg bent at the knee propped upwards and set between his legs, while his right hand almost entirely covered her inner thigh as it caressed her in a methodical up and down movement. She loved that. Sex was never her favourite thing as much as the petting and the affection. The fact that Charlie was physically impotent from the cocaine was actually in her favour. It was a contraceptive in itself, as well as the fact that if he got better he'd have to stay away from alcohol, be aware of his health and certainly develop a character and inner stamina from the experience capable of handling any conflict or obstacle: the perfect guy, go figure. Like the caterpillar to the butterfly he could go from the coke addict to a better man. It was hard for her to understand why anyone would try to deter her or any one from a relationship with someone that had all the potential to be something wonderful? People live their lives on a daily basis mindlessly investing time and energy into their future without guarantees, yet relationships aren't one of them. Next to death, people feared love more than anything else in the world as if the death of it, would actually kill them – how ironic was that? Charlie stopped caressing her and sunk himself comfortably under the covers. 'I'm going to walk around a bit – do you want to come?' she asked quietly. He shook his head and smiled politely at the same time. So she got up, showered and went out on her own.

It was a horribly windy and cool night. It was almost enough to deter her from going any further, but it seemed like a shame to be there and not walk around, or at least have a drink in the village after ten years. She thought of her friend and sent him a sms: "Guess where I am? Los Arcos de la Frontera!" and then stepped into a small place called "La Cueva" which was nothing less than a restored cave tucked inside the bedrock of the village with a few small tables and chairs, a small counter bar and Andalusia memorabilia hanging from the walls and the ceiling. Within minutes of ordering a small tapas and wine, her friend called. The call lasted a good fifteen minutes while they reminisced about their experience in the village ten years earlier. It was a feel good moment that left her feeling high until she got back to the hotel. It was about 10p.m. Still early enough to order something light to eat for Charlie, so she asked the front desk to prepare a sandwich plate for him. When she got back to the room Charlie was awake watching TV. He wasn't the least bit interested in her night out, but he was thankful for the food. By the time she'd showered and slipped into bed, he'd finished the sandwich plate and had stepped outside briefly for some fresh air. The view from their patio was a tremendous expansion of black night and stars over village lights that swooped down across the valley below. It was so cold however, that Charlie could hardly appreciate it, but at least managed to notice the stars: 'Lots of stars,' he said matter of fact. 'Yea, lots,' she murmured and fell asleep.

Four Noble Truths:
Dukkha – suffering is everywhere
Samudaya – there is a cause for suffering
Which is attachment or misplaced desire (tanha) rooted in ignorance
Nirodha – **t**here is an end of suffering, which is Nirvana
(The possibility of liberation exists for everyone)
Maggo – there is a path that leads out of suffering
Known as the Noble Eightfold Path
(Right view, right thought, right speech, right conduct, right vocation, right effort, right attention and right concentration).
BUDDHA

No body's perfect

The next morning was another story. Ugly. He was in a real ugly mood. Not surprising after his previous 24 hour binge. He was coming down which meant that the beast would come out in search for more and make him react unpleasantly during the following few days of withdrawal.

It was 11:00a.m. She was already up, been for breakfast downstairs and back to see if Charlie was awake. He was, dressed and sitting on the bed putting his shoes on.

'You know I don't like being taken advantage of – you know?' he snarled at her.

'Pardon?' she asked cautiously from the front door.

'¡La Palomar!' he exclaimed in a flamboyant way, 'do you know what a palomar is?' he asked her. She hadn't thought about it. 'Something related to pigeons?' she asked.

'A palomar,' he said as he stood up, 'is a cage for pigeons – homing ones to be precise and this room used to be a pigeon house!' he said with conviction. Michèle was delighted by the trivia unaware of where he was going with it. 'Oh really! I never realised, tha' – he cut her off.

'What did you think? That it was funny to bring me all the way to this remote cheap place and coop me up here like a pigeon in a cage so that you could seduce me last night like I was your puppet?

I feel violated and abused you know! If it wasn't for your wedding, I'd take the car and head back home right now! I am tired of your games and your manipulative ways! You know!' He ranted. She stood there momentarily in a deep freeze. 'Charlie, I asked you if you wanted to come out last night and you wanted to sleep instead. As for making you feel abused, that was not my intention. I'm sorry if I hurt you,' she said quietly. Although her real thoughts went along the lines of: *Feel used and abused by me? Not by the prostitute or your wife? You did the lines in front of me; I thought you were giving me a signal! It takes two to tango buddy and I didn't twist your arm!'* The moment brought her the déjà vu of them in the car after that day at the dentist's. She was not going to try and reason rather she simply pretended nothing was said: 'They have fresh orange juice downstairs,' she said nonchalantly. 'Ah, si?' he said. The change in behaviour was again remarkable from Doctor Jekyll to Mr. Hyde – all at a moment's notice. 'Yea, it's included in the price of the room,' she added stupidly. 'One would imagine that a Bed and Breakfast would,' he answered arrogantly. They checked out of "La Casa Grande" by noon. Charlie was less than affable and evidently wanted to get out of the village as soon as possible. The car ride to Cadiz was about an hour. Long enough for her to pensively go over events up until then and give Charlie quiet time to himself... *She felt guilty. She had dressed the part yesterday because she was hoping for some fool'n with him. Her subconscious had led her to believe that it was okay based on their trip to Paris. She had wanted to be better prepared on this trip than she had been when they were in Paris and the closest thing to sexy that she'd packed then, had been her long black skirt. It was also an attempt to get his attention back to her from V. As if dressing up kinky would remind him that Michèle could look the part too and suffice his needs without the coke. Gawd any excuse would do – how dumb was that?* Her thoughts railed-in at her: *'When it was least appropriate, you asserted advances to a guy who has been doing coke every day for a week or more? Of course he felt put into a corner! It certainly wasn't the time to provoke physical affirmation from him – Idiot! And of all places in a Palomar?! … IF that's a subtle hint that we're on the right track, I don't like the humour in it!,'* she shot-out to Life. She knew that it wasn't about anything more than the coke and V was simply related to it. *So when or how did she veer off of her Maggo?* She wondered. She felt like Charlie might, who couldn't explain why his memory would fail him right when he needed to remember. Freud would have an answer and she bet it was related to the cloaking spell of desire. She closed her eyes feeling more ashamed. Now she had a bigger problem. Charlie felt deceived by her. He would no longer feel confident with her motives. Worse, her little sexy escapade could associate her to prostitution and confuse his thoughts about her. Never mind what harm it might do to her chances of evolving more with him beyond rehab. Charlie was saturated in cocaine and she was trying sexual advances to manipulate him out of it? Worst of all, she'd seduced him when he was heavily under the influence, just like his wife had probably done from sheer frustration of waiting so long for him to get off the fence. That in spite of his being active, she took the bull by the horns, married him and gave birth to his son. '*Uugh, she was no better!*' groaned past her thoughts, '*at least his wife had the courage to give him a son!*' Everything about her and Charlie was supposed to be platonic yet she broke the rules because of his sexual rejection of her for a prostitute!? '*Wonderful 'Chèle, just wonderful!*' It had not been pre-meditated that way, but that's exactly what she'd done … It's like what Vladimir had said to her: "You're dangerous to yourself and to him." Yes, she agreed. If she did not stay focused the duality of her objectivity would turn subjective. '*Stay focused Michèle,*' she told herself … 'Charlie I'm really sorry about yesterday,' she suddenly said over the car noise. He offered her a nod; apology accepted.

A few minutes later they started up a conversation about the days when he used to travel and sell shoes. She listened intrigued to find out that he had travelled quite a bit on his own as a young man. Even while he was in a relationship, he was rarely around or dependent on it. She realised that Charlie had never really known what it was to be in a relationship with someone let alone how to manage one. The message was all about learning by doing, and it relieved a bit of her own misgivings about herself: nobody's perfect.

Chance never helps those who do not help themselves – SOPHOCLES.

Narconon

Once Charlie and Michèle arrived at Cadiz, they stopped into a bar for an early coffee, then checked into the hotel, slept until Charlie drove her to the church. The wedding came and went, during which time the only contact she'd had from Charlie came in a sms asking if there was a lot of food at the reception, to which she didn't reply. She got back at the hotel just before 3a.m. only to find out that the hotel did not have second room keys. So as to avoid waking up Charlie, she had the night concierge let her into the room. Needless to say the effort had been in vain because he woke up as soon as she closed the door. The room was dark, but daybreak was nearby giving the room a hue of soft grey light. While she got undressed Charlie followed the movement of her silhouette through the room while they chatted casually about the wedding and the food at the reception. It was all fine until she got into bed and Charlie turned away leaving his back facing her. It was harmless enough but somehow the influence of the cava she drank, or possibly the advent of her menstruation, or simply emotional blindness – whatever it was, resembling an addict deceived by its cravings, she once again reacted to the rejection. 'Charlie?' she dared lightly, 'why do you treat Vanesa better than me?' No reply. Gloated even more: 'You once said to me that I was pretty – has that changed?' Her voice sounded through the dimly lit room and dissipated without a reply. The next morning Michèle wanted to commit seppuku and told her self not to drink any more until after Charlie was gone. She was losing control of the feline in her. At breakfast Charlie was indifferent and irritable and when he finally spoke, it was to interrogate her: 'Who was the guy you came back with last night? I heard him outside the door,' he said indignantly.

'?? Charlie that was the concierge, th–'

'Nahhh, what do you think I'm stupid?' he cut her off defensively.

She was no longer vexed by his mood swings, especially since her behaviour had been even less acceptable. Instead she was tired and acutely aware of how deep his well was. They weren't touching bottom, yet she imagined that their shadows were. Though, what caused her the most anxiety was what the drug was doing to his mind every second that he was not at rehab. Cocaine is one of the cruellest drugs of all, because of its smooth and casual effect on the outside, while underneath lies the termite that gnaws at the brain slowly but surely, minute by minute, second after second, nonstop until the victim is mentally handicapped indefinitely, has Alzheimer's, or is dead from a physical overdose. At the rate that Charlie was going he was bordering on all the possibilities towards mental evaporation. 'Shall I meet you at reception?' she said side stepping his comments. She looked at him as he gave her an affirmative motion from his head, swallowed the last of his food and rolled up his napkin into a ball with the palms of his hands, all at the same time. She got up from the table and conferred to herself: *'I love this man.'* …

Narconon Mediterranean was an eye opener to say the least. Located on the outskirts of Seville in a dry open area with little life around it. Michèle associated its rundown appearance with that of the hotel-café in the film "Baghdad Café". She gave Charlie a quick look while he drove the car into the parking lot of the centre. He said nothing, but she could imagine what his thoughts were. She tried to conceal hers too. The place was really awful. Nothing like the newer centre in England or the latest one in the United States that she'd seen on the internet. The 2,000 euros suddenly seemed more about maintenance issues than the rehab programme itself. They got out of the car and were greeted by a small group of young adults sitting on the front steps, like high school students waiting for the class bell to ring. Michèle was instantly aware, as Charlie must have been, of the incongruity of his presence to the place. Inside the building was hollow and drab. The walls were in a faded peeling turquoise green, dotted with individual glass frames of diplomas, commemorative certificates of the centre and a few commemorative shots of staff and redeemed addicts. No one attended the front desk. There were two long halls that extended east-west from one another, where an evident sound of life was coming from one of the rooms along the west hall. It sounded like a man conversing over the telephone. Michèle looked at Charlie who suddenly seemed to be amused by the whole thing and smirked at her. She gave him a nod towards the sound down the hall. Charlie shrugged his shoulders.

'Shall I go knock on the door?' she asked.

'Don't know. I suppose they'll come,' he replied.

She stood there. It was ten minutes past their appointed time of meeting. She ignored Charlie's laissez-faire attitude and sauntered dubiously towards the room from where the voice was coming. When the voice ended the conversation, she also stopped in her tracks and took on an air of someone just waiting around. Then she heard the voice initiate another call. '*Okay, so the guy is waiting for us to make a presence,*' she thought. 'They'll come,' said Charlie almost aware of Michèle's thoughts. 'Charlie no worries. We've come all the way from Mayürqa you know,' she replied quietly, 'I'll just let him know that we're here.' So she did. She walked right up to the partly ajar door from where the man's voice could be heard and read the door label that said, "Director". Then tapped lightly on the door at the same time as she moved her head around its frame and smiled. He noticed her right away and waved his intention to get with her. Satisfied, she backed out of the doorway and headed back to Charlie: '¿Que?' he asked. *'Yea right, now you want to know,'* she thought, 'he's coming,' she said. Within ten minutes of the man's eager wave, he finally came out and led them both to his office. Everything about the man's office was about seventies wood panelling and meagre attempts at presenting a professional image of the centre and its programme. They spent about forty-five minutes chatting and then had a short tour of the centre. The pool outside was empty and filled with junk debris. The tennis court lacked a net. The bedrooms were glorified versions of hospital rooms in third world countries. The addicts that were there appeared to be from socially and economically challenged families. The TV room looked like a fraternity common room a few days after a party while the cafeteria was below ground level and frankly made prison look good. The highlight of the place were two sauna facilities where the first phase of the detox programme requires five hours of sauna daily, for six weeks. Furthermore, Narconon's programme did not use medication or drugs during the rehabilitation process and had a 70% success rate. The latter appearing to Michèle as being a generic rate of success shared by all the centres she'd looked at. Needless to say, neither Charlie nor Michèle needed to consider the place any further. Charlie was ready to leave before they'd even got started. Even Michèle knew that she would not feel at ease leaving Charlie alone in such a place; if she did, she'd have found a way to get a room next to him. However, the man was either very professional, or cared very much about his task because he managed to promote the centre and its name valiantly, despite its humble and disquiet appearances. The visit ended at reception. They shook hands with the man and departed back down the front steps and bid adieu to the small group still hanging out there. Once they got back into the car Charlie exclaimed: 'Aiii! – "The best centre for addiction is Hipócrates," by far!' he quoted from somewhere. Michèle said nothing for a moment. She did not know Hipócrates or its philosophy, but had no doubts about its prestige and tailored comforts for the wealthy and famous. At 7,000 euros a month where only 100 euros was really about the therapy sessions, it was a high-end business that catered to the privileged only. Charlie had already spent close to 13,000 euros the last time he was there, to no avail. After almost three months Hipócrates let him leave because he refused to follow the rules and insisted on leaving? Even she knew that the third month of rehab is one of the more delicate ones because it's precisely when the addict feels better and capable of taking on the world. So she didn't understand why the professionals at that place had not tried harder to dissuade him, except that they knew full well that he'd relapse and return, even though the centre underlines that second admittances are only permitted after "special consideration". '*Yea right,*' said her brain, '*it's all a guise for "show me the money".*' She was willing to bet that if Charlie decided to go back there a second time and decided to leave in his third month again, that they'd probably tie him to a chair before letting him go. By then, they would have met their 25,000 euro objective on, what Michèle decided to call their in-returning patients, while simultaneously taking advantage of Charlie's profile as being another success story. They knew his capacity to get better. Heck if she could see it, surely the professionals did too? Charlie simply fit the demographic forecast for their yearly budget plan. Gawd it vexed her to no end how a centre dedicated to helping addicts seemed to be taking advantage of their illness too. At 7,000 euros a month she felt little respect for the place. Charlie of course did not agree. He empathised with the professionals who'd worked with him and believed that their motives were for the well-being of all their patients. *'They do care Michèle. What you're saying isn't true,' he'd said to her during a dinner over "pa amb oli" one night. 'I didn't say that they didn't care Charlie. Only, I'm willing to bet that the altruism coming from the staff is vexed by the business end of it, that's all!' she answered. 'Nahhh,' he said emphatically and added, 'you're a teacher and you don't want your students to learn? If they don't pass their tests then whose fault is it?' he countered. 'Carles, anyone whose work promotes a social service wants to help individuals know the tools at large and inspire them to learn how to use them: not give them, to them. It's a joint effort between the teacher and the student to get where the student wants to go. However, although social service works from the heart, it needs money to meet its demand – you know?' she looked at him from across the table, 'Regardless of the profession, there is always some guesstimate about a student's potential and the logistics of even getting involved with that student. Heck, at exam time, many academies only accept to prepare those students who appear to have a chance at passing because if too many students don't pass, then their prestige as a good teaching institution is at risk of being challenged and therefore their economic benefits too,' she ended heatedly. 'Lo sé (I know),' he added casually. 'How does an academy know who has a better chance at success than the other, if the students are all there for the same reason?' He was playing the devil's advocate and she knew it. 'You don't,' she said annoyed at the truth to his comment, 'which to me is the important role of the maestro – the intuition and the motivation to keep the student alive and focused.' She exhaled. 'A good maestro wouldn't care about a student's rate of success compared with all the others, rather the student's rate of success compared with him or herself. If the teacher is good then any student is capable of getting there on the basis that everyone is his or her own benchmark for success,' she replied, 'and that's my point about Hipócrates. The business side of it, has taken over the virtue of that, is what I feel that's all ...'*

Narconon's philosophy on the other hand, literally appeared to be about having time for self-reflection and finding the source of the addiction rather than merely pacifying it like an aspirin does a headache. Their point was to find out why the need for the addiction arose and control the addiction from that point onwards. It made complete sense to Michèle. Even Asian culture supported the need to find the source of pain rather than the pain itself. It seemed to her that she and Charlie simply saw the wrong Narconon centre. It's shabby and rundown appearance contradicted its attempts to reach active addicts of Charlie's calibre, who will pay the centre that responds to the visual and egotistical senses first, before the illness. Hence in her opinion, Hipócrates was working well by that knowledge, but needed to avoid losing sight of its purpose in doing so ... '¿Que?' he said to her as he started up the car. 'Now you know where you *don't* want to end up,' she replied coolly. Charlie pulled out of the parking lot and headed for the airport. Michèle was pleased. Although the trip wouldn't be remembered with fond memories it met its purpose. Charlie was having a second chance at getting a full understanding of his options and limitations. The next time round he would have no excuses to relapse except his own desire to do so.

If you love something
Set it free
If it comes back, it's yours
If it doesn't, it never was.
RICHARD BACH

Freedom

Despite Michèle's inkling of small success Charlie's negative attitude towards her did not improve. At the airport he hardly spoke to her and on the flight back, he sat in the window seat with his body language completely turned to the window in a way that would have made Frosty the snowman next to her feel warmer. Unlike Paris, he was not attentive to her or receptive to her singular attempt at placing her hand on his lap. Hence, during the car drive back to Sa Ema, after Charlie inhaled from the butt of his cigarette, put down his window and threw it out the window, he declared: 'I think that we should end the formality of our friendship.' It was dark inside the Phedra with only the dashboard lights offering a hint to their presence in the car. The night was clear and the Phedra hummed with the wind it cut through. Charlie was already smoking another cigarette feverishly, giving her a sign that he was feeling a lot of anxiety. Still, she said nothing and really felt nothing. So she turned her head towards her window and looked out at a stationary starry sky while the night itself, blurred by in smeared yellow light trails equal to the Phedra's speed… *It's over now? Funny how he has the "courage" to end with me but he doesn't with Vannesa, or a divorce from his wife, despite an unfavourable fifteen years! He'll probably see V tonight. I am alerted psychologically again, by a perception on rejection from men who seek me, use me, receive me as a privilege then discard me for being "good." Hunt me, enjoy all the good stuff about me, but won't help me through the bad stuff? Accept my heart and then leave its carcass in the void. I am never allowed to be "bad" or wrong? Either charged for being "Miss Perfect" or convicted for revealing to them that they were wrong? I have to tolerate all their shit, but they won't tolerate mine? Then the ones who've stayed in the chase despite my resistance, actually find another reason not to have me when I finally do yield to them! Charlie? Please open your eyes and Re-cog-nise me. It's me – Michèle. You know me, but you fear me –Why? Did I hurt you badly once before? As long as you hurt, I hurt, because you and I are each other's "we"… Or do you let me go because unlike the ones you suffer by, you care about me? Your distance from me shares the same reason as the one you have for your son? Love? I don't know anymore. "I know nothing except the fact of my ignorance", so that makes me "wise"? Crap. Whose was that anyway? Socrates? I'm angry. I'm angry at his brothers – what happened to the divorce process? Why the delay? Why doesn't the wife pursue it? To protect Charlie's interests? – Bull shit, no way! Then Mitx who tells me that a divorce would make no difference because they've been so long without it?! Don't cure the problem because they're used to it? What the hell is THAT?!'* She shifted her eyes to the stars. *'Why am I here? What is it that I need to learn?'* … 'You know this is hard for me to do,' his words clotted her thoughts and she turned her head to him. She knew it was. He was not doing anything wrong. To the contrary; he was trying to do the right thing and he was. It was the second time that Charlie was letting her go and something told her that it was not the last. 'I agree with you,' she said tonelessly. He gave a slight appreciative nod to the affirmation and looked on at the night road ahead of him. The rest of the drive was quiet until he finally drove into his place. She collected her things put them into the Mini, gave him a kiss and a hug then quietly to his ear: 'Tot be (all good).' Then got into her car and drove away.

Michèle: 'Tot be.'
Grandpa: 'That day, he discovered that "Tot be," was her way of saying "I love you" and the day he realized he loved her too.'
Grandson: 'Hold it, hold it. What is this? Are you trying to trick me? Where's the dragon? Is this a kissing story?'
Grandpa: 'Wait, just wait.'
Grandson: 'Well, when does it get good?'
Michèle: 'Hear this now. I will always return for you.'
Charlie: 'How can you be sure?'
Michèle: 'This is true love – you think this happens every day? I told you I would come for you. Why didn't you wait for me?'
Charlie: 'Well... I tried.'
Michèle: 'Dark forces cannot stop true love. All they can do is delay it for a while.'
Miracle Max: 'You rush a miracle man, you get rotten miracles.'
'THE PRINCESS BRIDE' – SCRIPT ADAPTED

Charlie's princess knight

Journal: "The Dream – dare I write this? It is so wrong – yet I go there. It's not the same as the one about Jes, but it is just as difficult. I dream of Charlie loving me. I dream of him not ever wanting to lose me. I see and want his world to be shared with mine. Our look – our personalities, our chemistry, our independence and a need for love makes me wonder why this dream can only be so far away from reality. I dream that we are reunited. We live together, we work. He manages Sa Croix and maybe something else while I can help and maybe write. I dream that we are happy together and for once in our lives calm from the knowledge of having each other. He is "better" "stronger" and has improved his love with his son. His wife is his friend without being a threat; we are strong enough together to repel negativity. Sometimes we travel together, attend family events from time to time – we have twenty to thirty years to grow old together. Most of all too, I dream of how we evolve and flourish romantically and sexually. Both of us are satisfied and proud. I dream of an image of us together that is completely and honestly provoked by the unabated series of coincidences and events linking us together. Yet my thoughts and the energy behind them are alive with no place to go. It's about me. It's about Charlie. It's about Life and its evil ways of manipulating us all. I give thanks as often as I can. I try to appreciate life within, as often as I can – only to think and feel now that even "Life" or the "guardian angels above" manipulate me more than the devil itself. Ernest Hemingway believed that: "The best writing is certainly when you are in love." Tho' now, sentences are not working. Thoughts are all that I have. Again I ask: 'Why?' Killing me or dying would be such an ease while the fear of maybe having to come back here and go through it again – gawd that's worse. Indeed Hamlet, "Thus conscious does make cowards of us all," or braver for facing it. I want to write and learn Mayürqan for a year. I know that I have expressed this somewhere in a journal before. I know that I have had these thoughts before. I also know that I think of 40 as an important number. I remember Copenhagen last year, riding a bike and mentally asking questions to life when I clearly heard dad's voice say "40" to me. I laughed out loud because I imagined it so clearly that it was absurd. I think that the next two years are about work and building a life that I believe I would like to have; like the image of the Mini. It's all there, vague and unsure of whether it's all *too* idealistic. This is my vision by day more than by night, and probably just a *real* dream after all..."

> What you love is a sign from your higher self
> of what you are to do.
> SANAYA ROMAN

Russian roulette

March 25th? Five days gone by since her and Charlie had returned from Seville. Although they had not seen each other since Seville she had not remained idle with her thoughts about him. She'd gone over the options and thought up new strategies: Narconon Seville was definitely off the list as a possible rehab centre. Assistance from Charlie's family had become counter-productive simply because in the past six weeks since Charlie and Michèle had stopped trying the 24/7 together, it appeared to her that his family had also curtailed their efforts. It was as if they had resigned themselves to Charlie's already conceived routine of getting up, falling down, getting up and relapsing again. Granted, Charlie's addiction would forever challenge his stamina to live, but success and failure existed for everyone, not just the addict. "If you fall seven times then get up eight," was a Chinese proverb and the point was not to give up. A habit by definition never changes, yet one could learn how to make an ineffective one, productive. Charlie could live with his, provided he had the tools, the knowledge and the training. That the 24/7 was just a step towards Charlie having a fuller view of his options? Above all to her, it was simply another way of keeping the will to try, alive, while Mitx was chanting to her, 'Dejalo, dejalo (let him be, let him be).' Meanwhile Elisabet was still on Michèle's flank buzzing at her door for walks with Dasha, bringing her home cooked plates with time to chat about "things", inviting her to lunch and family get-togethers with a clear intention to get the latest information about Charlie. In return Elisabet offered a few bits and pieces about her life with the Serras and her clear definition of Charlie which to Michèle was never far from inaccurate. Everyone had a different experience with Charlie, but Michèle felt that hers was deeper and closer to the fuller being that he really was. They were so conditioned by appearances and little communication that they all lived in a world of misinterpreted perceptions. Including Charlie. Although, because of Charlie's straightforward strategy with his family, Michèle felt no reason to deny them small updates about his health. She often went out of her way to communicate his stages of highs and lows and even requested their advice about a few areas. However, the latter came to a full halt when Mitx simply didn't see any reason to keep at it. He was sitting comfortably sunk into his sofa with legs stretched out onto the coffee table while Michèle sat next to him in the black leather reclining chair: 'He'll go on like this until he can't get up anymore,' he said calmly. 'My brother and I went over to his place the other day with Elisabet because he won't yell at me when Belle is with us. We'll go back again but this time my brother is thinking of giving Carles an ultimatum and relinquishing his power of attorney, unless Carles makes a move to do something about his addiction,' he paused, 'DEJAlo (LEAVE him be),' he emphasized with exasperated affection. She sat there in silence for a moment trying to empathise with his reasons, rather than rebuttal against them. Plus too, he was being polite in addressing his views about his own brother, in his own house. In actual fact she had no purpose in being involved as she was, except that she believed in Charlie, cared for his family and had made an agreement with them to try getting him to rehab. They both loved the same flag but waved it differently. Elisabet walked into the living room just then and Michèle spoke: 'No puedo (I can't),' she said quietly. 'Forgive me Elisabet,' she said looking at her and then back to Mitx, 'I do not think your philosophy would remain the same if your youngest son was in the next room doing lines right now. If he impeded you from going into the room would you really respect his wishes, or would you enter the room any way possible and somehow haul him to rehab? I don't think either you or Elisabet would sleep until you found him help. Charlie is the same Mitx, except it's much more difficult to physically haul a 44 year old man than a 17 year old teenager. Time is only on our side if we respect it, and I just don't feel that letting time go by until he wakes up and smells the coffee, will work this time round.'

'It's that he doesn't want help, don't you see?' he replied.

'Si. Charlie doesn't want to get better,' added Elisabet. It might have been easier for Michèle simply because she had not been exposed to Charlie's addiction as long as they had. True too, they had done well surviving with Charlie's illness by reason of their self-interested culture and pragmatic love. Buddha might call it an intelligently selfish lifestyle off-kilter by too much egoism, while modern medicine would call it the codes of conduct for co-addict families. Either way, Charlie may not have given them the same attention as he had done to her, simply because they did not seek it. Hence by fault of their kindred relationship with him, they could not know him the way she did. 'Mitx – tell me when Charlie is most likely to tell the truth – during his depressive lows after the highs, or when he's feeling lucid?' 'When he's down of course and the highs are over and all his demons come to life as well as his reality,' he replied. She waited a second before going on, unsure if the words that would follow would be an infringement of Charlie's trust in her or not, but there was a need to defend herself: 'If Charlie told me that the life he has now is what he wanted then I would be happy to relax and hang out with him the way he is now, until Life decided otherwise..,' Mitx gave her a doubtful eye, 'but he has expressed to me more than once his desire to live – "quiero vivir" were h–', she was cut off. 'Really? He's never told us,' interrupted Elisabet. A negative vibe in Michèle flickered. She had shared too much already about her intimacy with Charlie and suddenly felt angry that his family was taking advantage of her willingness to keep them informed. 'Aii Michèle,' said Mitx lazily, 'I've already told you – the addict deceives and misleads people, they're like that.' She said nothing more. It might have been Mitx' way of protecting her, but there was little logic in that, simply because she felt he could still work with her in her efforts with Charlie. *Why not? What did he have to lose?* she was irritated. *"Russian roulette," she suddenly remembered. It was one of Charlie's analogies of how he felt about his life with cocaine and from what she'd gathered, he was right.* 'Why don't we just shoot him then, *like a horse with a maimed leg or a wolf gone mad? Fuck, it's an illness not a vendetta to hurt people.'* She stood up from the chair, smiled at them, and thanked them for their patience towards her. Then stepped over to Mitx and Elisabet gave them a polite kiss on the cheek and left; be what it might be, she cared about this family and had no frick'n clue why. Thereafter she called Hipócrates. The week before they'd gone to Seville she and Charlie had been sitting in the Phedra near the sea at Sa Ema, when she'd asked him if he might call Hipócrates to at least see if they would have him. Oddly enough he was willing to comply and called the man in charge of the therapy group in Menorca in order to get the telephone number of a therapist named Meralda, who Charlie apparently respected. The call was quick, but she paid attention for the details she wanted and wrote the name and number of Charlie's search in her own agenda. When Charlie finally got Meralda on line, he was delighted by the fact that she remembered him and that they might have a spot for him in one of the therapy groups, but would need to get back to him on that. 'As if they won't let you back Charlie,' huffed Michèle through the Phedra's passenger window. Charlie did not argue her words and merely paraphrased Meralda that the groups were going through transition and maybe he could join one in a few weeks. Well that would have been now. Such that, she'd begun her calls to Hipócrates the day after she and Charlie had returned from Seville. She was hoping to speak to Meralda in order to get some advice about his increasing state of debilitation and it took her three attempts before getting her on line. The first two were militant and unsympathetic calls requesting her name and the name of the patient she was calling for. She was reluctant to highlight Charlie's name, wasn't a family member and only had bits and pieces of information about his history at Hipócrates. So the first two tries ended unproductively. The final attempt was made with some aggressive tactics by using Meralda's name. The line had suddenly gone into a stand-off until they passed her through to Meralda. The tone in Meralda's voice was cool and direct. Michèle understood instantly why Charlie liked her; she was the tough kind with a heart that beat somewhere behind the professional armour. 'Si,' said the voice. It sounded like she was rushed and annoyed by the circumstances of the call. 'Hello Meralda – thank you for taking my call. My name is Michèle and I am a friend of Carles Serra. I believe you had him in one of your therapy groups last year?'

'Carles? Is he from Mayürqa?'

'Yes, yes.'

'Yes, he called me last week,' she confirmed.

'Yes that is right.'

'I called him back last week, but he didn't answer the phone.'

'Hmm yes. His dependency has increased to almost every day. Which is the purpose of my call. I wondered if you might tell me if there is any room for him to be admitted back to the centre?'

'What exactly is your relationship with him?'

She hesitated unsure how to answer the question. Her heart actually felt hurt at the cold reality that only Charlie was the keeper of her dedication to him; as far as his world was concerned, she had no title, not even a right to belong to him.

'I am just a friend of Charlie's and his family.'

'Does his wife know who you are?'

'We've never met formally, but she is aware of my involvement.'

'Listen, when Carles wants to speak to me he can call me. He has my number.'

'Yes. I understand, but I am concerned at how much he is taking right now. How can he call you if he can't even see straight? Might you consider calling him again? I intend to let him know that I have spoken to you. That might prompt his curiosity to speak to you.'

'Carles is an addict and a grown man – he can call me. Alright?'

'Yes fine. With all due respect, may I ask you why a centre of your calibre allowed him to leave so early the first time?'

'Our centre is ranked number one in Europe and is internationally acclaimed around the world. Our success rate is 80%! Carles did not wish to follow the rules of our programme.'

'Yes, I see. I simply thought your professionals would understand the addict better than the addict itself – O.K. Thank you for your time Meralda, sincerely. Thank you very much for taking my call.' Needless to say the call was not a warm and fuzzy one... *"Carles is an addict and a grown man,"* replayed in her mind, as if the definition of adulthood suddenly relinquished the right to receive the same attention a child would get in illness? *'I bet the Universe gets a kick out of that one,'* she mused to herself. Her call to Hipócrates turned out to be a timely one, because within three days of letting her go, Charlie showed up at her door with a take-away of paella from Sa Croix. She had not expected his visit, so when she opened the front door she squeaked: 'Ah!! Charlie? – Hi!!' The squeak domino affected to him, who also jumped slightly: 'Well you don't have to be scared,' he said slightly taken aback. He was dressed in his blue jeans and the French blue and white striped polo shirt. Hesitant and shy in his approach he handed her the rice: 'Here I brought you this,' he said gently. She was really happy to see him and it took every muscle in her body to impede her mouth from exploding with excited garble, so as not to scare him away. Their moment was brief, only long enough for her to put the paella away in the kitchen and ask how he was. The truth of the matter was, she had a few things to share with him and she was not sure when the right moment was going to be. It might have been that one, but she did not want to dampen it with heavy conversation vexed by the fact that his arrival was opportunistic. 'Charlie?' she said as they sat on the sofa, 'I want you to know that I called Hipócrates and spoke with Meralda,' she said cautiously. His face reacted slightly, but he asked: 'What did you talk about?'

'Nothing,' she answered, 'I inquired about admittance possibilities for you and she said that she tried to call you back unsuccessfully.'

'Yea I saw the missed call,' he said. 'I'll give her a call tomorrow,' he replied. She was relieved that he did not seem upset with her. 'Do you think you will go to "Cirque du Soleil" with us on Sunday?' she asked. Much like Charlie, his family at one time or another had mentioned to her their desire to travel and see new things, such that Michèle had bought tickets as a Christmas gift for Xisco and Maribel, Charlie and Mitx' family to see Cirque du Soleil in Barcelona. The problem was that it fell on Easter weekend and Mitx despite all talk, said that he no longer wanted to go because he would miss his favourite time of the year for Mayürqa's traditional Easter dishes. Elisabet however, came to the rescue and prepared a few dishes a week before their trip, so that he eventually changed his mind. 'No I don't think so,' replied Charlie. She did not think he would. He could hardly sit down for a moment let alone enjoy a trip to Barcelona and sit through a two hour show. If Maribel and Xisco had not been going, she would not have been enthusiastic about going either and would have stayed behind with Mitx eating Mayürqan meat pies. Charlie then suddenly got up quickly, and said: 'Auu! I'm going.' 'O.K.,' she said. With that, Charlie approached her and kissed her on the mouth. It was such a pleasant surprise she could only smile wide and stood there with her arms folded. 'Bye,' he said as he walked to the door. 'Bye,' she acted coolly. The moment left her feeling high and anxious at the same time. Regardless of his reasons or the source from where the kiss came, it was from Charlie and she felt re-affirmed again.

> There are no guarantees
> From the viewpoint of fear, none are strong enough
> From the viewpoint of love, none are necessary.
> EMMANUEL

Chance

"Bum bum bum" her telephone woke her up with a sms. She reached for her phone and noticed that it was close to 6a.m. When she flipped it open she saw that it was from Charlie and read: "¿Que haces? (What are you doing?)" She stared at it and knew intuitively that the message had not been meant for her. So she sent back: "Charlie?" knowing that it was enough to let him know of his mistake. She placed her phone back on the night table next to her. He'd obviously confused her number with V's or maybe another girl's, but her gut didn't think so. She wasn't sure if she should feel some virtue in the fact that he subconsciously had Michèle on his brain or slighted for being made aware of his intentions. Lying there face down on her pillow, she then realised too, that just before the sms had arrived, she had been dreaming, or having full conversations in her head with his brothers and the centre in Barcelona about Charlie? She was actually talking to a psychologist who was listening to her talk about her perspective on Carles and then of him and her beyond the rehab programme? … She shook her images out of mental sight, amazed that her brain could be so active at six in the morning and got up to pee. Sitting on the toilet she thought about Vladimir and what a super and talented guy he was and wished she felt the chemistry for him like she did for Charlie. Then again, was she confusing chemistry with a reaction to Charlie's rejection? Was it really rejection when one is overlooked because of an illness? It was so hard to keep her feelings objective and not take anything personally. Worse, she noted a sensation of jealousy creeping into her system carrying with it, an excuse that Charlie did not want Michèle, as well as a provocative suggestion that he did not even remember her anymore. She knew that he'd been out until 9:30a.m.

at C'an Colom on the Tuesday right after Seville. '*Does he look for her?*' asked Jealousy, '*did he find her?*' She'd actually driven to C'an Colom on that Tuesday to see. '*Where do they go?*' repeated Jealousy, '*where does she live? Maybe she's a high class prostitute?*' It would correlate with his style, tho' in C'an Colom she doubted it. '*She's probably a prostitute that he feels sorry for and trusts emotionally,*' poked Jealousy again. Whatever. She sighed. It was all too hard. Sad that he was no longer her friend. Didn't even ask about her. '*Charlie doesn't live here anymore,*' she thought, '*I tried. I really tried for him and for "us". I'm really attracted to his looks, his hands, lips, his brain and when you've tried it all and it doesn't work, it's okay to let go, just let it go. The "girlfriends" are fucking me up; I have to let go now. I know that I have received the best of him, but there has been a lot of yuck too. Just want his trust and friendship again. Don't care about the rest? Is that true or am I deceiving myself? Where is she and what does she look like? Not good that I ask ... Aii, going through a major bout of loneliness and my mind is a mess.*' She was miffed about herself, because she'd also come to the unequivocal conclusion that despite it all, she couldn't fight what she was feeling – confused or not. It's what she felt. That her arrival to Sa Ema for the time being seemed to be about what she was feeling. She wanted work, but not the conventional way, and she wanted to make between two thousand and twenty-five hundred euros a month. At least that's what she remembered having expressed somewhere in her latest journal, or was it the one from last summer? She reiterated in her head that forty was going to be an important number for her and the following two years were about work and building a life that she thought she would enjoy having. Again, like the Mini, it was vague – but there. Insecurity harassed her beliefs as all too ideal and unreal. Crazy? Not sure. She'd wanted 2005 to sow the seeds for her future. That everything from that year should have a longer or integral spot in her life – she hoped. Maybe from 2006 into 2007 she would find her work, be in love, maybe even loved back and her life then would be about its nurturing... She also felt? Imagined, or *knew?* That Charlie was it. Yet at the same time she was inhibited and reminded of specific truths: that possibly her portrait of him in her life was a misinterpretation of the real one. He was a cocaine addict and the odds of a full recuperation were very low. No one *really* believed, if at all, in his ability to curtail the addiction within a different lifestyle, nor did anyone really want him to. '*People,*' she exhaled. The unfortunate fact that many could still feel unwell by others' happiness, when it unsettled a truth about their own choices and their own lives that was not entirely satisfactory. Some will even look for a weak spot in others' happiness in order to give rise to their contented choices rather than simply embrace the others' happiness and benefit from it. She and Charlie had a right to be happy. Above all, they had a right to get there together. Yet Michèle was already harbouring anxiety about friends and family whose scepticism and resistance were too quick to remind Charlie of his illness and inhibit his confidence. Negative energy that she felt ill equipped to deal with while she was putting all of hers into Charlie. 'How dare they!' she muttered, feeling the anxiety bubble up more. 'People have a Right to be HAPPY!!' she sounded adamantly, but it wasn't enough and her mind went on: *Life wanted people to be happy! Because that kind of positive energy was what kept its world upside-up and alive!* 'He–llOo! Is anybody listening?!' she sounded again. Her mental hollering finally subsided and she reasoned: *there was no catch. The size of one's effort merely had to be the same size as one's problem and therefore desire, because the gift of happiness was so pure, it simply had to be earned. Those who managed to get there were not responsible for other people's happiness, but they could share theirs and be compassionate towards others by it* ... Even Charlie's family, despite all appearances, was still clannish in nature and cared for its members in such a way that no one's life was ever really independent from it. Compounded by the fact that Charlie did not, or should not love her or any woman, without a clear understanding of his personal issues: a sensitivity level that promoted an aversion to involvement and responsibility to others because he could and did take them seriously. Yet people could be fickle with their loyalties and that's what caused his emotional suffering; egocentric conversations with himself about people who'd manipulated him, women who'd played him, men who were "envious" of him, infected by an unhealthy love affair with his wife that inadvertently redirected him into placing his care-taking qualities into the wrong women because they temporarily satisfied his need to demonstrate and feel appreciated for his paternal capabilities as a provider and protector. As far as Michèle was concerned, the cure to Charlie's illness was a divorce that protected his relationship with his son, a new marriage and a daughter whom could all benefit from the intensity of his love. All that! Challenged by Charlie's fear of what sentimentality can do to a person if not respected: weaken ... 'But I F*EEL HIM*!!' she suddenly bellowed at the walls around her. She recalled the film "Mar Adentro" and how the quadriplegic Ramon Sampedro wished to die because he could not love the way he wanted to and how fear had been the terrible culprit that almost denied him his wish. Then there was that vision about her and Charlie that seemed so awfully impossible; why or where, did and does the hope come from? The horoscopes say: "To have faith and go with it," but how much of it was wrong like the relationships she'd had that did not last or go well before him? Or how much of it was actually a chance, prepared by those good and bad relationships for her to use and help her receive the love of her choice and therefore the one meant for her? 'Would God, the Universe, Life or Destiny really be so clever… or kind or fair?,' she whispered. '.. Please guide me right if I go left … Grant me more time, patience, faith and courage … and more sleep.'

PART IV

MICHÈLE VERSUS CHARLIE
A WARRIOR'S HEART

I shouldn't try what I'm gonna try
I shouldn't go where I'm gonna go
I shouldn't ask for what I'm gonna ask for
But I don't know better
I know I should go on, go on, go on
Don't stop!
I'm on a mission beyond all superstition
No need to worry, to fuss and cry
No need to go back and wonder why
I'm on a mission beyond all superstition
Yeah, cause I know, that you know
I know you know, I know you know
That you should
Go On!

'GO ON' – KEVIN JOHANSEN, LYRICS ADAPTED

> The new seed is loyal; takes root with greater force
> In the hollowest places.
> C.P. ESTÉS

I spy

5:30a.m., April 5th. C'an Colom sitting in the Mini parked up the street from Lady Veela's. She was sitting there actually feeling a sense of peace while waiting to see when Charlie would come out of the club. The Phedra was already there when she arrived at 5:15a.m. She was dressed in black track pants and her black sweat shirt with a hood that was oversized for her head and tended to fall just beyond the brow of her forehead, thereby bunching forward strawberry-blonde curls onto her face. Although her reason for wearing the sweatshirt was for warmth and comfort, the image of her circumstance made her feel like an undercover Nancy Drew doing it wrong, sitting in a bold yellow Mini. The early morning mist had started to dissipate as the day came into focus and she knew that bodies would soon start to filter out of the club. It was the fourth time that she had parked like this and was now pretty much on top of Charlie's routine at Veela's. It still seemed to follow a rhythm of heading out late on Tuesday nights into Wednesday mornings. The same seemed to be true for Sunday nights into Monday mornings, while occasionally on Thursdays he'd stay at Veela's after hours. He was more than a regular there, leading Michèle to think that he might have been managing another source of income from below that street corner. So that Charlie's imagery of squalor, rats and wells was understood considering that everything was below eye level and entertained people that were half his calibre intellectually. All "wannabe's" labelled as white trash by the less diplomatic individuals or victims of ignorance and exploitation by the more sympathetic ones. It would be easy for Charlie to feel important there, even though it was the squalor that took advantage of him and his illness. *Intelligence was such a difficult tool to conduct wisely*, she thought. *It had so much power because it was the ideal of the future. It saw through imagination which then transformed into reality. It was the power that allowed a positive evolution of mankind the chance to exist and to do it right, only if it was checked and on-kilter by its allied powers of love, patience and responsibility. Otherwise, intelligence on its own, was a creative weapon that was lethal, and killed...* She sat in the Mini pondering these thoughts because her own situation made her wonder about herself more than once. Once again, what the fuck was she doing sitting in the Mini waiting for Charlie? She was supposed to be an intelligent woman and although she could find ways to defend her position what was the point? He would only come out of the club, jump into the Phedra, fly back to his place, do a few more lines of coke on the little wooden table by the couch, ignore the mound of porno videos he already had sitting on top of the TV or stashed in his closet, then watch the new porno videos he'd picked up in Namacor, before heading to the club and finally sleep on the sofa by 9a.m. and move to his bed by 10 or 10:30a.m. How did she know all this? She was sitting on the passenger side of the Mini, her head pressed against the window staring down the empty street at the steps where people considered to be lost souls would start filtering out. 'Lost souls,' she mused to herself... *"All the lonely people, where do they all come from? – Aaahh look at all the lonely people.., where do they all come from?"* Her mind sang again with the Beatles and she hummed at the fact that she was probably one of them. Her behaviour would appear unethical if her purpose for being where she was, stemmed from a need to control Charlie and his activity with Vanesa. It also appeared simply pathetic that she would spend her time and lose sleep over a cocaine addict because it highlighted that she had nothing else better to do? That her buzz for the day was a perverse way of playing Nancy Drew by night and a princess knight by day? How ironic that the girl with the Mini was the one without a life? Even the rats and the squalor, as Charlie would often describe them, had more aromas in their shit than hers? How long had she been doing it for? It sort of crept up on her suddenly and recalled her experience with the Vietnam memorial she'd visited years earlier in Washington DC. She'd begun her walk from its zero mark and followed the names of all the soldiers engraved into the black marble "V" until she needed to step back for a better view, because her neck was feeling sore from having to crane it back, in order to see the names on the wall that had both suddenly increased in volume and in height. Without realising it the "V Memorial" had slowly grown out of proportion to her height by at a least a meter and she'd never even noticed. It is without a doubt one of the most successful works of art in its inescapable reminder of the war itself and to her a constant truth to the United States and the world, about the dichotomy of its nature. Regardless of the lessons, the American flag bears the symbol of the American eagle: an attractive, warm blooded, aggressive but beautiful predator. A creature that must go out every day looking for prey in order to maintain its nest and its need to exist, while the threat of its extinction, comes from within its own country. "Isn't it ironic," her mind flipped from the Beatles to Alanis Morissette. She sat there calmly reflecting on her latest behaviour over the past week ... *They were into April and it seemed to her that Charlie was approaching the climactic point of going through or missing the window of opportunity before it closed. If he took the window he would be on time for summer recuperation, his son's thirteenth birthday in the Fall and a successful closing of his year in 2005. He could do it. Her ambition for him had taken her over and because his sms communication to her had diminished tremendously, she'd begun to look in on him during her walks with Dasha. It had happened ever so casually but turned into a habit instantly. She'd discovered that it was possible to see Charlie's living room space and kitchen through the slits of the closed shutters that faced the sea. Her biggest anxiety at that point had been his high levels of cocaine consumption versus a possible haemorrhage to* the brain. Indeed her imagination had gone wild and yes, she was afraid of it happening without anyone around to tell. She saw so many similarities between him and her father whose cause of death from cancer was a blood clot to the brain. Hence, the occasional haemorrhaging that Charlie experienced in his right eye was an alarm of concern to her about the internal effects of the cocaine on him. Naturally, she was worried – he was a man of 44 not 22. It bothered her. He was deep into his well by then: shacked up in his place on his own, with all doors and windows closed up, refusing to see people without any way of getting to him, if he needed help. She understood too that his family had long progressed from such a fear and learned to live with it. If he died he died and it was true. Yet it was her first time round with him in this story, and he was older than he was in the past; and in all selfishness, she simply did not want him to die yet: it was her life too. So the week before, she'd become a "Peeping Tom." On her walks with Dasha in the morning and at night she would swing by Charlie's place and see if he was still alive. In the mornings she would check the Phedra first. If it was still warm then she knew that he'd been out until then. After that she would swing down by the sea and peek through the shutters to see if he was ok. The first few times, he was on the sofa while the TV flashed blue light through the shutter windows from the porno action on its screen. On the Tuesday morning she was up by 7a.m. and saw him doing lines from the little brown table before getting into his porno flicks. Nothing could be seen well except for brief glimpses of his feet or his arm or his face when he moved in a certain direction. It was enough for her that he was moving. At night it was enough to see the flashing blue light through the window shutters, a moving foot from the sofa, or him eating at the kitchen table. If he was not on the sofa she'd walk around to his bedroom window and listen for his snoring. All so nutty – so obsessed that she even told him about it and not because of a guilty conscious, rather because she did not want the risk of him finding out without her telling him first and unsettling trust issues between them; as if telling the truth would alleviate the punishment of consequence. The first time she'd done it was on the Monday morning – March 28th. Yet the funny thing was, even though she told him about it that same Monday afternoon, he did, nor said little to impede her from doing it again – as if he enjoyed the idea of her looking in on him? The only thing he did do, was place a few lawn-chair cushions on the floor against the bottom of the bay windows which obstructed the view through the shutters of the little table he did the coke on. So, that afternoon, she'd sent him a sms at 4p.m. asking him if she could drop by and see him. He didn't actually reply until 6p.m., but it was enough time for her to think up a reason for the visit: Madrid. When she got to his door and knocked he did not answer. So she sent him another sms: "Hi. It's me." Then he replied with, "Entra (enter)." She tried the door, but it was definitely closed so she walked to where the extra key was hidden and let herself in. Charlie was on the sofa, the TV was off and the little floor heaters were humming loudly from around the room: '¿Que?' he asked. 'Nada,' she answered, 'how are you?' The little brown table next to him was covered with cigarette ashes, the plastic cards he used to do lines with, a little green ashtray and all the literature that she had given him in the past few months: the report, the Capricorn horoscopes, the Asian and tarot zodiac articles for 2005, her birthday card with his sketch of the Champs de Elysée on it and a magazine folded open at an article that he must have been reading. It had only been five days since he'd popped by her place with the food from Sa Croix, yet she realised that she had not been in his place since they'd returned from Seville on the 20th. 'So?' she tossed at him as she took her spot in the Ikea chair. It amazed her how wonderfully comfortable she felt just being there with him, 'Have you had any thoughts about visiting the Narconon in Madrid? I know that Seville was pretty bad, but Madrid's appears a lot better on the internet and might share similar qualities with the new ones it has in the States – you know?' She kept on, 'We've still got the time, is what I think Charlie and if you think that you might go back to Barcelona it might be wise to go feeling absolutely certain, especially at 7,000 euros a month, no!?' she ended calmly. Charlie by then had lit a cigarette and remained slightly propped up on his back against cushions, smoking and listening to her with his gaze to the ceiling. The glass doors to the sea were now opaque from the closed shutters and reminded her of her initial reason for seeing him. 'What about TAVAD?' he asked. The mere fact that he even inquired about TAVAD meant that he had read through the report and refuelled her faith in him. 'Yea, did you call them?' Then with his right arm still across his chest and holding his cigarette in his fingers, he used his left hand to reach into his left shirt pocket and pulled out his cell phone. 'What's the number?' he asked in between puffs. 'I don't know,' she said, as she sat up and shuffled through the paper memorabilia on the little table until finally coming up with the report and the page on TAVAD. '902 100 197,' she relayed to him as he pressed the numbers into the phone. As he got ready for the call he started to search his shirt pocket and the wooden table for something. 'Tobacco?' she asked. He nodded. 'Maybe your room?' she asked again. He nodded again and then was interrupted by someone answering his call. So she got up and headed to his room to check. His voice trailed off into an incoherent gargle as she headed to his room. When she passed the little room where she sometimes slept, her eyes were caught by brilliant colours coming from the Valentine's card she'd given him a month before. Surprised that he still had it, she went into the room to look at it. It was just a silly handmade card made with vibrant Crayola oil glitter markers sitting on top of another card to him from his son, which for no apparent reason to her, transmitted goose bumps to her arms. She left the items in their spot and went looking for his cigarettes in his room, pushed the bedroom door open and saw the cigarette pack on the bedside table instantly, walked in, and then – (!?), her heart skipped a beat. On the wall above the little round table where the cigarette pack rested, were all the yellow sticky note messages Michèle had given him over the course of the past six months. She was shocked to discover that he not only still had them, he had pegged them on his wall by his bed. Needless to say that she was also awed at how many she had written for him! She counted fifteen and had never even noticed in the process. They were, in their moment, little motivational reminders for him that she had either stuck to the Phedra's windshield for him to find later, left on his bathroom medicine cabinet or the front door, if he had not been around. Her eyes scanned them quickly: "Life shrinks and expands according to one's courage." "Live the life you wish for tomorrow, today," "Fear is no object." "Poco que perder y mucho que ganar (Little to lose and everything to gain)." "Lv you" and so on. She pulled herself away and returned to the living room where Charlie's call had already ended. She handed him the pack. 'Gracias,' he said.

'De nada (your welcome),' she countered. 'So?' she prompted.

'Nah,' he said. 'It's only two days of body detox then the rest is psychological therapy for a minimum of six months,' he replied.

'How do they justify only two days of detox?' She questioned.

'I don't know. Something about a new method of natural medicine that relieves the anxiety and allows two days of detoxifying. I don't know ... Plus they don't have a residence which means I'd have to find a place in Madrid.'

'Might be cheaper that way no?' she offered.

'Maybe – but I don't like taking drug medicine you know..,' he countered.

His comment was a paradox to her. Yet she agreed. She was the first one to avoid drug-medicine unless it was absolutely necessary and really did not have faith in a cure for an addiction administered by a drug.

'What's the drug called?' she asked.

'I don't know – they don't tell you,' he said directly.

'They don't tell you!?' she said awe stricken.

'You can ask,' he added, 'they don't tell the patients,' he ended.

'What!? That's absurd Charlie!' she said feeling the hairs mounting on the back of her neck. Charlie too sensed her rising passion and allowed a brief smirk to appear across his mouth.

'Let me understand this correctly,' she started, 'an addict is supposed to be responsible for his or her own actions, while family and friends are not supposed to look out for an addict like they might for their children because they're likely to fall into co-addictive behaviour, even though it is understood that an addict has a maturity level of a twelve year old. Meanwhile a rehab centre of professionals that presumably understands the addict profile better than anyone, tells you to sign the dotted line while your head is in between emotional purgatory and hell without answering your questions about the drug treatment you will be under?! What the hell is that Charlie!? Total exploitation of an addict's illness that's what it is! Holy Jesus Christopher! Everyone wants to make a buck on you!' Her voice had raised a decibel and she was now standing up. 'Naahh,' he said in a soothing tone, 'tran-quii-la, tranquiiila (eea-sy eeeasy),' he continued calmly, having enjoyed her dramatic scene. She sat back into the Ikea chair both irked at abusive capitalist bullshit and tickled by Charlie's response to her. At least TAVAD's programme seemed to lean towards the psychological therapy more than the physical one. She exhaled audibly and looked at Charlie, who still had a look of amusement on his face, and inadvertently made her smile too. 'Ok, so what do you think then?' she asked subdued. He seemed unsure of what to say but finally answered: 'Well, I suppose we could check out Narconon in Madrid,' he said. Her mind raced. 'Alright,' she said in a controlled tone, 'if you want, I can call about flights and reserve tickets for the next week. They'll be cheaper that way... In the meantime maybe you could call them and see what day would be good for them?' she offered. 'Okay,' he said dryly. Her insides felt relieved and anxious. They would go to Madrid and she wanted to get the tickets right away before he had a change of heart, vexed by the fact that she still had to tell him about her peeping tom adventure that morning. 'Charlie?' her tone was inquisitive and apprehensive. With a slight turn of his head, he acknowledged her and then returned his sight at the ceiling. 'You might *want to put something across the shutters when you do lines,' she said casually. He shifted uneasily as if taking control of a rising tension. 'Why? Are you spying on me?' he asked. 'Well, I saw you this morning,' she said sidestepping the question. 'You don't even answer "O.K.," anymore to my sms messages, so it provoked me to check in on you and well yea, I looked through and saw you. That's all ... I'm sorry,' she said only slightly feeling guilty because in fact, she was not so sorry about looking in on him, as much as she was about being a pain in the ass to him. He said nothing for a moment. 'You know where the extra key is located,' he finally said. 'Yes, I thought about that, but you don't always put it back after you've used it,' she answered. .... 'Charlie,' she added, 'I even thought about keeping that sliding door unlocked,' she said pointing to the one next to the kitchen, 'but I didn't you know. You drink whiskey with the coke ... And my imagination runs wild and sees you lying on the couch, eyes wide and blood trickling down from your ears because of a brain clot and whose gonna know? How many days could go by before anyone really makes an effort to come in here? I don't want to feel guilty for not having peeped-in on you because it wasn't considered correct; that's for MY life Not yours. You tell people to stay away and they do, when I don't really believe that you mean it Charlie! Tell me that you want me to stop trying with you – tell me that you want this life and I will give you a kiss and a hug and go along with it ... I can't win Charlie but you can, and I'm willing to play this match with you as well as I can, but not without protecting MY conscious!' Her voice had risen again and this time Charlie listened silently with his arms crossed tightly across his chest. Pause. 'Answer my sms, a simple "O.K.," will do fine,' she ended quietly. Charlie turned his look to her and for a brief moment, contemplated her face intently. His face was serene and soft, while his eyes were intense on her; then he smiled lightly. '¿Que?' she said trying to overcome her attraction to him, 'are we still going to Madrid?' she asked pointedly. He nodded. She was relieved but still anxious by what she had just shared with him. She wasn't sure what the repercussions were just then, but she hoped her straight-forwardness strengthened his trust in her rather than weakened it. She couldn't be sure. It would be a tough call, even for her. She got up. 'Okay, I'm off,' she sounded. 'You're going?' he said a little surprised. 'Yup. I'll call the travel agent about Madrid. Try to call Narconon and ask them about the second week of April O.K.?' she asked. 'Okay,' he said. She stepped over to him, leaned in and said: 'Con permiso (with permission)' and kissed him on the mouth and left. Following that day it became a habit for her to swing by his place and peep in on him. Almost as if telling him had made it alright to do so. She'd thought about what he'd said about the extra key and convinced herself easily enough, that he was right. What was the point of seeing him near death on the sofa yet incapable of getting to him? So in that same week she went over to his place at six in the morning, touched the Phedra's warm engine, saw the blue light flashing through the shutter windows and then picked up the extra key in order to make a copy of it later in the morning. In retrospect, Murphy's Law arranged that on that same day Charlie had had a doctor's appointment in Juniper and had asked Mitx to wake him up at 10a.m. So that at 11:30a.m. on her way back from the key shop to Sa Ema they passed each other's car. She eradicated her concern that he might have noticed the key was gone; deciding that he was in too much of a hurry when he'd driven past her. Frankly too, so what? If he asked her, she'd tell him. So she put the extra key back in its spot and promised herself not to use the copy she had made unless there was an emergency. Plus she wouldn't tell Charlie about the extra key unless she actually used it outside the parameters of her promise; she saw no reason to tell him about it otherwise ...* She shifted from her thoughts to her current spot in the Mini. Parked outside of Lady Veela's, she understood her reasons for it all and wondered how many people would actually believe her? Outsiders would call it co- addiction. At this point she agreed, but what was co-addiction called when it was a calculated decision? How does one save a person drowning in a well without going into it? Especially if throwing in a rope doesn't help, when the victim is too wrapped up in the drowning? Instead, one would have to go into the well too and at least show the rope to the victim. Where was the line that removed the confusion between love and co-addiction? A parent who insists on being by a child's bedside, night and day when it is ill, is called love, or co-addiction? Sancho next to Don Quixote was loyal or a co-addict? Sam with Frodo in Lord of the Rings was brave or a crazy co-addict? Anyone who works in social assistance whether it be as a fireman, a policeman, or a sociologist for teenagers growing up in the ghetto, is virtuous and selfless or a co-addict? A label like co-addict was another word for co-dependency which in her mind suggested an unhealthy attachment to one person or family ... *That it was any one, who became obsessed with the need to care for and control an addiction thereby ignoring and denying one's own needs. Even told lies to protect the addict or upheld excuses for unacceptable behaviour and often blamed one's self for the addict's behaviour and attitude. Eventually the co-dependent individual becomes angry or bitter because he or she begins to feel unappreciated and used. So the co-addict tries harder to make the addict behave which only causes more disappointment.* "*Personality wise, the co-addict was someone often angry, full of self-pity, low self-esteem, needed validation from others, and often focused on solving other people's problems and pain while ignoring his or her own needs. Basically the individual changes to please others, experiences anxiety, depression, substance abuse, stress-related medical illnesses, remained in a primary relationship with an active substance abuser for at least two years without seeking help and continued to invest self-esteem in the ability to influence feelings and behaviour in both one's self and in others in the face of serious adverse consequences*" ... That was hers and a *Googled* understanding from a clinical point of view and in light of its definition, she was a co-addict along with every human being in the world that knew love and still felt lonely.

Everyone held these symptoms. Everyone. The point was knowing how to check them and direct them with intelligence when and if they ever came to surface. Charlie for example, like many, discovered that he had the illness later on in his life. Now he needed to learn how to manage it and *live* with it. In Asian culture, by reason of her birth date, she was a Black Dragon by day born into the year of the Red Horse. She thought about that … *In Asia, the symbol of dragons in general represented "spiralling DNA or the path into greater enlightenment. Dragons were referred to as the divine mythical creature that brought with them ultimate abundance, prosperity and good fortune. Their benevolence signified greatness, goodness and blessings and also symbolized power and excellence, courage and boldness, heroism, perseverance, nobility and divinity. A dragon overcame obstacles until success was its own. It was energetic, decisive, optimistic, intelligent and ambitious. Unlike the negative energies associated with Western Dragons, most Eastern Dragons were beautiful, friendly, and wise. They were the angels of the Orient and instead of being hated; they were loved and worshipped, for they controlled the rain, rivers, lakes, and seas. They were usually along seashores and riverbanks because most Eastern Dragons lived in water. Everything connected with Eastern Dragons was blessed. The Year of the Dragon, which took place every twelve years, was lucky such that present-day Oriental astrologers claimed that children born during Dragon Years enjoyed health, wealth, and long life. They were wise, but also vain and insulted when people did not honour their importance. They were also seen as the symbol of divine protection and vigilance as they were the ultimate representation of the forces of Mother Nature, the greatest divine force on Earth. Hence they were also regarded as the Supreme Being amongst all creatures. They had the ability to live in the seas, fly up to the heavens and coil up in the land in the form of mountains. Being the divine mythical animal, Dragons could ward off wandering evil spirits, protect the innocent and bestow safety to all that held its emblem. The Chinese Dragons in particular* were looked upon as the ultimate symbol of Good Fortune. Finally, their personality traits were self-confident and impulsive and consequently did not always listen to the advice of others. They were also perfectionists and set high standards for themselves, were strong and decisive dragons but not manipulative nor sly. They refused to deceive or compromise and failed to spot subversive intent. The Black Water dragon was less selfish and opinionated than the other Dragons. It was more inhibited and less power-hungry. It did have a tendency to be over-optimistic and needed to learn how to relinquish what was unfeasible so that it could concentrate its energies on the most rewarding endeavours. Such that, it could accept defeat without recriminations and made a good negotiator as it knew when, where and how to apply pressure...." Despite herself, the Black Water dragon was interestingly accurate in relation to where she was living and the fact that she actually spoke an Asian language. Even the church next to the bar-restaurant where she drank coffee in the mornings had two baby dragon gargoyles fixed to the church wall right over the bench on which she sometimes sat in order to take in some of the serenity of its surroundings. Not a big deal, except there are two benches to choose from and she had sat on the one under the dragons unaware of their presence. The only reason she'd finally noticed them, came when she and Dasha were walking past the church and an audible question from nowhere literally jumped into her head: "Wonder if those gargoyles are dragons?" She'd slowed the step of her walk, wondering why she'd thought of that and then as if to go with the flow of it all, walked over to look at the gargoyles more closely and, '*Oh* my Gawd! – they're baby dragons!?!' she'd exclaimed, 'Oh! My gawd! – whose going to believe me!?' she'd asked out load, while looking at Dasha and the trees surrounding them. Then, as if onto something, she went over to the other bench to see what the other gargoyles were. They looked like two menacing eels wrapped up with each other. Less interesting but somewhat relevant, because they were suggested animals under the Aquarian sign. 'Who is going to believe me?' she spoke out again into the cool blue morning air, then thought: *'Who cares? But holy cow! A fact is a fact – Here I am!'* Needless to say it had been another morsel for her, from who or what? What, psychological or energetic link made her suddenly think up, "wonder if they're dragons" at eight o'clock in the morning in the first place? Whatever it was, it made her sense that every piece of her and her life until then somehow fit together, in a way that her "here and now" were on track and slowly bringing into focus a puzzled image of her destiny. She pondered back to the Red Horse. It was said to be … *"The kaleidoscope of the mind that imparted light, colour and perpetual motion. It thought, saw and was moved by electric fluidity. Constant only in its inconsistency, it was unshackled by mundane holds, unchecked by sturdy binding goals. Incessant activity and searching may be to satisfy a deep-rooted desire to fit in. Paradoxically, a Horse felt a simultaneous yearning for independence and freedom that caused it to run unimpeded through virgin paths with an unconquered spirit that's soul was forever free. A person born in the year of the horse was said to be cheerful, popular and quick-witted; with a happy outlook, independent, subjective and self-centred. Such person had raw sex appeal rather than straight good looks. Earthy and warmly appealing, the person was very perceptive and talkative. The horse's changeable nature may lead it to be hot-tempered, rash and headstrong at times. It tended to come on very strong in the beginning of a relationship, craved love and intimacy, having an almost innate sense of romance and seduction, which was a double-edged sword since it often led it to feeling trapped. Hence the unpredictable horse could fall in love easily and fall out of love just as easily. In most cases the Horse left home early. If not, its independent spirit goaded it to start working, or to take up some career at an early age. An adventurer at heart, it was also noted for its keen mind, self-reliance, vivacity, energy, impetuousness and even brashness. The horse loved exercise both physical and mental. One could spot a horse by its rapid but graceful body movements, its animated reflexes and fast way of speaking. It responded quickly and could make snap decisions. Its mind worked at remarkable speed and whatever it might lack in stability and perseverance, it certainly made up for it, in being open-minded and flexible. Finally, The Fire or Red Horse was highly strung, powerful, inconsistent, alluring and motivated by strength of will and a nonconformist ..."* The definition made her smile, as it might easily have been confused with the astrological definition of the Aquarian woman. She was that too, with Capricorn as her moon. Thus meaning that her "air" sign was ruled by Saturn and Uranus. In general it was said that *Aquarians were sincere, altruistic, free and active individuals. As a fixed sign they literally tried to fix the social condition towards a healthier lifestyle, but had to be careful not to impede the freedom they wished to impart by trying too hard. Hence their keyword was friend and what made them tick was philanthropy. Usually quiet, but sometimes they could be extremely nervous or strained. They asked a lot from other people and when they were disappointed, they suffered and could bear a grudge against them. Aquarians could be vain; they loved compliments and never left anything to chance. They were intuitive, fanciful and critical. They could be good and pleasing friends as well as passionate lovers. They had lots of interests and creative ideas and were often suited to jobs such as poet, astronomer, actor, or pilot. The Aquarian woman tended to be nice, plain, curious and modern. She loved culture and travelling. She was always ready to help other people and to keep up with novelties. Her ideal man was brilliant, tolerant and educated. She shouldn't feel restrained within a house's four walls because she was essentially a free woman ..."*

.. Michele's mind raced on in her defence and concluded that any label could match her behaviour around Charlie. *In sports she was competitively relentless until the whistle blew. In fact when she played representative soccer for her city, she had been nominated Most Valuable Player and made captain of the team by virtue of her motivational skills, not her soccer skills which were nil. In her life, she was influenced by her father whose emotional ups and downs prepared her she felt, against co-addictive abuse. She had learned quickly to live her life to the fullest without being deterred by her own father's and brothers' challenges especially when cancer found him. At the age of fifteen she was already holding down two part-time jobs, playing soccer, making brown bag lunches for her brothers and getting by at high school. She left home for Japan at the age of nineteen, but stood by her father's side as closely as he would allow her to, while she studied around the world, worked around the world and loved her father like no other. She adapted his illness to her life with visits, phone calls, and words. They communicated often and when the whistle blew loudly she found the plane or the train and automobiles to get back to him because he had made it clear to her that he did not want it any other way. The night he died she had been in his hospital room – there, sitting in a stainless steel chair against a wall, slightly out of his view. She had flown in from Dubai because her brothers had given her the call. She had finally left his hospital room by ten at night and gone to her mother's place. Early the next morning the hospital called to say he had gone. The date was October 22nd, 1994...* Her mind paused again. The number suddenly appeared bold in her sight: 22. She huffed lightly at the reminder and went back to her mental debate on co-addiction versus love ... *In Charlie's case, he had told her that he wanted to live and the Black Water Dragon, the Red Horse, the Aquarian, the co-addict, the Teresa in her name, the love or just simply Michèle, was willing to help him get there. What did it matter why or how?* The end could not justify the means because there were no guarantees; the means had to justify the end and that translated to her as no holding back. Yes, the quiet wish to "grow old by his side" simmered silently within her. Her words were chosen carefully, because there was no desire to live with him in a conventional way. She was not conventional anyway. *Her man had to be elusive because she was elusive too. Charlie was not abusive in any way except by way of his illness which affected her by way of the prostitutes and the porno videos. Not his actual consumption of it. The addiction itself would never go away and would always simmer a risk of a relapse, but all relationships had the risk of infidelity and suffering – no? Just that Charlie's case made the risk higher and more imminent than others. Such that she felt clear about their match. Like a soccer game with a first half, a half time and a second half. It was about a year and she would play her position as well as possible; so that if she lost, she could feel no shame or regret to walk away. As far as she was concerned she was in the first half with Charlie. Then if he got to rehab, it would mean an intermission for them both. Life willing the second half might be about them evolving from their past together into a renewed experience of new beginnings ... it was dodgy. He would have to let her into his life before he might relapse again and that was conflicted by the fact that he would need time before he could allow himself to love without fear. So much time that its own duration might send him back to caring for prostitutes instead, because it was easier to care without love. He would need time to convince himself of a life and success without cocaine? How much time? Medicine suggested two to five years! Crazy. In light of a cocaine addict that was too long. What if she remained on the sidelines, letting him play his game but there, as a reminder not to give up until the whistle blew? There was fear from her part, because if Charlie did allow himself to evolve along with her, he might fall in love and then if he relapsed, his eventual death would not solely be from the cocaine but from his emotional sense of regret at having lost her; as she would not be able to sit by his sofa any more like she had the first time round. She would have to let him go. She felt certain of that. Primarily because nothing would be left to play after having played it so well in the first half together. She would let him go and love him from afar like she had done with Jes and her father. It was straight forward and no going back. That was her. The realisation of such to him, would make him suffer more thus make him more dependent on the relapse until possibly death do them part? Even if he got a divorce, he would always have his wife nearby because of his son but not Michèle …* She came out of her thoughts momentarily to focus on what she had just come across. His love for her could be an influential reason for his death, if she followed him too closely beyond rehab. Here came a new realisation about her love for Charlie: letting him go? Being his friend and letting go of her own selfish wish to grow old by him. Was that silly, or a co-addictive notion suggesting herself as a possible culprit to his possible death? Crazy thoughts about a time that did not even exist yet, or may never even surface? She had to think … *It was about intelligent love for both of them. Military? Military wives dealt with death every day their men went out to work. The wives of Formula 1 drivers also loved at the high risk of being widowed at a moment's notice. However death next to this kind of love was by reason of circumstance not affairs of the heart. Charlie could die by the circumstance of his addiction. This she accepted without qualms like the wives she had just thought of. Besides that, death was imminent for everyone; in direct ratio to every second that one lived. However, Charlie's love for any woman could increase his dilemma if he ever relapsed, by reason of the suffering he would feel from not being able to love her the way he wanted to? So a cocaine addict's plight was about not ever loving? Too sensitive too scared? While no one can ever love an addict in return, because a co-addict would feel responsible for an addict's demise, while a partner that does manage to adjust and live a full life with an addict had to accept being a possible reason for an addict's increased demise simply because the partner doesn't assimilate the addict's misery? Hence that was why Charlie kept his distance from his son and those he cared about – because he knew this and did not want them to love him too much, or suffer a sense of responsibility for his plight? A cocaine addict was a soldier in disguise? Was he in fact trying to manage his love responsibly the best way that he could? Can he be an addict and a co-addict at the same time, because he feels responsible for others' suffering too? All nonsense!? Suffering was everywhere. Trying to avoid it was like avoiding life. As long as there was love there would be suffering, because they were each other's counterpart? Wasn't that a Nirvana concept to mesh them together towards a neutral state of being? Maybe, but she preferred intensity. Would it not be better to die from cocaine having loved and been loved than not at all? Heck, maybe Charlie dies from a car accident – the way he drove the Phedra, it was not impossible. Maybe he lives until a hundred! Though she doubted it. Charlie suffered the occasional eye haemorrhaging and she suspected that was an alarm about something else going on inside of him. Crikey! Maybe she dies and all of her thinking is a waste of time!* She stopped thinking. Her head had gone too far. Death was something she thought about as much as she did about life, but sometimes she went too far. She refocused down the street at Veela's, suddenly feeling irritated about everything … *She did not believe in maintaining relationships that came to a standstill. Her romances in life were proof of that. Where several of them had ended because of her, not because of her partner. If anything, she chose relationships premature for longevity because of her need to evolve. She honestly believed that a person could experience everything one wanted in one life, if he or she respected the flow of time and change. The key was not to expect to have it all at the same time. So, if there was room to grow with Charlie, if in some destined way he was her other half, the years left to them would only be about twenty or thirty – enough to live the last leg of their lives, evolving with a shared plan, intensely without boredom and at no risk of wanting anything more because they would have "been there-done that" already. Again she pondered about her choice in him? It was a calculated choice as much as it was an emotional one. She was attracted to him; there was passion, spark and synergy. In her consideration of him she balanced the pros and cons of his birth date in relation to hers and noticed the results were in line with her thoughts. Maybe she was looking for them, but facts were facts. He was a Capricorn and in astrology not compatible with her sign in Aquarius. However, her ascendant was Capricorn. Her moon was his moon. Withstanding too, that the friends she trusted without question were also Capricorn. In Asian terms Charlie was a Green Wood Sheep born in the year of the White Rat. It meant that their physical core from the Red Horse and the White Rat were precisely polar from each other. He was an animal that thrived between 11p.m. and 1a.m. while hers was between 11a.m. and 1p.m.. He was December North and she was June South. Yet, yet, her innate core was the Black Water Dragon while his was the Green Wood Sheep. The Asian ideogram for her totem was water in male and his was wood in female, while the Black Dragon was an ally of the Rat and the Green Sheep was the ally of the Horse. In chart form on paper, their signs were a complete bi-polar match. In simpler terms, they were a perfect fit. More surprising too, was that the year of Charlie's Rat cycle had started in 1960 on her birth date January 28th – exactly seven years prior to her being born. So that it was hard for Michèle not to consider the possibility that she and Charlie were each other's halves. Then in pragmatic terms, he was professionally capable and independent, lightly travelled, intelligent and discreet. Despite the mendacity she saw in the culture, there was affection for his family and an undeniable series of coincidences between her and them, for which some kind of purpose for their encounter, simply existed. Before ever having known them, she'd already contemplated thoughts on growing old in Mayūrqa amongst a family, friends and the privileges of village infrastructure that made the metamorphous into old age a natural, almost un-inhibiting experience. Old age?– Her mind went off tangent, was a fact of life that made her circumstance seem logical and current issues like the death penalty, seem absurd? Everyone's life had a limitation to it and an opportunity to live it as well as one could, before it expired. Hence she did not understand the purpose behind Capital Punishment? In light of its definition, she assumed that the death penalty was about punishment by death for having committed a crime against the human race. Yet the ones who committed such hideous crimes were permitted to live an extended time, before dying under a lethal injection no more traumatic than what a needle was to a child. Why wasn't the sentence performed immediately thus denying criminals the opportunity to redeem themselves? It seemed to her that the death penalty was actually a favour to the worst criminals because it gave them a chance to redeem their conscious before death. Wasn't that what most people feared? The unknown beyond death more than death itself? The fear of dying before having a chance to make things right with one self, or others? People lived with this risk every day, why should criminals have time and opportunity to die at peace with themselves and the world, after their crimes? Wasn't it everyone's responsibility to try and be a good human being without the need of the death penalty to provoke it – how was it effective in reducing crimes? The state of California had at least six hundred people waiting on death row. If she were a criminal she would not waste her time with warm blooded crime. She'd commit whatever cold hearted crime was needed to get what she wanted and if caught, hope for death row. Otherwise, to go to jail for twenty-five years meant going back to a society that never really forgave anyway. It was ironic to her that the worst criminals had a greater chance for redemption on death row and getting away with murder, than the ones allowed to go free after fulfilling their sentences. It recalled her thoughts about a case in the United States, when Governor Arnold Schwarzenegger decided to uphold the execution of a man on death row. She had been giving an English class to one of Sa Croix' waitresses, a young lively girl of twenty-four, who talked about her passion for other cultures and her desire to travel; yet was already over-burdened with the village lifestyle of having a house, a car, and a boyfriend, who had a son of his own. She'd asked Michèle about her opinion on the controversy in California, because she was herself shocked that Capital Punishment was allowed to exist, let alone how awful Schwarzenegger and the United States were for having a man die after redeeming himself and even being nominated for the Nobel*

Prize? Michèle contemplated the young woman momentarily; how could she have answered? The young girl was from a village in Mayūrqa and knew nothing about the greater puddle. The bigger picture was her T.V. screen where everyone put their faith into learning about the truth and made an attempt at being well informed. Even Michèle could only speculate. Who were really the unethical ones? In Michèle's opinion it was not Schwarzenegger, rather the people and the bodies who'd nominated a man for the Nobel Prize and did not award it to him because it might have been in conflict with Capital Punishment's purpose to punish? To her, the fact of the matter was, the people of the state of California implemented a law of death as a deterrent against crime that could not be used nor manipulated into being a mere idle threat. It must be adhered to or not exist at all. That people can be so morally fickle in their views and so tiny in thought even though they are from the greater informed society? How easy it was to use Schwarzenegger as a way to remove shame from a law and a decision that had existed since before his arrival as Governor. A clever way to redirect people from the real issue. A man who took the opportunity to die at peace with himself, decided to use Capital Punishment wisely by living and contributing back to society with a book. In such a way to permit him to die in a good light with Life and possibly promote better energy towards the next one. He was in fact a very successful man in his own life because he did exactly what he'd wanted to do and was willing to pay the consequences; the truth in his heart at the time of his crime was real, because he'd known about Capital Punishment. The misdemeanour was attempting to pressure Schwarzenegger into pardoning the man from the death penalty so that he might receive the Nobel Prize. The man was on death row! And because of it, the elite bodies that be, would not justify giving him his right to earn the award before he died, even though Capital Punishment was the key ingredient towards his success in finding and demonstrating his self-redemption? Worse, he might have come to this life with the memory of a denied Nobel Prize, from his past life, which caused him to repeat his crime this time and give society a second chance, which of course it failed again, and therefore will be tested again in his next life, because he'll repeat his crimes until the Nobel prize is somehow granted to him? "Out there" 'Chèle,' *she told herself. However, that's what it was to her. In light of it all, a law like the death penalty actually appeared more humane to criminals than not. Such that it seemed true to her that the penalty of death was of little use as a deterrent to crime, in which case there had to be another way. The moral questions regarding man's unacceptable right to take the life of another had become rhetoric in today's world anyway. The new world was evolving with new intelligence and that would include the death of life in the process of getting it right. As far as she was concerned, that man on death row could not have been exonerated from the death penalty however, he should have been awarded the Nobel Prize, if his work had been deserving of it. If Capital Punishment was going to exist then do it. Stop the rhetoric of empathetic death. It was almost like the bodies that had implemented the law did not completely trust it themselves, because they afforded so much time before the sentence was completed; as if to suggest a margin of doubt and offer time to reverse a sentence in the case of their own possible error in judgement. As if its real motive was to act as a waiver to protect themselves, rather than to allot time to the criminal for personal redemption. Clearly, if there were flaws in the system, then society would just have to live with the guilt of its mistaken actions like criminals did too, because if a man nominated for a Nobel Prize was unable to avoid paying the price for his crimes, then neither should society. Pussyfooting around with the death penalty was bullpucky. Just do it, or don't do it at all ...* Her thoughts reverted to Charlie and she wondered why she shouldn't try attaining a brief life with Charlie if she too, like that man, was aware of the consequences? What if she also had a plan in the event that it did not work out? Her father's voice rang in, "God forbid if everyone did what they wanted",' to which her mind replied back: '*Or God forbid if everyone put a label on people's behaviour simply because they did not understand it, like it, or fear it. The heart was the truth, the way, the Universe, the right, even E.T.'s way HOME!, and God forbid anyone to impede that right because it was exactly that action which provoked resistance and social unrest – no? She grew up with fables like Beauty and the Beast and social teaching on loving what was inside a person more than what was on the outside, yet there she was, in love with Charlie's insides and being challenged for it, because people only knew him from his outside? In light of everything, if nothing evolved beyond her time with him then, she would have been the only one lucky enough to have known him so closely from the inside out. Perhaps that moment in time was the best moment with him? She also felt she knew when to stop, when to say no, when to let go. In Charlie's case it wasn't yet. She did not hide or throw away the coke she found in his jean pockets, she never fought with Charlie, or impeded his actions, neither did she ever have to lie on his behalf, she merely gave him food for thought. She merely stood by and made her presence known. She could. She still had the stamina and the whistle had not blown yet. That in itself was enough justification: her presence. She was sitting in her Mini like Nancy Drew under cover because it made her feel useful; lying in bed letting time go by, made her sensation of impotence seem greater than being nearby. Why do people stay by ailing loved ones – especially the ones in a coma or a state of non-reciprocal behaviour? If Charlie was aware of her presence he would either feel irritated by it, non-pulsed, or concerned but definitely aware of her presence, and the reminder when he couldn't keep track of time, that he had to make a move sooner than later towards his recuperation. He wanted to do so much and at 44 he still could, if he respected time…*

In hindsight, if she could have given the same energy to her own family she would have. However, her own brothers and mother were birds of the same feather. Love was about distance, freedom, and solidarity when called upon. She had wanted to stay in Canada yet it was her own mother who disregarded her own needs and like Michèle's father had done so many years before, set her daughter free because she did not want her, "37 year old daughter living with her mother yet; too young for that!" she'd said. Then Michèle took a year off from work in order to reassess her professional direction. She wanted to find peace with herself about Jesy. Elisabet had offered her a job in late January to teach English at the school where she worked in Artá and as crazy as it was Michèle had declined the offer. Her head space was not ready for classes yet. She thanked Elisabet seriously believing that the opportunity would come back to her for having been true to her gut feeling. Had she taken the post then, it would have been about social pressure when Michèle's heart still was not in line with her head. She would not have done well or lasted and possibly embarrassed Elisabet because of it. As a result, they thought she was silly, but they'd said the same too, when she'd told people that she wanted to live up north even though she didn't have a car or a job ... Her heart leaped suddenly at the appearance of bodies coming out of the club. She shifted her eyes quickly to the time on her phone that read 5:45a.m. The club was getting ready to close. One by one, men came out and found their cars quickly and drove away casually. One guy in particular got her attention because they'd made eye contact one night while she was parked in a different place closer to the club. He had parked in front of her and saw her while he got out of his car. He had curly hair and wore glasses and tended to get to the club just after it opened and took brief walks around the club every once in a while until the club closed at six o'clock ... One of the girls she'd seen with a boyfriend came out just in time for a white car to pull up and pick her up. She saw the two heads in the car meet for a kiss and then the car drove away. By 6:15 most of the girls had left the club either on foot or in groups packed into one car, but no sign of Charlie.

The Phedra stayed there, parked on its own. She got impatient and got out of the Mini to stretch her legs. While she stood there half leaning against the hood of the Mini, the guy with the glasses and curly hair came out of the club again and started his walk towards where she was parked. As he walked up closer to her, she felt nothing less than overtly conspicuous leaning against her Mini dressed in an oversized dark hoody at the break of dawn. So she flipped open her cell as if answering a sudden call and began to improvise a casually audible conversation in Spanish over the phone: 'Hi. I'm here. Where are you? About a half hour – how much longer do you need? Uhh huh…hmm yea, Okay, no worries I'll wait ….' In the meantime the guy with the curly hair and the glasses, walked right past her and disappeared left at the next corner street. She kept her improvised call going for a good few minutes more until she felt he wasn't going to come back. Then as soon as she closed her cell she saw him appear again at the bottom of the street where the club was and enter back inside. '*Who was he?*' she wondered. The morning air was damp and suddenly gave her a cool piercing chill through the sweatshirt. She stood up from her lean against the Mini, got back into the car, started the engine and waited for it to warm up … She smiled to herself in embarrassment at the fake call she had just made. Even more surprising was the ease with which she'd done it and despite herself actually had fun doing it. 'Gees get a life Michèle,' she laughed to herself. Then she felt awkward. She knew Charlie was about to find out that she was there. The guy with the curly hair and glasses was probably a casual walking look-out for the club, while it enjoyed clandestine activity inside. At least that's what she allowed her imagination to think. That and the fact that the guy certainly must have recognised her from the night before. If not, the Mini for sure. He would have gone inside and asked everyone including Charlie, if the Mini was waiting for any one. Then, as if her instinct had been right, Charlie suddenly came out with a rapid step, which she sensed was urged on by shame or irritation of his knowledge about her being there, crossed the street while selecting his car key from the many he had on a chain then jumped into the Phedra on his own and drove away. She sat there suddenly feeling tired and slightly ashamed herself. Why? Had he left early because of her? Had she impeded him from taking someone home with him? Had her presence been an irritating reminder to him about things he did not want to remember? Was her presence in that way a violation of his privacy and simply over the top unnecessary? Had her bull shit been any value at all? Yes. Would she do it again? Yes. It was the first half of the only match they would ever have together in that way, and she would not relent on the grounds of fickle social labelling and rhetoric until coach M inside her, blew the whistle and ended it for her.

M
W

Journal, Saturday April 2, 2005. *Was driving back from town this evening. Got to a roundabout and literally had a thought about Pope John Paul II? Followed by an instant whisper: "God Bless the Pope, a very good man." It was about 9:23 or 9:33pm at the time. Then later tonight, my friend Angie told me that he'd died today at 9:37pm?! Wow ...*

Charlie update: he sent me an sms on Wednesday asking me if I wanted to have a "pa amb oli" with him at the bar. I wasn't sure. In the end I replied 'O.K.' and went. Afterwards, I drove to C'an Colom to see if I might catch the Vanesa girl heading to work. I stayed out until 4:30a.m., without any luck. '*Geesus Michèle – It's not like she's going to walk by with a sign around her neck: "Hi I'm Vanesa"*.' Anyway, on my way back to Sa Ema I saw Charlie swing into his place, so I guessed he'd gone out afterwards too. Jealousy kicked in, least I hope that's *who* it was and suggested that she might have been with him instead of going to work. Maybe she spends more time with him than work and he pays her for the hours lost? Maybe they're past that now and hardly negotiate anything anymore except sharing the coke? Maybe yes maybe no – Why do I care to speculate? I keep having the same conversations with myself and don't understand why, when it's all the same. Am I concerned about the purpose or am I just jealous? Control? The V girl is a threat to Charlie's timeline for rehab? I want to know who she is so that I can *control* her, or manipulate her help for Charlie? '*Helllooo! Earth to Michèle again! She won't give a flying fuck about Charlie or your bright-eyed and bushy-tailed intent to help a hooker or an addict. Gawd, you are pathetic...*' He didn't go out Thursday night because he had a medical appointment in Juniper yesterday morning. Had I known, I wouldn't have gone back out to Veela's that night until 1:45a.m. Although I do enjoy that time to sit there with my silly sense of purpose, and just think. I realised while I was sitting there that I'm finding it hard to detach myself, or relax from it all at home. It all feels sour now. Charlie is at the point where he does not share or tell me anything anymore, but what bothers me more is that neither Mitx nor Elisabet gives me any feedback about anything. It seems like the only time they ever really approach me, is to find out if I know whether or not Charlie has taken money from Sa Croix, or if he's asked me for money, or what latest report I might have about him. In an absurd way, Charlie's detachment does me a favour by not testing my loyalty to him and my respect to his family's worries. Yet, they don't return the deference to me. I know I'm not family but honestly, what was the main reason I got involved in this in the first place? Who came up to the house more than once asking for English classes when I'd politely made it clear, I had thought, that I didn't want to give classes? Who sat with me at my table to discuss, in depth, ways to help Charlie? Wasn't this supposed to be a joint effort? My dark side feels as though Mitx experiences great satisfaction and enjoyment knowing that Charlie's deference has shifted back over to him? Mitx had been so expressive to ward me off from Charlie after he *let* me get involved. I don't think Mitx is concerned about me, as much as he might have felt some envy about my affection for Charlie and Charlie's deference to me, and now revels in our seemingly failed attempt? Because, God forbid if Charlie actually got past this, developed a chance with the "rubia" and made it to the same spot in life as his brothers, who unlike baby brother Charlie, had conformed to social pragmatics despite their truth? Above all, that it should happen by my presence and not by theirs, after so many years of doing it their way and thereby identifing their lack of pure faith. When did it solely become Charlie's and, or my crusade? As if Charlie's indifference to me proves Mitx right about the ugly nature of an addict? What if Charlie's indifference to me is about the obvious fact that I *am* involved and he's shifted his misery back to his brother and sister-in-law because they don't get into his face as much as I do, thus making it easier for him? Why aren't we using "Tough Love" in the same way, if the "Laissez-faire" method never worked? If Charlie's going to come in and out of people's lives while it serves his interests, then why aren't we doing the same with his life, which should serve a better interest for all including him? …Sigh. I can empathise with Mitx with the reasoning that he grew up when Franco was still alive. Compounded by the fact that he was the firstborn in his family, which automatically nominated him as the one to set the example of doing "the socially correct thing". Charlie on the other hand was the baby brother favoured by his mother, in a way that made him keenly sensitive to her and the emotional anxieties of caring for her men, and inadvertently conditioned Charlie to avoid being one of those men, by establishing a lifestyle cared for by a harem of women that requires a paternal commitment, not a sentimental one. Yet, he got married and now finds himself as the very product he wanted to avoid by virtue of his own son's sensitivity to his mother and what she must transmit to him through her suffering for the man she loves: Charlie. I see Charlie's sensitivity to his mother, parallel to mine towards my father, as well as the emotional turmoil Charlie experiences from the relationship with his wife, with that of my father's love for my mother. There was a period that lasted until my late twenties, when I did not enjoy being compared to her because I did not want to recognise an ability to make men suffer, like my father had suffered by his love for her. So I stood by him. I did not leave "like she had done", until the circumstance of my trip to Japan allowed me to. In hindsight, my mother also suffered greatly from my parents' separation. Especially when it became clear that the price of her decision included a high level of yielding to my father's emotional needs, if she really wanted to protect her children's emotional interests first. Few people understand what amount of courage is required to leave an unhealthy relationship, when children are involved. The one who leaves is often at risk at being controlled by the hurt of the one who is left behind, with emotional blackmail issues involving the children. My self-preserving reaction to my mother was distance. It was easier to live with my father, if I did not afford him a venue to think or inquire about my mother, or the possible enjoyment I might have had being with her, or the fact that she was happy in her new life. Naturally, my father knew this and despite his higher-self's attempt and sincere desire to embrace new beginnings too, was undermined by the emotional plight of forbidden love. As a result, my mother respected my way and loved me from a far while my father, in all the years that they were separated, never publicly expressed anything less than his utmost respect and regard for her ability to move on. His love and admiration for her was about all that. Time of course, turned in my mother's favour because her decision had been her truth. Both my brothers found her in their mid-teens, while she and I found each other after my father's death. A fact that I know made his rest a bit easier. Sigh. Separation is just no fun. I think of Charlie, who is still quite receptive to his mother's feelings and how the cocaine probably only compounds his guilt from having placed himself at the forefront of the very men he did not want to be among: men who cause women grief. In so much however, our memory of our parents' suffering is of course erroneous, because suffering is everywhere. It's not a reason brought on exclusively by the opposite sex. It's life and it's everyone's test, for the young and the old, to get over it and adapt it to one's desired life, regardless of what degree it's at. Some must live with cancer, a physical challenge, a natural disaster, a human or financial loss, failure, psychological turmoil, love. It's life's polarity of no pain no gain. No love no life; the human challenge to live a bit of both in the silver rather than the grey. Frankly too, if somebody really wants something, all the crap involved simply does not matter. People will tolerate living through home renovations for the bigger picture at the end of it, but few will tolerate the trials of a new relationship that aspires to something wonderful down the road. Ego gets in the way of that, which at least helps to highlight what one really wants as being capricious or not. People simply expect too much from one another too soon and won't wade through the crap to get to the glory. In my case, I perceive Charlie and I, as free spirited in the name of love and do not overtly take advantage of the opposite sex, which inadvertently draws it into our lives, because our sensitivity to it, can respond to emotional suffering when it asks us to. However, in doing so, we also maintain an elusive behaviour in order to reduce the risk of becoming the opposite sex's new scapegoat for suffering. The behaviour avoids guilt issues and allows us to be more straightforward, because we have no major consequences to lose. Meanwhile the act of being straightforward also permits us to test integrity by overtly revealing our imperfections as well as our qualities. Distance is also necessary, because the intensity of our deference can grow and create a level of expectation of the opposite sex too high for it to reciprocate. Thereby causing us to be slighted as a result of our own sensitivity and whether we wish it to or not, leaves a mark and acts as a reminder to us. Hence the only woman that Charlie may ever really love, is the one who stands by him because of him and not because he's a surrogate means to satisfying emotional voids; the former being an indefinite notion, not a fickle one. Hence he must be loved, not needed before he would be able to love back without the insecurity of falling victim to someone's emotional whims. Elisabet and his mother fit the bill to Charlie's dynamic because they are cared for by other men, while a woman like me is tested before he can also trust her love. In the meantime, his dynamic can intrude on Mitx' matrimony and any woman's attempt to care for Charlie, because it provokes Elisabet's deference to Charlie, but leaves it up to his brother to live out the commitments to her. Elisabet will never love another man more than her husband, yet her intention to care for Charlie as an extension of her love for Mitx can actually hurt her husband, when her care for Charlie resembles that of a surrogate wife who unintentionally places such care ahead of her primary role as Mitx' wife. Tho' Charlie's sporadic combustive presence might make Elisabet feel more appreciated and attractive by reason of having his "privileged" attention, it undermines his brother who is challenged by the routine of matrimony that dulls the senses, but in no way removes or reduces the fact that Mitx loves Elisabet and appreciates her more than Charlie ever could, because Elisabet is quite simply the woman of his life. In many ways her presence in Charlie's life, resembles that of the matriarchs', which appears to be about warding away women, except for the very one who hurts him: his wife. Mayürqans refer to them as "dragon mothers". Women who have been conditioned to keep their men by rendering them dependent on them, while the patriarchs in Charlie's life covet a soft level of envy at the attention he gets from the women regardless of his "bad behaviour". Either way, the entrenched presence of both genders in his life intimidates the right and the desire for another woman to care for him. Hence, any woman who wishes to be with Charlie must have enough confidence in herself and trust in Charlie to tolerate the females in his life including the ones that seek him at work, or in his night life. It would have to be a woman whose own independent character and lifestyle mirrored his own, in order to draw his attention to the same sensation of tolerance towards the many males in her life, and understand a love that is served with freedom and communication by reason of innate emotional loyalty and not co-dependency. Such that, she would have to be a woman, who despite her social charm with men, had a clearly reserved love and passion for one man, just like Charlie, whom I believe *does* when he loves a woman … Sigh, when I am feeling indignant I allow these conversations in my head to take their toll until I feel shame for even going there. How dare I place judgement calls on a family that's dynamics is probably healthier than ninety percent of most in the world. Above all, the same family that let me into their home and albeit accepted my help, did not ask for my opinions. How easy it is to look into other people's lives rather than our own. I've done the same with my brothers, my friends, anyone whom I care about. I get close and suddenly begin to see more than I wish to see. Like looking at a tree and automatically seeing straight through past the bark, the insects, its circles of time, right to its roots, its seed and finally the truth of its being rather than just accepting the knowledge from my eyesight that the forest behind it, is enough? As if I don't see with my eyes and use them instead as tools to avoid bumping into things while my sight comes from within? As corny as it may seem it's the truth and I sometimes wonder if I will have to live in the forest like a female Merlin. Nature is often my mentor and receives a higher level of respect from me when so few humans do. I'll hug a tree, talk to a snail, pick up a bird feather and take advice from the apparition of an unexpected animal more readily than I would from a human being. Heck, find me a wand and I'd be all set! The bottom line however, is that I need to care less about people and things, until I can figure out the balance in managing them; a lot like Charlie would have to do if he made it past rehab. Finally, if I have so much faith in who I think Charlie really is, then I should also know that if Charlie loved a woman he would go for her regardless of the matriarchs or the patriarchs in his life; that Mitx and Elisabet do maintain a strong relationship unthreatened by Charlie; that what I fear and presume to be accurate most likely isn't; further to what I have conjured up in my mind's eye, has most likely never even flirted with anyone's thoughts. In the end, it is I who has the problem because I am indignant from allowing myself to be used. I hate thinking that I'm adopting their suspicious and pessimistic ways of speculating about people. I'm starting to feel lonely, rejected, and used, and it's *not* coming from the outside.

Saying I love you
What would you say if I took those words away
Then you couldn't make things new
Just by saying I love you.
'MORE THAN WORDS' – EXTREME, LYRICS ADAPTED

Intense

Okay, what else? Car o.k. Dasha o.k. Family fine – thank you. Charlie? Do like mum can and just disconnect? Don't be so melodramatic. "Forget it." The V thoughts mess me up in a way that I don't think it's about Charlie anymore. Her presence feels like an evil spell between me and him because the cocaine alone is no longer the reason why he's still here. The more time he's around her the more he can't face himself in this world; the dark side hides his responsibilities, which removes the real dream that he wants and that he won't try to reach, because the task seems too overwhelming for him. The bitch – fuck her. Fuck the drug. Fuck his family that won't say, 'No' to him. Bullocks to him and his aversion to obligation, as if it were the answer to avoiding guilt. He flew by me this morning in the Phedra, while I was on my bike, as if the speed were putting distance between him and his demons. Maybe he was coming back after having left her at home. Maybe he's experiencing a new psychological high with her. Like one more girlfriend before he gets serious about rehab sort of thing? A naughty sense of privacy that they share that we could never have because I live above his brother's place? Yet to be with Charlie, is to accept his family in the picture too; contradicted by the fact that he keeps all segments of his life tremendously segregated from each other? Funny, I can relate to that too. Maybe he's enjoying a false sense of control with her, simply because he thinks that he doesn't have to worry about accountability or her feelings. Meanwhile time, is in fact taking over and they will inadvertently become closer and more vulnerable to each other, or until money or one of them runs out on the other? Here is when a prostitute loses out... I could talk to her. Just call her, or go into Veela's and ask for her directly. My concern is that I don't know her and she might not accept my altruism and then say something untrue to Charlie, if she felt my intent could threaten her financial or sentimental relationship with him. As his insecurities are overtly sensitive now, probably not a good idea. Charlie wouldn't be amused by it. Either way it wouldn't change anything and just leave me with egg on my face. Especially now, when neither one wants to be helped. Otherwise, I would talk to her. I'm sure that under it all, he likes her and certainly considers her as a friend, which is another reason I'd like to know her; better to know who he's with, than not at all. Besides, she's not evil and possibly just as unwell as Charlie. Maybe she really does care about Charlie and would help me in getting him to rehab? Or let me know if Charlie's in trouble or taken too much coke – like an insider? I wouldn't feel the need to watch Veelas at forsaken hours just to feel relieved that he's okay? Not. Would she be interested in a new profession? Maybe I could give her a few contacts from the cruise ships? Ha! Ships would love that! The thing too, is that he could look for her when and if he gets back from rehab? Plus his memory of her will be more positive than his recollection of me because she doesn't make him feel guilty? They can use cocaine and prostitution as the excuse for hurting each other when they finally do. Hence the sense of guilt they might feel, actually comes from people's unconditional love because their choice to use bad behaviour can no longer be blamed on anything more than themselves. In a nutshell, face to face with their personal misery. So, don't love your addict too much – it will only make him or her run the other way? True about anyone? Talk about character building. Makes me think that Charlie is in my life more for me, than me for him? Because similar to Charlie, I obviously have to love or care for people from a distance, while anyone's care that attempts to tame me too quickly or too closely, also alerts my timidness and makes me go the other way. Although I don't identify myself with co-addiction I don't doubt that I have some instinctual level of behavioural addiction. Really, who isn't an addict? I live every moment of my life intensely: working, playing, thinking, feeling, being mindless, social or solitary, loving, distancing, down-time, I am intense. So that I have to watch how I distribute my love because the caretaker in me can take over and smother both me and my object of interest. On one hand, I can feel indignant or hurt when people I care about, don't listen to my advice. How self-righteous is that? Then I suffer emotionally, when these same people make the same mistakes and wonder why? My ego also takes a beating because I sometimes want to say, "I told you so!" and never do, because in the end it's not up to me. Moreover, I know that there is a time and a place for everything and everyone. Yet the perfectionist in me, expects everyone else to be just as focused as I can be, to a point that I can be over-responsible and get possessively involved in the framework of another's life because it psychologically becomes a reflection of me, my world, my karmic responsibility and *my* self-esteem. I don't want to take responsibility for someone's suffering, if he or she does not try to give a hundred percent. The sensation of impotence tends to distance me from those I care for, when made to watch them live their life in a way that I feel could be improved or healthier for them. It's not that I think their way is misguided. Selfishly, the need to organise their chaos surfaces when it affects me negatively, and circumstance makes it hard to escape it. So I act on it and try to fix it, because my emotional state feels that it's about my life too, because "we're all connected." Talk about the pot calling the kettle black. As a result, I can distance myself from those I care about for months – like binging. People in the military or difficult professions probably manage something similar in order to keep themselves emotionally strong against falling into the void of sentimentality. In essence, I'm either in or out. Don't drug addicts do the same? Living at polar ends of emotion trying to satisfy the craving of a void? Everybody has a void. Mine probably started from an early age when I had six years as an only child before my first brother was born. At that time, my mother worked and both my parents were young and quickly oppressed by the confinements of marriage and family responsibilities. Such that I became sensitive to their feelings of entrapment by the unwanted responsibility of me. Then when my brothers arrived and my parents separated, the caretaker in me came out and I experienced prematurely the emotional anxieties and economic confinements of family responsibilities, without the official rights to the roles I managed. Thereby, I lacked the respect or emotional reward of affection an adult might experience in raising his or her own family. My caretaking was received with resistance because it was misdirected to my immediate family and not one of my own. Hence my memory of that experience has kept me weary of suddenly feeling physically restricted from leaving a situation, where my love doesn't feel valued or respected enough. Then, even though I recognise that "just because one doesn't love you the way you would like to be loved, doesn't mean that one doesn't love you", the estrangement can still cause me to drift from person to person, which may later invite an irrational fear of being considered fraudulent with my feelings, when in fact my own feelings probably misconceived others' estrangement to begin with— Augh deep! Thus similar to an addict? I've conditioned myself to love from afar. Then, like an addict who relapses, I can relapse from my discipline and experience a post-reaction from having binged too long on detachment by showing and needing affection too quickly, or excessively to the point of smothering people. The briefly-filled void for belonging, therefore goes empty again. Rather like a bucket with a hole in it. It's a vicious cycle. Hence like Charlie, I can maintain relationships with the emotionally protected, or society's underdog, because their challenges often make spiritually unbiased people out of them, and turn the insecurities of others into tools that help make them feel stronger; thus making the one with challenges feel useful and needed. Whereas the apparently "normal and stable" individuals by nature, would manage self-preservation too well to exercise self-involvement with someone that would complicate their lives. It's not wrong, but it indicates to me a lack of self-awareness of their own imperfections. I guess I find it hard to trust them. They may appear to be healthier people, but can eventually turn needy or dissatisfied with their lives as well, in a way that becomes unhealthy to themselves and detrimental to my health too. I simply love and flourish better with timid personalities that accept my love but do not, or cannot, use their challenges to abuse my caretaking abilities with emotional blackmail tactics against my need for me. Despite myself, my sense of responsibility would either keep me in their well fighting, or smother them. Hence because Charlie does not depend on my love, I'm not afraid to let my caretaker get involved; his emotional distance fuels desire in me rather than fear of entrapment. This type of devotion by its own nature does not feel superficial to me. However, like the Holy Grail, harder to earn and like a warrior's heart, only lives and dies for its master: love. I see or feel this because I am one of them. Similar to Charlie, love and distance are juxtaposed elements that have been conditioned into my personality and similar to Charlie, intimacy with one person would be the equinox of the two factors that we'd need in order to attain the balance of our being. Meanwhile, he gravitates to the prostitutes, the cocaine, his wife, things emotionally inferior to him. Things he can't love or shouldn't. While I deal with the "intelligently confused" ones who love me but can't, and therefore that fact protects me from feeling rejected because I can blame the illness. Both of us have an emotionally trumped-up waiver from getting hurt. More specifically, we trust the behaviour of a difficult or delinquent individual more readily in a relationship because this behaviour or delinquent lifestyle is already clearly defined. The degree of emotional disappointment is lighter when we are able to face anticipated betrayal without fear, because the preconceived knowledge would have already prepared us for it – at least in my case. In a different kind of relationship, my emotional state would coast on a false sense of emotional security, so that I would feel completely caught off guard if and when my partner inadvertently unintentionally betrays me. The unexpected shock to my super ego would stay with me longer, if not forever as a scar. I just live lighter by provisional preparatory skills simply because my life has been made acutely aware of separation and death since birth. I am gun shy. Likewise, a healthy relationship can suffer from my experience too, because my sensitivity to human nature already expects to be betrayed which eventually causes the poor guy to walk on egg shells and become insecure with himself. Hence even though relationships will always at one time or another hurt and disappoint, it feels easier for my timid nature to adapt to a difficult relationship up front rather than be caught by surprise by it down the road. As if developing an immune system against insecurity and mistrust issues quicker, rather than over a longer course of time, which does not even guarantee success anyway. Like death, if one got up every day expecting it, the fear would seem more manageable and life appreciated more intensely. I dunno. Healthier relationships usually know how to apologise and ease the pain faster than a difficult relationship would, but the tactic, like saying, "I love you" becomes abused. Whereas success in a relationship beyond its initial difficulties might flourish from having learnt how to overcome rhetorical tactics, address brass tactics in order to nurture better mileage and sincerity in the end. The only area of risk is if the difficulty continues without a positive evolution in sight and an inability to let go when all has been tried and tested. Masochism is not my idea of a good thing either. Sigh. In the end, the solution for Charlie more than myself remains in burning the waiver, reducing the distance between love and fear and maintaining a constant median between the intensity of our affection and the ability to distance ourselves from people we care about. It's about a balance again, which removes the automatic ability to get too emotionally involved in others' lives and thus avoid the sensation of rejection, while allowing our independent and elusive instinct to thrive without guilt— *Gawd intense!* Anyway, this realisation says to me that Charlie and I could miss the boat for each other by virtue of our emotionally timid personalities or live happily by each other, if we granted each other the Holy Grail of our love. Right now, Charlie does not trust my love under the guise of "Why would she love a cocaine addict?" Nor does he trust his ability to love "I can't and don't want to – I'm an addict" sort of thing. With the same token if Charlie did get well, I would probably put him to the same test: "Why does he want me now?"

Either way, why would anyone want to complicate his or her life when life in a regular relationship is hard enough? Yet do people ask this same question, when a person chooses to be with someone who is physically challenged? Yes, but when the answer is still yes, said person is respected for being virtuous or courageous? How is being with an emotionally challenged individual any different? I have to be some kind of an addict myself, or maybe an astrologer like the woman in the true life film "Shine", who chooses to leave a fiancé in order to marry a psychologically challenged pianist by reason of her astrological analysis, to justify my caring for Charlie? Otherwise my motives are either not altruistic, just a matter of wanting something else related to him, or simply a whim of wanting something I can't have? Charlie can justify a prostitute's interest in him for her financial needs or his family's by reason of blood ties, but why would a seemingly well-travelled, intelligent Canadian woman want to love or grow old by him? Shakespeare: "Love looks not with the eyes but with the mind." In my terms: because his core is real; equal to mine. Because I can learn more from him; because I trust his actions even when I do not immediately understand them. He has proven to me, to be wise and far more aware of things and life around him than he leads on. Regardless of his professional style, his addiction, or his selfish way with love – I simply respect the conviction with which he manages his Way. Enough that I can waiver my own in exchange for his and that to me is my truth, that I love him. Cupid can be blind at times, but like Robert Redford says in the film "Horse Whisperer", 'it didn't matter if it was right or wrong; I just loved her.' So, until my heart notifies me otherwise, all the rest doesn't matter, that's the key... Okay feeling better. Found out too, that Mitx and his other brother went over to see Charlie this afternoon, which relieved me from being the pain in the ass this time.

An entire life of masks
Who cares who it is, who cares who comes
24hrs with yesterday's face
The doors are open – 12hrs white, 12 hrs dark
That's the school – Sun to sun life goes by
One day begins and another ends
That is the story of dawn to dawn
An old street, a rancid square
Clean vagabonds with dirty hands – Woman perfuming the sidewalks
A leg enters with ripped tights – A hand full of gold without colour
Slowly they come, slowly they go
It's the pact on love.

[*Una vida entera llena de caretas/ Qué más da quien sea, qué más da quien venga/ 24 horas con cara de ayer/ Las puerta están abiertas/ 12 horas blancas, 12 horas negras/ Una tierna infancia una triste abuela/ esa es la escuela/ De sol a sol se pasa la vida / Un día empieza y otro termina/ Así es la historia de sol a sol/ Una calle vieja, una plaza añeja vagabundos limpios con las manos negras / mujeres caminando perfuman las aceras/ Unas piernas entran con las medias rotas/ Unas manos llenas de oro sin color/ Despacito llegan, despacito van/ Es el pacto del amor*]

'SOL A SOL' (DAWN TO DAWN) – CAFÉ QUIJANO, LYRICS ADAPTED

V
M

Monday April 4: *How incredible! – It WAS her on that very first night that I'd checked out Veelas! She walked right past the car – I knew I'd picked up on something from her. The one that walked slightly scraping the heels of her boots, the dark haired one. Incredible. It happened on the first night I was there! Here's me going to Veela's at absurd hours like five o'clock in the morning when all this time I'd already known who she was! Not only that! She's meee with dark hair!*

She woke up. When she looked at her clock it was 6:50a.m.!? Her mind was alert and awake. Why? Who just woke her up? Charlie? – Something going on with Charlie? Nonsense. Turnover and go back to sleep. Can't. '*I'm awake and now I'm wondering why?*' she thought to herself. '*What's the date? Monday April 4th. Nothing special; Dasha's awake too? Maybe she needs to go out?*' Daylight was coming into focus by the time she and Dasha had swung down to Charlie's for her routine peek-in. The morning was grey and windy from an overcast sky. Sa Ema remained asleep while the sea on the other hand, was already quite awake and lashing against the rocks along the small escarpment below Charlie's place. The Phedra was in sight, so that she expected to see nothing more than the flashing blue light from the TV screen or the outline of Charlie's frame sprawled along the sofa. She got to the white shutters crouched down into her usual position and peeked through the slits that offered her a dissected view of Charlie and the sofa area. He was sitting up against cushions at the head end of the sofa, with a cigarette in his right hand and his left arm bent at the elbow and propped behind his head on the sofa's back cushion. His head then turned slowly towards the T.V. to look at something, when a girl with jet black hair crossed in front of Michèle's eye level! It surprised her so much that she jerked back and almost fell backwards from her squatted position. A mixed sensation of nervous adrenalin and worry that the sudden movement might have caught their attention, ran through her. She quickly managed a level of composure to regulate her breathing, looked around self-consciously to see if the coast was still clear, and then looked back inside. The girl was about the same height with a slight build comparable to Michèle's. Long wavy black hair stereotypical of the Romanian girls Michèle remembered working with on ships. '*Oh my gawd it's her?*' she thought in amazement. It was the girl that had walked past the Mini while scraping the heels of her black leather boots along the pavement of the road, on that very first night she'd found Veelas. It was the one Michèle had felt a vibe for. Had it been just a passing sixth sense? A sensitivity to Charlie? Whatever it was, it was "V". She was dressed casually in a sporty light blue fitting sweater that Michèle associated with factory outlet sportswear stores and snug blue jeans that flared over her black heeled boots. She moved slowly with her arms crossed, as if to fend off the cold air in Charlie's place, while he silently watched her reach the sofa and sit down at the other end facing him. Everything moved in such a gentle manner that it was like watching a slow moving silent film. Despite Michèle's neurons' signal to leave while she still could, curiosity kept her captivated through her nervous system that had slightly paralysed her from moving in case it revealed her presence to them. Michèle observed the girl sit down on the sofa, turn her posture slightly to face the little wooden table that was next to the sofa, uncross her arms to move her hair away from her face and then bent over to presumably inhale some coke. Michèle could not see the table completely, let alone any coke because the cushions that Charlie had placed against the window, were still there; enough to lose the visual of the girl once she'd bent over. Instead she watched Charlie's reaction. He watched her with a lethargic look in his eyes, smoked from his cigarette and waited quietly while she inhaled the substance; like it was all a code of conduct to say nothing, chill out and take the drugs. Then she came back into Michèle's line of vision, crossed her arms again and leaned back against the opposite head of the sofa to take in the effect. They remained that way face to face without much movement. Possibly V was talking, but Michèle could not see that. Then Charlie said something to her and then, smiled. Jealousy flared through Michèle's system, which she quickly analysed as sadness, for they seemed quite comfortable with each other. Despite his womanising he was not a bed hopper. When he made choices he focused on them and as far as Michèle could calculate, they had known each other since before he'd met her. Then, from the periphery of her right eye, moving light caught her attention. She shifted her focus and saw two people approaching from down the hall that led to Charlie's bedroom. It was a guy and another girl. Michèle suspected they must have been doing their own thing in Charlie's room or simply just looking around because their body language was more abrupt and quicker than that of V or Charlie's relaxed one. The guy, who was hefty and could have been a bouncer for the club, placed a whisky glass of what appeared to be shimmering whisky inside, on the large oak table that was opposite from the TV. The girl was plain looking compared to V, but definitely had the svelte Eastern European features and a firmer body than V's. She too, casually dressed in jeans and wearing a light ski jacket cropped at the waist, was standing close to the little wooden table and talking to Charlie. '*Menudo fiesta de despedida* (quite a farewell party),' thought Michèle. She couldn't believe it. Charlie had broken his rules. He'd invited them to his place; something he'd suggested never having done before. The way the couple moved around it however, did appear to be their first time. Even V whose earlier languid movements from the kitchen, suggested that she might have been looking around too . Then suddenly Charlie's mood became more animated as he exchanged words with the other girl standing before him. Now sitting up on the sofa, he smirked and smiled a lot, as if enjoying from the girl, another one of his provocative reaction games. He then stood up with his cigarette balancing from his mouth, pulled out his wallet from his back jean pocket and retrieved the bills he wanted from it, before sitting back down on the sofa. Then, from a sitting position on the edge of it, extended his left arm out to the girl across from him and the right one to Vanesa next to him. She sat up to take the money and then hesitated in mid motion while Charlie's focus was still on the other girl. Michèle figured that the girl opposite him was not happy with the payment and would not take it. In fact she seemed to be defending her reasons as well as V's who didn't appear to say anything. Meanwhile Charlie was responding to the girl with a lightness in his posture that was all condescending, a goaded smirk and a flamboyant air from the way he waved around the bills in his hands as he conversed with her. As if he was saying: 'Nice try – take it or leave it.' The girl did not seem amused and Michèle quickly looked at V who seemed content to let the girl and Charlie come to terms on their own. The guy did not look impressed either; said a few words, but then avoided further involvement by turning his attention to the oak table. Finally, both V and the girl took the bills from Charlie's hands which looked to be about 70 euros each. V then stood up and disappeared from view. Charlie was still sitting down and presumably finishing his conversation with the girl. Then something inside Michèle instantly shifted: relief. A total sensation of relief. She had seen enough. These people, albeit not evil, had nothing to do with her – not even Charlie. It saddened her because unlike the others he was of the same calibre as she was, but his addiction and the world he lived by, really digressed him. One thing was the ability to befriend those of greater and lesser qualities than one's self and the other, was to behave at a level inferior to one's wisdom. Confucius' saying, "To be with those of equal or greater value to oneself" flashed through her mind. Worse, Charlie gave those people a false sense of status by being with them. She did not like what she saw from him: a good man lost in a quasi godfather role, making a complete buffoon of himself, being with people who had less education than him, yet made better than him on the basis that he was hosting them at his place. '*Te has puesto en un buen lio (Got yourself in good bind)*,' she thought to herself. Her thoughts raced through another corridor of her mind while her eyes followed the motion of the silent charade through the shutters. *It made his possible recuperation from rehab all the more difficult. It touched home. The memory was made and would always be recalled by his surroundings just like the memory of a sensitive person was easily recalled by scents, sounds, music and images. Recuperation from a drug seemed little different from that of a broken heart, a negative experience or personal shame? Was it solely about discipline, distance and change? Giving permission to Time and Space to invade the memory, long enough to create a new one? How dumb was that? Enough to be the story of mankind. Constantly creating in order to divert man from the process of learning and respecting the lessons from memory, because that accomplishment would inadvertently put an end to the subversive addiction to destroy. Like some addicts who don't want to give it up, much of mankind does not want to get better. It's too difficult – too overwhelming. Desire was an inherent ingredient in mankind not exclusive to addicts. Humans always relapsed into levels of bad behaviour because that's what being human was all about – self-improvement. Expecting an addict to abstain indefinitely was another case of the pot calling the kettle black. It was ironic to her that an addict might be considered to be at the bottom rung of self-development when in fact any human plagued by an addiction was probably closer to being a better human being if he or she could pull out of it and live life without it, because it would be a reflection of having attained a greater level of wisdom by virtue of having had the experience, having learned from it and still respecting it. 'Don't let Time and Space invade the memory without respecting it first,' she emphasised to herself. So that was the difference? The task was greater and more demanding of the addict, but among Life's innumerable exams the addict was bestowed the privilege of attempting to pass one, that would grant him or her the ability to reach a higher level of spiritual development in a shorter time than most. The world in itself would already be a better place if mankind didn't allow its mind to gravitate so closely to the universe's example of Black Holes without facing the memory bravely, learning from and then respecting its knowledge before it was removed from mental sight. Especially because the notion of "out of sight – out of mind" did not mean that the memory still did not exist. Nothing in the world was ever totally erased. Ever. The back up to the memory was far greater and far more difficult to remove: the heart. The common chip in all life that simply connected all and everyone together as far back as the inception of time. A sort of Univac of mankind's existence; all problems could be solved by it, but mankind's addiction to create a better world rather than itself, was the same rhetoric as an addict's belief that its behaviour was under control, increased productivity and therefore could dismiss the void it couldn't figure out how to fill, when the heart was the medium to finding the core and filling it ...* 'Listen to your heaaart..,' her thoughts mind-synced with Roxette and brought her back to the moment at hand. She went back to assessing the small group again. How easy it was for intelligence to fall into the well of ignorance and not vice versa and ... She caught herself. Immediately self-conscious of where she was and what she was doing too. Then suddenly hearing the kettle shouting back at the pot: "Et tu Brute!?!" Shame suddenly heated her ears. Withstanding that, there was also no reason to believe that neither one of the three visitors did not come from strong backgrounds like Charlie, although she doubted it. She'd been to Eastern Europe several times and life was indeed harsh there. The guy was not Mayürqan, but he looked more clear headed than Charlie did. Regardless, there was no need for her to peep anymore. It was all frankly pathetic and she wished Charlie into rehab then and there, away from home away from her. Then as fickle as an addict could be, her imagination briefly considered walking in on them. She knew where the extra key was and she had the extra one with her. She could just walk in, act like it was no big deal, introduce herself and hang out with them. What would Charlie care? Now she was caring less about his addiction and more about not being left behind by him. She caught herself again. What was that impulse; another reaction to rejection? It impressed her how her mindset could move in and out of rational as easily as the rhythm of the sea to the shore behind her. Dasha was getting antsy to move too. Then just as she was planning to slip away, Charlie stood up abruptly, retrieved his keys from the small table and got ready to leave. Her heart rate increased a few beats. She stood up quickly and remained by the shutters waiting to hear the front door close. 'Bang!' went the door, then the sounds of V's heels along the cement path followed by a few voices trailing away from her. She popped her head around the corner of the house just in time to see the guy and the girl walking ahead of V who hung back slightly for Charlie. Finally Charlie came whisking into view from the front entrance searching for his key to the car and marched on past V to the car causing Michèle's wave of jealousy to disappear. The realisation of it only amazed her at how easily Jealousy could be provoked, even by the aroma of someone else's poop if not kept in check, which she obviously hadn't done. She hopped down from her position next to the shutters and walked to the other side of Charlie's place in time to see V getting into the Phedra with Charlie and the other two driving off in an old Land Rover jeep. The Phedra pulled out of Charlie's driveway and sped past her and Dasha, leaving Michèle with another wave of sadness knowing that V sat in M's spot in the Phedra. In fact, if V's hair had been fair in colour, she could easily have been a younger version of Michèle rather than his wife, who was a cute woman with shoulder length blonde hair and a physical composition resembling a petite version of Brigitte Jones. It made her think that maybe she was Charlie's version of a day time prostitute. 'Crap Michèle, cut it out!' she mumbled to herself. She walked back home hoping to leave the thoughts that harassed her behind: *'Where were they going? To drop V off at home? A quick foreplay in the Phedra?'* Masochistic attempts at trying to provoke more waves of jealousy were unsuccessful giving her a sign that she really didn't care. She knew Charlie. He'd be interested in getting Vanesa home and being alone. If anything, Michèle sensed in herself, a feeling of detachment from him that suggested an end that she was not willing to accept yet. The same kind of feeling that arose when a friend or a family member exhausted all patience and desire to forgive or to keep in touch. That emotion of course eventually passed or was forgotten, which helped family members to survive each other. However in friendship, void of kinship, the emotion tested individuals at a higher level, on all the qualities needed for greater personal and social development. Above all one's ability to respect another unconditionally and thus putting into play Michèle's own understanding of a friend's true meaning:

"lover". Literally, the relationship between Latin's *amīcus,* "friend" and *amō,* "I love" was clear. As was the relationship between Greek's *philos,* "friend" and *phileō,* "I love". In English, it went back a millennium before the verb was evidently related to *friend.* When at that time, *frēond,* the Old English word for "friend", was simply the present participle of the verb *frēon,* "To love."

> Be slow to fall into friendship; but when thou art in
> continue firm and constant.
> SOCRATES

Frēon

She waited until he returned from wherever he'd been with V, before sending a text message to him asking if she could pop by. It was about 10a.m. when it was sent. She could have waited until late afternoon or evening to tell him, but she'd seen a lot that morning and selfishly wanted to get it off her chest sooner than later. Besides, he was awake then, probably on the sofa heading into his well of darkness in a way that he might not let her see him later on anyway. She walked over to his place before she got a reply, knocked on the front door and waited. She sent another sms: "Shall I use the key?" Finally a reply: "Yes." So she did, using the one she had for herself. The TV was flashing commercials without sound. Charlie was on the sofa under a fleecy blanket in a state of lethargic blankness, while the bowler glass with whiskey she'd seen the guy place on the oak table was still there. She also noticed that the cushions had been moved away from the window, while at the same time, the movement of someone walking-by outside, was detected from a flicker of natural light through the shutters. At that, her stomach sank in an instant. Charlie must have noticed her presence fixed to the other side of the shutters – No? He was just as observant as she could be – is that why he'd said nothing? Thank God! She'd told him. The cushions helped against other possible on-lookers, not solely against her? Holy cow – she didn't know whether to hug him or smack herself first. He let her play Nancy Drew if it made her feel better, while he'd turned a blind eye to it? ... '¿Que?' he asked with a sense of irritation. Her adrenalin about everything had risen in the few seconds that she'd realised so much, that it escaped through her mouth: 'Nada,' she replied with a heart rate of eighty beats per second. She was standing behind the Ikea chair she usually sat in, looking at Charlie who had changed his position on the sofa to have a better look at the apparent on-coming of her theatrics. 'Just that I wanted to ask you about the tickets to Madrid,' her arms moved here and there, 'I planned on asking you later today so that you could sleep and all, but I saw you this morning with your friends and Vanesa! – I was really surprised that you'd invited them here?' she was still on one breath, 'kind of broke one of your rules no? Was it a goodbye get together for you or something?' she stopped moving and took in a breath.

'Nah,' he said with a look of personal disgust on his face, 'the guy was a pain asking me to do the coke at my place so whatever, I said o.k.'

'Oh?' she said dryly. 'Well that sucks – kind of puts you between a rock and a hard place.'

'It doesn't do anything to me,' he retorted defensively. She knew her words provoked, but she went on. 'Charlie, I'm referring to your possible desire to get better. It just makes recuperation for you, when you get back, more challenging – or not?' she asked. He did not answer and reached for his cigarettes on the little table. 'Anyway,' she continued, 'I was really happy to see who she is. I almost came in to say hello and introduce myself.' He looked up at her with a smirk across his face. 'No really, what do you care if they know who I am. You already know that I watch you through the shutters ... Did you see me this morning?' She asked.

'No,' he said, 'how much did you see?' he asked. Her curiosity flashed: *What had she missed?* 'Everything, except the little table because you had the cushions across the bottom of the window.' No reply. 'You know Charlie I was surprised to see too, that V and I are quite similar physically and then completely intrigued by the fact that we're polar in the lifestyle you share with us; me with fair hair by the light of day and her with dark hair by night – funny huh? I was expecting someone more like your wife …' Her tone was purposely light and nonchalant, while trying to get her points across to him. 'It kind of made me sad to see her sitting in the Phedra with you – I sort of got possessive about that spot next to you. Still, now that I know who she is, you can have her.' Her words came out with conviction and in rapid fire. She was unloading and feeling better by it. Charlie said nothing. Then he asked: 'How do you know my wife?' 'I don't,' she replied, 'but I saw the photos from your parents' anniversary that she attended and you also showed me a CD jacket with a photo of her and her preschool students on it – remember?' He inhaled from his cigarette nodded slightly, all the while looking off into the distance. Then on a softer tone she inquired: 'Umm, I've reserved the tickets for the 12th, to Madrid. Are you okay with that?' He nodded. 'O.K. Can I collect them and then stop off at your office and ask your accountant to pay me for your ticket?' she asked carefully. 'Si,' he replied. 'Okay.., and uhm, sorry to be a pain Charlie, but maybe you could call Madrid to confirm our arrival on the 12th?' 'Okaaay,' he exaggerated. She wanted to prompt 'when' but thought better, and decided to get the tickets and just head over to the office once she had them. He'd said "O.K." and Charlie was still a man of his word. 'Ah, one more thing, I'm heading to the cleaners. Anything you want me to take for you?' 'Maybe,' he answered casually with a slight wave of his cigarette in his hand, 'there might be some shirts back there,' he said referring to the laundry room. She turned around, went to the laundry room and came back with a few shirts and jeans of his. 'These good?' she asked. He nodded. She smiled. 'Charlie? I apologise again for pouncing on you so early in the morning. I know I can be quite a motor mouth. Thank you for not being mad at me. It's all good.' She stepped over to him and gave him a kiss on the cheek. 'Bye,' she said. 'Bye,' he exhaled politely and she left.

> Oh, why do you look so sad?
> Tears are in your eyes – Don't be ashamed to cry
> Let me see you through –'Cause I've seen the dark side too
> When the night falls on you – You don't know what to do
> Nothing you confess – Could make me love you less
> So if you're mad, get mad
> Don't hold it all inside – Come on and talk to me now
> Hey, what you got to hide? – I get angry too, well I'm a lot like you
> When you're standing at the crossroads
> And don't know which path to choose
> Let me come along, 'cause even if you're wrong – I'll stand by you
> When the night falls on you and you're feeling all alone
> You won't be on your own
> Take me into your darkest hour and I'll not desert you
> I'll stand by you
> Won't let nobody hurt you
> I'll stand by you
> 'STAND BY YOU' – CARRIE UNDERWOOD, LYRICS ADAPTED

On guard for thee

She was driving the Mini back into the main entrance to Sa Ema when Charlie called her.

'Hi?' she said bringing the car to a slow stop.

'¿Donde estas? (Where are you?)' he asked rather darkly.

'Just coming into Sa Ema. Why?' she asked.

'I want to see you,' he said tonelessly. Something about his way was not positive to her.

'Um, okay. Give me about fifteen minutes, but are you mad at me or something?' she asked.

'Nah. Just come here,' he said again.

'O.K.,' and they hung up. When she got to the front door she had to knock because her arms were carrying a mound of Charlie's clothes she'd picked up when she'd gone to the cleaners to drop off their dirty stuff. Surprisingly enough he answered the knock without much delay. Like always, he opened the door gave her a polite smile and headed for his comfort zone either on the sofa or in bed. This time it was the sofa. 'Hey,' she said as she walked in, 'I picked up some of our laundry from the cleaners. Do you want me to put yours in your room?' she asked him from the door entrance. He turned his head towards her voice and said very curtly but calmly 'Gracias.' She took that as an okay and headed to his room to hang the clothes up. Once she got back to the TV room with him, she sat down into the Ikea chair. The mood in the room was stark and heavy. She assumed that Charlie had not moved much since her antic theatrics in front of him that morning. The air was heavy with tobacco smell and a subtle hint of Charlie's body odour. Natural light came into the room through the slits of closed shutters that highlighted stilled smoke above their heads and offered a sensation of dusk in the room close to the actual time of about 6 p.m. Charlie was lying on his left side along the sofa. Wearing a black t-shirt and black "Boss" boxer underwear while smoking his cigarette in such a methodical and eerie way that the image enhanced by his attractive features made her think of Marlon Brando's character as Colonel Walter E. Kurtz in the film "Apocalypse Now", who'd become "unsound" and turned into "a self-appointed god" during the Vietnam conflict. That, conjured up with Coppola's example of "the harrowing intersection of optimistic innocence" which felt slightly paralleled with her and her confrontation with Charlie's cocaine addiction. '*Crazy*,' she thought.

'¿Por qué me persigues? (Why are you following me?)' he hissed between inhales. Her stomach tightened. He was angry at her.

Enough time had gone by for the cocaine effects from that morning to dissipate and leave him wallowing in his squalid state of mind. She hardly moved or reacted and simply asked ever so quietly: 'What's the matter?'

'You know I don't like being controlled. You're trespassing on my privacy. That's illegal you know. What do you think I am? – Some kind of fool? I don't like being taken for granted or deceived,' he hissed again. Her sixth sense was alerted as she entered the battle field facing charly once again. She made an audible intake and release of air then spoke: 'Charlie – I am sorry for watching you. You are right of course, but it was not done to hurt you or make fun of you; if it had been I would not have told you about it. Besides, I thought you were letting me get away with it because you never told me not to, you know..,' she ended there. Letting his rhetoric on legalities go by as she stared at the white crust of cocaine embedded in the little wooden table next to him. It was amazing of course that he would feel used and deceived by her and not the world he did coke in. Probably because he simply could not understand her purpose with him; like what did she want from him? Too much unconditional love was too much for him? 'Look Charlie, you know what I want from you. I want you to follow through on your swing. It's not for me, albeit I'm no saint and of course my ego would feed well if you did. If you don't then fine, but please tell me so that I can stop spying on you and let you live the life that you want. O.K.? Otherwise respect the fact that I have made a commitment to you that I cannot deviate from, unless you make it clear to me that I can. *You* chose me Charlie and frankly you were not wrong by it. Stay with your instincts okay? Meanwhile, you could make it easy on us both and just focus on your swing you know. If not, the life you lead now is really not that bad at all. Partying until daybreak with the occasional tits and ass, you've even got a wife, have a son and a great family, you own a thriving business, you've travelled a bit, you choose to be alone because you are so surrounded by people and in old age you already have your parents' house and a village to die in. The only reason you might want to stop this lifestyle is because you're tired of it, or you want to decrease the likelihood of a premature death, or maybe just for the romantic but rewarding notion of seeing your son grow up and knowing his girlfriends? Shit, I dunno. However, if you got better, you could organise unresolved issues in your personal and professional life *your* way rather than the chaperons who manage you. Charlie "never say never" you know…You might *always* go back to cocaine, like people who go on and fall off diets, or return to restaurants after swearing "never again!" The *point* is to try and live one's better moments intensely, savour them, respect them and try to learn by doing as much as one can, so that if and when one falls it doesn't hurt as much; while the getting back up gets easier until some people don't even fall anymore, 'cause they eventually figure out how to avoid it. The "get back on the horse" theory – you know?' she paused briefly. 'Personally?' she resumed, 'it's about the fine line between life and death. I don't enjoy the idea of realising something important to me, too late. In your case, you could get better long enough just to tie up your pending issues, go back to the cocaine, die from it or from an elephant that suddenly lands on your head,' she hesitated slightly, seeing Charlie's eyes twinkle at her elephant comment, giving her sign that he was listening to her. 'Really Charlie, you never know these days.., but at least you would die at peace. That's all. Bla, bla, bla…' She ended feeling slightly tired of hearing her own voice. Sometimes she wondered why she cared to share her thoughts when people eventually figured it all out on their own anyway. Charlie said nothing for a moment. Then got up and walked to the kitchen. Michèle could hear him swing the fridge door open and pop open one of the many bottles of juice from within and swing the door closed. 'I want people to respect my privacy you know,' he said coming out of the kitchen. 'Do you know who really respects me?' he asked while standing in front of her. She hesitated a guess, but shook her head instead.

'My son,' he said, 'he respects me.'

'Yes he does Charlie, very much,' she added. 'Tho' I'm willing to bet that if he could drive he'd be in your face more than I am. That's why I think you have such a great window right now. Now's your opportunity to go to rehab and be with him right when he becomes a teenager this year and root a new level of respect from him before it grows past you,' she said cautiously. 'Especially then Charlie, in his teens your presence will have a greater effect on him than his mother's.'

'Yes, I know,' he breathed slightly calmer.

He walked over to the sofa and picked up a folded newspaper and brought it to her attention. 'Look at this and read the headlines,' he said putting a newspaper shot of a man standing next to a bicycle in front of a few traditional village homes and a few young boys in the background. She looked at the article. A man named Kevin Glass was apparently touring the world on his bike and had made a pit-stop in Mayürqa. She read the article more than once, but did not see the correlation between the man and Charlie. Then she looked more closely at the boys in the background. 'Is that your son?' she asked pointing at one of the boys in the photo. 'Si,' he affirmed irritated, 'my son gave me the photo a few weeks ago, when I'd gone to see him...'

By then Michèle was standing by the sofa still looking at the newspaper clip at the same time as Charlie's voice and body theatrics appeared to be gaining momentum as he dressed back into his jeans, put his red shirt over his black t-shirt and headed back to the kitchen: '...And that *man* Kevin Glass,' he stressed dramatically, 'was in my house when I arrived!'

'?? I don't understand Charlie – is he a friend of your wife's, does she speak English?' she enquired feeling somewhat perplexed.

'Are you kidding, my wife doesn't speak English. I got to the house and when she invited me in, she introduced me to him as her friend, you know...'

She watched him move around in the kitchen and proceed to prep the stove for cooking and then asked her more lightly: 'Are you hungry?'

'Uh, yea, okay,' she replied.

Something about Charlie's story didn't sit well with her. Was he jealous or hurt that another man was in the house with his son? 'Charlie, I'm sorry, what are you concerned about? Do you think it's jealousy of your wife and that man?' she asked ever so slowly.

'Nahh! She said that he was only a friend you know, but his bags had been there for a week and why would a guy travelling around the world on a bike stopover in Mayürqa for a week?' he asked indignantly. He was by then leaning over the stove stirring rice in a pot of heating water, 'You know my son is only twelve years old, but he's not dumb. He loves me you know and he's suffered a lot already for his age and seen *too* much between his mother and I you know.., too much.' The passion and the conviction in Charlie's words finally provoked his own anguish to reveal itself through his eyes from heavy teardrops of water that plopped onto the floor with only a few that hung tightly from the tip of his nose. He remained by the stove fully focused on his task of stirring the water that had come to a boil, while the bellowing steam from the pot seemed to give dimension to his misery. Michèle had moved and was leaning against the kitchen entrance wall from the TV room. Her spirit seemed to numb with his and left her at a loss for words. So she stood there silently and just said nothing for a moment. Her imagination of course had gone full speed ahead and began to conjure up all sorts of hypotheses about his son's suffering. *It was not the first time she had heard about it.* Both Mitx and Elisabet had alluded to a lot of the same and it led Michèle to think that Charlie and his wife might have had some severe arguments or clashes. That, or possibly the mother had transmitted her anger at Charlie to the child instead and that's what kept Charlie at bay from making any moves that could be unpleasant and provoke her. She then recalled Charlie's comment about his wife's sudden mood shift towards the boy in Paris and the scar on Charlie's head from an ashtray she'd apparently thrown at his head. In the end however, it was all hearsay and she really knew Didley Squat about any of that. Certainly too, the wife would have her own version. Still, end of all endings and beyond a reasonable doubt to Michèle, they were not a healthy pair. She sighed within. 'You know, my son is the goalie in football because that's what I played. His mother can play me in front of him, but I know he still respects me...' A semi notion was starting to come into focus that seemed to be about feeling indignant at being portrayed as the useless cocaine addict in the eyes of his son and the general entourage, while Charlie felt emotionally blackmailed by his wife? Why didn't she just tell him the truth and free them both from their scruples? He was being taken advantage of by using the cocaine addiction against him unfairly. Who is more in the wrong? The blind that steal or the ones who steal from the blind? Even at Sa Croix, Michèle had to make an effort to close her eyes. Although Charlie's staff management style left a better way to be desired it did not justify the behaviour of those who were trusted to care for his business, to steal from him. She saw it from the employees to the one's responsible for Sa Croix' accounting, never mind the ones who were permitted to abuse their family rights with him. Worse, was that Charlie was vaguely aware of it, but let it go by reason of his own imperfections, which turned into a life story of allowing the lines of being swindled versus being tolerant about being used, to unite as one. Welcome to the world of diplomacy. Canada instantly flirted past her heart and she suddenly missed her country very much and loved it for instilling in her the ability to live by respect and accept being tolerant in the face of social ignorance. Then her thoughts shifted completely from Charlie to her own shame at not being a better Canadian and standing her ground at home ... *There was nothing about her country that was not beautiful not even the cold. As cowardly as it was she flew to the warmer climates and avoided her country's national demise from its neighbour to the south. It seemed to her that ever since Pierre Eliot Trudeau stepped down from his role as Prime Minister, Canada had never been classier, smarter than or as confident as it was when he lived. Now its government was just another name for string puppet while Canadians were left to "Stand on guard for thee" practically on their own. They would too. She knew this. Odie in the end was a dog by nature and could chase the cat away if he had too ...* She looked at Charlie letting those thoughts assault her mind without much empathy at his despair ... *He could clean up his act, even for a short time and kick the ass out of those who were no better than he. At least Sa Croix was his and built by his own hands. She felt so on guard for him, while he was his own enemy and victim at the same time. Would she have to face him like the loyal dragon slayer in the film "Dragonheart" who had to slay his best friend, a dragon, in order for the dragon to get to its true destination? She hoped not because in light of all her observations of Charlie they could easily have been her own; she was a Black Water dragon remember? Leading her imagination to wonder if maybe Charlie was in fact the loyal dragon slayer* ... 'You know,' said Charlie darkly, 'I had forgotten something on my way to work one day and when I drove back home she was dressed in seductive women's lingerie. I asked her what she was doing and she said that she was trying on new clothes? She never wore any of the ones I bought for her. I asked her why and she was so evasive; I dunno!' he emphasised. Michèle was not sure where he was going or coming from. She prodded: 'Umm, Charlie, do you think she was with someone at the time?' 'I don't know, but Kevin Glass had visited the island before his world trip – you know?' he trailed off and stopped stirring the rice long enough to pull out a crumpled tissue from his jean pocket and blurt out, 'She's really *fucked* me up you know!' His anguish was tremendous and there was no way for Michèle to reach him. She could not hug him or even touch him. He stood there and blew his nose, wiped his mouth and used his hands to clear the tears from his face. There was so much pain in him. So much injustice directed at him because of his cool demeanour. The very armour he wore for protection was the very same that provoked his pain. It did not matter if his words were authentic or a misconception from his addiction, he was finally just letting it out. She decided to keep her reaction cool and simply moved to the cupboards and pulled the plates down to set the kitchen table. Charlie turned back to the stove and focused on the task of serving the rice soup. She sat down and Charlie brought the pot over to the table and ladled three portions of hot soup into her bowl first, then his. Put the pot back on the stove, sat down at the table with her and quickly deferred to her, 'It's hot,' before taking his spoon and starting. She sat their while the steam billowed up to her face, feeling a great amount of personal joy in spite of the circumstance of the moment. She had not expected her evening to turn out the way that it had. She loved his soup, loved being at the table alone with him and loved what she felt to be a comfort zone without words. 'Hmm. Thank you Charlie,' she said softly as she attempted her first spoonful of soup. She let a few moments go by before she finally decided to say something: 'Charlie?' she asked quietly, 'I have a question for you,' then took another sip of soup. By then Charlie had just finished wiping his hands on the napkins she'd placed on the table. He then reached for his cigarettes in his shirt pocket and for a lighter from the dozen that were lying on the table, gave her a quick glance, and asked,

'¿Que?,' then proceeded to flick-on the lighter and lit his cigarette. She smiled lightly and asked: 'Would the child you once were respect the adult that you've become?' He inhaled from his cigarette and leaned back in the chair looking at her with a mild look of perplexed concern in his eyes, '... And I say to you,' she continued confidently, 'yes... because of what you confirmed with me that your son loves you very much Charlie. In his eyes you are the cat's ass – no one, not even his mother can or will change that. If they tried, his loyalty to you would only entrench itself deeper. The only thing that could change it, is you and you have done nothing but suggest to me your intention to get well. We're going to Madrid because you want to – you know? Your intention is still true Charlie. The best part is that only you can change that – no one else.' She paused slightly then added: 'I'm not kissing your ass, but you're on track Charlie! Okay? That's it. Bla, bla, bla,' she said with a quick dismissive tone and got up and cleared the plates from the table. Charlie said nothing for a moment making her feel that she'd once again said too much. *'Whatever happened to "keep it simple", dummy?'* she mused to herself. Then almost upbeat, she heard Charlie say: 'Gracias Michèle.' 'For what?' she replied nonchalantly ignoring his meaning, 'you made dinner.' 'Leave the dishes,' he said getting up with obvious relief in his moves, 'I'll do them.' She would have rebutted, but she let it go. 'Okay. Thank you,' and went into the TV room, grabbed the remote control and quickly gave him a final glance before heading to her spot in the Ikea chair. He was already up to his elbows in suds, shirt cuffs rolled back and diligently balancing a cigarette from his mouth. She listened to a quiet rattle of pots and plates while methodically turning the ring that Charlie had given her from Paris, around the wedding finger of her right hand. Much like Charlie often did with his on his left hand that was from her trip to Dubai. It was a way to relax and let her thoughts go by, at least semi unnoticed. Although she had received a few gifts from Charlie at Christmas, the ring was by far the most cherished one. She turned and turned it, noticing that the mesh from the ring's links sometimes irritated her finger, making her move it with interval movements, over to her thumb and back to her finger where she liked it better. The hint of irritation from the ring actually bothered her because she managed to find a parallel between her difficult love for Charlie and the ring that did not fit entirely with ease. Plus the mesh had stretched a bit and she had almost lost it a few times from her finger, causing her to place it more often on her thumb which of course only stretched it further. It made her wonder if it was an indication about her relationship with Charlie. *It wasn't quite right. The gift, although from Charlie's sincere intention was given prematurely to her because it was not given under healthy circumstances. Therefore she hypothesised that she was bound to lose it, and Charlie would lose his too, because even though her energy in the giving was true, Charlie's was not in a clear state of mind. Thus making the exchange of their personal gifts a guise of the real thing. She went farther and imagined that maybe the rings symbolised a foreshadowing of what could be one day the real thing, but they would have to lose the rings in order to coincide with losing each other for a while, before they could find each other again and exchange such gifts with authentic sentimental value for each other ...* The realisation of this was a bitter sweet vision and made her give out a quiet exhale. Her relationship with Charlie was only the first phase of three and it had already been so intense. Time and space could take their toll and wipe out the memory, or if her instincts were true, then all she had to do was be patient, keep the faith and let the Universe do its thing ... That's *all*, she had to do.

Buck had a trick of love expression that was akin to hurt.
He would often seize Thornton's hand in his mouth and close so fiercely
That the flesh bore the impress of his teeth for some time afterward...
.. But the man understood Buck's feigned bite for a caress...
Faithfulness, devotion, things born of fire and a roof, were Buck's
Still, he retained his wildness and willingness
But because of his very great love, he could not steal from this man
Yet, from any other man, in any other camp
He did not hesitate an instant.
'THE CALL OF THE WILD'– JACK LONDON CHAPTER SIX 'FOR THE LOVE OF A MAN' – EXCERPT ADAPTED

For the love of a woman

Journal, April 5: *"No sé qué pretendes, pero dejar de aprovechar de mí, y no quiero más de tus besos falsos (Don't know what you're up to, but stop taking advantage of me, and I don't want any more of your fake kisses)"* – SMS CHARLY TO MICHÈLE.

We had lunch today at Sa Croix. Sitting at our regular table off to the far right corner of the entrance way from where Charlie can watch the activity on the floor. We ordered from the menu and then I asked him if he had known that I was at Veela's this morning. 'Well, I guessed it was you,' he said casually without much more to it than that. I smiled. 'I figured you would have. I saw the guy with the curly hair and glasses make a few walking rounds around the club more than once, I'm sure he noticed me too. Who is he anyway?' I asked flippantly.

'I don't know,' he said between bites of paella, 'he goes to the club – he's a bit unusual – I dunno,' he repeated, as if annoyed at wasting his time talking about someone he really cared less for.

'Oh,' I said. Then in an overly gregarious tone added, 'well I really felt silly you know, because I was there waiting for you, when I really just wanted to walk in there and say: 'Hi!' but figured that you really wouldn't have enjoyed that too much. So I just waited until I saw you leave and then I left too. You went pretty quickly,

like you were embarrassed about something, or was it because you just wanted to avoid my presence..?' I'd puffed-out my last two words, took in a breath and waited for his reply, but he did not react. Instead he said: 'I wouldn't have cared, but I don't think *you* would have enjoyed it.' Then asked with a focused tone: 'Why are you watching me?' I had to swallow the last of my food and took my time doing it in order to give him an adequate answer. He was annoyed by my presence and was doing a good job handling me, despite it. 'I suppose that it makes me feel that it keeps the focus on your possible decision to go to rehab, alive.' I said in a subdued manner. 'Like the lyrics in the song "California" from the CD you gave me that say: "Remind me when I can't remember",' I sighed, 'I dunno, something corny like that.' I ended while averting my eyes from him to my glass of water. Charlie leaned back from the table, wiped his hands in a crumpled napkin and reached for his cigarettes while sizing me up from my reply. He really did not know what to make of me, but I detected a mixed mood of affection and frustration from him towards me. Then tonight while I was driving home from Palma, I received a tough sms from Charlie at around eleven thirty that was on one hand directly cruel, and then on the other hand, confused. Something about my kisses being fake? My kisses aren't fake. I guess my affection confuses him. Kind of like a wild dog with its paw caught in a trap wanting help, yet so afraid of the helper. Then if the helper is successful in opening the trap long enough for the dog to remove its paw, and focus on its freedom, rather than attack the helper, it usually runs away free, leaving the helper unharmed and with the singular reward of having given the animal another chance to survive on its own...
'Hmfpt.'

Go ahead release your fears
You gotta be bad, you gotta be bold
You gotta be wiser
You gotta be hard, you gotta be tough
You gotta be stronger
You gotta be cool, you gotta be calm
You gotta stay together
'Cos all I know, all I know
Love will save the day.
'YOU GOTTA BE' – DES'REE, LYRICS ADAPTED

Bold

April 6: She went over to Charlie's just after three o'clock in the afternoon and he was not alone. Mitx had crossed paths with her earlier, on his arrival home from work and mentioned to her that he'd seen Charlie heading home at 8:30 that morning with a girl in the car with him. Then underlined that it was not the first time he'd seen him with her. 'Hmm, yes, I know,' she'd answered as a way to diffuse his attempt to redirect her. The truth was that she had suspected, but was not even sure if Mitx's truth was accurate. She knew Charlie had been going all out, but she had not sensed Vanesa as often as Mitx was suggesting. Anyway it didn't matter, but she felt that something had to be done. When she got to Charlie's front door she hesitated a moment: what was the motive behind the visit? Charlie was in his home more than likely hanging out with V doing coke and Michèle was about to invade their privacy. Not cool. Time and space had begun to flush out the purpose of getting Charlie out of the well and for a brief second she even considered doing nothing and letting it all go. Then pride caught up to her and reminded her that nobody was doing anything. If she let go like everyone else had, nothing in his life would change. Charlie had to run his course on his own but in a different way, than the last one he'd been running for the past fifteen years. Surely whatever she did could not be any worse for trying? She stood there at the door, heart beat picking up pace while she assessed her actions before their consequences. It was an extension to hanging-out in front of Lady Veelas at obscene hours just to make her presence felt. If she were a guardian angel she'd be on his shoulder night and day acting as his voice of reason whilst the cocaine would be a dressed up version of a little red V on his other shoulder taunting him to stay where he was. Her intentions were altruistic albeit excessive. In all frankness she wasn't going to be able to do anything else that day, even if she tried. Her focus was Charlie. She took in a deep breath and prepared to knock on the door and then quickly hesitated again. '*When in doubt don't do it?*' she thought to herself. The day was warm and she could feel the heat of the sun at the back of her neck at the same time as the white front door seemed to glare at her. She was not in doubt of her intention, but she was afraid that her impulse was too impulsive? '*Maybe wait a bit longer?*' she continued debating: '*What's the point of that?*' Now, or later, she wanted to irritate Charlie's moment with unwanted thoughts and recognition of where he was and what he was doing. Ah - Ha! There it was: the reason behind the purpose. Doing it then and there was better than later, when he'd be less impressionable. 'Okay okay,' she muttered to herself, while also thinking that even though people had their lives to live, destiny certainly had a knack for making people's paths cross when they had to. Hers and Charlie's certainly had. 'So like it, or lump it,' she whispered to herself, 'I'm going in!' The mental image of her own theatrics stimulated a small smile from her that minutely relieved her as she decided to send an sms to Charlie first. "Hi. I'm at your door can I come in?" No reply. She waited a bit more and sent another one: "It's me. May I come in?"

Still no reply. She started to feel anxious and knocked lightly on the door. Nothing. Then she tried again with a slightly firmer knock. Nothing. She finally buzzed the doorbell quickly in order to avoid hearing its sound, which did nothing more than highlight her intrusive behaviour even more. Then her phone flashed: "I prefer not."

'*Crap,*' she thought wryly, '*why bother asking him when you're not going anywhere until he lets you in?*' "Sorry Charlie. Can I just see that you're ok? It's for my relief not yours," she sent.

"I'm fine," he sent back.

'Uuugh!' She was about to enter troubled waters and mess up her altruism: "Charlie can I use the extra key? Just to pop my head in?" She was beside herself in disbelief at her insistence but it worked. The front door suddenly opened ever so slightly and only wide enough for her to see half of Charlie in the doorway: '¿Que Michèle?' he asked calmly.

'Hi. Can I come in for a bit?' she asked.

He was dressed in a white cotton shirt that fell loosely over his jeans and was open to the mid-section of his chest. The cuffs to the shirt were open and lightly rolled back, while he had his right hand gripping the door just slightly higher than his shoulder level. His face expressed lethargy across his features and there was a look of mild serenity in his eyes. He looked at her calmly, 'Another time o.k.,' he said.

'Charlie, just for a moment – I know she's here, it's no big deal.' He smiled slightly at her.

'Another time, okay..,' he said in a tone that bordered a slight plea. They stood there facing each other. She was really feeling badly about her conduct but could not find a way to back down.

'Charlie,' she hardly whispered, 'may I just step inside and then I'll go okay.' He looked at her with an obvious glimmer of mental suffering. Her heart sank even more. There she was pushing him to the limit, manipulating his own inability to tell her to piss off or even just close the door on her, just so she could finish her swing. Her altruism had already left and she wasn't even inside yet. 'Michèle what do you want to see? There's nothing here. I'm o.k.,' his tone was mild yet cool. If he wanted to smack her he was doing an incredible job of controlling it, in spite of his intoxicated state of mind. It was a stand-off between egos, because it really did not matter what happened, the only thing being tried was control. Who would give in first? So Michèle positioned herself for the draw and fired: 'Charlie I'm sorry. I really am. I will go away if you let me in for just a moment – really.' He was now leaning his weight more comfortably against the door and gave her an annoyed look, mixed with a complacent one that she assumed came from the cocaine. He really was induced yet he did not raise his voice at her or even criticise her verbally. He was so gentle that it made her behaviour stick out like an ugly sore thumb. Then, as if his ego found maturity before hers, he slowly removed his weight from the door, clicked his tongue between his teeth, gave her an exasperated look and opened the door wide enough for her to step inside the entrance way. 'Thank you,' she said lightly while her thoughts flushed her with guilt, shame and a bitter-sweet triumph all at the same time. She walked in and made a quick scan of the TV room before turning her back to it in order to focus her attention back to Charlie, who had not moved from his spot next to the open door. The scan was too quick and she did not see anything, or anyone to catch her attention. Once she turned around, she positioned herself next to the wall that faced the doorway which put her in an apex position from Charlie at the doorway and the one in the hall to his bedroom. Charlie stood with one leg crossed in front of the other while his right arm continued to hang over the open door. Light from the afternoon sun had boldly come into the hall area causing him to tilt his head slightly downwards, as if to avoid the glare in his eyes. He stood there like that in a waiting stance while Michèle stood there next to the wall without anything to say or do. She crossed her arms below her chest, then dropped them into clasped hands in front of her. She then realised that the hall door in front of her was closed when it was never closed. She stood there unable to move or do anything. As if her presence was all that she needed to impede whatever it was Charlie was doing. It was all so crazy. It wasn't like he was going to wrap up whatever it was that he was doing, fetch V from the bedroom where Michèle presumed she was and take her home. In a matter of moments Michèle would have to leave, he'd close the door and what would have been accomplished?

'O.K.,?' asked Charlie suddenly putting an end to the silence. 'You've seen okay?' he added giving a nod towards the door. She stood there, literally frozen. The moment became all too surreal for her. What was she doing there? She knew that she was pushing her luck, but as much as she knew that she had to go, her legs would not follow. Then the acute realisation that Vanesa was there too – just on the other side of the hall door, seemed to paralyse her even more. She looked at the door then at Charlie. 'Is she there?' she asked quietly. Charlie turned his head to face the open doorway with a hint of impatience in his look: 'No te preocupes (Don't worry),' he said in a calm matter of fact tone. She looked back at the closed hall door and sOo wanted to go through it. See or meet her. Her thoughts raced with hypotheses: '*Was she sleeping? High? Had he been entertained by her in the bedroom where Michèle and Charlie use to have long chats, or more than likely, they'd done their thing and Charlie had been on the sofa while she was resting in the bedroom when Michèle had knocked on the door? Was Vanesa even alone? Maybe it wasn't even her?*' Then she felt bad for the girl: '*Was Charlie like a papa snow? He could go to rehab and pay to get better and what of her? Left behind with a cocaine addiction?*' There lay another moment when the prostitute could lose out. Compassion for the girl suddenly found Michèle who was on the verge of heading straight through the door, finding Vanesa, introducing herself to her and offering her ways to live a different life. Oh how she wanted to, yet she couldn't out of deference to Charlie's already over taxed patience from her. 'Valee (okaay),' Charlie's tone was tired and irritated. Michèle quickly came out of her reverie of "Save the prostitutes!"

when in fact she was probably the one who needed saving. What seemed like an eternity was probably no more than five minutes. Finally, as a last attempt to re-instate the purpose to her visit she asked softly: 'Do you have feelings for her?' Charlie's arm seemed to swoop down from the door as he stood up on his own weight, looked down at the rings on his hand and while fidgeting with the one that Michèle had given him, darted a response: 'Nah.'

The reply was assertive and vexed, as if the sound of his own voice was enough to cause him frustration and annoyance at the reality of his current moment. He shifted his weight and looked out the front door with an obvious distaste for the moment on hand. Michèle said nothing for a second then saw his carry-on suitcase leaning up against the wall to the door. They were so close in getting there. 'Charlie,' she whispered evenly, '*why* are you *here*? What – *are* – you – doing?'… 'No lo sé (I don't know),' he said with a lost voice.

Silence fell between them while they stood across from each other, waiting for the moment to end. She looked at him from a standstill position. Feeling at once a great ache for him and a sudden need to leave, or forever live with the guilt that was beginning to fester inside her. There she was aggravating him in his own home, giving him the third degree after he'd allowed her to enter because she'd said that all she'd wanted, was to see that *he* was okay. He never shouted or yelled at her, just asked her nicely to leave. She glanced quickly at the suitcase and finally made her move to the doorway, stopped and turned gently to face Charlie who'd lined up behind her to close the door. 'Charlie,' she hesitated, 'my kisses are not fake.' A twinge of sensitivity flickered past his eyes and beyond his stare at her, to the day outside, 'I know,' he replied. Then as if given a final surge of courage she added: 'I will come here every day like a thorn in your butt – hate me or kill me, until that suitcase leaves this house with you.' Her tone was flat and nervous but came out coherently. Then she kissed his cheek, turned around and just before he disappeared behind the door she shouted emphatically: '¡Porque *me* ImPORTAS! (Because *You* MATTER to *me*!)' and walked back home.

If you have a dream, give it a chance to happen – RICHARD M. DEVOS.

The believer

Journal, April 7: *You're losing me from your life, from your reach. If only you were coherent enough to avoid letting it happen. You won't find anyone prepared to take you there and even lose you doing it. Someone will enjoy you in your wellbeing and it won't be me. [Me estás perdiendo de tu vida, de tu alcanzo. Y ojala que tenías la claridad de no dejar ello pasar. No encontraras nadie dispuesto a llevarte hasta ahí y demás perderte. Alguien disfrutara de tu bien estar y no será yo...]*

I told Charlie that I would go to his place every day until he and the suitcase left together for rehab. Great. Now I have to follow through; to the contrary it was just an idle threat? Or am I just looking for ways to be with him? Both I guess. I had another great coincidence today. I went to Palma in order to meet with a Japanese owner of a Japanese restaurant and it turns out he needs a replacement for his personal assistant who returned to Japan. He's also thinking about establishing a Japanese Cultural centre in Palma that maybe I could help him with. Plus, the Japanese player for Mayürqa's football team might get involved in its promotional activities. We haven't talked about salaries yet. We'll see. I also handed-in my CV to a few government ministries in Palma, a new Hotel on the east coast, called an English academy in Palma to see if they needed teachers and sent a follow-up email to ships about my job proposal idea for an office in Barcelona. So we'll see. Charlie? Ironic that while he is not well, the illness does however give him time to be with me, weakens his armour against sentimentality, humbles his fears, and makes him more sincere with his feelings, than when he could be after rehab. Sigh. I think part of my anxiety and one of the roots to my focus with Charlie is about money. I haven't figured out what to do, or how to make the money that I want out here, so until I do, I'm putting all my efforts into something that feels worthwhile. Life will tell me. Amusing how Charlie's issue makes people avoid their own problems. When he leaves they will feel a void – me in particular – and when he returns they will see their own shadows because his won't be around anymore. Least I hope not. Such that, I want him gone for a while, or else it won't make a difference to his pattern. We're supposed to go to Madrid on the 12th, to check-out Narconon. Please wherever he goes, make him go for at least five or six months! Lord don't be cruel. So cruel. Everything is possible. My wish is still the same: work, money, and then love. I have Carles and I think, feel? Believe it's there. It is too hard to deny the signs. How long? I don't know. I think that it's a possibility, or maybe Carles is just another lesson for me? Puff. In this God I will not change: he carries a Mont Blanc bag similar to mine. His racket and bike are similar to mine. We often dress in the same colours, or in the same style without knowing it. We live our lives similarly with sybaritic and sensitive personalities. Astrology and all the coincidences aside, we both have obsessive issues and I just *see* a reflection of his other half in me and mine in him. Frick and Frack at our best! Two lost souls searching. One blind, one deaf. Maybe down the road he returns from rehab, works, I work, and Dasha and his son are somewhere there in between? That this is my vision for and beyond 2006?! – Uh, hello out there? … Please make me a believer that is not a fool!

There were two people walking towards one another from opposite ends of a beach shore. There had been a terrific storm the night before and a zillion starfish washed up by the storm, covered the beach for as far as the eye could see. While the two walked along the shore, one of them was also picking up and returning as many of the star fish possible back into the sea. The latter could hardly get to them all and the effort of walking, bending and throwing looked tedious to say the least. When their paths finally met up, the first person asked: 'Why do you bother to throw the starfish back into the sea? There are miles and miles of starfish in front of you. Your efforts won't matter.' The second person listened politely, reaching down to throw another starfish back into the sea, then looked up at the voice of reason and kindly replied: 'Well, it mattered to that one.'

Madrid

April 12th

They got to Madrid airport without too much delay. Unlike Seville the trip thus far had been uneventful and the arrival much more pleasant and easy going. This time Charlie managed the car rental and got a car that was more to his liking than the little one they'd had in Seville. The morning was crisp and clear when they headed west from Madrid into the mountains of Guadarrama in order to visit the rehab centre that was there. It was a beautiful morning and the drive through Madrid and into its outskirts was a breath of fresh air for both of them. Charlie for the most part was calm, but vacillated easily between being congenial and irritated by her proximity to him on the trip. Still, she was feeling an incredible amount of freedom being away with him, just going with the ride and enjoying the scenery from the passenger side of the car. Charlie drove with his anxiety seemingly subdued by the blaring sound of the radio's music, muffled through the car's loud hum along the highway. Michèle stared out her window with a similar sense of tranquility at being in the car next to him, safe from all the negative energy that she felt surrounded them in Mayūrqa. Then as if to remind her, the ring from Charlie on her right hand began to irritate her index finger, causing her to move it to her thumb and fiddle with it while she stared out the window and noted the paradox of their moment that was seemingly okay, yet in direct opposition to the one they'd had the night before ... *It was about six o'clock when she and Charlie went to the cleaners to pick up their dry cleaning after having spent a few hours at Sa Croix during the lunch hour rush. When they got to the dry-cleaners, Charlie had to park the Phedra in a precarious spot so that she stayed in the car waiting for him. While she sat there it occurred to her that he'd left his mobile phone on the seat next to her. By then, she knew the password to get into it and had made a list of telephone numbers that she'd categorized as the black and the green lists of people in Charlie's agenda. It was something that she had prepared at the very beginning of their intense month together in January, when he'd allowed her to screen his calls. Since then, she had not been drawn to check his phone's activity until that morning in March, when he'd mistakenly sent her an sms that had been intended for Vanesa. As a result she'd looked at his phone's short message service twice without his permission in order to clarify her understanding of his increased relationship with V. At least that's what she'd told Charlie in the aftermath. The first time she'd done it, was while he was having a shower. She was hanging his dry cleaning in his bedroom cupboard when his phone alerted the arrival of an sms. She didn't even think twice and went over to the phone to see who it was from. "¿Que haces? V (What's up? V)" Needless to say she so wanted to answer on his behalf with a less than promising reply, but despite her impulse she was able to find reason and simply left the phone in its spot and waited for Charlie to come out of the shower. 'Umm Charlie?' she said once he came out, 'there is a message on your phone from Vanesa. I saw it while you were in the shower,' she said with trepidation. Without saying anything to her, his eyes darted quickly to the phone and then back to the cupboard where he began the task of choosing his clothes for that day. She took that as a sign and headed to the TV room leaving him with a quiet 'Lo siento (I'm sorry),' and waited for him there. The second time was nothing like the first* and seriously entered the realm of unethical behaviour, because she'd gone out of her way to check his phone so that she could assuage her own need for answers. It was one night, when Obsession finally usurped her reason and like a little girl of twelve, she allowed herself to do a very naughty thing. She slipped into his room while he was sleeping, quietly took his phone and went to the TV room to invade the phone's agenda. To her, that moment, was the pinnacle moment of when she was no longer acting in accordance with her creed of "Live and let Live"; no longer in line with her purpose to help, not even room for acquittal from any of the methods used and respected by "Tough Love". It was simply wrong and she realised that the harm that Charlie was susceptible to by his own friends and family had then included her. Who was in the well now? Above all, existed the shame at seeing that in light of the obvious exchange of sms between him, the "V" girl and the Pinocho woman from his village, the sms' that over-flowed and took up ninety percent of his phone's memory were from her. It appeared that the majority of them, if any, had not been deleted from as far back as November. Plus she knew that his exchange with V had been constant, yet it was obvious that Charlie had simply deleted them. Maybe to hide the fact, but even the messages from his wife and his family were not evident in proportion to the actual amount of communication between him and Michèle. Only hers and the ones from his son were still there. Her heart sank and pounded harder for him. She was really stricken with guilt and wanted to wake him up at that instant to tell him. She had really shot herself in the foot. What trust could Charlie ever afford in her then? Would he understand that it was a reaction to her involvement in getting him out of the same well that she had obviously gone into after him? Should she even tell him? Yes. Even if he could not trust her anymore that would be her price to pay, but she had to tell him to free her conscious and follow through with her truth. Like it or lump it, the damage was done and even though she'd try to mend it, the consequences were already on their way. Needless to say, she had a sleepless night. It was not until the *following morning that she managed to tell Charlie about her crime. 'Carles,' she began, 'I did something truly wrong yesterday.' He opened the pack of confectionery muffins and eyed her wearily. He was getting used to her naughty-good girl behaviour and making it obvious that he was getting tired of it. 'Venga (tell me),' he said with a cold air of disregard while he dunked one of the muffins into his coffee. 'I looked at your phone again while you were sleeping last night; even saying I'm sorry doesn't mean much does it?' she blurted. 'I would completely understand it, if you can't trust me anymore, but know that it wasn't to hurt you. I'm just a little obsessed by the V girl. You say that you have it all under control, but you're out almost every night and doing coke every day and inviting her to your place. Tell me you're on a major binge because you're getting ready to leave and I'll relax, but otherwise I'm not going anywhere – you know?' she'd decided to defend her case rather than make a plea for forgiveness. He finished the last of his coffee and muffins, wiped his hands and looked at her. 'I don't like you looking at my phone o.k.?' he said pointedly.*

'I understand. I wouldn't like it either,' she responded.

'So then, let it go okay – Let it go!' he raised a pitch on the last few words and got up to pay.

She never really replied, but told herself severely to abide by his request, even if it interfered with her hopes. Truth was, everything seemed to interfere with her plans to get him off ... Even Charlie was more relaxed about it than she was. She wanted it all done then and there, while everyone else was pussyfooting around and taking their sweet time doing it. So that there in the Phedra, she was tempted to check his phone once again. She reached for it and contemplated her reasons, then put it back on the seat where it had been and instantly felt relieved. As if she'd just broken a spell. She no longer cared. Besides too, what if Charlie had left it there to test her? Sure enough, when Charlie returned to the car the first thing he did was look at his phone. 'I didn't look at it,' she said casually, 'in case you were wondering.' He climbed into the car, gave her a sideway glance, 'I didn't say anything,' he smirked and they drove home. That night however, was not so congenial and the two of them had their first head to head stand-off over Michèle's unwillingness to leave his place and sleep at her place instead. She had somehow convinced herself that her presence was needed to dissuade Charlie from going out and possibly miss the plane to Madrid the following day. It was close to 11p.m. and Charlie was wearing little more than a black t-shirt, a pair of black fitting boxers and his slippers for whenever he got up from the sofa. Enough to suggest that he wasn't going anywhere and that Michèle's concerns were simply emotional. She was sitting in the Ikea chair dressed in her black sweats and the same black jumper with the hood that she wore when she parked out front of Veela's. They were quiet for the most part, while Charlie watched TV, smoked his cigarettes and Michèle vacillated between watching the TV and writing in her agenda. Finally he said, 'I'm going to bed.'

'Okay,' she said. He got up from the sofa and ever so subtly said: 'You can leave when you want.' Her stomach tightened slightly: 'Will my presence bother you if I stay?' she asked.

'A little,' he said evenly, as he headed down the hall to his bedroom. 'Alright,' she hesitated, 'may I hang out until you're asleep?' she tried, 'then I'll head home okay?'

The query had not been to his liking and he came back down the hall and headed to the kitchen for something to drink. 'Don't worry about tomorrow,' he said between gulps of juice, 'I'll get up.'

She did not know how to answer that. She knew that he was talking, but that the cocaine wouldn't cooperate and she simply wasn't able to believe it. There was a brief silence. Then Charlie headed to the front door behind her, opened it gallantly and gave her a definite indication to leave. 'Please,' he pronounced. She stayed in the Ikea chair unable to move or see him because her back was to the door. So from her spot in the chair, she turned her upper body to face him and saw the intensity of his wish searing from his eyes.

'Charlie,' she asked calmly, 'why do you want me to go?'

'Enough is enough Michèle,' he asserted, 'I'm tired of you manipulating me and taking advantage of me – you know?' The mood swing was quick and negative and she analysed his words and the impending moment rapidly. A craving might have crossed his thoughts, while he was on the sofa that was conflicted by her presence and simply felt irritated by her vigilance. Nonetheless, he was right about her tactics. Yet, even though he'd very politely and diplomatically asked her to leave, she would not obey him. It was like every ounce of her stubbornness and capacity for insubordination had grown to their mightiest size. He was plainly in his right, yet she felt a need to ensure their trip to Madrid the next day. Time was still on his side, but ever sooo slightly that she simply could not, or would not let it go by. The plane tickets were purchased at a discount price that made them non-refundable. Charlie was slipping, if not already there into an incoherent state that was sure to plunge him deeper into the well at a depth that would escape her reach for good. He had to keep moving, keep seeing and keep the focus of rehab in front of him. Above all she too, was getting tired and just didn't want to let go when they were so close. If he got to rehab that month, he'd still have five months before September arrived where so many of his quiet hopes were waiting for him...

'No. I can't,' somehow escaped from her lips.

'¡¿Porrr Qué?! (WhY)?!' he darted at her from his position by the door. He was standing with his right hand gripped at the top end of the open door, while his left arm swung in pendulum frustration at the exit. She had not meant to verbalise her thoughts and simply looked at him unmoving. '¡Venga! (Let's go!),' he repeated.

She had to do something, so she got up from the chair and moved to the sofa, so that she could see him better, and sat down again. Charlie was in an obvious state of bewildered fury at her. She could see it and felt confused by her own behaviour. What was she really doing apart from causing Charlie undeserved anguish? She cleared her throat softly *and offered:* 'Charlie, if you're not going out then great. Let me watch the end of this film and I'll go. Okay?' *He stared at her momentarily then let the door fly closed. Turned around and sauntered back to his room muttering to himself in exasperation:* 'This is UN-believable! I'm being accosted in my own home!' *He got to his room and shut the door loudly. Michèle remained motionless on the sofa for a moment while she gave her adrenalin and nerves a chance to level out. Finally, when it seemed that Charlie was not going to return, she leaned back into the sofa and proceeded to watch TV. Every muscle in her body however, was still on alert and she hardly moved or breathed for a bit longer until she felt that the friction between them had diffused. Now that he was gone she sensed her own desire to leave – as if the entire charade between them had been about ids and super egos and her desire to leave on her own good terms and not by his rejection. She sat there little proud of her actions that paralleled an image of her with that of the shrew from Shakespeare's "Taming of the Shrew". It was enough to convince herself to get up and go, having already satisfied Psychology that it would be on copacetic terms. Maybe Charlie was aware of this mental chip and had afforded her the solitude to do it on her own? That thought almost provoked a halt in her intention to leave, but she stood up all the same. Then, as if her thoughts had kept her idle for a fraction of a moment too long, she heard Charlie suddenly marching down the hall towards her:* 'I want you to leave please,' *he said emphatically. He hadn't waited long enough. This time he collected her black briefcase that was sitting open on the floor next to the Ikea chair, opened the door again and held the bag out to her. She looked at him. He was going out. She could tell:* 'Charlie?' *she said pleadingly.* 'Nah,' *he said,* 'here!' *then giving her the bag. It was hitting half past twelve and it occurred to her that his craving was in full demand. She had thirty minutes to weather the storm and if he still insisted afterwards, then she would go. At least that's what she told herself. If anything, Charlie was probably just as indignant, at not being able to go to bed on his terms in his own home. He'd given* her a chance to go without his insistence, but she'd missed the open window. The juxtaposition of her behaviour with his was remarkable. Who was in deeper, him or her? She rested the bag on the Ikea chair and without further ado for anything, let her passion go unchecked, blind all reason and as if she were a wound up car, suddenly walked towards him and past him in direction of his bedroom. The look of sheer relief and shock in his face were simultaneous with her movements. '¡¿Dondé vas?! (Where are you going?!),' he asked emphatically from the open door.

'I need to disconnect from there and think,' she answered as she walked steadfastly into his room. '30 minutes,' she hummed to herself. She heard the door bang closed and Charlie muttering in Mayürqan. 'Fine. You want me to go out? I'll go out. You can stay here on your own – O.K.!?' He ranted from the TV room. Touché. He was going to make it her fault if he went out. She stood strategically between the bedroom window behind her and the bed in front her with a full view of the hall before her. Her mind raced, her heart pumped and her hands were cold. She stood there in darkness with only the hall light to give definition of her presence in his room, lost in a reverie of what was going on between them and hardly capable of understanding it. The hood of her jacket had somehow found its way over her head, briefly comforting her and giving her a parabolic image of herself as little red riding hood in a black hood holding out in grandma's cupboard, while the injured wolf howled from the TV room. She stood still and said nothing. She just wanted her presence to be felt for the next twenty minutes. Charlie on the other hand was provoked by her silence and came up the hall towards the bedroom. 'You're in MY room. I want you out of my room,' he growled from the doorway. She obliged his request and walked right past him back to the TV room while she sensed Charlie following behind her. As she trotted back down the hall a paradoxical feeling of déjà vu swam across her stomach while her mind's eye laughed at the visual of her and Charlie doing a *"Tom and Jerry"* chase in his house. Then her super ego vexed her with the realisation of having possibly arrived at the same point that Charlie had already known with his wife? Was Michèle going to end up throwing an ashtray at him too? 'Gawd – fifteen more minutes!' she insisted to herself. When she got to the TV room, she veered into the kitchen, walked through it to the hall again, and headed back up to the bedroom. Charlie however stayed in the TV room. Silence. Then she heard the sound of Charlie's belt buckle clank as he proceeded to put his jeans on. He was heading out. She'd forced the issue too much and was about to pay for it. She watched him from her position behind the bed as he continued to get dressed and sound his final warning, 'Let's go!' and reached for her briefcase at the same ti–. 'Crash!'

Charlie had picked up her bag abruptly causing elements in the open bag to fall out onto the floor. One in particular was a mini tape recorder. 'Are you taping ME!?' he accused from down the hall… Life's volatility smacked her in the face. The thirty minute craving was no longer the issue. Now she was faced with blackmail and deceit issues by way of Charlie's perjured insinuations. Her heart sank and all adrenalin began to flood away from her system. Charlie came back to the bedroom and faced her from the other side of the bed. They stood there face to face at a loss for words with only the bed between them. Neither one of them wanted to hurt the other. Neither one of them wanted to attack or criticise the other. Still Charlie was the one being traumatised in his own home and now had more reason to doubt her because of the tape recorder. She looked at his eyes that were filled with rage and obvious hurt. He was really confused by her actions and her evasive antics were all to blame. She looked at him through the dark of the room and then at the bed that was now off limits to her and where Vanesa had only recently been. He'd become very guarded about the bedroom since his relationship with V signalling to her that much had gone on it the room and caused Michèle to feel oddly removed, when only months earlier it had been in the same bed where she and Charlie had chatted

together about her and how he had said it was "all under control"...
The physical stand-off between Michèle and Charlie and the issue of him being undermined by the female spell instantly recalled her memory to when she was seventeen and sharing a paradox situation with her father from the laundry room in the basement of their home ...
.. 'Go live with your mother!' he sounded at her.
'I don't want to live with my mother!' she countered.
'I'm asking you to live with your mother Michèle.' Her father's words were delivered with a mixture of vehement bile and valiant courage at trying to let go of something he loved. They were difficult years; her brothers had become more flexible and swung freely between their parents' homes until much of their belongings eventually shifted to their mother's place. It provoked an overwhelming sensation of injustice from her dad when he saw himself as the one dedicated to raising his kids, while their mother managed to get on with her life at his expense and still earn their sons' deference by way of her unrestricting lifestyle of live and let live. Even though he shared her mother's philosophy, he felt that such a right was still premature for two boys hardly into their teens. He was a man of great depth and perception, yet the boy in him came out; it was astonishing to see what chained love could do to a person. Her father had lived a life conflicted by an incessant whispering debate between his head and heart. His desire to get on with his life was clearer if not greater than her mother's yet his weakness lived in his conscious, his depth and confused love for a woman he so wanted to be freed from. He might have asked Michèle to leave with the sincere desire to be left alone, but the request to her had felt forced, as if an underlying one just wanted some sign of deference from his sons to him, acknowledging him as the one who stood by them. It was the caretaker's dilemma of needing some kind of affirmation against the shame of revealing the need. Even she needed to be freed from her devotion to her father, but she was waiting until another reason other than her mother, took her away. Such that she stood her ground faced her father and bore the slings and

arrows of his pain: 'You're an arrogant pain in the ass Michèle!' the stab went deep and her eyes stung with his words.

'I might be a pain in the ass,' she retorted, 'but I'm here!' she returned.

'You'd be better off at your mother's with your brothers,' he flew back at her.

'That's bull shit!' she darted back, 'I'll be better off when I'm able to live on my own; I'm not here just because of you okay. So you can vanquish that guilt from your system! It's the natural course of things daddy, that's going to send me away, not changing parental disciplines and you know it!' she challenged. 'How dare you,' she continued, 'act brave in front of me by testing my loyalties to you! How dare you dismiss your own truth that you have been a very good parent under very difficult circumstances daddy! If the guys hurt you by doing their own thing it is because they have become the human beings that you have wanted them to be: independent, self-assured, and honest! "Careful what you wish for" daddy because you got it! We're a reflection of your work and your ability to allow our mother into our lives daddy! So if I'm a pain in the ass it's because you gave me the courage to BE one!!' Her voice had risen to an all-time high to camouflage the hurt she'd felt from her dad's searing comment. She was truly angry and tired of his emotional bull shit. It was no lie that her reasons for staying with him also included motives that she'd assessed as being in her better interest. She was seventeen and needed to finish high school. Her dad's home was more conducive to live at than the place where her mother lived on the other side of town. Her jobs and school were closer to her dad's place than her mother's and above all, her mother was fine without her. That was her mother's unintentional gift: emotional independence. Love without a price. The energy was pure and shared without guilt. Although it bred a personal solidarity to oneself, it empowered strength and confidence too; living with her mother would have diminished those virtues between them, challenged her loyalty issues for her father

and over all have been more of a betrayal to herself than anyone else. He stood across from her by the dryer while she was standing on the penultimate step of the stairs that descended to the basement. 'I hate that woman for fucking with my life!' he hissed… She looked at her father and started to feel the tired effects of an abating adrenalin, turned around and headed back up the stairs while the sound of her voice trailed behind her: 'I'm sorry dad if I hurt you, but live what you've taught us – let go of the rest.' Then when she got to the top of the stairs she paused and stared back down the steps to him still standing by the dryer: 'We're living proof that you and mum have done well daddy. Feel good about that,' she ended calmly. That standoff with her father had ended with him taking off for a drive in his car while that interlude offered her a moment of great relief by going to her bedroom and letting her tears flow to alleviate her pent up anxiety long enough to make Alice in Wonderland's flood of tears look like a puddle. Her father's comment left her wondering if maybe her head-to-head with those she loved was a parable of her being an opinionated self-righteous pain in the ass? The notion was short lived however, because he returned a few hours later and invited her out for chicken wings. 'You don't have to dad,' she said feeling that his reasons were spurred on by guilt and not a real desire to have chicken wings with her. Her dad looked at her directly through clear brown eyes and with a slight smirk, knowing that it was now her game of cat and mouse. 'C'mon,' he said, and added coolly: 'Sometimes the truth hurts Michèle.' 'No kidding,' she replied while they both headed to the car feeling a sense of post-triumph and renewed synergy from their little battle of words in the basement …

'Michèle I want you to go,' Charlie's voice brought her back from her recollection to the reality of their moment. He'd kneeled one leg onto the bed and reached across to grab her left arm. The action of his minute force surprised her and even surprised him that he let go as soon as he'd done it. Nonetheless, it made it clear that things were getting out of hand. The two of them were in his room in pitch darkness except for the

hall light that highlighted their silhouettes near the bed. She was standing back against the window visible only by her hair that spiralled rebelliously from beneath the hood that covered it. She felt so petite standing in the shadows and terribly sad that she was causing Charlie so much anxiety too. Yet all logic took her by force and emotion aside, she stood by what she believed had to be done like a person who agrees to shoot a lamed horse. She looked at Charlie and shook her head ever so lightly within the confiniments of her black hood: 'Charlie,' she was hardly audible, 'I'm sorry. I can't go just yet. I promise to go in a few minutes. I just need to calm down – o.k.?' Her words seem to work and without saying anything more, he got up from his position on the bed with an air of fatigue in his gesture and returned to the TV room. She took in a deep breath pushed the hood back from her head and sent a mental request to Life for forgiveness, if she was in the wrong. Then she slowly walked back to the TV room too. He was back, sprawled out along the sofa, the tape recorder was on the table and she sat back into the Ikea chair. 'The tape recorder is for me, nothing else,' she said quietly. No reply. The time on her telephone read 1:15am. More than thirty minutes had gone by since their dance between rooms and Charlie was either resigned or simply calmer. Finally she spoke: 'I'm going now Charlie. Thank you for putting up with me; if you go out, no big deal. It would be good to try and leave here by 9a.m. tomorrow, otherwise just send me a sms alright.' He said nothing but nodded slowly, while his arms were tightly crossed to control his anger. She ignored it, got up, stepped over to him and gave him a kiss on the cheek. 'It's not about you o.k., it's about me,' she said gently. He'd remained silent, but she left feeling slightly better at having expressed herself and awed at the charades they had experienced when in the end she no longer cared if he went out or not. She'd have got her money for the plane ticket back from him and frankly, if it didn't matter to him, then why should she care!?... Because it did matter to him, and she knew it ... In hindsight Michèle was not happy about her behaviour. It entered the definition of co-addiction in a way that sent off alarm bells in her head. The need for Charlie to get away was no longer just for his benefit, but for both of them. 'Are you hungry?' he voiced over the noise in the car. She looked at the clock on the dashboard that read 1:30p.m. 'Sure,' she said, 'do you want to stop somewhere?' she sounded back. He gave her a nod and then said to her evasively while watching the traffic that he would turn off at the following exit where he felt corresponded with their final destination in Guadarrama. She affirmed his idea with a corresponding nod and the two of them watched the road intently as they drove off the main highway into a side road lined by mountain peaks and trees. They finally got to a round-about that displayed a sign indicating the way to Guadarrama town. Next to it was a restaurant called "El Cubano" that appeared to be a good place to stop and have lunch. It was warm and sunny when they stepped down from the car, coupled with natural surroundings that seemed to rejuvenate them both. In so much that despite Charlie's cloudy and negative state of mind, he still seemed to be enjoying the journey. They never talked about the night before, as if it had never happened or simply didn't matter, but Charlie had picked her up sharply at 9a.m. and they'd got to the airport without any of the mad rush they had experienced before. Michèle filed the memory of it away, as just another notch in strengthening their friendship, similar to the many ones she had with her childhood best friends and family, who had become her most important warriors in life. Conflict, she trusted, was not unhealthy if it was diffused constructively. It permitted the power of forgiving and apologising to be tested as well as one's own spiritual development. In the end it simply taught how to defend oneself, without fighting, much like the principles of martial arts. Her thoughts floated from the night before to the restaurant in front of them. Inside the place was empty while a small staff prepared its tables for the lunch rush. They were given a table with a wide window view of the road and the mountains behind it. The food was good and while they had lunch Charlie called the rehab centre to confirm directions and their arrival which was scheduled after lunch at 4p.m. At that point Charlie's behaviour was cool and critical. Michèle said very little to him. He seemed content to have her presence as long as she did not open her mouth. After lunch they headed into the town of Guadarrama, which was only ten minutes away from where they'd had lunch, so that once they got there, it was still early. They decided to park and went into one of the local bars for a coffee in order to kill some time. The bar shared similar traits with the one they'd been to in Alcalá de Guadaira when they'd been to Seville; high ceilings, with a long bar and lots of peanut shells on the floor. Then as if to offer a silver lining to Michèle's concerns about their trip, the woman behind the bar just happened to be married to a Canadian! Holy cow! The coincidence was just that, but well received by Michèle, who was willing to accept any kind of morsel that Life was still on her side. At half past three, they climbed back into the car and drove to the centre early, to ensure their arrival on time. When they finally found the place, Charlie parked the car under a few trees and the two of them stayed sitting there until it was time to meet the representative of the centre. 'What do you think?' she asked him. The place was definitely nicer and better located than the one they'd seen in Seville. It was a large house made out of whitewashed wood panelling, and adjoining bungalow buildings, with a modest but clean pool, snuggly situated in what appeared to be a good residential area at the base of the mountains. 'I don't know. It's nothing like Hipócrates,' he said casually. Both their car door windows were open and the air felt warm and invigorating. Charlie was comfortably stretched out in the driver's seat while she sat next to him on the passenger side. 'You know Charlie,' she began, 'maybe a place like this one is better for you. It's not luxury, but it will definitely make you think. Plus it's a bit farther away from Mayürqa? I dunno, what's that saying?' she pretended to search, '"all that glitters isn't gold?".'

'Nah,' he answered amused, 'all that is gold does not glitter.'

It was true that she was sceptical about Hipócrates. However her main point of contention was that Charlie made his own decision, convinced by his own arguments and her role as the devil's advocate. It seemed to be a nice way for him to wager things. He rarely if ever, made a decision or commitment that he did not follow through on. She knew this and hoped the next one he made would at least be an educated one rather than a frivolous one. By a few minutes to four she and Charlie sauntered down to the house entrance. The place was definitely not fancy. They crossed paths with a man slightly younger than Charlie who directed them to the reception area of the centre. As they passed the front gate area they scanned the premises, while Michèle watched Charlie's eyes give off a resigned glimmer that suggested that he'd already decided against the place. An open hut from the left of the entranceway appeared to be a gym with three stationary bikes that needed maintenance, two long mirrors, one with a crack in it, and the weights and barbells were scattered across the floor. The actual reception building resembled nothing less than a fraternity building. It had a common room with a shabby couch, a library that hosted one book shelf with bits and pieces of reading material and an office with nobody in it. Finally, a young blond woman similar to a petite Dolly Parton appeared and introduced herself as one of the centre's therapists. During that interview Charlie seemed more alert and relaxed than he was in Seville. Although it was clear that he had no intention of staying there he still asked questions about the centre and its methodology. There were books and workbooks for each patient. Class hours covered practical and theoretical life skills and philosophies. Above all the patient was asked to stay with the centre completely segregated from his or her life at home for at least three months.

Michèle liked it. There were books, and a desire to locate the source of the addiction; not just get over the addiction. Distance from life at home and self-reflection were the key tools and she liked it; never mind the fact that if it took her a lifetime to learn about herself; asking an addict to try it in six months was asking a lot. They left the place within a half hour of getting there, drove back to the airport, returned the car and still had time for a coffee by the gate before boarding. The trip went quite well for both of them. It was not until they got back to Mayürqa and into the Phedra that Charlie made a casual revelation that made Michèle's hopes sore: 'If I go to a place like that I might as well drive out to an empty field in the middle of nowhere, live there for six months on my own and its all the same!' he said sarcastically. 'Ding, ding, ding,' she responded softly, 'I don't care what Hipócrates says, it's medically too puritanical about addiction being solely a bio-chemical illness without an emotional reason. I think that there's always an emotional reason Charlie, 'cause that's what addiction feeds on! – No? I don't believe it's just a chemical imbalance, or a bad love affair with coke like you think. I know shit about shit but ask yourself, why you got involved with *her* in the first place?'

'I don't know,' he hesitated, 'I was attracted to her.'

'You only let attraction mess you up when you're missing something inside,' she conjectured.

'No lo sé (I don't know),' he sighed out as he focused his thoughts towards the road ahead of them. She said no more. He was going to Hipócrates – she could feel it, but their chat had somehow perturbed her. It somehow pointed the finger at her, as much as it did at him. Which was worse? Not knowing what the void was from, or knowing, and not being able to fill it?

Not all who wander are lost.
Frodo: I cannot do this alone.
Galadrial: This task was appointed to you
and if you do not find a way, no one will.
Frodo: I know what I must do, it's just that.., I'm afraid to do it.
Galadrial: You are a Ring-bearer, Frodo.
To bear a Ring of Power is to be alone.
Frodo: Go back, Sam. I'm going to Mordor alone.
Sam: Of course you are and I'm coming with you.
Frodo: I wish the ring had never come to me.
I wish none of this had happened.
Galadrial: So do all who live to see such times, but that is not for them to decide. All we have to decide is what to do with the time that is given to us. Remember Frodo, the ring will always try to get back to its master. It wants to be found. Your quest stands upon the edge of a knife. Stray but a little and it will fail. Yet hope remains, while the Company is true. There are other forces at work in this world Frodo, besides the will of evil and that is an encouraging thought.
'THE LORD OF THE RINGS: THE FELLOWSHIP OF THE RINGS – J.R.R. TOLKIEN. EXCERPT ADAPTED

The Ring

April 18th

She was driving back to Sa Ema from the airport after having changed their date of departure from the 18th to the 20th. Originally, she and Charlie were supposed to be in Barcelona that day. A few days after their trip to Madrid Charlie made his decision and gave Michèle the okay to purchase their plane tickets to Barcelona. 'Want to go with me and see the place?' he asked her from a sitting position on the sofa. She was really pleased by his offer. She wanted to go with him, but had not asked or alluded to it. 'I'll take care of the ticket,' he added. 'Well yea. I'd like to see the place,' she said coolly. 'I'll pay for my ticket 'cause it's my choice, but if you can cover the taxi fees that would be great.' He gave her a nod and that was that. He'd called Hipócrates on the Wednesday after Madrid to enquire about availability to which they said that they would call him back to let him know. Later that day she and Charlie had a coffee with his sister, who'd made an unexpected visit from Juniper to see him.

Then, the day after on Thursday, Hipócrates called Charlie to say that a patient was leaving and that Charlie could have that patient's spot as early as the upcoming Monday. Timing. It was all timing and Michèle could see that it was still on his side. It took Charlie a day to finally muster up the decision to call them and confirm his arrival on the 18th. When he gave Michèle the go ahead for the tickets, an excited energy impetuously soared inside her until it reached its limit just inside her mouth, where she decided to keep it a bay until they were actually on the plane to Barcelona. Even though he'd made the decision it was not enough to convince her to let up. So when Charlie went out that same night and did not return to Sa Ema until 9:30a.m. the next day, she was waiting for him in the Mini at the entrance-way; prepared with a pretext about his passport and a focused intent on making her presence an unwanted reality check for him, a soon as he drove in. Needless to say he was perturbed when he saw her and slowed down only because she flagged him down. When she got to the driver's window of the Phedra, Charlie had a tube glass filled halfway with what looked like a whiskey and cola mix, snuggled between his legs, while his body odour exuded the scent of sweet alcohol. He looked at her with a tired and heavy head while his eyes expressed nothing less than contempt at her. '¡Que!' he said sharply. She smiled and said: 'Nothing Charlie. I'm going to Palma to pick up the tickets and I couldn't find your passport at your place – is it in the door?' He eyed her sceptically then looked down at the driver's door and retrieved the passport for her. 'Thanks,' she said smiling at him. She'd known that it was there and he knew that she'd known. Yet despite her nerves and his obvious disdain with her, a rapid thought of herself as the girl who loved the Beast from the story "Beauty and the Beast" caught her by surprise and unintentionally provoked a smile to part her lips and the mental chip she needed to deflect his anger. Then as soon as she stood back from the Phedra, Charlie just drove off.

The next few days following that one, she acted cool on the outside, while butterflies in her stomach went on a 48hr flight that kept her anxiety levels at an all-time high. While the fact that Charlie had made the call remained a truth that she felt confident he would not back away from, he still spent no time in taking advantage of his final days going out at eleven at night and getting home the next day by nine or nine thirty in the morning. His plan of his departure should have been enough to relieve her. However instead, she was stimulated to be on a 24 hour alert mode by wonderful thoughts like '*Wouldn't it be ironic that just before he leaves he overdoses!*'

In the meantime she tried to keep herself distracted with other things, like getting the tickets and finishing the tape that had been in the tape recorder that Charlie had discovered in her briefcase the night before they'd left for Madrid. The tape was in fact a gift for Charlie for when and if he got to rehab. Initially, she'd come up with the idea of them taping their chats so that he could recall his dark moments as reminders whenever he might feel teased by a desire to relapse. However they shared little time together anymore and the prospects of Charlie ever wanting to face his past so directly once he got past it was probably expecting too much. So she forwent that idea and asked members of his family to tape individual messages to him as a "go get 'em" going away tape instead. The task had not been easy. No one showed the least bit of interest. Rather than just go for it, they resisted and offered feedback that he would not listen to it and that more than likely the rehab centre would not allow for it. Even if it was their way of side stepping shyness or keeping Michèle's hopes down to a minimum, it was a complete tug and pull until she convinced them to at least humour the idea and let Charlie and the rehab centre make their own decision about it later. In the end, Charlie's seventy-six year old mother would have taken up the entire "A" side of the tape, if his sister hadn't said so much too. Even Elisabet made a polite effort and went to the patio to tape her message. Once again the women in Charlie's life motivated him, and frankly, what man has not ever been? Even Christ had supposedly had *a close circle of women around him, especially one, Maria Magdalena, who was said to have been his most intimate disciple and advisor. She noticed it again. The dichotomy of women and their role in life, as mandated to them by Life. Suddenly the name of Christ and the man himself, seemed to highlight a pseudo significance to her: it was "Christopher", or "Christ-of-her" that appeared as being synonymous with "love" and "suffering". Where "her" could represent her dad's love for her mother, Charlie's relationship with his wife and overall any man's love for, or his suffering by, a woman … deep. Why? Her mind went into orbit and she saw "M" power on two legs or "W" power on its shoulders, suggest a need to have the stellar power of "Man" and "Woman" finely synchronized. It was "Yin-Yang" at its subtle best. Like it or lump it, the "M" and the "W" were one in the same. If the female spirit could give life then its antecedent spirit, the male one, could take it away. The checks and balances of Life were clear: if one spirit abused its power then the other could counter it. Leading her to wonder why individuals of opposite spirits, would wish for equal rights to such burdens of responsibility? The bottom line was to recognise the power of each one – not claim it. …*

All reverie aside, she also wondered if Charlie and his brothers practiced an innocent rivalry among themselves, where Charlie needed to defy the men in his life as the favoured baby brother while they enjoyed using it against him, because of their own inability to live independently as he did, even though they'd received the same support from women as Charlie had. Especially in adulthood, when the innocence of their tease, could turn into a quiet envy towards him and his ability to cordially live out the nature of his instincts, still be cared for by a little harem of women in a way that many men quietly imagine for themselves, but so few had the courage to realise by reason of its possible consequences. A lot of people talked about freedom, but were afraid to let go; maybe because a lot of people really don't know their truth. Notwithstanding that, few trusted it. Unaware that it was precisely that knowledge that albeit still provoked consequences, was often synonymous with temporary setbacks void of regret. It was the difference between living-out one's envy or living-out one's truth. At least that's what she hoped, because Charlie had sent her an sms on the 17th, letting her know that he was not going to leave on the 18th after all … *When she'd seen the message she replied: "Something up?" and he replied: "Yes." She went over to his place that afternoon and he explained to her that he wanted to see his son before he left. She did not know, if it was a delaying tactic on his part or not, but the reason was a valid one. 'Can you still go to Hipócrates on Tuesday then?' she asked. 'Yea,' he answered confidently, 'I'll give Meralda a call – she's partial to me.'* …

It had been frustrating to say the least. It meant that Michèle had to go to the airport the next day in order to change the date and possibly pay a penalty fee doing it. Never mind the fact that there were no guarantees of another flight. Worst of all, she expected that his family would take little time underlining their scepticism by telling her that they were right and that he wasn't going anywhere at all. She looked at Charlie, who was standing over by the bay windows with his back to her and looking out at the sea. If anything, what made her angry was them. They were not supporters, or maybe she was just frustrated as a whole and looking for a scapegoat for the fear and lack of control she was feeling from prostitutes, a divorced woman that communicated with him incessantly, family rhetoric and wife dramas. Her only manageable foes were the cocaine and herself, while the only silent partner she felt she had, was his son. 'Were you able to confirm the visit with his mother?' she asked carefully from behind him. 'Nah, she's not answering her phone,' he said dryly. She almost wished she hadn't asked. It would have stoked more anxiety in him for sure. It certainly did in her. She looked at him and wanted to give him a hug. It was Sunday afternoon and in a few days not only was Charlie's life going to change, but so was hers. She focused on him as if to take a mental shot for her memory: the light from outside was transparent and cast a soft hue around Charlie's silhouette. His posture was erect, while his hands were plunged deep into his jean pockets sending her a rapid visual of what she thought a Norman Rockwell would transmit of a tragic hero standing in a pensive mood. He was thin – Still attractive but very thin. His jeans no longer hugged his buttocks and his legs had shed their power from his thighs. He often stood in front of the bay window like that, as if searching for something or in expectation of something, to find him. He didn't speak, he just looked out, as if the time in front of the sea was the energy and the answer he needed to give him assurance and courage to follow through with whatever overwhelming plan was ahead of him. He was apprehensive; anxious. Decided, then cool with it all. He was Charlie before the storm. ... She turned into Sa Ema when it suddenly occurred to her that her ring from Charlie was not on her right hand. She looked at her left one. A slight nausea swam across her spirit as she slowed the Mini to a stop, sighed deeply like someone who'd just received an undesired but impending confirmation about something, and then as if it were standard protocol, began searching for it in the car. Nowhere. It was nowhere to be found. Neither on her, or anywhere in the car. Her state of mind went motionless for a moment as she stared past the passenger window into Spring's fields flushed with wild daisies and red poppies. Then, she let go and let her mind race backwards into time as an attempt to recall where she might have lost it, or taken it off; the airport? Palma downtown where she'd stopped for coffee? The bathroom? Where? Then it came to her like a bitter sweet recollection. She'd slipped it off her finger and placed it on her lap in order to avoid getting it caught in her hair when she'd tied it back. The visual came in clearer by the second making her realise that her mind must have been really distracted. She'd probably tied her hair and then proceeded to start the car, headed into Palma without remembering about the ring on her lap. She more than likely lost it, when she'd got out of the car for coffee. The ring was in Palma, lying somewhere in the street where she'd parked. She wanted to scream, but nothing came out. She wanted to cry, but her system went dry instantly. She was emotionally void from the sensation of irreversible finality. She'd lost the ring. She was neither surprised nor comforted by her thoughts. Had she projected its loss or was it a premonition? '*Fuck fuck, fuck,*' she thought, but even the emphasis on swearing did not satisfy. She was hollow. An urge to drive back to Palma crossed her mind, but it was getting late. Besides, her expectation of losing the ring was connected to something more than just its loss: she was going to lose Charlie. Her imagined prophecy that Charlie would be next to lose his ring came back to her. *Then, if he got past rehab the true test of her lip-service to him would begin, when it would be up to Charlie, feeling like a toad in his sobriety and no longer handsome from the cocaine, to ask her for the same kiss that he'd requested in December 2004. Like the frog that just needed to accept being loved as the toad he thought he was, to having the confidence to ask her for a kiss, only to instantly discover that he was a prince.* A slight smile broke from her dramatic conjectures. In many ways losing the rings might have been a symbolic way of keeping their cocaine experience together, behind them. While giving them the freedom to move forward towards reaching their personal quests, together or not. Yet in spite of her conclusions, the ring still made her feel an obsessive need to find it and she considered going to Palma early the next morning to retrace her steps. She started up the Mini and typed an sms to Charlie: "I've got the tickets. Wednesday morning," then sent it hoping at the same time that he'd been able to see his son that day. Then she drove-on to her place where she still had to get ready for an invitation to a Chinese dinner with Mitx and Elisabet. It was Monday April 18th, 2005. They were all going out to celebrate Mitx and Elisabet's son's seventeenth birthday,

Charlie was going out with his friends to say goodbye and Michèle's ring was probably lost somewhere for good. With any luck, she thought wryly, Charlie's ring would be too.

Discovering
The light and the shadow of your life
I allowed my heart to beat for you
Relieved for having at least brushed by you
In this life
As you must be too
For having found and caressed perhaps
The woman of your soul.
[*A conocer la luz y la sombra de tu vida/ Deje que mi corazón lata para ti/ Aliviada de haberte rozado en esta vida/ Como tú lo debes de ser también/ Por haber encontrado y acariciado la mujer, tal vez/ De tu alma*]
'MUJER DE TU ALMA' (WOMAN OF YOUR SOUL) – M.

Sa M de Farrutx

Farrutx' M

April 19, 8:20 p.m. She's sitting on the ledge outside the open bay windows from Charlie's TV room that positions her in front of the sea and the mountains beyond. She is sitting there with agenda and pen on her lap while Charlie is on the sofa enjoying the view of the sea beyond them. This time together is theirs and possibly their last. She feels this and the knowledge of this makes her senses all the more acute and attentive to the moment. The dishes are done, the place is tidy and his clothes are dry-cleaned, while the carry-on by the door is on standby to be packed for Charlie's departure to Hipócrates the next day. *May he go, may this year be his! – may it be so!* She feels well. Inspired by the beautiful closing of the day. The sea is very calm and she can hear it ever so lightly as it washes into shore, over the rocks and laps back unto itself again. The sound reminds her of other places where she has lived before and makes her wonder again, how she ever got to, never mind found Sa Ema de Farrutx? The sky is into dusk offering a cotton candy coloured blue canvas with wisps of pink cotton candy clouds stretched in wads across it. She also hears a cricket, or is it a frog in the background? A blended aroma of sweet grass and dry seaweed sweeps by them on a casual breeze and makes its presence known within the white cotton curtains that flutter independently here and there between the TV room and the open windows. The mountains do not move. They are solid and strongly blended with ash-grey and red-purple colours; partly groomed with a layer of moss green flora. They are there in the distance, silent, majestic and unmoving, defined by a jagged profile that ever so slightly resembles a serene woman lying on her back and casually dips into the apex of an "M" centred between her breast and her belly. It's all so pretty. So tranquil. So well. It is dusk by virtue of the pink and yellow hues of daylight. A cool night is approaching while spring is already here.

Fall down to the ground so deep; you think you won't get out
But with the months you realise; you get up and start again
And the force of falling a lot, then back to getting up
You see that things don't change
Except you're already not, who you were before
So I've already been 5 or 6; now I'm he who thinks
I don't want to think what tomorrow brings
My thoughts always look into the present
Don't conjugate other tenses, of what I'll do
What I'm not going to do
So today or maybe tomorrow; I'll be here or I'll be there
I'll be a piece of the universe that doesn't notice the passing of time
That which I do in every instant, is the effort that overwhelms me
I don't want to think on what will happen tomorrow
Jump at each instant – It's unique; it won't repeat itself
And it tells me to jump; not to think about all that will come
That a pencil never draws
Without a hand.

[Caus a terra molt avall, – Croixs que no te'n sortiràs / Però amb els mesos te n'adones que tornes a començar / I a força de molt caure – i de tornar–te a aixecar / Veus que les coses no canvien però ja no ets qui eres abans / Doncs he estat ja cinc o sis, – i sóc el que ara tinc/ No vull pensar en el que arribarà demà./ I per què els meus pensaments, que sempre viuen en present/ No conjuguen altres temps – que el "ja faré el que no vaig fer"/ Doncs avui o potser demà seré aquí o seré per allà/ Seré un tros de l'univers, que no nota el pas del temps/ El que faig a cada instant – és la força que em fa gran/ No vull pensar – en el que arribarà demà/ Llenca't, cada instant – És únic no es repetirà/ I diu que em llenci/ Que no pensi en tot el que vindrà/ Que un llapis mai no/ Dibuixa sense una mà.]

'LLENÇAT' (JUMP) – LAX'N BUSTO, LYRICS ADAPTED

El Paso

The step

'Charlie do you know the story about the Man and the boy?' she asked him while they were hanging out at his place. He lightly shook his head. 'Well, a man and a boy were standing at the edge of a chasm looking out as far as their eyes could see, when the boy asked the man: 'How wide is a chasm?' The man replied: 'Jump and find out.' 'It's a chasm!' exclaimed the boy, to which the man answered: '"*Don't be afraid to take a big step if one is indicated; you can't cross it in two small jumps."' So the boy with all his might put all his effort towards one big jump *and LEAPED forward! ... Only to land instantly and discover that it was not so wide, after all.'* – **DAVID LLOYD GEORGE.*

Wednesday April 20th. 2005. 7a.m. – 'Charlie?' she whispered from behind his bedroom door. 'Charlie?'… Nothing save for the deep rhythm of his breathing. 'Charl*ie*?' she whispered again.

A movement. 'Charlie, it's 7a.m., it's time to wake up,' she added slightly more audibly. Michèle had been awake off and on since 5a.m. She'd slept at Charlie's place in the extra room, but the advent of the day's agenda had kept her nervous and unable to sleep well. Charlie had returned from his farewell get together around 9:30 in the morning on Tuesday, and had stayed-in all day and night after that. Michèle had arrived at his place close to 6:30p.m. that Tuesday evening, and the two of them just hung out casually, until she finally went to bed at 10p.m. Although Charlie seemed to have been satiated by his farewell and the afternoon with his son on Monday, Michèle still remained on alert until she finally heard the quiet sound of his breathing hum from beyond his bedroom door. It must have been about 1:30a.m when she finally heard it. Until then Charlie had stayed pretty much close to the sofa; responding to an incessant number of messages and calls to his phone, that according to him were mostly by the pinocho woman and only a few from Vanesa. Then she heard a few more calls that sounded as though they were from the pinocho woman again, another few from friends, while the rest were conversations with his mother and his family. Finally into late evening, a sms arrived from Elisabet to Michèle's phone offering the two of them "a good trip." '*Thank you for Isa,*' she'd thought to herself, as she sent off a "Thank you" reply.

Up until that moment, little if any moral support had been directed her way, making those few words well appreciated. Charlie had been pretty much quiet the whole time. Sometimes he got up to fish something from the kitchen, or to organise the CDs that were on the larger table by the TV. He watched TV, stood by the bay windows staring out at the sea, lay on the sofa, cleared his nose and smoked his cigarettes in a methodical silence that compared to a warrior's contemplative moment before going into battle. Everything was set to go. By 7p.m. she'd asked for Charlie's permission to set out his clothes and things for him to peruse before packing; he still had not done anything related to that and the following morning at 7a.m. was going to be too late. She would normally have gone with his flow, but he was neither here nor there in thought. So that her desire to get it all done then and there, antagonised his tranquillity, but she simply did not want to go through a repeated version of last minute dramas with him, if it could be avoided, as Charlie would probably end up organising and doing at his own pace anyway. Hipócrates was a good example of that: it had told him Monday and in the end he had decided to go on the Wednesday. That was Charlie. He was a focused individual even with a fogged up head and his decision to go on the Wednesday was in fact wise by reason of the final details he'd wanted and managed to tie up before his departure. That was her experience with him. He did things his way and if he could help it, rarely deviated from his word. This time, however, she didn't want to take any chances that he or the addiction would delay them to the point of aborting their mission. By the time she'd finally gone to bed, Charlie had offered little concern about her choices and suggestions to him about the packing, so that she'd managed to prep one large and one carry-on suitcase for his stay in Barcelona:

'Which black shoes do you want,' she'd asked him?

'It doesn't matter,' he'd answered plainly.

'Charlie – please...,' she'd said softly.

'Okay those ones,' he'd replied from his spot on the sofa.

'Okay, how many shirts?' She'd returned with her options in hand, 'two of each colour? – Ok?'

'Ok,' he'd said. 'If possible,' he'd added politely, 'can you pull out a blue pair of summer pants and my white cotton shirt?'

'Yup, already got 'em,' she'd answered. It still hadn't ceased to amaze her at how much of their clothing resembled each other's. Never mind that they enjoyed the same smart-casual styles, but they even had the same kinds of summer cotton pants and shirts and in the same colours too. Even her white shirt which was a man's shirt could have been a perfect swap for Charlie's. Clothing trends were pretty generic across the globe, so it really was not a big deal except for a small realisation that the clothing items were purchased before they'd ever met; lifestyles and years apart from each other...

..'Charlie..? Wake up okay...it's 7a.m.,' she repeated lightly through the door.

'What time is it?' he asked groggily.

'It's sev'– ten after seven,' she corrected. Her heart had begun to pump. They were still on time, but Charlie still had to shower, get dressed and finalise his inspection of the packing all by 8a.m. when they had to be on the road. She was already dressed. Black blouse, black dress pants and black ankle boots highlighted by a silver watch, which used to be accompanied by the silver ring from Charlie. She'd gone to Palma the day after losing it and had had no luck finding it; neither at the airport nor the other places that she'd been to the day before. Her only sense of relief at the time came with the possibility that someone else had found it and was enjoying it with renewed energy from having found such a cool ring. Otherwise she was still missing it. 'C'mon Charlie,' she resumed, 'you can do it,' she said. It was hard. Asking Charlie to get up at 7a.m. in the morning with the level of cocaine that was saturated into his system was like asking someone to casually come out of coma. In fact, much of the first few weeks of rehab were about nothing more than isolation, sleep and more sleep. He turned over onto his back and stared at the ceiling waiting for some of his fog to clear. 'What time is it?' he asked again.

'I'm not sure now – a quarter past seven?' she answered from the doorway.

'Look at the phone,' he said. She brushed past the open door and looked at his phone on the side table next to him. 'Yup. 7:15,' she confirmed.

'No puedo Michèle (I can't),' he said seriously. Her insides began to react. The stomach was tightening while her adrenalin had already made her hands go cold.

'Si que puedes Charlie (Yes you can Charlie),' she answered slowly, 'go slow. We're on time .., baby steps o.k.,' she asserted lightly.

'Nahhh – there's no time, I still have to shower,' he groaned.

'Charlie it's only 7:20,' she replied dryly, 'you've done your thing with everyone, made your decision: "Dicho. Hecho (Said and done)," right? – c'mon, Up!' she said in a soft but firm tone.

He'd made himself more comfortable bringing the flannel blankets up over his entire body just under his nose and stared blankly into the air. Michèle stared at the wall behind his bed covered in the yellow sticky notes he'd saved from her since they'd met in November. Her eyes scanned them rapidly trying to find one that she could use, but they'd all been expressed already. She stood there next to his bed, the two of them quiet while simultaneously feeling the anxiety in her, start to bubble. 'Charlie,' she began almost inaudibly, 'I'm very sorry, but there is nothing that you have decided thus far that you have not followed through on your own.., but if we *miss* the plane today, it *will* be the worst day of your life! Get up please, c'mon.' The tone in her voice had moved to a low and quiet growl. Only the stress on *please* alleviated its temperature slightly but nothing more. Her lack of sleep from the night before was turning into the straw on the verge of breaking the camel's back. She was tired, irritable and suddenly very angry and very willing to go into a full communicative battle with him. The warning in her voice must have transmitted well to him because he dully replied with, 'Okay, give me ten minutes.' Her stomach relaxed a little. 'Ok,' she replied coolly and left him alone. It was 7:40 when she heard the clatter of Charlie's belt buckle tell her that he was finally dressed. Then she heard him go out of his room and head into the guest room where the two suitcases she'd prepped were laid open on the bed. Naturally Charlie had to add and or remove things, causing anxiety levels in both her and Charlie to exude into the air and finally combust on impact! '¡Jo*d*er! (Damn!),' he swore emphatically. The little carry-on was suddenly emptied and tossed to the floor because Charlie couldn't fit another pair of shoes in it: 'There's, NO ROOM! In this!!' he exclaimed. 'Use the other suitcase!' he stated in an annoyed but calmer tone. Michèle's jaw tightened as she refrained from saying anything and went for the bigger suitcase. '*He's nervous,*' she spoke to herself, '*he's got a month's worth of white shit in his system – it's a big day today; we're both stressed and tired – hooold on,*' she tried to reason with herself. 'Charlie I was trying to keep your luggage light – you know,' she voiced tersely while he repacked his things. He said nothing and tried to focus on the packing like someone suffering from a very bad hangover and migraine headache at the same time. Then he went back to his bedroom to get more shirts and for some reason decided to change from the navy one that he was wearing to a black one, such that the two of them were both dressed in the same colour and style. She said nothing but enjoyed the subtlety of it. He finally returned to the packing in the guest room while Michèle scanned the bedroom a final time noticing that he had left behind the brown ring box she'd given him from Dubai, the sticky notes on the wall and his son's photo on the side table. She brought the box and the photo to him and he accepted the photo but not the box. It stung her a little, but in all practicality the box was not needed. Besides, he still had the ring she'd given him. So she returned the box to the bedroom and started to make the bed to keep herself calm. It was ten to eight and time to go. Then fate made its call and a sms sounded from his phone on the table. Without even thinking she picked it up and saw V's message: "¿Que haces? (What's up?) Bombon." '*Bombon!?*' her eyes glowered at the word "Bombon" while her heart felt a twinge and her ego drew up arms. Bombon was a way of saying someone was stunning or lovely. '*He calls her his Bombon!?*' Her fatigue clashed with her anger and came out in an act of complete emotional behaviour. Suddenly being a "bombon" was better than being a "flower". She glared at the wall pasted with the yellow sticky notes and felt the sting of rejection inside her, take over Super-ego's attempt to stop her from doing what she'd regret later – It was too late. She took down every one of the little notes, hesitating only slightly to place them in his brown ring box, but then surrendering to evil and crunching them all up into a ball and throwing them into the garbage! Then she marched back into the room to an unexpecting Charlie and roared ever so fiercely: '¡Toma! (Here!),' and planted the brown box and his phone on the bed. 'I may not be your "*BOMBON*",' but you might show some deference to the one who is next to you!' Then stormed back to his bedroom where she immediately felt disgusted with her feline display of jealousy. This was not the way she wanted the day to evolve. Above all Charlie was sincerely oblivious to all of that! Prostitutes, pinochos, bombons, yadi-yadi-ya, were nothing more to him than whimsical play for his ego; not his heart and she knew that! '*Augh!*' She sat there in disgust with herself for a few seconds, until Charlie finally appeared in the doorway. '¿Vamos? (Ready?),' he said calmly.

'Si. Let's go,' she answered in a subdued voice and they headed out. They loaded the Mini, dumped the trash, swung by Mitx and Elisabet's to say goodbye then stopped off at Sa Croix for a quick coffee and a bit of money. '¿Vais de negro hoy? (Going black today?),' queried one of the young waitresses when she noticed that both Charlie and Michèle were dressed in black. Charlie said nothing, but Michèle was amused by the morsel; glad that she hadn't been the only one who'd noticed. By 8:15a.m., they were back on the highway. Their flight was at 9:05 and it normally took Michèle forty-five minutes from Juniper to Palma, which was the main reason why she'd wanted to get an early start, so that she could avoid the pressure of having to drive at the speed of light like Charlie and the Phedra were so accustomed to doing. '*Go Mini go!*' she chanted in her head, '*zoom like a bee!*' So they did. The little Mini left a smear of yellow and black wind behind it, as it drove ferociously between stone hedged walls, along winding narrow roads and arrogantly overtook law abiding drivers on the highway! Even Charlie appeared to be slightly disconcerted at Michèle's obvious lack of patience for even the politest driver. 'Tr*an*qu*ii*la,' he said to her calmly, while fidgeting with the ring she'd given him. She gave him a sideway glance; how come he could drive like a bat out hell but not her? Still it was enough to make her feel self-conscious and she slowed down only slightly. 'Charlie,' she sounded over the hum of the car and the crackle of music from the radio, 'I want to apologise for my antics this morning.' She glanced at him quickly, but he said nothing and stayed focused on the ring. 'I'm afraid I let my emotions get the better of me. Even though I understand the logistics to all *that*, I'd like to think that my presence in your life has a bit more importance to you than Vane–'

'Por supuesto (Of course),' he interrupted tersely. It's what she wanted to hear, but the result from it only made her feel weaker about herself for provoking it from him, when she didn't have to: she knew it did. Worse, they'd had the conversation before. Why couldn't she have stopped after "sorry" and left it at that? 'Ugh, Charlie now I feel embarrassed for making you underline it for me.' 'Don't worry about it,' he said with disregard and stared out the window. She kept quiet, but continued to cross-examine herself in her head: '*He's the one with the major challenge ahead of him, yet I'm the one being emotional and loading it off on him. Yuck.*'

'Have you got my passport?' he asked suddenly.

'Your passport?' she said surprised. 'No. Do you not have it with you?' she asked.

'Nope. I couldn't find it yesterday morning,' he answered.

'Uff Charlie. I wasn't aware of that. Where was the last place you think you had it?' she enquired as she focused on the traffic before her. He sort of gave a small cackle, 'well, I had dinner with friends at Jaume's in C'an Colom and I had it then, or–'

'You had dinner at Jaume's Monday night? What time were you there!?' she asked surprised again. 'About eleven or so,' he answered.

'We were *right* next door at the Chinese for the birthday dinner!' she exclaimed.

'Yea,' he affirmed, 'I thought I'd recognised my brother's car.

'Wow Charlie, what a coincidence!' she said, 'I'm surprised that I didn't see you. I was right there, just before we went into the Chinese, because I saw one of Jes' old neighbours having dinner on Jaume's patio. He's –'

'You mean the little man with the drinking problem?' he smiled a bit.

'Yea, that's him. His name is Miquel. Sweet guy. He used to come by the house in Sichus to see Jesy.

'Yea, I saw him too. We invited him for a coffee at our table,' he said casually.

She'd seen Miquel while she was heading for dinner with the Serras and simply went over to greet him. He was terribly thin since the last time she'd seen him standing in Jes' kitchen almost four years earlier. The fact that she and Charlie should run into him at the same time at such an unsuspecting place made the hairs on her neck stand: Jesy was nearby and she and Charlie were definitely sharing a channel of something between them … 'After that we went to a few clubs in Alcudia – it could be there too,' he added dryly. Her thoughts evaporated. She glanced over at Charlie knowing already what clubs he was referring to, so didn't ask. Instead she tagged: 'Well you have your citizen card with you, right?'

'Yea,' he said.

'Okay then, so no problem with the flight. Don't worry about the passport Charlie, I'm sure you'll get it back.'

'Hmfpt,' he smirked unconvinced, then exhaled, 'Aiii Michèle.'

They swung into the departure's area on two wheels at 8:50a.m.! There was no time to park the car, so in one complete eloquent motion: left the car in the Short Term parking zone, kissed the ring on her finger that was from her dad, whispered thanks to the Mini, Jes and her Grandma for getting them there safely and left a note with her cell number and expected time of return in view on the dashboard!

'No llegaremos (We won't make it),' said Charlie as Michèle hopped out of the car and paced aggressively towards the automatic doors.

'Si que llegaremos (Yes we will!),' she tossed back.

'Aii, Michèeele,' he droned at a cool pace behind her.

'C'mon Charlie I've already got the boarding cards!'

It was hell. The P.A. system aggressively sounded their names throughout the airport, Charlie displayed a non-pulsed air of concern even though she felt that more was probably going on inside him than he let on, but as long as she was doing well with the theatrics, he was content to watch. She was in full trot to the gate thinking that if it were possible to turn her stomach inside out, it would have displayed a tragic image of a million butterflies reacting to the poison of stress she was feeling! What was she worried about anyway? There really was no rush and plenty of planes to choose from. Fear. Fear that Charlie would use it as an excuse to try another day, miss the jump and then hesitate even more from the failure of having missed it. Her mind raced with probabilities enough to distract her stress from the current moment and suddenly find herself in front of the gate face to face with a flight attendant who actually gave her a polite smile. ... 9a.m.,Charlie caught up to them, handed in his boarding card with a mild look of defeated apprehension, replaced quickly by a soft smirk on his face, as if to say, *Déjà* vu? ... '¿Que?' she tried to bite.

'Nada,' he said, and the gates to the chasm behind them closed.

LE DÉNOUEMENT

I've got bad news – It wasn't a coincidence
I wanted it to happen to us
And you, you let it happen
I don't want you to forgive me and don't ask me for forgiveness
Don't deny that you looked for me
None of this, none of this was a mistake
Nothing and none of this was in error – Mistakes are not chosen
For good or for bad I didn't fail when you came
And you, you didn't want to fail
I learned the difference between luck and chance
Who watches you and who goes for it
None, none of this
But none of this
Was a mistake.
[Tengo una mala noticia – no fue de casualidad/ yo quería que nos pasara... y tú, y tú/ Lo dejaste pasar No quiero que me perdones – y no me pidas perdón/ No me niegues que me buscaste/ Nada nada de esto – nada de esto fue un error/ Los errores no se eligen/ Para bien o para mal- no fallé cuando viniste/ Y tú, y tu/ No quisiste fallar/ Aprendí la diferencia entre el juego y el azar/ Quien te mira y quien se entrega/ nada nada de esto/ nada de esto fue un error]
'NADA FUE UN ERROR'– COTI, LYRICS ADAPTED

Go! Charlie go!

Everything from that moment onwards fell into place nicely. Hipócrates is without question the epitome of an exquisite five star hotel for people fallen ill by the very thing they expect will cure them: wealth. The entrance was monitored by video camera, the reception area was flanked by a lovely open garden full of green and exotic plants, a few water fountains, a grape-vine tarp over a set of twentieth century benches with soft music coming from hidden speakers in the ground. The reception staff was polite and formal, although the space around them felt stuffy even despite its airy modern layout, decorated with large ikebana displays set in the centre of a few large tables. Charlie would receive maid and laundry service, three meals a day prepared by a professional chef, have access to an incredibly luxurious spa and gym facility, and attend therapy sessions once or twice a day; a few times a week. Other than that, the atmosphere was simply sterile and ostentatious. 'Quite a place Charlie,' she said to him while they waited to be escorted to his room. As if aware of the sarcasm in her tone he replied, 'Yes it is, but in two weeks I'll be tired of the food and bored stiff.' She understood his comment. The life she'd lived on cruise ships had been a privileged one, kept in check by the intensity of the work she did. Otherwise, she could not have appreciated it as much as she had. It was another contradiction about people who complain about work, but when they retire try to fill their time with things to do. It reminded her of the saying that work wasn't work if one liked what one was doing. Being active and doing was a natural process of living, so one might as well work at making a living by something that called for one's passion – no? The only trouble was that money culture was interrupting that natural flow every day and making the primitive era from the hunting and gathering generations seem like the golden one.

Charlie's room was nothing less than a very generic but aesthetically attractive room, fully equipped with two single beds, colour

TV, CD player with stress relief CDs to choose from, two arm chairs, a classic writer's desk that Michèle yearned to break-in, a well sized bathroom with telephone, a tub equipped with water jets for light jacuzzi action and a long marble counter with wonderful little soap and shampoo samples to choose from; all joined to a private hardwood balcony with a charming little table and two chairs on it. Two young nurses, friendly and professional in appearance, had escorted them to the room. There, they began to explain the rules and the methodology of the centre and the rehabilitation programme to Charlie and Michèle at the same time as they unpacked his things. Charlie was already aware of the formalities so that Michèle was the only one really paying attention: no calls in or out for the first six days of internship. After that, Charlie could make all the calls that he wanted while only family and approved persons could call him. Although it was recommended that nobody call and just let him be. Charlie would have to spend the first forty eight hours confined to his room, following that he would begin his therapy sessions and would not be permitted to leave the hotel for the next six weeks at which time privileges would be discussed. Visitation rights were on Saturdays and were permitted to commence ten days after the patient checked-in. Therapy sessions were on Fridays for family members and then couples. People permitted to visit, who did not live in Barcelona, could spend a night in a room in the hotel while couples could share the patient's room without charge. 'So you can stay here when you visit,' said one of the nurses referring to Charlie's room. Michèle smiled at the nurse's faux-pas, gave a quick look at Charlie who remained focused on his ring fiddling and said: 'Well I suppose that will depend on Charlie.' The nurse understood Michèle's nuance quickly and said: 'Naturally it's up to him.' 'Si, we'll see,' he added. It was hoped that a patient would stay a minimum of three months and as long as six, if one was going to do it right. Then it was recommended that the patient live in the village nearby for a few months before returning home. The whole process suggested at least six months for any of the patient's investment to be worthwhile. Michèle listened intently, asking questions here and there, noticing at times a slight lack of confidence in their delivery that disconcerted her. One girl spoke and the other emptied and searched Charlie's belongings thoroughly. Every pocket on his clothing was pulled inside out, his shoes were turned upside down and manually searched, his sundries were opened and inquired about, as well as his music player whereas sharp objects like disposable razors, nail scissors and clippers were confiscated. Then came the cross examination of all the reading material that had been packed: Charlie's Spanish-English Oxford Dictionary, the English study materials Michèle had supplied him with, the astrological articles for that year, a few flight magazines, several books and a newspaper. Then last of all, the nurse pulled out the brown ring box Michèle had so vehemently planted on the bed that morning and caused him to pack it. A flush of guilt washed over Michèle. Finally, Charlie was requested to meet with his doctor and one of the nurses escorted him down to the clinic. In the meantime, Michèle waited in the room while the other nurse finished the process of unpacking, briefed Michèle on the rest of the visit's procedures and then left the room. She sat there in solitude and looked around her. Something about the place did not sit well with her. She tried to feel differently, but her instincts were nervous. Perhaps it was because she was confused by the methodology. Everything had been confiscated from Charlie's things except the "DaVinci Code," his electric razor and his lighter. They'd confiscated all the reading and study materials, including little Buddha but left him with a 26" TV in his room that would expose him to everything considered to be taboo just in the commercials alone. She saw little difference between his position on the couch back home and the one he would find on the bed in the hotel room. Withstanding that there was a gift shop in the hotel where he was permitted to charge new magazines and books to his room, if he wanted. He could make all the calls that he wanted from the hotel, but would be charged hotel rates. The last time Charlie checked-out, his phone bill was close to six hundred euros. It was understood that there was a need for Charlie to be responsible for his own actions including his impulses, but in the first six weeks of rehab when he was at his weakest, she felt that he ought to be completely isolated from all exterior influences and people and left to hibernate into himself. The centre seemed to share the view, yet removed his opportunity to study English, read books that offered him unique philosophies about life and left him with "The DaVinci Code" instead; the book with the most likelihood of stimulating Charlie's memory and cravings. They took away the disposable razors, but left him with his cigarettes and lighter. The contradictions made her nervous. '*Relax Chèle, they're the professionals – have faith that they know what they're doing,*' she said to herself. She felt fear. Like a rabbit that knows that something is amiss but can't do anything about it. The place reeked of manipulation and mendacity. Her mind whirred up a recollection of Crichton's "The Firm" further fuelling her imagination to consider that the rooms were monitored by hidden cameras and phone calls were tapped. That's how uneasy she felt. The books that had been confiscated probably questioned the puritanical outlook by medical science. Charlie even had to sign a confidential contract with the centre that removed all liability from it. In fact it wasn't the contradictions that made her uneasy or her scepticism about its methodology, but her inability to see, if at all, any direct or beneficial purpose that served Charlie's recuperation, when the benefits to the company were all too visible to her. She tried to change her chip: '*Whoa there missy – ease up now,*' she thought soberly to herself. Charlie chose the place and she ought to have more faith that they knew more than she did. Above all, it was up to Charlie and it did not matter where he went. With that thought she felt reassured and confident by her faith in him. She just didn't like feeling that he was being taken advantage of, even by the Hotel. The door opened and Charlie and the nurse walked into the room. '¿Que?' she directed at Charlie. 'Okay it's your turn,' said the nurse to Michèle, 'I'll take you down now, and then bring you back to say goodbye,' she added kindly. 'Oh?! Okay,' acknowledged Michèle with a pleased tone. In light of Hipócrates list of restrictions, she had not anticipated an interview with the doctor too. The clinic area, unlike the hotel area upstairs, offered Michèle a moment of relief from her fears. In this area the walls displayed full sized frames of photos that promoted examples of reaching out, love and support, while the therapists and doctors she observed walking-by transmitted care about their work. Despite the business side of things, the people that Charlie would be in direct contact with, appeared to be sharp and sincere. The doctor who greeted Michèle was formal and polite, while her manner with Michèle was empathetic and kind. 'Okay, I've spoken with Carles. As you know it is not the first time that he has been here. The good thing is, this time he knows what he needs to do, but more importantly what he shouldn't do, if he really wants to make his effort worthwhile,' she said calmly. Michèle liked her instantly; finally someone on the same page as her. 'You understand that Charlie must be completely removed from everyone and everything for a long period of time – that it would be better if no one including yourself contacted him for a long time?' she asked her directly. 'Absolutely,' responded Michèle, 'or longer, if he chooses to stay here or go to China! – I'd be happy with that too!' she added enthusiastically and meaning every word she'd said. 'Now,' the doctor enquired, 'explain to me you relationship with Carles. Do you know about his personal life?' The question, Michèle felt, was a test. Charlie and the doctor would have already talked about her and stipulated the relationship that they had had. 'Charlie and I are friends. We embarked on a trial period of detoxification at home that lasted eleven days until he relapsed. It consisted of me and him spending close to 24hours daily together doing a routine that included the gym, changing his phone number, giving me his phone and car keys at night, going out or just hanging out together, ..' At this point the doctor's facial expression reacted slightly, making Michèle think that their trial was considered foolish. *Had it been? Had everything they'd done been considered a joke at her expense? While she firmly believed in every step they took; every little morsel of success they had had in getting to rehab within two and a half months of their trial – not three, nor six nor a lifetime but two months! Surely his family would not have allowed it to go the way it had, if they hadn't been serious about it too..?* Something inside her hurt at the possibility of this, but she continued: 'So by definition of the word, we were a pair. After a month we stopped that effort and used the following two months considering his options, including visits to a few other clinics before Charlie decided to return here. Charlie's older brother and sister-in-law are the owners of the flat where I live and they live downstairs from me, while Charlie's wife has been made aware of my presence. Although we have never met, she once communicated through Charlie her appreciation for our efforts. It's all been very straightforward,' she concluded. 'Well,' said the doctor, 'it is obvious that your relationship together has been very intense. You both need a break and some time to relax. However, would you be interested in attending the therapy sessions here? There are two; one for couples and one for families. You can't attend the family one but in light of your experience with Carles, you might consider the one for couples?' Michèle wanted to burst. It was everything she'd hoped would happen. Charlie's recuperation she felt, had to be different including the way he performed it. Despite her own feelings about him, the ones towards his purpose were still stronger and she simply believed that her continued presence in his life was still important in helping him to relocate his self. She wanted to attend the therapy, both for him and herself as well. He'd shared so much with her already and because much of his dilemma was in his relationship with his wife, maybe therapy sessions with Michèle would help shed light on things. She wanted so much for it to happen that her anxiety bubbled. It was the first time that she was truly feeling supported. Someone was offering to help her and Charlie in the same way that she believed to be right. *'Thank you God,'* she thought. 'I'd be very happy to attend the therapy sessions with Carles, however it would be up to Carles and his wife,' she answered.

'Well, Carles does not want to see his wife; they'd tried therapy with a personal therapist before his admission here and it was unproductive.' She paused. 'I don't think he'll mind your presence at therapy,' she offered.

'Oh,' said Michèle quietly. She'd known about the therapy sessions that Charlie and his wife had tried and how clearly he was against trying again. '...I think you should know,' she began, 'that I was quite persistent about his departure for rehab, especially in the last two months, when I think I highlighted co-addictive behaviour, such that I think the therapy would be good for me too. However, I just don't want my presence in Carles' life's to turn into a negative sensation for him or get stuck in his memory with the cocaine. I'd rather avoid that,' she responded.

'Okay,' said the doctor, 'the first session is on the 29th, we'll call you to confirm. Have you anything else that you'd like to tell me?'

'Yes. A tape was made for Carles that has messages on it from members of his family and I wondered if he might receive it later, when more time as gone by?'

'Well,' said the doctor, 'it's not policy to permit it, but if you hand it to the nurse she will pass it on to his therapist, who will listen to it and decide the viability of giving it to him or not.' It wasn't the answer Michèle wanted to hear but expected it, and said: 'That's fine. Thank you,' and added, 'may I confirm my telephone number with you?'

'Yes of course, I have it here,' said the doctor, referring to some digits on a note-pad.

'Yes, that's correct. How do you know which calls to pass on to Carles – anyone can say they are family?'

'Yes. We refer to a list. If the telephone number does not correspond with an approved number then we don't accept the call.'

'I see,' said Michèle, 'I have a similar list from the month we spent together, may I offer a few numbers to you that have been very active in Carles' phone lately?'

'Absolutely.'

Michèle gave the telephone numbers that belonged to V, the woman from the village and two other ones that were related to buying cocaine. Truth be known the only one she felt was going to try calling from that list was the woman from the village, who had the best likelihood of finding out where Charlie was. 'May I ask you to inform Carles that I have given these numbers to you – I intend to let Carles know before I go, but just in case I can't...' she trailed off.

'Don't worry I shall tell him,' she reassured.

'O.K. then. Thank you very much for your time. I sincerely appreciate it.'

They stood up from their chairs and shook hands. 'Okay Michèle. We'll see you in a few weeks then, goodbye.' The nurse who'd escorted her the first time was waiting for her outside the doctor's door and escorted Michèle back to Charlie's room. There, he handed Michèle his telephone, house keys and wallet for safe keeping because he could not keep them at the hotel. 'Charlie I gave the doctor these numbers from your phone,' she said indicating them to him from her agenda. Then she collected the rest of her things and turned to face Charlie who was standing in front of the bed next to her. They were both very tired and emotionally drained. She looked at him, and suddenly noticed his height over her small frame...

'O.K., – I'm off.'

'O.K,' he said.

Neither one of them wanted to make a dramatic exit. She reached up to him and gave him a hug and he complied. It was the second hug she'd received from him and it was just as good as the first one had been. His cologne eased her senses and brought her voice to whisper: 'Adelante soldado (Steadfast soldier).' She then kissed him lightly on the cheek and turned for the door. 'Se buena (Be good),' his voice trailed, just before the heavy hotel door clicked shut behind her.

She was escorted back to reception where a limo-cab was waiting to take her back to the airport. Once she got into the back seat of the car, an immense sense of relief and sadness waved in and out of her system at the same time. It was Wednesday, April 20th, 2005. Everything about the date's constitution was related to her and Charlie. Everything. Including the fact, it also happened to be the same date that her paternal grandmother had passed away seven years earlier. 'Hmft, "*with every death there is a birth*",' voiced the memory, to which Michèle responded lightly, 'I hope so… Go! Charlie, *go*.'

I realized quickly when I knew I should
That the world was made up of this brotherhood of man
For whatever that means
So I cry sometimes – When I'm lying in bed
Just to get it all out – What's in my head
And I am feeling a little peculiar
So I wake in the morning and I step outside
Take a deep breath and I get real high
And scream at the top of my lungs – What's going on?
And I say, hey, hey? – What's going on?
I try, oh my God do I try
I try all the time, in this institution
I pray, oh my god do I pray – I pray every single day for a revolution
So I take a deep breath and I get real high
Trying to get up that great big hill of hope
For a destination.
'WHAT'S GOING ON' – 4 NON BLONDES, LYRICS ADAPTED

What's going on?

The nine days leading up to the 29th were nothing less than an interlude comparable to the calm before a storm. While Charlie was about to face his demons at Hipócrates, so too was Michèle at Sa Ema de Farrutx. It was hard not to notice how much of their personal challenges seemed to parallel each other's. Especially at the prelude of their recuperation, when Michèle felt that her personal stamina was still alive but not entirely well. Her mind's focus was still on Charlie, while daily events felt tested and tried as early as her arrival back to the airport that night when she discovered that the Mini had been towed from the temporary parking lot to the car pound. On one hand she was lucky because pound was in walking distance, which helped her more, when the consequence of the matter was a ninety euro fee. She did not have the amount on her, but was able to walk back to Arrivals and withdraw cash from an automated teller machine, which just happen to have exactly ninety-two euros left in her account. Once she got the Mini back, delighted that the experience was not as harrowing as it might have been in a big city airport, she drove directly to Alcudia and then C'an Colom to see about Charlie's passport. The clubs in Alcudia were closed, but the restaurant in C'an Colom wasn't.

'Hi,' she said to one of the waiters.

'Hi!?' he said at once recognising her from another time when she'd been there with Charlie and before she could even ask, 'your friend left his passport here the other night.'

'Oh, really!' she was delighted, 'it's here then? That's why I've come by.'

'Si, si, just a moment,' he said, then bellowed across the floor to a colleague standing behind the counter, 'where's that passport we picked up the other night?' The passport was intact including the money and notes that were inside it. Despite the expense of time and gas the search had been successful within a few hours of looking for it. That same night she checked-in with Elisabet and Mitx about Charlie and Hipócrates. Then picked up Dasha from her place and slept at Charlie's where she felt more at home than she had been feeling above Mitx and Elisabet's place. It was her moment of separation and bereavement from Charlie, comparable to the one she had experienced when Jesy had died. She simply needed to be alone with the things she'd felt closest to: Dasha and Charlie. The next day she intuitively woke up early and cleaned the place from top to bottom. Kitchen, bathrooms, floors, bay windows and all. Even came across a gold plated bracelet in the laundry room as well as a long strand of black hair in Charlie's bed that she presumed had been Vanesa's. The discoveries did nothing more than give Michèle a wonderful sensation of relief and pride in herself. Tears plopped intermittently from her eyes onto her cheeks like plump raindrops on petals. It was her moment, and she allowed every bit of personal motivation to hug her and the love she felt for Charlie. They'd done it. He was gone and all of *that* was now in the past. Every moment of his future was already a better memory for his past – Did anyone care? Time would tell. She dried her face, then proceeded to sort and pack Charlie's things in bags and boxes. The whole day was therapeutic to say the least and by late evening she went back to her place leaving no.4 by the sea clean, organised, packed and ready for any sudden decisions regarding the place where Charlie wasn't living anymore. Then she drove to Charlie's parents' place and handed his mother the keys to Charlie's Phedra and the flat.

'Thank you very much,' she told Michèle from the doorway of her home, 'won't you come in?' she asked.

'No, no, thank you,' replied Michèle. Charlie's mother was obviously moved by her son's departure.

'Thank you,' she emphasised again. Then with a slight waver in her voice, 'It was because of you, he went. I, we, did not think he was going to go,' she ended in emotion.

'Naah,' answered Michèle firmly, 'Charlie went on his own accord. I just assisted a bit – really.'

Then ever so hushed, almost inaudibly the mother continued, 'My grandson came by yesterday and his mother asked me who Carles went with and I didn't have the heart to tell her, so I said he went alone… She is a nice girl and she has so many troubles of her own you know–,' she trailed off. Michèle was not sure if it was an apology or a confession but answered: 'It's okay Mrs Serra. However telling her the truth would be better for her in the long run, you know…' What was she going to say? Michèle was a woman and any comments about the wife or the relationship between she and Charlie would automatically be held against her as self-interested motives. Such wisdom had to be imparted from the family that didn't appear to promote the notion, or his friends, who obviously cared more about being in his good graces than about him. 'O.K.!' Michèle pronounced firmly, 'I'm off – don't worry about Carles, we just have to leave him alone now,' she said getting into the car. 'Yes, yes,' replied his mother assertively and Michèle believed her. She knew his mother was faithful to his needs and his heart and for that reason Michèle initially appreciated her. A few days later Charlie's parents buzzed at her door and asked if she would mind accompanying them to his place, so that they could collect his belongings. It would seem that the family had already been in touch with Charlie regarding the affairs of his place and work. She couldn't believe it. Her reaction from within was instant: *'If it were so important to get Charlie's approval could they not have waited a month? At least some time for the fog in his head to lift and give him some decision making space? Wasn't Hipócrates monitoring calls? Was it so urgent to save one month's rent and move his things by May 1st? Wasn't that what "power of attorney" was all about? To make decisions when the one being represented can't make any decisions? When Charlie was in the well everyone told me to 'let him be, let him be' and then when he's finally in rehab everyone wants to get in touch with him? What bull shit is that!?'* Her thoughts whirred with darkness. Not only had she been clear about her activist role while he had been home, she was equally clear about her passive role while he was away: *'NOW is the time to let him be, NOT before!'* she thought adamantly to herself. *'FuuucK.'* Anger was beginning to spoil her sense of victory. It wasn't over yet she could see. A new battle was on the horizon and it was going to be greater than the one she'd faced against cocaine: family. She looked at the elderly couple before her. She really did like these people. They were from another time and another way of doing things. They were kind, polite and trusted their children to guide them through the new world that was invading their Mayūrqa. 'Mr. Serra,' she smiled politely, 'I think you have an extra key to Carles' place on his car keys.' 'Yes, we have it here, but we did not want to go over without asking you first,' he admitted. The gesture was welcomed more than it should have been, but it felt like Charlie's parents were the only ones to openly respect the relationship that she and Charlie had shared. Their words of gratitude gave her a lift that felt shameful at the same time. Had there been just a drop of verbal encouragement from the others, who had openly promoted her involvement with Charlie, her self-confidence would have remained enough to satisfy her, but her energy reserves were low. So it was his parents from the generation of silence and stiff upper lip who had, and it was worth more in weight to her, than if it had come from those whom she felt could have said something. In the end it was the parents who correctly respected Charlie's interests the way he would have done and had. So the three of them went over to his place. Needless to say his parents were overwhelmed by the order and preparation that she had left on standby. There was little for them to do except decide on whether or not to take all of his things or just his clothing, because they were not entirely clear if Charlie's place was going up for rent or not. Michèle sensed confusion in their hearts as to whom they should adhere to: their sons' convictions or to the woman whom Charlie had obviously done well by. Not long after their arrival to the flat, the oldest of Mitx and Elisabet's sons happened-by and hung out in the TV room until his grandparents left, causing Michèle to wonder if he had been advised to chaperone the interlude between her and his grandparents. 'Do you think we should rent this place?' asked Charlie's dad.

'I don't know. I think that's up to Charlie, but I believe one of the steps towards recovery is a change of lifestyle including the home – no?' she answered while glancing over at their grandson.

'Yes. That's what they say, but what if he comes back early? It won't make any difference where he lives,' they offered. 'Yes I agree, that's why I think he's supposed to be left alone for a while, so that he can make these decisions on his own – you know. He needs to be responsible for himself and his past actions. Maybe let him lose a month's rent, as part of the consequences. Then in a month's time, see what he says,' she suggested.

'My sons say that he can't afford to pay another month's rent,' replied the father.

   Michèle's senses were alerted, so she replied: 'I don't know what to say to you both. Your sons have a better understanding of Carles' financial affairs than I do. Besides, if they have already spoken to Charlie and he has said O.K., then I think we should go with that.' Her answer had tapped out the last of her energy reserves. She was truly feeling annoyed inside. How could they expect Charlie to make any clear decisions about anything at such a preliminary stage of his recuperation? – *Geesus*! She suddenly felt challenged by forces that she could not see nor locate – only feel. Now that the dirty work was done and left on Charlie's memory as being largely related to her, they could regain the reins that they'd relinquished at the time of battle and gain Charlie's favour without ever having placed themselves at risk. It was like "wham bam thank-you mam, we'll take control from here." She tried to pacify the anger, so that she could hear the other voice, which spoke with a deeper understanding; it was his family who simply didn't want to feel indebted to her anymore, or who recognised that Charlie's decision to go as well as he had, was largely managed without them. That by all rights, Charlie was back to being a family issue, not hers. That's how the family unit still worked in deep Mayürqa and in most of Spain: the clan is at once a great shelter, protector of its members and protagonist of its members. However, it was also the culprit that was often guilty of treason in their absence, abused its family rights, could take advantage of its members' fortune, disrupt their personal relationships, as well as handicap personal development with a simple reminder of the family's need to come first. In the end, a simple case of the indefinite dichotomy of the love-hate issues that existed in family in general and that can persecute many until death do them part. Michèle knew this from her own experience, and it would seem that she still had a lot to learn about it and herself. She cared very much about Charlie and his family in a way that was beyond her control, yet it seemed as though she still had a phase to go through exempt from Charlie: his family. It was going to be her next test. Charlie's had already begun and so was hers. She went to bed that night and whispered to Life: '*When will it all end? This emotional battle to earn what I feel is mine? Have I been so wrong? But they are in my destiny. How do polar halves unite back as one if their divided core is a reflection of the other? Why do you make it so hard – or is it that? I still need to learn from my weaknesses before I am permitted to move on, if at all? Is it about training my patience to respect the time line of my visions? How to be intelligently selfish and focus on my gifts without guilt? I am in serious financial debt. Although I'm in it because of a quiet plan, even Oprah would not be impressed. I need my faith to work in tandem with my patience and considering your track record with me, that is kind of unfair – no? What am I supposed to do? Sigh. My lip service is being tested isn't it? It's my own test to myself. I quote the wisdom of others to Charlie with the help of past experience, but now I have to demonstrate my trust in you, in a culture that has nothing to do with my upbringing or experiences. Okay then. May the tools and emotional wisdom that my family and life in Canada afforded me protect me against my own ignorance and fear. May my insecurities created from my past be snubbed by my faith in me and the knowledge that they don't have to be repeated. May I motivate me without arrogance or abuse my faith in you. May I learn their language and understand them better rather than be frustrated or take it to heart. May I learn how to care without caring too much...May your test be fair and the people you've chosen to teach me, at least be kind. May I not disappoint you. Above all, keep me strong, please and I'll find the way, and thank you for your protection. I know you've been there when I've strayed the wrong way.*'

On the 23rd of April Michèle bought her plane tickets for the therapy session with Charlie on the 29th. It was a week away and made the tickets slightly more affordable and flexible. If Hipócrates called her to cancel the session, she'd still be able to postdate the tickets to another time up to 24hrs of the original departure date. On the 27th she hadn't heard from them and called the centre. Everyone she might have spoken too was unavailable at the time so she left a message requesting that someone return her call with a reply about the 29th. That evening she heard Elisabet talking to Charlie from the front patio. It bothered her. The six day ban on personal calls had been lifted, but she'd quietly hoped that everyone would have just left him alone. However it wasn't just that. Something was beginning to fester in her and she realised with time that much of Charlie's inability to get out of his dilemma was because of family. Like pet owners who feed their dogs left-overs and rich foods, or parents who express their love with extravagant gifts and actions of generosity – a misdirected love that seeks to be loved by trying to earn it by reason of their own lack of faith in themselves that their work as caretakers was well done. In the end, the victim is inadvertently the one being manipulated. On the morning of April 28th Michèle called Hypócrates again and waited for someone to answer... *She knew that the centre had not called back because something had been changed. She was vexed. She could have and probably should have let it go. While it seemed hypocritical of her to be disconcerted about his family's preliminary contact with him when she was anticipating therapy sessions with him as early as the following day. Yet, yet, the sessions had been brought to her attention. Plus Hypócrates was an internationally recognised centre that surely understood the virtues of direct communication? Even if it was only about keeping worried family and friends at bay so that it could do its work effectively, they could at least get someone to respond to her call. Otherwise, the impropriety only provoked her need to know what was going on. Especially after the doctor had prompted her to return even before Michèle had suggested the idea, confirming to her that her ideas about Charlie's needs* were not so hypothetical at all. It was a part of his recovery and as far as she was concerned Charlie's process had just begun, as well as hers. She needed help too. She had questions too. Charlie's arrival there was just the first phase, but there was still his interlude away and then his return. At least a year in total from when they'd begun in January, if not from the day he got there on the 20th and then some. She no longer wanted to be the activist, but the passive part of his recuperation. A sort of prototype while the professionals communicated with them along the way. Was that so wrong? Like a football season there was more than one match to win before getting to the finals. Yet now that one little match had been won, people were changing the players and she felt like she was being benched. What was going on? ... A receptionist from the centre finally came over the phone line and told her that no-one was able to take her call. So she asked if Charlie would speak to her. There was a slight pause while her telephone number was checked and surprisingly enough it was among the accepted numbers. Her stomach went tight as she prepared to talk to the one person she could talk to and shouldn't talk to at the same time. Why hadn't Hypócrates just called her back to clarify? The call went through and Charlie answered:

'¿Si?'

'Hi,' she said.

'Hi.' His voice was subdued and lethargic. She didn't like noticing that, coupled by her own anxiety at having to bother him and ask the things that she'd tried to confirm on her own without him.

'How's things?' they asked each other.

'Well you know..,' they replied.

'Charlie I'm calling because I wanted to know if you're okay with the therapy session tomorrow?'

'Tomorrow?' he asked, 'I don't think Mitx and Elisabet are coming until next week.'

'Oh,' she said, 'I'm referring to the one with me. Didn't the doctor ask you about it?'

'What doctor?' he asked again.

'The one I met last week. She suggested that we try a few sessions together. If it goes well great and if not, well we tried it as something different from your last time there, you know –?'

Her long explanations bothered her because she could tell that Charlie was still in a mental state of uncertainty and indecisiveness and she hated being among those who wasn't making it any easier for him.

'I don't know anything about that Michèle, but if she told you to come then come.'

It was the answer that she'd wanted to hear but didn't sit well with her, because the help was coming from the patient who needed to be left alone, while friends and family including her tried to subdue their own needs.

'Well, okay,' she exhaled.

'Ahh,' he hesitated, 'have you still got a key to my place?' he asked.

'Yup,' she answered, 'me and your parents.'

'Okay,' and added cordially, 'if you have a moment could you go over there and take my CDs, the bags in the cupboard and a box from the shelf, before my family goes over there to empty the place?'

'Absolutely. So you decided to give up the place?'

'My brothers say that I should, what do you think?' he asked.

She hadn't expected that. The decision had been made when it was too soon to even be going there. What was the hurry? If they wanted to give deference to Charlie about his place why couldn't they just wait a month? *Bull Shit! Just bull shit!* her mind flared. 'Well Charlie,' she answered, 'you'll move eventually anyway no?'

'Hmm,' he complied.

'Anything else?' she asked.

'No, thank you,' he answered.

'Okay Charlie, go get 'em, and I'm terribly sorry for the call. I was unable to get a reply from the centre.'

'Don't worry about it. They don't tell you anything around here,' he said seemingly irritated by the fact.

'Okay, then do your thing – bye.'

'Bye,' he softened and their call ended.

The bags that Charlie had referred to were the ones that belonged to his wife that he still had to return to her on his own. The CDs were many and Michèle found the box on the shelf that appeared to be for a hair-dryer. It wasn't until she started packing the CDs and opened the hair-dryer box to fit a few of the CDs in it an–'OH! My GawD! 'Oh!–my–gawD!!' she screeched repeatedly jumping up and down and all around. She really hadn't expected the content to be what it was. She then stopped her theatrical dance a foot away from the bed and craned her neck over the box hesitantly to look at it again, 'Oh My gawd! Oh my gawd!' she resumed, skipping back and forth half cackling, half hysterical. 'It's a gun! There's a gun in the box!' she chanted to herself trying to calm down: 'Is it Charlie's? Or is he holding it for someone? Is it legal? Worse – Is it loaded? It should have a safety on it – right?' She sounded to no one in the room. Even Dasha wasn't there to justify her reason for direct speech. The fact that Charlie had a gun in his room really wasn't that unusual to her at all. She had known about other people with drug problems and even soldiers, who'd returned from war and sometimes slept with a gun, because they suffered from paranoia. No, the real issue was that she did not enjoy having it close to her. It felt like a negative item that did nothing less than invite fear into the home. What to do? She was in financial debt – maybe she could sell it? Although, it wasn't hers to sell. Where to put it? She kept herself entertained with questions, while she stuffed the box with kitchen towels so that the gun could not budge within it. Then she closed the box and taped its lid. Once she got the items to her place she put them all together in a larger box inside a cupboard in her office. Everything was labelled, classified and organised. The location of the gun however, put her into a bit of a tizzy as she tried to find the right spot for it. She didn't like having it inside the flat so she opted to place in inside Dasha's travel cage on the veranda. Then she worried that maybe temperature changes would affect it, causing her imagination to trump up the possibility that it could cause something inside it to combust or explode. She finally ended up putting the box on a high shelf like Charlie had done, pushed it to the back of the same cupboard where the other box was located, closed the cupboard doors and forgot about them. Then that evening close to six o'clock Charlie called her. His therapist told him to inform her that she was not permitted to attend therapy with him because they were not an item. She was sincerely shocked at the way she was being informed. Charlie had mentioned the therapy session to his therapist who simply advised against it because they were not a couple. Then she made Charlie call her, instead of calling and talking to Michèle directly herself. If Charlie was supposed to be anxiety free it wasn't going to happen like that.

'Charlie,' she asked, 'was her decision based on your suggestion. Would you rather not see me for a while? I completely understand if you don't,' she said.

'Nahh. I don't know why she said it,' he added.

She believed him. If he didn't want to see her he would have told her. 'Then, I don't understand. It's almost seven o'clock at night and my flight is tomorrow,' she said.

'Have you already got the tickets?' he asked.

'Yes, but that's beside the point,' she said.

'Well come then,' he said, 'if you have the tickets than you can't change them – don't worry about it.'

'Charlie, I don't want to get on their bad side you know.'

'Don't be silly,' he said. There was a pause … 'Okay,' she replied at last and they said goodbye.

So, she went to Barcelona to meet Charlie at the rehabilitation centre for the rich and famous and almost didn't get there. The "couple therapy" session was from 7p.m. until 9:30 p.m., every week on Fridays. She'd waited a week for the centre to call her and confirm the session but it didn't. That should have been sign enough. However, she'd bought her plane tickets for the Friday departure and a Saturday morning return with reference to the information sheet she'd been given from the centre on the day that Charlie and she had arrived. Needless to say, she wanted to do the therapy sessions with Charlie and not just for him but for herself too. She wanted to learn more about it. She needed to ask questions and share her perspective on Charlie's dilemma as well as be told how much of it was co-addict behaviour versus a rational one. She thought she could contribute to his recovery per the intense experience they had had. If the sessions turned out to be counterproductive, then at least they'd have known from trying something that had never been tried. Heck it had worked so far, why stop then? Most of all, she was still confused by the centre's programme. If Charlie was supposed to be left alone, incognito, then she was all for it, but he was allowed to have visitors and attend therapy sessions with his family within ten days of his arrival. Not even the other centres they'd visited recommended that. Furthermore, if her speculations were so wrong, she felt someone could have at least told her so. She never claimed to be an expert on the issue. The whole thing had been a walk-and-discovery experience. The anxiety at not hearing from the centre was slightly relieved at expressing it on paper; she wrote and wrote, like she had always done, since the age of thirteen, when pen and paper became a way for internal peace. She had to. Her mind, her thoughts would not be still. She really felt the therapy was it. When she finally felt sedated, she found herself looking at an eight paged report on her personal perspective of Charlie's problem with cocaine and how he might attain a full recovery. It was ludicrous of course. Her head space at the time was fully emotional and frustrated. Certainly though they could peruse it. Maybe there was something in it worth noticing? In hindsight, her need to get it all out felt like a push. She never once felt like she was trying. Above all, more importantly to her, was the understanding that Charlie's recuperation at the end of the day was always up to him. Like every child should have a right to an education, he had a right to see and know what his possibilities were before making his choices, especially if someone was willing to show him. People learned about themselves and their options during their lifetime – how could anyone expect people who suffer from any addiction to mature at the same rate on their own, with a shorter grandfather clause? *'Nobody "gets there" completely on their own – Nobody,'* is how she felt.

After Charlie had given her the okay to attend therapy with him, she still wasn't relaxed. She did not want to show up at the centre as a rebel against the system. She wanted to work with it not against it. Despite her fears, Michèle still reminded herself that Hypócrates knew what it was doing, and that the picture was bigger than what she could see. So that morning on her way to the airport she tried more than once to call the centre and talk to someone. She finally got the nurse, who'd escorted her to the doctor's office that first day they'd arrived, to have a therapist call her back before her flight at half past one. By half past twelve she was at the airport and finally received a call. The woman at the other end of the line was toneless and impatient. Michèle could only assume that she was being perceived by the woman as being like everyone else who tried to share their views about how to manage their patients; albeit, she would have respected their rules if they had been communicated consistently. 'Thank you for your call,' said Michèle. 'What exactly can I help you with?' questioned the woman. 'I'm calling to ensure that the centre is aware of my arrival today for a therapy session with Carles Serra at 7:30pm,' she replied. 'Did he not communicate with you yesterday that his therapist declined your presence?' she asked. 'Yes he did. That is why I am calling. There seems to be a misunderstanding somewhere. I bought plane tickets because his doctor suggested that we try the sessions,' she offered.

'Which doctor are you referring to?' she interrogated.

'Carles',' she said. There was a pause, which suggested to her that communication had not been relayed well between the doctors and the therapists. 'Mam, I do not wish to disrespect the rules. Perhaps I may visit today and see how it goes? If not, I've written a report that may be of interest to the staff and Carles about our experience, and Carles' dilemma with the cocaine.' 'There is no dilemma,' the woman growled, 'he's been an addict since the first day he drank a beer. He's an alcoholic first, then a drug addict. It's all related. There are no reasons for his addiction. It's not emotional, it's an illness in his biochemistry!' she asserted. Michèle waited a second before saying more: 'What do you suggest then?' she asked hearing the P.A. system announce her flight. 'You can come to the therapy session, but you may not stay over. You'll have to fly back tonight,' the woman was curt. 'Fine,' said Michèle, 'thank you very much,' and they hung up. She got on the plane feeling slightly better at having confirmed her arrival, but still quite anxious that what she was doing was possibly counterproductive to Charlie. She was no longer sure and only somewhat alleviated by a silly horoscope blurb that she'd read the night before in her email inbox that said: "Don't let authority figures undermine your instincts." Then when she got to the airport in Barcelona, she took a cab to the hotel and discovered that the driver's name also happened to be Carles. He dropped her off by 2:30p.m. and they agreed to have him pick her up at 9:45p.m. to take her back to the airport that night. She walked into the centre *right* when Charlie was heading into an elevator. He saw her when he'd turned around just before the doors closed. She was early. They were not meant to see each other until 3p.m., so she sat in the lobby area and waited. Five minutes later he appeared, and she noticed instantly that they were both wearing white shirts. He'd gained weight and his head was clean shaven. He was a different looking man already, but when he spoke to her it was Charlie. 'I wanted to brush my teeth', he said. 'No worries,' she said, 'I'm early. If you're not supposed to be here, then come back down at three – I'm good.' He seemed relieved by her words because he did not hesitate to agree and they met twenty minutes later in the same place. Truth be known, she was nervous. The uncertainties about her arrival had really taxed her. When he came back down he asked her if they could go to the spa. He'd lost the ring she'd given him that morning and thought it might be there. The news about the ring caught her off guard but did not surprise her. She knew he was going to lose it, but hadn't expected it to happen so soon. Nonetheless, his guess had been right about the ring's location and they managed to retrieve it from the spa reception. In her own imaginative way she thought he'd forgot it in the same way that she kept forgetting hers until she finally lost it that day in Palma. Clearly, the rings to her, symbolised the intimidated love between them: it was there, but they couldn't have it under the circumstances and were unsure if they ever could; Charlie more than her. So that her arrival that day caused him anxiety in such a way that he probably played on and off with it until eventually losing it, albeit temporarily. After that they went to the café-bar and had a coffee outside on the patio where other patients and their family and friends were also visiting. They were calmer there; at least she was until he told her that they weren't going to have the therapy session together: 'Why Charlie!?' she tried to ask as calmly as possible. 'Because' he conjectured, 'we're not a couple – are we?' He was confused and frankly so was she! 'What is their definition of being a couple?' she asked. 'We have to have lived together and experienced the problems of addiction and co-addiction,' he said. She stared at him and said nothing. They'd only spent six intense months together, that's all. Nonetheless, there was the real issue that he was married and that if he wanted couple therapy he could do it with his wife. Even though she did not feel that his therapy should be about their marriage as much as why he did cocaine. 'Did you get the things from my place?' he asked. 'Yes.' 'Had you known what was in the box?' he continued. She smiled big at the memory of her discovery of it. 'Nope,' she said, 'but I sure had a good surprise when I did,' she laughed and went into the theatrics of telling him her story, which lasted about five minutes and made them both laugh.

As it turned out, the gun had been given to him much before they'd ever met when he had been worse off than he had been with her. All the paranoia had finally got to him, such that someone he knew had given him a gun. It had been in his closet ever since, but he had been worried about alarming his parents. 'No doubt,' she said to him with a smirk. Then she gave him a play-by-play about the trip back to Palma after they had checked him into Hypócrates. How she got the car out of the vehicle impound at the airport and retrieved his passport in C'an Colom, all in the same night. When she finally ended her theatrical rendition of the waiters and all, Charlie asked her about the impound's fee, but Michèle dismissed his concern to pay her back simply because she'd known the risks when she'd parked the car there in the first place... 'But thank you. A few more things Charlie,' she continued casually, 'your friend from the village was calling your phone non-stop since you left, so I deleted her calls, her number, as well as Vanesa's and a few others from your phone and turned it off. It's also got a new pin to get into it. I wrote the telephone numbers down, in case you feel you want them when you get home,' she ended. Charlie said nothing, which said enough to her. She knew it was not up to her to control his agenda. She'd recognised too that she'd probably done it out of an emotional reaction to keep her role as his guardian, when it had never been her role in the first place. Telling him was another "bad girl, good girl" symptom that caught her when she'd gone into the well after him in March. Hence another reason why she felt a desire to talk to someone. Finally, at a quarter past four a short energetic woman in her mid-fifties came into the café and gregariously greeted everyone who knew her.

'Hello Carles – is this Michèle?' she asked him with a twinkle in her eyes.

'Si si,' he replied with a smile.

'Pleased to meet you,' she said shaking Michèle's hand.

'Pleasure.' Michèle returned. Then like a nervous rabbit the woman skirted further introductions and headed back to the coffee bar. 'Um, I'm sorry Charlie, who was that?'

'She's my therapist.'

'The one who –,'

'Okay Michèle I'm ready!' interjected the woman, 'shall we go?' Then moved rapidly for the door.

'Go?' muttered Michèle. It was all so fast. She had no idea if she was going to see Charlie later or not. She wanted to say goodbye but had to follow the therapist who was quickly disappearing from her sight. She managed a quasi-head turn back to Charlie who was conversing with another patient and simply oblivious to it all. It was all a whirr to her and she truly felt like she was being manipulated and distracted on purpose. She finally caught up to the woman who directed her to an office and closed the door behind them. 'Okay Michèle, what can I do for you?' The question was delivered as briskly as was her movement to get behind the desk before them and sit down onto the swivel chair before her. 'I'm sorry, I am not clear on who you are,' said Michèle calmly. 'I'm the head of the department here and Carles' therapist. I've been working here for over thirty years and know my work well,' she underlined. Her demeanour was unnecessarily aggressive. Furthermore, her introduction felt defensive when Michèle had not even suggested anything contrary to her professional abilities. 'Well, I appreciate your time,' said. Michèle, 'my intention was to attend a therapy session with Carles today. It had been cleared by two of your staff,' she added. The older woman looked surprised and a bit annoyed at the incongruities from within the staff's communication. 'Well,' she said, 'I'll brief them about our meeting later. Michèle, you have to understand that Carles is ill. There is no other reason. It's like cancer and right now he is in intensive care,' she explained. The phone suddenly rang and the little woman answered it and attended to it for a good five minutes. In the meantime, Michèle watched her and collected her thoughts. She was quite aware of cancer. Her father died from it when she was twenty seven and although it was an illness, she had reason to believe that a lot of it was provoked by the emotional debates her dad had often suffered between his head and heart. She watched the woman before her and felt sad that there seemed no way to compromise with her. She was doing her job by way of facts, figures and her experience, while Michèle was relying on instincts, energy and her own experience too. Brian Weiss of course came to her thoughts instantly. Why couldn't scientific medicine and holistic philosophy work together? The woman finally ended the call and kindly humoured Michèle's questions a good hour longer than the twenty minutes she'd probably had in mind: 'I wondered why or what professional reasons your therapist in Menorca might have had to allow Carles' wife attend their group sessions when he had been clear about not wishing to see her the whole time that he had been here the first time? Carles suggested to me that neither his wife nor the therapist had even asked him about it? Is the therapist-patient relationship different in recuperation?' ... The woman gave her a polite smile and calmly said, 'I was not aware of that. The group leader in Menorca is not a therapist. He gives group sessions to recovering addicts like himself. As he lives in Menorca he was an option for Carles to go to. I will make a note of that and give him a call,' she said sincerely. The breadth of incongruities was beginning to make Michèle nervous. '*How,*' she wondered swiftly, '*was it possible that Charlie could pay so much money and not be offered a professional for therapy sessions in extended recovery? Had his wife tried to attend them in Menorca because Carles had refused to see her in Barcelona?*' It only made Michèle feel stronger about his need to do couple therapy; either with her or his wife. The answers to his problem seemed to be woven somewhere in his relationship with women and sentimentality. While Charlie simply feared the emotional trip getting there to highlight it. She was then told that all the therapists at Hypócrates had been addicts too, such that they were presumed experts on how addicts thought: 'We're spoiled, selfish and irresponsible people,' said the woman. 'We've always had our butts wiped and we don't care about others. Carles is a womaniser, an alcoholic, a gambler, married with a son and doesn't care about anyone except himself,' she said curtly. Michèle watched her eyes and listened to her tone. The woman's manner wasn't for real. It was all sincerely a tough General's speech that had little effect on Michèle. Thirty years dedicated to the same work was remarkable, but it also made people insular in their thinking. The woman had already classified Michèle as a nice girl who'd been taken for a ride and landed into co-addiction, because she could not understand why Michèle had dedicated so much time to Charlie. While Michèle wondered why a recovered addict who dedicates a life to helping other addicts was considered a professional and nothing else? She continued with her inquiries including some clarification about the books, to which the woman explained that Charlie had to decide what books or philosophies he wanted to read rather than be influenced by any. Michèle agreed, but suggested that he might still see the materials and discard what he wanted. That she could not see the difference between having the books in his room or the 26" TV that he chose his programming from? The director contemplated Michèle for a brief moment. 'You have to understand that after this visit you can't see Carles for a very very very verrrrry long time,' she said with a firm but warm tone. 'I understand that,' said Michèle. 'Why am I the only one on the list?' she asked. You don't have any ties with him. You need to go home and forget about him. Think about yourself and move on,' she concluded. '*His family lives below me – not exactly an easy task,*' she thought to herself. Never mind that, the realisation that they would cut out a "good thing" in his life and keep the same crap to regurgitate the same shit around and within him, antagonised her deeply. All that she had was the report but by then, it felt so inept, amateur and completely out in left field, trying to consider the root to why he felt comforted by cocaine. Much of it suggesting a dilemma from a sensitive personality versus the emotional sense of blackmail he felt by biased cultural restraints and the only woman whom he'd ever really committed to. She was coming from the "love" perspective when maybe Charlie really was just another dodgy guy that had taken her for a ride. She wasn't sure any more about anything. 'He just needs to learn how to love and be loved,' she said, noticing how corny it all sounded, 'I thought my experience with him might complement his rehabilitation programme. I recognise the importance of separating myself from Carles, however we've come this far together and in such good time too. We need time away from each other, which coincides with the therapy sessions that are only once a week and we don't have to attend them all; perhaps once a month? Wouldn't the novelty of that, keep the focus alive?' she questioned. 'If not, how would you suggest that I get over Carles or deal with his addiction, if I am not permitted assistance from the professionals?' she asked candidly. 'I know myself too well and it's better to wean me from the issue than segregating me from it. Just this conversation alone is well appreciated,' she explained. The woman wavered slightly: 'I will read your report.' Michèle was reluctant: 'Well thank you, but it's not necessary. It feels rather silly now,' she added. 'Nonsense; you worked hard at it. I'll look it over,' replied the woman. Michèle handed it to her, no longer feeling sure. 'I have Carles' too, may I give it to him?' 'No, no,' the woman shook her head vehemently. Then she got up from the swivel chair behind the desk and escorted Michèle to the door. 'You are an intelligent woman,' said the woman as she placed her hand on the door handle, then directly asked: 'Do you love him?' Michèle heard the word "intelligent" first and recognised that she'd heard it once before from Charlie, suddenly sensing that it carried an aura of intimidation to it; as if it put her in a league where the Michèles and the Charlies should not or could not be together. It made her sad, because her unfortunate need to communicate did not make her intelligent, it made her vulnerable. She shifted moist eyes from the woman's focus on her, understanding that the question was out of deference to Charlie, not to her. The woman in front of her, despite her rough attempts was just as sensitive as he was, because they were from the same experience. That what she was really asking was if Michèle's love was confused with a whimsical affection that could dissipate with time and hurt him later. It was about insecurities asking "how long will you love" versus "it's not long enough" and Michèle thought ever so fleetingly that if their answer to addiction was about being hard with love, then Charlie's armour would only become harder after having loosened it so much already.

She hesitated. She did not wish to share her feelings with the woman after the circumstance of their talk. 'I care about him very much,' she answered instead. 'Ah then, you don't love him,' replied the woman gregariously, suddenly becoming very warm, as if relieved from her own doubts, and landed Michèle a hug: 'Take care of yourself.' Followed by another contradiction: 'Maybe you can see Carles sooner – you never know.' Michèle was truly perplexed: 'Where do I go now?' 'Home,' replied the woman. 'May I say goodbye to Carles first?' she asked. 'It's not necessary,' replied the woman. They shook hands and Michèle thanked the woman sincerely for her time. Despite the contradictions, the rules and the fact that she was not related to Charlie, the interview with the veteran and head therapist of Hypócrates, had been appreciated. When she heard the door to the office close behind her, she noticed once again the large black and white framed photographs of hands reaching out to one another, hung along the reception wall. Then her father and their code of honour on how life was too volatile to deny what she was feeling, simultaneously waved across her mind's memory and without even second guessing it, proceeded directly to Charlie's room, to say goodbye. '¿Que?' he said, while he found his new position on the bed and she found hers in the sofa chair. They chatted calmly about her interview with his therapist, which included her mention to him about the tape and the report that she'd handed to his therapists. Then just before heading out, Charlie went over to the little fridge in his room and pulled out a white plate with a piece of lemon pie on it: 'Au,' he announced with the plate in his hand, 'I have to go to therapy now. This is for you,' he said casually, and placed it into her hands, 'I know you like these things.' They gave each other the Spanish kisses and then he left. She stared at the pie, moved by the gesture and smiled. Although she loved homemade pastries and coffee ice cream, it was her dad who loved the lemon and key lime pies. Needless to say, she ate the morsel in three bites flat, then headed down to reception.

The heart knows things the mind cannot understand – UNKNOWN.

Destination: B Magic
April 29th, 2005

She walked over to reception just after five thirty, concerned about the taxi driver Carles who was meant to pick her up at 9:30p.m. She tried to contact him using the telephone number that was on the receipt he'd given her, however the dispatch was unable to assist her in locating him without his car number. She felt terrible. The only thing she managed to do was leave him twenty euros in an envelope with a note and her telephone number on it. She then asked reception if someone from the desk could go down to the corner at 9:30p.m. in order to hand it to him. The staff complied, no problem. After that, she enquired about transport to the airport, to which she was asked if she would mind sharing the limo-cab with another guest, who was also heading to the airport. Her peripheral vision then noticed the back of a very slight woman calmly sauntering to the garden area that Michèle intuitively felt was the other guest. It turned out that it was and neither she nor the woman, had a problem with sharing the ride. The woman was very thin. Dressed in a waist length navy blue denim evening sport jacket, funky jeans and open-toed wide heeled summer shoes. A Hermés scarf was draped around the collar of the jacket, while two Gucci bags dangled from her left arm. Every finger on both hands was adorned with jewellery, loose bangles chimed from her wrists and her hair was a silver grey colour that was pulled back into a short pony tail. At a distance her delicate profile reminded Michèle very much of her mother's. At a closer glance, Michèle's physical impression of the woman was of someone who had survived through a lot, was spiritually guided, slightly hippy, led a privileged lifestyle and whose overall physical sketch reminded her a lot of southern Miami or California. The cab was going to take twenty minutes to arrive, so the woman went over to one bench and Michèle headed over to another one where Charlie and she had been only a few hours earlier. She deviated only momentarily when she saw a white rose bush that instantly recalled her maternal grandmother's voice: 'Stop and smell the roses' So she did, but they had no smell. She finally sat down, in a contemplative mood; feeling happy to just sit; okay to go and satisfied with the visit. It was up to Charlie now. She'd done her thing. She was still feeling uneasy but erased it with her confidence in him. He could do it. It didn't matter where he was, Michèle knew he could do it. She observed the woman sitting on the other bench seemingly reading a newspaper. She looked pensive and calm. Michèle was feeling the same and quite empty too. The limo-cab arrived contrasted against a driver that was wearing a casual short-sleeved T-shirt and jeans. Together the woman and Michèle sat in the back seat and were driven off to the airport. After a few minutes, a polite and slow conversation between them began. 'Are you Spanish?' asked the woman after hearing Michèle question the driver on their expected time of arrival.

'Oh, no,' she smiled, 'I'm not.'

'No I didn't think so, but your accent is hard to place,' she said kindly.

'Yes. I've been told. I'm Canadian,' she said.

'Ah, then you speak English,' she confirmed.

'Yes, that's right.'

'May I assume you speak French too?' she continued gently.

Michèle smiled politely, 'Yes.'...

'I love Canadians,' she added, 'I was there thirty years ago in Toronto – is that where you're from, or Québec?' Michèle was not really in the mood to talk, but the woman's manner was so gentle that she responded, albeit timidly, to her comments. 'Hmm, yes, I was born in Toronto but raised in Québec.' B, as Michèle eventually called her, shared an ability with languages like she did, such that they found their medium and conversed mostly in English. 'Are you flying to Madrid too?' she asked.

'No, Mayürqa,' she replied.

'Oh I love Mayürqa,' she said, 'I was there a few years back when I wanted to open a marine wild life centre for dolphins, but it never got off the ground. It's a nice place. I love the sun and beach, but my favourite is Miami. I go there a lot. I really love South Beach to just sit there on my own. I get my energy from there,' she smiled warmly.

'Yes, I know South Beach,' said Michèle, 'the company I used to work for has its head office next door.' ... Then, ever so tactfully the woman inquired: 'We're you staying at the hotel?'

The area that neither of them was sure to talk about but wanted to, finally surfaced. '

No,' said Michèle, 'I was visiting a friend.'

'I left my daughter there,' volunteered the woman, 'we checked-in today. It seems like a good place...' She seemed anxious for an answer.

'Well, I'm sure they know more than I do,' Michèle tried, 'but I didn't find much warmth in it. A bit too sterile for me,' she admitted.

'Yes, I know what you mean,' said B, 'they took most of my daughter's things away but left her with "The DaVinci Code" and "Angels and Demons" books.' Then as if adapted to the pattern of their chat gave Michèle another hopeful glance…

'Um.., yes, they did the same with my friend. Took away a little book of Buddha quotes, but left him with the DaVinci code and a 26 inch television.'

Despite their cultural differences, a smirk on B's face suggested that she'd picked up on the wry tone.

'I dunno,' continued Michèle, 'but I tend to lean on the emotional side of the problem while they seem to be purely scientific about it. Have you ever heard of Brian Weiss? He's –'

'Oh yes!' B cut her off and with a big smile continued, 'I saw him in Madrid.'

'Really?' added Michèle. 'I wanted to see him in Barcelona, but tickets were sold out.'

'I liked his seminar, it was very interesting. Have you ever read any of Paulo Coello books?'

'Yes. Only a few though.'

'He's a very nice man,' said B, 'I met him one day when I passed a book store in Miami and suddenly decided to go in, and there he was. We chatted for a bit and now exchange contact once in a while. It was a nice encounter,' she added. B's words were carefully chosen and not pretentious at all, even though the moment she'd described was far from casual, and she had not related the experience to coincidence or chance but as an encounter.

'"Encounter",' repeated Michèle, 'I like your choice of wording. It's refreshing. Not really the kind of lingo that can be used with every one.'

'Oh yes it can,' B answered directly. 'You know my daughter is at the centre, because she saw an article and photo about the centre in a magazine, exactly like the one I'd found and given to her exactly one day after she had seen the article. Then I noticed that her room number sums up to the total of my favourite number seven.' B's timid manner from before had been quickly replaced by a very confident one. Michèle listened to her with goose bumps on her arms. She had a woman in the car with her who read from life as much, if not more, than she could do. Never mind the fact that "7" was significant to Michèle as well.

'Are you by chance Aquarian?' continued B.

'Yes,' said Michèle.

'Ah, two of my most favourite people are Aquarians – my husband and my son,' she said.

Michèle wondered if she was having a surreal moment. The list of symmetrical coincidences between them was simply over the top too much. Had someone been listening to their conversation it would have been rated as an esoteric attempt to get everyone on the bandwagon. The funny thing is, no one who feels or talks about these occurrences wants to be perceived that way or even label it as anything more or less than natural. It is just an unavoidable truth that cannot be denied when such moments find people, or when people can see it. … The two of them conversed on, then they chatted and then they shared some more. Both had felt that same sense of confusion and emptiness when they walked out of Hypócrates and both felt that the physical and scientific truth of a problem could not be entirely solved without spiritual understanding. That the emotional and mental together were the ingredients to help overcome any illness. 'Mucho mucho amor (lots and lots of love),' rhymed B as they neared the airport. They were definitely feeling better by the same feather and it wasn't like they were the only ones who believed in it. Great athletes, famous writers, music groups, blog pages and book stores were filled with such information, yet the world still seemed unaware of it.

Once they got to the airport to check-in there was a slight undercurrent feeling of whether or not they should end the encounter. As if concerned that the moment might be damage by too much of it. Michèle still had to see if she could change her flight to an earlier one while B checked into her flight to Madrid. As it turned out Michèle's flight to Mayürqa was changed to the same time as B's flight for Madrid. B had gate 21 and Michèle had gate 22. Needless to say that they were both on a roll and noticed the sum of the gates' digits was seven. They went for a coffee. After the waitress took their order, B placed a plastic pencil bag holder on their table and emptied its contents into her bag. 'I want to give you this,' she said. Michèle was embarrassed. She didn't want anything. The meeting with her had been therapeutic enough. 'I insist,' said B.

Michèle stared at the multi coloured bag and began to focus on the artwork of characters and symbols that decorated it. 'Oh my goodness!?' she blurted, 'these are Japanese frogs!?' 'Yes,' replied B, delighted at Michèle's enthusiasm, 'I collect them.' Then Michèle really noticed B's Gucci bags and realised that the charms hanging from them were indeed frogs. 'I have a company called "Mucho Mucho Amor",' she explained. The logo on this key chain is a heart with the eyes of a frog facing one another like it were reflecting upon itself. In Maya culture "mucho" also means frog and is the symbol for self-reflection and love.' 'Wow B, I had not noticed. You see I speak a little Japanese. These symbols on the bag are katakana for weather words,' she tried to explain as unpretentiously as possible. B's eyes flickered and her mouth smiled: 'Boy, I'm really glad we met – you know.' 'Yea, I feel answered,' said Michèle using the lingo. 'Yes, me too,' B replied.

As they got ready to head to their gates of departure a man approached their table and ever so politely and inaudibly asked B a few questions to which she nodded self-consciously in reply. 'It's a sincere pleasure to meet you,' he said shaking her hand with a wide smile and giving Michèle a cordial look before leaving them. Nothing was asked, nor said about that and the two of them headed off to their departure gates. Once they got to the gate they exchanged contact details and took a photo of each other from their cell telephones. Then while they waited for flights to be called B showed Michèle the photos from the album she had brought for her daughter, while Michèle offered some of hers from her phone. It was truly interesting. Both had winter shots from home, Michèle's from Canada and B's in Germany that could have been interpreted as one and the same place, not missing either that B's dogs had Japanese names. They talked and talked freely about what they saw and believed about energy and its ambiguities. Confident that its power through them and others somehow helped to keep the world upside up. They also decided that Charlie and B's daughter were going to meet because their own meeting had been too obvious to deny. B was noticeably happier and relieved and Michèle truly felt that the "signs" were in favour of her and her daughter, as well as for herself; as if there was an invisible line of support for Charlie that was not purely her own. It was a "good feeling" connection. As though the timing of their meeting had been all under control in order to recharge their batteries before they were meant to physically go on their own separate ways again. Michèle's flight was called first. They hugged and said goodbye. That encounter with B had been a nice reminder to her about the chain of preceeding events that got her there to begin with and that it was almost denied by exterior influences that had not been entirely supportive of her. Yet, even if she had not made it, Life would have arranged for another one with someone else carrying the same feather; of this she felt certain. B collected frogs, while people gave Michèle frog memorabilia. She didn't know why, but B was not the first. Even Elisabet had given her a silver one when she first arrived. Then there were other token reminders, like the pewter guardian angel that was given to her by a guest just before she'd ended her final ship contract and when buying a car that year hadn't even been a full thought yet; a finger puppet that was given to her by one of the directors from that same contract that is none other than a smiling flower. Naturally, she had been reminded of it when circumstances one day led Charlie to calling her a "flower" and made her think that the kind words were not just coming from Charlie. Not denying either that post B, she suddenly "noticed" all the references to flowers and frogs in her home that had been given to her over the years. Withstanding that, ever since Jes' death she'd been collecting feathers. He used to pick them up and she simply associated them with his presence. Then while she was trying to find some artwork on the internet about female Merlins, the link mistakenly took her to a photo of a drawing of a young Caucasian woman dressed in prehistoric hunting attire with a feather in her hair, who could seriously have been a younger version of her mother. The adage "birds of a feather flock together", made her wonder if there was something more to be said about feathers? North American Indians did. It was all so crazy. However the series of linked events that brought her to taking a cab with B were real and in some mystical way, not about a meeting with Charlie but rather, a private meeting with Life and another one of its feathers. That in some shape or form people like B and Michèle could communicate in the same *Life* dialect, such that a morsel moment like the one they had shared, was Life's way of keeping its language alive. It all seemed so religious and terribly absurd and how she wished that it didn't. Yet, how else to describe knowing about the overwhelming energy of a power that is out there? How much music and literature was required? Open your eyes, what *do* you *see*? *'Respect your life; don't oppose it,'* she reminded herself, and the plane took off.

The next morning she instinctively woke up and whispered a, 'Good morning' to both B and Charlie. Then she and Dasha walked past Charlie's place and discovered that the area around it was being prepped for excavation repairs that were going to last until midsummer. Timing. Charlie's timing to leave on the 20th was so well calculated without even trying. *'He's one of us,'* she chuckled, still on her high from the day before. Elisabet and Mitx had also informed her of their intention to move his things out on May 1st, making her sudden need to clean and collect his things the week before seem all the more timely. Finally, she received a call from B late that afternoon: 'I had to call,' she explained, 'last night my flight was delayed until they got another plane to Madrid. *Guess* what the captain's name was?' she practically squeaked.

'I don't know,' replied Michèle.

'Manolo, Manolo Amores (Manolo Love)!'

When we all give the power – We all give the best
Every Minute of an hour – Don't think about a rest
When you all get the power – You all get the best
When everyone gives everything – And every song everybody sings
Then it's life
When we all feel the power
When the feeling of the people – Is the feeling of the band
Every minute of the future – Is a memory of the past
'Cause we all gave the power – We all gave the best
Life is life.
'LIFE IS LIFE' – OPUS, LYRICS ADAPTED

Roof Top

Saturday, April 30th, 2005. She looked at the night of blue stars and black space above her. Focused on his name and ever so carefully whispered: 'Charlie, yes–you–*Can*… I love you.'

L'APERITIU
水曜 29年 9月13日 [1]

Wednesday, September 13, 2017 (5) [2]
Sa Croix on a breezy equinoctial evening
Just before sun and dusk take their leave
A priceless view from everyone's table on the terrace
A crisp cold glass of white wine
Two *Quely* biscuits
Pen on paper scribbling away
Sorting out her classes for the next year
The sudden honk from the carpark, in time she looks up to see
A confident silver machine, gliding in on three wheels
It's Carles at the helm and a fine looking young man at 25
Wearing the same black T as his dad
Sitting in the front at Carles' side!

...

---

[1] L'Aperitiu is Catalan for *the appetizer*.
The year 2017 is the 29th year of the reigning Emperor of Japan, also known as the *Heisei* era meaning "Achieving Peace" or "Peace everywhere".

[2] Carles (2) and son (5) equal (7): 2+5+7 =14, (5).

ADDENDUM

THE FIRST HALF: PART III
MICHÈLE VERSUS CHARLY

Plan I: The Proposed Agenda for Rehab

Return to Barcelona – Short term 2 to 3 months
- Enough time to reach a level of coherency and energy to take on personal and professional affairs.
- Personal and professional affairs can be maintained while you are away due to the provisional support system that already exists.

Possible conflicts
- Higher risk of immediate relapse.
- Incompletion of projects due to possible relapse.
- Fees while away 6 months: 12,000 euros – 18,000 euros.
- *Greater possibility of success, if rehab is done outside of Mayürqa for a longer time period. Between 6 to12 months.
- *Consider terminating rental contract or move personal items to storage, or family while away.
- Fee: minimum 36,000 euros or more depending on where and how much time is dedicated to rehabilitation.

Rehab centres – long term options
- Hotel Hipócrates – Barcelona:7,000 euros/month.
- Easier to adapt to, due to previous experience.

- Already familiar with its programme and staff.
- Previous knowledge of margin of success might impress the will to follow programme rules.
- Close to Mayürqa and family.
- Centre offers a village to live in during second phase of rehab.
- Platform to live abroad 6 to12 months less difficult.
- Easy to move personal belongings from Mayürqa to Barcelona.

Possible conflicts

- Familiarity might remove the novelty and desire from the rehabilitation.
- Difficult to set up professional prospects in Barcelona.
- Maybe too close to home, family and negative influences.
- High expenses to incur while living second phase of rehab in Barcelona.
- Provisional professional support system for Sa Croix would need reviewing if rehab is more than six months.

TAVAD – Advanced treatment for addiction – Madrid

- More than 20 years of experience.
- Several press releases and reports from Spanish press media about the success of its programme.
- Advanced technology and treatment.
- Comfortable and modern facilities.
- Detoxification 100% success rate; 76% success after one year of rehab for males up to 57 years of age or 18 years of consumption.
- Provisional professional support system for Sa Croix would need reviewing if rehab is more than six months.
- Easy to move personal belongings from Mayürqa to Madrid.
- More information on internet.
- Contacts: 902 100 197 / No. 8 Fuentelarrreina Ave. Madrid.

Possible conflicts
- Farther from home. Little information about the medication and treatments.
- 5,000 euros for one year without room and board. Physical intern only two days. Includes medical treatment and therapy sessions in Madrid.
- Difficult to set up professional prospects in Madrid.
- Phone call to the centre received evasive answers to inquiries and asked too many survey questions.
- Expenses to extend therapy in Madrid unknown – facilities if any unknown.
- Provisional professional support system for Sa Croix would need reviewing, if rehab is more than six months.

Narconon: American base, Arizona – several international/European centres
- Since 1966 – founder was formerly sentenced to prison.
- Has a lot of experience and popularity in the US.
- Might have scientology undercurrents in its methodology.
- In California / Arizona – It would be possible to live there 6 months – take advantage of the novelty of being in America. Cheaper with respect to money exchange; very nice facilities and location; room to travel around later; Narconon is apparently the pioneer of rehab centres for addiction.
- Beautiful new centre in Canada Oklahoma – state of the art centre.
- There are currently 3 centres in Spain: Madrid (2), and Andalucía – "The Mediterranean" (only 3 years old) located in Alcalá de Guadaira Seville.
- "The Mediterranean" has a 75% success rate with 70 rooms – 902 101 501.
- In the UK 44 1424 420 036 – New, modern, English language.

Possible conflicts
- Spain easier for move, but Seville not as easy as Madrid or Barcelona.
- Little information about the medication and treatments however internet information suggests none is used.
- Cost 2,500 euros for first three months.
- Not guaranteed a private room.
- Farther from Mayürqa – transport expenses higher.

Live abroad 6 to 12months – Dubai / Menorca / Canaries / Canada/ US
- This option invites change of scenery and ideas and your thoughts about your professional and personal life after rehab. Maybe leads to professional expansion beyond Mayürqa. The physical distance from Mayürqa might make secondary challenges of recuperation easier to handle.

Dubai – high standard of living
- Great professional development possibilities between Mayürqa and Dubai.
- Contacts and social references are available.
- Far from everything – adds experience and new adventure to life.
- Best place to intimidate drug abuse.

Possible conflicts
- Possible culture shock.
- Might need to go with someone.
- Lots of traffic, far from home, Sa Croix needs a long term provisional plan without you.

Menorca – similar to and next door to Mayürqa
- Adaptable, cheaper, closer but more remote than the mainland, same culture etc.

Possible conflicts
- Sa Croix needs a long term provisional plan without you.
- Very high winds at winter and extremely quiet during off-season.
- Close to home and negative influences.

The Canaries – similar to Balear islands
- Good place to set up a personal and professional lifestyle if desired.
- Has support group centres like "Project Man".
- New contacts and people.
- Far but not as expensive – Easier for family to visit.

Possible conflicts
- Variable temperatures.
- Might need to go with someone.
- Sa Croix needs a long term provisional plan without you.

Canada / US
- Experience American culture.
- Practice languages.
- Business development opportunities.
- "Project Man" centres exist for extended therapy sessions.
- Professional contacts and social references available.

Possible conflicts
- Cold – depending on location.
- Work permit / Visa required.
- Far / Expensive for family to visit.
- Might need to go with someone.
- Sa Croix needs a long term provisional plan without you.

Plan II: Extended rehabilitation – Proposed return agenda
(If you return to Mayürqa after the first phase of rehabilitation)

- Follow through on the swing – Begin with removing as much of the negative influences from the last chapter as possible: Telephone numbers, social contacts, new address.
- Family should re-adapt their preconceived patterns about you and themselves.
- Live with someone or near people who can support your recuperation process.
- Manage some time with positive people.
- Sign up for group therapy sessions, sports, gym.
- Initiate new business ideas.
- Manage a full-time day-to-night schedule in order to promote sleep at night.
- Consider sorting personal agenda, new house, move the old olive tree.
- Don't deviate or break the rhythm of the rules you follow, for a good while. Even when you are feeling better.
- Professional development projects post-short term rehab (2 to 3 months).

Colonia de San Pedro bar/restaurant – possibilities
- Good location – infrastructure – fully equipped.
- High revenue potential without the need of heavy P.R. media.
- Sa Croix – staff and start up support.
- Precedence from Sa Croix supports easier start up and preparation.

Possible conflicts
- Too many rules and standards assigned by the Club's shareholders.
- Questionable clauses in the contract: 3.7 / 3.8 / 3.10 / 3./12.
- Little time to meet closing date for bid submission.

Sa Croix possibilities: A
- Return – ready to re-position staff morale, renovate economic status of the business.
- Change staff, Sa Croix image, organise accounting.
- In other words as if it were a new business. Work each day morning until night.

Possible conflicts
- Sa Croix has been around for 14 years. Its charm has been harmed for the last 5 to 6 years, from the stories and gossip around your personal life.
- The pressure from local gossip and expectation could cast a shadow over initial motivation and provoke a relapse after only a few months of rehab.
- Sa Croix largely related to the past might be difficult to move on – You would have to be well recuperated mentally to do it. More rehab time away before heading back would be better.

Sa Croix – New manager: B
- Hindsight after 14 years Sa Croix has maintained good client retention despite its challenges. Even possibly until its rental agreement expires nine years from now. Such that a new manager who is completely independent from Sa Croix' history placed in charge of human resource issues, staffing, overall restaurant management while you could manage more P.R. with the clients on the floor without the weight of administrative or staff issues. Also change the energy of gossip into a better direction. Would give you more time to be away on rehab – the new manager could use your old place in Mayürqa while you are away.
- With or without rehab it's a good suggestion.
- Offers more time to be away and recupe better and stronger.
- Need to interview potential candidates well.
- A new manager would alleviate the staff and level of disorganisation

on the floor.
- Can be used as a reason to get better sooner than later if you wish to eventually manage the place on your own.

"Juniper Station" – possibilities
- Building is already yours. Therefore there is an indefinite amount of time to develop a new business there. Meanwhile it's a great asset.
- Great location.

Possible conflicts
- After only 2 to 3 months – Money, health, lack of morale.

Personal issues after 2 to 3 – months of rehab
- Divorce – Better ability to manage the process. This option is feaseable to do while away on rehab.
- Divorce could be a healthy decision for everyone: husband, wife, son.
- Might give the sensation of having closed a major part of cocaine chapter.
- Could enable guidelines for consistent behaviour among everyone.
- Upon returning – Desire and ability to improve father/son relationship. Maybe more willingness to get more involved in son's life.
- *Formal terms of agreement could be a good way to communicate with each other respectively and reduce conflictive situations.

Possible conflicts
- 2 to 3 months is little time to directly face the above mentioned suggestions without a high risk of relapsing. More than 3 months of rehab would offer a better level of lucidity and confidence.
- Less prone to the concept of "failure".

Relationship
- A positive relationship is a reachable goal only if both individuals have the will and desire to try.
- Requires starting with a courting initiative.
- Weekly psychological therapy sessions – personal and couple therapy.
- Both individuals prepared to work together on, pride issues, humility, confidence; communication, listening skills and respect.
- Live together only if both individuals agree and accept the above mentioned suggestions.
- Understand the possibility like any couple – there is no guarantee of duration. Therefore be able to continue at a mature level of communication, unconditional care, without negative restrictions, no obligation or conditional ties. End with respect for one another. Patience, time, courage.

Plan III
- Stay in Mayürqa – Little possibility of success if cocaine consumption is not reduced.
- Per the last 14 years there is little to support or faith from people in your life.
- In addition rules and regulations would have to be incorporated into your daily agenda that restrict your movement around bad influences which are pretty much everywhere.
- Need to involve someone to help. Need to attend group sessions and therapy.
- Join social clubs, or sports.
- Fee: until you've recuperated, your personal economic condition is a minimum of 2000euros a month on activities surrounding cravings alone.

APPENDIX

RESOURCES[3]

LADYBUG: THE FIRST HALF
1. About Mozart, Ultima Hora newspaper, January 30, 2006.
2. Aquarius, definition of zodiac, Google.
3. Art of War, Sun Tzu, Oxford Uniersity Press, 1971.
4. Asian horoscopes – Horse & Sheep, definition of... Google.
5. Capricorn, definition of...zodiac www.Astrocentre.msn.com, September 26, 2005.
6. Co-addict, definition of... Google.
7. Friend, definition of ... www.answers.com/topic/friend.
8. Friend, definition of... Google: WORD HISTORY EXCERPT.
9. Más Platón y menos Prozac, Lou Marinoff, PURESA,S.A. 2004.
10. Memoirs, Christopher Short, November 9, 1989.
11. Morir no es lo peor que te puede pasar, Elisabet Menéndez periodista, Mujer de hoy magazine, March 26 to April 1, 2005 issue, page 38.
12. Mujer de hoy magazine, Javier Sadabá, July 9 to July 15, 2005 issue.
13. Mujer de hoy magazine,September 16 to September 23, 2005 issue.
14. Nursery rimes, Google: Thomas Guthrie Anstey.
15. Oxford Pocket Dictionary of Current English, Oxford University Press, Amen House, London, fourth edition1952.
16. Oxford Universal Dictionary On Historical prInciples, Little

William, Oxford University Press Amen House London, third edition 1955.
17. The Call of the Wild, Jack London, "For the love of a man", chapter six.
18. The Faithful Gardener: A Wise Tale About That Which Can Never Die, Clarissa Pinkola Estés, Millenium 2003.
19. The Lord of the Rings: The Fellowship of Rings, (excerpt adapted) JRR Tolkien.
20. The Scapegoating of Mary Magdaline, by Judd and Jason Speak Out, Wednesday April 19, 2006.
21. Vidas Privadas, Javier Sábada philosopher, Mujer de hoy magazine July 9 to July 15, 2005 issue, page 16.
22. Astro Internet, Hotmail, 2005; www.fortunecity.com/greenfield/ecolodge/197/rat.html.

QUOTES

LADYBUG: THE FIRST HALF

1. Albert Camus, PART II
2. Albert Einstein, PART I, II
3. Anais Nin, INDUCTION
4. André Gide, PART I
5. Anonymous, PART I, II, III
6. Antonio Machado, PART II
7. Arab Proverb, PART I
8. Buddha, PART II, III
9. C.P. Estés, PART IV
10. Charlie, PART III
11. Chinese Proverb, PART II
12. CMS, PART II, IV
13. David Lloyd George, PART IV
14. Doc Childre, PART II
15. Elisabet, PART I
16. Elmer Leterman, PART I
17. Emmanuel, PART III
18. English Proverb, PART III
19. Étienne de Grellet, PART III
20. Franklin P. Jones, PART III
21. H. Jackson Brown, JR., PART I
22. H. L. Mencken, PART III
23. Henry Wadsworth Longfellow, PART I
24. Heraclitus, PART II
25. Hugh MacLennan, PART I
26. Japanese Proverb, INDUCTION
27. Jerome K Jerome, PRECURSOR

28. Jiminy Cricket (Pinocchio, Walt Disney), INDUCTION
29. John A. Shedd, PART II
30. Laozi, PART II
31. Leo Buscagliaer, PART II
32. M, INDUCTION, PART, II, IV,
33. Mahatma Ghandi, PART II
34. Mary Pickford, PART II
35. Meaning of Elisabet , PART II
36. Rainer Maria Rilke, PART I
37. Ralph Waldo Emerson, PART II
38. Ray Charles, PART II
39. Richard Bach, PART III
40. Richard M. Devos, PART IV
41. Robert Redford, 'HORSE WHISPER' PART IV
42. Saint Teresa's Prayer, PART I
43. Sanaya Roman, PART III
44. Sócrates, PART IV
45. Sophocles, PART III
46. T.S. Eliot, PART I
47. The Proncess Bride, PART III
48. Vladimir, PART I
49. Walt Disney, INDUCTION, PART I
50. Wolfgang Amadeus Mozart, PART I

SONG TITLES RUNNING ORDER

INDUCTION:
1. The power of love – Franky Goes to Hollywood
2. Maneater – Hall & Oates
3. Private dancer – Tina Turner
4. All you need is love – Beatles
5. Timing – Kevin Johansen

THE FIRST HALF:
6. It's my life – Bon Jovi

PART I:
7. Viva España – Instrumental
8. Over the rainbow – Judy Garland
9. Mariposa – Oreja de Van Gogh

PART II:
10. Estoy harto – Guillermo
11. California – Mikel Erentxun
12. Fuego en el fuego – Eros Ramazzotti
13. La vie en rose – Patricia Kas
14. Give a little bit – Supertramp
15. Imagine – John Lennon
16. Corazón espinado – Santana
17. She's got the look – Roxette
18. Unchain my heart – Ray Charles
19. Falso amor – Unión

20. Sex bomb – Tom Jones
21. Cumbiera intelectual – Kevin Johansen

PART III:
22. Leave your hat on – Randy Newman
23. El cielo no entiende – OBK
24. Daisy – Kevin Johansen
25. Don't think of me –Dido
26. Sexual healing – Marvin Gaye

PART IV:
27. Go on – Kevin Johansen
28. More than words – Extreme
29. Sol a sol – Café Quijano
30. I'll stand by you – Carrie Underwood
31. You gotta be – Des'Ree
32. Llençat – LaxN Busto

LE DÉNOUEMENT:
33. Nada fue un error – Coti
34. What's up? – 4 Non Blondes
35. Life is life – Opus
36. Candombito – Kevin Johansen

SONG TITLES (ALPHABETICAL ORDER)

LADYBUG: THE FIRST HALF
1. All you need is love – Beatles, Lyrics INDUCTION
2. California – Mikel Erentxun, Lyrics PART II
3. Candombito – Kevin Johansen, Instrumental BOOK II
4. Corazón espinado – Santana, Lyrics PART II
5. Cumbiera intelectual – Kevin Johansen, Lyrics PART II
6. Daisy – Kevin Johansen, Lyrics PART II
7. Don't think of me – Dido, Lyrics PART III
8. El cielo no entiende – OBK, Lyrics PART IV
9. Estoy harto – Guillermo, Lyrics PART II
10. Falso amor – Unión, Lyrics PART II
11. Fuego en el fuego – Eros Ramazzotti, Lyrics PART II
12. Give a little bit – Supertramp, Lyrics PART II
13. Go on – Kevin Johansen, Lyrics PART IV
14. I'll stand by you – Carrie Underwood, Lyrics PART IV
15. Imagine – John Lennon, Lyrics PART II
16. Its my life – Bon Jovi, Lyrics PRECURSOR
17. La vie en rose – Patricia Kas, PART II
18. Leave your hat on – Randy Newman, Lyrics PART III
19. Life is life – Opus, Lyrics LE DÉNOUEMENT
20. Llençat – LaxN Busto, Lyrics PART IV
21. Maneater – Hall & Oates, Lyrics INDUCTION
22. Mariposa – Oreja de Van Gogh, Lyrics PART I
23. More than words – Extreme, PART IV
24. Nada fue un error – Coti, Lyrics LE DÉNOUEMENT
25. Over the rainbow – Judy Garland, Lyrics PART I

26. Private dancer – Tina Turner, Lyrics INDUCTION
27. Puff the magic dragon – Mamas and the Papas, Lyrics PART II
28. Sex bomb – Tom Jones, Lyrics PART II
29. Sexual healing – Marvin Gaye, Lyrics PART III
30. She's got the look – Roxette, Lyrics PART II
31. Sol a sol – Café Quijano, Lyrics PART IV
32. The power of love – Franky Goes to Hollywood
    Lyrics INDUCTION
33. Timing – Kevin Johansen, Lyrics INDUCTION
34. Unchain my heart – Ray Charles, Lyrics PART II
35. Viva España – PART I
36. *Way we were – Barbara Streisand, Lyrics PART I
37. What's up? – 4 Non Blondes, Lyrics LE DÉNOUEMENT
38. *When the saints go marching in – Louis Armstrong
    Lyrics PART I
39. You gotta be – Des'Ree, Lyrics PART IV

SONG ARTISTS AND WRITERS

1. Beatles, **LENNON**, All you need is love
2. Beatles, **McCARTNEY**, Let it be
3. Bon Jovi, **JON BON JOVI, RICHIE SAMBORA, MAX MARTIN**, It's my life
4. Café Quijano, **MANUEL, OSCAR, RAÚL QUIJANO**, Sol a Sol
5. Carrie Underwood, **CHRISSIE HYNDE**, I'll Stand by You
6. Coti, **COTI**, Nada fue un error
7. Des'Ree, **DESIRÉE ANNETTE WEEKS**, You Gotta Be
8. Dido, **DIDO**, Don't Think of me
9. Dido, **ibid**, Here with me
10. Dido, **ibid**, Honestly ok
11. Dido, **ibid**, My lover's gone
12. Dido, **ibid**, Take my Hand
13. Dido, **ibid**, This land is mine
14. Dido, **ibid**, White Flag
15. Enya, **MICHAEL CRETU, KUO YING-NAN, KUO HSIU-CHU**, The Return to Innocence
16. Eros Ramazzotti, **EROS RAMAZZOTTI**, Fuego en el fuego
17. Extreme, **GARY CHERONE, NUNO BETTENCOURT**, More than words
18. Fool's Garden, **PETER FREUDENTHALER, VOLKER HINKEL**, Yellow lemon tree
19. 4 Non Blondes, **LINDA PERRY**, What's Up?
20. Franky Goes to Hollywood, **HOLLY JOHNSON, PETER GILL, MARK O-TOOLE, BRIAN NASH**, The Power of Love

21. Guillermo, **GUILLERMO**, Estoy Harto
22. Hall & Oates, **SARA ALLEN, DARYL HALL, JOHN OATES**, Maneater
23. John Lennon, **JOHN LENNON**, Imagine
24. Judy Garland, **EDGAR YIPSEL HARBURG**, Over the Rainbow
25. Kevin Johansen, **KEVIN JOHANSEN**, Candombito
26. Kevin Johansen, **ibid**, Cumbiera intelectual
27. Kevin Johansen, **ibid**, Daisy
28. Kevin Johansen, **ibid**, Go On
29. Kevin Johansen, **ibid**, Hindueblues
30. Kevin Johansen, **JACQUES PRÉVERT, JOSEPH COSMO**, La Chanson de Prévert (Les Feuilles Mortes – original song.)
31. Kevin Johansen, **ibid**, Timing
32. Kyu Sakamoto, **ROKUSUKU EI**, Sukiyaki (Hitori Bocchi)
33. Lax'n'Busto, **LAX'N'BUSTO**, Llençat
34. Luz Casal, **GLORIA VARONA**, No me importa nada
35. Macy Gray, **MACY GRAY, JEREMY RUZUMNA, JINSOO LIM, DAVID WILDER**, I Try
36. Madonna, **MADONNA, PATRICK LEONARD**, Frozen
37. Peter, Paul and Mary, **PETER YARROW, LEONARD LIPTON**, Puff the Magic Dragon
38. Manà, **JUAN GABRIEL**, Se me olvidó
39. Marvin Gaye, **MARVIN GAYE, ODELL BROWN, DAVID RITZ**, Sexual Healing
40. Mikel Erentxun, **JESÚS MARÍA CORMÁN**, California
41. Navajita Plateá con Alba Moli, **ANTONIO DE LOS RÍOS MADRILES**, Noches Bohemia
42. OBK, **MIGUEL ARJONA**, El cielo no entiende
43. Opus, **EWALD PFLEGER, NIKI GRUBER, HERWIG RÜDISSER, KURT-RENE PLISNIER**, Life is Life
44. Oreja de Van Gogh, **XABIER SAN MARTIN**, Mariposa

45. Patricia Kas, **ÉDITH PIAF, MARGUERITE MONNOT**, La vie en rose
46. Randy Newman, **RANDY NEWMAN**, Leave your hat on
47. Ray Charles, **TEDDY POWELL, BOBBY SHARP**, Unchain my heart
48. Robbie Williams, **ROBBIE WILLIAMS**, Feel
49. Robin Williams, **ibid**, Angels
50. Roxette, **PER GESSLE**, She's got the look
51. Santana, **SANTANA**, Corazón espinado
52. Santana, **ROB THOMAS, ITAAL SHUR**, Smooth
53. Seguridad Social, **BRUNO LOMAS**, Ven sin temor
54. Shakira, **SHAKIRA**, Inevitable
55. Shakira, **ibid**, Ojos Asi
56. Shakira, **ibid**, Que Vuelves
57. Shakira, **SHAKIRA, LUIS F. OCHOA**, Sombra de Ti
58. Shakira, **ibid**, Sordomuda
59. Shakira, **ibid**, Tú
60. Supertramp, **ROGER HODGSON, RICK DAVIES**, Give a little bit
61. Taxi, **TAXI**, Tu Oportunidad
62. Tina Turner, **MARK KNOPFLER**, Private dancer
63. Tom Jones, **MOUSSE T., ERROLL RENNALLS**, Sex Bomb
64. Unión, **ED COBB**, Falso amor (Tainted Love – original song.)
65. Barbara Streisand, **ANDREW LLOYD WEBBER, TREVOR NUNN**, Memories
66. Luis Armstrong, **LUIS ARMSTRONG**, When the Saints Go Marching In

BOOKTRACK
THE FIRST HALF

PLAYLIST I
1. It's my life – Bon Jovi, Lyrics PRECURSOR
2. The power of love – Franky Goes to Hollywood, Lyrics INDUCTION
3. Mariposa – Oreja de Van Gogh, Lyrics PART I
4. Timing – Kevin Johansen, Lyrics INDUCTION
5. California – Mikel Erentxun, Lyrics PART II
6. La vie en rose – Patricia Kas, PART II
7. Fuego en el fuego – Eros Ramazzotti, Lyrics PART II
8. Daisy – Kevin Johansen, Lyrics PART II
9. Corazón espinado – Santana, Lyrics PART II
10. Sex bomb – Tom Jones, Lyrics PART II
11. Cumbiera intelectual – Kevin Johansen, Lyrics PART II
12. Estoy harto – Guillermo, Lyrics PART II
13. El cielo no entiende – OBK, Lyrics PART IV
14. Go on – Kevin Johansen, Lyrics PART IV
15. Sol a sol – Café Quijano, Lyrics PART IV
16. Llençat – Lax'n'Busto, Lyrics PART IV
17. Nada fue un error – Coti, Lyrics LE DÉNOUEMENT
18. What's up? 4 Non Blondes, Lyrics LE DÉNOUEMENT
19. Life is life – Opus, Lyrics LE DÉNOUEMENT

PLAYLIST II: EXTENDED VERSION
1. Viva España – PART I
2. She's got the look – Roxette, Lyrics PART II
3. Maneater – Hall & Oates, Lyrics INDUCTION

4. <u>Leave your hat on</u> – Randy Newman, Lyrics PART III
5. <u>Private dancer</u> – Tina Turner, Lyrics INDUCTION
6. <u>Don't think of me</u> –Dido, Lyrics PART III
7. <u>Falso amor</u> – Unión, Lyrics PART II
8. <u>All you need is love</u> – Beatles, Lyrics INTRODCTION
9. <u>Imagine</u> – John Lennon, Lyrics PART II
10. <u>*O Canada anthem</u>, PART II
11. <u>Give a little bit</u> – Supertramp, Lyrics PART II
12. <u>Over the rainbow</u> – Judy Garland, Lyrics PART I
13. <u>*Puff the magic dragon</u> – Mamas and the Papas, PART II
14. <u>Unchain my heart</u> – Ray Charles, Lyrics PART II
15. <u>Sexual healing</u> – Marvin Gaye, Lyrics PART III
16. <u>You gotta be</u> – Des'Ree, Lyrics PART IV
17. <u>More than words</u> – Extreme, PART IV
18. <u>I'll stand by you</u> – Carrie Underwood, Lyrics PART IV
19. <u>Wind beneath my wings</u> – Bet Midler, Lyrics DEDICATION

*Lyrics not listed

[3] To the writers, poets, songwriters and music artists: to your words, your lyrics, your Work – Thank you for being there.

DEDICATION

It must be cold there in my shadow
To hardly have sunlight on your face
Yet you seem content to let me shine
It's still your way
You've always walked a step behind
So I'm the one with all the glory
While you're the one with all the strength
A beautiful face without a name – for so long
A beautiful smile to hide the pain
I know I've given this to you once before
"Machine to machine"
So this is just to remind you
That you're still my hero
It might appear to go unnoticed
But I've got it all here in my heart
I want you to know – I know the truth
Of course I do – Impossible without you
Fly away – You've let us fly so high
Thank you very much for your help
Until we meet again
You know we'll have a good time then!
We love you.

THE WIND BENEATH MY WINGS' – BETTE MIDLER
LYRICS ADAPTED

Christopher Shaw Michael Short
November 10, 1940 – October 22, 1994
A.K.A. Dad Short.

LADYBUG

BOOK II
THE INTERMISSION

CPSIA information can be obtained
at www.ICGtesting.com
Printed in the USA
LVOW03s0348261217
560802LV00002B/213/P

9 781681 815107